The
Art Teacher's
BOOK OF LISTS

Helen D. Hume

PRENTICE HALL
Paramus, New Jersey 07652

Library of Congress Cataloging-in-Publication Data

Hume, Helen D., 1933-
   The art teacher's book of lists / Helen D. Hume.
      p.   cm.
   ISBN 0-13-758814-3 (p). — ISBN 0-13-517756-1 (s)
   1. Art—Miscellanea. I. Title.
   N7438.H86 1988
   702—dc21   97-36644
                      CIP

FRONT COVER: Matisse, Henri. *The Red Studio.* Issy-les-Moulineaux (1911). Oil on canvas, 71¼″ × 72¼″ (181 × 219.1 cm). The Museum of Modern Art, New York. Mrs. Simon Guggenheim Fund. Photograph © 1997 The Museum of Modern Art, New York.

Printed in the United States of America

10 9 8 7 6 5 4 3

ISBN 0-13-517756-1 (S)

ATTENTION: CORPORATIONS AND SCHOOLS

Prentice Hall books are available at quantity discounts with bulk purchase for educational, business, or sales promotional use. For information, please write to: Prentice Hall, 240 Frisch Court, Paramus, NJ 07652. Please supply: title of book, ISBN number, quantity, how the book will be used, date needed.

PRENTICE HALL
Paramus, NJ 07652

On the World Wide Web at http://www.phdirect.com

PRENTICE-HALL INTERNATIONAL (UK) LIMITED, *LONDON*
PRENTICE-HALL OF AUSTRALIA PTY. LIMITED, *SYDNEY*
PRENTICE-HALL CANADA INC., *TORONTO*
PRENTICE-HALL HISPANOAMERICANA, S.A., *MEXICO*
PRENTICE-HALL OF INDIA PRIVATE LIMITED, *NEW DELHI*
PRENTICE-HALL OF JAPAN, INC., *TOKYO*
PEARSON EDUCATION ASIA PTE. LTD., *SINGAPORE*
EDITORA PRENTICE-HALL DO BRASIL, LTDA., *RIO DE JANEIRO*

To my beloved Jack and
my wonderful, supportive family.

ACKNOWLEDGMENTS

Art Educators are a sharing group of people, not only with their students, but with each other! Over the years of attending National Art Education Conventions, I have been privileged to meet and learn from creative and inspired art educators who have introduced new materials and shared new approaches to old techniques.

My grateful appreciation to friends and colleagues, art teachers Timothy Smith, Mary Ann Kroeck, Lauren Davis, Sue Trent, Bonnie Enos, Beth Goyer, LuWayne Younghans, Luci McMichael, Cheryl Venet, Suzanne Walker, Betty Schermen, my education students at Florissant Valley Community College, and apprentice art teachers at Webster University. A special note of gratitude to colleague John Dunivent, who shared his expertise as a photo collector and researcher of photography, and was kind enough to read and advise. Special thanks to John Baker, film and video producer/director, who shared technical advice on video production. The Education staff at the St. Louis Art Museum, including Kate Guerra, Sue Hooker, Cheryl Benjamin, Joanlee Ferarra, Barbara Decker-Franklin, Carlene Fullerton, and Education Director Beau Vallance have all contributed to my education, appreciation, and knowledge in the field. Art Specialists Loretta Schaffer (formerly in the Special School District) and Jeanne Manley, current art-coordinator of the St. Louis County Special School District have been generous in sharing ideas for teaching special populations with me and my teacher-in-training classes.

In doing research for this *Book of Lists,* I have become more aware than ever how much the atmosphere of a library contributes to the happy feeling I have whenever I am reading and writing about art. From the time I can remember, I have enjoyed libraries and have considered librarians my friends—and my respect has increased as they have shown their expertise in helping me locate just the right resource. I would especially like to thank the staff of the St. Louis Library Fine Arts Room: Tim Willman, Mary Frechette, and Tim Gebauer, who have been tireless in helping me search for just the right resource. The St. Louis Art Museum library and staff, especially Clare Vasquez and Cheryl Vogler under the direction of Stephanie Sigala, have introduced me to the many tools available on the computer, as well as helping me locate current resources. Other librarians who have assisted me are Nancy Bender of the Laumeier Sculpture Garden, Carol Callahan of the Florissant Valley Community College Library, the staff of the St. Louis County Library, and the librarians at Parkway West High School: Paula Lucas and Barbara Kellams.

Others who have been especially helpful are Pat Sanders, Folk Art Section of the National Endowment for the Arts in Washington, DC, Jeanne Bond, Executive Director, and Glenn Harper, Director, of the International Sculpture Center in Washington, DC, and Carn Luciarelli, Permissions Editor of the National Art Education Association.

I would like to express my gratitude to members of the production staff at Prentice Hall and their associates who have helped in pulling the book into final form, in particular Project Editor Mariann Hutlak, Nancy Marcus Land of Publications Development Company, and Barbara Palumbo of Prentice Hall, a computer whiz who has helped me with several problems. Copy editor Diane Turso has again demonstrated her wide-ranging knowledge. The role of the editor as sounding board has never been as important to me as in writing this book. Connie Kallback and Win Huppuch have become friends over the years of publishing my books, and their unerring judgment has helped to keep me on the right track.

ABOUT THE AUTHOR

Helen D. Hume has been an art teacher for thirty years and has taught art at all levels (including General Art, Advanced Placement Art History, Photography, Crafts, Sculpture, Painting and Drawing, and Design and Ceramics). Her experience has been in public schools in the Parkway School District and in private International Schools in Antwerp Belgium and São Jose Dos Campos, Brazil. She teaches Education and Art Education courses at Florissant Valley Community College in St. Louis County, Missouri, and serves as a supervising teacher for apprentice art teachers at Webster University.

She studied painting at Het Vrij Atelier in Antwerp, Belgium, and has undergraduate and graduate degrees from Webster University, specializing in painting, photography, sculpture, and printmaking. She has done numerous presentations at National Art Education Association State and National Conventions, as well as presentations to fellow art educators at the St. Louis Art Museum. She was a team member and writer for the "Curriculum for the 21st Century" Project for the state of Missouri. She is a member of the Art Section of the St. Louis Artists' Guild, and currently is a member of the Executive Board and Secretary of the Board of Governors. She travels extensively, and has always had an interest in architecture and art history. Her previous three books: *A Survival Kit for the Secondary School Art Teacher, Art History and Appreciation Activities Kit,* and *American Art Appreciation Activities Kit* have also been published by Prentice Hall or its subsidiaries.

ABOUT THIS RESOURCE

This book of lists is a resource where one can quickly find information about specific artists, art materials, art history, museums, or disciplines. It is a general art reference book, and is basically *Everything You Always Wanted to Know About Art and Didn't Know Who to Ask* (and some things you didn't even *know* you didn't know).

Choices of lists were based on personal experiences as an art specialist. For example, as a substitute teacher every day for a full year, I appreciated having on hand some of the one-day lesson plans that are included here. As a university teacher of "Art for Elementary Teachers" I'm aware that these teachers may offer their students the only formal art experience they will ever have. I share research results with these teachers-in-training that show the positive impact of art in the curriculum on student achievement in other disciplines. As a beginning (and still learning art specialist), I remember what it is like to try to learn about materials and what one can do with them. As a traveler, my lists have to include interesting places and regional architecture. As an artist, I seem to continue to learn many things the hard way.

The book is written with many different purposes in mind. One is as a memory jogger. While there are probably few words and names in the vocabulary or pronunciation lists that are not familiar to teachers, these may serve to clarify when needed. The experienced art teacher knows that there is really nothing new in art—that it has all been done before. What is exciting about art though, is the creative interpretation students, colleagues, and fellow artists develop when they are working with traditional materials and techniques. Simple innovations sometimes give wildly new twists to the same old thing. Some of these original approaches to materials are listed in the *Things to Do* lists. For art teachers, these lists of activities and ideas in all media are so brief that they simply serve as reminders.

Of particular value to teachers of art, history, or interdisciplinary courses are the many reproducible pages such as the *Time Lines of Art and Culture, Egyptian, Chinese, and Japanese Dynasties, Elements and Principles of Art, Architectural Elements,* and *Careers in Art.* Tips on portfolio preparation, how to photograph artwork, writing for publication, and resources for art publications and materials are useful background information. Current art education theory is featured, including a sample lesson plan and grading criteria.

An effort has been made to include examples of artworks, architectural examples, museums, and cultural assets throughout the world and especially the North American continent. For art-minded travelers, these lists may give interesting "things to see" during holidays.

The book is divided into ten sections arranged in logical sequence, with the section *For the Teacher* near the front, and *Museums* at the rear. The introductory chapter, *All About Art* features lists of 100 Famous: Paintings, "Buildings," Photographs, Art Objects, and Sculptures. Other lists in that chapter are *What Did It Sell For?* (a list of auction prices for famous paintings), and resources for slides, posters, art publications, and materials. *Art History,* which is the basis for teaching art, is also near the front. Separate chapters: *Materials and Things to Do with Them, Painting, Sculpture, Architecture, New Technology* (such as photography, video, and the copy machine), *Folk Art and Crafts,* include vocabularies, materials and equipment, and suggestions for "Things to Do" in each of these media.

As an avid reader, I prefer a plot, but also find myself (when reading books on art) often going immediately to the back of a book to get information in list format. As a researcher and teacher of art history, I've tried to share the things that I have found to be profound, interesting, useful, and fun.

CONTENTS

SECTION 3   For the Art Teacher

SECTION 4   Art Materials and Things to Do with Them

SECTION 5   Painting, Drawing, and Printmaking

SECTION 6   Sculpture

SECTION 7   Architecture

SECTION 8   Fine Crafts and Folk Art

SECTION 9   Technology and Art: Photography, Video, Computer Graphics, and the Copy Machine

SECTION 10   Museums

SECTION 1
ALL ABOUT ART

List 1–1   Quotations About Art

"(Art is) . . . a product of the untalented, sold by the unprincipled to the utterly bewildered."

—AL CAPP, SPEAKING ON ABSTRACT ART

"Ah, good taste! What a dreadful thing! Taste is the enemy of creativeness."

—PABLO PICASSO

"Fine Art is that in which the hand, the head, and the heart of man go together."

—JOHN RUSKIN

"Of all lies, art is the least untrue."

—GUSTAVE FLAUBERT

"Sir, when their backsides look good enough to slap, there's nothing more to do."

—PETER PAUL RUBENS

"What garlic is to salad, insanity is to art."

—AUGUSTUS SAINT-GAUDENS

"The true function of art is to . . . edit nature and so make it coherent and lovely. The artist is a sort of impassioned proofreader, blue-penciling the bad spelling of God."

—H. L. MENCKEN

"Art doesn't transform. It just plain forms."

—ROY LICHTENSTEIN

"All the really good ideas I ever had came to me while I was milking a cow."

—GRANT WOOD

"My American image is made up of what I have come across, of what was 'there' in the time of my experience—no more, no less."

—THOMAS HART BENTON

"A man throws himself out of the fourth-floor window: if you can't make a sketch of him before he gets to the ground, you will never do anything big."

—EUGENE DELACROIX

"Any art communicates what you're in the mood to receive."

—LARRY RIVERS

"How important are the visual arts in our society? I feel strongly that the visual arts are of vast and incalculable importance. Of course I could be prejudiced. I *am* a visual art."

—KERMIT THE FROG

List 1–2   Art Definitions

Abstract Expressionism   a New York 1940s' painting movement that rarely featured a subject; sometimes called action painting

abstract   not realistic, though often based on an actual subject

academic art   art that follows proscribed rules; not experimental

acanthus   a plant with a large leaf, frequently represented on columns, friezes, and moldings

acrylic   pigment in a plastic binder medium; water-based paint that adheres to most surfaces

aerial perspective   the effect of distance or atmosphere shown through haziness or changes in color

aesthetic   the science of the beautiful in art; defined by visual, moral, social, and contemporary standards

alla prima   paint applied to canvas in one coat instead of applied layer by layer

altarpiece   a religious work of art placed behind the altar of a Christian church

American Scene Painting   (usually) paintings of the rural Midwest during the 1920s and 1930s

analogous colors   colors closely related on a color wheel, e.g., red, red–orange, yellow

ankh   Egyptian symbol for life

applied art   design principles applied to functional objects such as furniture and metalwork

aquatint   an etching technique consisting of sprinkling a metal plate with powdered resin and heating it to adhere, creating a dense or lightly granulated effect

arabesque   decorative technique that uses curving plant forms; frequently used in Islamic art

archaic art   Greek sculpture or vases from 620 to c. 500 BC; ancient art

Armory Show   an exhibit in New York in 1913 that introduced Paris-based Modernism to America

Art Deco   applied design from the 1920s and 1930s derived from French, African, Aztec, and Chinese motifs

Art Nouveau   an 1890s' asymmetrical decorative style featuring sinuous forms based on objects found in nature

artifact   hand-made object that represents a particular culture or period

Arts and Crafts movement   a return to the hand-made decorative arts during the 1930s

Ash Can school   paintings of everyday life in the city done by a group of painters of realism

asymmetrical   different on either side of a central axis

atmospheric perspective   (in painting) the change in color of objects in the distance

avant garde   at the forefront of new developments in art

balance   equilibrium in a composition, either symmetrical or asymmetrical

Barbizon school   French landscape artists who worked near Barbizon, France, c. 1835–1870

baren   a flat, round Japanese device that is used in printmaking in lieu of a mechanical press

Baroque   detailed, swirling composition, diagonal lines, unusual viewpoints; period from mid-sixteenth to mid-eighteenth centuries

bas-relief   low-relief sculpture that projects slightly from a background

basilica   a long building that today is used as a Christian church; in Roman times, a public place

bat   a block of plaster of Paris that clay is placed on to speed drying

batik   dyed textile or paper that has a wax resist pattern applied with molten wax

batten   a narrow, thin strip of wood used for a variety of purposes in art, e.g., ceramics or framing

Bauhaus   a design school that existed in Weimar, Germany, from 1919 to 1933 until it was closed by the Nazis

Beaux-arts   a tradition of the nineteenth and twentieth centuries following principles of the French Academy

bench-hook   a wood or metal device to prevent linoleum from slipping while it is being cut

biomorphic   art based on irregular abstract forms found in nature

bisque (or biscuit ware)   dull, fired ceramic clay before glazing

List 1–2 Continued

Blaue Reiter, Der (The Blue Rider)   a group of avant-garde German Expressionists

blockbook   fifteenth-century books in which the text and illustration were cut from the same block of wood

Book of Hours   illuminated Medieval books with prayers for specific times of the day

Book of the Dead   painting and hieroglyphics on a papyrus scroll, placed in an Egyptian tomb

brayer   a rubber roller used to apply ink in printmaking

breakfast piece   seventeenth-century Dutch still life that showed an interrupted meal

bronze   an alloy of copper and tin used for sculpture

Brücke, Die (The Bridge)   German Expressionist painters from Dresden working c. 1905

burin   an engraving tool with a diamond shape for carving deep lines in metal

burnish   to polish or rub to make something shiny

Byzantine   stylized religious art of the Eastern Roman Empire from 330–1453 AD

Calligraphic Expressionism   dripping or pouring paint onto a canvas

calligraphy   fine handwriting in ink with a quill, reed pen, or brush; follows specific rules or designs

camera obscura (dark room)   a darkened box used as a drawing aid in the sixteenth century

campanile   Italian word for a bell tower; sometimes freestanding such as *The Leaning Tower of Pisa*

caricature   character studies that usually exaggerate one or more features

cartoon   full-scale drawing for tapestry or wall painting; or a humorous or satirical drawing

cartouche   a lozenge shape that surrounds Egyptian names; or a frame of the same shape

carving   a subtractive method of sculpture; taking away wood or stone

caryatid   a carved female figure that substituted for a column to support a roof

casting   reproducing—in plaster, bronze, or plastic—an original piece of sculpture made of clay or a similar material

cave art   prehistoric art found in caves

Celtic art   art produced from c. 450 BC to c. 700 AD by the Celts; mostly portable objects

center-of-interest   the largest, lightest, darkest, or most important part of a composition

ceramic   any object made of clay and fired

chalice   a cup used in Christian observances that has a foot and a stem, often made of precious materials

chalk   calcium carbonate, used in gesso, mixed with colored pigment to make pastels

chiaroscuro   the use of light and shadow to create a focal point or mood

classical   originating in Greece and Rome; represents unadorned beauty

cloisonné   an Asian technique for fusing ground glass to a metal surface decorated with thin metal strips

codex   cut-sheet manuscript rather than a scroll; bound into book form

collage   a grouping of different textures, objects, and materials glued down

colonnade   a series of columns at regular intervals supporting a roof or arches

colossal order   freestanding or attached columns or pilasters that rise through several stories

column   round or square support for a roof

complementary colors   colors at the opposite sides of a color wheel, such as red/green or yellow/violet

composition   the manner in which the forms, lines, and colors of an artwork are arranged

Constructivists   a Russian group of artists who wished to reflect modern machinery and technology; working c. 1913

Contemporary art   generally defined as art produced during the second half of the twentieth century

conté   a chalk stick available in black, gray, white, bistre (brown), and sanguine (red)

contour   an outline drawing of a form or object

List 1–2   Continued

contrapposto   an S-curve or twist of the human figure caused by placing the weight on one foot

crenellation (battlement)   the upper story of a castle that has openings for archers alternating with solid walls

cromlech   a circle of upright stones (dolmens) such as *Stonehenge*

crosshatch   to create differences in value through a crossed series of parallel lines

Cubism   natural forms changed by geometrical reduction

cuneiform   characters written on clay tablets by the Mesopotamians; a precursor to hieroglyphics

design   the organization of line, form, color, value, texture, and space in an eye-pleasing arrangement

diptych   two painted panels that are usually hinged together

Doge   a ruler or governor of Venice and Genoa

dome   a vaulted roof, usually round or elliptical

donor   a client or patron of an artist who donates the work to an institution; in altarpieces the donor and family were often included in the painting

drawing   usually a work in pen, pencil, or charcoal on paper

dry-brush   a technique used with wet media applied with an almost-empty brush

drypoint   a printmaking method in which line is drawn with a sharp pointed tool, creating burrs on the printing plate

earthworks   a deliberate moving of earth and change in natural topography designed by artists

easel   a support for an artist's canvas during painting

eclecticism   the borrowing of a variety of styles from different sources and combining them

element   artistic design considerations such as color, line, texture, shape or form, and space

elongated   the deliberate vertical distortion of a figure; a form of stylization

embossing   to raise a relief design on the surface of paper through pressure

emphasis   a design principle that gives dominance to a particular area through color, size, or repetition

enamel   fuse glass powder to a metal surface through heating at high temperatures

encaustic   pigment mixed with melted wax and resin, then applied to a surface while hot

engraving   cutting a line into a metal or wood plate for printmaking

entablature (architrave, frieze, and cornice)   the structure above columns in Classical architecture

etching   design scratched in a wax resist on a plate, then removing metal through immersing in an acid bath; used in printmaking

Expressionism   the painting of feelings, sometimes with recognizable images, often totally abstract

figure   the human or animal form used in creating art; e.g., figure-drawing

firing   placing ceramic ware into a special oven and heating at high temperatures until it is mature

foreshortening   the technique of distortion in perspective (e.g., of the human figure) in order for the subject to appear three-dimensional

fresco   the technique of painting into freshly laid plaster; e.g., *The Sistine Chapel*

frieze   the decoratively carved or painted band at the top of a wall

frottage   textural rubbing on paper done with crayon, oil, or pencil

Futurism   an Italian art movement that tries to show the rapid movement of machinery

genre   a form of realistic painting of people that depicts ordinary events of the day; not religious, historical, or mythological

gesso   an underpainting medium made of glue, plaster of Paris or chalk, and water

gild   a thin coat of gold leaf applied to the surface of a painting, frame, or architecture

glaze   (in ceramics) a glass-like coating that makes ceramics waterproof; (in painting) to build up transparent layers of paint

List 1–2   Continued

golden section   a proportion (in painting) of roughly 8 to 13 that was considered by Renaissance masters to express perfect visual harmony

Gothic   all medieval art produced during the period between mid-twelfth and early fifteenth centuries

gouache   a watercolor medium made more brilliant by the addition of finely ground white pigment

grisaille (literally gray)   a painting in shades of gray, sometimes on the outside of an altarpiece

highlight   a light area that represents the reflection of light (as in the eye of a model)

horizon line   the distant view where sky meets water or land at the artist's eye level

Iconic Expressionism   a style in which the painting is dominated by a form, usually centralized

illumination   the decoration of manuscript pages, often with gold leaf and brilliant colors

illustration   an artwork developed to accompany a story, advertisement, or written text

impasto   the thick, textured build-up of a picture's surface through repeated applications of paint

Impressionism   an outdoor painting technique that shows the changing effects of light and color

intaglio   damp paper pressed into the inked etched or engraved lines of a metal printing plate

Italian Renaissance   revival of classical art, literature, and learning based on humanism

kitsch   artwork, often mass-produced, that goes beyond good taste

kore   stiffly standing archaic Greek female sculpture, clothed

kouros   archaic Greek male figure, unclothed

landscape   a scenery painting; also includes the cityscape or seascape

linear perspective   a technical system that allows depth to be shown on a two-dimensional surface

lithography   a printmaking method in which a metal plate or stone is drawn on with an oily crayon that resists water, while holding the ink for printing

lost-wax (cire perdue)   a method of creating a wax mold of a sculpture, then heating the mold to melt out the wax, and replacing it with molten metal

maquette   a small three-dimensional model for a larger piece of sculpture

mandorla   an almond-shaped background, enclosing the figure of a sacred figure in a *glory* of light

medium   the material that is used in an artwork; e.g., watercolor, oil, pastel

megalith   a block of stone basically unchanged, but sometimes arranged in lines or circles of standing stones

mihrab   a small niche in a mosque wall (qibla) that shows the direction of Mecca

mobile/stabile   terms coined to describe work created by Alexander Calder: the *mobile* is a hanging, movable sculpture; the *stabile* rests on the ground, but may also have moving parts

modeling   (in sculpture) transforming clay or wax into a form; (in painting) varying the colors to suggest a three-dimensional quality

monochromatic   a color scheme that involves different values of a single color

monotype   a method of printmaking done by applying pigment to glass, metal, or plastic and transferring to paper

mosaic   design or picture created by imbedding stones or pieces of glass on a floor, vault, or wall

mural   a continuous painting made to fill a wall

naturalism   reality-based painting

nonobjective   an abstract artwork not based on anything in reality

odalisque   term used to refer to a painted reclining woman, from the word for a Turkish harem slave

oil paint   a powdered pigment held together with oil

onion dome   a bulbous, pointed dome frequently seen in Byzantine architecture

palette   a board on which an artist mixes paints; certain colors used by a specific artist

List 1–2   Continued

papyrus   marsh plant from which paper was first made in Egypt; a scroll painted on this material

parchment   thin tanned animal hide (often kid or lamb), used for illuminated manuscripts

pastel   pigment held together with a binder and pressed into stick form (dry or oil-pastel)

perspective   a formal method of creating a three-dimensional effect on a two-dimensional surface

pigment   powdered earth, minerals, and chemicals, ground and mixed with a binder such as oil

plein air   loose, fluid painting done outdoors, capturing effects of light and air

pointillism (divisionism)   the application of pure color in small dots, allowing the eye to mix (such as red and blue dots side by side, which the eye sees as violet)

polychrome   many colored

polyptych   a painting that consists of more than three panels hinged together

Pop Art   objects from commercial art and the popular culture transformed into artworks

primary colors   red, yellow, and blue; may be mixed to make other colors but cannot themselves be mixed from other colors

print   a work of art (usually on paper) created from a "plate" that has been transformed through a technique such as engraving, etching, or woodcut and then inked and transferred to paper

Psalter   a book of Psalms thought to have been written by King David

putti   nude male infants, often with wings, used in Classical and Renaissance painting; cherubs

realism   an artist's attempt to portray a subject as accurately as possible

romanticism   a type of painting that idealizes images; often with surrealistic or imaginative compositions

saturated color   hues undiluted with white, consequently deep and intense

secondary colors   green, violet, and orange; the colors obtained by mixing primary colors

sfumato   a soft, smoky, hazy appearance with blurred images

stenciling   applying paint to a wall or cloth surface through a hole cut in metal or oiled cardboard

still-life (nature morte)   a composition featuring inanimate objects such as food or flowers and vases

stylize   to abstract a form, leaving it simpler, yet recognizable

tempera   pigment, mixed with water or egg yolk to apply

tenebrism   an effect such as chiaroscuro, with most figures in shadow, yet others in a shaft of light

texture   the tactile quality of the surface

tone   harmony in colors and values in an artwork

tracery   decorative ornamental stone or wood patterns used between pieces of glass or on walls

triptych   a painting done in three sections hinged together

trompe l'oeil (fool the eye)   a painting so real that you want to touch the objects

values   differences in the lightness or darkness of a hue

vanishing point   a term used in perspective; all lines lead to this point which may be on or off the canvas

vellum   thinned calf-hide, prepared for writing

wash   pigment diluted with water and applied to a painting surface to give a translucent effect

watercolor   pigment mixed with a binder and applied with water to give a transparent effect

woodcut   a print made when the surface of a block of wood is transformed through cutting, then inked and transferred to paper

List 1–3   Pronunciation Guide

ARTISTS

Albers, Josef: **al** burrs, josef

Bosch, Hieronymus: bosh, her **on** i mus

Botticelli, Sandro: bot tee **chel** lee, **san** dro

Boucher, François: boo **shay,** frahn swah

Braque, Georges: brock, zhorzh

Brueghel, Pieter: **Broy** ghel, peter

Caravaggio, Michelangelo: car a **vod** jo, mike el an jel o

Cezanne, Paul: say **zan,** paul

Chagall, Marc: shah **gall,** mark

Chardin, Jean Baptiste: shar **dan,** zhon bahteese

Chirico, Giorgio de: **kee ree** co, georgee-o dee

Dali, Salvador: **dah** lee, sal va dor

Daumier, Honore: dough mee eh, on o ray

David, Jacques Louis: dah **veed,** zhock loo ee

Degas, Edgar: day **gah,** ed gar

Delacroix, Eugene: della crwah, u-gen

Dufy, Raoul: doo **fee,** rah ool

Durer, Albrecht: **dure** er, al brekt

Eyck, Jan van: ike, yon van

Fragonard, Jean Honore: frag o nar, zhan on o ray

Gauguin, Paul: go **ganh,** paul

Gericault, Jean Louis: **zhay** ree co, zhon loo ee

Giorgeone: george **oh** nay

Giotto di Bondone: **jot** toe dee bon doe nee

Gogh, Vincent van: go, vin cent van

Goya, Francisco de: **goy** ah, frahn cees co day

Greco, El: **greck** o, ell

Gris, Juan: greece, whahn

Grunewald, Mathis: **grewn** vahlt, **mah** tis

Holbein, Hans: **hole** byne, hahns

Ingres: **ann g**'r

Klee, Paul, clay, paul

Kokoschka, Oskar: ko **kosh** ka, oh-scar

Kollwitz, Kathe: **call** vits, ka ty

Leonardo da Vinci: lay o **nar** doe da vin chee

Leyster, Judith: **lie** ster, **joo** dith

Manet, Edouard: mah **nay,** aid wahr

Mantegna, Andrea: mon **tane** ya, an dray a

Martini, Simone: mar **tee** nee, see mon ee

Massaccio: ma **sotch** o

Matisse, Henri: mah **teess,** on ree

Medici, Giuliano de: **may** de chee, jool **yah** no de

Medici: **may** de chee

Michelangelo (Buonarroti): mee chel **an** jel o (bwoe na **rot** tee)

Millet, Jean Francois: mill **ay,** zhahn frahn swah

Mondrian, Piet: moan dree **ahn,** peet

Monet, Claude: mo **nay,** clowd

Picasso, Pablo: pea **kass** o, pab lo

Pollaiuolo, Antonio: paul eye woe lo, an **tone** ee o

Poussin, Nicolas: poos **an,** neek o lahs

Raphael: rafe ee ul

Redon, Odilon: r'dawn, o dee lawn

Renoir, Pierre-Auguste: ren **wahr,** pee air-oh **goost**

Rivera, Diego: ree **vay** ra, dee ay go

Rouault, Georges: roo **oh,** zhorzh

Rousseau, Henri: roo **sew,** on ree

Ruisdael, Jakob van: ryes **doll,** yah cob van

Seurat, Georges: sir ah, zhorgh

Toulouse Lautrec, Henri de: too **looze** low trek, on ree de

Velazquez, Diego: vay **las** kez: dee **ay** go

Vermeer, Jan: ver **mare,** yahn

Warhol, Andy: **wohr** hohl, andy

Watteau, Jean Antoine: wah **toe,** zhon on twon

TECHNIQUES

casein, case-een

chine collé: sheen cole ay

cloisonné: cloy zon **nay**

gesso: jess o

gouache: gwahsh

intaglio: in **towl** yo

trompe l'oeil: trome **p'loil**

MISCELLANEOUS

Art Nouveau: ar **nu** vo

Bauhaus: **bough** house

Beaux-Art: bows ar

Champs Elysees: shahns ay lee **zay**

chiaroscuro: key **are** o skoo ro

douanier: dwahn yay

fauve: fove

genre: **jahn** reh

magi: may-jigh

Notre Dame: notrah dahm

objet d'art: obe **zhay** d ar

plein air: play-**nair**

putti: **put** ti

List 1–3   Continued

MISCELLANEOUS (cont.)

Savonarola: sav o na roll a
sfumato: sfoo **mah** to
triptych: **trip** tick
Uffizi: you **feet** zee

TITLES OF PAINTINGS

Der Blaue Reiter: dehr blah way right er
Grand Jatte La: grahnd **jhot**
Guernica: **gwere** nee ka
Icarus: **ik** are us
Lascaux: lass **ko**

Las Meninas: lahs men een yahss
Les Demoiselles d'Avignon: lay dem wah zel **dahv** een yone
Mona Lisa: moan a **lees** a
Montefeltro, Federigo da: mon te **fell** tro, fay day **ree** go dah
Mont Sainte-Victoire: mawn sant veek twah
Moulin Rouge: moo lan roozh
Pieta: pea eh **tah**
Primavera, La: pree ma **vay** ra lah
Sabine: **say** byne

List 1–4   Artists' Birthdays

JANUARY

1 Bartolomé Esteban Murillo, 1618
   Paul Revere, 1735
   Alfred Stieglitz, 1864
2 Ernst Barlach, 1870
3 August Macke, 1887
   Jack Levine, 1915
4 Marsden Hartley, 1877
5 Yves Tanguy, 1900
6 Gustave Doré, 1832
7 Albert Bierstadt, 1830
10 Barbara Hepworth, 1903
11 A. Sterling Calder, 1870
12 John Singer Sargent, 1856
   Jusepe Ribera, 1588
13 Jan van Goyen, 1596
14 Berthe Morisot, 1841
   Henri Fantin-Latour, 1836
18 Antoine Pevsner, 1886
19 Paul Cezanne, 1839
22 Francis Picabia, 1879
23 Edouard Manet, 1832
24 Robert Motherwell, 1915
26 Kees van Dongen, 1877
28 Jackson Pollock, 1912
   Claes Oldenburg, 1929
29 Barnett Newman, 1905
   Peter Voulkos, 1924
30 Bernardo Bellotto, 1720
31 Max Pechstein, 1881

FEBRUARY

1 Thomas Cole, 1801
3 Norman Rockwell, 1894
4 Fernand Leger, 1881
   Manuael Alvarez Bravo, 1902
8 Franz Marc, 1880
   John Ruskin, 1819
11 William H.F. Talbot, 1800
   Kazimir Malevich, 1878
12 Max Beckmann, 1884
   Eugene Atget, 1857
13 Grant Wood, 1892
15 Charles François Daubigny, 1817
17 Raphaelle Peale, 1774
18 Louis Comfort Tiffany, 1848
   Max Klinger, 1857
20 Elie Nadelman, 1882
   Ansel Adams, 1902
21 Constantin Brancusi, 1876
22 Rembrandt Peale, 1778
   Horace Pippin, 1888
23 Tom Wesselmann, 1931
24 Charles Le Brun, 1619
24 Winslow Homer, 1836
25 Pierre A. Renoir, 1841
26 Honoré Daumier, 1808
27 Joaquin Sorolla, 1863
   Marino Marini, 1901
29 Balthus, 1908

MARCH

1 Oscar Kokoschka, 1886
   August Saint-Gaudens, 1848
3 Arnold Newman, 1918
4 Sir Henry Raeburn, 1756
5 Giovanni Battista Tiepolo, 1696
6 Michelangelo Buonarroti, 1475
7 Piet Mondrian, 1872
   Milton Avery, 1893
8 Anthony Caro, 1924
9 David Smith, 1906
11 Charles Lock Eastlake, Jr., 1836
13 William Glackens, 1870
   Alexej von Jawlensky, 1864
14 Reginald Marsh, 1898
   Diane Arbus, 1923
16 Rosa Bonheur, 1822
17 Kate Greenaway, 1846
   François Girardon, 1628
18 Adam Elsheimer, 1578
19 Josef Albers, 1888
   Georges de La Tour, 1593
   Albert Pinkham Ryder, 1847
20 George C. Bingham, 1811
   Jean Antoine Houdon, 1741
21 Hans Hofmann, 1880
22 Anthony van Dyck, 1599
   John Frederick Kensett, 1816
23 Juan Gris, 1887
24 John Smibert, 1688
   William Morris, 1834
   Edward Weston, 1886
25 Gutzon Borglum, 1867
27 Ludwig Mies van der Rohe, 1886
   Edward Steichen, 1879
28 Grace Hartigan, 1922
30 Francisco de Goya, 1746
   Vincent van Gogh, 1853
31 William Morris Hunt, 1824
   John La Farge, 1835

APRIL

2 Max Ernst, 1891
3 Henry van de Velde, 1863
4 Grinling Gibbons, 1648
   Edward Hicks, 1780
5 Jean Honoré Fragonard, 1732
6 Raphael, 1483
   Gustave Moreau, 1826
   René Lalique, 1860
7 Gerard Dou, 1613
8 Cornelis de Heem, 1631
9 Eadweard Muybridge, 1830
   Victor Vasarely, 1908
10 Kenneth Noland, 1924
11 Gustav Vigeland, 1869
12 Robert Delaunay, 1885
   Imogen Cunningham, 1883
13 Thomas Jefferson, 1743
   James Ensor, 1860
15 Leonardo da Vinci, 1452
   Charles Willson Peale, 1841
   Theodore Rousseau, 1812
16 Elisabeth Vigee-Le Brun, 1755
18 Max Weber, 1881
   Ludwig Meidner, 1884
20 Joan Miró, 1893
   Daniel Chester French, 1850
22 Odilon Redon, 1840
23 J.M.W. Turner, 1775
24 Willem de Kooning, 1904
   Bridget Riley, 1931
25 Karel Appel, 1921
   Cy Twombly, 1928
26 Eugene Delacroix, 1798
   Dorothea Lange, 1895
27 Samuel F.B. Morse, 1791

MAY

1 Benjamin Henry Latrobe, 1764
   George Inness, 1825
4 Frederic Edwin Church, 1826
6 Ernst Kirchner, 1880
8 Alphonse Legros, 1837
13 Joseph Stella, 1877
   Georges Braque, 1882
15 Jasper Johns, 1930
18 Walter Gropius, 1883
19 Jacob Jordaens, 1593
   Gaston Lachaise, 1882
20 William Thornton, 1759
21 Albrecht Durer, 1471
   Henri Rousseau, 1844
22 Mary Cassatt, 1844
   Marisol, 1930
23 Franz Kline, 1910
24 Emanuel Leutze, 1816
25 Wil Barnet, 1911
27 Georges Rouault, 1871
30 Alexander Archipenko, 1887
31 Ellsworth Kelly, 1923

JUNE

1 Red Grooms, 1937
3 Raoul Dufy, 1877
5 Thomas Chippendale, 1718
6 Diego Velasquez, 1599
  John Trumbull, 1756
7 Paul Gauguin, 1848
8 Sir John Everett Millais, 1829
  Frank Lloyd Wright, 1867
9 Pieter Saenredam, 1597
10 Gustave Courbet, 1819
  André Derain, 1880
11 John Constable, 1776
  Julia Margaret Cameron, 1815
12 Annie Albers, 1899
13 Christo, 1935
14 Margaret Bourke-White, 1906
16 Jim Dine, 1935
17 Charles Eames, 1907
18 Robert W. Weir, 1803
19 Thomas Sully, 1783
20 Kurt Schwitters, 1887
21 Henry Tanner, 1859
23 Carl Milles, 1875
24 Robert Henri, 1865
25 Sam Francis, 1923
  Antonio Gaudi, 1852
27 Philip Guston, 1913
28 Peter Paul Rubens, 1577
29 Robert Laurent, 1890

JULY

2 André Kertész, 1894
3 John Singleton Copley, 1738
  Jean Dubuffet, 1901
4 William Rush, 1756
5 Jean Cocteau, 1889
7 Marc Chagall, 1887
8 Käthe Kollwitz, 1867
9 David Hockney, 1937
10 Camille Pissarro, 1830
  J.M. Whistler, 1834
  Georgio de Chirico, 1888
12 Amedeo Modigliani, 1884
  Andrew Wyeth, 1917
14 Gustav Klimt, 1862
15 Rembrandt Harmensz van Rijn, 1606
16 Sir Joshua Reynolds, 1723
  Charles Sheeler, 1883
17 Camille Corot, 1796
  Lyonel Feininger, 1871
  Berenice Abbott, 1898
18 Gertrude Käsebier, 1852
19 Edgar Degas, 1834
20 Lazló Moholy-Nagy, 1895
22 Edward Hopper, 1882
  Alexander Calder, 1898
24 Alex Katz, 1927
25 Thomas Eakins, 1844
26 George Catlin, 1796
  George Grosz, 1893
28 Beatrix Potter, 1866
  Marcel Duchamp, 1887
29 Hiram Powers, 1805
  Eastman Johnson, 1824
30 Giorgio Vasari, 1511
  Henry Moore, 1898
31 Erich Heckel, 1883

AUGUST

2 John Sloan, 1871
  Arthur Dove, 1880
4 John Twachtman, 1853
5 George Tooker, 1920
  Naum Gabo, 1890
7 Emile Nolde, 1867

AUGUST (cont.)

8 Andy Warhol, 1931
10 William M. Harnett, 1848
  Reuben Nakian, 1897
11 Martin Johnson Heade, 1819
12 George Bellows, 1882
13 George Luks, 1867
17 Larry Rivers, 1923
19 Gustave Caillebotte, 1848
  Bradley Walker Tomlin, 1899
20 Eliel Saarinen, 1873
  Eero Saarinen, 1910
21 Asher Durand, 1796
  Aubrey Beardsley, 1872
22 Jacques Lipchitz, 1891
  Henri Cartier-Bresson, 1908
24 George Stubbs, 1724
  Alphonse Mucha, 1860
27 Man Ray, 1890
28 Morris Graves, 1910
29 J.A.D. Ingres, 1780
30 Jacques Louis David, 1748
  Theo van Doesburg, 1883
31 Georg Jensen, 1866

SEPTEMBER

1 Yasuo Kuniyoshi, 1893
2 Romare Bearden, 1914
3 Louis Sullivan, 1856
4 Oskar Schlemmer, 1888
6 Horatio Greenough, 1805
7 Grandma Moses, 1860
  Jacob Lawrence, 1917
10 Sir John Soane, 1753
12 Ben Shahn, 1898
13 Robert Indiana, 1928
15 Antoine Louis Barye, 1795
16 Jean Arp, 1887
  Carl André, 1935
18 Mark de Suvero, 1933
21 Hans Hartung, 1904
23 Paul Delvaux, 1897
25 Francesco Borromini, 1599
  Mark Rothko, 1903
26 Theodore Gericault, 1791
  Lewis W. Hine, 1874
28 Caravaggio, 1573
  Frederick William MacMonnies, 1863
29 François Boucher, 1703

OCTOBER

1 Claes Berchem, 1620
  Larry Poons, 1937
3 Pierre Bonnard, 1867
4 Giovanni Battista Piranesi, 1720
  Jean François Millet, 1814
  Frederick Remington, 1861
6 LeCorbusier, 1887
9 Frank Duveneck, 1848
10 Antoine Watteau, 1684
  Benjamin West, 1738
  Alberto Giacometti, 1901
12 Al Held, 1928
15 John Vanderlyn, 1775
  Ralph Blakelock, 1847
17 Childe Hassam, 1859
18 Canaletto, 1697
19 Umberto Boccioni, 1882
20 Aelbert Cuyp, 1620
  Sir Christopher Wren, 1632
21 Katsushika Hokusai, 1760
22 Robert Rauschenberg, 1925
25 Pablo Picasso, 1881
  Arshile Gorky, 1904
27 Roy Lichtenstein, 1923

OCTOBER (cont.)

28 Andrea della Robbia, 1435
  Francis Bacon, 1909
30 Alfred Sisley, 1839
31 Jan Vermeer, 1632
  Meindert Hobbema, 1638
  Richard Morris Hunt, 1827

NOVEMBER

1 Benvenuto Cellini, 1500
  Antonio Canova, 1757
2 Jean Baptiste Chardin, 1699
3 Walker Evans, 1903
4 Gerrit van Honthorst, 1590
5 Philips Koninck, 1619
  Washington Allston, 1779
  Raymond Duchamp-Villon, 1876
7 Francisco de Zurbaran, 1598
8 Charles Demuth, 1883
9 Stanford White, 1853
10 William Hogarth, 1697
  Sir Jacob Epstein, 1880
11 Paul Signac, 1863
  Edouard Vuillard, 1868
12 Auguste Rodin, 1840
14 Claude Monet, 1840
  John Steuart Curry, 1897
15 Georgia O'Keeffe, 1887
  Wayne Thiebaud, 1920
17 Agnolo Bronzino, 1503
  Isamu Noguchi, 1904
18 Louis Daguerre, 1787
20 Paulus Potter, 1625
21 René Magritte, 1898
23 José Orozco, 1883
24 Henri de Toulouse-Lautrec, 1864
  Cass Gilbert, 1859
26 George Segal, 1924
27 José de Creeft, 1884
28 William Blake, 1757
  Morris Louis, 1912
29 James Rosenquist, 1933
30 Andrea Palladio, 1508
  Adriaen van de Velde, 1636

DECEMBER

2 Georges Seurat, 1859
  Otto Dix, 1891
3 Gilbert Stuart, 1755
4 Wassily Kandinsky, 1866
5 Walt Disney, 1901
6 Frederic Bazille, 1841
7 Gian Lorenzo Bernini, 1598
  Stuart Davis, 1894
8 Aristide Maillol, 1861
  Diego Rivera, 1886
9 Roy deCarava, 1919
10 Adriaen Van Ostade, 1610
11 Mark Tobey, 1890
12 Edvard Munch, 1863
  Helen Frankenthaler, 1928
15 David Teniers II, 1610
  George Romney, 1734
  Oscar Niemeyer, 1907
17 Paul Cadmus, 1904
18 Willem van de Velde II, 1633
  Paul Klee, 1879
20 Pieter de Hooch, 1629
21 Masaccio, 1401
22 Max Bill, 1908
23 John Marin, 1870
24 Joseph Cornell, 1903
  Ad Reinhardt, 1913
25 Paul Manship, 1885
  Raphael Soyer, 1899
30 W. Eugene Smith, 1918
31 Henri Matisse, 1869

List 1–5   Elements of Art

Line

Line is the path of a moving point. Following are some variations in line:

vertical   horizontal   diagonal   curved   angular   zig zag   bent

straight   interrupted   thick   thin   parallel   cross-hatched   spiral

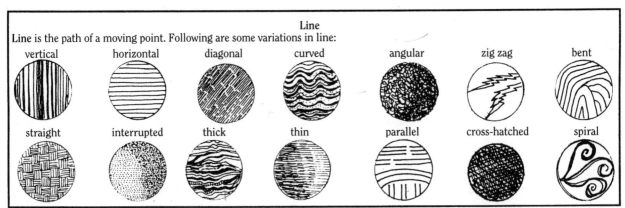

Form: 3-D: height, width, and depth
Shape: 2-D: the area enclosed by an outline

realistic
geometric
abstract form
idealized form
naturalistic
nonrepresentational
amorphous form
biomorphic

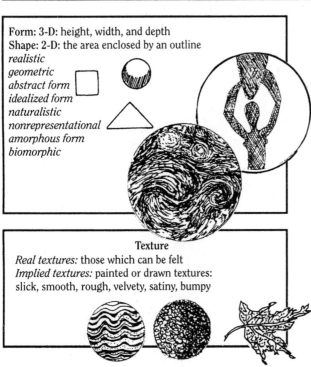

Texture

Real textures: those which can be felt
Implied textures: painted or drawn textures:
slick, smooth, rough, velvety, satiny, bumpy

Value

Value: differences in a hue or neutral ranging from the lightest to the darkest, for example, white to black.

Space

Space organizes elements in a composition.

shallow: *actual:*
little perspective   control of size, color, overlapping

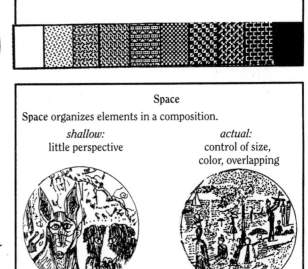

Color

Hue
pure color

primary colors
red, blue, yellow

secondary colors
violet, orange, green

complementary colors
opposites on color wheel

Color Wheel

analogous colors
side by side

cool colors
violet, green, blue

warm colors
red, yellow, orange

neutral colors
gray, black, white, brown

monochromatic
variations of one hue

Tone
grayed color

Shade
hue plus black

Tint
hue plus white

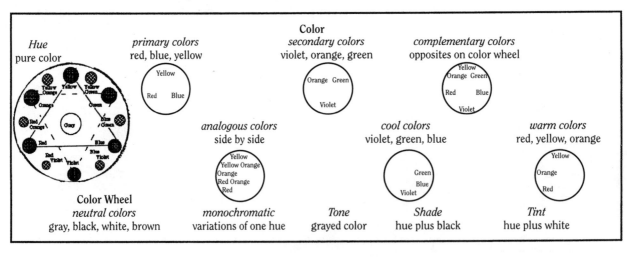

List 1–6   Principles of Design

According to National Visual Arts Standards, the principles of design are: repetition, balance, emphasis, contrast, and unity.

Repetition

Repetition is the use of line, color, or a motif, in more than one place in a compostion.
Pattern is created through a repetitious use of the same element to create an overall design.

Rythm is the repeated use of similar elements such as color, line, or shape—the smooth transition from one part to another.

Balance

Balance is the equillibrium of various elements in the work of art.
symmetrical or formal balance. equal balance on each side of an imaginary middle line.
asymetrical or informal balance. balance achieved through unequal distribution on each side of an imaginary middle line

Emphasis

Emphasis is given to a center-of-interest, which might be the largest, brightest, or lightest subject.

Contrast

Contrast shows differences between the elements of art, which are: line, color, shape, value, space, and texture.

Unity

Unity is the harmony of all the visual elements in a composition.
Proportion is the pleasing relationship of all parts to each other and to the whole of the design.
Variety consists of differences in scale, surface, line, value, and shape that give interest to a composition.

List 1–7   100 Famous Paintings

A "Top 100" list is based on the opinions of many writers and art historians. Paintings may be the artist's most famous painting rather than his or her "best." Some artists whose lifework includes many acknowledged masterpieces may have only one listed. It is not possible, of course, to include all the works that deserve to be on such a list.

1. Arcimboldo, Giuseppe, *Winter,* 1563, Kunsthistorisches Museum, Vienna
2. artist unknown, *The Ascension of Mohammed,* 1539, British Library, London
3. artist(s) unknown, *Lascaux Cave,* c. 15,000–13,000 BC, Lascaux, France
4. Beckmann, Max, *Acrobats,* 1939, St. Louis Art Museum, Missouri
5. Bellini, *The Doge,* c. 1501, National Gallery, London
6. Bonheur, Rosa, *The Horse Fair,* 1853–1855, Metropolitan Museum of Art, New York City
7. Bosch, Hieronymus, *The Garden of Earthly Delights,* 1500, Prado, Madrid
8. Botticelli, Sandro, *Birth of Venus,* c. 1480, Uffizi Gallery, Florence
9. Botticelli, Sandro, *Primavera,* 1477–1478, Uffizi Gallery, Florence
10. Brueghel, Pieter, *Peasant Dance,* c. 1567–1568, Kunsthistorisches Museum, Vienna

Drawn from *American Gothic,* 1930, Grant Wood, The Art Institute of Chicago

11. Brueghel, Pieter, *The Blue Cloak (Netherlandish Proverbs),* 1599, State Museum, Berlin
12. Campin, Robert (Master of Flemalle?), *The Merode Altarpiece,* c. 1425–1428, Metropolitan Museum of Art, New York City
13. Caravaggio, Michelangelo de, *Bacchus,* 1589, Uffizi Gallery, Florence
14. Caravaggio, Michelangelo de, *Calling of St. Matthew,* c. 1599–1600, S. Luigi dei Francesi, Rome
15. Cassatt, Mary, *Emmie and Her Child,* 1889, Wichita Art Museum, Kansas
16. Cezanne, Paul, *Mont Sainte-Victoire,* 1885–1887, Metropolitan Museum of Art, New York City
17. Cimabue, (Cenni di Peppi), *The Madonna of the Angels,* c. 1275, Louvre, Paris
18. Clouet, Jean, *Portrait of Francis I,* 1524, Louvre, Paris
19. Copley, John Singleton, *Brook Watson and the Shark,* 1782, Detroit Institute of Arts, Michigan
20. Courbet, Gustave, *The Artist's Studio,* 1855, Musée d'Orsay, Paris
21. Cranach, Lucas, *Adam and Eve,* 1528, Uffizi Gallery, Florence
22. Daumier, Honore, *The Third-Class Carriage,* c. 1862, Metropolitan Museum of Art, New York City
23. David, Jacques Louis, *Death of Marat,* 1793, Musées Royaux des Beaux-Arts de Belgique, Brussels
24. Degas, Edgar, *The Glass of Absinthe,* 1876, Musée d'Orsay, Paris
25. de Kooning, Willem, *Woman II,* 1952, Museum of Modern Art, New York City
26. Delacroix, Eugene, *Liberty Leading the People,* 1830, Louvre, Paris
27. Demuth, Charles, *I Saw the Figure 5 in Gold,* 1928, Metropolitan Museum of Art, New York City
28. Duchamp, Marcel, *Nude Descending a Staircase #2,* 1912, Philadelphia Museum of Art, Pennsylvania
29. Durer, Albrecht, *Self Portrait in a Fur Coat,* 1471, Alte Pinakothek, Munich
30. Dyck, Anthony van, *Portrait of Charles I at the Hunt,* 1635, National Gallery, London
31. Eddy, Don, *New Shoes for H,* 1973–1974, Cleveland Museum of Art, Ohio
32. Eyck, Jan van, *Giovanni Arnolfini and His Bride,* 1434, National Gallery, London
33. Eyck, Jan van, *The Mystic Lamb Altarpiece,* 1432, Church of St. Bavo, Ghent, Belgium
34. Flack, Audrey, *Marilyn* (Monroe), 1977, University of Arizona Museum of Art, Tucson
35. Gainsborough, Thomas, *Jonathan Buttall: The Blue Boy,* c. 1770, Henry E. Huntington Library and Art Gallery, San Marino, California
36. Gauguin, Paul, *Fatata te Miti* (By the Sea), 1892, National Gallery of Art, Washington, DC

List 1–7   Continued

37. Gericault, Theodore, *The Raft of the Medusa,* 1818–1819, Louvre, Paris
38. Ghirlandaio, Domenico, *An Old Man and His Grandson,* c. 1480, Louvre, Paris
39. Giorgeone (Barbarelli), *Pastoral Concert,* c. 1510, Louvre, Paris
40. Giotto (di Bondone), *Arena Chapel,* 1305–1306, Padua, Italy
41. Goes, Hugo van der, *Portinari Altarpiece,* 1476, Uffizi Gallery, Florence
42. Gogh, Vincent van, *Irises,* 1889, Metropolitan Museum of Art, New York City
43. Gogh, Vincent van, *The Starry Night,* 1888–1889, Museum of Modern Art, New York City
44. Goya, Francisco, *Naked Maja, Clothed Maja,* 1800, Prado, Madrid
45. Goya, Francisco, *The Executions of the 3rd of May,* 1808, Prado, Madrid
46. Greco, El, *View of Toledo,* 1600–1610, Metropolitan Museum of Art, New York City
47. Hals, Frans, *The Jolly Toper,* 1627, Rijksmuseum, Amsterdam
48. Harnett, William Michael, *After the Hunt,* 1885, California Palace of the Legion of Honor, San Francisco
49. Hobbema, Meindert, *A View on the High Road,* 1665, National Gallery, London
50. Hokusai, Katsushika, *The Great Wave Off Kanagawa,* 1823–1829, Metropolitan Museum of Art, New York City
51. Holbein, Hans, *The Ambassadors,* 1533, National Gallery, London
52. Homer, Winslow, *Inside the Bar, Tynemouth,* 1883, Metropolitan Museum of Art, New York City
53. Hopper, Edward, *Early Sunday Morning,* 1930, Whitney Museum of American Art, New York City
54. Ingres, Jean-Auguste-Dominique, *Napoleon on His Throne,* 1806, Musée de l'Armee, Paris
55. Johns, Jasper, *Target with Four Faces,* 1955, Museum of Modern Art, New York City
56. Kahlo, Frida, *Self Portrait with Monkey and Parrot,* 1942, Collection of IBM Corp., Armonk, New York
57. Leonardo da Vinci, *Mona Lisa,* 1503–1506, Louvre, Paris
58. Leonardo da Vinci, *The Last Supper,* c. 1495, Santa Maria delle Grazie, Milan
59. Lichtenstein, Roy, *Mural with Blue Brushstroke,* 1986, Equitable Life Assurance Society Building, New York City
60. Lorenzetti, Ambrogio, *Good Government in the City,* 1338–1340, Palazzo Pubblico, Sienna
61. Manet, Edouard, *Bar at the Folies Bergere,* 1882, Courtauld Institute, London
62. Manet, Edouard, *Le Dejeuner sur l'Herbe* (Luncheon on the Grass), 1863, Musée d'Orsay, Paris
63. Martini, Simone, *Christ Carrying the Cross,* c. 1340, Louvre, Paris
64. Masaccio, Tomaso, *The Tribute Money,* 1427, Santa Maria del Carmine, Florence
65. Matisse, *Luxe, Calme et Volupte,* 1904–1905, Musée d'Orsay, Paris
66. Matisse, *The Dance,* 1909–1910, The Hermitage, St. Petersburg, Russia
67. Memling, Hans, *Shrine of St. Ursula,* c. 1430, St. Jan's Hospice, Bruges, Belgium
68. Michelangelo, *Sistine Chapel,* 1508–1512, Vatican, Rome
69. Mondrian, Piet, *Composition with Red, Yellow and Blue,* 1922, Rijksmuseum, Amsterdam
70. Monet, Claude, *Impression Sunrise—Le Havre,* 1872, Musée Marmottan, Paris
71. Monet, Claude, *Rouen Cathedral, Sunset,* 1905, Museum of Fine Arts, Boston, Massachusetts
72. Munch, Edvard, *The Scream,* 1893, National Gallery, Oslo, Norway
73. Picasso, Pablo, *Guernica,* 1937, Prado, Madrid
74. Picasso, Pablo, *Les Demoiselles d'Avignon,* 1907, Museum of Modern Art, New York City
75. Pollock, Jackson, *Number 1 (Lavender Mist),* 1950, National Gallery of Art, Washington, DC
76. Raphael, *School of Athens,* 1510–1511, Stanza della Segnatura, Vatican, Rome
77. Raphael, *The Alba Madonna,* c. 1509, National Gallery of Art, Washington, DC
78. Rembrandt Harmensz van Rijn, *The Night Watch,* 1642, Rijksmuseum, Amsterdam
79. Renoir, Auguste, *Luncheon of the Boating Party,* 1881, Phillips Collection, Washington, DC
80. Reynolds, Joshua, *Mrs. Siddons as the Tragic Muse,* c. 1789, Henry E. Huntington Library and Art Gallery, San Marino, California

List 1–7 Continued

81. Rivera, Diego, *The Liberation of the Peon,* 1931, Philadelphia Museum of Art, Pennsylvania
82. Rousseau, Henri, *The Dream,* 1910, Museum of Modern Art, New York City
83. Rubens, Peter Paul, *The Descent from the Cross,* c. 1612, Cathedral, Antwerp, Belgium
84. Ruisdael, Jacob van, *Mill at Wijk by Duurstede,* c. 1670, Rijksmuseum, Amsterdam
85. Sargent, John Singer, *Lady X,* 1884, Metropolitan Museum of Art, New York City
86. Seurat, Georges, *Sunday Afternoon on the Island of La Grande Jatte,* 1884–1886, Art Institute of Chicago, Illinois
87. Tanner, Henry Ossawa, *The Banjo Lesson,* c. 1893, Hampton Institute, Virginia
88. Titian, *Bacchus and Ariadne,* c. 1560, National Gallery, London
89. Toulouse-Lautrec, Henri, *The Moulin Rouge,* 1892, Art Institute of Chicago, Illinois
90. Tung Ch'i-ch'ang, *River and Mountains on a Clear Autumn Day,* 1555–1636, Nelson-Atkins Museum of Art, Kansas City, Missouri
91. Turner, J.M.W., *The Slave Ship,* 1840, Museum of Fine Arts, Boston, Massachusetts
92. Uccello, Paolo, *Battle of San Romano,* 1327, Uffizi Gallery, Florence
93. Velasquez, Diego, *Las Meninas,* 1656, Prado, Madrid
94. Vermeer, Jan, *Allegory of the Art of Painting,* c. 1670–1675, Kunsthistorisches Museum, Vienna
95. Watteau, Antoine, *Pilgrimage to Cythera,* 1717, Louvre, Paris
96. West, Benjamin, *The Death of General Wolfe,* 1770, National Gallery of Canada, Ottawa
97. Weyden, Rogier van der, *Descent from the Cross,* c. 1435, Prado, Madrid
98. Whistler, James McNeill, *Arrangement in Gray and Black No. 1: The Artist's Mother,* 1871, Louvre, Paris
99. Wood, Grant, *American Gothic,* 1930, Art Institute of Chicago, Illinois
100. Yen Li-Pen, *The Thirteen Emperors,* 7th century AD, Museum of Fine Arts, Boston, Massachusetts

Drawn from *Washington Crossing the Delaware,* 1851, Emanuel Gottlieb Levtz, Metropolitan Museum of Art, New York City

List 1–8   100 Famous Sculptures

These sculptures are among the hundreds of famous sculptures throughout the world, and are selected because they are representative of certain time periods in the history of sculpture.

1. Apollonius of Athens, *Apollo Belvedere,* 1st century BC, Vatican Museum, Rome
2. artist unknown, *Apollo of Veii,* c. 515–490 BC, Villa Giulia, Rome
3. artist unknown, *Boy Removing a Thorn* (Spinario), c. 200 BC–AD 27, Capitoline Museums, Rome
4. artist unknown, *Human-Headed Winged Lion,* 883–859 BC, Metropolitan Museum of Art, New York City
5. artist unknown, *Colossal Head, Olmec,* c. 800 BC, Museo de Antropologia, Jalapa, Mexico
6. artist unknown, *Buddha,* 386–535 AD, Louvre, Paris
7. artist unknown, *Calf Bearer,* c. 570 BC, Acropolis Museum, Athens
8. artist unknown, *Charioteer of Delphi,* c. 470 BC, Delphi, Greece
9. artist unknown, *Colossal Statues of Ramesses II,* 1275 BC, Abu Simbel, Egypt
10. artist(s) unknown, *Colossi of Memnon,* 1411–1375 BC, Egypt
11. artist unknown, *Constantine the Great,* c. AD 314, Capitoline Museums, Rome
12. artist unknown, *Cycladic Figure of a Seated Man Playing a Harp,* 2400–2200 BC, National Museum, Athens
13. artist(s) unknown, *The Descent of the River Ganges from Heaven,* 10th century AD, Mamallapuram, India
14. artist(s) unknown, *Elgin Marbles (Parthenon sculptures),* attributed to Phidias, c. 438–432 BC, British Museum, London
15. artist unknown, *Equestrian Statue of Marcus Aurelius,* AD 165, Capitoline Museums, Rome
16. artist unknown, *Four Horses,* c. 330 BC, Church of San Marco, Venice
17. artist unknown, *Gate of the Lions,* 1250 BC, Mycenae, Greece
18. artist unknown, *Gudea, King of Lagash,* 2141–2122 BC, British Museum, London
19. artist unknown, *Head of Queen Olokun,* Ife, c. 11th–15th centuries AD, British Museum, London
20. artist unknown, *Head of the King of Ife,* 13th century, British Museum, London
21. artist unknown, *Hippopotamus,* 20th–18th centuries BC, Cairo Museum, Egypt
22. artist unknown, *Ivory Panel with Archangel,* c. 5th century AD, British Museum, London
23. artist unknown, *Kore* (young girl), c. 530 BC, Acropolis Museum, Athens
24. artist unknown, *Kritios Boy,* c. 480 BC, Acropolis, Athens, Greece
25. artist unknown, *Laocoön,* 1st century BC, Vatican, Rome
26. artist unknown, *Leopard,* Benin, 16th–17th centuries, British Museum, London
27. artist unknown, *Little Admiral,* c. 1750, Old State House, Boston, Massachusetts
28. artist unknown, *Minoan Snake Goddess,* 1600 BC, Museum, Heraklion, Crete
29. artist unknown, *Nefertiti,* c. 1375–1357 BC, State Museums, Berlin
30. artist unknown, *Poseidon (Zeus?) of Artemision,* 460 BC, National Museum of Athens, Greece
31. artist unknown, *Prajnaparamita,* goddess, c. 1300, Museum Nasional, Jakarta, Indonesia
32. artist unknown, *Prince Rahotep and His Wife Nofret,* c. 2580 BC, Egyptian Museum, Cairo
33. artist unknown, *Rampin Head,* c. 560 BC, Louvre, Paris
34. artist unknown, *Sarcophagus from Ceveteri,* c. 520 BC, Louvre, Paris
35. artist unknown, *She-Wolf,* c. 500–480 BC, Capitoline Museums, Rome
36. artist(s) unknown, *Sphinx,* c. 2500 BC, Giza, Egypt

David, 1501–1504, Michelangelo

List 1–8   Continued

37. artist unknown, *Stele from Sounion,* 460 BC, National Museum of Athens, Greece
38. artist(s) unknown, *Stone images,* 17th century or earlier, Easter Island
39. artist(s) unknown, *Tomb Figures,* Qin Dynasty, 221–207 BC, Xian, China
40. artist unknown, *Tomb Figure of a Horse,* 618–906 AD, Art Institute of Chicago, Illinois
41. artist unknown, *Venus de Milo,* c. 100 BC, Louvre, Paris
42. artist unknown, *Venus of Willendorf,* c. 25,000–20,000 BC, Kunsthistorisches Museum, Vienna
43. artist unknown, *Winged Victory of Samothrace* (Nike), c. 200 BC, Louvre, Paris
44. Bernini, Gianlorenzo, *Apollo and Daphne,* 1622–1624, Villa Borghese, Rome
45. Bernini, Gianlorenzo, *The Ecstasy of St. Theresa,* 1645–1652, Sta. Maria della Vittoria, Rome
46. Boccione, Umberto, *Unique Forms of Continuity in Space,* 1913, Museum of Modern Art, New York City
47. Bourgeois, Louise, *Nature Study (Dog),* 1984, Whitney Museum of American Art, New York City
48. Brancusi, Constantin, *Bird in Space,* 1912, Philadelphia Museum of Art, Pennsylvania
49. Brancusi, Constantin, *Mlle. Pogany (Version II),* 1919, Solomon R. Guggenheim Museum, New York City
50. Butterfield, Deborah, *Horse #6-82,* Dallas Museum of Art, Texas
51. Calder, Alexander, *Circus,* 1932, Whitney Museum of American Art, New York City
52. Calder, Alexander, *Flamingo,* 1974, Federal Center Plaza, Chicago, Illinois
53. Canova, Antonio, *Pauline Borghese as Venus,* 1805–1807, Borghese Gallery, Rome
54. Christo (Javacheff), *Surrounded Islands, Biscayne Bay,* 1983 (temporary), Biscayne Bay, Florida
55. Cornell, Joseph, *Medici Slot Machine,* 1942, Solomon R. Guggenheim Museum, New York City
56. Degas, Edgar, *Little Dancer of Fourteen Years,* 1840–1845, St. Louis Art Museum, Missouri
57. de Huy, Renier, *Baptismal Font,* 1107–1118, St. Barthlemy, Liege, Belgium
58. Donatello, *David,* 1425–1430, Museo del Bargello, Florence
59. Donatello, *Equestrian Monument of Erasmo daNarn: (Gattamelata),* 1445–1450, Piazza del Santo, Padua, Italy
60. Flavin, Dan, *Pink and Gold,* 1968, Museum of Contemporary Art, Chicago, Illinois
61. French, Daniel Chester, *Minute Man,* 1889, Concord, Massachusetts
62. Gabo, Naum, *Head of a Woman,* 1916–1917, Museum of Modern Art, New York City
63. Ghiberti, Lorenzo, *The Gates of Paradise,* c. 1435, East Doors, Baptistry, Florence
64. Giacometti, Alberto, *Tall Figure,* 1947, Hirshhorn Museum and Sculpture Garden, Washington, DC
65. Graves, Nancy, *Zaga,* 1983, Nelson-Atkins Museum of Art, Kansas City, Missouri
66. Hanson, Duane, *Tourists,* 1970, Glasgow Art Gallery, Scotland
67. Hepworth, Barbara, *Pendour,* 1947, Hirshhorn Museum and Sculpture Garden, Washington, DC
68. Hosmer, Harriet, *Zenobia,* 1858, Metropolitan Museum of Art, New York City
69. Houdon, J. A., *Thomas Jefferson,* 1785, New York Historical Society, New York City
70. Johns, Jasper, *Ale Cans,* 1960, collection, Dr. Peter Ludwig, New York City
71. Keinholz, Edward, *The State Hospital,* 1966, Moderna Museet, Stockholm
72. Lipchitz, Jacques, *Man with Guitar,* 1916, Museum of Modern Art, New York City
73. Maillol, Aristide, *The River,* 1939–1943, Norton Simon, Inc., Foundation, Los Angeles, California
74. Maillol, Aristide, *Venus with Necklace,* 1918–1928, St. Louis Art Museum, Missouri

Colleoni Monument, 1483–1488, Andrea del Verrocchio, Venice

List 1–8   Continued

75. Marini, Marino, *Little Horse and Rider,* 1949, Hirshhorn Museum and Sculpture Garden, Washington, DC
76. Marisol Escobar, *The Family,* 1962, Museum of Modern Art, New York City
77. Matisse, Henri, *Back 1,* 1909; *Back II,* 1913; *Back III,* 1916–1917; *Back IV,* 1930; Hirshhorn Museum and Sculpture Garden, Washington, DC
78. Matisse, Henri, *La Serpentine,* 1909, Hirshhorn Museum and Sculpture Garden, Washington, DC; also Museum of Modern Art, New York City
79. Michelangelo, *Moses,* c. 1513–1515, St. Peter in Chains, Rome
80. Michelangelo, *Pieta,* 1498–1499, St. Peter's Basilica, Vatican, Rome
81. Michelangelo, *David,* 1501–1504, Galleria del'Accademia, Florence
82. Modigliani, *Head,* 1915, Museum of Modern Art, New York City
83. Moore, Henry, *Draped Seated Woman,* 1957–1958, Hebrew University, Jerusalem
84. Moore, Henry, *King and Queen,* 1952–1953, Hirshhorn Museum and Sculpture Garden, Washington, DC
85. Myron, *The Discobolus,* c. 450 BC, National Museum, Rome
86. Nadelman, Elie, *Hostess,* 1918, Hirshhorn Museum and Sculpture Garden, Washington, DC
87. Naumburg Master, *Uta of Naumburg,* c. 1250–1260, Patrons' Gallery, Naumburg Cathedral, Germany
88. Nevelson, Louise, *An American Tribute to the British People,* 1960–1965, Tate Gallery, London
89. Oldenburg, Claes, Lipstick Ascending on Caterpillar Tracks, 1969, Yale University Art Gallery, New Haven, Connecticut
90. Picasso, Pablo, *Head of Fernande Olivier,* 1909, Hirshhorn Museum and Sculpture Garden, Washington, DC
91. Pollaiuolo, Antonio, *Hercules and Antaeus,* c. 1475, Museo Nazionale, Florence
92. Remington, Frederic, *The Bronco Buster,* 1895, St. Louis Art Museum, Missouri
93. Rodin, Auguste, *Balzac,* 1897, Rodin Museum, Paris
94. Rodin, Auguste, *The Burghers of Calais,* 1884–1888, Calais, France, and Rodin Museum, Philadelphia, Pennsylvania
95. Rogers, Randolph, *Nydia, the Blind Girl of Pompeii,* 1895, Pennsylvania Academy of Fine Arts, Philadelphia
96. Segal, George, *Cinema,* 1963, Albright-Knox Art Gallery, Buffalo, New York
97. Sluter, Claus, *Well of Moses,* 1395–1403, Chartreuse de Champnol, Dijon, France
98. Smith, David, *Cubi XIX,* 1964, Tate Gallery, London
99. Smithson, Robert, *Spiral Jetty,* 1970, earthwork (now gone), Great Salt Lake, Utah
100. Verrocchio, Andrea del, *Equestrian Monument of Bartolomeo Colleoni,* c. 1483–1488, Venice

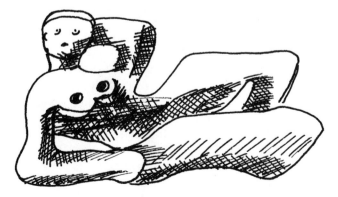

Drawing after *Reclining Figure,* Henry Moore, 1946–1947, Collection Henry R. Hope, Bloomington, Indiana

List 1–9   100 Famous "Buildings"

Although some of these "buildings" did not have a roof, most of these famous structures did serve to accommodate people (living or dead).

1. Alberti, Leon Battista, *Palazzo Rucellai,* 1444–1459, Florence
2. artist(s) unknown, *Church of the Holy Apostles,* 14th century, Salonica, Greece
3. artist(s) unknown, *Diocletian's Palace,* AD 300, Split, Croatia
4. artist(s) unknown, *Durham Cathedral,* begun 1093, Durham, England
5. artist(s) unknown, *Kailasa Temple,* Ellora, 8th century AD, Maharashtra, India
6. artist(s) unknown, *Machu Picchu Fortress Ruins,* Inca, 16th century, Peru
7. artist(s) unknown, *Alcazar,* 14th century, Seville, Spain
8. artist(s) unknown, *Angkor Wat Temple-Mountain,* 1113–1150, Angkor, Cambodia
9. artist(s) unknown, *Arch of Constantine,* AD 312, Rome
10. artist(s) unknown, *Audience Hall of the Temple,* c. 500 BC, Persepolis, near Baghdad, Iraq
11. artist(s) unknown, *Basilica of Saint Ambrogio,* late 11th and 12th centuries, Milan
12. artist(s) unknown, *Basilica of St. Denis,* c. 1135–1144, Paris
13. artist(s) unknown, *Borgund Church,* c. 1150, Borgund, Norway
14. artist(s) unknown, *Chartres Cathedral,* 1140–1220, Chartres, France
15. artist(s) unknown, *Chateau of Chambord,* c. 1526–1544, France
16. artist(s) unknown, *Chichen Itza,* 12th century AD, Yucatan, Mexico
17. artist(s) unknown, *Colosseum,* 72–80 AD, Rome
18. artist(s) unknown, *Erechtheum, Portico of the Caryatids,* 421–405 BC, Athens
19. artist(s) unknown, *Escorial,* 1563–1584, Madrid, Spain
20. artist(s) unknown, *Forbidden City,* begun 1406, Beijing, China
21. artist(s) unknown, *Forum Romanum,* 78 BC–AD 608, Rome
22. artist(s) unknown, *Funerary Temple of Queen Hatshepsut,* 1504–1483 BC, Thebes, Egypt
23. artist(s) unknown, *Great Wall of China,* unified 210 BC, may be seen near Beijing, China
24. artist(s) unknown, *Kutub Minaret,* AD 1200, Delhi, India
25. artist(s) unknown, *Library of* Celsus *(façade),* AD 135, Ephesus, Turkey
26. artist(s) unknown, *Mausoleum of Galla Placidia,* c. AD 420, Ravenna, Italy
27. artist(s) unknown, *Mont Saint Michel,* 1203–1264, Mont Saint Michel, France
28. artist(s) unknown, *Mosque of Cordoba,* 8th-9th centuries, Cordoba, Spain
29. artist(s) unknown, *Palace at Knossos,* c. 1500 BC, Crete
30. artist(s) unknown, *Pantheon,* 118 BC–AD 25, Rome
31. artist(s) unknown, *Pisa, Leaning Tower and Cathedral* complex, c. 1063–1173, Pisa, Italy
32. artist(s) unknown, *Pont du Gard,* 27 BC–AD 14, Roman aqueduct, Nîmes, France
33. artist(s) unknown, *Puerta del Sol,* 1200, Toledo, Spain
34. artist(s) unknown, *Pyramids of Giza,* 2530–2470 BC, Giza, Egypt
35. artist(s) unknown, *San Vitale Church,* 526–547 AD, Ravenna, Italy
36. artist(s) unknown, *St. Basil's,* 1554–1560, Moscow, Russia
37. artist(s) unknown, *St. Mark's Cathedral,* begun 1063, Venice, Italy
38. artist(s) unknown, *Stonehenge,* c. 2000 BC, Salisbury Plain, Wiltshire, England
39. artist(s) unknown, *Stupa at Borobudur,* 8th century AD, Java, Indonesia
40. artist(s) unknown, *Stupa of Sanchi,* 1st century AD, India
41. artist(s) unknown, *Taj Mahal,* 1630–1650, Agra, India
42. artist(s) unknown, *Temple of Athena Nike,* c. 427 BC, Athens
43. artist(s) unknown, *Temple of Bacchus,* 2nd century AD, Baalbek, Lebanon
44. artist(s) unknown, *Temple of Poseidon,* c. 550 BC, Paestum, Italy
45. artist(s) unknown, *Temple of Heaven,* 15th century, Beijing, China
46. artist(s) unknown, *Temple of Horus,* Edfu, 327 BC, Egypt
47. artist(s) unknown, *Temple of Horyu-ji,* Asuka period, begun AD 607, Nara, Japan

Stonehenge, c. 2000 BC, Salisbury Plain, Wiltshire, England

© 1998 Prentice Hall

List 1–9   **Continued**

48. artist(s) unknown, *Temple of Quetzalcoatl,* 770–829 AD, Teotihuacan, Mexico
49. artist(s) unknown, *Temple of Rameses II,* c. 1257 BC, Abu Simbel, Egypt
50. artist(s) unknown, *Temple of Tirukalikunram,* South India
51. artist(s) unknown, *The Alhambra, Court of the Lions,* Moorish, 1333–1354, Granada, Andalusia, Spain
52. artist(s) unknown, *Toledo Cathedral,* 1732, Toledo, Spain
53. artist(s) unknown, *Treasury of Atreus* (Beehive tomb), c. 1300–1250 BC, Mycenae
54. artist(s) unknown, *Tula Ruins,* 12th–13th centuries, Toltec, near Mexico City
55. Barry, Sir Charles, *Houses of Parliament,* 1836–c. 1860, London
56. Bernini, Gianlorenzo, *Colonnade of St. Peter's,* begun 1656, Rome
57. Borromini, Francesco, *San Carlo alle Quattro Fontane,* 1665–1667, Rome
58. Bramante, Donato, *Tempietto, San Pietro in Montorio,* 1502, Rome
59. Brunelleschi, Filippo, *Cupola of Santa Maria del Fiore* (Cathedral), 420–436, Florence
60. Burlington, Lord/William Kent, *Chiswick House,* 1725–1729, London
61. Eiffel, Alexandre-Gustave, *Eiffel Tower,* 1889, Paris
62. Garnier, Charles, *Opera House,* 1861–1875, Paris
63. Gaudi, Antoni, *Church of the Sagrada Familia,* 1883–1926, Barcelona, Spain
64. Gaudi, Antoni, *Casa Mila,* 1905–1910, Barcelona, Spain
65. Gropius, Walter, *Bauhaus,* 1925–1926, Dessau, Germany
66. Hood, Raymond, *McGraw Hill Building,* 1930, New York City
67. Ictinus and Callicrates, *Parthenon,* 447–432 BC, Acropolis, Athens, Greece
68. Imhotep, *Pyramid of King Djoser,* c. 2630 BC, Sakkara, Egypt
69. Isidore of Miletus and Anthemius of Tralles, *Hagia Sophia,* 532–537 AD, Istanbul
70. Jefferson, Thomas, *Monticello,* 1772, near Charlottesville, Virginia
71. Le Corbusier, Charles-Edouard, *Notre Dame du Haut,* 1955, Ronchamp, France
72. Le Corbusier, Charles-Edouard, *Villa Savoie,* 1929–1931, Poissy, France
73. Le Vau, Louis, and Jules Hardouin Mansart, *Versailles,* c. 1669, France
74. Le Vau/Lebrun/Claude Perrault, *Louvre,* east front, 1667, Paris
75. Lisboa, Antonio Francisco, *Church of São Francisco,* 1766–1794, Ouro Preto, Brazil
76. Matisse, Henri, *Chapel of the Rosary,* 1950–1951, Vence, France
77. Michelangelo (Buonarroti), *Cupola of St. Peter's,* 1546–1564, Rome
78. Michelangelo (Buonarroti), *Medici Chapel, Church of San Lorenzo,* 1524–1534, Florence
79. Nash, John, *Royal Pavilion at Brighton,* 1815, Brighton, England
80. Nervi, Pier Luigi, *Palazzetto dello Sport,* 1956–1957, Rome
81. Neumann, Balthasar, *Church of Vierzehnheiligen,* 1743–1771, Vienna
82. Neumann, Balthasar, *Wurzburg Palace,* 1720–1724, Wurzburg, Germany
83. Niemeyer, Oscar, *Palace of the National Congress,* 1960, Brasilia, Brazil
84. Olivera, Mateus Vicente de, *Queluz Palace,* 1747–1752, Lisbon, Portugal
85. Palladio, *Villa Rotunda,* 1567, near Vicenza, Italy
86. Paxton, Sir Joseph, *Crystal Palace,* 1851, London (destroyed)
87. Prandtauer, Jakob, *Melk Monastery,* 1702–1738, Melk, Austria
88. Richardson, Henry Hobson, *Marshall Field Warehouse,* 1885–1887, Chicago, Illinois
89. Saarinen, Eero, *Jefferson Arch,* c. 1965, St. Louis, Missouri
90. Saarinen, Eero, *Dulles International Airport,* 1958, Washington, DC
91. Soufflot, Jacques Germain, *Pantheon (Ste. Genevieve),* 1755–1792, Paris
92. Sullivan, Louis, *Carson, Pirie, Scott Store,* 1899, Chicago, Illinois
93. Utzon, Jorn, *Opera House,* 1956, Sydney, Australia
94. van der Rohe, Mies, *Seagram Building,* 1958, New York City
95. Vanbrugh, Sir John, *Blenheim Palace,* 1705–1724, Oxfordshire, England
96. Vignon, Alexander-Pierre, *Church of the Madeleine,* 1806–1843, Paris
97. Von Erlach, Johann Fischer, *Karlskirche,* 1716–1737, Vienna, Austria
98. Wren, Christopher, *Saint Paul's Cathedral,* 1675–1710, London
99. Wren, Christopher, *College of William and Mary,* 1695–1702, Williamsburg, Virginia
100. Wright, Frank Lloyd, *Falling Water,* 1936, Bear Run, Pennsylvania

St. Basil's Cathedral, 1554–1560, Moscow

List 1–10   100 Famous Art Objects

This list could include thousands of art objects, but this is a representative list of objects that are mostly in museums and considered to be outstanding examples.

1. Antimenes painter, *Heracles and the Nemean Lion,* Greek vase, c. 520 BC, British Museum, London
2. artist unknown, *Animal Head from the Oseberg Ship-Burial,* c. 825 AD, University of Antiquities, Oslo, Norway
3. artist unknown, *Antependium* (frontal altar) of Henry II, early 11th century, Cluny Museum, Paris
4. artist unknown, *Arms of Peru,* Chimu culture, c. 1200–1300, Miguel Mujica Gallo Museum, Lima, Peru
5. artist unknown, *Barbarini Ivory,* c. 527, Louvre, Paris
6. artist(s) unknown, *Battle Between Darius and Alexander,* 4th century BC, Muzeo Nazionale, Naples
7. artist unknown, *Benin Bronze Panel,* c. AD 1500, British Museum, London
8. artist(s) unknown, *Book of Kells,* 8th century AD, Trinity College, Dublin
9. artist unknown, *Blackamoor with Matrix of South American Emeralds,* c. 1724, Gemaldegalerie, Dresden, Germany
10. artist unknown, *Bracelet,* Persian, 10th–11th centuries, Los Angeles County Museum of Art, California
11. artist unknown, *Buddha Enthroned,* 10th century, Kimbell Art Museum, Fort Worth, Texas
12. artist unknown, *Bulls Head on a Harp,* 2500 BC, Egyptian Museum, Cairo
13. artist unknown, *Bust of Tiberius,* 1st century AD, Pitti Palace, Florence
14. artist unknown, *Chalice of Abbot Suger,* c. 1140, National Gallery of Art, Washington, DC
15. artist unknown, *Code of Hammurabi.* c. 1930–1888 BC, Louvre, Paris
16. artist unknown, *Court of the Emperor Justinian* (mosaic) 6th century AD, San Vitale, Ravenna, Italy
17. artist unknown, *Court of the Empress Theodora* (mosaic) 6th century AD, San Vitale, Ravenna, Italy
18. artist unknown, *Cross of Princely Crowns,* 13th–15th centuries, Treasury of Wawel Cathedral, Cracow, Poland
19. artist unknown, *The Cyrus Cylinder,* 539 BC, British Museum, London
20. artist(s) unknown, *Dead Sea Scrolls,* c. 100 BC–AD 68, Israel Museum Hakirya, Jerusalem, Israel
21. artist(s) unknown, *Blue Delft Collection,* 1560–1800, Rijksmuseum, Amsterdam
22. artist unknown, *Emerald Topkapi Dagger,* 1746–1747, Ottoman, Topkapi Palace Museum, Istanbul, Turkey
23. artist unknown, *Feather Crown of King Montezuma,* c. 1500, Ethnological Museum, Vienna
24. artist unknown, *Flute Player* (Benin), 15th–16th centuries, British Museum, London
25. artist unknown, *Geese of Meydum* (frieze), c. 2600 BC, Cairo
26. artist unknown, *Geometric Amphora,* 800 BC, National Museum, Athens
27. artist unknown, *Gold Beaker,* 1200–1000 BC, Archaeological Museum, Teheran, Iran
28. artist unknown, *Gold Cradle,* 17th century, Topkapi Palace Museum, Istanbul, Turkey
29. artist unknown, *Gold Crown with Two Pendants,* 5th–6th centuries, National Museum of Korea, Seoul
30. artist unknown, *Gold Man from Gaul,* late 4th to early 5th centuries, Dumbarton Oaks, Washington, DC
31. artist unknown, *Gold Mask of King Tutankhamen,* 1362–1253 BC, Egyptian Museum, Cairo
32. artist unknown, *Gold Rhyton,* 5th century BC, Archaeological Museum, Teheran, Iran
33. artist(s) unknown, *Grand Condé Rose Diamonds,* 1621–1686, Condé Museum, Chateau of Chantilly, France
34. artist(s) unknown, *Great Bed of Ware,* late 16th century, Victoria and Albert Museum, London
35. artist(s) unknown, *Guelph Treasure,* c. 1579, State Museums, Berlin
36. artist unknown, *Head of Buddha,* 4th–5th centuries, Victoria and Albert Museum, London
37. artist unknown, *Horse Biting Its Leg,* Sung Dynasty, 960–1260 AD, Collection, King Gustaf VI Adolf of Sweden
38. artist unknown, *House Model,* Han Dynasty, 206 BC–AD 221, Nelson-Atkins Museum of Art, Kansas City, Missouri
39. artist unknown, *Imperial Crown* (Crown of Otto), School of Reichenau, c. 962, Museum of Art History, Vienna

List 1–10   **Continued**

40. artist(s) unknown, *Imperial Coach of the Viennese Court,* 18th century, Kunsthistorisches Museum, Vienna
41. artist unknown, *Ivory Panel with Archangel,* c. 5th century AD, British Museum, London
42. artist(s) unknown, *Koran Collection,* 1436–1520, Topkapi Palace Museum, Istanbul, Turkey
43. artist(s) unknown, *Lady with the Unicorn Tapestries,* 1509–1515, Cluny Museum, Paris
44. artist unknown, *Lady Wen-Chi's Return,* 12th century, Museum of Fine Arts, Boston, Massachusetts
45. artist(s) unknown, *Lindisfarne Gospels,* c. AD 698, British Museum, London
46. artist unknown, *Lorsch Bookcover,* 9th century, Victoria and Albert Museum, London

47. artist unknown, *Lothar Cross,* end of 10th century, Treasury of the Royal Palace, Aachen, Germany
48. artist unknown, *Lotus Bowl,* c. 1107–1127, The National Palace Museum, Tapei, Taiwan
49. artist unknown, *Lycurgus Cup,* 4th century, British Museum, London
50. artist unknown, *Lyre with Gold Bull's Head,* c. 2500 BC, Baghdad, Iraq
51. artist unknown, *Mask of Agamemnon,* 1580–1550 BC, National Museum of Athens
52. artist(s) unknown, *Mildenhall Treasure,* 4th century, British Museum, London
53. artist(s) unknown, *Mosaic of the Good Shepherd,* Mausoleum of Galla Placida, 5th century AD, Ravenna, Italy
54. artist unknown, *Mummy Cartonnage of Amen-Nestawy Nahkt,* c. 1000 BC, St. Louis Art Museum, Missouri
55. artist unknown, *North Transept Rose Window,* c. 1230, Notre Dame de Chartres, Chartres, France
56. artist unknown, *Order of the Golden Fleece,* c. 15th century, Residence Palace, Munich
57. artist unknown, *Crown of the Holy Roman Empire,* c. AD 962, Kunsthistorisches Museum, Vienna
58. artist unknown, *Pala d'Oro,* 976–1209, Cathedral of St. Mark, Venice
59. artist unknown, *Palace Ladies Hunting from a Pavilion,* 1760–1770, Cleveland Museum of Art, Ohio
60. artist unknown, *Palette of King Narmer,* c. 3000 BC, Egyptian Museum, Cairo
61. artist(s) unknown, *Pergamon Altar of Zeus,* 180 BC, State Museums, Berlin
62. artist unknown, *Portland Vase,* c. 1st century AD, British Museum, London
63. artist unknown, *Ram Caught in a Thicket,* c. 2600 BC, British Museum, London
64. artist unknown, *Reliquary of the Head of the Emperor Charlemagne,* c. 1350, Cathedral Treasury, Aachen, Germany
65. artist unknown, *Rosetta Stone,* 196 BC, British Museum, London
66. artist unknown, *Sarcophagus of Djedkhonsouioufankh* (mummy cover), c. 660–525 BC, Louvre, Paris
67. artist unknown, *Scythian Stag, Scythian Panther,* c. 7th–6th centuries BC, Hermitage, St. Petersburg, Russia
68. artist unknown, *Stone Calender,* 1450–1500, Museum of Archaeology, Mexico City, Mexico
69. artist unknown, *Studley Bowl,* c. 1400, Victoria and Albert Museum, London
70. artist(s) unknown, *Sutton Hoo Treasure,* 7th century, British Museum, London
71. artist(s) unknown, *Throne of Tutankhamen,* c. 1350 BC, Egyptian Museum, Cairo
72. artist unknown, *Tres Belles Heures du Duc de Berry* (five pages attributed to Van Eyck), 15th century, Turin, Italy
73. artist unknown, *Trojan Gold Diadem,* Bronze age, Pushkin Museum, Moscow
74. artist(s) unknown, *Turquoise Throne of Murat III,* Topkapi Palace Museum, Istanbul, Turkey
75. artist unknown, *Two-headed Serpent,* Aztec, 15th century, British Museum, London
76. artist(s) unknown, *Vaphio Cups,* c. 1500 BC, National Museum, Athens
77. artist unknown, *The Wilton Diptych,* c. 1395, National Gallery, London

List 1–10   Continued

78. Bey, Sinan and others, *Miniatures Collection,* 13th–18th centuries, Topkapi Palace Museum, Istanbul, Turkey

79. Castagno, Andrea del, *Shield of David,* 1420–1457, National Gallery of Art, Washington, DC

80. Cellini, Benvenuto, *Saltcellar,* 1539–1564, Museum of Art History, Vienna

81. Cellini, Benvenuto?, *Rospiogli Cup,* 16th century, Metropolitan Museum of Art, New York City

82. Chizhevski, Gregory, *Royal Gates,* 1784, Church of the Nativity of the Mother of God, Kiev, Russia

83. Dali, Salvador, *The Royal Heart,* c. 1952, The Owen Cheatham Foundation, New York City

84. Dieux, Jacques, *Sevres Bowl,* 1792, Getty Museum, Los Angeles, California

85. Euphronios (painter)/Euxitheos (potter), *Red-Figured Calyx-krater: Sleep and Death Lifting the Body of Sarpedon,* c. 515 BC, Metropolitan Museum of Art, New York City

86. Fabergé, Peter Carl, *Easter Egg,* 1912, Museum of Fine Arts, Richmond, Virginia

87. Gutenberg, Johannes, *Gutenberg Bible,* 1456, British Museum, London

88. Hiroshige, Utagawa, *Fifty-three Stages of the Tokaido Shono,* c. 1834, Museum of Fine Arts, Boston, Massachusetts

89. Limbourg Brothers, *Les Tres Riches Heures du Jean, Duc de Berry,* 1413–1416, Musée Condé, Chantilly, France

90. Martinez, Maria and Julian, *Black Vase,* 1929, The Indian Art Center of California, Studio City

91. Ordhi, Muwajd el, *Celestial Globe,* c. 1279, The Municipal Mathematics Room, Dresden, Germany

92. Pan painter, *Lekythos with Artemis and a Swan* (Greek), c. 409 BC, Hermitage, St. Petersburg, Russia

93. Perkhin, Mikhail, *Golden Egg Decorated with Enamel and Diamonds,* 1902, Fabergé workshops, Armoury Chamber, Moscow, Russia

94. Queen Mathilde and her attendants, *Bayeux Tapestry,* end of 11th century, Bayeux, France

95. Reimer, Hans, and Munich Masters, *St. George and the Dragon,* c. 1590, Residence Palace, Munich

96. Reutlingen, Hans von, *Imperial Gospel Book,* 9th century, Museum of Art History, Vienna

97. Revere, Paul, *Liberty Bowl,* 1768, Museum of Fine Arts, Boston, Massachusetts

98. Stothard, Thomas, *The Wellington Shield,* Victory, 1822, Wellington Museum, Apsley House, London

99. Stradivari, Antonio, *Violin,* 1644–1737, Metropolitan Museum of Art, New York City

100. Vyner, Robert, *Crown of St. Edward,* 1667, Crown Jewels of England, London

List 1–11   100 Famous Photographs

These 100 greatest photographs are examples of many photographers' frequently reproduced works. Many are represented in several collections, though only one location is listed.

1. Abbot, Berenice, *El at Columbus and Broadway,* New York City, 1929, Art Institute of Chicago, Illinois
2. Adams, Ansel, *Moonrise Over Hernandez,* 1941, Collection of the Ansel Adams Trust, San Francisco, California
3. Adams, Ansel, *Winter Sunrise, Sierra Nevada, from Lone Pine, California,* 1944, Center for Creative Photography, University of Arizona, Tucson
4. Arbus, Diane, *Identical Twins, Cathleen and Colleen, 1967, Roselle, New Jersey,* Metropolitan Museum of Art, New York City
5. Annan, Thomas, *Close No. 31, Salt Mkt.,* c. 1868, St. Louis Art Museum, Missouri
6. Atget, Eugene, *The Reflecting Pool of the Park at Sceaux,* 1925, Bibliothèque Nationale, Paris
7. Atget, Eugene, *Ragpicker,* 1899–1900, Museum of Modern Art, New York City
8. Avedon, Richard, *Juan Patricio Lobato, Carney, Rocky Ford, Colorado, 8/25/80,* collection of the artist
9. Bourke-White, Margaret, *The Kremlin, Moscow, Night Bombing by the Germans,* 1941, Hallmark Photographic Collection, Kansas City, Missouri
10. Brassai, (Gyula Halasz), *Bijou of Montmarte,* 1933, Museum of Modern Art, New York City
11. Brady, Mathew, *Abraham Lincoln,* 1864, National Archives, Washington, DC
12. Bravo, Manuel Alvarez, *How Small the World Is,* 1942, Center for Creative Photography, University of Arizona, Tucson
13. Callahan, Harry, *Detroit Street Scene,* 1943, Art Institute of Chicago, Illinois
14. Cameron, Julia Margaret, *Alice Liddell as Pomona,* 1872, Metropolitan Museum of Art, New York City
15. Cameron, Julia Margaret, *Call, I Follow; I Follow, Let Me Die,* c. 1867, Royal Photographic Society, Bath, England
16. Capa, Robert, *Naples,* 1943, Art Institute of Chicago, Illinois
17. Capa, Robert, *Soldier at the Moment of Death, Spanish Civil War,* 1936, International Center of Photography, New York City
18. Carava, Roy de, *Dancers, New York,* 1956, St. Louis Art Museum, Missouri
19. Cartier-Bresson, Henri, *Behind the Gare Saint-Lazare, Paris,* 1932, St. Louis Art Museum, Missouri
20. Cartier-Bresson, Henri, *Siphnos, Greece,* 1961, collection of Magnum Photos, Inc., New York City
21. Close, Chuck, *Self-Portrait/Composite/Sixteen Parts,* 1987, Pace/MacGill Gallery, New York City
22. Coburn, Alvin Langdon, *Williamsburg Bridge,* 1909, University of Texas, Austin
23. Cunningham, Imogen, *Two Callas,* 1929, The Imogen Cunningham Trust, Berkeley, California
24. Daguerre, Louis, *Collection of Shells and Miscellany,* 1839, Conservatoire Nationale des Arts et Metiers, Paris
25. Daguerre, Louis, *A Portrait of Charles L. Smith,* 1843, International Museum of Photography at George Eastman House, Rochester, New York
26. Eakins, Thomas, *Nude Broad Jumping,* 1884–1885, The Library Company of Philadelphia, Pennsylvania
27. Edgerton, Harold, *Milk Drop Coronet,* 1936, Hallmark Photographic Collection, Kansas City, Missouri
28. Eggleston, William, *Tallahatchie County, Mississippi,* 1972, Museum of Modern Art, New York City
29. Evans, Frederick H., *A Sea of Steps, Wells Cathedral: Stairs to the Chapter House and Bridge to Vicar's Close,* 1903, Royal Photographic Society, Bath, England
30. Evans, Walker, *View of Railroad Station, Edwards, Mississippi,* 1936, San Francisco Museum of Modern Art, California
31. Fox Talbot, William Henry, *The Game Keeper,* c. 1843, National Museum of American History, Smithsonian Institution, Washington, DC
32. Fox Talbot, William Henry, *Sailing Craft,* c. 1844, Science Museum, London
33. Frank, Robert, *Parade, Hoboken,* New Jersey, 1955, Museum of Modern Art, New York City

List 1–11   Continued

34. Friedlander, Lee, *Colorado,* 1967, Museum of Modern Art, New York City
35. Frith, Francis, *The Great Pyramid at Giza, From the Plain,* 1859, Library of Congress, Washington, DC
36. Frith, Francis, *Fallen Colossus,* c. 1858, Janet Lehr, Inc., New York City
37. Gardner, Alexander, *Home of a Rebel Sharpshooter, Gettysburg,* 1863, Library of Congress, Washington, DC
38. Gardner, Alexander, *Abraham Lincoln,* 1865, National Portrait Gallery, Smithsonian Institution, Washington, DC
39. Gilbert Proesch and George Passmore, *The Decorators,* 1978, Morton G. Neumann Family Collection
40. Gilpin, Laura, *Sunburst, the Castillo, Chichen Itza,* 1932, Amon Carter Museum, Fort Worth, Texas
41. Groover, Jan, *Untitled* (still life), 1988, Robert Miller Gallery, New York City
42. Hine, Lewis, *Bowery Mission Bread Line,* 1906, Museum of Modern Art, New York City
43. Hine, Lewis, *Powerhouse Mechanic,* c. 1925, Hallmark Photographic Collection, Kansas City, Missouri
44. Hockney, David, *Pearblossom Hwy., 11–18 April 1986,* #2, collection of the artist
45. Iturbide, Graciela, *Mujer angel,* 1979, Center for Creative Photography, University of Arizona, Tucson
46. Käsebier, Gertrude, *Baron Adolf de Meyer,* 1903, Museum of Modern Art, New York City
47. Kertész, André, *Satiric Dancer,* 1926, collection of Nicholas Pritzker
48. Kertész, André, *Chez Mondrian,* 1926, Art Institute of Chicago, Illinois
49. Kruger, Barbara, *Untitled (Use Only as Directed),* 1988, St. Louis Art Museum, Missouri
50. Lange, Dorothea, *Migrant Mother, Nipomo, California,* 1936, Oakland Museum, California
51. Lartigue, Jacques-Henri, *Paris, Avenue des Acacias,* 1912, Museum of Modern Art, New York City
52. Lartigue, Jacques-Henri, *My Hydroglider with Propeller,* 1904, Association des Amis de J.-H. Lartigue, Paris
53. Leibovitz, Annie, *John Lennon and Yoko Ono, December 8, 1980, Rolling Stone* cover, 1981
54. Leibovitz, Annie, *The Blues Brothers,* 1979, *Rolling Stone* cover, February
55. Levitt, Helen, *New York,* c. 1942, Museum of Modern Art, New York City
56. Mapplethorpe, Robert, *Tulips,* 1977, Museum of Modern Art, New York City
57. Martin, Paul, *Woman Raking,* 1893, Victoria and Albert Museum, London
58. Meyerowitz, Joel, *Bay Sky Series, Provincetown,* 1977, Hallmark Photographic Collection, Kansas City, Missouri
59. Michals, Duane, *Giorgio de Chirico at Home Near the Spanish Steps,* 1972, collection of the artist
60. Mili, Gjon, *Pablo Picasso Drawing Minotaur with Light,* 1950, *Life* Magazine, Time Inc.
61. Moholy-Nagy, Laszlo, *Berlin Radio Tower,* c. 1928, Art Institute of Chicago, Illinois
62. Muybridge, Eadweard, *Nude Men, Motion Study,* 1877, Museum of Modern Art, New York City
63. Nadar (Gaspard-Felix Tournachon), *Sarah Bernhardt,* 1859, International Museum of Photography at George Eastman House, Rochester, New York
64. Niepce, Joseph Nicephore, *View from His Window at La Gras,* 1827, University of Texas, Austin
65. Newman, Arnold, *Igor Stravinsky,* 1946, collection of the artist
66. O'Sullivan, Timothy H., *Black Canyon, Colorado River, From Camp 8, Looking Above,* 1871, Getty Museum, Los Angeles, California
67. Penn, Irving, *Man in White/Woman in Black,* 1971, collection of the artist
68. Penn, Irving, *Woman with Umbrella, New York,* 1950, Hallmark Photographic Collection, Kansas City, Missouri
69. Porter, Eliot, *Dark Canyon, Glen Canyon,* 1965, Art Institute of Chicago, Illinois
70. Ray, Man, *Rayogram,* 1923, Museum of Modern Art, New York City
71. Ray, Man, *Mrs. Henry Rowell,* c. 1929, Art Institute of Chicago, Illinois
72. Riis, Jacob, *In the Home of an Italian Rag-Picker, New Jersey,* c. 1889, Museum of the City of New York
73. Sander, August, *The Earthbound Farmer,* 1910, Museum of Modern Art, New York City
74. Sheeler, Charles, *Stairwell,* 1914, Museum of Modern Art, New York City

List 1-11   **Continued**

75. Sherman, Cindy, *Untitled Film Still #16,* 1978, Hallmark Photographic Collection, Kansas City, Missouri
76. Simmons, Laurie, *Walking Camera (Jimmy the Camera),* 1987, St. Louis Art Museum, Missouri
77. Skoglund, Sandy, *Radioactive Cats,* 1980, St. Louis Art Museum, Missouri
78. Sleet, Moneta, *Story Hour, St. Louis, Missouri,* 1991, St. Louis Art Museum, Missouri
79. Smith, W. Eugene, *Tomoko in the Bath,* Museum of Fine Arts, Boston, Massachusetts
80. Smith, W. Eugene, *Untitled* (Three soldiers with the Spanish Guardia Civil), 1950, Center for Creative Photography, University of Arizona, Tucson
81. Steichen, Edward, *Flatiron Building,* 1904, Metropolitan Museum of Art, New York City
82. Steichen, Edward, *Charles Chaplin,* 1925, International Museum of Photography at George Eastman House, Rochester, New York
83. Stieglitz, Alfred, *Hands, Georgia O'Keeffe,* 1920, Metropolitan Museum of Art, New York City
84. Stieglitz, Alfred, *The Steerage,* 1907, St. Louis Art Museum, Missouri
85. Strand, Paul, *Photograph, New York (Blind Woman),* 1916, Metropolitan Museum of Art, New York City
86. Strand, Paul, *Wall Street,* 1915, Canadian Center for Architecture, Montreal, Canada
87. Strand, Paul, *Church Gateway, Mexico,* 1933, St. Louis Art Museum, Missouri
88. Sudek, Josef, *Chair in Janacek's House,* 1972, Getty Museum, Los Angeles, California
89. Uelsmann, Jerry N., *Untitled,* 1976, Metropolitan Museum of Art, New York City
90. Uelsmann, Jerry N., *Small Woods Where I met Myself,* 1967, Hallmark Photographic Collection, Kansas City, Missouri
91. Warhol, Andy, *Marilyn Monroe,* 1967, Museum of Modern Art, New York City
92. Warhol, Andy, *Elvis,* 1963, Australian National Gallery, Canberra
93. Watkins, Carleton E., *The Valley from Mariposa Trail, Yosemite, California,* 1863, collection of Daniel Wolf, Inc., New York City
94. Weegee, *The Critic,* 1943, Hallmark Photographic Collection, Kansas City, Missouri
95. Wegman, William, *Red/Grey-Grey/Red,* 1982, Museum of Modern Art, New York City
96. Weston, Edward, *Nude,* 1936, International Museum of Photography at George Eastman House, Rochester, New York
97. Weston, Edward, *Pepper,* 1930, Los Angeles County Museum of Art, California
98. Weston, Edward, *Shell,* 1927, Center for Creative Photography, University of Arizona, Tucson
99. White, Minor, *Pacific, Devil's Slide, California,* 1947, Museum of Modern Art, New York City
100. Winogrand, Garry, *Circle Line Ferry, New York,* 1971, Museum of Modern Art, New York City

List 1–12   What Did It Sell For?

While one should never judge the quality of a work of art by its price, the prices for various artworks sold at auction are still newsworthy. It has been hundreds of years since some works were on the market, and they are virtually priceless. The art market has its ups and downs, as has the popularity and consequently the value of paintings by specific painters. In general the artworks listed are oil paintings. Titles are sometimes translated to English. Dates are given where available. Some of these prices were obtained from the *International Art Prices* computer file, which is updated annually.

Artist	Year Sold	Price at Auction	Title and Year of Artwork
Bacon, Francis	1994	$ 353,500	*Self Portrait—Diptych,* 1977
Bartolommeo, Fra	1996	22,500,000	*Rest on the Flight into Egypt with Saint John the Baptist,* 1509
Beckmann, Max	1994	1,496,350	*Quapi auf Blau mit Butchy,* 1943
Bellows, George	1995	2,862,500	*Easter Snow,* 1915
Bellows, George	1995	1,377,500	*Dock Builders,* 1916
Boucher, François	1994	291,970	*Une Dame a sa Toilette,* c. 1738
Calder, Alexander	1994	1,817,500	*Constellation,* 1960
Cassatt, Mary	1996	3,700,000	*In the Box,* c. 1880
Carraci, Anibale	1994	2,202,500	*Boy Drinking,* c. 1580
Cezanne, Paul	1997	50,000,000	*Still Life, Flowered Curtain and Fruit,* 1900
Cezanne, Paul	1994	28,602,500	*Nature Morte: les Grosses Pommes,* c. 1890–1894
Cezanne, Paul	1996	1,989,000	*Les Baigneurs,* c. 1890
Cezanne, Paul	1996	11,002,500	*La Cote du Galet, à Pontoise,* c. 1879–1881
Dali, Salvador	1995	3,522,500	*Swans Reflection of the Elephants,* 1937
Degas, Edgar	1995	4,950,000	*Woman in the Tub,* 1884
Degas, Edgar	1993	7,042,500*	*Danseuses Se Baissant (Les Balerines),* 1885
Degas, Edgar	1996	11,882,500	*Young Dancer at 14* (bronze), 1878–1881
de Kooning, Willem	1989	18,800,000	*Interchange,* 1949
de Kooning, Willem	1996	15,600,000	*Woman,* 1949
Disney, Walt	1995	29,900	Celluloid from *Cinderella,* 1950
Gauguin, Paul	1989	24,200,000*	*Mata Mua—in Olden Times,* 1892
Gauguin, Paul	1995	28,692,370	*Tahitiennes pres d'un Ruisseau,* c. 1891
Gogh, Vincent van	1990	82,500,000*	*Portrait du Dr. Gachet,* 1890
Gogh, Vincent van	1990	26,400,000	*Autoportrait,* 1888
Gogh, Vincent van	1987	53,900,000	*Irises,* c. 1889/1890
Gogh, Vincent van	1993	57,000,000	*Wheat Field with Cypresses,* 1889
Gogh, Vincent van	1995	24,500,000	*Sous-Bois,* 1890
Greco, El	1995	2,312,500	*Christ on the Cross in a Landscape with Horseman,* late 16th century
Hassam, Childe	1994	5,502,500	*The Room of Flowers,* 1894
Hicks, Edward	1994	486,500	*Peaceable Kingdom of the Branch,* c. 1830
Johns, Jasper	1994	68,500	*Savarin* (lithograph), c. 1977
Johns, Jasper	1988	7,040,000	*White Flag,* 1955–1958
Johns, Jasper	1995	2,800,000	*Winter,* 1986
Kahlo, Frida	1995	3,192,500	*Autoretrato con Chango y Loro,* 1942
Klimt, Gustave	1994	11,662,500	*Dame mit Facher,* c. 1917–1918
Lichtenstein, Roy	1995	2,532,500	*Kiss II,* 1962
Lichtenstein, Roy	1995	2,477,500	*I . . . I'm Sorry,* 1966
Lichtenstein, Roy	1995	1,600,000	*Emeralds,* 1961
Lichtenstein, Roy	1989	5,500,000	*Torpedo . . . Los,* 1963
Manet, Edouard	1989	26,000,000*	*La Rue Mosnier aux Drapeaux,* 1878

List 1–12   Continued

Artist	Year Sold	Price at Auction	Title and Year of Artwork
Manet, Edouard	1990	16,500,000*	*Le Banc, le Jardin de Versailles,* 1881
Mapplethorpe, Robert	1994	63,250	*Calla Lily,* 1987
Matisse, Henri	1994	13,752,500	*La Vis* (gouache & cut paper), 1951
Matisse, Henri	1995	14,852,500	*Hindoue,* 1923
Modigliani	1995	5,942,500	*Portrait de Jeanne Hebuterne,* 1919
Mondrian, Piet	1994	5,612,500	*Composition No. 8,* 1939–1942
Monet, Claude	1994	7,504,300	*Peupliers au Bord de la Epte, Effet du Soir,* 1891
Monet, Claude	1996	6,500,000	*Les Meules, Giverny, Effet du Matin,* c. 1889
Monet, Claude	1995	3,742,500	*Vue de l'Eglise de Vernon,* 1883
Monet, Claude	1989	14,300,000*	*Le Parlement, Coucher de Soleil,* 1904
Monet, Claude	1992	12,100,000*	*Le Bassin aux Nympheas (waterlilies),* 1919
Monet, Claude	1996	4,600,000	*Nympheas,* 1908
Munch, Edvard	1996	7,702,500	*Girls on a Bridge,* c. 1902
Picasso, Pablo	1989	47,850,000	*Yo Picasso,* n.d.
Picasso, Pablo	1994	4,402,500	*Femme et Enfants au Bord de la Mer,* c. 1932
Picasso, Pablo	1995	29,152,500	*Angel Fernandez De Soto,* 1903
Picasso, Pablo	1995	18,200,000	*Le Miroir,* 1932
Pollock, Jackson	1989	10,500,000	*Number 8,* 1950
Prendergast, Maurice	1995	1,432,500	*On the Shore,* after 1907
Remington, Frederic	1993	1,212,500	*Coming Through the Rye,* 1902
Renoir, Pierre-Auguste	1994	6,712,500	*Women in a Garden,* 1872–1873
Renoir, Pierre-Auguste	1990	78,100,000*	*Au Moulin de la Galette,* 1876
Rivera, Diego	1995	3,082,500	*Ball in Tehuantepec,* 1928
Rubens, Peter Paul	1995	882,500	*Portrait of the Young Anthony Van Dyck,* 1615
Sargent, John Singer	1994	7,592,500	*Spanish Dancer,* c. 1880
Sargent, John Singer	1996	11,112,500	*Cashmere,* 1908
Signac, Paul	1994	897,496	*La Place aux Herbes,* 1908
Smith, David	1995	1,982,500	*Three Circles and Planes* (sculpture), c. 1957
Warhol, Andy	1995	1,058,500	*Let Us Now Praise Famous Men,* 1963
Warhol, Andy	1989	31,900	*Campbell's Soup Can,* 1985
Warhol, Andy	1996	376,500	*Soup Can,* 1962

*Price includes 10% commission.

List 1–13 Auction House Addresses

CALIFORNIA

Butterfield and Butterfield, 220 San Bruno Ave., San Francisco, 94103
Butterfield and Butterfield, 7601 Sunset Blvd., Los Angeles, 90046

ILLINOIS

Dunning's, 755 Church Rd., Elgin, 60123
Hanzel Galleries, 1120 South Michigan Ave., Chicago, 60605
Leslie Hindman Auctioneers, 215 W. Ohio St., Chicago, 60610

MICHIGAN

DuMouchelle Auction Galleries, 409 E. Jefferson, Detroit, 48226

MISSOURI

Selkirk's, 7447 Forsythe Blvd., St. Louis, 63105

NEW YORK

Christie's, 502 Park Ave., New York City, 10022
Grisebach, 120 E. 56th St., #635, New York City, 10022
Sotheby's, 1334 York Ave. at 72nd St., New York, 10021
Swann Galleries, Inc., 104 East 25th St., New York City, 10010

PENNSYLVANIA

Freeman/Fine Arts, 1808–1810 Chestnut St., Philadelphia, 19103

OTHER

Villa Grisebach Auktionen, Munich, Cologne, Berlin, Great Britain, Vienna, Israel, Caracas

List 1–14   Movies and Plays About Artists

MOVIES

Gainsborough, Thomas, *Kitty,* 1945

Gauguin, Paul, *Gauguin the Savage* (film made for TV), 1980

Gauguin, Paul, *The Moon and Sixpence,* 1942

Gauguin, Paul, *Wolf at the Door,* 1987

Gautier, Henri, *Savage Messiah,* 1972

Gogh, Vincent van, *Vincent* (Australian movie: paintings shown while letters are read), 1987

Gogh, Vincent van, and Gauguin, Paul, *Lust for Life,* 1956

Goya, Francisco, *The Naked Maja,* 1959

Greco, El, *El Greco,* 1966

Michaelangelo, *The Agony and the Ecstasy,* 1965

Modigliani, Amedeo, *The Lovers of Montparnasse,* 1957

O'Keeffe, Georgia, and Alfred Stieglitz, *Steiglitz Loves O'Keeffe,* 1996

Picasso, Pablo, *The Adventures of Picasso* (Swedish comedy), 1978

Picasso, Pablo, *The Mystery of Picasso* (French), 1955

Picasso, Pablo, *The Picasso Summer,* 1969

Picasso, Pablo, *Surviving Picasso,* 1996

Picasso, Pablo, *Picasso at the Lapin Agile,* 1996

Rembrandt Harmensz van Rijn, *Rembrandt,* 1936

Rothko, Mark, *The Rothko Conspiracy* (film made for TV), 1983

Toulouse-Lautrec, *Moulin Rouge,* 1953

Warhol, Andy, *I Shot Andy Warhol,* 1996

PLAYS

Art, London play about collectors and friendship, 1997

Basquiat, Jean-Michel, Andy Warhol, and Julian Schnabel, *Basquiat,* 1996

Seurat, Georges, *Sunday in the Park with George* (musical play), 1984

Spencer, Stanley (English painter, 1871–1959), *Stanley,* 1996

Drawn from *The Maquette for "Way Down East,"* 1978, Red Grooms, Hirshhorn Museum and Sculpture Garden, Washington, DC

List 1–15   Fiction About Art and Artists

Maugham, Somerset, *The Moon and Sixpence* (about Paul Gauguin), Heritage Press, 1940

Sollers, Philippe, *Watteau in Venice, 1944,* Charles Scribner and Sons, 1994

Stone, Irving, *Lust for Life* (life of Vincent van Gogh), Doubleday, 1954

Stone, Irving, *The Agony and the Ecstasy* (about Michelangelo), Doubleday, 1961

FICTION ABOUT ARCHITECTS

Boll, Heinrich, *Billiards at Half-Past Nine,* McGraw Hill, 1962

Colegate, Isabel, *The Summer of the Royal Visit,* Knopf, 1992

Dickens, Charles, *Martin Chuzzlewit,* Knopf, 1994

Ferber, Edna, *So Big,* Doubleday, 1924

Galsworthy, John, *The Man of Property,* Scribner, 1987

Greene, Graham, *A Burnt-out Case,* Viking, 1961

Lively, Penelope, *City of the Mind,* Harcourt Brace Jovanovich, 1991

Rand, Ayn, *The Fountainhead,* Penguin Books, 1943

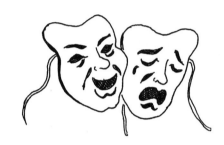

FICTION ABOUT ART, GENERAL

Francis, Dick, *To the Hilt,* P. G. Putnam's Sons, 1996

Hoving, Thomas, *Masterpiece,* Simon and Schuster, 1986

McCarthy, Mary, *Cannibals and Missionaries,* Harcourt Brace Jovanovich, 1979

Stassinopoulos Huffington, Ariana, *Picasso: Creator and Destroyer,* Simon & Schuster, 1988

FICTION ABOUT ART COLLECTORS

Davies, Robertson, *What's Bred in the Bone,* Viking, 1995

Hoving, Thomas, *Discovery,* Simon & Schuster, 1989

Krentz, Jayne Ann, *Grand Passion,* Pocket Books, 1994

Wharton, Edith, *False Dawn,* short story published in *Wharton E.,* Old New York Publishers, 1928

FICTION ABOUT ART CRITICS

Morrow, James, *City of Truth,* St. Martin's Press, 1992

ABOUT ART DEALERS

Banks, Oliver T., *The Rembrandt Panel,* Little, Brown, 1980

MacInnes, Helen, *Prelude to Terror,* Harcourt Brace Jovanovich, 1978

West, Morris L., *Masterclass,* St. Martin's Press, 1991

Woods, Stuart, *Imperfect Strangers,* HarperCollins, 1995

FICTION ABOUT ART FORGERY

Banks, Oliver T., *The Rembrandt Panel,* Little, Brown, 1980

Davies, Robertson, *The Lyre of Orpheus,* Viking, 1989

Davies, Robertson, *What's Bred in the Bone,* Viking, 1995

Gaddis, William, *The Recognitions,* Penguin Books, 1993

Hoving, Thomas, *Masterpiece,* Simon & Schuster, 1986

ART GALLERIES AND MUSEUMS

Brown, Rita Mae, *Venus Envy,* Bantam Books, 1993

List 1–15   Continued

ABOUT ART OBJECTS

Archer, Jeffrey, *A Matter of Honor,* Simon & Schuster, 1986

James, Henry, *The Spoils of Poynton,* Houghton, 1896; republished in *The Complete Tales of Henry James,* Lippincott, 1962–1965

Johnson, Velda, *The Etruscan Smile,* Dodd Mead, 1977

FICTION ABOUT PAINTERS

Aiken, Conrad, *Conversation; or Pilgrim's Progress,* Duell, Sloan & Pearce, 1940

Cary, Joyce, *The Horse's Mouth,* Harper, 1950

Clark, Mary Higgins, *A Cry in the Night,* Pocket Books, 1993, © 1982

Colwin, Laurie, *Family Happiness,* Knopf, 1982

Durrell, Lawrence, *Clea,* Dutton, 1961

Eden, Dorothy, *The Vines of Yarrabee,* Coward McCann, 1969

Farmer, Philip Jose, *Riders of the Purple Wage,* republished in the *Classic Philip Jose Farmer, 1952/1964,* Crown Publishers, 1984

Gallico, Paul, *The Snow Goose,* Doubleday, 1959

Godwin, Gail, *Violet Clay,* Random House, 1978

Graham, Winston, *The Walking Stick,* Collins, 1967

Gray, F. du Plessix, *World without End,* Simon & Schuster, 1981

Hemingway, Ernest, *Islands in the Stream,* Scribner, 1970

Ishiguro, Kazuo, *An Artist of the Floating World,* Faber, 1986

James, Henry, *The Europeans,* Oxford University Press, 1985

Kipling, Rudyard, *The Light That Failed,* Doubleday, 1899

Krantz, Judith, *Mistral's Daughter,* Thorndike Press, 1982

Lofts, Nora, *The Day of the Butterfly,* Doubleday, 1979

Mason, Richard L., *The World of Suzie Wong,* World Publishing Co., 1957

Momaday, N. Scott, *The Ancient Child,* Doubleday, 1989

Murdoch, Iris, *Nuns and Soldiers,* Viking Press, 1980

Nathan, Robert, *Portrait of Jennie,* Knopf, 1939

Potok, Chaim, *The Gift of Asher Lev,* Alfred A. Knopf, 1990

Potok, Chaim, *My Name is Asher Lev,* Knopf, 1972

Roberts, Kenneth Lewis, *Northwest Passage,* Doubleday, 1937

Sarton, May, *Joanna and Ulysses,* W.W. Norton & Company, 1963

Siddons, Ann R., *Hill Towns,* HarperCollins, 1993

Styron, William, *Set This House on Fire,* Random House, 1960

Wharton, William, *Dad,* Knopf, 1981

White, Patrick, *The Vivisector,* Cape, 1970

Whitney, Phyllis A., *The Golden Unicorn,* Doubleday, 1976

FICTION ABOUT PAINTINGS

Banks, Oliver T., *The Caravaggio Obsession,* Little, Brown, 1984

FICTION ABOUT SCULPTORS

Hawthorne, Nathaniel, *The Marble Faun,* New American Library, 1987, © 1961

Hesse, Hermann, *Narcissus and Goldmund,* Farrar, Straus & Giroux, 1968

James, Henry, *Roderick Hudson,* Houghton, Mifflin & Co., 1917

Piercy, Marge, *Summer People,* Summit Books, 1989

Walters, Minette, *The Sculptress,* St. Martin's Press, 1993

List 1–16   Art Magazines

The *Standard Periodical* Directory, published by Oxbridge Communications, Inc., is in most library reference rooms and lists hundreds of current publications. The following art-related magazines were selected because they are well-established and have a large circulation.

African Arts, African Studies Center, University of California, Los Angeles, 405 Hilgard Ave., Los Angeles, California 90024-1301

Airbrush Action, 1985 Swarthmore Ave., PO Box 2052, Lakewood, New Jersey 08701

American Art (Smithsonian Studies in American Art), Rizzoli International, 300 Park Ave. South, New York, New York 10010

American Artist, BPI Communications, Inc., 1515 Broadway, 14th Floor, New York, New York 10036

American Art Therapy Association Newsletter, 1202 Allanson Rd., Mundelein, Illinois 60060-3808

American Ceramics, 9 E. 45th St., New York, New York 10017-2403

American Craft (formerly *Craft Horizons*), American Craft Council, 72 Spring St., New York, New York 10012-4019

American Indian Art Magazine, 7314 E. Osborn Dr., Sta. B, Scottsdale, Arizona 85251-6148

American Photo (formerly *American Photographer*), Hachette Filipacchi Magazines, Inc., 1633 Broadway, New York, New York 10019-6741

Aperture, Aperture Foundation, Inc., 20 E. 23rd St., New York, New York 10010

Architecture, BPI Communications, Inc., 1515 Broadway, New York, New York 10036

Architectural Digest, Condé Nast Publications, Inc., 350 Madison Ave., New York, New York 10017-3136

Architectural Record, McGraw-Hill, 1221 Avenue of the Americas, 36th Floor, New York, New York 10020-1095

Architectural Review, Audit House, Field End Rd., Eastcote, Ruislip, Middlesex, HA49 BR, United Kingdom

Art Bulletin, College Art Association, Inc., 275 Seventh Ave., New York, New York 10001

Art in America, Brant Publications, Inc., 575 Broadway, New York, New York 10012-3230

Art Education Journal, National Art Education Assn., 1916 Assn. Dr., Reston, Virginia 22091-1590

Art of the West, Duerr & Tiemey Ltd., 15612 Highway 7, Sta. 2335, Minnetonka, Minnesota 55345-3551

Artforum, Artforum International Magazine, 65 Bleeker St., New York, New York 10012-2466

Artist's Magazine, F & W Publications, 1507 Dana Ave., Cincinnati, Ohio 45207-1056

Art Journal, College Art Association, Inc., 275 Seventh Ave., New York, New York 10001

ARTnews, Artnews Associates, 48 W. 38th St., New York, New York 10018-6238

Arts & Activities, 591 Camino de la Reina, Suite 200, San Diego, California 92108-3104

Art & Antiques, 3 E. 54th St., New York, New York 10022

Arts New York, Box 1215, Cooper Station, New York, New York 10276-1215

Canadian Art, Canadian Art Foundation, 6 Church St., 2nd Floor, Toronto, Ontario, M5E 1M1, Canada

Canadian Forum, Canadian Forum, 804-251 Laurier Ave. West, Ottawa, Ontario, K1P 5J6, Canada

Carnegie Magazine, 4400 Forbes Ave., Pittsburgh, Pennsylvania 15213-4007

Ceramics Monthly, 735 Ceramic Pl., Westerville, Ohio 43086

Darkroom & Creative Camera Techniques (formerly *Darkroom Techniques*), Preston Publishers, 7800 N. Merrimac Ave., Niles, Illinois 60714-3426

Draw Magazine, Whiz Bang Graphics, 43 Ankara Ave. #98, Brookville, Ohio 45309-1207

Fine Art Magazine, Sunstorm Arts Publishing Co., Inc., 1014 Drew Ct., Ronkonkoma, New York 11779

Glass Art, PO Box 260377, Littleton, Colorado 80126-0377

Handwoven, Interweave Press, Inc., 201 E. 4th St., Loveland, Colorado 80537-5601

Illustrator, Art Instruction Schools, 500 S. 4th St., Minneapolis, Minnesota 55415-1592

Metalsmith, Society of North American Goldsmiths, 5009 Londonberry Dr., Tampa, Florida 33647

Metropolis, Bellerophon Publications, Inc., 177 E. 87th St., New York, New York 10128-2268

© 1998 Prentice Hall

List 1–16   Continued

Native Peoples, The Arts and Lifeways, Media Concepts Group, Inc., 5333 North Seventh St., Suite C-224, Phoenix, Arizona 85014

OnLine Design, Online Design Publications, Inc., 2261 Market St. #331, San Francisco, California 94114-1600

Paintworks, MSC Publishing, Inc., 243 Newton Sparta Rd., Newton, New Jersey 07860-2748

Popular Ceramics, Jones Publishing Inc., N7450 Aanstad Rd., PO Box 5000, Iola, Wisconsin 54945-5000

Popular Photography, 1633 Broadway, New York, New York 10019

Portraits, Holland & Edwards Publishing, Inc., 250 Mercer St., Apt. A-203, New York, New York 10012-1144

Progressive Architecture, Penton Publishing, 600 Summer St., Stamford, Connecticut 06904

School Arts, 50 Portland St., Worcester, Maine 01608-2099

Sculpture Magazine, International Sculpture Center, 1050 17th St., NW, Washington, DC 20036-3587

Sculpture Review, National Sculpture Society, 1177 6th Ave., 15th Floor, New York, New York 10036-2705

Shutterbug, Patch Publishing, 5211 S. Washington Ave., Titusville, Florida 32780

Southwest Art, Cowles Magazine, Inc., 4 High Ridge Pk., Stamford, Connecticut 06905

Studies in Art Education, National Art Education Assn., 1916 Assn. Dr., Reston, Virginia 20191-1590

Studio Potter, Studio Potter, Inc., PO Box 70, Goffstown, New Hampshire 03045-0070

U.S. Art (Midwest Art), MSP Communications, 220 S. 6th St., Sta. 500, Minneapolis, Minnesota 55402-4501

Watercolor Magic, F & W Publications, 1507 Dana Ave., Cincinnati, Ohio 45207-1056

Wildlife Art News, Pothole Publications, Inc., PO Box 16246, Saint Louis Park, Minnesota 55416-0246

List 1–17   Visual Art Resources and Publishers

These resources should be willing to send a catalogue or list of available art resources upon request.

A & F Video, PO Box 264, Geneseo, New York 14454 **(books and videos)**

Arthur Schwartz & Co., 234 Meads Mt. Rd., Woodstock, New York 12498 **(art techniques)**

Alarion Press, Inc., PO Box 1882, Ft. Collins, Colorado 80306-1882 **(timelines, art history projects, videos, workbooks)**

Art Book Catalogue, 32 Shell Ave., Milford, Connecticut 06460

Art Image Publications, Inc., PO Box 568, Champlain, New York 12919-0568

ARTNews for Students, ARTNews, 48 West 38th Street, New York, New York 10018-6211

Arts & Activities, 591 Camino de la Reina, Suite #200, San Diego, California 92108-3104

Crizmac—Art and Cultural Education Materials, PO Box 65928, Tucson, Arizona 85728-5928

Crystal Productions, PO Box 2159, 1812 Johns Dr., Glenview, Illinois 60025-6159

Dale Seymour Publications, 200 Middlefield Rd., Menlo Park, California 94025

Davis Publications, Inc., 50 Portland St., Worcester, Massachusetts 01608-2099

DK Publishing, Inc., (Dorling Kindersley), 95 Madison Ave., New York, New York 10016

Dover Publications, 31 E. 2nd St., Mineola, New York 11501

Getty Center for Education in the Arts, PO Box 909, 112 South Washington, Douglas, Michigan 49406-1909

Gibbs Smith Publisher, PO Box 667, Layton, Utah 84041

Glencoe/McGraw Hill, 936 Eastwind Dr., Westerville, Ohio 43081

J.L. Hammett Co., PO Box 9057, Braintree, Massachusetts 02185-9057

Heinemann, 361 Hanover Street, Portsmouth, New Hampshire 03801-3912

Knowledge Unlimited, PO Box 52, Madison, Wisconsin 53707-0052

List 1–17 Continued

Lakeshore Learning Materials, PO Box 6261, Carson, California 90810

Modern Learning Press, PO Box 167, Rosemont, New Jersey 08556-0167

Prentice Hall/Simon & Schuster, 240 Frisch Court, Paramus, New Jersey 07652

Scholastic, Inc., 555 Broadway, New York, New York 10012-3999

Grove's Dictionaries Inc., 150 Fifth Ave., Suite 916, New York, New York 10011 **(The Dictionary of Art)**

Sax Arts & Crafts, Visual Art Resources Catalogue, PO Box 51710/Dept. SA, New Berlin, Wisconsin 53151

School Arts, 50 Portland Street, Worcester, Massachusetts 01608-2099

Shambhala Publications, Inc., Horticultural Hall, 300 Massachusetts Avenue, Boston, Massachusetts 02115

Teaching PreK–8, PO Box 182, Columbus, Ohio 43216-0182

Townsend Outlook Publishing, 20 E. Gregory Blvd., Kansas City, Missouri 64114

University of Illinois Press, 1325 South Oak St., Champaign, Illinois 61820

University of New Mexico Press, 1720 Lomas Blvd., NE, Albuquerque, New Mexico 87131-1591 **(art and photography books)**

University of Washington Press, PO Box 50096, Seattle, Washington 98145-5096

Walter Foster Publishing, Inc., 23062 La Cadena, Laguna Hills, California 92563-1352

West Educational Publishing, 620 Opperman Drive, PO Box 64779, St. Paul, Minnesota 55164-0779

Wild Berry Learning Systems, Rt. 3, Box 224A, Buckhannon, West Virginia 26201

Wilton, PO Box 302, Wilton, Connecticut 06897

Woodstocker Books division of Arthur Schwartz & Co., Inc., 234 Meads Mountain Road, Woodstock, New York 12498-1016

List 1–18   Resources for CD-ROM and Art Videos

A & F Video, PO Box 264, Geneseo, New York 14454

Alarion Press, Inc., PO Box 1882, Ft. Collins, Colorado 80306-1882

Art Instruction Software, 38 Balsam Dr., Medford, New York 11763

ArtsAmerica Inc., 12 Havemeyer Pl., Greenwich, Connecticut 06830

Broderbund Software, 500 Redwood Blvd., Box 6121, Novato, California 94948

Clearvue/eav, 6465 N. Avondale Ave., Chicago, Illinois 60631-1996

Crizmac, PO Box 65928, Tucson, Arizona 85728-5928

Crystal Productions, Box 2159, Glenview, Illinois 60025

M. Doggett Videos, 29909 Robin Rd., Plano, Texas 75007

L & S Video, Inc., 45 Stornowaye, Chappaqua, New York 10514-2321

Media for the Arts, 73 Pelham St., Newport, Rhode Island 02840

National Gallery of Art, Publications Mail Order Department, 2000B South Club Drive, Landover, Maryland 20785

The Roland Collection, 1344 South 60th Ct., Cicero, Illinois 60650

Sax Visual Art Resources Catalogue, 2405 S. Calhoun Rd., PO Box 51710, New Berlin, Wisconsin 53151-0710

Video Classroom Series, PO Box 1352, Dept. 4, West Chester, Pennsylvania 19380-0022

Western ITV, 1438 North Gower, Box 18, Los Angeles, California 90028

List 1–19   Poster and Print Resources

These distributors have catalogues or lists, which they should send upon request.

Alarion Press, Inc., PO Box 1882, Ft.Collins, Colorado 80306-1882

Arti Grafiche Ricordi, Via Quaranta, 44, 20139 Milano (Italy)—American Distributor, Imaginus, Inc. (address below)

Art Education/Nordevco, PO Box 542, South Plainfield, New Jersey 07080 **(multicultural art prints)**

Art Image Publications, Inc., PO Box 568, Champlain, New York 12919

Art Visuals, PO Box 925, Orem, Utah 84059 **(timelines, modern art styles, multicultural sets, women artists)**

Crizmac, PO Box 65928, Tucson, Arizona 85728-5928

Crystal Productions, Box 2159, Glenview, Illinois 60025

Imaginus, Inc., 51 Harpswell St., Brunswick, Maine 04011-2549

Knowledge Unlimited, PO Box 52, Madison, Wisconsin 53707-0052

Modern Learning Press, PO Box 167, Rosemont, New Jersey 08556-0167

Museographs, The Lazar Group, Inc., 3043 Moore Ave., Lawrenceville, Georgia 30244

New York Graphic Society, PO Box 1469, Greenwich, Connecticut 06836

Parent Child Press, PO Box 675, Hollidaysburg, Pennsylvania 16648-1675

Sandak, 180 Harvard Ave., Stamford, Connecticut 06902 (or 1633 Broadway, 6th Floor, New York, New York 10019-6785)

Shorewood Fine Art Reproductions, 33 River Rd., Cos Cob, Connecticut 06807

University Prints, 21 East St., Winchester, Massachusetts 01890

List 1–20   Slide Resources

American Library Color Slide Co., Inc., American Archives of World Art, PO Box 5810, Grand Central Station, New York, New York 10163-5810

Davis Publications, Inc./Rosenthal Art Slides, 50 Portland St., Worcester, Massachusetts 01608-2099

Education Department, St. Louis Art Museum, Forest Park, St. Louis, Missouri **(slide kits and individual slides from the collection)**

Department of Education Resources/Extension Programs, 6th St. and Constitution, NW, Washington, DC 20565-0001

National Gallery of Art, Publications Mail Order Department, 2000B South Club Dr., Landover, Maryland 20785

Sandak, 180 Harvard Avenue, Stamford, Connecticut 06902 (or 1633 Broadway, 6th Floor, New York, New York 10019-6785)

School Arts, 50 Portland St., Worcester, Massachusetts 01608

Universal Color Slide Company, 8450 South Tamiami Trail, Sarasota, Florida 34238-2936

List 1–21   General Art Supply Resources

These established companies carry almost any supplies needed for art and art education, including books, painting, sculpture, printmaking, paper, etc. Most of them will supply a catalogue on request.

Binders Discount Art Center (formerly Co-op Artists' Materials), PO Box 53097 Atlanta, Georgia 30355

Cardinal Arts & Crafts, PO Box 626, Elk Grove Village, Illinois 60009-0626

Dick Blick Art Materials, PO Box 1267, Galesburg, Illinois 61401-1267

J. L. Hammett Company, One Hammett Place, PO Box 859057, Braintree, Massachusetts 02185-9057

Nasco Arts & Crafts, 901 Janesville Ave., Ft. Atkinson, Wisconsin 53538-0901 (and PO Box 3837, Modesto, California 95352-3837)

R.B. Walter, 1185 Corporate Dr. West, Arlington, Texas 76005

Sax Arts & Crafts, 2405 S. Calhoun Road, PO Box 51710, New Berlin, Wisconsin 53151-0710

School Specialty (formerly Chaselle Arts & Crafts) 1000 N. Bluemound Dr., Appleton, Wisconsin 54913

S. & S. Arts and Crafts, Mill Street, Dept. 2021, Colchester, Connecticut 06415

Triarco Arts & Crafts, 14650 28th Ave. North, Plymouth, Minnesota 55447–4821

United Art & Education Supply, Box 9219, Fort Wayne, Indiana 46899

Utrecht Manufacturing Corp., 33 Thirty-Fifth St., Brooklyn, New York 11232

Welsh Products, Inc., PO Box 845, Benicia, California 94510

List 1–22 Specialty Art Supply Resources

Aztek Airbrush (division of Testor Corporation), 620 Buckbee St., Rockford, Illinois 61104-4835

Badge-A-Minit, Ltd., Box 800, LaSalle, Illinois 61301

Badger Air Brush Company, 9128 W. Belmont Ave., Franklin Park, Illinois 60131-2895

Bemiss-Jason Corporation, 37600 Central Ct., Newark, California 94560 **(paper, yarn, equipment)**

Binney & Smith, Inc., 1100 Church Lane, PO Box 431, Easton, Pennsylvania 18044-0431 **(all Crayola products, Model Magic® brushes)**

Brooks & Flynn, Inc., PO Box 2639, Rohnert Park, California 94927-2639 **(everything for the fabric artist)**

Compleat Sculptor, Inc., 90 Van Dam St., New York, New York 10013

Crafty's Featherworks, Inc., PO Box 370, 2010 North Airport Rd., Overton, Nevada 89040

Createx, 14 Airport Park Rd., East Granby, Connecticut 06026 **(poster and fabric color)**

Dharma Trading Co., PO Box 150916, San Rafael, California 94915 **(fiber arts supplies)**

Dixon Ticonderoga Company, 2600 Maitland Center Pkwy., Suite 200, Maitland, Florida 32751-4160 **(Prang® products, ColorArt® products)**

Ed Hoy's International, 1620 Frontenac Rd., Naperville, Illinois 60563-1762 **(supplies for stained glass and glass fusing)**

Empire Berol USA, Brentwood, Tennessee 37027 **(Primacolor® products)**

Fiskars, Inc., 3100 Dundee Rd., Suite 801, Northbrook, Illinois 60062 **(special scissors)**

Fletcher-Terry Company, 65 Spring Lane, Farmington, Connecticut 06032 **(mat cutting and framing equipment)**

General Pencil Company, 3160 Bay Rd., Redwood City, California 94063

Gold's Artworks, 2100 N. Pine, Lumberton, North Carolina 28358 **(papermaking supplies)**

Grumbacher, 100 North St., Bloomsbury, New Jersey 08804-3092 **(brushes, paints)**

Harrisville Designs, Center Village, PO Box 806, Harrisville, New Hampshire 03450 **(yarns, looms, and other weaving supplies)**

Hunt Manufacturing Company, One Commerce Square, 2005 Market Street, Philadelphia, Pennsylvania 19103-7085 **(pen points, ink)**

Jiffy Foam, Inc., PO Box 3609, Newport, Rhode Island 02840 **(Balsa-foam for carving)**

Koh-I-Noor, Inc./Grumbacher, 100 North St., Bloomsbury, New Jersey 08804-3092 **(technical drawing pens, brushes)**

Logan Graphic Products, 1100 Brown St., Wauconda, Illinois 60084-1192 **(mat cutters)**

Marvel Brush Company, PO Box 382, Hartsdale, New York 10530-0382

The Moll Company, PO Box 2816, Mansfield, Ohio, 44906 **(heavy-duty easels made of metal pipe)**

Museum Stamps (Fine Art Distributors), PO Box 693, Manhattan Beach, California 90266

OMYA Color, 142 Berkeley St., Boston, Massachusetts 02116 **(Artmache® and Plastiro® air-dry modeling clays)**

Polaroid Education Program, 72 Elizabeth St. #3, Salt Lake City, Utah 84102

Pro Chemical & Dye Inc., Box 14, Somerset, Massachusetts 02726

RIT Dye/The Softness Group, 381 Park Avenue South, New York, New York 10016

Riverside Paper Company, PO Box 179, 110 N. Kensington Dr., Appleton, Wisconsin 54912-0179

Sanford-Faber Corporation, 1711 Washington Blvd., Bellwood, Illinois 60104-1988 **(Design® art markers and pencils, Prismacolor® colored pencils)**

Scratch-Art Company, PO Box 303, Avon, Massachusetts 02322-0303

Silkpaint Corporation, Box 18, Waldron, Missouri 64092-0018

Swest, Inc., 11090 N. Stemmons, Dallas, Texas 75229-4544 **(jewelry and casting equipment)**

Tandy Leather Company, 1400 Everman Pkwy., Ft. Worth, Texas 76140-5006

Walker Display Incorporated, 250 South Lake Ave., Duluth, Minnesota 55802 **(display systems)**

Whittemore Durgin, Box 2065 AD, Hanover, Massachusetts 02339 **(stained glass supplies)**

List 1–22   Continued

CERAMICS

Aardvark Clay & Supplies, 1400 E. Pomona St., Santa Ana, California 92705-4812

AMACO (American Art Clay Co., Inc.), 4717 W. 16th St., Indianapolis, Indiana 46222-2598 **(kilns, wheels, slab rollers and hand extruders, carts, equipment)**

American Art Clay Company, 4717 W. 16th St., Indianapolis, Indiana 46222-2598

A.P. Green Industries, Inc., Green Blvd., Mexico, Missouri 65265

A.R.T. Studio Clay Company, 1555 Louis Ave., Elk Grove Village, Illinois 60007

Brent, 4717 W. 16th Street, Indianapolis, Indiana 46222 **(electric wheels)**

Creative Paperclay Company, 1800 South Robertson Blvd., Suite 907, Los Angeles, California 90035

Geil Kilns Company, 1601 W. Rosecrans Ave., Gardena, California 90249-3021

Great Lakes Clay & Supply Company, 120 S. Lincoln Ave., Carpentersville, Illinois 60110-1703

Hartman, 373 Poplar Road, Honey Brook, Pennsylvania 19344 **(foam board manufacturing)**

Mid-South Ceramic Supply, 12330 4th Ave. North, Nashville, Tennessee 37208-2714

Minnesota Clay USA, 8001 Grand Ave. South, Minneapolis, Minnesota 55404-4347

Orton, The Edward Orton Jr. Ceramic Foundation, PO Box 460, Westerville, Ohio 43081 **(pyrometric cones, vent systems, autofire controllers)**

Sheffield Pottery, Inc., U.S. Route 7, Box 399, Sheffield, Massachusetts, 01257

Skutt Ceramic Products, Inc., 2618 SE Steele St., Portland, Oregon 97202-4691

Spectrum Glazes, Inc., #33-40 Hanlan Rd., Woodbridge, Ontario, L4L 3P6, Canada

Vent-A-Kiln Corporation, 621 Hertel Ave., Buffalo, New York 14207

PAINTS

Chroma Acrylics, Inc., 205 Bucky Dr., Lititz, Pennsylvania 17543

Createx Colors, 14 Airport Park Rd., East Granby, Connecticut 06026

DEKA-Decart, Inc., Box 309, Morrisville, Vermont 05661-0309

DecoArt, PO Box 327, Stanford, Kentucky 40484 **(all-purpose acrylic paint)**

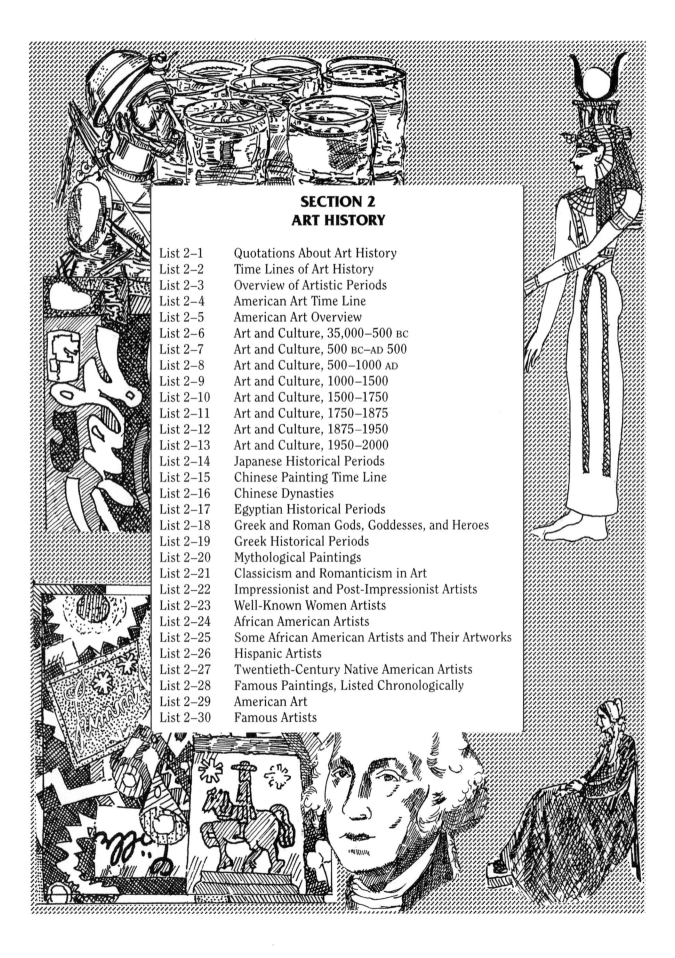

SECTION 2
ART HISTORY

List 2–1 Quotations About Art History

"Rembrandt painted about 700 pictures—of these, 3,000 are in existence."

—Wilhelm Bode

"I like to make an image that's so simple you can't avoid it, and so complicated you can't figure it out."

—Alex Katz

"You are lost the instant you know what the result will be."

—Juan Gris

"A portrait is a painting with something a little wrong with the mouth."

—John Singer Sargent

"Art is long and time is fleeting."

—Henry Wordsworth Longfellow

"I would not cast off my illness, for there is much in my art that I owe to it."

—Edvard Munch

"A good portrait . . . has more than just accurate features. It has some other thing."

—Alice Neel

"I skirmish and battle with the sun. And what sun here! . . . One would have to paint with gold and gems."

—Claude Monet

"As a painter I shall never signify anything of importance. I feel it absolutely."

—Vincent van Gogh

"As the old saying goes, good work, good pay."

—Giotto

"It does not matter how badly you paint, so long as you don't paint badly like other people."

—George Moore: *Confessions of a Young Man*

"I've been 40 years discovering that the Queen of all colours is black."

—Auguste Renoir

"You should keep on painting no matter how difficult it is, because this is all part of experience, and the more experience you can have, the better it is—unless it kills you, and then you know you have gone too far."

—Alice Neel

List 2–2   Time Lines of Art History

PREHISTORIC PERIOD
Venus of Willendorf, c. 25,000 BC

THE OLD STONE AGE
50,000–10,000 BC Paleolithic Period
10,000–3000 BC

Cave Paintings

IRON AGE,
1400 BC

Stonehenge, c. 2000 BC

EGYPT
2940–2134 BC Old Kingdom
2040–1640 BC Middle Kingdom
1550–1070 BC New Kingdom

Sphinx, 2530 BC

Nefertiti, 1365 BC

HISTORIC PERIOD
4000–2000 BC

Ram Caught in a Thicket, 3000 BC

Pyramids, 2530–2470 BC

SUMERIA
3500–2500 BC

ASSYRIA
1000–612 BC

Bull, 2800–2600 BC

CHINA

Yang Shan and Long Shan cultures
7000–4000 BC

Great Wall of China, 214 BC

JAPAN
Jomon culture, 5000 BC   Yayoi culture, c. 3000 BC

2300–1100 BC Mycenae
1100–700 BC Geometric Period
735–650 BC Orientalizing Phase
700–400 BC Archaic
480–323 BC Classical
323–30 BC Hellenistic

GREEK ART
2800–100 BC

Parthenon, 448–432 BC

AGEAN
2000–1800 BC

MINOAN
1100 BC

Snake Goddess,
1550 BC

Nike of Samothrace, 200–190 BC

She-Wolf, 500 BC

ETRUSCAN ART
700–300 BC

Apollo from Veii, 510 BC

ROMAN ART
750 BC–AD 476

200–27 BC Republic of Rome
200–476 AD Late Imperial
AD 476 End of Western Roman Empire

Colosseum, 72–80 AD

BYZANTINE ART
500–1453 AD Byzantine Empire

Hagia Sofia, 532–537 AD

ASIAN ART

2205–1766 BC Hsia Culture
1122–770 BC Chou Dynasty
618–907 AD T'ang Dynasty
960–1280 AD Sung Dynasty
1368–1644 AD Ming Dynasty
1644–1900 AD Qing Dynasty

REPUBLIC OF CHINA
1911–1949 AD

PEOPLE'S REPUBLIC OF CHINA
1949–Present

T'ang Dynasty

Benin Art

AFRICAN AND ISLAMIC ART

500 BC–AD 500 Nok Culture
570–632 AD Life of Mohammed
800–1550 AD Kingdom of Mali
1100–1500 AD Classical Life Art
AD 1500 Classical Benin Art

MIDDLE AGES
400–1000 AD

Oseberg Ship–Burial, 825 AD

ROMANESQUE
1000–1150 AD
Bayeux Tapestry, 1073–1083 AD

Pisa, 1153–1283 AD

GOTHIC
1100–1400 AD

Chartres, 1140–1175 AD

List 2–2   Continued

1350–1600 Northern Renaissance
1400   International Style
1400–1450 Early Renaissance
1495–1520 High Renaissance
1525–1600 Mannerism

RENAISSANCE ART
1250–1600

Arnolfini Portrait, 1434,
Jan Van Eyck

Florence Cathedral
1296–1436

Mona Lisa, 1503–1505
Leonardo da Vinci

David, 1504
Michelangelo

Qing (Ching) Dynasty, China
1644–1911

St. Paul's Cathedral
Wren, 1675–1710

The Jolly Toper
1627, Frans Hals

BAROQUE
1590–1750

Ecstasy of St. Theresa, Bernini
1645–1652

Karlskirche, Vienna
1715–1737

ROCOCO
1700–1800

NEOCLASSICISM
1770–1820

Monticello, Thomas Jefferson
1770–1782

ROMANTICISM
1800–1850

The Opera House
Paris, 1861–1874

The Fifer, 1866
Edouard Manet

REALISM
1850–1880

Cassatt

The Thinker,
Rodin

IMPRESSIONISM
1886–1920

Eiffel Tower
1889

POST-IMPRESSIONISM
1886–1910

Toulouse-Lautrec, 1899

Van Gough
1889

THE AMERICAS

NORTH AMERICA
AD 1000-present

Quilting
1620 onward

San Estevan, NM, 1629

NATIVE NORTH AMERICAS
AD 100–present

Burial Mounds
100–400

Rock Engravings
c. 1150

Olmecs, 1500–1000 BC

MESO-AMERICA
Nazca, 300 BC–AD 700

Anasazi
700–1750

SOUTH AMERICA

Classic Maya, 300–900

Inca, 1200–1530
Macchu Picchu, 1450–1500

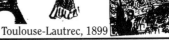

MODERN ART

1880–1910 Art Nouveau
1905–1907 Fauvism
1890–1940s Expressionism
c. 1908   Futurism
1930–1960 Abstraction
1922–1940 Surrealism

CUBISM
1907–1920

Georgia O'Keeffe

MODERNISM
1913–1945

SOCIAL REALISM
1920–1940

Edward Hopper

ABSTRACT EXPRESSIONISM
1945–1960

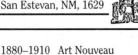

Alexander Calder

CONTEMPORARY ART

1970s   Conceptual Art
1960s–
  present Feminist Art
1960s   Minimalist Painting

POP ART
1950–1960

Claes Oldenburg

Robert Indiana
1966

COLOR FIELD
1950–present

Frank Ghery
1994

PHOTOREALISM
1960–1975

POST MODERN
1960s–present

Deborah Butterfield
1985

List 2–3   Overview of Artistic Periods

PREHISTORY

Prehistory simply means that there was no *written* history. The Chinese, Egyptian, Indian, Mesopotamian, and Sumerian civilizations developed in great river valleys from 35,000–15,000 BC. It was not until the discovery of the *Rosetta Stone* in 1799 by scholars who accompanied Napoleon to Egypt, and its translation in 1821, that Egyptian Hieroglyphs could be accurately translated. Among the oldest European discoveries were grave artifacts such as the *Venus of Willendorf* approximately 30,000 years old, and cave paintings from 15,000 to 10,000 BC.

WESTERN ART

The historic period of Western art began in Egypt approximately 4000–2000 BC, and moved from Egypt through Greece, to Southern Europe, then Northern Europe, and eventually to the Americas. Egyptian art was *unified,* meaning that paintings and sculpture complemented the architecture for which they were specifically designed. The more closely an Egyptian artist could follow the "rules" of art, the more the work was admired. The discovery of King Tutankhamen's tomb in 1922 provided historians with the first tomb that had not been opened first by grave robbers; therefore, it gave a much more complete view of the life of the pharaohs.

GREEK ART

Greek art almost paralleled Egyptian art. Greek art evolved from stiff, rigid human forms to classical sculptures such as the *Discus Thrower* and architecture such as the *Acropolis.* Throughout the centuries, Neo-Classical revivals based on Greek and Roman art continue to surface in painting, sculpture, and architecture. Not one Greek painting survived (it is presumed because of earthquakes), although the paintings on Greek vases show us how sophisticated it might have been. Greek influence spread to Italy, where it greatly affected the development of Etruscan and Roman art.

ETRUSCAN, ROMAN, AND EARLY CHRISTIAN ART

Etruscan, Roman, and Early Christian art developed from approximately 750 BC–AD 400. The Roman empire fell in AD 476, but its influence was widespread, as Romans occupied Egypt and North Africa, Great Britain, and portions of Northern and Southern Europe. Roman sculpture reflected the Greek influence, and wall paintings probably were similar to those of the Greeks. Roman architecture gave us such innovations as the amphitheater, arch, atrium, groin vault, concrete, organized city planning, and apartment houses.

BYZANTINE EMPIRE

The Byzantine Empire from 323 to 1453 AD began with the move of Roman Emperor Constantine to Istanbul (first called Byzantium, then Constaninople). Early Byzantine church decoration was notable for rich mosaics made of brilliantly colored pieces of glass. The mosaic figures were stiff; frontal, with large staring eyes, unsmiling features, and long, narrow faces. Later Byzantine panel painting featured religious figures, usually placed against gold backgrounds (these were called icons). The greatest Byzantine architectural innovation was the pendentive, which enabled a rounded dome to be placed on square pillars.

ART OF THE MIDDLE AGES

Art of the Middle Ages refers to the time between classical antiquity and modern times. The fifth to thirteenth centuries were referred to sometimes as the "Dark Ages." This time was primarily notable for manuscript illumination, grave goods (such as elaborately carved burial ships for northern kings), carved ivory book covers, beautiful metalwork reliquaries (to house the relics of saints), and jewelry. In 1073, the first artwork known to be created by women was the *Bayeux Tapestry,* created by Queen Matilda and her court to commemorate the Battle of Hastings. Architecture was considered by some to be the great artistic contribution of this time, with the growth of churches such as the *Palace Chapel of Charlemagne* at Aachen, Germany begun in AD 792.

ROMANESQUE PERIOD

The Romanesque Period from AD 1000 to 1150 reflected the Roman influence in the building of churches. The vaulted ceilings and long nave were reminiscent of the Roman marketplace. An intense period of church building commenced in approximately 1100, when great groups of people made pilgrimages across Europe to Santiago de

List 2–3   Continued

ROMANESQUE PERIOD (cont.)

Compostelo in Spain. Large churches were needed to accommodate them. Architecture, stained glass, stone carving, manuscript illumination, jewelry, and reliquaries all were dedicated to the glory of a Christian god. The sculptures of people were elongated and quite "wooden," as if the human form were nonexistent under the outer clothing. Favorite subjects were the lives of the saints, crucifixion scenes, allegories of the months, and zodiac signs. Everything the Greeks had learned about sculpting the human form seemingly was forgotten.

GOTHIC ART

Gothic art, which was from approximately 1100 to 1400, came to its glory through its beautiful churches, with their heaven-reaching spires and glowing stained-glass windows. Although use of the barrel and groin vaults began in Romanesque times, it wasn't until the flying buttress (support) was perfected that churches could rise to previously-unknown heights. Gothic churches are particularly distinguished by the use of ribbed vaults, pointed arches, a high nave, and clerestories with jewel-like stained glass. Carvings, jeweled reliquaries, paintings, and sculpture were mostly based on the Christian religion, although they reflected the Eastern influence (brought back by the Crusaders from their travels to the Middle East). In 1348, the black death (bubonic plague) decimated half of Europe. The artwork that decorated churches was created to instruct a population that was basically illiterate. Illuminated manuscripts and portraits were produced with the patronage of the church and the aristocracy.

NORTHERN RENAISSANCE ART

Northern Renaissance (1350–1600) art was sometimes considered late Gothic, rather than Pre-Renaissance. As artists traveled more and brought back innovations in style and technique, an international style evolved. Elongated, stylized figures, luxurious fabrics, and crowded scenes were typical. Paintings became more portable and affordable by the merchant class as well as royalty and the aristocracy. Jan van Eyck is credited with introducing the use of oil as a painting medium.

ITALIAN RENAISSANCE ART

Italian Renaissance art is generally acknowledged to be from 1400 to 1520, and was based on the principles developed by the Greeks. The age of Humanism had arrived. Renaissance philosophers, writers, scientists, and artists based their principles on science and math as they knew it. Leonardo da Vinci felt that even the human form might be based on geometric principles. Renaissance architecture displayed geometric forms and symmetry. The Renaissance actually began with the *Arena Chapel* frescoes of Giotto in 1305, which were based on real people who showed emotion, and whose clothing appeared to cover human forms. Giants of art such as da Vinci, Michelangelo, Raphael, and Botticelli created enduring masterpieces during this "rebirth."

MANNERISM

Mannerism closely followed the High Renaissance. Artists chose to depart from the faithfulness to nature that characterized the Renaissance, and instead elongated and distorted the human figure, using harsh, vivid colors for emotional impact. El Greco was among the best-known artists of this period.

BAROQUE ART

Baroque art (1590–1750) developed almost as a reaction to the discipline of Renaissance art, and was intended to appeal to the emotions of the viewer. It was everything the Renaissance was not, in painting, sculpture, and architecture. In place of geometrically developed composition, Baroque paintings were notable for swirling intensity, strong diagonals, brilliant coloration, dramatic contrasts, and an emotional intensity. Patrons continued to be the church, the aristocracy, the government, and now the wealthy merchant class, which purchased paintings for their homes. As in the Renaissance, many magnificent artists became notable in the field of art. Among these were Rubens, Rembrandt, Vermeer, Bernini, Velazquez, and Caravaggio.

ROCOCO ART

Rococo art (1700–1800) applies to the decorative arts of the time of Louis XV of France. It featured designs based on naturalistic forms such as plants, rocks, shells, and flowers. It has come to mean the excessive use of ornament in the decorative arts.

List 2–3   Continued

THE "ISMS"

Neoclassicism (1770–1820), Romanticism (1800–1850), Realism (1850–1880), Impressionism (1870–1905), Art Nouveau (1880–1910), Post-Impressionism (c. 1880–1900s), Symbolism (1880–1900), and Expressionism (c. 1890) were the first of the many "isms" to emerge from the Renaissance. Trends in the world of painting, sculpture, and architecture seemed to swing from naturalistic (romantic) to classical (restrained), and back again to naturalistic. Many of these trends came from the ideas of the writers and philosophers of the time. Painters and sculptors reacted in their work to what was happening around them. American painting was beginning to reflect what was being done in Europe, as the best American painters still went to Europe to complete their studies. Many artists, because of their long lives, spanned many "schools" of painting.

BARBIZON SCHOOL

This group of landscape painters took their name from the village of Barbizon near Fontainebleau, where they settled and painted. They preferred to paint in their studios, as opposed to the Impressionists, who painted outdoors whenever possible.

SYMBOLISM

The Symbolist painters attempted to represent the mystical and occult in their paintings, as literary and poetic Symbolists of their epoch were also doing in their writing. Their approaches to paintings varied greatly, though they favored peasant scenes. Favorite subjects were death, disease, and sin.

PRE-RAPHAELITES

Between 1848–1910, a group of young English painters adopted the name Pre-Raphaelites in the hopes of recapturing a simpler time (before Raphael/academic training). Their work reflected nature in minutely detailed landscapes and allegories.

MORE "ISMS"

Fauvism (1905–1907), Cubism (1907–1920), Futurism (1908–1918), Dada (1916–1922), Realism (1920–1940), Surrealism (1922–1940s), German Expressionism (1910–1932), and Modernism (c. 1920–1945) brought painting and sculpture into the modern world. It appeared rules were made to be broken, and color, form, and reality were all distorted to reflect the artists' viewpoint. The Armory Show in New York in 1913 brought European trends to America, effectively ending the naturalistic trends of the Hudson River School and the Ash Can School (naturalism at its most romantic, and its most brutal). Technical advances in the use of iron allowed skyscrapers to be built, and these reflected other artistic trends of the time. Art Deco (c. 1930s) architecture once again was *unified,* with sculpture and decorative motifs complementing the architecture.

ARTE POVERA

This largely Italian movement (c. 1969) used junk objects in composition, a form of rebellion against materialism.

TWENTIETH-CENTURY TRENDS

Pop Art (1950s–1960s), Op Art (1960s), Abstract Expressionism (1945–1960), Hard Edge, Shaped, and Color Field Painting (1950–1960s), Photorealism (1960–1975), Minimal Art (1960s to present), Conceptual Art (1970s to present), Feminist Art (1970s to present), and Appropriationist Art (using other people's artwork—1970s to present) are all trends since mid-twentieth century. Artists in some societal groups retain the identity of their unique cultures, while others reflect their ethnic backgrounds through contemporary subjects. The artwork reflects the diversity of the population.

POST-MODERN

For a time New York seemed to dominate the art world, but as in the Renaissance when artists traveled and began an international trend, an international art developed. Artists the world over are influenced by what they see happening in other cultures. The art of the late twentieth century does not seem to have any one dominant trend, but includes many means of expression such as continued Photorealism, Appropriationism, Graffiti Art, Neo-Classicism, Neo-Expressionism, Neo-Conceptualism, Earth Art, and New Feminism. In the era of rapid worldwide communication, it would be surprising if change were *not* occurring as frequently in the field of art as it is everywhere else.

List 2–4   American Art Time Line

NATIVE AMERICAN ART
100–present

Burial Mounds
100–400

Mimbres Pot
1000–1200

California Basketmakers,
c. 1500

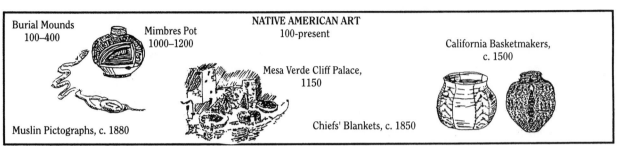

Mesa Verde Cliff Palace,
1150

Muslin Pictographs, c. 1880

Chiefs' Blankets, c. 1850

AMERICAN ART
1600–1800

1610   Alphabet Sampler
1705–1750 Robert Feke
1738–1820 Benjamin West

Scrimshaw

Independence Hall, c. 1751

Quilting

Monticello, 1768–1809

Edward Hicks, 1780–1849

Paul Revere, 1735–1818

AMERICAN ART
1800–1900

1790–1820   Federal Period
1820–1860   Greek Revival
1830–1875   Gothic Revival
c. 1880–1910 Art Nouveau

William Harnett, 1848–1892

George Catlin, 1796–1872

Audubon's Birds of America, 1827

Frederick Remington, 1861–1909

Louis Sullivan, 1856–1924

Winslow Homer, 1836–1910

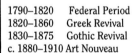

Whistler, 1834–1903

Henry Ossawa Tanner, 1859–1937

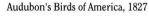

AMERICAN ART
1900–1950

1900–1920 Ash Can School
1905–1917 Photo Secession
1913   Armory Show
1915   American Modernism
c. 1925   Art Deco
1920–1940 Realism
from 1915 Precisionism

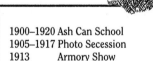

Jacob Lawrence

Georgia O'Keeffe

Armory Show,
1913

Edward Hopper

1919–1929 Harlem Renaissance
1930s   American Scene Painting
1930s   Works Progress Administration

AMERICAN ART
1950–present

1945–1965 Pop Culture
1960s   Op Art
c. 1960   Hyper Realists
late 1960s–
   present Feminist Art
1960s–
   present Post Modern
1960s   Conceptual Art
1970s on New Realism

Alexander Calder

Robert Rauschenberg

Keith Haring

List 2–5   American Art Overview

HUDSON RIVER SCHOOL

This was a group of painters (c. 1825–1875) whose work reflected their pride in the beauty and grandeur of the American landscape. The second generation of this "school" were sometimes called "luminist artists" because of their treatment of light.

ROCKY MOUNTAIN SCHOOL

This term was applied to Western artists (c. 1858–1900) who painted views of the frontier and Rocky Mountains in a similar manner to the Hudson River School.

WESTERN PAINTERS

These painters illustrated frontier life including Indian scenes, landscape, and army life.

AMERICAN IMPRESSIONISM

It began a little later (late nineteenth century) than French Impressionism and lasted into the twentieth century. In paintings of such Impressionists as "The Ten," forms were more solid in appearance, and there was less concern with light.

THE TEN

Most of this group of painters (1898–1919) had studied in Europe and reflected the popularity of Impressionism in Paris. Their first exhibition, "Ten American Painters," was in 1898, and they continued to show together for 20 years.

TROMPE L'OEIL PAINTERS

A number of Americans, including William Michael Harnett, John Frederick Peto, and Raphaelle Peale were virtuosos of "deceiving the eye" through their extremely realistic paintings (c. 1876–c. 1900).

THE EIGHT (THE ASH CAN SCHOOL)

They began as the Philadelphia Realists (where most of them had been newspaper artists), then moved to New York, and became the New York Realists. Their paintings (1900–1920) realistically depicted daily life in the American urban environment, specializing in people on crowded streets and at the park, theaters, and entertainment spectacles.

DADA

This (c. 1916) movement began in France as a revolt against World War I. It fostered creativity by rebelling against traditional forms of logic, art, and culture.

FUTURISM/CUBISM

Futurist/Cubist painting (c. 1909) was primarily a European movement, but a few painters attempted to show the pace and movement of American cities with fractured prisms of light.

PHOTO SECESSION

This (1905–1917) movement was headed by photographer Alfred Stieglitz. Exhibitions in his Gallery 291 spearheaded the modern movement in the United States.

SYNCHROMISM

Synchromist paintings (1913–1918) were filled with swirling, colorful shapes, that were softly painted and modeled.

ART DECO

Art Deco (c. 1925) referred to applied design that was primarily popular during the 1930s. It was used in buildings, furniture, decorative objects, jewelry, typefaces, and book bindings.

List 2–5   Continued

PRECISIONISM

Precisionist painters (1915–onward) were sometimes called Cubist-Realists or the Immaculates. Their paintings were frequently based on photography—transforming cities, the industrial landscape, and machinery to flattened shapes and strong shadows, stripped of detail almost to the point of abstraction.

GROUP F.64

A group of 1930s San Francisco photographers shared the belief that a photograph should not try to imitate a work of art, but simply be what it was—a black-and-white image of the finest possible sharpness and clarity.

AMERICAN SCENE PAINTING

American Scene painters in the 1930s thought that American art needed its own typically American subjects and scenes. There is little difference between the terms American Scene painters and Regionalists, and some of the painters are identified with both schools.

REGIONALISM

The 1930s Regionalists painted people at work, American legends, and landscapes, preserving in their paintings the atmosphere and lifestyles of different areas of the country.

THE BAUHAUS

This group was prominent in Germany from 1919–1933. When the Nazis closed the Bauhaus School in Dessau, Germany, in 1933, many Bauhaus artists were displaced and immigrated to the United States. They established a short-lived American Bauhaus in Chicago in 1938.

HARLEM RENAISSANCE

During the (1919–1929) Harlem Renaissance, African American artists in all the art forms received recognition. Writers, musicians, painters, sculptors, dancers, and actors portrayed the African American experience in their art, with far-reaching results. Many young African American artists were recruited to paint murals by the government during the depression.

FEDERAL ARTS PROJECTS

During the 1933–1943 depression, the Federal Government formed a number of different agencies to aid artists. Among these were PWAP (Public Works of Art Project), the WPA (Works Progress Administration), and the FSA (Farm Security Administration).

SOCIAL REALISM

The early 1930s–1940 Social Realists used their art to comment on the plight of poor or oppressed Americans. In 1936 they formed an Artists' Congress for the purpose of fighting facism, social inequities, and economic depression through their art.

MAGIC REALISM

Magic Realist painters (c. 1943) peopled their imaginary worlds with extreme, realistic representations of people.

ABSTRACT EXPRESSIONISM

Abstract Expressionists (1943–1960) conveyed emotion through their method of applying paint to canvas—whether it was random mark-making or specific, repeated forms.

HAPPENINGS

"Happenings" (performance art) in the late 1950s sometimes involved the audience and art or found objects. These spontaneous theatrical presentations were usually nonverbal, and often unplanned.

HARD-EDGE

With the creation of polymer paints, new techniques were possible in 1958–1960s. Masking tape applied to canvas enabled artists to make straight edges. Paintings were not always rectangular, but sometimes shaped to the

List 2–5   Continued

HARD-EDGE (cont.)

pattern of the painting. Hard-Edge referred to (usually brightly-colored geometric) paintings where colors were not blended into one another, but were next to each other.

COLOR FIELD PAINTING

In Color Field paintings (1960s), which usually involved few colors, large unprimed canvases were stained with acrylic paints without the use of strong tonal contrasts or visible brushstrokes.

MINIMAL ART

"Minimal Art" was a term that applied to a number of art movements, including Op Art, Color Field Painting, Serial Imagery (related works in a series), Hard-Edge painting, and the shaped canvas from the 1960s to the present. It sometimes featured the use of high-tech materials such as neon, plastic, and metals. Artworks were stripped to the essence, purposely devoid of any "artist's touch."

OP ART

These 1960s artists used devices such as high contrast, shape, and color to create optical illusions. Moiré patterns or geometric shapes in contrasting colors create the illusion of movement.

POP ART

Pop Art (1945–1965) reacted to the emotional quality of Abstract Expressionism through the use of banal consumer products as themes. The techniques often were direct copies of advertising techniques such as the Benday dot, or comic book styles.

CONCEPTUAL ART

Conceptual art (1970 to present) is often more an idea of art rather than an actual artwork. Sometimes it is written about or drawn, but not always executed. The result is that the location of the artwork is sometimes in the mind of the viewer.

PHOTOREALISM OR HYPERREALISM

These 1967–1977 artists had as their subject the everyday environment as seen through the eye of a camera. Photorealist artists tended to specialize, with one doing signs, another faces, or another still-lifes.

EARTH ART (OFTEN CALLED ENVIRONMENTAL ART)

Earth Art (1968 to the present) began when artists used a "new" medium—piles of rocks or dirt to form installations in galleries. The materials might be shaped by chance (such as a heap of sand), or by an artist (a circle of rocks arranged on a museum floor). Ultimately artists went to out-of-the-way places to create their (often impermanent) artworks. Drawings, films, and photographs of the work-in-progress were exhibited and sold.

FEMINIST ART

A movement (late 1960s to present) of women artists who combined female "subjects" with female objects such as quilts, fibers, and ceramics, to make a statement about feminism.

FUNK ART

Funk Art (1950–1960s) originated in the San Francisco Bay area. Although painters founded the movement, sculptural techniques and assemblage soon took over. Taboo subjects and materials that would not normally be considered suitable for art, became art.

NEO-EXPRESSIONISM

Neo-Expressionism (1975–present) was basically a German movement, but a number of American artists are considered part of the movement.

POST-MODERN

Post-Modernism (1960s to present) seems to include many "Neos" such as Neo-Classicism, Neo-Expressionism, Neo-Conceptualism, Neo-Romanticism, Neo-Dadism, Neo-Surrealism, New Perceptualism, New Realism, New Image Art, New Left, etc. In other words, everything old is new again!

List 2–6　Art and Culture, 35,000–500 BC

35,000–5000 BC	5000–3000 BC	3000–2000 BC	2000–1000 BC	1000–500 BC
VISUAL ART AND ARCHITECTURE Cave Paintings, Peche Merle, France, c. 35,000 BC Venus de la Corne, c. 25,000 BC	Narmer's Palette, c. 3000 BC Potter's Wheel, 3200 BC Egyptian Kingdoms, 3500–100 BC	King Zoser Step Pyramid, 2630 BC Great Pyramid of Cheops, 2528 BC Great Sphinx, c. 2500 BC Mycenae, 2300–1100 BC	Queen Hapshepsut's Funerary Temple, 1480 BC Tutankhamen, c. 1340 BC Chinese Painting, 1028 BC Shang Dynasty, 1766–1122 BC	Scythian Stag, 7th–6th century BC Etruscan, 750–200 BC Greek Dipylon Vase, 800–700 BC Charioteer of Delphi 500 BC
GOVERNMENT AND CULTURE	Japan, Jomon Culture, 5000 BC	Japan, Yayoi Culture, c. 3000 BC	Chou Dynasty, 1122–256 BC	Mexico, Olmec Culture, 850–150 BC
LITERATURE		Sumerian Cunieform writing, c. 3500 BC	First Chinese dictionary, 1100 BC Oldest Sanskrit literature, 1500 BC	Homer's *Illiad & Odyssey*, 750 BC Sappho, Greek Poet, c. 700 BC India, *Diamond Sutra* Scroll, 868 BC
SCIENCE Use of fire, c. 12,000 BC Egyptian calendar, c. 5000 BC	Middle East, Sundial, c. 3500 BC China, Egypt, Irrigation, c. 3150 BC	Egypt's 365-day calendar, 2772 BC India, Peru, Egypt, cotton produced, c. 2500–2000 BC	Iron Age, 1400 BC China, Silk production, 1500 BC Egypt, Papyrus, 1500 BC	China, Woodblock printing, 618 BC ·
MUSIC	Egypt, Harps & flutes, 4000 BC China, Bamboo pipes c. 3000 BC	China, 5-tone scale, c. 2500 BC Denmark, trumpets, c. 2000 BC	Hittites: Guitar, lyre, trumpet, c. 1500 BC Syria, musical notations, c. 1300 BC	Babylon: 7-tone scale, c. 800 BC Pythagoras introduces the octave, c. 600 BC Sumeria, earliest recorded music, 800 BC
WORLD EVENTS Jordan, Wall of Jericho, 7000 BC Yang Shan, Long Shan Culture, 7000–4000 BC	Sumerians, 3500–2000 BC Woven cloth, c. 5000 BC	Chinese observed eclipse of the sun, 2155 BC Temple at Edfu, c. 230 BC	Hammurabi's code of Law, 1290 BC Trojan War, 1185 BC Israelites leave Egypt, 1250 BC	David, King of Israel, 1000–960 BC Confucius, 551–479 BC Greek Alphabet

List 2–7   Art and Culture, 500 BC–AD 500

500–300 BC	300–100 BC	100 BC–AD 100	100–300 AD	300–500 AD
VISUAL ARTS AND ARCHITECTURE Africa, Nok Culture, 500 BC–AD 500 *Greek Theater,* Epidaurus, 400 BC Greek sculptor Phydias, c. 500–432 BC *Temple of Athena-Nike* 427–424 BC	Nike of Samothrace, 190 BC Greek sculptor Praxiles, c. 350–330 BC *Venus de Milo,* c. 140 BC Persia, Susa, *Bull Capitol,* 486–423 BC	Rome, *Pantheon,* AD 18–25 Pompeii, *Villa of the Mysteries,* 100 BC Roman, *Pont du Gard,* 1st century AD	Rome, *Trajan's Column,* AD 114 *Baths of Caracalla,* 212–216 AD China, Eastern Han, 2nd century AD America, Ohio, Serpent Burial Mound, 10–400 AD	*Arch of Constantine,* 312–315 AD *Emperor Constantine,* 306–337 AD *Diocletian's Palace,* Split, Croatia, AD 300 Peru, Colima Culture, 200 BC–AD 300
GOVERNMENT AND CULTURE Egypt, Ptolemaic Period, 332–30 BC	Mound Builders, Ohio Valley, 100 BC–AD 400 Nazca, Peru, 300 BC–AD 700	Mexican Zapotec and Monte Alban cultures, 200 BC–AD 200 Han Dynasty, 206 BC–AD 220	London founded, AD 43	End of Western Roman Empire, AD 476 MIssissippi Valley Culture, 450–500 AD
LITERATURE Euripedes, 484–406 BC Aristotle, 384–322 BC Socrates, 470–399 BC Plato, 428–348 BC	Hindu, *Bhagavad Gita,* c. 200 BC Roman poet Horace, 65–8 BC	First four books of *New Testament,* c. 70–100 AD Roman poet Ovid, 43 BC–AD 18	Chinese calligraphy, AD 175 Greek historian Plutarch, 47–120 AD	
SCIENCE Hippocrates, c. 400 BC	Hipparchus, trigonometry, c. 140 BC Euclid, deductive mathematics, c. 300 BC	China, paper making, c. AD 100 China, magnetism, c. AD 80	Native American production of potoato, tobacco, corn, chocolate, and tomatoes 100–500 AD	India, algebra used, c. AD 500 India, decimal system, c. AD 500
MUSIC Greek choral music, c. 500 BC Pindar, Greek musician, 520–477 BC	Aristotle's Musical Theory, c. 340 BC			Greek Melodos' hymns, AD 500 Peru, flutes, horns, tubas, drums, AD 450
WORLD EVENTS Buddha, 552–480 BC Prince Perspolis, 5th–4th cent., BC	Rosetta Stone, 195 BC Great Wall of China, c. 214 BC Laocoon, 200 BC Republic of Rome, 200–27 BC	Romans made first stone bridge, 100 BC Jesus of Nazareth, Christianity, 1–30 AD Pompeii, Vesuvius erupts, AD 79	Constantinople founded, AD 330	Maya Civilization, AD 470 Emperor Justinian, 483–565 AD

List 2–8   Art and Culture, 500–1000 AD

	500–600 AD	600–700 AD	700–800 AD	800–900 AD	900–1000 AD
VISUAL ARTS AND ARCHITECTURE	*Hagia Sophia,* 532–537 AD Earliest Chinese scroll landscape, AD 535 Japan, *Horyuji Temple,* AD 595	T'ang Dynasty, 618–906 AD England, *Purse,* Sutton Hoo, c. AD 655 *Book of Kells,* 760–820 AD India, Gupta Period, 320–600 AD	Classic Maya Art, 300–900 AD India, *Cave Temple at Ellora,* AD 700 T'ang Dynasty, c. AD 725	*Animal Head,* Oseberg Ship-Burial, AD 825 *Great Mosque at Samarra,* AD 848–852 India, *Mamallapuram,* early 8th century AD	al-Azhar Mosque, Cairo, AD 970 Kingdom of Mali, 800–1550 AD 2nd Pueblo Period, Southwestern U.S., AD 900 *Mosque of Cordoba,* AD 900
GOVERNMENT AND CULTURE	Byzantine Empire, 500–1453 AD	Mayan Culture, AD 600 Japan, Asuka Period, 552–645 AD Japan, Nara Period, 645–784 AD	Japan, Early Heian Period, 784–897 AD		Mexico, Olmec, Classic Period, AD 1000 Peru, Chimu Culture, 900–1465 AD
LITERATURE	Epic poem, *Hero and Leander,* AD 550	Library at Alexandria, AD 640 China, book printing, AD 600		*Utrecht Psalter,* AD 832	
SCIENCE	India, decimal system, AD 595	India, concept of 0, c. AD 600 China, cast iron, AD 618	Egypt, sugar grown, AD 710 France, Crossbow used, AD 851	Alfred the Great, 24-hour measurment system, AD 886	China, Canal locks invented, AD 980
MUSIC	China, orchestras formed, AD 619		Germany, France, England, Gregorian Church Music, AD 750		Winchester Cathedral organ, AD 980
WORLD EVENTS	Mohammed, 570–632 AD Emperor Justinian, 483–565 AD Paracas in Peru, AD 500	Mohammed's flight to Medina, AD 622 Jerusalem, *Dome of the Rock,* AD 691 Baghdad founded by Muslims, AD 762	First Olympics, AD 776	Charlemagne, 742–814 AD First Holy Roman Emperor	Ottonian Rule, 900–1150 AD Leif Ericson arrived in America, AD 1000 Sung Dynasty, 960–1280 AD

List 2–9   Art and Culture, 1000–1500

1000–1100	1100–1200	1200–1300	1300–1400	1400–1500
VISUAL ARTS AND ARCHITECTURE *Bayeux Tapestry,* 1067–1083 Yoruba Kingdoms founded, 1000 Native American, Anasazi, 700–1750	Chartres Cathedral, c. 1210–1236 *Abbot Suger's Chalice,* 1147 Native American *Deer Mask,* 800–1400 Kamakura Period, Japan, 1185–1333	Giotto di Bondone, c. 1266–1337 Notre Dame, Paris, c. 1250 Classical Ife Art, 1100–1500 Lion Court, Alhambra Palace, 14th century	Northern Renaissance, 1350–1600 *Tres Riches Heures,* Limburgh Brothers, 1400–1430 *Temple of Heaven,* Forbidden City, 1420	Colleoni, Verrocchio, 1483 Classical Benin Art, c. 1500 Botticelli's *Venus,* 1480
GOVERNMENT AND CULTURE William the Conquerer, 1028–1087	Saladin, Syrian Commander of Egypt, 1138–1193 Peru, Inca, 1200–1530	China, Yuan Dynasty (Mongol), 1271–1368	Japan, Muromachi Period, 1333–1573	Peru, Macchu Picchu, Inca 1450–1500
LITERATURE Omar Khayyam, 1027–1123	*Reynard the Fox* fable, 1176	*Magna Carta,* 1215 *Roman de la Rose,* 1225	Boccacio's *Decameron,* 1348–1353 Geoffrey Chaucer, 1340–1400 Petrarch, Italian Poet, 1304–1374	Printing press, movable type, 1450 Gutenberg's Bible, 1454 Erasmus, 1511
SCIENCE	China, Rocket, 1100 China, Gunpowder, c. 1150	Eye glasses, 1285 Roger Bacon invented magnifying glass, 1250 Nitric Acid, 1287	Jan Van Eyck, Oil painting perfected, 1395–1441 Wire, 1410 Metal cannon, 1326	Lunar nautical navigation, 1474 Leonardo's drawing of a flying machine, 1493
MUSIC Berno, Books on Musical Theory, 1008 Guida de Arezzo, 995–1050	Secular music begins, 1100 France, Troubador musicians, 1125	Dresden, Boys choir founded, 1220 Choral *Passion,* 1250	Paris Musician's Guild, 1330–1773 Pope forbids use of counterpoint in church music, 1322	First printed music, 1465
WORLD EVENTS First Christian Crusade, 1096–1099 Duncan of Scotland killed by Macbeth, 1040	*Tower of London,* 1078–1300 *Mesa Verde Cliff Palace,* 1150	Marco Polo, 1271 Sienna University founded, 1203 India, Shiva Nataraja, 12th century	Beginning of Hundred Years' War, 1337 England, Black Death, 1361	*Sun Stone,* Aztec calendar, 1450–1500 Joan of Arc, 1412–1431 Columbus sails to West Indies, 1492 Martin Luther, 1483–1546

List 2–10   Art and Culture, 1500–1750

	1500–1550	1550–1600	1600–1650	1650–1700	1700–1750
VISUAL ARTS AND ARCHITECTURE	High Renaissance, 1495–1520 *David*, Castagno, 1450 Bramante's *Tempietto*, 1502	Baroque, 1590–1750 Andrea Palladio, 1508–1580 Mexico City, *Cathedral*, 1563 Constantinople, *Blue Mosque*, 1557	Judith Leyster, *The Jester*, 1609–1660 Agra, India, *Taj Mahal*, c. 1635 Benin Culture Japan, Edo Period, 1614–1868	Rococo Art in Europe, 1697–1764 Rembrandt's *Polish Rider*, 1655 Borromini's *San Carlo allo Quatro Fontana*, 1665–1667	*St. Paul's Cathedral*, 1675–1710 *Voltaire Seated*, Houdon *Independence Hall*, c. 1751 *Pompei* and *Herculaneum* discovered, 1745
GOVERNMENT AND CULTURE Pissarro conquers Peru, 1533		Kingdom of Asante, 1600	China, Qing (Ching) Dynasty, 1644–1911	Quakers settled, 1668	
LITERATURE François Rabelais, 1494–1553 Erasmus' *Colloquia*, 1519		William Shakespeare, 1564–1616 Cervantes' *Don Quixote*, 1605–1615 Christopher Marlowe, 1564–1593	King James version of the *Bible*, 1611		*Guilliver's Travels*, 1726 Benjamin Franklin's *Poor Richard's Almanack*, 1732 *Candide*, 1694–1778
SCIENCE Nostradamus, Astrologer, 1503–1566 Pistol, 1540		Mercator's navigation map, 1569 Modern calendar, 1582	Galileo's astronomical telescope, 1609 Logarithms, 1614 Thermometer, 1616 Geometry, 1637 Barometer, 1643	Isaac Newton's *Theory of Gravity*, 1684 Halley's Comet, 1682 Bacteria identified, 1683 Fahrenheit, 1686–1736	Steam engine, 1712
MUSIC		Bartoleme Spolone, Madrigal composer, 1529–1586 Violin developed, 1553	Antonio Stradavari's violins, 1644–1737 Claudio Monteverdi, 1567–1643	George Frideric Handel, 1685–1759 Antonio Vivaldi, 1678–1741 Johann Sebastian Bach, 1685–1750	Bartolomeo Christofori, Pianoforte, 1709 Franz Joseph Haydn, 1732–1809
WORLD EVENTS Anglican Church, 1534 Cortez brings horses to America, 1519 John Calvin, 1509–1564		Hernando de Soto discovers Mississippi River, 1541 Spanish Armada defeated, 1588 Galileo, 1564–1642 Henry VIII, 1491–1547	Dutch East India Company, 1602 Jamestown, VA, 1607 Santa Fe, NM, 1610 Plymouth Rock, 1620 Harvard founded, 1636	Marquette and Joliet explore Mississippi River, 1673 Massachusetts, witches hanged, 1692 Pennsylvania founded by William Penn, 1681	Captain Kidd hanged in London, 1701 George Washington, 1732–1799 The *Alamo*, 1744

List 2–11   Art and Culture, 1750–1875

1750–1775	1775–1800	1800–1825	1825–1850	1850–1875
VISUAL ARTS AND ARCHITECTURE Mount Vernon, 1759–1769 *George Washington,* Gilbert Stuart, 1755–1828 *George Washington Crossing the Delaware,* Leutz, 1851	George Catlin, 1796–1872 John J. Audubon, 1785–1851 *Birds of America,* 1827 Edward Hicks, 1780–1849	Africa, Zulu people, c. 1800 Strickland, *Merchant's Exchange,* 1822	Mary Cassatt, 1845–1926 James Abott McNeill, Whistler, 1834–1903 Edgar Degas, 1834–1917	Louis Sullivan, 1856–1909 Frederic Remington, 1861–1909 Henri Matisse, 1869–1964 Japan, Meiji Restoration, 1868
GOVERNMENT AND CULTURE American Revolutionary War, 1775–1783	Declaration of Independence, July 4, 1776 French Revolution begins, 1789	War of 1812 Simon Bolivar, Battle of Waterloo, 1815	USA war with Mexico, 1846 Trail of Tears, 13,000 Cherokees sent to Oklahoma, 1839	War Between the States, 1861–1865 Lincoln assassinated, 1865
LITERATURE William Wordsworth, 1770–1850 *Encyclopedia Britannica,* 1770	*Common Sense,* 1776 *The Rights of Man,* Thomas Paine, 1890	*Pride and Prejudice,* Jane Austen, 1813 Charles Dickens, 1812–1870	*Little Women,* Louisa May Alcott, 1832–1888 Tolstoy, 1828–1910	*War and Peace,* 1864 *Great Expectations,* Charles Dickens, 1861 *Uncle Tom's Cabin,* Stowe, 1851/52
SCIENCE Ben Franklin's kite experiments, 1752 Priestley and Rutherford discover nitrogen, 1772	Steam engine, James Watts, 1769 Hydrochloric acid, Joseph Priesley, 1775 Cotton gin, Eli Whitney, 1793	Electricity, 1800	Daguerrotype, 1839 Telegraph, Samuel F.B. Morse, 1844	*Origin of the Species,* Darwin, 1859 Pasteur's theory of germ fermentation, 1861 Periodic Law of Elements, 1869
MUSIC Wolfgang Amadeus Mozart, 1756–1791 Ludwig von Beethoven, 1770–1827	*Beggar's Opera,* 1750 Frans Schubert, 1797–1828	Frederic Chopin, 1810–1849 Franz Liszt, 1811–1886 Giuseppe Verdi, 1813–1901	Johann Strauss, 1825–1899 Johannes Brahms, 1833–1897 Peter Tchaikovsky, 1840–1893	Claude Debussy, 1862–1918 Richard Strauss, 1864–1949 Scott Joplin, 1868–1917
WORLD EVENTS Boston Massacre, 1770 Boston Tea Party, 1773	Cook discovers Hawaii, 1778 Constitution of USA, 1787	Louisiana Purchase, 1803 Cherokee written alphabet, 1821	Queen Victoria crowned, 1837 California, Gold Rush, 1849	Pony Express, 1860 USA buys Alaska, 1867 Women's Suffrage, 1869 Transcontinental Railroad, 1870 Barnum's Circus, 1871

List 2–12   Art and Culture, 1875–1950

1875–1900	1900–1920	1920–1930	1930–1940	1940–1950
VISUAL ARTS AND ARCHITECTURE Art Nouveau, 1880–1910 George Caleb Bingham, 1811–1879 Post-Impressionism, 1886–1920 Rodin's *The Thinker,* 1880–1900	Fauvism, 1905–1907 Cubism, 1907–1920 Armory Show, 1913 Picasso's *Old Blind Gutiar Player,* 1903 Futurism, 1908 *Seated Woman,* 1901 Aristide Maillol 1861–1944 *The Old King,* 1937 Georges Rouault, 1871–1958	Bauhaus, 1925 Dada, Surrealism, 1916–1922 Max Beckmann, 1920 *Reclining Figure,* Henry Moore, 1926 Harlem Renaissance, 1919–1929	*Flying Dragon,* 1975 Alexander Calder, 1898–1976 Georgia O'Keeffe, 1887–1986 *American Gothic,* 1930 Grant Wood, 1892–1942	Abstract Expressionism, 1945–1960 Pop Culture, 1945–1965 Claes Oldenberg, b. 1929 *Horse and Rider,* Marino Marini, 1949 Robert Rauschenberg, b. 1925 Andy Warhol, 1927–1987
GOVERNMENT AND CULTURE Battle of Little Big Horn, 1876 Boxer Rebellion in China, 1900	Russian Revolution, 1917 Republic of China, 1912–1949 Archduke Ferdinand killed, 1914	Panama Canal, 1904 League of Nations, 1920	Japan invades Manchuria, 1931 People's Republic of China, 1949 Spanish Civil War, 1936	World War II, 1941–1945 UN founded, 1946 NATO founded, 1949
LITERATURE Robert Frost, 1874–1963 Mark Twain, *Tom Sawyer,* 1876	A. Conan Doyle, *Hound of the Baskervilles,* 1902 John Steinbeck, 1902–1968	F. Scott Fitzgerald, *The Great Gatsby,* 1925 Mona van Duyn, poet, 1921	Ernest Hemingway, *The Sun Also Rises,* 1926 *For Whom the Bell Tolls,* 1940	*Watch on the Rhine,* Lillian Hellman, 1940 *Blood, Sweat, and Tears,* W. Churchill, 1941
SCIENCE Telephone, 1876 Lightbulb, 1879 Linotype, 1886 Contact Lens, 1887 Aspirin, 1899	Marie and Pierre Curie, Radium, 1902 Einstein's Theory of Relativity, 1905 Wasserman, Test for syphilis, 1906	Penicillin, Alexander Fleming, 1928 Nylon, Neoprene, Carothers and Colins, 1932	Jet engine, 1936 Photocopier, Chester Carlson, 1938	Fermi splits the atom, 1942 Computer, 1944
MUSIC George Gershwin, 1898–1937 Louis Armstrong, 1890–1971	Ragtime Jazz, 1901 Billy Holiday, 1915–1959 John Cage, 1912–1992 L. Bernstein, 1918–1990	Los Angeles Symphony, 1919 *Showboat,* Jerome Kern and Oscar Hammerstein, 1927	Bessie Smith, 1894–1937 Cole Porter, 1893–1964	Nat King Cole, 1919–1965 Aaron Copland, 1900–1990
WORLD EVENTS Hull House founded, 1889 AFL (American Federation of Labor), 1885 Pancho Villa, 1878–1923 Gas auto engine, 1885	Wright Brothers, 1903 Pure Food & Drug Act, 1906 Model T Ford, 1908 Gene theory, 1910 Leica camera, 1914 World War I, 1918 India, Ghandi, 1920	Grand Old Opry, 1924 Income tax, 1913 Prohibition, 1920 Stock market crash, 1929 Lindbergh flies solo across Atlantic, 1927	CCC (Civilian Conservation Corps), 1933 WPA (Works Progress Administration), 1935 Great Dust Bowl, 1936	Atomic Bomb, World War II ends, 1945 India, British rule ends, 1947 Israel established, 1948

List 2–13   Art and Culture, 1950–2000

	1950–1960	1960–1970	1970–1980	1980–1990	1990–present
VISUAL ARTS AND ARCHITECTURE	Pop Art, 1950s and 1960s *Geodesic Dome,* 1960 *Head,* Roy Lichtenstein, 1966 Guggenheim Museum, 1959 Frank L. Wright, 1867–1959	Feminist Art, 1960s to 1970s *Giant Hamburger,* Claes Oldenburg, 1969 *Cubi XVIII,* David Smith, 1964 Marisol b. 1930 *Homage to a Square,* Josef Albers, 1963	*Tourists,* Duane Hanson, 1970 Jasper Johns, 1968 *Goldfish Bowl,* Roy Lichtenstein, 1978	Portland Public Service Building, Michael Graves, 1981 *Atiyah,* Deborah Butterfield, 1986	*American Center,* Frank Gehry, 1994 Shingle Style Revival, Robert A.M. Stern, 1991 *Raven Mask,* Joe Bolton, 1992
GOVERNMENT AND CULTURE Queen Elizabeth, 1952 European Common Market, 1957		Chinese Cultural Revoltuion, 1965–1968 Vietnam War, 1965–1973	Watergate, Nixon resigns, 1973–1974 Egypt, Aswan Dam, 1970 US Bicentennial, 1976	China, Tianamen Square, 1989	Gulf War, 1991 Argentina invades Falkland Islands, 1992 Hong Kong reverts to China, 1997
LITERATURE Nobel Prize to William Faulkner, 1950 J.D. Salinger's *Catcher in the Rye,* 1951		Harper Lee, *To Kill a Mockingbird,* 1961 Steinbeck, *Travels with Charlie,* 1962 William Faulkner, *The Reivers,* 1963	*The Right Stuff,* Thomas Wolfe, 1975	*The Color Purple,* Alice Walker, 1983 *Lonesome Dove,* Larry McMurtry, 1986 *Satanic Verses,* Salman Rushdie, 1988	Nobel Prize to Toni Morrison, 1993 Frank McCourt, *Angela's Ashes,* 1997
SCIENCE Measles vaccine, 1953 Hydrogen bomb, 1954 Polio vaccine, Jonas Salk, 1955 Space launch, 1957		Laser, 1960 First human heart transplant, 1967	EPA (Environmental Protection Agency), 1972 First test–tube baby born, 1978	AIDS diagnosed, 1982 Artificial heart, 1982 DNA fingerprinting, 1986	Computer Technology, Internet, 1997 Cloning of a sheep, 1997 Successful Mars Expedition, 1997
MUSIC Sergey Prokofiev, 1891–1953		The Beatles, 1962 Hard Rock, Jimi Hendrix, 1968	*Jesus Christ Superstar,* 1971 Elvis Presley died, 1977	Beatle John Lennon shot, 1980 Compact disk player, 1984	Dizzy Gillespie dies, 1993
WORLD EVENTS *Brown vs. Topeka Board of Education,* 1954 USSR's Sputnik, 1957 Alaska and Hawaii achieve statehood, 1959 OPEC, 13 nations, 1960		J.F. Kennedy assassinated, 1963 Six-day war in Israel, 1967 Martin Luther King, Robert Kennedy, assassinated, 1968 US astronauts land on the moon, 1969	Charles Manson, 1971 Busing approved for integration, 1971 *Roe vs. Wade,* 1973 Women admitted to military academies, 1975 Wounded Knee, 1973 First space lab, 1973	First woman Supreme Court Justice, 1981 Columbia space shuttle, 1981 *A Nation at Risk,* report on schools, 1983 Olympics in LA, 1984	Berlin Wall, 1961–1990 Sexual harassment, 1991 Watts riots, 1992 World Trade Center bombed, 1993 Balkan hostilities, 1992 OJ Simpson trial, 1995

List 2–14   Japanese Historical Periods

Jomon	5000 BC
Yayoi	3000 BC
Prehistoric period	ended AD 552
Asuka period	552–645
Nara period	645–784
Heian period	784–1185
Early Heian	784–897
Middle and Late Heian	897–1185
Kamakura period	1185–1333
Muromachi period	1333–1573
Momoyama period	1573–1614
Edo, or Tokugawa period	1614–1868
Meiji Restoration	1868–1912
Modern times	1912–present

List 2–15   Chinese Painting Time Line

1027–256 BC, Chou	Chinese painting makes its first appearance
206 BC–AD 220, Han	Introduces style that later becomes known as traditional Chinese technique
220–580 AD, Six Dynasties Era	Painting on scrolls first appears
618–906 AD, T'ang	"Golden Age" of Chinese art; advances in painting
960–1280 AD, Sung	"Golden Age" of landscape painting
1368–1644 AD, Ming	The collecting and restoration of older, traditional works become fashionable
1644–1911 AD, Qing (Ch'ing)	Painting continues to be main form of expression for the literary class

Drawn from *Landscape After a Song by Yang Hung-hsui "The Clearing Sky, The Fading Rainbow and The Red Glow of Sunset,"* 1621–1624, Tung Ch'i-ch'ang, Nelson-Atkins Museum of Art, Kansas City, Missouri

List 2–16   Chinese Dynasties

Neolithic Period	c. 7000–1600 BC	Liao Dynasty	916–1125
Yanshao Culture	5000–2000 BC	Sung (Song)	960–1280
Longshan Culture	3000/2500–1500 BC	Northern Sung	960–1127
Hsia (Xia)	2205–1766 BC	Southern Sung	1127–1279
Shang Dynasty	c. 1600–1027 BC	Jin Dynasty	1115–1234
Zhou (Chou)	1122–770 BC	Yuan (Mongol) Dynasty	1271–1368
Western Zhou	1027–771 BC	Ming Dynasty	1368–1644
Eastern Zhou	770–256 BC	Hungwu	1368–1398
Period of Spring and Autumn	770–475 BC	Jianwen	1398–1402
Warring States Period	475–221 BC	Yongle	1403–1424
Qin (Ch'in)	221–207 BC	Hongxi	1425
Han Dynasty		Xuande	1426–1435
Western (former) Han	206 BC–AD 9	Zhengtong	1436–1449
Xin	9–25 AD	Jingtai	1450–1456
Eastern (later) Han	25–220	Tianshun	1457–1464
Six Dynasties Period	220–580	Chenghua	1465–1487
Three Kingdoms Period	220–265	Hongzhi	1488–1505
Tsin (Jin)	265–420	Zhengde	1506–1521
Western Jin	265–316	Jiajing	1522–1566
Eastern Jin	317–420	Longqing	1567–1572
Northern Dynasty		Wanli	1572–1620
Northern Wei	386–534	Tiachang	1620
Eastern Wei	534–550	Tianqi	1620–1627
Western Wei	535–556	Chongzhen	1628–1644
Northern Qui	550–557	Qing (Ch'ing)-(Manchu) Dynasty	1644–1911
Northern Zhou	557–581	Shunzhi	1644–1661
Southern Dynasty		Kangxi	1662–1722
Song	420–479	Yongzheng	1723–1735
Qi	479–502	Qianlong	1735–1795
Liang	502–557	Jiaqing	1796–1820
Chen	557–589	Daoguang	1821–1850
Sui Dynasty	589–618	Xianfeng	1851–1861
Tang (T'ang) Dynasty	618–906	Tongzhi	1862–1874
Five Dynasties and Ten Kingdoms	906–960	Guangxu	1875–1908
Later Liang	907–923	Xuantong	1908–1911
Later Tang	923–936	Republic of China	1912–1949
Later Jin	936–947	People's Republic of China	1949–present
Later Han	947–950		
Later Zhou	951–960		

List 2–17   Egyptian Historical Periods

Predynastic Period

Badarian	6100–3800 BC
Naqada I, Amratian	3800–3600 BC
Naqada II, Early Gerzean	3600–3400 BC
Naqada III, Late Gerzean	3400–3100 BC
Dynasty o, Late Predynastic	3100–2920 BC

Dynastic Period, Ruler(s)	**Capital City**	**Time Period**
Early Dynastic Period: Old Kingdom		2940–2134 BC
Dynasties 1 and 2, King Narmer (Menes)	Thinis	2940–2649 BC
Dynasty 3, Kings Zoser, Snefu	Memphis	2649–2575 BC
Dynasty 4, Cheops, Chefren, and Mycerinus	Memphis	2575–2465 BC
Dynasty 5, Userkaf, Sahura, Niuserra, Unas, et al.	Memphis	2465–2323 BC
Dynasty 6, Kings Teti, Pepi I, et al.	Memphis	2323–2150 BC
First Intermediate Period		2134–2040 BC
Dynasties 7 and 8, many kings, short reigns	Memphis	2150–2134 BC
Middle Kingdom		2040–1640 BC
Dynasties 9 and 10	Heracleopolis	2134–2040 BC
Dynasty 11, Count of Thebes, Menuhotep	Thebes (Preunification)	2134–2040 BC
Dynasty 11	Thebes (Postunification)	2040–1991 BC
Dynasty 12, Kings Amenemhat, Sesostris	Thebes	1991–1783 BC
Second Intermediate Period		1640–1532 BC
Dynasties 13–17, 50 rulers, Sebekhotep, Neferhotep, et al.		1783–1640 BC
Dynasty 13	Thebes	1783–1640 BC
Dynasty 14, Xoite rulers		ends 1640 BC
Dynasties 15 and 16, Hyksos kings		1640–1532 BC
Dynasty 17, Ahmose I	Thebes	1640–1550 BC
New Kingdom (Empire)		1550–1070 BC
Dynasty 18, Amenophis I, Tuthmosis I, II, and III, Hatshepsut, Akhenaten, Tutankhamen, Horemheb	Diospolis, Luxor, and Karnak	1550–1307 BC
Dynasty 19, Harmhab, Seti I, and Ramesses I and II	Tomb at Abu Simbel Diospolis	1307–1196 BC
Dynasty 20, Ramesses III, IV, and V	Diospolis	1196–1070 BC
Third Intermediate Period (Post Empire)		1070–332 BC
Dynasty 21	Tanis	1070–945 BC
Dynasty 22, Sheshonk, Petubastis, Osorkon, Takecloth		945–745 BC
Dynasty 23	Tanis	745–712 BC
Dynasty 24, Psamtik	Sais	724–712 BC
Dynasty 25, Ethiopian Kings		712–664 BC
Dynasty 26, Saite Kings: Necho, Apries	Sais	664–525 BC
Dynasties 27 to 30, Persian kings		525–343 BC
Ptolemaic Period		332–30 BC
Alexander the Great	Alexandria	332–323 BC
Macedonian dynasty		332–304 BC
Ptolemies I–XV, Cleopatra (last of the Ptolemies)		304–30 BC
Roman Domination		30 BC–AD 395

List 2–18   Greek and Roman Gods, Goddesses, and Heroes

This list includes most of the well-known gods, goddesses, and heroes of the Greek and Roman cultures. Stories about the gods were perpetuated as explanations of the universe, and they were given many very human characteristics. From ancient times the stories have been interpreted in literature and art.

THE TITANS	**THE TITANESSES**
Oceanus	Tethys, goddess of the sea/fertility
Coeus	Theia
Crius	Themis, justice
Hyperion	Mnemosyne, memory/remembrance
Iapetus	Phoebe
Chronus	Rhea, mother of Zeus

THE OLYMPIANS

Greek Name (Roman Name)

Zeus(Jupiter)	ruler of the gods, god of the sky; symbol: thunderbolt and lightning
Hera (Juno)	goddess of marriages, wife of Zeus
Aphrodite (Venus)	goddess of love and beauty
Apollo (Apollo)	god of the sun, truth (reason), archery, music, medicine, and prophecy
Ares (Mars)	god of war
Artemis (Diana)	goddess of the hunt, twin sister of Apollo, guardian of women
Demeter (Ceres)	goddess of the underworld/agriculture
Hades (Pluto)	ruler of the underworld
Hermes (Mercury)	messenger of the gods
Hestia (Vesta)	goddess of the family and home
Pallas Athena (Minerva)	goddess of wisdom and war; patroness of artisans
Poseidon (Neptune)	ruler of the sea; carried a magic trident

OTHER GODS

Acacesius	benefactor of mankind, deliverer from evil
Amphitrite	wife of Poseidon, goddess of the sea
Asklepios (Aesculapius)	god of healing
Atlas	superhuman strength; carried the world on his shoulders
Chronus (Saturn)	god of time
Dionysus (Bacchus)	god of wine
Eos (Aurora)	goddess of dawn
Epimetheus	cousin of Zeus; slow-witted
Eros (Cupid)	god of love
Fortuna	goddess of fate (fortune)
Hephaistos (Vulcan)	god of fire
Hygeia	goddess of health
Menoetius	arrogant, brutal, evil man
Nike (Victoria)	goddess of victory
Pan (Faunus)	god of the shepherds; half-human/half-goat
Pandora	when she opened the box, she released all the plagues against mankind
Persephone (Prosperine)	goddess of the underworld

List 2–18   Continued

OTHER GODS (cont.)

Priapus	god of fertility
Prometheus	cousin of Zeus; clever
Psyche	goddess of the soul

ZEUS'S WIVES AND LOVES

Alcmene	mother of Hercules and Semele
Demeter (Ceres)	mother of Persephone
Europa	sister of Cadmus; the mother of famous sons (with Zeus)
Eurynome	mother of the three "graces": Aglaia, Euphrosyne, Thalia
Harmonia	possibly the mother of the nine Muses
Hera (Juno)	mother of Ares, Hebe, Eileithyia, and Hephaestus (not Zeus's daughter)
Io	mother of Epaphus
Leto	mother of Artemis and Apollo
Maia	mother of Hermes
Metis	Zeus swallowed her before she could give birth; Zeus's first wife
Mnemosyne	associated with memory; mother of the nine Muses
Semele	mother of Dionysus
Themis	mother of the "hours": Thallo, Auxo, Carpo; and the "fates": Clotho, Lachesis, Atropos

HEROES (HALF-HUMAN/HALF-DIVINE)

Atalanta	female hero who hunted with other heroes for the Calydonian boar
Bellerophon	ordered to kill the fire-breathing monster (the Cimera); mounted on Pegasus
Cadmus	founder of the city of Thebes
Deucalion and Pyrrha	sole survivors of the flood that Zeus brought to destroy a wicked world
Hercules	completed twelve tasks to atone for a crime his father committed
Io	female ancestor (with Zeus) of Heracles (Hercules)
Jason	leader of the heroes of the ship "Argo" in search of the Golden Fleece
Oedipus	unknowingly killed his father and married his mother
Peleus	father of Achilles
Perseus	killed Medusa, one of the Gorgons
Terminus	god of boundaries
Theseus	kin of Heracles, King of Athens, sailed with Jason on the "Argo"

HEROES OF THE TROJAN WAR

Odysseus (Ulysses)	hero of the *Iliad,* king of Ithaca; creator of the Trojan Horse
Achilles	greatest of the Greek warriors
Aeneas	forefather of the Romans
Agamemnon	commander of the Greeks, brother-in-law of Helen
Ajax	second to Achilles in valor and beauty
Hector	enemy of Achilles
Menelaus	descendant of Atreus
Patroclus	
Priam	

List 2–18   Continued

OTHERS

Three Furies (punished those who escaped justice)

Alecto

Megara

Tisiphone

Three Fates (spun the threads of human destiny)

Atropos (Morta)

Clotho (Nona)

Lachesis (Decuma)

Three Graces (goddesses of the social arts)

Aglaia

Euphrosyne

Thalia

Nine Muses (sisters; daughters of Zeus)

Calliope	muse of epic poetry; chief of the muses
Clio	muse of history
Erato	muse of love poetry
Euterpe	muse of lyric poetry
Melpomene	muse of tragedy
Polyhymnia	muse of sacred poetry, mime
Terpsichore	muse of dance
Thalia	muse of comedy
Urania	muse of astronomy

Gorgons (The three winged sisters)

Euryale

Medusa

Stheno

List 2–19   Greek Historical Periods

MEDITERRANEAN ART

Aegean, Early Cycladic	1800–2000 BC
Greek-speaking tribes on the mainland	2000 BC
Mycenae	2300–1100 BC
Minoan	2000–1100 BC

GREEK VASE TIME PERIODS

Geometric Period, *Dipylon Amphora,* 8th century BC, Athens	850–700 BC
Orientalizing Phase, *Owl Perfume Jar,* c. 650 BC, Corinth	700–600 BC
Black Figured (Archaic), *Heracles Strangling the Nemean Lion,* c. 525 BC	650–480 BC
Red Figured, *Lapith and Centaur,* c. 490–480 BC	c. 530 BC
Classical	480–323 BC
Red-Figure, *Eos and Memnon,* c. 490–480 BC	
White Ground, *Mistress and Maid,* 440–430 BC	

GREEK SCULPTURE TIME PERIODS

Archaic, *Kouros,* c. 600 BC, Metropolitan Museum of Art, New York City	700–480 BC
Classical, *Kritios Boy,* c. 480 BC, Acropolis Museum	480–323 BC
Hellenistic, *Dying Gaul,* c. 230–220 BC, Capitoline Museums, Rome	323–30 BC

GREEK ARCHITECTURE TIME PERIODS

Geometric Period, timber and mud-brick buildings	c. 750 BC
Archaic Period, (Doric), *Temple of Apollo,* Corinth	c. 540 BC
Classical Period, (Doric, Ionic)	c. 480 BC
Hellenistic Period, (Ionic, Corinthian),	323–30 BC
Altar of Zeus, c. 175 BC, Pergamon	

List 2–20   Mythological Paintings

Myths were a favorite subject of painters and sculptors, giving them an opportunity to paint figures, yet maintaining the approval of the church.

Aenas Fleeing from Troy, Barocci, 1598, Villa Borghese, Rome

Angelica and the Hermit, Peter Paul Rubens, 1620–1625, Kunsthistorisches Museum, Vienna

Angelica, Jean-Auguste-Dominique Ingres, 1819, Museu de Arte, São Paulo, Brazil

Apollo and Daphne, Nicolas Poussin, 1664, Louvre, Paris

Apollo and Daphne, Nicolas Poussin, c. 1627, Alte Pinakothek, Munich

Apollo Pursuing Daphne, Giambattista Tiepolo, c. 1755–1760, National Gallery of Art, Washington, DC

Apollo-Bacchus, Nicolas Poussin, 1626, Nationalmuseum, Stockholm

Artemis and a Swan, Pan Painter, c. 480–450 BC, Hermitage, St. Petersburg, Russia

Ascanius Shooting the Stag, Claude Lorraine, 1682, Ashmolean Museum, Oxford, England

Atalanta and Hippomenes, Guido Reni, c. 1620, Museo Nationale di Capodimonte, Naples

Atalanta and Meleager, Jacob Jordaens, c. 1628, Prado, Madrid

Bacchanal of the Andrians, Titian, 1523–1525, Prado, Madrid

Bacchanal, Peter Paul Rubens, 1630, Nationalmuseum, Stockholm

Bacchanal, Nicolas Poussin, c. 1630, Prado, Madrid

Bacchus and Ariadne, Titian, 1523, National Gallery, London

Youthful Bacchus, Caravaggio, c. 1589, Uffizi Gallery, Florence

Calumny of Apelles, Sandro Botticelli, c. 1495, Uffizi Gallery, Florence

Concert Champetre, Titian, 1510–1511, Louvre, Paris

Cupid Complaining to Venus, Lucas Cranach, c. 1530, National Gallery, London

Danae, Titian, 1553–1554, Prado, Madrid

Danae, Antonio Corregio, c. 1534, Villa Borghese, Rome

Dance in Honor of Priapus, Nicolas Poussin, 1638–1640, Museu de Arte, São Paulo, Brazil

Diana after her Bath, François Boucher, 1742, Louvre, Paris

Diana and Actaeon, Titian, 1556–1559, National Gallery of Scotland, Edinburgh

Diana and her Nymphs, Peter Paul Rubens, 1635–1640, Prado, Madrid

Diana as a Huntress, Fontainebleau School, c. 1550, Louvre, Paris

Diana, Resting, François Boucher, 1742, Louvre, Paris

Drunken Silenus, Anthony van Dyck, c. 1620, Gemaldegalerie, Dresden

Flora, Quentin Metsys, 1561, Nationalmuseum, Stockholm

Saskia as Flora, Rembrandt, 1635, National Gallery, London

Fortune, Guido Reni, 1623, Vatican, Rome

Ganymede, Rembrandt, 1635, Gemaldegalerie, Dresden

Ganymede, Antonio Corregio, c. 1534, Kunsthistorisches Museum, Vienna

Garden of Love, Peter Paul Rubens, 1632–1634, Prado, Madrid

Hercules at the Cross-Roads, Carracci, c. 1596, Museo Nationale di Capodimonte, Naples

Io, Antonio Corregio, c. 1534, Kunsthistorisches Museum, Vienna

Judgment of Paris, Lucas Cranach the Elder, 1530, Staatliche Kunsthalle, Karlsruhe, Germany

La Primavera, Sandro Botticelli, c. 1475–1478, Uffizi Gallery, Florence

Landscape with Ariadne, Carlo Saracini, c. 1608, Museo Nationale di Capodimonte, Naples

Landscape with Orpheus and Eurydice, Nicolas Poussin, 1650, Louvre, Paris

Landscape with Salmacis and Hermaphroditus, Carlo Saracini, c. 1608, Museo Nationale di Capodimonte, Naples

Landscape with the Nymph Egeria, Claude Gelee (Lorraine), 1669, Museo Nationale di Capodimonte, Naples

List 2–20   Continued

Laocoon, El Greco, c. 1608, National Gallery of Art, Washington, DC

Leda, Tintoretto (Jacopo Robusti), 1580–1585, Uffizi Gallery, Florence

Leda and the Swan, Antonio Corregio, c. 1534, Staatliche Museen Dahlem, Berlin

Mars and Venus United by Love, Paolo Veronese, c. 1570, Metropolitan Museum of Art, New York City

Mars, Giovanni Guercino, c. 1660, Apsley House, London

Mercury and Argus, Peter Paul Rubens, 1635–1638, Gemaldegalerie, Dresden

Midas and Bacchus, Nicolus Poussin, c. 1625, Alte Pinakothek, Munich

Nymph and Shepherd, Titian, 1570–1575, Kunsthistorisches Museum, Vienna

Nymph of the Source, Lucas Cranach the Elder, after 1537, National Gallery of Art, Washington, DC

Painting, Giovanni Pelligrini, 1725–1730, Accademia, Venice

Pallas and Centaur, Sandro Botticelli, c. 1482, Uffizi Gallery, Florence

Pardo Venus, Titian (Tiziano Vecellio), 1560, Louvre, Paris

Primavera, Sandro Botticelli, c. 1477, Uffizi Gallery, Florence

Rape of Europa, Cavalier d'Arpino, 1607–1608, Villa Borghese, Rome

Rape of Europa, Francesco Zuccarelli, 1740–1750, Accademia, Venice

Rinaldo Abandoning Armida, Giambattista Tiepolo, 1745, Art Institute of Chicago, Illinois

Sacred and Profane Love, Titian, c. 1514, Villa Borghese, Rome

Salmacis and Hermaphroditus, Bartholomeus Spranger, c. 1590, Kunsthistorisches Museum, Vienna

Saturn, Peter Paul Rubens, 1636–1637, Prado, Madrid

Saturn Devouring his Children, Francisco de Goya, 1819–1823, Prado, Madrid

Tempest, Giorgione, 1506–1508, Accademia, Venice

The Bathers, Jean-Honoré Fragonard, c. 1765–1770, Louvre, Paris

The Birth of Venus, Peter Paul Rubens, 1636–1638, Musées Royaux des Beaux-Arts de Belgique, Brussels

The Birth of Venus, Sandro Botticelli, c. 1480–1485, Uffizi Gallery, Florence

The Death of Actaeon, Titian, 1559, National Gallery, London

The Departure from Cythera, Jean-Antoine Watteau, 1717, Louvre, Paris

The Dream of Antiope, Antonio Corregio, c. 1530, Louvre, Paris

The Fall of Icarus, Pieter Brueghel the Elder, 1567–1578, Musées Royaux des Beaux-Arts de Belgique, Brussels

The Fall of Icarus, Peter Paul Rubens, 1636–1638, Musées Royaux des Beaux-Arts de Belgique, Brussels

The Fall of Icarus, Carlo Saracini, c. 1608, Museo Nationale di Capodimonte, Naples

The Feast of the Gods, Giovanni Bellini, 1514, National Gallery of Art, Washington, DC

The Flaying of Marsyas, José de Ribera, 1630, Musées Royaux des Beaux-Arts de Belgique, Brussels

The Intervention of the Sabine Women, Jacques Louis David, 1797, Louvre, Paris

The Judgment of Paris, Peter Paul Rubens, 1632–1635, National Gallery, London

The Judgment of Paris, Peter Paul Rubens, 1638–1639, Prado, Madrid

The Kingdom of Flora, Nicolas Poussin, 1631, Gemaldegalerie, Dresden

The Rape of Proserpina, Rembrandt, 1628–1629, Staatliche Museen Dahlem, Berlin

The Rape of the Sabine Women, Nicolas Poussin, 1626–1637, Metropolitan Museum of Art, New York City

The Spinners, Diego Velasquez, c. 1657, Prado, Madrid

The Three Graces, Peter Paul Rubens, 1638–1640, Prado, Madrid

The Feast of Venus, Peter Paul Rubens, c. 1635, Kunsthistorisches Museum, Vienna

The Garden of Venus, Titian, 1518–1519, Prado, Madrid

Sleeping Venus, Paul Delvaux, 1944, Tate, London

The Toilet of Venus, Diego Velasquez, 1806, National Gallery, London

List 2–20 Continued

The Triumph of Venus, François Boucher, 1740, Nationalmuseum, Stockholm
Venus and Adonis, Titian, 1553, Prado, Madrid
Venus and Adonis, Paolo Veronese, c. 1550–1575, Prado, Madrid
Venus and Adonis, Abraham Janssens, c. 1620, Kunsthistorisches Museum, Vienna
Venus and Adonis, Jacopo Amigoni, c. 1745, Accademia, Venice
Venus and Cupid with an Organist, Titian, 1545–1548, Prado, Madrid
Venus and Cupid, Lucas Cranach the Elder, 1509, Hermitage, St. Petersburg, Russia
Venus and Mars, Sandro Botticelli, 1485–1490, National Gallery, London
Venus and Mars, Piero di Cosimo, 1498, National Gallery, London
Venus and Mars, Carlo Saracini, c. 1608, Museu de Arte, São Paulo
Venus and the Organ Player, Titian, c. 1550, Prado, Madrid
Venus Bandaging the Eyes of Cupid, Titian, c. 1565, Villa Borghese, Rome
Venus Consoling Love, François Boucher, 1751, National Gallery of Art, Washington, DC
Venus with a Mirror, Titian, 1488–1490, National Gallery of Art, Washington, DC
Venus with Mercury and Cupid, Coreggio, mid 1520s, National Gallery, London
Venus, Cupid, Folly, and Time, Agnolo Bronzino, c. 1540, National Gallery, London
Venus, Love and Jealousy, Agnolo Bronzino, 1545–1546, National Gallery, Budapest, Hungary

List 2–21 Classicism and Romanticism in Art

Art does not develop independently of the time in which it is created, but often reflects the philosophies of writers, scientists, the church, and the government. Throughout history, architecture, sculpture, and painting seem to go back and forth between periods of classicism and romanticism.

"Classical" describes certain periods of Greek and Roman art. The term represents the best or most typical example of its kind, with excessive decoration removed, leaving the essence. In art, it has come to mean the opposite of Romantic. Romantic art appeals to the emotions, and it is often characterized by energetic swirling lines and shapes. A new, perfect Greek temple would be considered classical, whereas its *ruin* might be considered romantic.

PERIODS IN ART THAT WERE CONSIDERED "ROMANTIC"

Early Christian
Byzantine
Migration
Medieval
Romanesque
Gothic
Baroque
Rococo
Romanticism
Post-Impressionism
Art Nouveau
Fauvism
Dadaism
Expressionism
Fantasy Art
Abstract Expressionism

PERIODS IN ART THAT ARE CONSIDERED "CLASSICAL"

Classical Greek art
Hellenistic Greek art
Roman art
Late Gothic art
International Style
Early Renaissance
High Renaissance
Mannerism
Neoclassical art
Realistic art
Impressionism
Post-Impressionism
Cubism
Abstraction
Art Nouveau
Op Art
Surrealism
Light Art
Post-Modernism

List 2–22   Impressionist and Post-Impressionist Artists

ORIGINAL IMPRESSIONISTS

Cassatt, Mary (1844–1926). Cassatt frequently painted portraits of women and children, using pastels or oils. The only American who exhibited with the Impressionists, some of her work resembled the Japanese woodcuts so popular at the time.

Degas, Edgar (1834–1917). Degas mostly worked in pastels. Subjects often were ballet dancers and horses. He used dramatic lighting and short, parallel, diagonal strokes. He sculpted clay, using the same "sketchy" approach.

Manet, Edouard (1832–1883). Manet used dramatic contrast, often depicting people in a "snapshot" effect. His work was basically realistic, and he sometimes used a neutral background and flat colors.

Monet, Claude (1840–1926). Monet used pastel colors, using smallish strokes of color. He painted people early in his career, but mostly did landscapes and waterlilies later.

Morisot, Berthe (1841–1895). Morisot painted portraits and interiors, but ultimately painted out-of-doors with the Impressionists and exhibited with them.

Pissarro, Camille (1830–1903). Pissarro was the eldest of the Impressionists, known for his city and country landscapes. He also spent a time experimenting with pointillism.

Renoir, Pierre Auguste (1841–1919). Renoir was a portrait artist, frequently painting members of his family, flowers, Mediterranean landscapes, and holiday scenes.

POST-IMPRESSIONISTS

Bonnard, Pierre (1867–1947). Bonnard was known as an "Intimiste" because of his interest in painting domestic interior scenes in (sometimes) Fauvist colors.

Cezanne, Paul (1839–1906). Cezanne used patches of color, concentrating on relationships of forms and patterns. His work was considered a major influence in Cubism.

Gauguin, Paul (1848–1903). Gauguin's work was distinguished by bright, often unrealistic colors and patterns; and flat areas of color.

Gogh, Vincent van (1863–1890). van Gogh used vivid colors applied in a thick impasto; swirling brush marks distinguished his paintings. He sold only one painting in his lifetime.

Matisse, Henri (1869–1954). Matisse had several facets to his art—his sure use of line; bright, unrealistic colors reflecting his association with the Fauves; the paper cut-outs that he did in his old age; and his sculpture.

Redon, Odilon (1840–1916). Redon isolated the face against a plain background, then filled in around the edges of the picture plane with flowers.

Rodin, Auguste (1840–1917). Although not working with light and color as the painters did, Rodin made an "Impressionistic" breakthrough with his unfinished, sketchy, surface.

Rousseau, Henri (1844–1910). Rousseau, the "Douanier" (customs official), painted "jungle scenes" based on what he had seen at the Paris Botanical garden. His work was frequently surrealistic.

Seurat, Georges (1859–1891). Seurat worked in what he called "divisionism" (pointillism), small dots of color placed closely together and "mixed by the eye." He died at a young age, therefore completing few large paintings.

Sisley, Alfred (1839–1899). Sisley's work was at times almost indistinguishable from that of Monet. He specialized in landscapes, mostly doing scenes in and around Paris.

Toulouse-Lautrec, Henri (1864–1901). Lautrec often painted in cafes. He used pastels in short, slanted, parallel strokes on a tan background, allowing the strokes to show through.

Vuillard, Edward (1868–1940). Vuillard specialized in domestic scenes that rendered flat planes and contours using the bright colors of Gauguin and some of the Fauves.

List 2–23   Well-Known Women Artists

This list is of well-known women in all fields of art such as painting, sculpture, photography, crafts, and architecture.

AMERICA

Abakanowicz, Magdalena, 1930
Abbott, Berenice, 1898–1991
Albers, Anni, 1899–1994
Arbus, Diane, 1923–1971
Attie, Dotty, 1938
Aycock, Alice, 1946
Baca, Judith Francisca, 1946
Bacon, Peggy, 1895–1987
Bartlett, Jennifer, 1941
Beaux, Cecilia, 1855–1942
Benglis, Linda, 1941
Bishop, Isabel, 1902–1988
Bontecou, Lee, 1931
Bouguereau, Elizabeth Jane Gardner, 1837–1922
Bourgeois, Louise, 1911, b. France
Bourke-White, Margaret, 1904–1971
Brown, Joan, 1938–1990
Brownscombe, Jennie Augusta, 1850–1936
Butterfield, Deborah, 1949
Butterworth, Elizabeth, 1949
Cassatt, Mary, 1844–1926
Catlett, Elizabeth, 1915
Chicago, Judy, 1939
Chryssa, 1933
Cordero, Helen, 1915–1994
Cunningham, Imogen, 1883–1976
Dahl-Wolfe, Louise, 1895–1989
Daw, Leila, 1940
de Kooning, Elaine, 1920–1989
Duckworth, Ruth, 1919
Edelson, Mary Beth, 1934
Eiosenman, Nicole, 1963
Falkenstein, Claire, 1908
Fish, Janet, 1938
Flack, Audrey, 1931
Forrester, Patricia Tobacco, 1940
Frank, Mary, 1933
Frankenthaler, Helen, 1928
Frey, Viola, 1933
Friedlander, Lee, 1934
Fuller, Meta Vaux Warrick, 1877–1968

Gillespie, Dorothy, 1920
Gilpin, Laura, 1891–1979
Goldin, Nan, 1953
Goodacre, Glenna, 1939
Graves, Nancy, 1940–1995
Hale, Ellen Day, 1855–1940
Hamilton, Ann, 1956
Hardin, Helen, 1943–1984
Hartigan, Grace, 1922
Hesse, Eva, 1936–1970, b. Germany
Hoffman, Malvina, 1887–1966
Holt, Nancy, 1938
Holzer, Jenny, 1950
Hosmer, Harriet, 1830–1908
Hu, Mary Lee, 1943
Huntington, Anna Hyatt, 1876–1973
Hurd, Henriette Wyeth, 1907–1997
Jacobi, Lotte, 1896–1990
Jaudon, Valerie, 1945
Jessup, Georgia Mills, 1926
Jones, Lois Mailou, 1905
Käsebier, Gertrude, 1852–1934
Kelly, Mary, 1941
Kent, Corita, 1918–1986
Kozloff, Joyce, 1942
Krasner, Lee, 1908–1984
Kruger, Barbara, 1945
Lange, Dorothea, 1895–1965
Lavenson, Alma, 1897–1989
Leibovitz, Annie, 1949
Levine, Sherrie, 1947
Levitt, Helen, 1918
Lewis, Edmonia, 1845–c. 1909
Lewis, Lucy, 1897–1992
Lewis, Samella, 1924
Lin, Maya, 1959
Linhares, Judith, 1940
Longman, Evelyn Beatrice, 1874–1954
Low, Mary F. MacMonnies, 1858–1946
Mangold, Sylvia Plimack, 1938
Marisol (Escobar), 1930, b. Colombia
Mark, Mary Ellen, 1940

List 2–23   Continued

AMERICA (cont.)

Martin, Agnes, 1912

Martinez, Maria Montoya, 1887–1980

Matthiasdottir, Louisa, 1917

Mears, Helen Farnsworth, 1872–1916

Mitchell, Joan, 1926–1992

Morgan, Julia, 1872–1957

Moses, Anna Mary Robertson (Grandma), 1860–1961

Murphy, Catherine, 1946

Murray, Elizabeth, 1940

Natzler, Gertrud Amon, 1908–1971

Neel, Alice, 1900–1984

Nevelson, Louise, 1899–1988

Nilsson, Gladys, 1940

O'Keeffe, Georgia, 1887–1986

Peale, Anna Claypoole, 1791–1878

Peale, Sarah Miriam, 1800–1885

Pepper, Beverly, 1924

Perry, Lilla Cabot, 1848–1933

Pfaff, Judy, 1946

Pindell, Howardena, 1943

Pinney, Eunice, 1770–1849

Prophet, Nancy Elizabeth, 1890–1960

Ringgold, Faith, 1930

Rothenberg, Susan, 1945

Saar, Alison, 1956

Saar, Betye, 1926

Sauer, Jane, 1937

Savage, Augusta, 1892–1962

Schapiro, Miriam, 1923

Sherman, Cindy, 1954

Skoglund, Sandy, 1946

Sleigh, Sylvia, 1935

Smith, Jaune Quick-to-See, 1940

Smith, Kiki, 1954

Spencer, Lilly Martin, 1822–1902

Spero, Nancy, 1926

Stephens, Alice Barber, 1858–1932

Tafoya, Margaret, 1904

Tanning, Dorothea, 1913

Thomas, Alma, 1891–1978

Truitt, Anne, 1921

Van Ness, Beatrice Whitney, 1888–1981

von Wiegand, Charmion, 1900–1983

Vonnoh, Bessie Potter, 1872–1955

Walking Stick, Kay, 1935

Warashina, Patti, 1940

Weems, Katherine Lane, 1899–1990

Whitney, Anne, 1821–1915

Whitney, Gertrude Vanderbilt, 1877–1942

Wildenhain, Marguerite, 1896–1985

Wilke, Hannah, 1940–1993

Willson, Mary Ann, 1810–c. 1840

Wood, Beatrice, 1893

Wright, Patience Lovell, 1725–1786

Zorach, Marguerite Thompson, 1887–1968

BELGIUM

Peeters, Clara, 1594–after 1657

CANADA

Rockburne, Dorothea, 1934

ENGLAND

Beauclerk, Diana, 1734–1808

Butler, Elizabeth Thompson, 1846–1933

Cameron, Julia Margaret, 1815–1879

Carrington, Leonora, 1917

Hepworth, Barbara, 1903–1975

John, Gwendolen, 1876–1939

Osborn, Emily, 1834–c. 1909

Potter, Beatrix, 1866–1943

Riley, Bridget, 1931

Siddall, Elizabeth, 1829–1862

Whiteread, Rachel, 1963

FRANCE

Abbema, Louise, 1858–1927

Bashkirtseff, Marie, 1859–1884, b. Russia

Bonheur, Rosa, 1822–1899

Claudel, Camille, 1864–1943

Gerard, Marguerite, 1761–1837

Haudebourt-Lescot, Antoinette Cecile Hortense, 1784–1845

Labille-Guiard, Adelaide, 1749–1803

Laurencin, Marie, 1885–1956

Loir, Marie Anne, c. 1715–1769

Messager, Annette, 1943

Morisot, Berthe, 1841–1895

Navarre, Marie-Genevieve, 1737–1795

Saint-Phalle, Niki de, 1930

Valadon, Suzanne, 1865–1938

Vallayer-Coster, Ann, 1744–1818

Vigee-Lubrun, Marie Louise Elizabeth, 1755–1842

List 2–23   Continued

GERMANY

Hoch, Hannah, 1889–1978
Kollwitz, Kathe, 1867–1945
Merian, Maria Sibylla, 1647–1717
Modersohn-Becker, Paula, 1876–1907
Munter, Gabriele, 1877–1962
Stolzl, Gunta, 1897–1983
Van Schurman, Anna Maria, 1607–1678

THE NETHERLANDS

Leyster, Judith, 1609–1660
Ruysch, Rachel, 1666–1750

ITALY

Brooks, Romaine, 1894–1970
Anguisciola, Sofonisba, 1528–1625
Carriera, Rosalba, 1675–1752
Gentileschi, Artemisia, 1593–c.1652/3
Fontana, Lavinia, 1552–1614
Sirani, Elisabetta, 1638–1665

MEXICO

Kahlo, Frida, 1907–1954

PORTUGAL

Rego, Paula, 1935

RUSSIA

Delaunay, Sonia Terk, 1885–1979
Exter, Alexandra, 1882–1949
Goncharova, Natalia, 1881–1962
Popova, Lyubov, 1889–1924
Stepanova, Varvara, 1894–1958

SCOTLAND

Blackadder, Elizabeth, 1931
Redpath, Anne, 1895–1965

SWITZERLAND

Bailly, Alice, 1872–1938
Kauffman, Angelica, 1741–1807
Oppenheim, Meret, 1913–1985, b. Germany
Taeuber-Arp, Sophie, 1889–1943

List 2–24   African American Artists

This list includes sculptors, painters, architects, and folk artists. Dates may vary significantly depending upon the publication.

Adkins, Terry, 1953
Alston, Charles H., 1907–1977
Andrews, Benny, 1930
Artis, William E., 1914–1977
Ausby, Ellsworth, 1942
Bailey, Herman Kofi, 1931–1981
Bailey, Malcolm, 1947
Bannister, Edward M., 1828–1901
Barthé, Richmond, 1901–1989
Basquiat, Jean Michel, 1960–1987
Bearden, Romare, 1911–1988
Beasley, Phoebe, 1943
Benoit, Rigaud, 1911–1987
Biggers, John T., 1924
Billops, Camille, 1933
Blackwell, Tarleton, 1956
Bolling, Leslie G., 1898–1958
Bowling, Frank, 1936
Bowser, David Bustill, 1820–1900
Bradford, David, 1937
Brown, Everald, 1917
Brown, Grafton Tyler, 1841–1918
Buchanan, Beverly, 1940
Burke, Selma, 1900–1995
Burke-Morgan, Arline, 1950
Burroughs, Margaret T., 1916
Campbell, Elmer S., 1906–1971
Carraway, Arthur, 1927
Carter, Allen D., 1947
Casey, Bernard T., 1939
Catlett, Elizabeth, 1915
Chandler, Dana, 1941
Chase-Riboud, Barbara, 1936
Chaplin, John G., 1828–1907
Clark, Claude, Sr., 1914
Clark, Edward, 1926
Clark, Irene, 1927
Coleman, Floyd, 1937
Colescott, Robert H., 1925
Conwill, Houston, 1947
Cortor, Eldzier, 1916
Craig, Burlon ("B.B."), 1914
Crichlow, Ernest, 1914
Crite, Alan Rohan, 1910
Cruz, Emilio, 1937
Davis, Alonzo Joseph, 1942
Davis, Bing W., 1937
DeCarava, Roy, 1919
Delaney, Beauford, 1901–1979
Delaney, Joseph, 1904–1991
Dempsey, Richard W., 1919–1987

Drawn from Poster Design . . .
Whitney Exhibition, 1974,
Jacob Lawrence, Terry Dinten-
fass, Inc., New York City

DePillars, Murry, 1938
Dial, Richard, 1955
Dial, Thornton, Jr., 1933
Donaldson, Jeff, 1932
Douglas, Aaron, 1898–1979
Douglass, Robert M., Jr., 1809–1887
Driskell, David, 1931
Duncanson, Robert Stuart, 1823–1872
Edmondson, William, c. 1870–1951
Edwards, Melvin, 1937
Eversley, Fred, 1941
Feelings, Tom, 1933
Ferguson, Amos, 1920
Flemister, Frederick, 1916
Fletcher, Mikelle, 1945
Fuller, Meta Vaux Warrick, 1877–1968
Gammon, Reginald, 1921
Gilliam, Sam, 1933
Gordon, Russell T., 1936
Gorleigh, Rex, 1902–1987
Goss, Bernard, 1913–1966
Grigsby, Eugene, Jr., 1918
Gudgell, Henry, 1826–1899
Hammons, David, 1943
Hampton, Phillip J., 1922
Harper, William, 1944
Hayden, Palmer C., 1893–1973
Henderson, William, 1943
Henry, Gregory A., 1961
Hicks, Leon, 1933
Hoard, Adrienne, 1949
Hobbs, G.W., Reverend, flourished 1784
Hollingsworth, Alvin C., 1928
Honeywood, Varnett, 1950
Hudson, Julien, active 1831–1844
Hughes, Manuel, 1938
Hunt, Richard, 1935
Hunter, Clementine, 1880–1988
Hutson, Bill, 1936
Jackson, Suzanne, 1944
Jackson-Jarvis, Martha, 1952
Johnson, Daniel, 1938
Johnson, Joshua, c. 1765–c. 1830
Johnson, Malvin Gray, 1896–1934
Johnson, Marie E., 1920
Johnson, Sargent Claude, 1887–1967
Johnson, William Henry, 1901–1970
Jones-Hogu, Barbara, 1938
Jones, Benjamin, 1942
Jones, Lois Mailou, 1905
Joseph, Clifford R., 1927

List 2–24 Continued

Joseph, Ronald, 1910
Keene, Paul, 1920
Lacy, Jean, 1932
Lark, Raymond, 1939
Lawrence, Jacob, 1917
Lee, Ron, 1951
Lee-Smith, Hughie, 1915
Le Va, Barry, 1941
Lewis, Edmonia, 1845–c. 1909
Lewis, Norman, 1909–1979
Lewis, Samella, 1924
Locke, Alain Leroy, 1886–1954
Logan, Juan, 1946
Love, Edward, 1936
Loving, Alvin D., Jr., 1935
Manigault, Mary, c. 1910
Marshall, Kerry James, 1955
Mason, Phillip Lindsay, 1939
Mayhew, Richard, 1924
Maynard, Valerie, 1937
Miller, Dave, Jr., 1903–1977
Miller, Dave, Sr., 1872–1969
Miller, Thomas, 1945
Mills, Priscilla (P'lla), 1918–1964
Mitchell, Dean, 1957
Montgomery, Evangeline J., 1933
Moorhead, Scipio, active 1770s
Morgan, Clarence, 1950
Morgan, Norma G., 1928
Mosely, Jimmie, 1927
Motley, Archibald J., Jr., 1891–1981
Olugebefola, Ademola, 1941
Oubre, Hayward, 1916
Overstreet, Joe, 1934
Owens-Hart, Winnie R., 1949
Pajaud, William E., 1925
Parks, James Dallas, 1907
Patterson, Edna J.
Perkins, Marion M., 1908–1961
Phillips, Bertrand, 1938
Phillips, Charles James, 1945
Philpot, David, 1940
Pierce, Elijah, 1892–1984
Pigatt, Anderson, 1928
Pindell, Howardena, 1943
Pippin, Horace, 1888–1946
Pogue, Stephanie, 1944
Porter, Charles Ethan, 1847–c. 1923
Porter, James A., 1905–1971
Powell, Georgette Seabrook, 1916
Powers, Harriet, 1837–1911
Primus, Nelson A., 1842–1916
Prophet, Nancy Elizabeth, 1890–1960
Purifoy, Noah, 1917
Puryear, Martin, 1941

Reason, Henry, 1817–c. 1850
Reid, Robert, 1924
Richardson, Earl Winton, 1913–1935
Rickson, Gary, 1942
Riddle, John, 1933
Ringgold, Faith, 1930
Roberts, Lucille Malkia, 1927
Rogers, Sultan, 1922
Rose, Arthur, 1921
Russell, Gordon, 1932
Ryder, Mahler, 1937–1992
Saar, Alison, 1956
Saar, Betye, 1926
Saunders, Raymond, 1934
Savage, Augusta, 1892–1962
Scott, John T., 1940
Scott, Joyce J., 1948
Scott, William Edouard, 1884–1964
Searles, Charles, 1937
Sebree, Charles, 1914–1985
Seifert, Charles Christopher, 1871–1949
Shabaka, Onajide, 1948
Sills, Thomas, 1914
Simmons, Philip, 1912
Simms, Carroll H., 1924
Simpson, William H., 1818–1872
Sleet, Moneta, Jr., 1926
Smith, Albert Alexander, 1896–1940
Smith, Vincent, 1929
Stevens, Nelson, 1938
Stout, Renee, 1958
Tanner, Henry Ossawa, 1859–1937
Thomas, Alma W., 1891–1978
Thompson, Robert, 1936–1966
Traylor, Bill, 1854–1947
Van Der Zee, James, 1886–1983
Walker, Annie E., 1855–1929
Warburg, Eugene, 1826–1859
Ward-Brown, Denise, 1953
Waring, Laura Wheeler, 1887–1948
Washington, James W., Jr., 1911
Webster, Derek, 1934
Weems, Carrie Mae, 1953
Wells, James Lesesne, 1902–1993
West, Pheoris, 1950
White, Charles, 1918–1979
Williams, Pat Ward, 1949
Williams, William T., 1941
Wilson, Edward N., 1925
Wilson, Ellis, 1899–1977
Wilson, John Woodrow, 1922
Woodruff, Hale A., 1900–1980
Wright, Bernard, 1938
Young, Milton, 1935

List 2–25 Some African American Artists and Their Artworks

Alston, Charles, *The Family,* 1955, Whitney Museum of American Art, New York City

Andrews, Benny, *Black,* 1971, collection of the artist

Bannister, Edward Mitchell, *Landscape,* 1882, Museum of Art, Rhode Island School of Design, Providence

Bannister, Edward Mitchell, *Sabin Point, Narragansett Bay,* 1885, Brown University, Providence, Rhode Island

Barthé, Richmond, *The Boxer,* 1942, Metropolitan Museum of Art, New York City

Bearden, Romare, *The Intimacy of Water,* 1973, St. Louis Art Museum, Missouri

Bearden, Romare, *The Prevalence of Ritual: Baptism,* 1964, Hirshhorn Museum and Sculpture Garden, Washington, DC

Biggers, John, *Shotguns, Third Ward,* mural, 1987, Christia V. Adair Park, Harris County, Texas

Biggers, John, *Starry Crown,* 1987, Dallas Museum of Art, Texas

Brown, Everald, *Instrument for Four People,* 1986, National Gallery of Jamaica, Kingston

Brown, Grafton Tyler, *Grand Canyon of the Yellowstone from Hayden Point,* 1891, The Oakland Museum, California

Catlett, Elizabeth, *Malcolm X Speaks for Us,* 1969, Museum of Modern Art, New York City

Catlett, Elizabeth, *Sharecropper,* 1968, National Museum of American Art, Washington, DC

Cortor, Eldzier, *Southern Gate,* 1942–1943, National Museum of American Art, Washington, DC

Douglas, Aaron, *The Negro in the African Setting,* Panel 1, 1934, New York Public Library, New York City

Duncanson, Robert Stuart, *The Blue Hole, Flood Waters, Little Miami River,* 1851, Cincinnati Art Museum, Ohio

Duncanson, Robert Stuart, *The Land of the Lotus-Eaters,* c. 1861, His Majesty's Royal Collection, Stockholm

Edmondson, William, *Turtle,* limestone, 1940, collection of Mr. and Mrs. Robert L. Gwinn

Ferguson, Amos, *Polka Dot Junkanoo,* 1984, collection of Geoffrey Holder, New York City

Ferguson, Amos, *Untitled (Mermaid),* 1983, Intl. Folk Art, Museum of New Mexico, Santa Fe

Hayden, Palmer, *John Henry on the Right, Steam Drill on the Left,* 1947, collection of Museum of African Art, Los Angeles, California

Johnson, Malvin Gray, *Self-Portrait,* 1934, National Museum of American Art, Washington, DC

Johnson, Sargent Claude, *Mask,* 1935, San Francisco Museum of Modern Art, California

Johnson, Sargent Claude, *Forever Free,* 1935, San Francisco Museum of Modern Art, California

Johnson, William Henry, *Street Musicians,* c. 1940, Oakland Museum of Art, California

Johnston, Joshua, *Portrait of a Cleric,* c. 1805, Bowdoin College Museum of Art, Brunswick, Maine

Jones, Ben, *Stars II* (15 elements), 1983, collection of the Newark Museum, New Jersey

Jones, Lois Mailou, *Parade des Paysans,* 1965, collection of Max Robinson, Washington, DC

Jones, Lois Mailou, *Symbols d'Afrique II,* 1983, collection of the artist

Lacy, Jean, *Little Egypt Condo/New York City,* 1987, collection of the artist

Lawrence, Jacob, *Builders #1,* 1972, St. Louis Art Museum, Missouri

Lawrence, Jacob, *Migrants Cast Their Ballots,* 1974, St. Louis Art Museum, Missouri

Lawrence, Jacob, *The Migration of the Negro,* Panel 1, 1940–1941, Phillips Collection, Washington, DC

Lee-Smith, Hughie, *Two Girls,* 1966, New Jersey State Museum, Trenton

Lewis, Edmonia, *Hagar,* 1869, National Museum of American Art, Washington, DC

Lewis, Norman, *Yellow Hat,* 1936, collection of Ouida B. Lewis, New York City

Lewis, Samella, *Boy With a Flute,* 1968, collection of the artist

Love, Edward, *Mask for Mingus,* welded steel, 1974, collection of the artist

Miller, Dave, Sr., *Talisman,* wood, 1940, collection of the estate of David Miller, Jr.

Motley, Archibald, Jr., *Chicken Shack,* 1936, Harmon Foundation Collection, National Archives, Washington, DC

Phillips, James, *Spirits,* 1986, collection of Michael D. Harris

List 2–25   Continued

Pigatt, Anderson, *Caught in the Middle Earth,* wood and paint, 1970, New York Public Library, New York City

Pippin, Horace, *The Holy Mountain,* 1944, Hirshhorn Museum and Sculpture Garden, Washington, DC

Porter, James A., *Woman Holding a Jug,* 1930, Fisk University, Nashville, Tennessee

Primus, Nelson A., *Lizzie May Ulmer,* 1876, Connecticut Historical Society, Hartford

Prophet, Nancy Elizabeth, *Congolais,* 1931, Whitney Museum of American Art, New York City

Richardson, Earl, *Negro Pharaoh,* 1934, New York Public Library, New York City

Rogers, Sultan, *Man in Striped Necktie,* 1988, University of Mississippi, University

Rogers, Sultan, *Walking Stick,* wood, 1985, University of Mississippi, University

Savage, Augusta, *Gamin,* 1930, New York Public Library, New York City

Scott, William Edouard, *When the Tide Is Out,* c. 1931, Harmon Foundation Collection, National Archives, Washington, DC

Searles, Charles, *Dancer Series,* 1976, collection of Dr. and Mrs. Maurice Clifford, Philadelphia

Stout, Renee, *Fetish #1,* 1988, Dallas Museum of Art, Texas

Tanner, Henry Ossawa, *Banjo Lesson,* 1893, Hampton University Museum Collection, Hampton, Virginia

Tanner, Henry Ossawa, *The Thankful Poor,* 1894, collection of Dr. William and Dr. Camille Cosby, Malibu, California

Thomas, Alma W., *Light Blue Nursery,* 1968, National Museum of American Art, Washington, DC

Warrick, Meta Vaux Warrick, *Richard B. Harrison as "De Lawd,"* c. 1935, Howard University Gallery of Art, Washington, DC

White, Charles, *Take My Mother Home,* 1957, collection of Dr. Richard Simms, Harbor City, California

Wilson, Ed, *Jazz Musicians,* 1982–1984, Douglass High School, Baltimore, Maryland

Wilson, Ellis, *Field Workers,* date unknown, National Museum of American Art, Washington, DC

Wilson, Ellis, *Haitian Funeral Procession,* c. 1950s, Amistad Research Center, Tulane University, New Orleans, Louisiana

Woodruff, Hale, *Poor Man's Cotton,* 1934, Newark Museum, New Jersey

Woodruff, Hale, *Golden State Life Insurance Murals,* 1948–1949, Los Angeles, California

List 2–26   Hispanic Artists

HISPANIC/AMERICAN

Abizu, Olga, 1924, b. Puerto Rico

Abularach, Rodolfo, 1923, b. Guatemala

Aguirre, Emilio

Alfonzo, Carlos, 1950–1991, b. Cuba

Algaze, Mario, 1947

Almaraz, Carlos, 1941–1989, b. Mexico

Amezcua, Consuelo (Chelo) Gonzalez, 1903

Alpuy, Julio, 1919, b. Uruguay

Aragon, José Rafael, active 1826–1850

Archuleta, Felipe, 1910–1991

Azeceta, Luis Cruz, 1942, b. Cuba

Baca, Judith Francisca, 1946

Blanco, Eloy, 1933

Briseno, Rolando, 1952

Buzio, Lidya, 1948, b. Uruguay

Canas, Maria Martinez, 1960

Casas, Melesio (Mel), 1929

Castillo, Consuelo Méndez, 1952

Cervantez, Pedro, 1915

Chavez, Edwardo, 1917

Chavez, Joseph A., 1938

Chavez, Margaret Herrera, 1912

Chavez, Ray, 1938

De Montes, Roberto Gil, 1950, b. Mexico

Espada, Ibsen, 1952

Fernandez, Rudy, 1948

Frigerio, Ismael, 1955, b. Chile

Garcia, Antonio, 1901

Garcia, Rupert, 1944

Garza, Carmen Lomas, 1948

Gomez, Glynn, 1945

Gonzales, Julio, 1876–1942, b. Spain

Gonzales, Patricia, 1958, b. Colombia

Gonzalez, Ruben, 1923

Graham, Robert, 1938, b. Mexico

Gronk (Glugio Gronk Nicandro), 1954

Healy, Wayne Alaniz, 1949

Herrera, Carmen, 1915, b. Cuba

Herrón, Willie, 1951

Jimenez, Luis, 1940

Juarez, Roberto, 1952

Lam, Wilfredo, 1902–1982, b. Cuba

Lasansky, Mauricio, 1914, b. Argentina

Lebron, Michael, 1954

Linares, Victor, 1929

López, Felix, 1942

López, Graciela Carrillo, 1949

López, José Dolores, 1868–1937

López, Michael, 1938

López, Yolanda M.

Lujan, Gilbert Sanchez, 1940

Marín, Augusto, 1921

Marisol (Marisol Escobar), 1930, b. Venezuela

Martinez, Alfredo Ramos, 1875–1946

Martinez, Cesar Augusto, 1944

Martino, José Antonio Torres

Martorell, Antonio, 1939, b. Puerto Rico

Marzan, Gregorio, 1906, b. Puerto Rico

Matta (Roberto Sebastian Antonio Matta Echaurren), 1911, b. Chile

Medellin, Octavio, 1907

Mendoza, Tony, 1941

Montoya, Jose, 1932

Morales, Raphael Colon, 1942

Moroles, Jesus Bautista, 1950

Neri, Manuel, 1930

Palomino, Ernesto, 1933

Pena, Amado, 1943

Perez, Irene, 1950

Perez, Pedro, 1951, b. Cuba

Ponce de Leon, Michael, 1922

Quesada, Eugenio, 1927

Ramirez, Joel Tito, 1923

Ramirez, Martin, 1885–1960, b. Mexico

Roche, Arnaldo, 1955, b. Puerto Rico

Rodríguez, Patricia, 1944

Rodriguez, Peter, 1926

Romero, Frank, 1941

Ruiz, Gilberto, 1950

Salinas, Porfirio, 1912

Sánchez, Alex, 1946

Sierra, Paul, 1944, b. Cuba

Soto, Jorge, 1947

Stand, Luis, 1950, b. Colombia

Tanguma, Leo, 1941

Tapia, Luis, 1950

Torres-Garcia, Joaquin, 1874–1949, b. Uruguay

List 2–26   Continued

HISPANIC/AMERICAN (cont.)

Trevino, Rudy, 1945
Tufino, Nitza, 1949
Valdadez, John, 1951
Velazquez, Juan Ramon, 1820–1902
Villa, Estaban, 1930

MEXICO

Gerzso, Gunther, 1915
Izquierdo, Maria, 1902–1955
Kahlo, Frida, 1907–1954
Lazo, Agustin, 1898–1971
Merida, Carlos, 1891–1984
Orozco, José Clemente, 1883–1949
Ramos-Martinez, Alfredo, 1875–1946
Rivera, Diego, 1886–1957
Romero, Carlos Orozco, 1896–1984
Romo, José Luis, 1953
Ruiz, Gilberto, 1950
Siqueiros, David Alfaro, 1896–1974
Tamayo, Rufino, 1899–1991
Toledo, Francisco, 1940

Zarraga, Angel, 1886–1946
Zuniga, Francisco, 1911

SPAIN

Dali, Salvador, 1904–1989
Goya, Francisco, 1746–1828
Greco, El, 1541–1614
Gris, Juan, 1887–1927
Miró, Joan, 1893–1983
Murillo, Bartolomé, 1617–1690
Picasso, Pablo, 1881–1973
Ribera, Jusepe, 1588–1652
Tapies, Antoni, 1923
Velasquez, Diego, 1599–1660
Zurbaran, Francisco de, 1598–1664

OTHER

Botero, Fernando, 1932, Colombia
Oller, Francisco Manuel, 1833–1917, Puerto Rico
Otero, Alejandro, 1921–1990, Venezuela
Portinari, Candido, 1903–1962, Brazil

The Flower Carrier, 1935, Diego Rivera, San Francisco Museum of Modern Art

List 2–27   Twentieth-Century Native American Artists

This list includes well-known Native Americans whose work may be representative of a particular family or group of artists. The work of most Native American artists of previous centuries is not identified by name. Tribal affiliations and birthdates are included where available. If only one name is given, a second name in parentheses may be a family name. Some tribes have different names in the United States and in Canada, and these distinctions are given. Examples are Blackfeet (U.S.)/Blackfoot (Canada); Eskimo (U.S.)/Inuit (Canada); Chippewa (U.S.)/Ojibwa (Canada).

Abeyta, Narcisco, 1918, Navajo
Abeyta, Tony, 1965, Navajo
Aguilar, José Vincent, 1924, San Ildefonso/Picuris
Amiotte, Arthur Douglas, 1942, Oglala/Lakota Sioux
Anderson, Troy, 1948, Cherokee
Angeconeb, Allen, 1955, Ojibwa
Annesley, Robert, 1943, Cherokee
Ashevak, Kenojuak, 1927, Inuit
Ashoona, Mayoreak, 1946, Inuit
Ashoona, Pitseolak, 1904–1983, Inuit
Atencio, Gilbert, 1930–1995, San Ildefonso
Awa, Tsorej, 1898–1955, San Ildefonso
Bales, Jean, 1946, Iowa
Battles, Asa, 1923, Choctaw
Beardy, Jackson, 1944–1984, Cree/Saulteaux/Ojibwa
Beaver, Fred, 1911–1980, Creek
Beck, Clifford, 1946, Navajo
Beeler, Joe, 1931, Cherokee
Begay, Harrison, 1917, Navajo
Begay, Keats, c. 1920, Navajo
Begay, Shonto W., 1954, Navajo
Big Lefthanded, active c. 1905–1912, Navajo
Bird, JoAnne, 1945, Sisseton Sioux
Biss, Earl, Jr., 1947, Crow/Chippewa
Black Owl, Archie, 1911–1992, Cheyenne
Blue Eagle, Acee, 1907–1959, Creek/Pawnee
Bosin, Blackbear, 1921–1980, Kiowa/Comanche
Boyer, Bob, 1948, Metis
Bradley, David, 1954, Chippewa/Sioux
Broer, Roger L., 1945, Oglala/Lakota Sioux
Cannon, T.C., 1946–1978, Caddo/Kiowa/Choctaw
Cardinal-Schubert, Joane, 1942, Peigan
Chee, Robert, 1938–1972, Navajo
Cia, Manuel Lopez, 1937, Navajo
Collins, Adele, 1908, Chickasaw
Cordero, Helen, 1915–1994, Cochiti Pueblo
Crumbo, Woodrow W., 1912–1989, Potawatomi/Creek
Cutschall, Colleen, 1951, Oglala/Rosebud Sioux
Da, Tony, 1940, San Ildefonso
Danay, Richard Glazer, 1942, Mohawk
David, Neil R., Sr., 1944, Hopi

Davis, Jesse E., 1921–1976, Cheyenne
Debassige, Blake R., 1965, Ojibwa
Denetsosie, Hoke, 1919, Navajo
DesJarlait, Patrick, 1921–1973, Chippewa
DesJarlait, Robert, 1946, Red Lake Chippewa
Dewey, Wilson, 1915–1969, San Carlos Apache
Dick, Cecil, 1915–1992, Cherokee
Dishta, Duane, d. 1992, Zuni
Emerson, Anthony Chee, 1963, Navajo
Fadden, John, 1938, Mohawk
Fife, Phyllis, 1948, Creek
Fonseca, Harry, 1946, Maidu
Gawboy, Carl, 1943, Chippewa
Geionety, R.W., 1950, Kiowa
Glazer-Danay, 1942, Mohawk
Goodbear, Paul, 1913–c. 1940, Cheyenne
Gorman, Carl Nelson, 1907, Navajo
Gorman, Rudolph Carl (R.C.), 1932, Navajo
Goshorn, Shan, 1957, Cherokee
Gray, Gina, 1954, Osage
Grummer, Brenda Kennedy, Potawatomi
Halsey, Minisa Crumbo, 1942, Creek/Potawatomi
Haney, Enouch Kelly, 1940, Seminole/Creek
Hardin, Helen, 1943–1984, Santa Clara Pueblo
Harjo, Benjamin, Jr., 1945, Seminole/Shawnee
Havard, James, 1937, Choctaw/Chippewa
Heap of Birds, Edgar, 1954, Cheyenne/Arapaho
Henderson, Kathy, 1954, Cherokee
Herrera, Joe Hilario, 1923, Cochiti
Herrera, Velino, 1902–1973, Zia
Hessing, Valjean McCarty, 1934, Choctaw
Hill, Joan, 1930, Creek/Cherokee
Hill, Rick, 1950, Tuscarora
Hokeah, Jack, 1902–1969, Kiowa
Honewytewa, Louis Calvin, 1930, Hopi
Houser, Allan, 1915–1994, Chiricahua Apache
Howe, Oscar, 1915–1983, Yankton Sioux
Ingram, Jerry, 1941, Choctaw/Cherokee
Jacobs, Arnold, 1942, Iroquois/Onondaga

List 2–27 Continued

Jemison, G. Peter, 1945, Cattaraugus Seneca

Johns, David, 1948, Navajo

Jones, Ruthe Blalock, 1939, Delaware/Shawnee/Peoria

Kabotie, Fred, 1900–1986, Hopi

Kabotie, Michael, 1942, Hopi

Keahbone, George, 1916, Kiowa

Kenojuak (Ashevak), 1927, Inuit

Kimball, Yeffe, 1914–1978, Osage

Kuka, King, 1946, Blackfeet

LaPena, Frank, 1937, Nomtipom/Wintu

Larsen, Mike, 1944, Chickasaw

Lewis, Lucy, 1897–1992, Acoma

Little Turtle, Carm, 1952, Apache/Tarahumarqa

Lomahaftewa, Linda, 1940, Hopi/Choctaw

Lomakema, Milland, Sr., 1941, Hopi

Longfish, George, 1942, Seneca/Tuscarora

Lucy (Qinnuayuak), 1915–1982, Inuit

Manygoats, Betty, 1945, Navajo

Martinez, Crescencio, c. 1879–1918, San Ildefonso

Martinez, Julian, 1897–1943, San Ildefonso

Martinez, Maria Montoya, 1887–1980, San Ildefonso

Martinez, Santana R., birthdate unknown, Tewa/San Ildefonso

McCombs, Solomon, 1913–1980, Creek

Medina, Rafael, 1929, Zia

Mikkigak, Qaunak, 1932, Inuit

Mirabel, Eva, 1920–1967, Santa Fe

Momaday, Al, 1913–1981, Kiowa

Montileux, Dan, 1968, Oglala Sioux

Montoya, Tommy, birthdate unknown, San Juan

Mootzka, Waldo, 1903–1940, Hopi

Mopope, Stephen, 1898–1974, Kiowa

Morez, Mary, 1946, Navajo

Morrisseau, Norval, 1931, Ojibwa

Murdock, Cecil, 1913–1954, Kickapoo

Nailor, Gerald, 1917–1952, Navajo

Namingha, Dan, 1950, Hopi

Nampeyo, 1860–1942, Hopi/Tewa

Naranjo, Louis, 1932, Chochiti

Naranjo, Michelle Tsosie, 1959, Santa Clara/Navajo/Laguna/Mission

Naranjo-Morse, Nora, 1953, Santa Clara

Nevaquaya, Doc Tate, 1932, Comanche

Odjig, Daphne, 1919, Ojibwa

Orduno, Robert, 1933, Gabrielino

Padilla, Fernando, Jr., 1958, Navajo/San Felipe

Paladin, David Chethlahe, 1926–1984, Navajo

Palmer, Dixon, 1920, Kiowa/Choctaw

Pena, Tonita, 1893–1949, San Ildefonso

Pitaloosie (Saila), 1942, Inuit

Pitsiulak, Oopik, 1946, Inuit

Poitras, Jane Ash, 1951, Plains Cree

Polelonema, Otis, 1902–1981, Hopi

Pootoogook, Napachie, 1938, Inuit

Quintana, Ben, 1923–1944, Cochiti

Quoyavema, Al, 1938, Hopi

Ray, Carl, 1943–1978, Cree

Red Bear, Martin, 1947, Oglala Sioux

Red Star, Kevin, 1943, Crow

Reid, Bill, 1920, Haida

Sahmie, Ida, 1960, Navajo

Sakyesva, Harry, 1921, Hopi

Sampson, William, Jr., 1933–1987, Creek

Saul, C. Terry, 1921–1976, Choctaw/Chickasaw

Scholder, Fritz, 1937, Luiseno

Seabourn, Bert, 1931, Cherokee

Seabourn, Connie, 1951, Cherokee

Shelton, Peter, Jr., 1920s, Hopi

Smith, Jaune Quick-To-See, 1940, Salish/Cree/Shoshone

Smith, Kevin Warren, 1958, Cherokee

Stewart, Susan, 1953, Crow/Blackfeet

Stone, Willard, 1916–1985, Cherokee

Suazo, Jonathan Warm Day, Taos

Summers, Diosa, Santa Clara

Tafoya, Margaret, 1904, Santa Clara

Tafoya, Teofilo, 1915, Santa Clara

Tahoma, Quincy, 1921–1956, Navajo

Tailfeathers, Gerald, 1925–1975, Blood (Blackfoot)

Talaswaima, Terrance, 1939, Hopi

Taulbee, Dan, 1924–1987, Comanche

Tiger, Jerome, 1941–1967, Creek/Seminole

Toledo, José Rey, 1915–1994, Jemez

Toppah, Herman, 1923, Kiowa

Tsinajinnie, Andrew, 1916, Navajo

Tsosie, Nelson, 1961, Navajo

Tunnillie, Ovilu, 1949, Inuit

Tuttle, Frank, 1957, Maidu/Yurok/Wailaki

Two-Arrows, Tom, 1920, Onondaga

Velarde, Pablita, 1918, Santa Clara

Vigil, Arthur, 1955, Santo Domingo

Vigil, Romando, 1902–1978, San Ildefonso

Vigil, Tomas, c. 1889–1960, Tesuque

Walkingstick, Kay, 1935, Cherokee/Winnebago

West, Richard W. (Dick), 1912, Cheyenne

Whitehorse, Emmi, 1956, Navajo

Whitethorne, Baje, Sr., 1950, Navajo

Yazz, Beatien (Jimmy Toddy, Sr.), 1928, Navajo

Yazzie, James Wayne, 1943–1969, Navajo

Youngman, Alfred, 1948, Chippewa/Plains Cree

List 2–28   Famous Paintings, Listed Chronologically

MIDDLE AGES

artist unknown, *Madonna,* sixth–seventh centuries, Sta. Francesca Romana, Rome

artist unknown, *St. Matthew the Evangelist,* AD 800, British Museum, London

Illuminated Manuscripts

artist unknown, *Lindisfarne Gospels,* c. 700, British Library, London

artist unknown, *The Book of Kells,* c. 760–820, Trinity College, Dublin

artist unknown, *The Gospel Book of Charlemagne,* c. 800–810, Kunsthistorisches Museum, Vienna

artist unknown, *Gospel Book of Otto III,* c. 1000, Bavarian State Library, Munich

artist unknown, *Tres Riches Heures du Jean, Duc de Berry,* 1413–1416, Limbourg Brothers, Musée de Condé, Chantilly, France

ROMANESQUE

artist unknown, *Initial R with St. George and the Dragon,* twelfth century, Citeux, France

artist unknown, *St. John the Evangelist (Gospel Book of Abbot Wedricus),* c. 1147, Societé Archeologique, Avesnes, France

artist unknown, *St. Luke Washing the Feet of Peter, Gospel Book of Otto III,* c. 1000, Bavarian State Library, Munich

artist unknown, *Virgin and Child Enthroned,* c. 1130, Metropolitan Museum of Art, New York City

GOTHIC

artist unknown, *Belleville Breviary,* c. 1323–1326, Bibliothèque Nationale, Paris

artist unknown, *Wilton Diptych,* c. 1377–1413, National Gallery, London

PRE-RENAISSANCE

Francesca, Piero Della, *Discovery and Proving of the True Cross,* c. 1460, St. Francesco, Arezzo, Italy

Giotto, *Arena Chapel,* 1305–1306, Padua, Italy

Masaccio, *Tribute Money,* c. 1427, Brancacci Chapel, Florence

NORTHERN RENAISSANCE

Bosch, Hieronymus, *Garden of Earthly Delights,* 1500, Prado, Madrid

Goes, Hugo van der, *Portinari Altarpiece,* 1476, Uffizi Gallery, Florence

Grunewald, Mathias, *Crucifixion,* 1524, Badische Kunsthalle, Karlsruhe, Germany

Master of Flemalle (Robert Campin?), *Merode Altarpiece,* 1425–1428, Cloisters Collection, Metropolitan Museum of Art, New York City

Eyck, Hubert and Jan van, *Ghent Altarpiece,* 1432, Church of St. Bavo, Ghent, Belgium

Eyck, Jan van, *Giovanni Arnolfini and His Bride,* 1434, National Gallery, London

Weyden, Rogier van der, *Descent from the Cross,* 1435, Prado, Madrid

RENAISSANCE

Alberti, Leone Battista, *S. Andrea,* 1470, Mantua, Italy

Arcimboldo, Giuseppe, *Winter,* 1563, Kunsthistorisches Museum, Vienna

Botticelli, Sandro, *Madonna of the Magnificat,* c. 1483, Uffizi Gallery, Florence

Botticelli, Sandro, *Birth of Venus,* c. 1480, Uffizi Gallery, Florence

Leonardo da Vinci, *Last Supper,* 1495–1498, Sta. Maria delle Grazie, Milan

Leonardo da Vinci, *Mona Lisa,* 1503–1506, Louvre, Paris

Lorenzetti, Ambrogio, *Good Government in the City,* 1338–1340, Palazzo Pubblico, Sienna, Italy

List 2–28   Continued

RENAISSANCE (cont.)

Luca, Signorelli, *Madonna and Child,* 1490, Uffizi Gallery, Florence

Mantegna, Andrea, *St. Sebastian,* c. 1455–1460, Kunsthistorisches Museum, Vienna

Masaccio, *Holy Trinity with the Virgin and St. John,* 1425, Sta. Maria Novella, Florence

Michelangelo, *Holy Family,* 1506, Uffizi Gallery, Florence

Michelangelo, *Sistine Chapel,* 1508–1512, Vatican, Rome

Perugino, Pietro, *Delivery of the Keys,* 1482, Vatican, Rome

Raphael, *Madonna of the Chair,* 1515–1516, Pitti Palace, Florence

Raphael, *School of Athens,* 1510–1511, Stanza della Segnatura, Vatican, Rome

BAROQUE

Caravaggio, *Calling of Saint Matthew,* c. 1599–1600, St. Luigi dei Francesi, Rome

De La Tour, Georges, *Newborn,* 1630, Musée des Beaux-Arts, Rennes, France

Gentileschi, Artemisia, *Judith with the Head of Holofernes,* c. 1625, Detroit Institute of Arts, Michigan

Hals, Frans, *Banquet of the Officers of the Saint George Guard Company,* 1616, Frans Hals Museum, Haarlem,
    The Netherlands

Heda, Willem Claesz, *Still Life,* c. 1648, Fine Arts Museum of San Francisco, California

Leyster, Judith, *Boy with Flute,* 1630, National Museum, Stockholm

Poussin, Nicolas, *Holy Family on the Steps,* 1648, National Gallery of Art, Washington, DC

Rembrandt Harmensz van Rijn, *The Night Watch,* 1642, Rijksmuseum, Amsterdam

Ribera, Jusepe de, *Boy With a Clubfoot,* c. 1642, Louvre, Paris

Rubens, Peter Paul, *Garden of Love,* c. 1638, Prado, Madrid

Ruisdael, Jacob van, *View of Haarlem,* c. 1670, Mauritshuis, The Hague

Steen, Jan, *The World Upside Down,* c. 1663, Kunsthistorisches Museum, Vienna

Velasquez, Diego, *Las Meninas,* 1656, Prado, Madrid

Velasquez, Diego, *Triumph of Bacchus,* c. 1628, Prado, Madrid

Vigeé-Lebrun, Elizabeth, *Marie Antoinette and Her Children,* 1788, Museé National du Chateau de Versailles,
    Paris

Watteau, Jean-Antoine, *A Pilgimage to Cythera,* 1717, Louvre, Paris

BAROQUE PORTRAITURE

Dyck, Anthony van, *Portrait of Charles I in Hunting Dress,* 1635, Louvre, Paris

Rembrandt van Rijn, *Self Portrait,* 1659, National Gallery of Art, Washington, DC

Rubens, Peter Paul, *Henry the IV Receiving the Portrait of Maria de Medici,* 1621–1625, Louvre, Paris

DUTCH BAROQUE STILL LIFE

Claesz, Pieter, *Still Life,* 1643, St. Louis Art Museum, Missouri

Heda, Willem Claesz, *Still Life,* 1634, Boymans-van Beuningen Museum, Rotterdam

van der Ast, Balthasar, *Flowers,* 1622, St. Louis Art Museum, Missouri

DUTCH BAROQUE STREET SCENES AND INTERIORS

Berckheyde, Gerrit, *Haarlem,* 1638, Rijksmuseum, Amsterdam

Hooch, Pieter de, *A Country Cottage,* c. 1665, Rijksmuseum, Amsterdam

van Der Heyden, Jan, *View of the Martelaarsgracht in Amsterdam,* 1637, Rijksmuseum, Amsterdam

Vermeer, Jan, *Street in Delft,* c. 1660, Rijksmuseum, Amsterdam

Vermeer, Jan, *The Allegory of the Art of Painting,* 1666, Kunsthistorisches Museum, Vienna

Vermeer, Jan, *View of Delft,* c. 1662, Mauritshuis, The Hague

List 2–28   Continued

BAROQUE GROUP PORTRAITURE

Hals, Frans, *Banquet of the Officers of the Saint George Guard Company,* 1616, Frans Hals Museum, Haarlem, The Netherlands

Hals, Frans, *The Women Regents of the Old Men's Almshouse,* c. 1664, Frans Hals Museum, Haarlem, The Netherlands

Rembrandt Harmensz van Rijn, *The Anatomy Lesson of Dr. Tulp,* 1632, Rijksmuseum, Amsterdam

Rembrandt Harmensz van Rijn, *The Syndics of the Drapers' Guild,* 1662, Rijksmuseum, Amsterdam

Velasquez, Diego, *Las Meninas,* 1656, Prado, Madrid

BAROQUE LANDSCAPES

Rembrandt Harmensz van Rijn, *The Omval,* 1645, Bibliothèque National, Paris

Rembrandt Harmensz van Rijn, *Three Trees,* 1643, Metropolitan Museum of Art, New York City

NEO-CLASSICAL

David, Jacques Louis, *Coronation of Napoleon and Josephine,* 1805–1807, Louvre, Paris

Ingres, Jean-Auguste-Dominique, *Comtesse d'Haussonville,* 1845, Frick Collection, New York City

ROMANTIC

Constable, John, *Stoke-by-Nayland,* 1844, Art Institute of Chicago, Illinois

Delacroix, Eugene, *Greece on the Ruins of Missolonghi,* 1826, Musée des Beaux-Arts, Bordeaux, France

Delacroix, Eugene, *Tiger Hunt,* 1854, Musée d'Orsay, Paris

Gericault, Theodore, *Mounted Officer of the Imperial Guard,* 1812, Louvre, Paris

Goya, Francisco, *The Third of May,* 1814–1815, Prado, Madrid

Turner, J.M.W., *Rain, Steam, and Speed,* 1844, National Gallery, London

Turner, J.M.W., *The Slave Ship,* 1840, Museum of Fine Arts, Boston, Massachusetts

REALISTIC

Daumier, Honoré, *The Third Class Carriage,* c. 1850, Metropolitan Museum of Art, New York City

Eakins, Thomas, *The Gross Clinic,* 1875, Jefferson Medical College, Philadelphia, Pennsylvania

Homer, Winslow, *The Croquet Game,* 1866, Art Institute of Chicago, Illinois

Homer, Winslow, *The Morning Bell,* 1866, Yale University Art Gallery, New Haven, Connecticut

Millet, Jean Francois, *The Sower,* c. 1850, Museum of Fine Arts, Boston, Massachusetts

Whistler, James, *Nocturne in Black and Gold,* 1871, Detroit Institute of Arts, Michigan

IMPRESSIONIST AND POST-IMPRESSIONIST PORTRAITS

Cassatt, Mary, *Lady at the Tea Table,* 1885, Metropolitan Museum of Art, New York City

Cassatt, Mary, *La Loge,* c. 1882, National Gallery of Art, Washington, DC

Cezanne, Paul, *Self-Portrait,* 1877, Bayerische Staatsgemalde Collection, Munich

Cezanne, Paul, *The Woman with a Coffee Pot,* 1890–1894, Musée d'Orsay, Paris

Degas, Edgar, *Singer with Glove,* 1878, Fogg Art Museum, Harvard University, Cambridge, Massachusetts

Gauguin, Paul, *Girl with Mango,* 1892, Baltimore Museum of Art, Maryland

Gogh, Vincent van, *Self-Portrait,* 1899, private collection, New York

Manet, Edouard, *Le Moulin de la Galette,* 1876, Musée d'Orsay, Paris

Manet, Edouard, *The Fifer,* 1866, Musée d'Orsay, Paris

Manet, Edouard, *The Reading,* 1868, Musée d'Orsay, Paris

Matisse, Henri, *Decorative Figure Against an Ornamental Background,* 1925, Museé National d'Arte Moderne, Paris

Matisse, Henri, *Lady in Blue,* 1937, collection of Mrs. John Wintersteen, Philadelphia, Pennsylvania

List 2–28   Continued

IMPRESSIONIST AND POST-IMPRESSIONIST PORTRAITS (cont.)

Monet, Claude, *Madame Gaudibert,* 1868, Musée d'Orsay, Paris

Rouault, Georges, *The Old King,* 1937, Museum of Art, Carnegie Institute, Pittsburgh, Pennsylvania

Seurat, Georges, *Woman with Parasol,* 1884, Emil G. Buehrle Collection, Zurich

IMPRESSIONIST LANDSCAPES

Boudin, Eugene, *The Beach at Trouville,* 1863, Ittleson Collection, New York

Manet, Edouard, *Dejeuner sur l'Herbe (Luncheon on the Grass),* 1863, Musée d'Orsay, Paris

Monet, Claude, *Rouen Cathedral in Fall Sunlight,* 1892–1893, Museum of Fine Arts, Boston, Massachusetts

Monet, Claude, *Water Lilies,* c. 1920, Carnegie Institute, Pittsburgh, Pennsylvania

Monet, Claude, *Impression Sunrise—Le Havre,* 1872, Musée Marmottan, Paris

Monet, Claude, *The River,* 1868, Art Institute of Chicago, Illinois

Pissarro, Camille, *The Orchard,* 1877, Musée d'Orsay, Paris

POST-IMPRESSIONIST PAINTINGS

Cezanne, Paul, *Mont Ste. Victoire,* 1885–1887, Courtauld Institute Galleries, London

Gauguin, Paul, *Vision After the Sermon,* 1888, National Gallery of Scotland, Edinburgh

Gauguin, Paul, *The Day of the God,* 1894, Art Institute of Chicago, Illinois

Gogh, Vincent van, *The Starry Night,* 1888, Museum of Modern Art, New York City

Munch, Edvard, *Melancholy,* c. 1891, National Gallery, London

Redon, Odilon, *Ophelia Among the Flowers,* 1905–1908, National Gallery, London

Rousseau, Henri, *The Dream,* 1910, Museum of Modern Art, New York City

Rousseau, Theodore, *Tropical Storm with a Tiger,* 1891, National Gallery, London

Seurat, Georges, *Bathers at Asnieres,* 1883–1884, National Gallery, London

MODERN ART

Davis, Stuart, *Report from Rockport,* 1940, collection of Mr. & Mrs. Milton Lowenthal, New York City

Demuth, Charles, *Buildings, Lancaster,* 1930, Whitney Museum of American Art, New York City

Demuth, Charles, *I Saw the Figure 5 in Gold,* 1928, Metropolitan Museum of Art, New York City

Duchamp, Marcel, *Nude Descending a Staircase,* 1912, Philadelphia Museum of Art, Pennsylvania

Hopper, Edward, *Nighthawks,* 1942, Art Institute of Chicago, Illinois

Kokoschka, Oscar, *Self-Portrait,* 1913, Museum of Modern Art, New York City

Lawrence, Jacob, *Jukebox,* 1946, Detroit Institute of Arts, Michigan

Modigliani, Amedeo, *Gypsy Woman with Baby,* 1919, National Gallery of Art, Washington, DC

Mondrian, Piet, *Composition in Line and Color,* 1913, Rijksmuseum Kroller-Muller, Otterlo, The Netherlands

Picasso, Pablo, *Les Demoiselles d'Avignon,* 1907, Museum of Modern Art, New York City

FAUVES

Derain, André, *Pool of London,* 1906, Tate Gallery, London

Matisse, Henri, *The Green Stripe* (Mme Matisse), 1905, Royal Museum of Fine Arts, Copenhagen

SURREALISM

Chagall, Marc, *I and the Village,* 1911, Museum of Modern Art, New York City

Chagall, Marc, *Self Portrait with Seven Fingers,* 1912, Stedelijk Museum, Amsterdam

Chirico, Giorgio de, *Nostalgia of the Infinite,* 1913, Museum of Modern Art, New York City

Chirico, Giorgio de, *The Disquieting Muses,* 1916, Gianni Mattioli Foundation, Milan

Duchamp, Marcel, *The Large Glass,* 1915, Philadelphia Museum of Art, Pennsylvania

List 2–28   Continued

SURREALISM (cont.)

Dali, Salvador, *The Persistence of Memory,* 1931, Museum of Modern Art, New York City

Ernst, Max, *Elephant of the Celebes,* 1921, Museum of Modern Art, New York City

ART SINCE MID-CENTURY

Bacon, Francis, *Head Surrounded by Sides of Beef,* 1954, Art Institute of Chicago, Illinois

Close, Chuck, *Linda,* 1975–1976, Akron Art Museum, Ohio

de Kooning, Willem, *Woman I,* 1950–1952, Museum of Modern Art, New York City

Estes, Richard, *Prescriptions Filled (Municipal Building),* 1983, private collection

Flack, Audrey, *Marilyn (Vanitas),* 1977, University of Arizona Museum of Art, Tucson

Frankenthaler, Helen, *Mountains and Sea,* 1952, National Gallery of Art, Washington, DC

Johns, Jasper, *Target with Four Faces,* 1955, Museum of Modern Art, New York City

Kiefer, Anselm, *Burning Rods,* 1984–1987, St. Louis Art Museum, Missouri

Kiefer, Anselm, *March Heath,* 1984, Van Abbemuseum, Eindhoven, The Netherlands

Mathieu, Georges, *Capetians Everywhere,* 1954, Musée National d'Art Moderne, Centre Georges Pompidou, Paris

Neel, Alice, *Andy Warhol,* 1970, Whitney Museum of American Art, New York City

Neel, Alice, *Red Grooms and Mimi Gross, No. 2,* 1967, Robert Miller Gallery, New York City

Paik, Nam June, *TV Buddha,* 1974, (Video installation), Stedelijk Museum, Amsterdam

Pollock, Jackson, *Autumn Rhythm (Number 20),* 1950, Metropolitan Museum of Art, New York City

Rego, Paula, *The Dance,* 1988, Tate Gallery, London

Richter, Gerhard, *Atelier,* 1985, Staatliche Museen, Nationalgalerie, Berlin

Rollins, Tim, *+ K.O.S. Amerika IV,* 1986–1987, Saatchie Collection, London

Rosenquist, James, *House of Fire,* 1981, Metropolitan Museum of Art, New York City

Rothenberg, Susan, *Mondrian Dancing,* 1985, St. Louis Art Museum, Missouri

Warhol, Andy, *Marilyn Diptych,* 1962, Tate Gallery, London

List 2–29   American Art

AMERICAN COLONIAL PAINTINGS

artist unknown, *Mrs. Freake and Baby Mary,* 1674, Worcester Art Museum, Massachusetts

artist unknown, *Pocahontas,* c. 1616, National Portrait Gallery, Washington, DC

Feke, Robert, *Family of Isaac Royall,* 1741, Harvard Law School, Cambridge, Massachusetts

Feke, Robert, *Self Portrait* (date unknown), Museum of Fine Arts, Boston, Massachusetts

Greenwood, John, *Sea Captains Carousing in Surinam,* c. 1758, St. Louis Art Museum, Missouri

Hesselius, Gustavus, *Tishcohan,* 1735, Historical Society of Pennsylvania, Philadelphia

Le Moyne, Jacques, *Saturiba, the Indian Chief, and Rene Laudonniere at Ribaut's Column,* 1564, New York Public Library, New York City

Smibert, John, *The Bermuda Group,* 1729, Yale University Art Gallery, New Haven, Connecticut

White, John, *Indians Fishing,* 1585, British Museum, London

PAINTINGS OF THE AMERICAN REVOLUTIONARY PERIOD

Copley, John Singleton, *Paul Revere,* 1768–1770, Museum of Fine Arts, Boston, Massachusetts

Peale, Charles Willson, *The Staircase Group,* 1795, Philadelphia Museum of Art, Pennsylvania

Peale, Charles Willson, *Washington After Trenton,* 1767, Metropolitan Museum of Art, New York City

Pratt, Matthew, *The American School,* 1765, Metropolitan Museum of Art, New York City

Revere, Paul, *The Bloody Massacre,* 1770, Library of Congress, Washington, DC

Stuart, Gilbert, *George Washington,* 1796, Museum of Fine Arts, Boston, Massachusetts

Stuart, Gilbert, *The Skater,* 1782, National Gallery of Art, Washington, DC

Trumbull, John, *Death of General Mercer at the Battle of Princeton,* 1777, Yale University Art Gallery, New Haven, Connecticut

Trumbull, John, *The Declaration of Independence,* 1786–1794, Yale University Art Gallery, New Haven, Connecticut

Trumbull, John, *The Surrender of Cornwallis at Yorktown,* 1817–1820, United States Capitol, Washington, DC

West, Benjamin, *Penn's Treaty with the Indians,* 1772, Pennsylvania Academy of the Fine Arts, Philadelphia

West, Benjamin, *The Death of General Wolfe,* 1771, Royal College, London; and National Gallery of Canada, Ottawa

PAINTINGS OF NATIVE AMERICANS AND THE WEST

Catlin, George, *Buffalo Bull's Back Fat, Head Chief, Blood Tribe,* 1832, American Museum, Washington, DC

Catlin, George, *Tal-lee, a Warrior of Distinction,* 1834, American Museum, Washington, DC

Eastman, Seth, *Travelling Tents of the Sioux Indians Called a Tepe,* 1847–1849, St. Louis Art Museum, Missouri

King, Charles Bird, *Young Omahaw, War Eagle, Little Missouri, and Pawnees,* 1821, Smithsonian Institution, Washington, DC

Wimar, Charles F., *Chief Billy Bowlegs,* 1861, St. Louis Art Museum, Missouri

AMERICAN PAINTINGS, c. 1800–1850

Allston, Washington, *The Rising of a Thunderstorm at Sea,* 1804, Museum of Fine Arts, Boston, Massachusetts

Audubon, John James, *Great Blue Heron,* 1821, Mercantile Library, St. Louis, Missouri

Bingham, George Caleb, *Fur Traders Descending the Missouri,* 1845, Metropolitan Museum of Art, New York City

Bingham, George Caleb, *Raftsmen Playing Cards,* 1847, St. Louis Art Museum, Missouri

Cole, Thomas, *View from Mount Holyoke, Massachusetts, after a Thunderstorm—The Oxbow,* 1836, Metropolitan Museum of Art, New York City

Leutz, Emanuel Gottlieb, *Washington Crossing the Delaware,* 1851, Metropolitan Museum of Art, New York City

Ryder, Albert Pinkham, *Moonlit Landscape,* 1819, Museum of Fine Arts, Boston, Massachusetts

List 2–29   Continued

AMERICAN NARRATIVE PAINTING

Copley, John Singleton, *Watson and the Shark,* c. 1782, Detroit Institute of Arts, Michigan

Homer, Winslow, *Prisoners from the Front,* 1866, Metropolitan Museum of Art, New York City

Peale, Charles Willson, *Exhuming the Mastodon,* 1806–1808, Peale Museum, Baltimore, Maryland

Quidor, John, *The Legend of Ichabod Crane,* c. 1828, Yale University Art Gallery, New Haven, Connecticut

Quidor, John, *The Money Diggers,* 1832, Brooklyn Museum, New York

Quidor, John, *The Return of Rip Van Winkle,* c. 1849, National Gallery of Art, Washington, DC

Wimar, Charles F., *The Buffalo Dance,* 1860, St. Louis Art Museum, Missouri

HUDSON RIVER SCHOOL PAINTINGS

Cropsey, Jasper Francis, *Autumn on the Hudson River,* 1860, National Gallery of Art, Washington, DC

Durand, Asher B., *Kindred Spirits,* 1849, New York Public Library, New York City

Kensett, John F., *White Mountain Scenery,* 1859, New York Historical Society, New York City

VICTORIAN PAINTINGS

Eakins, Thomas, *The Gross Clinic,* 1875, Jefferson Medical College, Philadelphia, Pennsylvania

Homer, Winslow, *The Croquet Game,* 1866, Art Institute of Chicago, Illinois

Homer, Winslow, *The Morning Bell,* c. 1866, Yale University Art Gallery, New Haven, Connecticut

Sargent, John Singer, *Lady X,* 1884, Metropolitan Museum of Art, New York City

Sargent, John Singer, *Mrs. George Swinton,* 1896, Art Institute of Chicago, Illinois

Sargent, John Singer, *Portrait of Lady Agnew,* c. 1892–1893, National Galleries of Scotland, Edinburgh

Tanner, Henry Ossawa, *The Banjo Lesson,* c. 1893, Hampton Institute, Hampton, Virginia.

Whistler, James Abbott McNeill, *Arrangement in Gray and Black, No. 1: The Artist's Mother,* 1871, Musée d'Orsay, Paris

Whistler, James Abbott McNeill, *Nocturne in Black and Gold: Falling Rocket,* c. 1874, Detroit Institute of Arts, Michigan

AMERICAN IMPRESSIONISM

Benson, Frank, *Sunlight,* 1909, Indianapolis Museum of Art, Indiana

Cassatt, Mary, *The Bath,* 1891, Art Institute of Chicago, Illinois

Hassam, Childe, *Allies Day, May 1917,* 1917, National Gallery of Art, Washington, DC

Hassam, Childe, *The Union Jack, New York, April Morn,* 1918, Hirshhorn Museum and Sculpture Garden, Washington, DC

Paxton, William, *The Front Parlor,* 1913, St. Louis Art Museum, Missouri

Tarbell, Edmund, *Across the Room,* 1899, Metropolitan Museum of Art, New York City

THE ASH CAN SCHOOL

Bellows, George, *Cliff Dwellers,* 1913, Los Angeles County Museum of Art, California

Bellows, George, *Stag at Sharkey's,* 1909, Cleveland Museum of Art, Ohio

Glackens, William, *Hammerstein's Roof Garden,* 1901, Whitney Museum of American Art, New York City

Glackens, William, *The Green Car,* 1910, Metropolitan Museum of Art, New York City

Henri, Robert, *New York Street in Winter,* 1902, National Gallery of Art, Washington, DC

Henri, Robert, *The Masquerade Dress,* 1911, Metropolitan Museum of Art, New York City

Luks, George, *Mrs. Gamely,* 1930, Whitney Museum of American Art, New York City

Prendergast, Maurice, *Central Park,* 1908–1910, Metropolitan Museum of Art, New York City

Sloan, John, *Hairdresser's Window,* 1907, Wadsworth Atheneum, Hartford, Connecticut

Sloan, John, *Sunday, Women Drying Their Hair,* 1912, Addison Gallery of American Art, Phillips Academy, Andover, Massachusetts

List 2–29   Continued

MODERNISM

Davies, Arthur B., *Intermezzo,* 1915, Graham Gallery, New York City

Dove, Arthur, *Nature Symbolized—Connecticut River,* 1911, Indiana University Art Museum, Bloomington

Duchamp, Marcel, *Nude Descending a Staircase, No. 2,* 1912, Philadelphia Museum of Art, Pennsylvania

Morgan, Russell, *Four Part Synchromy No. 7,* 1914–1915, Whitney Museum of American Art, New York City

Stella, Joseph, *Battle of Lights, Coney Island,* 1914, Yale University Art Gallery, New Haven, Connecticut

Stella, Joseph, *Brooklyn Bridge,* 1917, Yale University Art Gallery, New Haven, Connecticut

Weber, Max, *Chinese Restaurant,* 1915, Whitney Museum of American Art, New York City

Weber, Max, *Rush Hour, New York,* 1915, National Gallery of Art, Washington, DC

DADA

Duchamp, Marcel, *Fountain,* 1917, New York Independents Show, collection of Louise and Walter Arensberg, New York

Duchamp, Marcel, *The Bride Stripped Bare by Her Bachelors, Even* (The Large Glass), 1915–1923, Philadelphia Museum of Art, Pennsylvania

THE 1920s

Demuth, Charles, *Acrobats,* 1919, Museum of Modern Art, New York City

Dove, Arthur, *Fog Horns,* 1929, Colorado Springs Fine Arts Center, Colorado

Marin, John, *Maine Islands,* 1922, Phillips Collection, Washington, DC

O'Keeffe, Georgia, *New York Night,* 1928–1929, Nebraska Art Association, Sheldon Gallery, Lincoln, Nebraska

PRECISIONIST PAINTINGS (CUBIST/REALIST)

Davis, Stuart, *House and Street,* 1931, Whitney Museum of American Art, New York City

Hopper, Edward, *Early Sunday Morning,* 1930, Whitney Museum of American Art, New York City

Sheeler, Charles, *Classic Landscape,* 1931, St. Louis Art Museum, Missouri

Stella, Joseph, *The Bridge,* 1920–1922, Newark Museum, New Jersey

SOCIAL REALIST PAINTINGS

Gorky, Arshile, *The Artist and His Mother,* 1926–1929, Whitney Museum of American Art, New York City

Hopper, Edward, *Nighthawks,* 1942, Art Institute of Chicago, Illinois

Marsh, Reginald, *Twenty Cent Movie,* 1936, Whitney Museum of American Art, New York City

Shahn, Ben, *The Passion of Sacco and Vanzetti,* 1931–1932, Whitney Museum of American Art, New York City

AMERICAN SCENE PAINTERS/REGIONALISTS

Benton, Thomas Hart, *The American Historical Epic,* 1924–1927, Nelson-Atkins Museum of Art, Kansas City, Missouri

Burchfield, Charles, *Sun and Rocks,* 1950, Albright-Knox Art Gallery, Buffalo, New York

Soyer, Moses, *Artists on W.P.A.,* 1935, National Museum of American Art, Washington, DC

Wood, Grant, *Dinner for Threshers,* 1934, Whitney Museum of American Art, New York City

HARLEM RENAISSANCE PAINTINGS

Douglas, Aaron, *Aspects of Negro Life*: *From Slavery Through Reconstruction,* 1934, New York Public Library, New York City

Fuller, Meta Vaux Warrick, *Ethiopia Awakening,* 1914, New York Public Library, New York City

Hayden, Palmer, *The Janitor Who Paints,* 1939–1940, National Museum of American Art, Washington, DC

Johnson, William H., *Young Man in a Vest,* c. 1939–1940, National Museum of American Art, Washington, DC

Jones, Lois Mailou, *Les Fetiches,* 1938, National Gallery of American Art, Washington, DC

Woodruff, Hale, *The Mutiny Aboard the Amistad, 1839,* 1938–1939, from the Amistad Mutiny Mural, Talladega College, Alabama

List 2–29   Continued

PAINTINGS FROM THE 1940s, 1950s, AND EARLY 1960s

Burchfield, Charles, *The Sphinx and the Milky Way,* 1946, Munson-Williams-Proctor Institute, Utica, New York

de Kooning, Willem, *Queen of Hearts,* 1943–1946, Hirshhorn Museum and Sculpture Garden, Washington, DC

de Kooning, Willem, *Woman and Bicycle,* 1952–1953, Whitney Museum of American Art, New York City

Frankenthaler, Helen, *Blue Territory,* 1955, Whitney Museum of American Art, New York City

Johns, Jasper, *Target with Four Faces,* 1955, Museum of Modern Art, New York City

Johns, Jasper, *White Flag,* 1955, Kunstsammlung Nordheim-Westfalen, Düsseldorf

Kline, Franz, *Mahoning,* 1956, Whitney Museum of American Art, New York City

Lichtenstein, Roy, *Dreaming Girl,* 1963, Museum of Modern Art, New York City

Rauschenberg, Robert, *Monogram,* 1955–1959, Moderna Museet, Stockholm

Rauschenberg, Robert, *Retroactive I,* 1964, Wadsworth Atheneum, Hartford, Connecticut

Rothko, Mark, *Centre Triptych for the Rothko Chapel,* 1966, Rothko Chapel, Houston, Texas

Tooker, George, *The Subway,* 1950, Whitney Museum of American Art, New York City

Warhol, Andy, *Marilyn Monroe Diptych,* 1962, Tate Gallery, London

PAINTINGS SINCE 1965

Diebenkorn, Richard, *Ocean Park No. 122,* 1980, Museum of Fine Arts, Houston, Texas

Dine, Jim, *Blue Clam,* 1981, Museum of Contemporary Art, Chicago, Illinois

Estes, Richard, *Times Square at 3:53 pm, Winter,* 1985, private collection

Fish, Janet, *Eight Water Glasses Under Fluorescent Light,* 1974, private collection, New York City

Frankenthaler, Helen, *The Other Side of the Moon,* 1995, Knoedler Gallery, New York City

Hockney, David, *A Bigger Splash,* 1967, private collection, London

Holzer, Jenny, *Protect Me from What I Want,* 1988, LED display, Picadilly Circus, London

Rothenberg, Susan, *Holding the Floor,* 1985, Sperone Westwater Gallery, New York City

Stella, Frank, *Guadalupe Island, Caracara,* 1979, Tate Gallery, London

Stella, Frank, *Jarama II,* 1982, National Gallery of Art, Washington, DC

Tansey, Mark, *Action Painting II,* 1984, Montreal Museum of Fine Arts, Quebec, Canada

Drawn from *George Washington,* 1796,
Gilbert Stuart, The Saint Louis Art Museum

List 2–30   Famous Artists

A number of artists may have their names listed several times because their work spanned several "periods" of art, or they immigrated to another country. Until Gothic times, few artists were known by name. While most of these artists are painters, a few are also photographers or sculptors.

PRE-RENAISSANCE (LATE GOTHIC), c. 1250–1470

Italy

Angelico, Fra, c. 1400–1455

Bellini, Jacopo, c. 1400–1470

Castagno, Andrea del, c. 1421–1457

Cimabue, 1251–1302

Duccio, 1255–c. 1319

Fabriano, Gentile, c. 1370–1427

Francesca, Piero Della, c. 1416–1492

Gaddi, Taddeo, c. 1300–1366

Giotto di Bondone, c. 1266–1337

Gozzoli, Benozo, c. 1420–1497

Lippi, Fra Filippo, c. 1406–1469

Martini, Simone, 1315–1344

Masaccio, Tommaso, c. 1401–1428

Pollaiuolo, Antonio del, 1432–1498

Uccello, Paolo, 1397–1475

Veneziano, Domenico, c. 1410–1461

Verrocchio, Andrea del, c. 1435–1488

Germany

Schongauer, Martin, c. 1450–1491

The Netherlands (Flemish and Dutch)

Bosch, Hieronymus, c. 1450–1516

Bouts, Dieric, d. 1475

Brueghel, Pieter, the elder, c. 1525–1569

Campin, Robert, 1375–1444

David, Gerard, c. 1450–1516

Eyck, Jan van, c. 1390–1441

Goes, Hugo van der, c. 1440–1482

Heemskerck, Maerten van, 1498–1574

Limbourg brothers, Paul, Herman, and Jean, active 1380–1416

Memling, Hans, c. 1430–1494

Weyden, Rogier van der, c. 1399–1464

RENAISSANCE, 1450–1520

Italy

Bellini, Gentile, c. 1429–1507

Bellini, Giovanni, c. 1431–1516

Botticelli, Sandro, 1444–1510

Bramante, Donato, 1444–1514

Correggio, Antoni Allegri, c. 1489–1534

del Sarto, Andrea, 1486–1530

di Cosimo, Piero, 1462–1521

Francesca, Piero Della, 1420–1492

Ghirlandaio, Domenico, 1449–1494

Giorgione, Giorgio da Castelfranco, 1478–1510

Leonardo da Vinci, 1452–1519

Mantegna, Andrea, 1431–1506

Michelangelo, Buonarroti, 1475–1564

Perugino, Pietro, c. 1450–1523

Raphael, Sanzio, 1483–1520

Verrocchio, Andrea del, 1435–1488

MANNERISM, 1525–1600

Italy

Anguisciola, Sofonisba, 1528–1625

Arcimboldo, Giuseppe, 1527–1593

Bronzino, Agnolo, 1503–1572

Cellini, Benvenuto, 1500–1571

Fiorentino, Rosso, 1495–1540

Giorgione, c. 1478–1510

Palladio, Andrea, 1508–1580

Parmigianino, 1503–1540

Pontormo, 1494–1556/57

Tintoretto, Jacopo, 1518–1594

Titian (Tiziano Vecellio), c. 1485–1576

Vasari, Giorgio, 1511–1574

Veronese, Paolo, 1528–1588

France

Clouet, François, c. 1522–1572

Clouet, Jean, c. 1486–1541

Germany

Altdorfer, Albrecht, c. 1480–1538

Baldung, Hans, c. 1484–1545

Cranach, Lucas, 1472–1553

Dürer, Albrecht, 1471–1528

Elsheimer, Adam, 1578–1610

Grunewald, Matthias, c. 1470–1530

Holbein, Hans, the younger, 1497–1543

List 2–30   Continued

MANNERISM, 1525–1600 (cont.)
Spain

Greco, El (Domenikos Theotocopoulos), 1541–1614

BAROQUE, 1590–1750
Flanders

Brueghel, Jan, 1568–1625
Dyck, Anthony van, 1599–1641
Jordaens, Jacob, 1593–1678
Rubens, Peter Paul, 1577–1640
Teniers, David, the younger, 1610–1690

France

De La Tour, Georges, 1593–1652
Le Nain, Louis, 1593–1648
Lorrain, Claude, 1600–1682
Poussin, Nicolas, 1594–1665

Italy

Bernini, Gianlorenzo, 1598–1680
Carracci, Annibale, 1560–1609
da Caravaggio, Michelangelo, 1571–1610
Gentileschi, Artemisia, 1593–1653

The Netherlands

Avercamp, Hendri, 1585–1634
Claesz, Pieter, 1590–1661
Cuyp, Aelbert, 1620–1691
Hals, Frans, 1580–1666
Heda, Willem Claez, 1594–1680/2
Heem, Jan Davidsz. de, 1606–1683
Hobbema, Meindert, 1638–1709
Hooch, Pieter de, 1629–1684
Rembrandt Harmensz van Rijn, 1606–1669
Ruisdael, Jacob van, 1628–1682
Saenredam, Pieter, 1597–1662
Steen, Jan, 1626–1679
van Ostade, Adriaen, 1610–1685
Vermeer, Jan, 1632–1675
von Honthorst, Gerrit, 1590–1656

Spain

Greco, El, 1541–1614, b. Greece
Murillo, Bartolomé, 1618–1682
Ribera, Jusepe, 1588–1652
Velasquez, Diego, 1599–1660
Zurbaran, Francisco de, 1598–1664

ROCOCO, c. 1700–1800
America

Feke, Robert, c. 1707–1752
Greenwood, John, 1727–1792
Hesselius, Gustave, 1682–1755
Smibert, John, 1688–1751

England

Hogarth, William, 1697–1764

France

Boucher, François, 1703–1770
Chardin, Jean-Battiste-Simone, 1699–1779
Falconet, Etienne-Maurice, 1716–1791
Fragonard, Jean-Honoré, 1732–1806
Watteau, Jean-Antoine, 1684–1721

Italy

Bellotto, Bernardo, 1721–1780
Canaletto, Giovanni Antonio Canal, 1697–1768
Guardi, Francesco, 1712–1793
Longhi, Pietro, 1702–1785
Tiepolo, Giambattista, 1696–1770

NEOCLASSICISM, 1770–1820
America, 1750–1790

Bulfinch, Charles, 1763–1844
Copley, John Singleton, 1738–1815
Earl, Ralph, 1751–1801
Greenough, Horatio, 1805–1852
Jefferson, Thomas, 1743–1826
Peale, Charles Willson, 1741–1827
Revere, Paul, 1735–1818
Rush, William, 1756–1833
Stuart, Gilbert, 1755–1828
Trumbull, John, 1756–1843
West, Benjamin, 1738–1820

England

Blake, William, 1757–1827
Raeburn, Sir Henry, 1756–1823
Reynolds, Sir Joshua, 1723–1792

France

Canova, Antonio, 1757–1822
Corot, Jean Baptist Camille, 1796–1875
David, Jacques Louis, 1748–1825

List 2–30   Continued

NEOCLASSICISM, 1770–1820 (cont.)

France

Greuze, Jean Baptiste, 1725–1805

Ingres, Jean, 1780–1867

Vigee-LeBrun, Elizabeth, 1755–1842

Spain

Goya, Francisco, 1746–1828

ROMANTICISM, c. 1800–1850

America

Bingham, George Caleb, 1811–1879

Hicks, Edward, 1780–1849

Levtz, Emanuel Gottlieb, 1816–1868

England

Constable, John, 1776–1837

Gainsborough, Thomas, 1727–1788

Romney, George, 1734–1802

Turner, J.M.W., 1775–1851

France

Delacroix, Eugene, 1798–1863

Gericault, Theodore, 1791–1834

Millet, Francois, 1814–1875

Moreau, Gustave, 1826–1898

BARBIZON SCHOOL, 1840s

Daubigny, Charles-Francois, 1817–1878

Diaz, Narcisse Virgile, 1807–1876

Dupre, Jules, 1811–1889

Millet, Jean-François, 1814–1875

Jacque, Charles-Emile, 1813–1894

Rousseau, Theodore, 1812–1867

Troyon, Constant, 1810–1865

REALISM, c. 1850–1880

America

Eakins, Thomas, 1844–1916

Homer, Winslow, 1836–1910

France

Boudin, Eugene, 1824–1898

Corot, Jean Baptiste, 1796–1875

Courbet, Gustave, 1819–1877

Daumier, Honoré, 1808–1879

Fantin-Latour, Henri, 1836–1904

Houdon, Jean Antoine, 1741–1828

Germany

Friedrich, Caspar David, 1774–1880

Japan

Hiroshige, Ando, 1797–1858

Hokusai, Katsushika, 1760–1849

AMERICAN WESTERN PAINTERS, c. 1800–1850

Audubon, John James, 1785–1851

Bodmer, Karl, 1809–1893

Catlin, George, 1796–1872

Eastman, Seth, 1808–1875

Johnson, Eastman, 1824–1906

King, Charles Bird, 1785–1862

Remington, Frederic, 1861–1909

Russell, Charles, 1864–1926

Ryder, Albert Pinkham, 1847–1917

Wimar, Charles F., 1828–1862

AMERICAN PAINTING, 1800–1870

Allston, Washington, 1779–1843

Audubon, John James, 1785–1851

Peale, Raphaelle, 1774–1825

Peale, Rembrandt, 1778–1860

Peale, Titian Ramsey II, 1779–1885

Quidor, John, 1801–1881

Sully, Thomas, 1783–1872

THE HUDSON RIVER SCHOOL (AMERICAN), c. 1825–c. 1875

Church, Frederick Edwin, 1826–1900

Cole, Thomas, 1801–1848

Cropsey, Jasper Francis, 1823–1900

Doughty, Thomas, 1793–1856

Durand, Asher, 1796–1886

Fisher, Alvan, 1792–1863

Inman, Henry, 1802–1846

Inness, George, 1825–1894

Morse, Samuel F.B., 1791–1872

PRE-RAPHAELITE BROTHERHOOD (ENGLISH), 1848–1910

Brown, Ford Madox, 1821–1893

Collinson, James, 1825–1881

Hunt, William Holman, 1827–1910

Millais, John Everett, 1829–1896

Rossetti, Dante Gabriel, 1828–1882

Rossetti, W. M., 1829–1919

List 2–30   Continued

PRE-RAPHAELITE BROTHERHOOD (ENGLISH), 1848–1910 (cont.)
Stephens, F. G., 1828–1907
Strudwick, John Melhuish, 1849–1937
Woolner, Thomas, 1825–1892

ROCKY MOUNTAIN SCHOOL (AMERICAN), c. 1860–1890
Bierstadt, Albert, 1830–1902
Hill, Thomas, 1829–1908
Keith, William, 1839–1911
Moran, Thomas, 1837–1926
Wimar, Charles F., 1828–1862

IMPRESSIONISM, c. 1870–1905
America
Butler, Theodore E., 1861–1936
Cassatt, Mary, 1845–1926
Hassam, Childe, 1859–1935
Perry, Lilla Cabot, 1848–1933
Robinson, Theodore, 1852–1896

France
Degas, Edgar, 1834–1917
Manet, Edouard, 1832–1883
Monet, Claude, 1840–1926
Morisot, Berthe, 1841–1895
Pissarro, Camille, 1830–1903
Renoir, Auguste, 1841–1919

Spain
Sorolla y Bastida, Joaquin, 1863–1923

POST-IMPRESSIONISM, c. 1886–1920
France
Bonnard, Pierre, 1867–1947
Caillebotte, Gustave, 1848–1894
Cezanne, Paul, 1839–1906
Gauguin, Paul, 1848–1903
Matisse, Henri, 1869–1954
Redon, Odilon, 1840–1916
Rodin, Auguste, 1840–1917
Rousseau, Henri, 1844–1910
Seurat, Georges, 1859–1891
Signac, Paul, 1863–1935
Sisley, Alfred, 1839–1899
Toulouse-Lautrec, Henri, 1864–1901
Vuillard, Edward, 1868–1940

The Netherlands
Gogh, Vincent van, 1863–1890

Norway
Munch, Edvard, 1863–1944

TROMPE L'OEIL (AMERICAN), c. 1880s
Harnett, William Michael, 1848–1892, b. Ireland
Peale, Raphaelle, 1774–1825
Peto, John Frederick, 1854–1907

SYMBOLISM (FRANCE), 1880s–1890s
Gauguin, Paul, 1848–1903
Moreau, Gustave, 1826–1898
Puvis de Chavanne, Pierre, 1824–1898
Redon, Odilon, 1840–1916

VICTORIAN ART, 1870–1900
America
Beaux, Cecelia, 1855–1942
Currier, Nathaniel and Ives, James, active 1835–1907
French, Daniel Chester, 1850–1931
Hosmer, Harriet, 1830–1908
LaFarge, John, 1835–1910
Parrish, Maxfield, 1870–1966
Ryder, Albert Pinkham, 1847–1917
Saint-Gaudens, Augustus, 1848–1907
Sargent, John Singer, 1856–1925
Tanner, Henry Ossawa, 1859 -1937
Tiffany, Louis Comfort, 1848–1933
Ward, John Quincy Adams, 1830–1910
Warner, Olin Levi, 1844–1896
Whistler, James McNeill, 1834–1903

NABIS (FRENCH), 1890s
Bernard, Emile, 1868–1941
Bonnard, Pierre, 1867–1947
Denis, Maurice, 1870–1943
Gauguin, Paul, 1848–1903
Maillol, Aristide, 1861–1944
Serusier, Paul, 1863–1927
Vuillard, Edward, 1868–1940

ART NOUVEAU, c. 1880–1910
Austria
Klimt, Gustave, 1862–1918
Mucha, Alphonse, 1860–1939

List 2–30   Continued

ART NOUVEAU, c. 1880–1910 (cont.)
England
Beardsley, Aubrey, 1872–1898

EXPRESSIONISM, 1905–1925
Austria
Kokoschka, Oscar, 1886–1980
Schiele, Egon, 1890–1918

Belgium
Ensor, James, 1860–1949
Permeke, Constant, 1886–1952

France
Rouault, Georges, 1871–1958

Germany
Beckmann, Max, 1844–1950
Dix, Otto, 1891–1969
Feininger, Lyonel, 1871–1956
Grosz, George, 1893–1959
Heckel, Erich, 1883–1970
Kirchner, Ernst Ludwig, 1880–1938
Kollwitz, Käthe, 1867–1945
Macke, August, 1887–1914
Marc, Franz, 1880–1916
Modersohn-Becker, Paula, 1876–1907
Nolde, Emil, 1867–1956

Italy
Modigliani, Amedeo, 1884–1920

Norway
Munch, Edvard, 1863–1944

Russia
Kandinsky, Wassily, 1866–1944
Malevich, Kasimir, 1878–1935
Soutine, Chaim, 1894–1943
von Jawlensky, Alexei, 1864–1941

Switzerland
Klee, Paul, 1879–1940

THE TEN (AMERICAN), 1898–1918
Benson, Frank W., 1861–1951
Chase, William Merrit, 1849–1916 (a replacement)
De Camp, Joseph R., 1858–1923
Dewing, Thomas W., 1851–1938

Hassam, Childe, 1859–1935
Metcalf, Willard L., 1853–1925
Reid, Robert, 1862–1929
Simmons, Edward, 1852–1931
Tarbell, Edmund C., 1862–1938
Twachtmann, John Henry, 1853–1902
Weir, J. Alden, 1852–1919

THE EIGHT OR THE ASH CAN SCHOOL (AMERICAN), 1900–1920
Davies, Arthur B., 1862–1928
Glackens, William, 1870–1938
Henri, Robert, 1865–1929
Lawson, Ernest, 1873–1939
Luks, George, 1866–1933
Prendergast, Maurice, 1859–1924
Shinn, Everett, 1873–1958
Sloan, John, 1871–1951

DIE BRÜCKE (GERMAN), 1905
Bleyl, Fritz, 1880–1966
Kirchner, Ernst, 1880–1938
Nolde, Emil, 1867–1956
Pechstein, Max, 1881–1955
Schmidt-Rottluff, Karl, 1884–1976

FAUVISM, 1905–1907
Belgium
Dongen, Kees van, 1877–1968
Vlaminck, Maurice, 1876–1958

France
Braque, Georges, 1882–1963
Derain, André, 1880–1954
Dufy, Raoul, 1877–1953
Matisse, Henri, 1869–1954
Rouault, Georges, 1871–1958

Germany
Heckel, Erich, 1883–1970

PHOTO SECESSION (AMERICAN), 1905–1917
Dove, Arthur, 1880–1946
Hartley, Marsden, 1877–1943
Marin, John, 1870–1953
O'Keeffe, Georgia, 1887–1986
Steichen, Edward, 1879–1973
Stieglitz, Alfred, 1864–1946

List 2–30   Continued

CUBISM, 1907–1920s

France

Archipenko, Alexander, 1887–1964, b. Russia
Braque, Georges, 1882–1963
Delaunay, Robert, 1885–1941
Duchamp, Marcel, 1887–1968
Leger, Fernand, 1881–1955
Lipchitz, Jacques, 1891–1973
Villon, Jacques, 1875–1963

Spain

Gris, Juan, 1887–1927
Picasso, Pablo, 1881–1973

FUTURISM, 1909–1919

America

Feininger, Lyonel, 1871–1956
Stella, Joseph, 1877–1946

Italy

Balla, Giacomo, 1871–1958
Boccioni, Umberto, 1882–1916
Severini, Gino, 1883–1966

DER BLAUE REITER (GERMAN), 1911

Kandinsky, Wassily, 1866–1944
Macke, August, 1887–1914
Marc, Franz, 1880–1916

SYNCHROMISM (AMERICAN), 1913–1918

Macdonald-Wright, Stanton, 1890–1973
Morgan, Russell, 1886–1943

PRECISIONISM, 1915–PRESENT

Demuth, Charles, 1883–1935
Sheeler, Charles, 1883–1965

DADA, 1916–1922

America

Ray, Man, 1890–1977

France

Arp, Jean, 1887–1966
Brancusi, Constantin, 1876–1957, b. Romania
Duchamp, Marcel, 1887–1968
Picabia, Francis, 1879–1953

Germany

Grosz, George, 1893–1959
Schwitters, Kurt, 1887–1948

DE STIJL (THE NETHERLANDS), 1917

Mondrian, Piet, 1872–1944
Rietveld, Gerrit Thomas, 1888–1964
van Doesburg, Theo, 1883–1931
Vantongerloo, Georges, 1886–1965

CONSTRUCTIVISM (RUSSIAN), 1920

Gabo, Naum, 1890–1977
Kandinsky, Wassily, 1866–1944
Lissitzky, El, 1890–1941
Malevich, Kasimir, 1878–1935
Pevsner, Anton, 1886–1962
Popova, Lyubov, 1899–1924
Rodchenko, Alexander, 1891–1956
Tatlin, Vladimir, 1885–1953

GERMAN BAUHAUS, 1920–1933

Bayer, Herbert, 1900–1985
Breuer, Marcel, 1902–1981
Gropius, Walter, 1883–1969
Kandinsky, Wassily, 1866–1944
Klee, Paul, 1879–1940
Mies van der Rohe, Ludwig, 1886–1969
Moholy-Nagy, Laszlo, 1895–1946, b. Hungary

AMERICAN BAUHAUS, 1937

Albers, Josef, 1888–1976
Feininger, Lyonel, 1871–1956
Gropius, Walter, 1883–1969
Hofmann, Hans, 1880–1966
Moholy-Nagy, László, 1895–1946, b. Hungary
Mies van der Rohe, Ludwig, 1886–1969

SURREALISM, 1922–1940

America

Blume, Peter, 1906–1992
Cornell, Joseph, 1903–1972
Ray, Man, 1890–1977
Tobey, Mark, 1890–1976

Belgium

Delvaux, Paul, 1897–1994
Magritte, René, 1898–1967
Tanguy, Yves, 1900–1955

England

Carrington, Leonora, 1917

France

Dubuffet, Jean, 1901–1985

List 2–30   Continued

SURREALISM, 1922–1940 (cont.)
Germany
Ernst, Max, 1891–1975

Italy
Chirico, Giorgio di, 1888–1978

Mexico
Kahlo, Frida, 1907–1954

The Netherlands
Escher, Maurits C., 1898–1972

Russia
Chagall, Marc, 1887–1985

Spain
Dali, Salvador, 1904–1988
Miró, Joan, 1893–1983

Switzerland
Giacommetti, Alberto, 1901–1966
Klee, Paul, 1879–1940

MAGIC REALISM, C. 1925
America
Albright, Ivan Le Lorraine, 1897–1983
Blume, Peter, 1906–1992

Belgium
Magritte, Rene, 1898–1967

HARLEM RENAISSANCE, 1919–1929
Alston, Charles, 1907–1977
Bearden, Romare, 1914–1988
Biggers, John, 1924
Douglas, Aaron, 1899–1979
Fuller, Meta Vaux Warrick, 1877–1968
Gilliam, Sam, 1933
Hayden, Palmer, 1890–1973
Johnson, William H., 1901–1970
Jones, Lois Mailou, 1905
Lawrence, Jacob, 1917
Lewis, Samella, 1924
Motley, Archibald, Jr., 1891–1981
Savage, Augusta, 1892–1962
Tanner, Henry, 1859–1937
Van Der Zee, James, 1886–1983
Woodruff, Hale, 1900–1980

**AMERICAN SCENE PAINTING, REGIONALISM,
1920s–1930s**
Bellows, George, 1882–1925
Benton, Thomas Hart, 1889–1975
Curry, John Steuart, 1897–1946
Jones, Joe, 1909–1963
Soyer, Isaac, 1907–1981
Soyer, Moses, 1899–1974
Soyer, Raphael, 1899–1987
Wood, Grant, 1892–1942
Wyeth, Andrew, 1917

REALISM, 1920–1940
America
Beaux, Cecelia, 1855–1942
Bellows, George, 1882–1925
Burchfield, Charles, 1893–1967
Davis, Stuart, 1894–1964
Demuth, Charles, 1883–1935
Hopper, Edward, 1882–1967
Kane, John, 1860–1932
Marin, John, 1870–1953
Marsh, Reginald, 1898–1954
Moses, Anna Mary (Grandma), 1860–1961
O'Keeffe, Georgia, 1887–1986
Pippin, Horace, 1888–1946
Rockwell, Norman, 1894–1978
Shahn, Ben, 1898–1969
Sheeler, Charles, 1883–1965
Wyeth, N. C., 1882–1945

France
Utrillo, Maurice, 1883–1955

Mexico
Orozco, Jose Clemente, 1883–1949
Rivera, Diego, 1886–1957
Siqueiros, David A., 1896–1974
Tamayo, Rufino, 1899–1991

SOCIAL REALISM, 1930s–1940
Evergood, Phillip, 1901–1975
Hirsch, Stefan, 1899–1964
Hopper, Edward, 1882–1967
Lawrence, Jacob, 1917
Shahn, Ben, 1898–1969

PAINTER OF SOUTHERN LIFE
Gwathmey, Robert, 1903–1988

List 2–30   Continued

AMERICAN MODERNISM, 1930s
Davis, Stuart, 1894–1964
Demuth, Charles, 1883–1935
Diller, Burgoyne, 1906–1965
Dove, Arthur, 1880–1946
Feininger, Lyonel, 1871–1956
Hartley, Marsden, 1877–1943
Hofmann, Hans, 1880–1966
Kuhn, Walt, 1880–1949
Lachaise, Gaston, 1882–1935
Nadelman, Elie, 1882–1946, b. Poland
O'Keeffe, Georgia, 1887–1986
Sheeler, Charles, 1883–1965
Tobey, Mark, 1890–1976
Tooker, George, 1920
Weber, Max, 1881–1961

GROUP F.64, 1930s
Adams, Ansel, 1902–1984
Cunningham, Imogen, 1883–1976
Edwards, John Paul, 1883–1958
Noskowiak, Sonya, 1900–1975
Swift, Henry, 1891–1960
Van Dyke, Willard, 1906–1986
Weston, Edward, 1886–1958

FEDERAL ARTS PROJECTS, 1933–1943 (5,000 ARTISTS EMPLOYED DURING DEPRESSION)
Adams, Ansel, 1902–1984
Evans, Walker, 1903–1975
Lange, Dorothea, 1895–1965

ABSTRACT EXPRESSIONISM, c. 1940–1970
America
Avery, Milton, 1893–1965
Baziotes, William, 1912–1963
Calder, Alexander, 1898–1976
Cornell, Joseph, 1903–1972
Davis, Stuart, 1894–1964
de Kooning, Elaine, 1920–1989
de Kooning, Willem, 1904–1997
Flavin, Dan, 1933–1996
Francis, Sam, 1923–1994
Gorky, Arshile, 1904–1948
Gottlieb, Adolph, 1903–1974
Graves, Morris, 1910

Guston, Philip, 1913–1980
Hofmann, Hans, 1880–1966
Kline, Franz, 1910–1962
Krasner, Lee, 1908–1984
LeWitt, Sol, 1928
Martin, Agnes, 1912
Motherwell, Robert, 1915–1991
Nevelson, Louise, 1899–1988
Newman, Barnett, 1905–1970
Pollock, Jackson, 1912–1956
Reinhardt, Ad, 1913–1967
Rivers, Larry, 1923
Rothko, Mark, 1903–1970
Smith, David, 1906–1965
Stella, Frank, 1936
Still, Clyfford, 1904–1980
Thomas, Alma, 1891–1978
Tobey, Mark, 1890–1976

England
Bacon, Francis, 1909–1992, b. Ireland
Hepworth, Barbara, 1903–1975
Moore, Henry, 1898–1986

France
Brancusi, Constantin, 1876–1957, b. Romania
Delaunay, Robert, 1885–1941
Dubuffet, Bernard, 1901–1985

Germany
Bill, Max, 1908–1995

Italy
Burri, Alberto, 1915–1995
Modigliani, Amedeo, 1884–1920

The Netherlands
Appel, Karel, 1921
Mondrian, Piet, 1872–1944

Russia
Kandinsky, Wassily, 1866–1944
Lissitsky, El, 1890–1941
Malevich, Kasimir, 1878–1935

Switzerland,
Giacometti, Alberto, 1901–1966

List 2–30   Continued

ART INFORMEL (EUROPE), 1940s–1950s
France
Balthus (Balthasas Klossowski de Rola), 1908
de Stael, Nicolas, 1914–1955
Dubuffet, Jean, 1901–1985
Klein, Yves, 1928–1962

Germany
Hartung, Hans, 1904–1989

Italy
Burri, Alberto, 1915–1995
Fontana, Lucio, 1899–1968

Spain
Tapies, Antoni, 1923

POP ART, 1945–1965
America
Bengston, Billy Al, 1934
Bontecou, Lee, 1931
Diebenkorn, Richard, 1922–1993
Dine, Jim, 1935
Goode, Joe, 1937
Indiana, Robert, 1928
Johns, Jasper, 1930
Lichtenstein, Roy, 1923
Marisol (Escobar), 1930
Oldenburg, Claes, 1929
Ramos, Mel, 1935
Rauschenberg, Robert, 1925
Rosenquist, James, 1933
Ruscha, Edward, 1937
Warhol, Andy, 1930–1987
Wesselman, Tom, 1931

England
Blake, Peter, 1932
Hamilton, Richard, 1922

Italy
Fontana, Lucio, 1899–1968
Mazoni, Piero, 1913

Switzerland
Oppenheim, Meret, 1913–1985, b. Germany

OP ART, c. 1965
America
Anuszkiewicz, Richard, 1930
Davis, Ron, 1937
Poons, Larry, 1937

England
Riley, Bridget, 1931

France
Vasarely, Victor, 1908

Israel
Agam, Yaacov, 1928

FUNK ART, 1950–1960s
Arneson, Robert, 1930–1993
DeForest, Roy, 1930

COLOR FIELD PAINTING, 1950s–1960s
America
Francis, Sam, 1923–1994
Frankenthaler, Helen, 1928
Kelly, Ellsworth, 1923
Liberman, Alexander, 1912, b. Russia
Louis, Morris, 1912–1962
Newman, Barnett, 1905–1970
Noland, Kenneth, 1924
Rothko, Mark, 1903–1970
Stella, Frank, 1936
Still, Clyfford, 1904–1980

NEW REALISM, 1950s–PRESENT
America
Fish, Janet, 1938
Levine, Jack, 1915
Neel, Alice, 1900–1984
Segal, George, 1924
Trova, Ernest, 1927
Wyeth, Andrew, 1917
Wyeth, Jamie, 1946

HYPERREALISM, c. 1965–1977
America
Bechtle, Robert, 1932
Close, Chuck, 1940
Eddy, Don, 1944

List 2–30   Continued

HYPERREALISM, c. 1965–1977 (cont.)
America

Estes, Richard, 1932
Flack, Audrey, 1931
Hanson, Duane, 1925–1996
Pearlstein, Philip, 1924

CONCEPTUAL ART, 1970–PRESENT
America

Borofsky, Jonathan, 1942
Holzer, Jenny, 1950
Serra, Richard, 1939

England

Gilbert and George (Gilbert Proesch, 1945; George
    Passmore, 1942)

Germany

Beuys, Joseph, 1921–1986

The Netherlands

Dibbets, Jan, 1941

VIDEO ART

Allen, Terry, 1943
Finlay, Ian Hamilton, 1925
Graham, Dan, 1942
Hill, Gary, 1951
Nauman, Bruce, 1941
Paik, Nam June, 1932, b. Korea
Viola, Bill, 1951

POST-PAINTERLY ABSTRACTION, 1964

Held, Al, 1928
Kelly, Ellsworth, 1923
Louis, Morris, 1912–1962
Noland, Kenneth, 1924
Olitski, Jules, 1922, b. Russia

ENVIRONMENTAL ART, 1968–PRESENT
America

Andre, Carl, 1935
Aycock, Alice, 1946
Chin, Mel, 1951
Christo (Javacheff), 1935, b. Bulgaria
Guillebon, Jeanne-Claude, 1935, b. France
Harrison, Newton, 1932

Heizer, Michael, 1944
Holt, Nancy, 1938
Johanson, Patricia, 1940
Lin, Maya, 1960
Oppenheim, Dennis, 1938
Pepper, Beverly, 1924
Roloff, John, 1947
Smithson, Robert, 1938–1973
Warhol, Andy, 1928–1987

England

Goldsworthy, Andy, 1956
Long, Richard, 1945

The Netherlands

Dibbets, Jan, 1941

HAPPENINGS, LATE 1950s

Dine, Jim, 1935
Grooms, Red, 1937
Kaprow, Allan, 1927
Oldenburg, Claes, 1929
Whitman, Robert, 1935

FEMINIST ART, LATE 1960s–PRESENT

Chicago, Judy, 1939
Fish, Janet, 1938
Flack, Audrey, 1931
Frank, Mary, 1933
Graves, Nancy, 1940–1995
Hamilton, Ann, 1956
Holzer, Jenny, 1950
Kruger, Barbara, 1945
Levine, Sherri, 1947
Neel, Alice, 1900–1984
Ringgold, Faith, 1930
Saar, Betye, 1926
Schapiro, Miriam, 1923
Sherman, Cindy, 1954

MINIMALISM, 1960s AND 1970s

Bell, Larry, 1939
Judd, Donald, 1928–1994
Marden, Brice, 1938
Martin, Agnes, 1912, b. Canada
Rothko, Mark, 1903–1970
Serra, Richard, 1939

List 2–30   Continued

**LATE TWENTIETH CENTURY (POST-MODERN,
NEO-EXPRESSIONISM, NEO-CONCEPTUALISM),
1965–PRESENT**

America

Artschwager, Richard, 1924
Baldessari, John, 1931
Bartlett, Jennifer, 1941
Basquiat, Jean-Michel, 1960–1988
Benglis, Linda, 1941
Borofsky, Jonathan, 1942
Brooks, Ellen, 1946
Casebere, James, 1953
DeForest, Roy, 1930
Divola, John, 1949
Estes, Richard, 1936
Fischl, Eric, 1948
Fish, Janet, 1938
Flavin, Dan, 1933–1996
Frey, Viola, 1933
Gantz, Joe, 1954
Gillespie, Gregory, 1936
Golub, Leon, 1922
Gonzales-Torres, Felix, 1957–1996
Groover, Jan, 1943
Haring, Keith, 1958–1990
Hockney, David, 1937
Holzer, Jenny, 1950
Horn, Rebecca, 1944
Kahn, Wolf, 1927
Kasten, Barbara, 1936
Koons, Jeff, 1955
Kruger, Barbara, 1945
Levine, Sherrie, 1947
Mangold, Robert, 1957
Marden, Brice, 1938
Mitchell, Joan, 1926–1992
Morris, Robert, 1931
Murphy, Catherine, 1946
Nicosia, Nic, 1951
Nilsson, Gladys, 1940
Nutt, Jim, 1938
Paschke, Ed, 1939
Pearlstein, Philip, 1924
Pfaff, Judy, 1946
Ringgold, Faith, 1930

Rothenberg, Susan, 1945
Salle, David, 1952
Samaras, Lucas, 1936
Scharf, Kenny, 1958
Schnabel, Julian, 1957
Sherman, Cindy, 1954
Skoglund, Sandy, 1946
Smith, David, 1906–1965
Smith, Kiki, 1954
Smith, Tony, 1912–1980
Stella, Frank, 1936
Tansey, Mark, 1949
Twombly, Cy, 1929
Vallance, Jeffrey, 1955
Wegman, William, 1943
Witkin, Joel-Peter, 1939
Wofford, Philip, 1935

Belgium

Alechinsky, Pierre, 1927

England

Blake, Peter, 1932
Freud, Lucian, 1922

France

Balthus (Balthasas Klossowski de Rola), 1908
Klein, Yves, 1928–1962

Germany

Baselitz, Georg, 1938
Beuys, Joseph, 1921–1986
Haack, Hans, 1936
Kiefer, Anselm, 1945
Polke, Sigmar, 1941
Richter, Gerhard, 1932

Italy

Burri, Alberto, 1915–1995
Clemente, Francesco, 1952
Cucchi, Enzo, 1950

Japan

Funakoshi, Katsura, 1950
Morimura, Yasumasa, 1951

Other

Botero, Fernando, 1932, b. Colombia

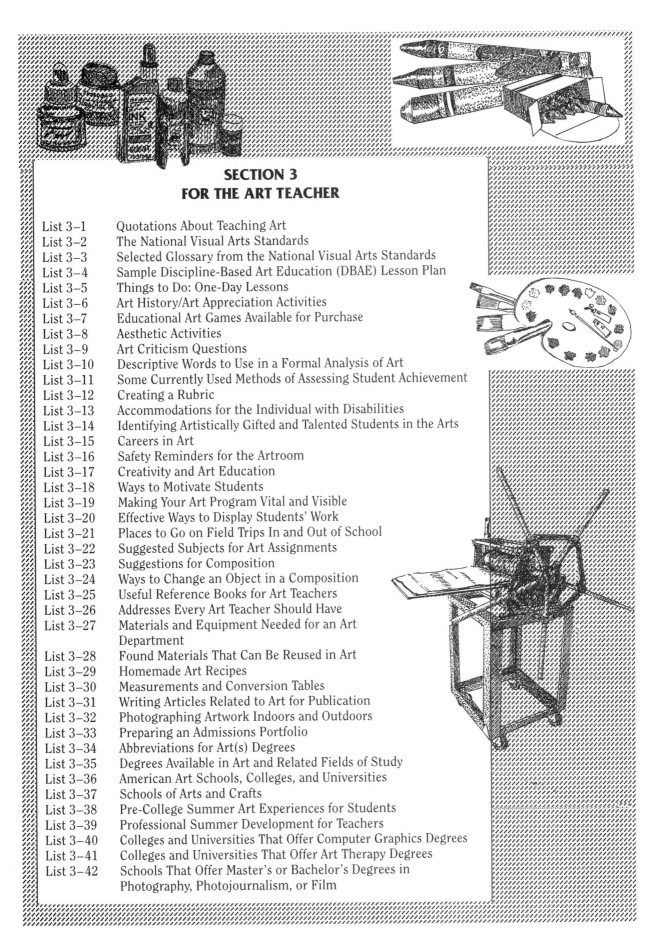

SECTION 3
FOR THE ART TEACHER

List 3–1   Quotations About Teaching Art

"I am afraid that the young, seeing in my work only the apparent facility and negligence in the drawing, will use this as an excuse for dispensing with certain efforts which I believe necessary."

—Henri Matisse

"Every child is an artist. The problem is how to remain an artist once he grows up."

—Pablo Ruiz Y Picasso

"Art is a way of expression that has to be understood by everyone, everywhere."

—Rufino Tamayo

"Teachers open the door, but you must enter by yourself."

—Chinese proverb

"Art does not reproduce what we see. It makes us see."

—Paul Klee

"The artist must train not only his eye but also his soul."

—Wassily Kandinsky

"The sculptor, and the painter also, should be trained in all these liberal arts: grammar, geometry, philosophy, medicine, astronomy, perspective, history, anatomy, theory of design, arithmetic."

—Lorenzo Ghiberti, c. 1440–1450

"Perhaps the greatest value of art teaching is that the pupil may later have something to unlearn."

—Charles Sheeler

"Any art communicates what you're in the mood to receive."

—Larry Rivers

"Art is either plagiarism or revolution."

—Paul Gauguin

"A painting is never finished—it simply stops in interesting places."

—Paul Gardner

"How you do your work is a portrait of yourself."

—Author unknown

"When I sit down to make a sketch from nature, the first thing I try to do is to forget I have ever seen a picture."

—John Constable

"You can never do too much drawing."

—Tintoretto

"What we have is given by God and to teach it to others is to return it to him."

—Gianlorenzo Bernini, c. 1665

List 3–2   The National Visual Arts Standards

The Goals 2000: Educate America Act was passed by Congress in 1993. A National Standards Visual Arts Task Force consisting of National Art Education Officers, regional and division leaders, and K–12 teachers reviewed drafts for national standards that specify the art knowledge and skills students should achieve in their K–12 schooling in art education. Achievement Standards specify the understandings and levels of achievement that students are expected to attain in the competencies, for each of the arts, at the completion of grades 4, 8, and 12. These standards are not mandatory, but optional for school districts and states.

The following Content Standards specify what students should know and be able to do in the arts disciplines:

1. Understanding and applying media, techniques, and processes.
2. Using knowledge of structures and functions.
3. Choosing and evaluating a range of subject matter, symbols, and ideas.
4. Understanding the visual arts in relation to history and cultures.
5. Reflecting upon and assessing the characteristics and merits of their work and the work of others.
6. Making connections between visual arts and other disciplines.

They should be able to communicate at a basic level in the four arts disciplines—dance, music, theater, and the visual arts. This includes knowledge and skills in the use of the basic vocabularies, materials, tools, techniques, and intellectual methods of each arts discipline.

They should be able to communicate proficiently in at least one art form, including the ability to define and solve artistic problems with insight, reason, and technical proficiency.

They should be able to develop and present basic analysis of works of art from structural, historical, and cultural perspectives, and from combinations of those perspectives. This includes the ability to understand and evaluate work in the various arts disciplines.

They should have an informed acquaintance with exemplary works of art from a variety of cultures and historical periods, and a basic understanding of historical development in the arts disciplines, across the arts as a whole, and within cultures.

They should be able to relate various types of art knowledge and skills within and across the arts disciplines. This includes mixing and matching competencies and understandings in art-making, history and culture, and analysis in any arts-related project.

List 3–3   Selected Glossary from the National Visual Arts Standards

aesthetics   a branch of philosophy that focuses on the nature of beauty, the nature and value of art, and the inquiry processes and human responses associated with those topics

analysis   identifying and examining separate parts as they function independently and together in creative works and studies of the visual arts

art criticism   describing and evaluating the media, processes, and meanings of works of visual arts, and making comparative judgments

art elements   visual arts components, such as line, texture, color, form, value, and space

art history   a record of the visual arts, incorporating information, interpretations, and judgments about art objects, artists, and conceptual influences on developments in the visual arts

art materials   resources used in the creation and study of visual art, such as paint, clay, cardboard, canvas, film, videotape, models, watercolors, wood, and plastic

art media   broad categories for grouping works of visual art according to the art materials used

assess   to analyze and determine the nature and quality of achievement through means appropriate to the subject

context   a set of interrelated conditions (such as social, economic, political) in the visual arts that influence and give meaning to the development and reception of thoughts, ideas, or concepts and that define specific cultures and eras

create   to produce works of visual art using materials, techniques, processes, elements, and analysis; the flexible and fluent generation of unique, complex, or elaborate ideas

expression   a process of conveying ideas, feelings, and meanings through selective use of the communicative possibilities of the visual arts

expressive features   elements evoking affects such as joy, sadness, or anger

ideas   a formulated thought, opinion, or concept that can be represented in visual or verbal form

organizational principles   underlying characteristics in the visual arts, such as repetition, balance, emphasis, contrast, and unity

perception   visual and sensory awareness, discrimination, and integration of impressions, conditions, and relationships with regard to objects, images, and feelings

process   a complex operation involving a number of methods or techniques, such as the addition and subtraction processes in sculpture, the etching and intaglio processes in printmaking, or the casting or constructing processes in making jewelry

structures   means of organizing the components of a work into a cohesive and meaningful whole, such as sensory qualities, organizational principles, expressive features, and functions of art

techniques   specific methods or approaches used in a larger process; for example, gradation of value or hue in painting or conveying linear perspective through overlapping, shading, or varying size or color

technologies   complex machines used in the study and creation of art, such as lathes, presses, computers, lasers, and video equipment

tools   instruments and equipment used by students to create and learn about art, such as brushes, scissors, brayers, easels, knives, kilns, and cameras

visual arts   a broad category that includes the traditional fine arts such as drawing, painting, printmaking, sculpture; communication and design arts such as film, television, graphics, product design; architecture and environmental arts such as urban, interior, and landscape design; folk arts; and works of art such as ceramics, fibers, jewelry, works in wood, paper, and other materials

visual arts problems   specific challenges based in thinking about and using visual arts components

This glossary is taken from *The National Art Education Association News* of June, 1994. Copyright 1994 by THE NATIONAL ART EDUCATION ASSOCIATION. Reprinted with permission.

List 3–4   Sample Discipline-Based Art Education (DBAE) Lesson Plan

PROJECT TITLE:

AMOUNT OF TIME NEEDED:

MEDIUM:

ART ELEMENTS AND PRINCIPLES:

MATERIALS:

STUDENT PERFORMANCE

Primary goal/objective(s):

The student/learner will:

Discipline-Based Art Education (DBAE)

Art History:

Art Production:

Art Perception (aesthetics) relates to beauty/ quality:

Criticism (student's response to own work and that of others):

TEACHING STRATEGIES*

1. establish set (focus attention)
2. state explicit objectives/purpose
3. give information (provide input)
4. model: visual & verbal demonstrations
5. check for understanding
6. guided practice
7. independent practice
8. closure

* Modifications of M. Hunter Model

1.

2.

3.

4.

5.

6.

7.

8.

EVALUATION (should relate to goals)

RESOURCES (books, films, notes)

List 3–5   Things to Do: One-Day Lessons

- Bring in a piece of fruit such as an apple or orange. On one piece of paper, draw it whole, then sliced vertically or crosswise, with seeds or with a bite out of it. Use several different views.
- Bring in a sack full of twigs, and have students select and draw one as if it were a giant tree.
- Cut out a 5-inch triangle or rectangle of colored paper and lay it on a white background. Cut shapes into the edges of the colored paper, and fold them outward from the original shape. Carefully glue the geometric shape and the cutouts onto the background.
- Do a life-size or larger pencil drawing of an ordinary object such as crumpled paper, paper bag, soft-drink can, piece of popcorn, or candy wrapper in extreme detail.
- Do a surrealist project by writing a list of nouns (e.g., ice-cream cone, shoe, bicycle), verbs (e.g., running, skating, swimming), and adjectives (e.g., muscular, thin, checkered). Select one or two of each, then make a cut-out composition of the nouns, changing them according to the other words chosen. Use varied colors of white and fluorescent typing paper and black marker.
- Draw a series of eyes in as many different ways as you can think of, or a series of noses or mouths.

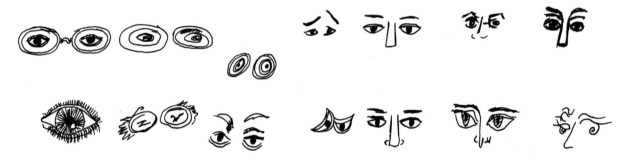

- Draw yourself, a friend, or family member at the workplace (even if it is doing dishes at home).
- Give students plastic cleaners' bags (or kraft paper) and twine and have them wrap an object in an artistic manner.
- Loosely paint watercolor on paper and, while it is wet, press leaves into the background, adding extra paint around the edges of the leaves. Leave for a bit, then remove. Repeat. Emphasize the use of dark and light values.
- Make a small drawing based on aboriginal art by dipping the end of an eraser into tempera or acrylic paints, and stamping these colors onto the drawing. The themes of aboriginal art often are based on day-to-day experiences to do with hunting or travel to various places.
- On a 5 × 7-inch card, do a self-portrait in the pointillist (dot) technique with markers.
- On one piece of paper, use fine-line black marker to realistically draw your hand in five different areas in different positions.
- Select a small corner of the room and do a perspective line drawing of it.
- Stack stools, chairs, or boxes, and use a viewfinder to select a small portion to draw, running the drawing off the edges.
- Use a ball-point pen to do drawings of your own hand holding something. Use cross hatching or dots to show shadows.
- Use a fine-line marker to doodle on a 12 × 18-inch piece of white paper, spacing various types of marks. Then make a jungle scene, incorporating the doodle marks into animals, plants, and flowers.
- Use a fine-line marker to draw the inside of your locker, your closet, or your room.
- Using ink, make a forest scene using a variety of mark-making instruments such as sticks, cotton swabs, cotton balls, bamboo, the stick end of a brush, a feather with the end shaped, match sticks, toothpicks, broken popsicle sticks.
- Using newspaper and masking tape, a group of students may "dress" one of its members in a Colonial costume.
- With colored pencil, draw something small and personal such as a wallet and cards, contents of purse, keys.

List 3–6   Art History/Art Appreciation Activities

INDIVIDUAL ACTIVITIES

- In looking at modern art, which often does not have a subject, "scan" the painting by first simply stating what is there; then look for the Elements (the sensory properties such as line, color, texture, form, and space) and Principles of Art (the formal properties) such as repetition, rhythm, variety, center-of-interest, balance; then the medium used by the artist; and the mood or meaning.

- Look at a painting or poster, then verbally **invent** a history; tell something about how the artist was feeling when it was painted, why the curator of a museum bought this particular painting rather than one you might like better, something about the subject. (Most of what is known about the *Mona Lisa* is speculation.)

- Look at slides or photos of Classical Greek sculpture such as *The Discobolus* (Discus Thrower), and become aware of the triangles, the negative space, and the diagonals. With another sculpture point out contrapposto (the S-curve), the way the weight rests on one foot, forcing the hip to be higher on that side. Try to do this yourself.

- Place several posters on the wall. Select one, and specifically write all the colors used, all the textures, and describe the edges of shapes. Take down the posters, and use pastels, markers, or watercolors to make a picture of an entirely different subject, using the colors, textures, and edges you have written about.

- Project a slide onto the wall and study it for one minute. Turn it off. On a 9 × 12-inch sheet of paper, reproduce the painting from memory, using watercolor.

- Select a Renaissance reproduction. Place tracing paper on top of it and lightly trace the main groups. Then use a ruler and compass to draw geometric figures for analyzing the composition.

- Write about the three works of art you would purchase if price were absolutely no object. This would be the beginning of a "personal art collection." Talk about the choices.

GROUP ACTIVITIES

- Divide into groups of three or four. Each group selects a poster to analyze according to the Elements and Principles of Art.

- Divide postcards and reproductions among several groups. The groups sort these into two portions, giving a "name" to each portion. Then they start over and divide the reproductions into four portions, again naming each portion.

- Each group selects a famous painting with figures, then mimics the poses in the artwork. Get back into a large group and have each group interpret its painting while others guess what it is.

- Each person should try to draw what he or she perceives as the ugliest building in town. Then talk about whether it should be torn down or saved and restored. Why?

- Groups are given postcards and reproductions and asked to be curators at a museum, trading items that do not fit into their particular "department." When they have a collection, then the paintings must be arranged for display.

- Have people call out nouns (such things as car, flower, sky, clouds, house, painting, etc.) as one person writes. Divide these into art and nonart.

- Put a group of posters on the wall. Have each person write a diamante (diamond-shaped) poem about one poster; the person then reads the poem to the group who must guess which poster it was about. A diamante poem is: *line 1,* a one-word equivalent of the picture; *line 2,* an action phrase; *line 3,* a simile or metaphor; *line 4,* a single-word summation.

- Groups try to find several paintings that are based on mythology, and then tell the myth that is behind the painting.

- Groups write their definitions of what art is. Based on the definitions, decide whether these items are art: a shell, a printed coffee mug, a photograph, a ragged pair of treasured jeans, a printed T-shirt, a film poster, a magazine advertisement. Discuss what art is.

List 3–7   Educational Art Games
Available for Purchase

These games are available in many museum shops or in catalogues of art supplies.

Art Bits® Card game
Art Memo Game
Art Rummy
Artdeck® Mexican Artist Playing Cards
Artdeck® African Artifacts Playing Cards
Artdeck®, 52 paintings on a deck of playing cards
Artpack
Double-Deck Illusions Cards

Impressionist Memo Game
Izzi 2® Game
National Gallery of Art Lotto Game
National Gallery of Art Rummy Game
Nature in Art Quiz (National Gallery of Art,
   Washington, DC)
Where Art Thou

List 3–8   Aesthetic Activities

According to the German philosopher Alexander Baumgarden, "Aesthetics is the science of the beautiful." In seeking the answers to a specific question such as "What is art?" or "Is this art?" or "Is this beautiful?" one often ends up with more questions than answers. Because a reaction to art is such a personal thing, there simply aren't absolute answers that would be valid for all time periods and cultures.

TEACHER GUIDELINES FOR AN AESTHETIC DISCUSSION

1. Avoid questions that contain their own answers.
2. Encourage people to play "devil's advocate" by presenting counter arguments.
3. Give "wait time" after asking a question and before moving on to the next one.
4. Play off one person's answer against another. For example, "Do you agree with him/her?"
5. Suggest people be open minded to viewpoints different from their own.
6. After an extended discussion, sometimes try to come up with a consensus.

SAMPLE QUESTIONS TO ASK IN AN AESTHETIC DISCUSSION

- Can advertising provide an example of good art? Propaganda?
- Can an object found in nature be considered a work of art?
- Do you need to know the artist's intention to appreciate the artwork?
- Does an artwork have to be beautiful?
- If it is manufactured in quantity, does that make it less art than something that is one-of-a-kind?
- In the future how will you decide for yourself whether something is art?
- Is a copy of an artwork as much a work of art as the original? If not, why not?
- Is there a way we can tell what an artwork means?
- Might an artwork speak more to one segment of society than to another, yet still be an artwork?
- Should we all agree on what is beautiful?
- What do you mean by that? Give me an example.
- What is the difference between an abstract painting made by an elephant or chimpanzee and one made by a human?
- What is the difference between art and craft?
- What makes one thing beautiful, and another similar item (such as a sofa) ugly?
- Who decides what an artwork is?
- Without an artist to create it, is there art?

AESTHETIC ACTIVITIES

- Discuss what people think might be masculine or feminine art. What would be considered masculine characteristics? Which would be feminine? Would one be more or less feminine/masculine if one preferred one type of art over another?

List 3–8   Continued

AESTHETIC ACTIVITIES (cont.)

- First as an individual, then as a group, define what is considered art in your own culture. Then, looking around your immediate surroundings, identify something that everyone can agree is art.
- Have people post construction-paper tokens on a grouping of posters as follows: green rectangle, the one they think cost the most money; white hand, the one that was the most work; red heart, the one they think their mother would love the most; blue ribbon, the one they think a museum curator might buy or a judge would award "best of show."
- *Pair/Share:* Two students analyze a group of objects and decide whether it is art, then present their opinions to the larger group for dissection and discussion.
- Put two slides or posters side by side for comparison. Write things that are different and things that are the same, and analyze each according to medium, style, content, and the elements and principles of art.
- Talk about the aesthetics of cars: Which old ones were the funniest? Which would they buy if money were no object? Which ones are considered "classic" cars? What are some exterior changes they would make in cars of today? Which colors do they consider really terrible for a car? Can a car be considered a work of art?

List 3–9   Art Criticism Questions

Part of Discipline-Based Art Education is criticism. Too often, students think this means that people will say bad things about their art. The purpose of criticism is to get students to look at their own art and that of other people (students and professionals) analytically. They should be able to talk about the composition using terms such as the elements and principles of art. A critique need not last very long. It can often be an effective way of concluding a project. Of course, a critique of a portfolio would be much more intensive. Here are some sample questions that can get conversations about art going.

FOR A FORMAL ANALYSIS OF A WORK OF ART BY A KNOWN ARTIST

- Close your eyes. Keep them closed. When you open them, remember what the first thing is that you notice. Why did you see it first? (color, size, location)
- Describe the colors. Are they bright? muted? grayed? garish? pretty? soft? pastel? clashing?
- Do you feel an emotion when you look at this work of art?
- Find how the artist leads your eye through the painting.
- Find where the artist used repetition of color or a shape.
- Let's talk about this picture in terms of the elements and principles of art.
- Look at this painting. Describe the edges. Are they fuzzy? soft? hard? blurry? blended? no edges?
- Show me variety in line in this picture.
- Squint through your eyelashes. Notice if the artist used differences in value. Show me the darkest, the lightest, the brightest areas.
- What about lines? Are they thick? thin? curvy?
- What emotion do you think the artist might have been trying to show when this was created?
- What kinds of shapes do you see here? Are they geometric, or amorphous?
- Which of the elements (line, shape, color, value, or texture) do you think is most dominant in this artwork?

SAMPLE QUESTIONS FOR HELPING STUDENTS ANALYZE THEIR OWN WORK AND THAT OF FELLOW STUDENTS

- Would someone be willing to talk about your own work?
- Which of these artworks uses line (shape, color, form, space) most effectively?
- Which of these meets the goals of the project best? (A goal might have been variety, creativity, etc.)
- Which one of these shows the greatest differences in value . . . the most contrast?
- Does this remind you of the work of any artist whose work you have seen?
- If you could make one change in your own artwork, what would you do?
- If you were a curator and you could buy one of these artworks for the collection of your museum, which one would it be? Why?
- In talking about your own work of art, what would you have done if you had had more time?
- What were you trying to show through the style you used?

List 3–10   Descriptive Words to Use in a Formal Analysis of Art

ELEMENTS OF ART

Line

blurred
broken
controlled
curved
diagonal
freehand
fuzzy
horizontal
interrupted
meandering
ruled
short
straight
thick
thin
vertical
wide

Texture

actual
bumpy
corrugated
flat
furry
gooey
leathery
prickly
rough
sandy
shiny
simulated
smooth
soft
sticky
tacky
velvety
wet

Colors

brash
bright
calm
clear
cool
dull
exciting
garish

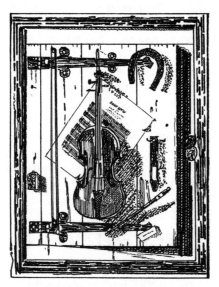

Drawn after *Still-Life Violin and Music,*
1888, William Michael Harnett, The Metropolitan Museum of Art, New York City

grayed
multicolored
muted
pale
polychromed
primary
saccharine
secondary
subdued
sweet
warm

Shape/Form

amorphous
biomorphic
closed
distorted
flat
free-form
full of spaces
geometric
heavy
light
linear
massive
nebulous
open
organic

Value

dark
light
medium

Space

ambiguous
deep
flat
negative/positive
open
shallow

Principles of Art

balance
contrast
emphasis
harmony
pattern
repetition
rhythm
unity
variety

THEMES IN ART

adoration
children
circus
cityscape
earth, air, fire, and water
farming festivals
gardens
grief
history
hunting
landscape
love
music
mythology
narrative of historic occasions
portraiture
processions
religion
seascape
storytelling
theater
war

List 3–10   Continued

MEDIA (MATERIALS)

Two-Dimensional

chalk
colored pencil
conté
egg tempera
found materials
gouache
ink
oil
pastel
pencil
photograph
print
tempera
vine charcoal
watercolor

Three-Dimensional

bronze
clay
fibers
found materials
marble
metal
mixed media
papier-mâché
plaster
stone
wood

TECHNIQUE

architecture
batik
carving

ceramics
collage
crafts
glassblowing
jewelry making
metalwork
modeling
mosaics
painting
photography
printmaking
repoussé
sculpture
weaving

STYLE OR PERIOD

abstract
classical
genre
historical
literary
naive
narrative
nonobjective
primitive
realistic
romantic
Renaissance

**CHARACTERISTICS OF
CLASSICAL ART**

balanced
calm
clean outlines
conservative

controlled
cool
decorous
detached
dignified
elegant
formal
intellectual
rational
serious
simple
symmetrical
traditional
tranquil

**CHARACTERISTICS OF
ROMANTIC/EMOTIONAL**

asymmetrical
blurred outlines
conveys a mood
dynamic
emotional
expressive
extreme emotions
man not at center
mysterious
nature at center
otherworldly
personal to the artist
sad
spiritual
strong diagonals
swirling
unrestrained

List 3–11   Some Currently Used Methods of Assessing Student Achievement

THE TEACHER

compares artwork to pre-stated objectives

looks for progress

looks for originality

observes the student at work (process)

tests for knowledge of vocabulary, techniques, and facts

THE STUDENT

fulfills an agreed-upon contract

shows evidence of preparation and planning

makes a self-evaluation of work

THE STUDENT AND TEACHER

evaluate the student portfolio together

List 3–12   Creating a Rubric

Art teachers have always used specific standards for grading, but we might have been unaware that we were creating a *rubric*. It is a term that comes from the Language Arts curriculum. Simply, it means that you decide what is required to make an A, B, C, D, or F, by how well the student meets your predetermined objectives. For example, if 30 points might be given for a project that took 30 minutes, it could contain 10 points for originality, 5 points for use of color, 10 points for use of the entire page, and 5 points for balance. This list contains some criteria you might use.

communicates well with the teacher

completes work within a specific period

creates personally expressive work

demonstrates a positive attitude

demonstrates consistently high quality of work

demonstrates growth

does creative problem solving

explores several options

has a personal involvement in subject

has good work habits

helps classmates to succeed

is not deterred by degree of difficulty or complexity of project

is open-minded to stylistic differences

makes a sincere effort

makes connections to other knowledge

makes regular reflective journal entries

meets contractual agreement (if any)

participates in group activities and critiques

perseveres

reacts to criticism appropriately

satisfies the restrictions of the problem

selects appropriate media for expression

shows dependability

shows good craftsmanship

shows self-satisfaction with quality of work

takes personal and group responsibility

takes risks

uses class time effectively

uses higher-level thinking skills

uses materials and equipment responsibly

uses resources effectively

RUBRIC FOR GRADING ART

100 95 90%	89 85 80%	79 75 70%	69 65 60%	59% and below
A	B	C	D	F
Excellent	Above Average	Average	Below Average	Unsatisfactory
Outstanding	Very Good	Good	Needs Improvement	Poor
Exemplary	Acceptable	Not YetAcceptable	Barely acceptable	Unacceptable

ELEMENTS OF DESIGN: LINE, TEXTURE, COLOR, SHAPE/FORM, VALUE, SPACE
PRINCIPLES OF DESIGN: REPETITION, BALANCE, EMPHASIS, CONTRAST, UNITY

A: Planned carefully, made several sketches, and showed an awareness of the elements and principles of design; chose color scheme carefully, used space effectively.

B: The artwork shows that the student applied the principles of design while using one or more elements effectively; showed an awareness of filling the space adequately.

C: The student did the assignment adequately, yet it shows lack of planning and little evidence that an overall composition was planned.

D: The assignment was completed and turned in, but showed little evidence of any understanding of the elements and principles of art; no evidence of planning.

F: The student did the minimum or the artwork was never completed.

CREATIVITY/ORIGINALITY

A: The student explored several choices before selecting one; generated many ideas; tried unusual combinations or changes on several ideas; made connections to previous knowledge; demonstrated outstanding problem-solving skills.

B: The student tried a few ideas before selecting one; or based his or her work on someone else's idea; made decisions after referring to one source; solved the problem in a logical way.

C: The student tried one idea, and carried it out adequately, but it lacked originality; substituted "symbols" for personal observation; might have copied work.

D: The student fulfilled the assignment, but gave no evidence of trying anything unusual.

F: The student showed no evidence of original thought.

EFFORT/PERSEVERANCE

A: The project was continued until it was as complete as the student could make it; gave effort far beyond that required; took pride in going well beyond the requirement.

B: The student worked hard and completed the project, but with a little more effort it might have been outstanding.

C: The student finished the project, but it could have been improved with more effort; adequate interpretation of the assignment, but lacking finish; chose an easy project and did it indifferently.

D: The project was completed with minimum effort.

F: The student did not finish the work adequately.

CRAFTSMANSHIP/SKILL/CONSISTENCY

A: The artwork was beautifully and patiently done; it was as good as hard work could make it.

B: With a little more effort, the work could have been outstanding; lacks the finishing touches.

C: The student showed average craftsmanship; adequate, but not as good as it could have been, a bit careless.

D: The student showed below-average craftsmanship, lack of pride in finished artwork.

F: The student showed poor craftsmanship; evidence of laziness or total lack of understanding.

GROUP COOPERATION/ATTITUDE

A: The student worked toward group goals, effectively performed a variety of roles in group work, followed through on commitments, was sensitive to the feelings and knowledge level of others, willingly participated in necessary preparation or work for classroom.

B: The student participated enthusiastically, followed through on commitments, performed more than adequately, assisted in preparation and cleanup.

C: The student mostly allowed others in the group to make all the decisions, did his or her share of work adequately, assisted in preparation and cleanup when asked.

D: The student allowed others to do most of the work, did participate minimally, did the minimum amount.

F: The student was part of the group, but did almost nothing toward group goals, did a minimal amount of preparation and cleanup.

List 3–13   Accommodations for the Individual with Disabilities

Part of teaching is to make accommodations for every student because each one is so different. As with all students, keep trying until you learn what works for that student. These instructions for accommodations for the student with disabilities are from my personal experience and from Loretta Schafer and Jean Manley, Art Specialists from the Special School District of St. Louis County, Missouri.

ADAPTIVE METHODS FOR WORKING WITH THE PHYSICALLY AND BEHAVIORALLY DISABLED

- A smile, a friendly touch on the forearm, a wink, a handshake, or a thumbs-up sign, are all nonverbal ways to say "you're on the right track."
- Allow a student to work in a secluded area if it is easier for concentration.
- Allow extra time for a student who needs it.
- Assign different students to help a disabled student when you see it is needed; both students gain from this.
- Find something positive to say about the efforts each student is making.
- Make eye contact and call the student by name.
- Offer choices of media; if a student isn't comfortable painting, oil pastel would be a good substitute.
- Teach with a variety of teaching methods: written, oral presentation, and demonstration. Particularly at the secondary level, have the student take more and more responsibility for his or her own learning, as you are preparing many of these students for the work world or university, and they should learn to ask questions if they do not understand something.
- Break activities into shorter tasks rather than giving a long list of instructions.

BEHAVIORALLY CHALLENGED STUDENTS

- Appoint such a student as your special helper to pass out or count supplies.
- Especially for students with behavioral problems, offer praise freely.
- Explain rules and expectations, and consistently follow them.
- Emotionally disturbed students may find it soothing to work with clay.

VISUALLY IMPAIRED OR BLIND STUDENTS

- Add fine sand to paint to help a visually impaired student comprehend a design.
- Allow them to touch your hands as you are working.
- Call them by name and let them know you are talking to them.
- For coloring work, use a glue gun to make an outline. The student can feel the outline and apply color within it.
- Identify the location of something by using the clockface direction. For example, "the wire is at 1:00."
- Make size comparisons in relation to the student's own size. For example, "the length of your hand." When describing something, discuss texture, weight, smell, size, volume.
- Suggest the student tape a lecture if it will be quite detailed.
- Tape screenwire (plastic or metal) to a piece of cardboard. When this is placed under a crayon drawing, the visually impaired student can feel the wax that is left.
- Tell them you are moving on before you walk away.
- Use a normal speaking voice.
- Visually impaired students may find it rewarding to work with clay, even learning to throw on the wheel.
- Work with materials that have a tactile sensation.
- Place such things as water containers, crayon box, and paint containers in a ring made of a roll of masking tape taped to the table (or tape a frame made of stretcher strips in place on the table).

DEAF OR HEARING IMPAIRED STUDENTS

- Assign a student note taker if you will be lecturing or give the student copies of your lecture.
- In working with a deaf or hearing impaired student, it is similar to working with a foreign student who does not speak English well, but understands many words.
- Make sure your face is visible to the student when you talk.
- Touch the student on the arm to get his or her attention.
- Write notes or a few words if necessary, or even draw what you mean on a piece of paper, then throw it away. Remember not to draw on the student's work, but on a separate piece of paper.

List 3–13   Continued

GENERAL SUGGESTIONS

- Add warm water to powdered clay or premixed clay, if a student does not like the feel of cold clay.
- Allow students to tear rather than cut paper if necessary.
- Cutting may be easier if someone holds the paper vertically and the student cuts from bottom to top.
- For younger children, finger painting can be done on a cafeteria tray with liquid starch mixed with powdered paint, or use chocolate pudding instead.
- Glue may have to be put into a soft plastic dispenser such as a plastic hairdressing dye bottle. Glue sticks and roll-on glue are especially useful.
- If the student cannot control scissors, hold the student's hand firmly, with your thumb placed on the student's entire palm below the thumb while he or she is cutting.
- Large painting surfaces are preferable for students who have orthopedic or gross motor problems. Tempera now comes in refillable marker applicators for ease of use.
- Scissors with double grips will allow a teacher's or "buddy's" hand to guide while the student cuts. Snip-loop scissors work for students with motor difficulties.
- Some students could learn to cut with an X-acto® knife under controlled conditions.
- Tape paper on the table so the student doesn't have to hold it in place.
- Use paste jars that come with applicators.
- Wheat paste may need color and warm water added to make it more appealing to some youngsters.
- When teaching some young children to use only one finger for pasting, make a hole in a sock to allow only one finger through.

List 3–14   Identifying Artistically Gifted and Talented Students in the Arts

This list includes the theories of many art educators as to what a "gifted and talented art student" will show.

often begins drawing at a young age

demonstrates early-on mastery of advanced drawing techniques

develops a personal style in early grades of school

shows the ability and desire to draw more detail than average

shows the ability to think of many ideas

has the ability to stay with a task longer than many other students

demonstrates greater-than-average persistence

can discuss the meaning of his or her own art or that of others

considers questions of aesthetics

demonstrates originality within a given assignment

frequently has a higher-than-average IQ

has the ability to look at things from several different aspects

often recalls or imagines things in photographic detail

has the interest, motivation, and desire to do art

is able to create and analyze space in art (spatial relationships)

is multidimensional

is technically skilled

makes art that personally means something

Drawn from *Elisha Hurlbut House*, pre-1790, Winthrop Chandler

List 3–15   Careers in Art

administrator   director of an art gallery or museum; dean of art school; art director; fund-raiser; public relations

architecture   architect; drafter; city planner; interior designer; interior architect; lighting consultant; restoration planner; architectural renderer; model maker

art education   art specialist; art supervisor; art school teacher; artist-in-residence; media specialist; art therapist; museum educator; textbook author; art historian; art lecturer; researcher

computer graphics   animator; graphic designer; advertising artist; cartoonist; aviation consultant; weather graphics

designer   furniture; textiles; interiors; store windows; wallpaper; gift items; store displays; housewares; autos; bookplates; industrial designs; theatrical designer; toy designer

fashion   shoes and boots, fabrics, hats, babies' and children's clothes, coats, dresses, hosiery, handbags, accessories, jewelry; pattern maker; fashion illustrator; fashion copywriter; fashion editor/writer; fashion show coordinator; fashion merchandiser; fashion art director for an advertising firm; theatrical costumer; hair stylist; color consultant; window decorator

fine artist and craftsperson   sculptor; painter; ceramist; weaver; potter; jewelry-maker; metalsmith; glassblower and designer; engraver; etcher; woodworker; mold maker; muralist; performance artist; police sketch artist; printmaker

graphic design   outdoor advertising, greeting cards, typefaces, billboards, logos; layout artist; letterer; art editor; book, newspaper, magazine, or brochure designer; book cover designer; silk-screen artist; cartographer; computer graphics specialist; paste-up artist; letter design; sign painter; corporate art director

historian   auction house cataloguer, writer, lecturer, researcher; gallery owner or assistant; art librarian; curator; museum educator; museum director

illustrator   children's books; medical journals; fashion ads; cars; compact disc covers; greeting cards; technical and scientific designs; medical illustrator; botanical drawings; advertising; courtroom artist; animator; cartoonist; colorist; editorial illustrator; technical illustrator

industrial and business   product design; package design; furniture design; automobiles and airline equipment; factory layout; interior design; heavy equipment design; safety clothing and equipment design; stencil design; sports equipment design; decorative metalwork design; art director; design consultant; color consultant; model maker; sign painter; window trimmer; tool designer; renderer

museum   curator; art education specialist; art historian; purchasing agent for bookstore; art appraiser; director; conservator; restorer; archaeologist; display artist/designer; librarian; museum photographer; editor; writer; public relations; researcher; graphic designer; publication permissions; public relations; museum exhibit designer; archivist; audio-visual librarian; auction house cataloguer

photography   medical illustrator; photo journalist; fashion photographer; museum photographer; newspaper or magazine photographer; architectural photographer; aerial photographer; studio, industrial, food, fine art, crime scene photographer; portrait photographer; darkroom technician; illustrator; industrial photographer

theater   lighting designer; set designer; costumer; program designer; make-up artist; graphic artist; puppetmaker

video and film   film director; producer; editor; video operator; courtroom video operator; art director; cinematographer; animator; lighting consultant; set designer; special effects person; computer graphics

varied careers   colorist; lithographer; art materials manufacturer's representative

writer   public relations; art critic; author of books about art; art historian; art book copy editor; researcher for writers

List 3–16   Safety Reminders for the Artroom

Many tools and materials may be used for secondary students that are completely inappropriate for students younger than 12 years old. AP (Approved Product) and CP (Certified Product) are seals given by the Art and Craft Materials Institute and should appear on any consumables used for students under 12. Simply be aware of hazards, make students aware of unsafe practices, and frequently check yourself to see if you are following safety recommendations.

GENERAL GUIDELINE

- Review "Material Safety Data Sheets" (MSDS) that often come with art products.

CLEANLINESS

- Avoid unnecessary ceramic dust by having students wipe tables with wet sponges.
- If working with clay, try to have the floor damp-mopped each evening.
- Keep materials in cupboards, on shelves, or covered when not in use.
- Keep a printing press covered to prevent dust or injuries.
- Keep tools organized, clean, and dust free.

SAFE PRACTICES

- Carefully store (and count after each class) tools that have sharp edges.
- Consider taking a first-aid course from the Red Cross.
- Cutters are necessary to the teaching of art. Give frequent instructions in proper and safe use. Do not leave small cutting tools out; rather, get them out as needed. Select the appropriate cutting equipment for the age group that will use it.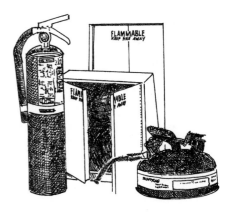
- Do not leave staple guns lying around. Students feel they must test them.
- Give older students instruction in the proper use of a paper cutter.
- Give specific instructions for use of X-acto® knives, scissors, razor blades, and electrical tools such as electric drills, grinders, saws, and hot plates.
- If there is an accident, send for the nurse or have the student *escorted* to the nurse (the student could faint on the way).
- Include safety instructions as part of a lesson for anything that might remotely present a problem.
- Instruct students to always use the proper tool for a job (not cutting wire on the paper cutter, for example).
- Keep a first-aid kit available in case the school nurse is not on duty or for an immediate emergency.
- Keep electrical equipment in good condition through a regular maintenance inspection.
- Make sure you know how to use a fire extinguisher, and check the expiration date regularly.
- Never operate machinery without proper guards in place.
- Post safety instructions to remind students of safe practices.
- Send students outside the building if there is a need to spray anything.
- Students must push sleeves above elbows, and remove all jewelry when working with electrical tools.
- Students who are working with electrical tools must have hair tied back from face.
- Use bench hooks when working with linoleum- or wood-cutting tools.
- Use grounded (three-pronged) extension cords rated for the appropriate wattage for the purpose.
- Use heat-resistant rather than asbestos gloves.
- Use safety goggles and/or masks when sculpting or operating machinery.

List 3–16   Continued

MATERIALS

- Avoid lacquer thinner, benzene, turpentine, paint stripper, varnish remover, and aerosol sprays.
- Be aware that fixatives for pastels or charcoal may be toxic. Spray outside.
- Check for a safety seal on permanent markers for classroom use, particularly for students under 12 years old.
- Do not allow students younger than 12 to use rubber cement or Duco® cement.
- Dust masks should be worn to mix dye, powdered pigment, or powdered clay and glazes.
- Flammable liquids are acetone, benzene, ethyl alcohol, gasoline, toluol, and turpentine.
- Follow school district waste-disposal policies.
- Have a place for everything and everything in its place.
- Have adequate ventilation when using wheat paste; it may have toxic preservatives. Check label for AP seal of approval
- Inventory existing supplies and check labels for toxicity, and AP and CP labels. Throw away old materials if you are uncertain of toxicity.
- Substitute odorless mineral spirits for turpentine.
- Use disposable gloves for activities that require solvents.
- Use gloss polymer medium in place of varnish. If you must use varnish, take it outside for spraying.

SURROUNDINGS

- Check for adequate general ventilation to handle fumes, odors, and dust.
- Floor drainage may be a necessity in some classes.
- For electrical equipment such as a band-saw or drill press, mark the floor with colored tape for a safety zone.
- Have a fire-resistant cabinet for keeping solvents, and store only small quantities in clearly marked cans.
- Have a self-closing can to hold solvent-soaked rags for disposal.
- Have adequate lighting.
- Have electrical outlets tested on a routine maintenance schedule.
- Have kiln ventilate to the outside (canopy hood is the safest).
- Have sufficient electrical outlets to avoid using extension cords whenever possible.
- Keep floors clean and traffic patterns free of obstacles.
- Mark differences in floor level (steps or platforms) with yellow tape.

List 3–17   Creativity and Art Education

The following attitudes, beliefs, and tactics are a combination of ingredients that promote creativity:

- a desire to work hard and at the edge of one's abilities and knowledge
- a willingness to drop unproductive ideas and temporarily set aside stubborn problems
- a willingness to persist in the face of complexity, difficulty, or uncertainty
- a willingness to take risks and expose oneself to failure or criticism
- a willingness to suspend judgment so that all possibilities can be considered
- a belief in one's own standards of evaluation and the use of those standards to judge the worth of one's ideas or work
- a desire to do something because it's interesting or personally challenging to pursue
- a desire to go beyond the obvious and break from habitual thinking
- an ability to use various tactics to reframe ideas and problems in order to generate new perspectives
- an ability to find relationships between different ideas or events
- an ability to concentrate effort and attention for long periods of time
- a belief in doing something well for the sake of personal pride and integrity

---

From *Creativity and Art Education: A New Look at an Old Relationship* by Craig Roland, NAEA Advisory, Fall 1991, by THE NATIONAL ART EDUCATION ASSOCIATION. Reprinted with permission.

List 3–18   Ways to Motivate Students

artist-in-residence
books
demonstration
dramatization
exhibitions
field trips
films
have students write poetry
have students write a story to illustrate
interactive video
invite adults from the community
photocopies from books (laminated)

photos from magazines
professional guest artists
reading
recall of personal experiences
relate artwork to their lives
slides
still-life objects
student examples
students' personal photographs
students teach each other about an artist
videos

List 3–19   Making Your Art Program Vital and Visible

- Send home a *Newsletter* (at least twice a year) or add a column in the principal's newsletter:

  . . . Be specific about where students can take outside art lessons.

  . . . Find appropriate quotes about art to include.

  . . . Give an explanation of what was learned in a specific lesson.

  . . . Include information about art students' achievements.

  . . . Include jokes about art.

  . . . Invite parents to your once- or twice-yearly school exhibitions.

  . . . Mention museum exhibitions in nearby large cities (get on museum mailing lists by phoning the museum).

  . . . Mention upcoming school exhibitions.

  . . . Talk about the achievements of graduates.

- Act as a resource person to your fellow educators.
- Help your librarian select outstanding art resources by giving suggestions on current books.
- Join your National Art Education Association. Attend a state or national art conference; it is a great way to meet fellow art educators. Consider presenting something related to your program at the convention.
- Become aware of gender issues, making sure you treat both sexes equally. Teach about non-Western traditions.
- Develop an interdisciplinary lesson with a colleague.
- Discuss careers in art with your students. When a student shows a special interest in art, give special encouragement to that student. Try to stay in contact with those students who do go on to careers in art.
- Encourage your students to tutor an art class of younger students, or to help in an after-school art program.
- Establish a Principal's Collection, selecting one artwork a year. Have it beautifully framed, complete with brass plaque with the student's name, grade, and year.
- Exhibit your students' work outside the school at public locations within the community.
- Give some assignments that are applicable to the real world.
- Personally create a work of art that is not just a "sample." Talk with your students about your own experiences in creating art.
- Gear your departmental philosophy to the reality of the modern classroom, students, and facilities.
- Invite guest speakers to your classes.
- Involve parents as helpers or resource persons.
- Involve your students in evaluating their own art.
- Join a local group of artists or an art association.
- Learn about the advances in materials and equipment appropriate to what you teach.
- Make a monumental artwork for a big wall of ceramic, found-object sculpture, or tapestry; or have students paint a mural.
- Offer teachers, administrators, and counselors leftover artwork for their classrooms or offices. Place a rotating student exhibition in the main office and halls.
- Participate in a yearly exhibition in a bank or place where the general public will see it. If you can persuade the bank to give prizes, send photos to a local paper featuring the winners and their work. Other places where people would see your students' artwork are: business lobbies, a large recreational complex, indoor shopping mall, art museum lobby, libraries, school district administrative offices, and meeting rooms.
- Participate in your annual regional Congressional High School Competition.
- Participate in Youth Art Month (March) in your state, or have a local Youth Art Month celebration.
- Provide opportunities for students to work in a group.
- Send an article about a student or your program to a magazine such as *School Arts* and *Arts and Activities* (see suggestions in List 3–31 for writing such an article).
- Start an art club or National Art Honor Society (Junior and Senior Highs). Contact the NAEA about further information.
- Have fund-raisers to earn enough to give an annual art scholarship, or to purchase some special piece of equipment for your department.
- Subscribe to art magazines, or check them out from the library.
- Take your classes on field trips.
- Time an exhibit for when parents will be in the building for another purpose (such as enrollment).

List 3–20   Effective Ways to Display Students' Work

Most of these models may be made with 30 × 40-inch or 40 × 60-inch foamcore® (which may be purchased in white, black, or colors at hobby shops or through art suppliers). These can be held together with 3-inch wide plastic tape made especially for that purpose. The display boards shown with legs are stapled to frames made of 1 × 2-inch lumber with triangular reinforced corners, which may be painted black prior to applying the boards. Corrugated cardboard may be substituted for foamcore®, but will not last as well.

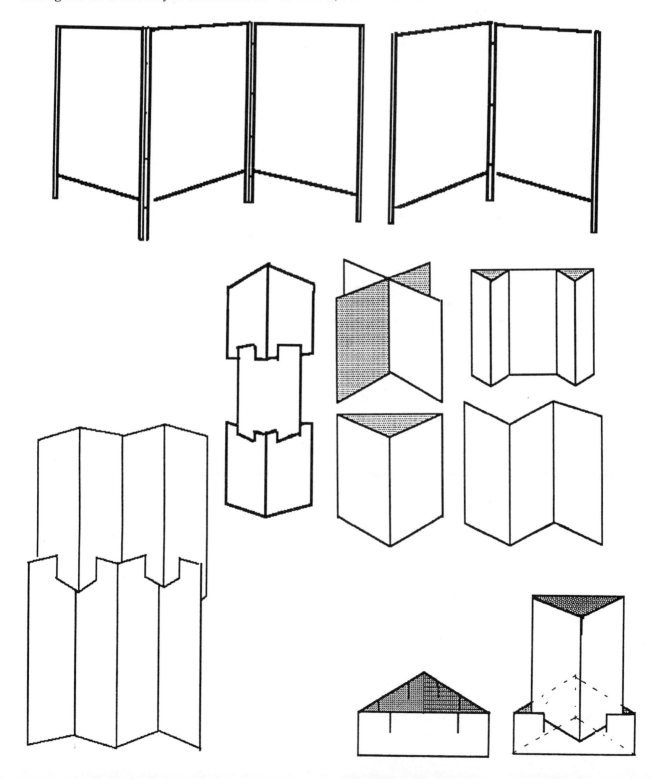

List 3–21   Places to Go on Field Trips In and Out of School

Both large cities and small towns have places for sketching, photographing, and observing the surroundings. Often sketches may be brought back to the studio for painting. If all else fails, take students to other areas of the school building to have an "in-school field trip."

OUT-OF-SCHOOL FIELD TRIPS

aquarium	botanical garden	seashore
art museum	florist's greenhouse	Victorian houses
artist's studio	graphic design studio	zoo
bicycle shop	grocery store	
book store	pond, pool, river, lake	

IN-SCHOOL FIELD TRIPS

art storage closet	home economics kitchen	parking lot
behind the scenes (stages)	industrial arts machinery area	science classroom
cafeteria	inside of your locker	science equipment area
computer lab	library	sewing classroom
custodian's closet	music classroom	
gymnasium equipment room	outdoors	

List 3–22   Suggested Subjects for Art Assignments

after a tornado	formal garden	school of fish
among corals	four seasons	ship on the ocean floor
amusement park	friends at the beach	snowy day
animal kennels	games	summer vacation
animals	impressions of video games	sunset
antique shop	in the countryside	the forest
arctic animals	in the fabric shop	the sound of music
beach with pebbles	in the kitchen	three of a kind
beans (assorted)	in the science room	toys
before a storm	kaleidoscope	tree
bridges	King Tut's tomb	tropical birds
buildings	landscape	tropical plants
butterflies	last person on Earth	two of a kind
camping	light in early morning	video game patterns
carnival	merry-go-round	view of your home from the air
carpet designs	misty morning	view of your park from the air
city buildings	monumental miniature	walking in the rain
country store after a flood	mood	waterfall
crossing the Antarctic	palaces	what my closed eyes see
factory	reflections in the water	with the dolphins
favorite place	roots	workbench details
fireworks in the sky	rubber masks	zoo experience
flower stall	saguaro cacti	

List 3–23   Suggestions for Composition

THINGS TO DO FOR BETTER COMPOSITION

These are suggestions that won't fit all assignments, but serve as reminders for students when they are working on a composition.

- Break up the background.
- Distribute the weight of objects.
- Don't let subjects just float in the air.
- Draw a line one inch inside the edges of the paper to keep the table clean and to define the edges.
- Let your drawing run outside the line sometimes, or off the page.
- Draw lines behind people instead of at their feet.
- Draw people the way you see them.
- If you use a bright color in one spot, repeat it in a small area someplace else.
- Repeat a shape sometimes in different size or color.
- Rule of thirds: divide the paper like a tic-tac-toe grid and place your main subject at an intersection.
- Try to have your subject at least as large as your hand so it can be seen at a distance.
- Use all the space.
- Use different thicknesses and qualities of line; for example, thick, thin, curvy.
- Use light and dark areas.
- Use texture or pattern to make a work more interesting.
- Use your own ideas.

THINGS TO AVOID

Students instinctively feel the need to fill corners, often using familiar symbols. Discussions of other ways to completely fill space exist. You can draw your own list of things to avoid, using the familiar red circle outline with a slash drawn through it that is used for traffic signals. Here are some suggestions to get you started.

an *uninterrupted* horizontal or vertical line

balloon trees

drawing things right to the bottom of the paper

putting heaviest things at the top of the paper

putting your subject exactly in the middle

rainbows

smiley faces

stick figures

suns in corners

List 3–24   Ways to Change an Object in a Composition

add something
change direction
change the color
combine it with other shapes
cut, flip, and paste
divide it
make a different background
make it larger
make it smaller
make it three-dimensional

miniaturize it
multiply it
"pour" it into a different format
put a hole in it
repeat it
slice it
soften it
substitute something else for a portion of it
take part of it away
turn it a different direction

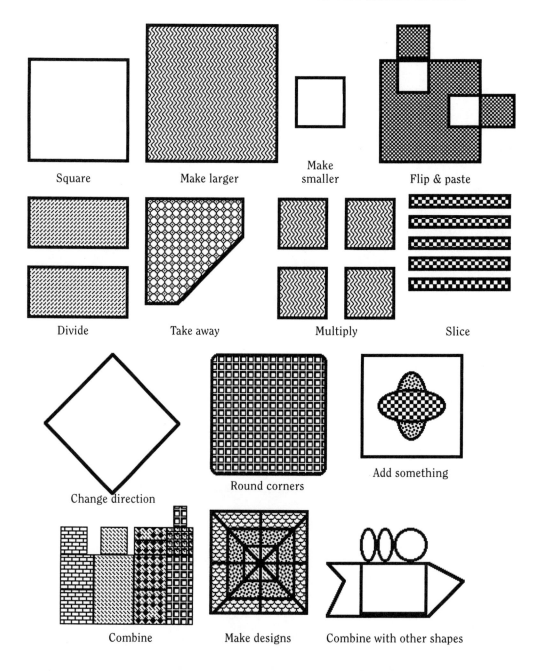

Square   Make larger   Make smaller   Flip & paste

Divide   Take away   Multiply   Slice

Change direction   Round corners   Add something

Combine   Make designs   Combine with other shapes

List 3–25   Useful Reference Books
for Art Teachers

American Art Directory, 1997–1998, 56th edition (R. R. Bowker, New Providence, New Jersey)

Animals, 14190 Copyright Free Illustrations (Dover Publications, New York, 1979)

Cerrito, Joan (editor), *Contemporary Artists* (St. James Press, Detroit, Michigan, 1996)

Chilvers, Ian, Harold Osborne, Dennis Farr, *The Oxford Dictionary of Art* (Oxford University Press, New York, 1994)

Fagin, Gary, *The Artist's Complete Guide to Facial Expressions* (Watson-Guptill, New York, 1990)

Feldman, Edmund Burke, *Varieties of Visual Experience,* 3rd edition (Harry N. Abrams, Inc., New York, 1987)

Fleming, John, Hugh Honour, Nikolaus Pevsner, *The Penguin Dictionary of Architecture* (Penguin Books, London, 1966, 1991)

Gair, Angela, *Artist's Manual, A Complete Guide to Painting and Drawing Materials and Techniques* (Chronicle Books, San Francisco, 1996)

Hartt, Frederick, *Art: A History of Painting, Sculpture and Architecture,* 3rd edition (Harry N. Abrams, Inc., New York, 1989)

Hobbs, Jack and Richard Salome, *The Visual Experience* (Davis Publications, Worcester, Massachusetts, 1991)

Hogarth, Paul, *The Artists' Manual: Equipment, Materials, Techniques* (Mayflower Books, New York, 1980)

Janson, H. W., *History of Art,* 5th edition (Harry N. Abrams, Inc., New York, 1995)

Kershaw, David, *The Beginner's Guide to Portrait Painting* (Chartwell Books, Inc., Secaucus, New Jersey, 1994)

Levy, Vic, *The Beginner's Guide to Figure Drawing* (Chartwell Books, Inc., Secaucus, New Jersey, 1993)

Lowenfeld, Viktor and W. Lambert Brittain, *Creative and Mental Growth,* 8th edition (Macmillan Publishing Co., New York, 1987)

Lucie-Smith, Edward, *Dictionary of Art Terms* (Thames and Hudson, London, 1984)

Mayer, Ralph, *A Dictionary of Art Terms and Techniques,* 2nd edition (HarperCollins, New York, 1969, 1991)

Mayer, Ralph, *The Artists' Handbook of Materials and Techniques,* 5th edition (Viking/Penguin, New York, 1991)

Page, Hilary, *Color Right from the Start, Progressive Lessons in Seeing and Understanding Color* (Watson-Guptill, New York, 1994)

Saur, K.G., *International Directory of Arts, 1997/98 edition,* 23rd edition, (Munich, 1997: auctioneers, restorers, art periodicals, numismatics, antiques, museums and public galleries, Universities and academic colleges, international)

Saur, K.G., *Museums of the World* (Reed Reference Publishing Co., Munich, 1995)

Skokstad, Marilyn, *Art History* (Harry N. Abrams, Inc., New York, 1995)

Strickland, Carol, and John Boswell, *The Annotated Mona Lisa, A Crash Course in Art History from Prehistoric to Post-Modern* (Andrews and McMeel, Universal Press Syndicate Company, Kansas City, Missouri, 1992)

The Twentieth Century Art Book (Phaidon Press, Limited, London, 1996)

Turner, Jane, editor, *The Dictionary of Art,* 34 volumes (Macmillan Publishers, Ltd., London; Groves Dictionaries, Inc., New York, 1996)

Winters, Nathan B., *Architecture Is Elementary* (Gibbs Smith, Salt Lake City, Utah, 1986)

List 3–26   Addresses Every Art Teacher Should Have

- Getty Education Institute for the Arts, 1200 Getty Center Drive, Los Angeles, California 90049-1683; *ArtsEd-Net* at http://www.artsednet.getty.edu
- National Art Education Association, 1916 Association Drive, Reston, Virginia 20191-1590
- The Art Institutes International, c/o Art Institute of Pittsburgh, 300 Sixth Avenue, Suite 80, Pittsburgh, Pennsylvania 15222
- Youth Art Month, c/o Council for Art Education, ACMI, 100 Boylston Street, Suite 1050, Boston, Massachusetts 02116

List 3–27   Materials and Equipment Needed for an Art Department

GENERAL EQUIPMENT

Art Display Area

bulletin board
ceiling hooks
locking glass display cases
movable display boards or easels

Departmental

electric hot plate
extension cords
face shields
goggles
ladders
light box
mannequins, hardwood
photo flood lights and stands (at least 2)
posters (general overview of art)
skeleton, miniature
skeleton, plastic full-sized human
slide projector
slide storage
staple guns and staples
staple removers
storage for supplies
VCR
video monitor

General Art Classroom

chairs or stools
drying rack
ladder
large scissors
large-size paper cutter
lockable storage

opaque projector
overhead projector
paper cutter
shades or blinds for darkening room
sink (not in a corner)
sketch boards, masonite
storage (adjustable) for paintings
table easels
tables
tote trays
wastebaskets or large trash containers
workbench with vise at each corner
writing board (or chalkboard)
yardstick (preferably metal)

Student Tools and Supplies

brushes
metal rulers
pen holders and pen points
protractors
rulers
scissors and holder
X-acto® knives

Consumables

charcoal
clay
conté crayons
crayons
drawing paper
erasers
glue
markers

List 3–27   Continued

Consumables (cont.)

masking tape
newsprint
paints
paper towels
pastels
pencils
polymer medium
soap
sponges
string
tagboard, all sizes
tempera
tissue paper
watercolor paper
watercolors

Ceramics Room Supplies

bats
batten boards
brushes
ceramic clay
ceramic glazes
decorating wheels
elephant ear sponges
heat-resistant gloves
kiln
kiln decorating wheels
kiln furniture
kiln shelves
needle tools
paper towels
plaster or masonite
plastic for wrapping pots
rolling pins
shelving for drying pots
sponges, clean-up
spray booth
tools: loops, scrapers, needles

wire
work tables

Painting and Drawing Room Supplies

brushes
drawing boards
easels
materials for still life
mirror tiles (1 per person)
paper storage area
stools
tables
varieties of cardboard
varieties of paint
varieties of paper

Photography Room Supplies

cameras
changing bags
darkroom
developing tanks
developing trays
dry-mount press
enlargers
grain focusers
light box
negative carriers
paper cutters
photo-flood lights
screen for slides
sinks
slide projector
Speed-easels®
squeegee
tables
timers
tongs
tripods
work tables

List 3–28   Found Materials That Can Be Reused in Art

Art teachers have always known about recycled materials, and fortunately today's students are also conscious about conserving materials. Here is a list of recyclables. Parents are often happy to send things to you.

acorns	pine cones
baby food jars	plastic drink bottles
bottle tops	plastic margarine tubs
boxes of all sizes and shapes	plastic soda bottles
broomsticks	plastic squeeze bottles
brown paper bags	ribbon
buttons	roll-on bottles (empty)
cardboard cartons	rope
cardboard tubes	rubber from inner tubes
clock parts	rug samples
cloth scraps	sand
coat hangers	sandpaper
corks	scrap leather
corn husks	scrap paper (maps, gift wrap, foil)
cotton swabs	screens (window)
doilies	sheet plastic
dowels	sheets (old)
driftwood	shells
egg cartons	straws
embroidery thread	string
feathers	Styrofoam cups and lids
flowers, dried	Styrofoam meat trays
flowers, silk	tile (kitchen or acoustic)
glass	tongue depressors
housepaint	toothbrushes
linoleum samples	toothpicks
magazines	wallpaper sample books
metal Band-Aid® boxes	whole egg shells, empty
metal scraps	wrapping paper
mirrors	yarn
newspaper	
oatmeal containers	
paper bags	
paper towels	
pencil stubs	

List 3–29 Homemade Art Recipes

TRANSFER LIQUID FOR MAGAZINE PHOTOS

Apply liquid, place photo face down on clean paper, and rub on back with the bowl of a spoon.

½ cup turpentine

2 cups water

small sliver of soap

recent newspaper or magazines

sheets of clean paper

SAWDUST MODELING MATERIAL

sawdust

3 cups wheat paste

1 cup water

GLUE

2 cups skim milk

4 teaspoons vinegar

4 teaspoons baking soda

2 tablespoons warm water

Heat milk and vinegar until lumpy; strain out the liquid and save the lumps. Add the water and smash in the baking soda with a fork, then force the glue through the sieve into a container. Let it rest for 24 hours; then stir and use.

MODELING DOUGH #1

3 cups flour

1 cup salt

1 cup water

3 tablespoons salad oil

food coloring

MODELING DOUGH #2

1 cup flour

1 cup warm water

2 teaspoons cream of tartar

1 teaspoon oil

¼ cup salt

Mix over medium heat until smooth; knead.

BAKER'S CLAY

4 cups flour

1 cup salt

1½ cups water

Roll out ¼ inch thick and cut into shapes. Bake in 200° oven until hard (from 10 minutes to 1 hour, depending on the size).

CORNSTARCH CLAY

2 cups baking soda

1 cup cornstarch

1½ cups water

Cook until thick over a low flame.

GESSO #1

One part rabbit-skin size (glue) to 15 parts water, soak overnight.

Heat size in a saucepan (do not boil).

Add plaster of Paris, stirring until it is the consistency of heavy cream.

GESSO #2

1½ oz. rabbit-skin glue (powder or granules)

1¼ pints water

powdered chalk (whiting)

Soak the glue overnight in water, then heat in a double boiler, stirring and adding whiting until it is the consistency of heavy cream.

List 3–30   Measurements and Conversion Tables

ENGLISH/AMERICAN MEASUREMENTS

Length

12 inches = 1 foot
36 inches = 3 feet
3 feet = 1 yard
144 square inches = 1 square foot
1,296 square inches = 9 square feet
9 square feet = 1 square yard

Liquid Measures

8 ounces = ½ pint (1 cup)
16 ounces = 1 pint (2 cups)
32 ounces = 2 pints (4 cups)
2 pints = 1 quart
4 quarts = 1 gallon
128 ounces = 8 pints
128 ounces = 4 quarts
128 ounces = 1 gallon
1 gallon of water weighs 8⅓ pounds
1 pint of water weighs +/− 1 pound

Angular Measures

1 octant = 45°
1 sextant = 60°
1 quadrant = 90°
1 semicircle = 180°
1 circle = 360°

METRIC SYSTEM EQUIVALENTS

Length (in meters)

1 millimeter (mm) = 0.001 meter
1 centimeter (cm) = 0.01 meter
1 decimeter = 0.1 meter
1 meter (m) = 10 decimeters
1 decameter = 10 meters
1 hectometer = 100 meters
1 kilometer = 1000 meters

Weight (in grams)

1 milligram = 0.001 gram
1 centigram = 0.01 gram
1 decigram = 0.1 gram
1 gram
1 decagram = 10 grams
1 hectogram = 100 grams
1 kilogram = 1,000 grams

WEIGHT AND MASS CONVERSION

To convert	to	multiply by
pounds	grams	453.6
pounds	kilograms	45.
grams	ounces	0.0353
grams	pounds	0.0022
ounces	grams	28.35
ounces	pounds	¹⁄₁₆
kilograms	ounces	35.27
kilograms	pounds	2.3
fluid ounces	milliliters	29.57
fluid ounces	liters	0.03
fluid ounces	gallons	¹⁄₁₂₈
liters	pints	2.11
liters	quarts	1.06
liters	U.S. gallons	0.26
gallons	Imperial gallon	0.833
gallons	liters	3.785
gallons	ounces	128.
gallons	milliliters	3,785.4

LENGTH CONVERSIONS

To convert	to	multiply by
inches	millimeters	25.4
inches	centimeters	2.54
inches	meters	0.0254
meters	inches	39.37
meters	feet	3.28
meters	yards	1.09
meters	centimeters	100.
centimeters	inches	0.3937
centimeters	feet	0.0328
millimeters	inches	0.03937
millimeters	feet	0.00328
feet	centimeters	30.48
feet	meters	0.305

TEMPERATURE CONVERSIONS

To convert Centigrade to Fahrenheit, multiply by 9, divide by 5, and add 32.

To convert Fahrenheit to Centigrade, subtract 32, multiply by 5, and divide by 9.

List 3–31   Writing Articles Related to Art for Publication

Art Teachers share theories, concepts, and projects with each other through writing for the National Art Education publications or professional magazines such as *School Arts* and *Arts and Activities*. This list is a result of a presentation by editors of these publications at the 1997 National Art Education Conference. Because editors' addresses change from time to time, check the journals themselves for current mailing addresses for manuscripts.

WRITING FOR *ARTS AND ACTIVITIES* AND *SCHOOL ARTS*

These two magazines prefer articles written in a conversational style, containing theory, practical applications, and ideas. It is suggested that you look at earlier issues to get an idea of style and layout. Both of these magazines will send a brochure with specific writing suggestions upon request.

School Arts: a two-page spread preferred, including photos. However, give enough information to make things clear.

Arts and Activities: a two-page spread (500–1000 words) preferred, including photos.

Suggestions

- Include a cover page with the title of the article, your name, school address and phone number, and home address and phone number.
- Send two copies of a double-spaced, typed manuscript, including one set of original photos, and a photocopied set.
- Number each page in the upper right-hand corner. Use 10- to 12-point font on the computer (or typewriter). Do not use a fancy format, but underline where you want italics.
- Resources and references should be included where appropriate.
- Include a self-addressed stamped envelope for return of reviewed copies.
- Check spelling on the computer (or dictionary).
- Have a colleague read your article for clarity and conciseness before submitting.
- Suggest how projects and ideas could be adapted for the classroom teacher.
- Avoid long quotations.
- If you don't take good photos, have someone do it for you.
- Submit an article to only one magazine. If it is rejected, *then* send it to another.
- You may send the article on $3\frac{1}{2}$-inch disk, including hard copy as well.
- Use gender-free terms such as "student(s)" or "craftsperson(s)" as much as possible.
- If you are using hazardous materials or equipment, include safety reminders.
- Avoid using brand names of products.
- Be aware that ethnic projects should not trivialize cultural groups.
- Adaptations to different grade levels might be included.

Photographs and Artwork

- Small flat artwork may be sent, but photos are preferred.
- Keep the photos simple—one or two students, one artwork—clear and sharply focused.
- High-contrast black-and-white photos, color prints, or slides may be sent (slides give the best color reproduction).
- Place slides and photos in plastic sleeves.
- Do not write on the backs of photographs; use self-adhesive labels instead.
- If you wish something cropped, use light grease pencil or tissue overlay.
- Include a separate caption sheet with the student(s)' name, your name, and other information.
- Number the captions to correspond with the number on the back of the photo.

List 3–31   Continued

Appropriate Themes and Projects

architecture

art curriculum and assessment (all levels)

art history and appreciation activities

back-to-school projects

ceramics

computer graphics

connecting with the environment

DBAE (Discipline-Based Art Education) suggestions

end-of-year activities

integrating art with other disciplines

involving parents and community in art projects

low-budget tips

classroom organization and management

paint and two-dimensional projects

paper (collage, cutting, sculpture)

three-dimensional projects

WRITING FOR RESEARCH-BASED MAGAZINES

These journals include historical and philosophical research-based articles, applications of theory, assessment, curriculum, Discipline-Based Art Education, etc. For future specific information, a brochure and addresses for where to send manuscripts may be requested from the NAEA.

Art Education, The Journal of the National Art Education Association: 3,000 words. Article to be of professional interest to members of the Association (not lesson plans). Send an abstract of no more than 500 words that gives the central point, theme, and agenda. Send three copies, one with title page, two others with no title page. Include references, according to the *Publication Manual of American Psychological Association,* 4th edition (1994).

Studies in Art Education, a Journal of Issues and Research: Twenty pages (approximately 5,000 words). Submit four copies. Do not send photographs or artwork.

NAEA Advisory: This is "aimed at translating research and theory into practice for the K–12 NAEA member." Three to five pages double spaced, including references, 600–700 words. Include references, according to the *Publication Manual of American Psychological Association,* 4th edition (1994).

Translations: From Theory to Practice: These articles may be based on "demographics, conceptual foundations, curriculum instruction, contexts, student learning, evaluation, or teacher education." 2,500 words, including references according to the *Publication Manual of American Psychological Association,* 4th edition (1994).

List 3–32   Photographing Artwork Indoors and Outdoors

Artwork may be photographed in different lighting situations, using either natural light or tungsten lighting. Equipment recommended is an 18% gray card (available at a photo shop), tripod, photo floodlamps (3200 K), and cable release (to prevent camera shake). If photographing small work, you may need a macro lens or close-up rings (magnifying filters). This method also works for photocopying artwork from books.

GENERAL SUGGESTIONS

- To avoid unnecessary borders, take within the border of the artwork if possible.
- Photograph the artwork on a black matte background such as paper or felt to "mask" it rather than putting tape on the slide edges (which sometimes causes them to stick in slide carousels).
- If the shape does not fit within a rectangle, use two L-shaped pieces of heavy black paper or matboard (approximately 4 inches wide) and put around the edges.
- When photographing artwork, take a reading on a gray card to ensure accurate color.

TO FILM INDOORS

- Use slide film for tungsten lighting (Ektachrome® 160 ISO is recommended).
- Outdoor slide film may be adapted for use with tungsten lighting by using a blue (80B) filter.
- Use two tungsten photo floodlights (3200 K) with reflectors.
- Place the floodlights at the height of the artwork at a 45-degree angle, between the camera and the artwork.
- Look through the viewfinder to see if there is glare on the artwork, or if one side appears brighter than another. If so, adjust the floodlights, even possibly moving them almost to the wall to eliminate glare.
- Place the gray card in front of the artwork and take a reading, filling the lens so all you see is gray card (even if you have to walk in close to take a reading and then back off to take the photo). The gray card "reads" approximately the same as the palm of your hand, adjust the camera to that reading, then take the photo. The reading may show an underexposed or overexposed photo, but trust the gray card to give true colors. You may prefer to "bracket" the exposures, taking one at the exact reading, another overexposed, and a third underexposed.

TO FILM OUTDOORS

- Use daylight slide film, 100 or 200 ISO.
- Follow general suggestions above.
- Choose a calm day.
- Work in evenly lit shade.

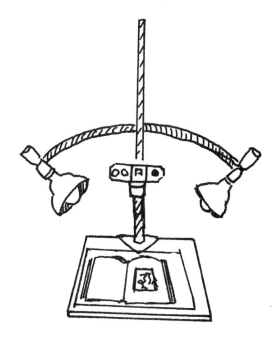

List 3–33   Preparing an Admissions Portfolio

Regional Portfolio Days are held countrywide at which various art schools and universities send representatives to critique portfolios and talk with students about college options. Quality and originality are far more important than quantity when showing a portfolio.

Portfolios for admission to an art school often are presented through slides. It is better not to send original artwork for evaluation because then nothing in it is available to show during that period. Instead, make two or more sets of slides that can be sent out at the same time. Submit 15 to 20 slides in a slide sleeve. Use an arrow to indicate the top of the slide, and write on the slide mount the student's name, the year the work was done, the medium, and the dimensions of the work. Also include a list of the slides with this same information.

SUGGESTIONS

- At least half of the portfolio should show drawing from life.
- Avoid obvious "class assignments."
- Do not include copy work.
- Include a variety of drawing, color, and design.
- Include a well-filled sketchbook if you have it.
- Include examples of original and creative problem solving.
- Include figure drawing as part of a complete composition.
- Include slides of three-dimensional work.
- Photographs and 3-D should not be more than one-third of the work.
- Show evidence of training in the use of perspective.

APPROPRIATE MEDIA

chalk
charcoal
colored pencil
computer graphics
conté
crayon
designs with colored paper
ink and ink wash
jewelry
magic marker
mixed media
paint: oil, acrylic, watercolor
pastel or oil pastel
pencil
photography
pottery
printmaking
sculpture
three-dimensional work

SUBJECT MATTER OR TREATMENT

poster designs
fabric designs
still-life
reflections
several views of the same subject
figure drawing
drawing of crumpled paper, cloth, or wrapped object
use of positive/negative space in artwork

cubistic drawing of a figure or still-life object
surrealistic treatment of space
abstraction from a real object
contour and gesture drawings
drawings of dreams or private fantasies
collage techniques combined with drawing
metamorphosis of an object through a series of drawings

List 3–34   Abbreviations for Art(s) Degrees

An *Associate* degree is offered by two-year undergraduate programs in the visual arts. A *Bachelor of Arts* normally takes four years for completion. A *Bachelor of Fine Arts* requires 60 to 90 credit hours in art, and 30 to 60 credit hours in academic requirements for a total of 120 hours. A *Master of Fine Arts* requires 30 to 40 credit hours in studio art, and 20 to 30 credit hours in "distributive requirements" for a total of 60 credit hours. A *Doctoral* degree is not presently offered in the visual arts, except in Art History. A certificate or diploma is given for attendance and completion of a specific course or number of classes at an institution.

ASSOCIATE DEGREES

AA	Associate of Arts
AAS	Associate of Applied Science
AFA	Associate of Fine Arts
AOS	Associate of Occupational Studies
AS	Associate of Science
C	Certificate of completion of study

BACHELOR DEGREES

ABpA	Bachelor of Applied Art
ABT	Bachelor of Arts in Teaching
BA, AB	Bachelor of Arts
BAE	Bachelor of Art Education
BAEd	Bachelor of Arts in Education
BApS	Bachelor of Applied Science
BArch	Bachelor of Architecture
BCA	Bachelor of Creative Arts
BEd	Bachelor of Education
BFA	Bachelor of Fine Arts
BFAEd	Bachelor of Fine Arts Education
BGD	Bachelor of Graphic Design
BID	Bachelor of Industrial Design
BIntArch	Bachelor of Interior Architecture
BLandArch	Bachelor of Landscape Architecture
BLArch	Bachelor of Landscape Architecture
BS	Bachelor of Science
BSAEd	Bachelor of Science in Art Education
BSD	Bachelor of Science in Design
BSEd	Bachelor of Science in Education
BSPA	Bachelor of Science in Professional Arts
BUP	Bachelor of Urban Planning
BVA	Bachelor of Visual Arts

FIVE-YEAR COMBINED DEGREES

BA/BFA	Bachelor of Arts/Bachelor of Fine Arts
BFA/MAT	Bachelor of Fine Arts/Master of Teaching
BS/BFA	Bachelor of Science/Bachelor of Fine Arts

MASTER DEGREES

MA	Master of Arts
MAAH	Master of Arts in Art History
MAAT	Master of Arts in Art Therapy
MAE	Master of Education
MAEd	Master of Arts in Education
MArch	Master of Architecture
MAT	Master of Art Therapy
MAT	Master of Arts in Teaching
MDes	Master of Design
MFA	Master of Fine Arts
MID	Master of Industrial Design
MLandArch	Master of Landscape Architecture
MS	Master of Science
MSArch	Master of Science in Architecture
MST	Master of Science in Teaching

OTHER

O	Other degree
EdD	Education doctorate
PhD	Doctor of philosophy
X	Diploma, Canada

List 3–35 Degrees Available in Art and Related Fields of Study

The College Blue Book, Degrees Offered by College and Subject, published by Simon & Schuster, Macmillan, and Prentice Hall International, is updated annually and available in most library reference rooms. It has a complete listing of degrees by specialty and the schools where they may be earned.

ARCHAEOLOGY

ARCHITECTURE

Architectural & Building Engineering Technology
Architectural & Civil Engineering Technology
Architectural & Environmental Design
Architectural Construction
Architectural Design
Architectural Design & Construction
Architectural Design Technology
Architectural Drafting
Architectural Engineering
Architectural Engineering Technology
Architectural Graphics
Architectural History
Architectural History & Urban Development
Architectural Science
Architectural Studies
Architectural Technology
Architecture
Architecture & Planning
Architecture & Structural Engineering
Architecture & Urban Planning

ART

Animation	Collage	Direction	Music
Archaeology	Commercial Art	Ethnic Art Studies	Music Education
Assemblage	Communication	Fresco	Papermaking
Automotive Design	Conceptual Art	Furniture Design	Photography
Basketry	Conservation	Graphic Communication	Technology
Blacksmithing	Copywriting	Media	Transportation Design
Calligraphy	Creative Writing	Mural Design	Education
Children's Programs	Design	Museology	

ART HISTORY

Art History	Art History & Librarian-ship	Art History & Religion	Art Marketing
Art History & Appreciation		Art History & Studio Art	Art Production
Art History & Archaeology	Art History & Museum Studies	Art in Business	Art Theory & Practice
Art History & Criticism		Art Management	Art Therapy

ARTS

Arts & Crafts	Arts & Sciences	Arts in Religion
Arts & Humanities	Arts Administration Management	Arts Management
Arts & Letters	Arts for Children	Arts, General
Arts & Science Program	Arts in Christian Education	

COMPUTER GRAPHICS

CRAFTS

Crafts	Crafts Management

ADVERTISING

Creative Advertising

PHOTOGRAPHY

Creative Photography	Photographic Technology	Photography & Multimedia
Photographic Illustration	Photography	Photojournalism
Photographic Science	Photography & Film	

List 3–36   American Art Schools, Colleges, and Universities

This list includes two-year schools, art institutes, liberal arts colleges, and state universities, all of which offer specialized training for the visual artist. Most offer BA, BFA, and many offer an MFA degree. *No attempt has been made to list all the schools in the United States that offer degrees in art.* This is simply a list of schools that have well-known art programs. *The College Blue Book* and *The International Directory of the Arts* are updated yearly and offer current information about art programs. Nondegree programs are available from community colleges, artists guilds, and art workshops.

ALASKA

Alaska Pacific University, 4101 University Dr., Anchorage 99508

University of Alaska at Anchorage, 2533 Providence Ave., Anchorage 99504

ALABAMA

Auburn University, 101 Biggin Hall, Auburn 36849

Stillman College, 3601 15th St., Tuscaloosa 35403

University of Alabama at Birmingham, 900 13th St., South Birmingham 35294

ARIZONA

Arizona State University, Matthews Center and Nelson Fine Arts Center, Tempe 85287

Grand Canyon College, 3300 W. Camelback Rd., Phoenix 85061

Northern Arizona University, Box 6021, Flagstaff 86011

Phoenix Community College, 1202 W. Thomas Rd., Phoenix 85013

University of Arizona, Speedway and Park Ave., Tucson 85721

CALIFORNIA

Academy of Art College, 625 Sutter, San Francisco 94108

Art Center College of Design, 1700 Lida St., Pasadena 91109

Art Institute of Southern California, 2222 Laguna Canyon Rd., Laguna Beach 92651

Association of Independent Colleges of Art & Design, 3957 22nd St., San Francisco 94114

Brooks Institute of Photography, 801 Alston Rd., Santa Barbara 93108

California College of Arts and Crafts, 5212 Broadway, Oakland 94618

California Institute of the Arts 24700 McBean Pkwy., Valencia 91355

Idyllwild Arts Academy, PO Box 38, Idyllwild 92549-0038 (degrees earned through USCLA)

Otis/Parsons School of Art and Design, 2401 Wilshire Blvd., Los Angeles 90057

San Francisco Art Institute, 800 Chestnut St., San Francisco 94133

University of California, 238 Kroeber Hall, Berkeley 94702-1800

University of California at San Diego, Visual Arts Department, La Jolla 92093-0327

University of Southern California, School of Fine Arts, Watt Hall 104, Los Angeles 90089-0292

COLORADO

Colorado Institute of Art, 200 E. Ninth Ave., Denver 80203

Rocky Mountain College of Art & Design, 6875 East Evans Ave., Denver 80224

University of Colorado at Boulder, Department of Fine Arts, Boulder 80309-0318

CONNECTICUT

Hartford Art School, University of Hartford, 200 Bloomfield Ave., West Hartford 06117

University of Bridgeport, 126 Park Ave., Bridgeport 06601

Yale University School of Art, 180 York St., New Haven 06520-8242

DISTRICT OF COLUMBIA

Corcoran School of Art, 500 17th St. NW, Washington, DC 20006-4899

The American University Art Department, 4400 Massachusetts Ave. NW, Washington, DC 20016

FLORIDA

Art Institute of Fort Lauderdale, 1799 SE 17th St., Fort Lauderdale 33316

New World School of the Arts, University of Florida, 300 Northeast Second Ave, Miami 33132-2297

Ringling School of Art and Design, 2700 N. Tamiami Trail, Sarasota 34234-5812

University of Miami, PO Box 248106, Coral Gables 33124-4410

List 3–36   Continued

GEORGIA

Art Institute of Atlanta, 3376 Peachtree Rd. NE, Atlanta 30326

Atlanta College of Art, 1280 Peachtree St. NE, Atlanta 30309-3582

Savannah College of Art & Design, PO Box 3146, Savannah 31402-3146

School of Visual Arts/Savannah, 110 East President St., Savannah 31401

HAWAII

University of Hawaii at Manoa, 2535 The Mall, Honolulu 96822

ILLINOIS

Blackhawk Mountain School of Art, 6600 34th Ave., Moline 61265 (two-year)

Columbia College, 600 S. Michigan Ave., Chicago 60605

Northern Illinois University, DeKalb 60115

School of The Art Institute of Chicago, 37 S. Wabash, Chicago 60603

Southern Illinois University at Carbondale, Carbondale 62901-4301

Southern Illinois University, Dept. of Art and Design, Edwardsville 62025

University of Illinois, Urbana-Champaign, 408 E. Peabody Dr., Champaign 61820

INDIANA

Herron School of Art, Indiana University, 1701 N. Pennsylvania St., Indianapolis 46202

IOWA

Drake University, 25th and University Ave., Des Moines 50311

Iowa State University, 158 College of Design Bldg., Ames 50011-3092

University of Iowa, School of Art and Art History, Iowa City 52242-1706

KANSAS

Kansas State University, Art Building, Manhattan 66506

University of Kansas, School of Fine Arts, 300 Art and Design Bldg., Lawrence 66045

Wichita State University, 1845 Fairmount, Wichita 67260-0067

KENTUCKY

Berea College, College Station, Berea 40404

LOUISIANA

Loyola University, 6363 St. Charles Ave., New Orleans 70118

Tulane University, 1229 Broadway, New Orleans 70118

MAINE

Maine College of Art, 97 Spring St., Portland 04101-3933

MARYLAND

Maryland College of Art & Design, 10500 Georgia Ave., Silver Spring 20902

Maryland Institute College of Art, 1300 W. Mt. Royal Ave., Baltimore 21217

University of Maryland, College Park 20742

MASSACHUSETTS

Art Institute of Boston, 700 Beacon St., Boston 02215

Boston University, School for the Arts, 855 Commonwealth Ave., Boston 02215

Massachusetts College of Art, 621 Huntington Ave., Boston 02115

Montserrat College of Art, Box 62, Beverly 01915

School of the Museum of Fine Arts, 230 The Fenway, Boston 02115

University of Massachusetts, Amherst, Box 32510, Amherst 01003-2510

MICHIGAN

Center for Creative Studies, College of Art and Design, 245 E. Kirby St., Detroit 48202-4034

Kendall College of Art and Design, 111 Division Ave. North, Grand Rapids 49503-3194

University of Michigan School of Art, 2000 Bonisteel Blvd., Ann Arbor 48109-1069

MINNESOTA

Minneapolis College of Art & Design, 2501 Stevens Ave. S., Minneapolis 55404-4347

University of Minnesota, Department of Art, 208 Art Bldg., 216 21st Ave. S., Minneapolis 55455

MISSOURI

Kansas City Art Institute, 4415 Warwick Blvd., Kansas City 64111-1874

St. Louis Community College at Florissant Valley, 3400 Pershall Rd., St. Louis 63135

Washington University, School of Art, One Dr., St. Louis 63130

Webster University, 470 E. Lockwood Blvd., St. Louis 63119-3194

List 3–36   Continued

NEW MEXICO

Institute of American Indian Arts, College of Santa Fe Campus, Santa Fe 87501

NEW YORK

Art Students' League of New York, 215 W. 57th St., New York 10019

Cooper Union School of Art, Cooper Sq., New York 10003

Cornell University, College of Art, Architecture and Planning, Ithaca 14853

Fashion Institute of Technology, 227 W. 27th St., New York 10001-5992

Long Island University (C.W. Post Campus), Brookville 11548

Parsons School of Design, 66 Fifth Ave., New York 10011

Pratt Institute, 200 Willoughby Ave., Brooklyn 11205

Munson Williams Proctor Institute School of Art, 310 Genesee St., Utica 13502

New York Academy of Art, 111 Franklin St., New York 10013

Rochester Institute of Technology, One Lomb Memorial Dr., Rochester 14623

School of Art and Design at Alfred University, PO Box 765, Alfred 14823

School of Visual Arts, 209 East 23rd St., New York 10010-3994

Sotheby's Institute (Graduate Level), 1334 York Ave., New York 10021

Syracuse University School of Art and Design, 202 Crouse College, Syracuse 13244-1010

Woodstock School of Art, Inc., PO Box 338 W., Woodstock 12498

NORTH CAROLINA

East Carolina University School of Art, E. 5th St., Greenville 27834

North Carolina State University, PO Box 7701, Raleigh 27695-7701

Saint Mary's College Art Dept., 900 Hillsborough St., Raleigh 27611

Sawtooth Center for Visual Design, 226 N. Marshall St., Winston-Salem 27101

University of North Carolina at Asheville, University Heights, Asheville 28804

University of North Carolina at Chapel Hill, 101 Hanes Art Center, Chapel Hill 27514

University of North Carolina at Greensboro, 2000 Spring Garden St., Greensboro 27412

OHIO

Art Academy of Cincinnati, 1125 St. Gregory St., Cincinnati 45202

Cleveland Institute of Art, 11141 East Blvd., Cleveland 44106

Columbus College of Art and Design, 107 N. Ninth St., Columbus 43215

Ohio University School of Art, 528 Siegfred Hall, Athens 45701-2979

OREGON

Oregon School of Arts & Crafts, 8245 SW Barnes Rd., Portland 97225

Pacific Northwest College of Art, 1219 Southwest Pk., Portland 97205

PENNSYLVANIA

Art Institute of Philadelphia, 1622 Chestnut St., Philadelphia 19103

Art Institute of Pittsburgh, 526 Penn Ave., Pittsburgh 15222

Carnegie Mellon University, Department of Art, Pittsburgh 15213-3890

Drexel University, College of Design Arts, 32nd & Chestnut Sts., Philadelphia 19104

Moore College of Art and Design, 20th and The Pkwy., Philadelphia 19103

Pennsylvania Academy of the Fine Arts, 118 N. Broad St., Philadelphia 19102

Pennsylvania School of Art and Design, 204 North Prince St., Lancaster 17603

Tyler School of Art, Temple University, Beech & Penrose Aves., Philadelphia 19126

University of the Arts, 320 South Broad St., Philadelphia 19102

University of Pennsylvania Graduate School of Fine Arts, 205 South 34th St., Philadelphia 19104-6312

RHODE ISLAND

Rhode Island College, Providence 02908

Rhode Island School of Design, Two College St., Providence 02903-2787

TENNESSEE

Memphis College of Art, 1930 Poplar Ave., Overton Pk., Memphis 38104-275

Memphis State University, Administration 215, Memphis 38152

List 3–36   Continued

TEXAS

Art Institute of Dallas, 2 N. Park East, 8080 Park Lane, Dallas 75231-9959

Art Institute of Houston, 1900 Yorktown, Houston 77056

Sam Houston State University, Huntsville 77341

San Antonio Art Institute, 6000 North New Braunfels, San Antonio 78209

Southern Methodist University, Dallas 75275

University of Houston, Houston 77204-4893

University of North Texas, PO Box 5098, Denton 76203

UTAH

Brigham Young University, B-509 Harris Fine Arts Center, Provo 84602

VERMONT

University of Vermont, Colchester Ave., Burlington 05405-0064

VIRGINIA

Virginia Commonwealth University, 325 N. Harrison St., Richmond 23284

WASHINGTON

Art Institute of Seattle, 2323 Elliott Ave., Seattle 98121-1642

Cornish College of the Arts, 710 East Roy St., Seattle 98102

WISCONSIN

Milwaukee Institute of Art and Design, 273 E. Eric St., Milwaukee 53202

OTHER

Ontario College of Art, 100 McCaul St., Toronto, Ontario, Canada, M5T 1W1

List 3–37   Schools of Arts and Crafts

Alberta College of Art & Design, 1407–1414 Ave., NW, Calgary, Alberta, Canada, T2N 4R3

American Stained Glass Institute, Ghost Ranch Conference Center, Albuquerque, New Mexico 87501

Arrowmont School of Arts and Crafts, PO Box 567, 556 Parkway, Gatlinburg, Tennessee 37738

Blackhawk College, 34th Ave., Moline, Illinois 61265

Brookfield Craft Center, Route 25, PO Box 122, Brookfield, Connecticut 06804-0122

Cranbrook Academy of Art (Graduate School for the Fine Arts), 500 Lone Pine Rd., Box 801, Bloomfield Hills, Michigan 48013

Haystack Mountain School of Crafts, PO Box 518, Deer Isle, Maine 04627

Instituto Allende, Box 85AA, San Miguel de Allende, Guanajuato, Mexico 37700

Kutztown University of Pennsylvania, Kutztown, Pennsylvania 19530

Massachusetts College of Art, 621 Huntington Ave., Boston, Massachusetts 02115

North Texas State University, PO Box 5098, Denton, Texas 76203

Nova Scotia College of Art and Design, 5163 Duke St., Halifax, Nova Scotia B3J 3J6

Oregon School of Arts & Crafts, 8245 SW Barnes Rd., Portland, Oregon 97225

Pasadena City College, Pasadena, California 91103

Penland School of Crafts, Penland Road, Penland, North Carolina 28765

Pilchuk School, 315 2nd Ave. South, Seattle, Washington 98104

Purdue University, West Lafayette, Indiana 47907

Sam Houston State University, Huntsville, Texas 77341

Sawtooth Center for Visual Design, 226 N. Marshall St., Winston-Salem, North Carolina 27101

Tamarind Institute, 108 Cornell Ave., SE, Albuquerque, New Mexico 87106

University of Illinois at Urbana, 408 E. Peabody Dr., Urbana/Champaign, Illinois 61820

University of Maryland, College Park Campus, College Park, Maryland 20742

Virginia Commonwealth University, 325 N. Harrison St., Richmond, Virginia 23284

List 3–38   Pre-College Summer Art Experiences for Students

Arrowmont School of Arts and Crafts, PO Box 567, Gatlinburg, Tennessee 37738
Art Institute of Boston, 700 Beacon St., Boston, Massachusetts 02215
Art Institute of Dallas, 8080 Park Lane, Two North Park, Dallas, Texas 75231
Art Institute of Fort Lauderdale, 1799 Southeast Seventeenth St., Fort Lauderdale, Florida 33316-3000
Art Institute of Houston, 1900 Yorktown, Houston, Texas 77056
Art Institute of Philadelphia, 1622 Chestnut St., Philadelphia, Pennsylvania 19103-5198
Art Institute of Phoenix, 2233 W. Dunlap Ave., Phoenix, Arizona 85021
Art Institute of Pittsburgh, 526 Penn Ave., Pittsburgh, Pennsylvania 15222
Art Institute of Seattle, 2323 Elliott Ave., Seattle, Washington 98121-1642
Art Institute of Southern California, 2222 Laguna Canyon Road, Laguna Beach, California 92651
Art Workshops of Vermont, Box 57S, Chittenden, Vermont 05737
Atlanta College of Art, 1280 Peachtree St. NE, Atlanta, Georgia 30309-3582
Boston University Tanglewood Institute, 855 Commonwealth Ave., Boston, Massachusetts 02215
Brookfield Craft Center, Route 25, PO Box 122, Brookfield, Connecticut 06804-0122
Chautauqua School of Art, PO Box 1098, Dept. AS, Chautauqua, New York 14722
Cleveland Institute of Art, 11141 East Blvd., Cleveland, Ohio 44106
Colorado Institute of Art, 200 E. 9th Ave., Denver, Colorado 80203
Columbus College of Art and Design, 107 North Ninth St., Columbus, Ohio 43215
Crizmac Art and Cultural Education Materials, PO Box 65928, Tucson, Arizona 85728-5928
Fallingwater, PO Box R, Mill Run, Pennsylvania 15464
Fashion Institute of Technology, 7th Ave. at 27th St., New York, New York 10001
Fine Arts Work Center, 24 Pearl St., Provincetown, Massachusetts 02657
Haystack Mountain School of Crafts, PO Box 518, Deer Isle, Maine 04627
Illinois Institute of Art at Chicago and Schaumberg, 350 North Orleans, Chicago, Illinois 60654
Interlochen Center for the Arts, PO Box 199, Interlochen, Michigan 49643-6321
Kansas City Art Institute, 4415 Warwick Blvd., Kansas City, Missouri 64111-1874
Maine College of Art, 97 Spring St., Portland, Maine 04101
Marie Walsh Sharpe Art Foundation, 711 N. Tejon, Suite B, Colorado Springs, Colorado 80933
Maryland Institute, College of Art, 1300 Mount Royal Ave., Baltimore, Maryland 21217
Massachusetts College of Art, 621 Huntington Ave., Boston, Massachusetts 02149
Milwaukee Institute of Art and Design, 273 E. Erie St., Milwaukee, Wisconsin 53202
Minneapolis College of Art and Design, 2501 Stevens Ave. South, Minneapolis, Minnesota 55404
Montserrat College of Art, 23 Essex St., Beverly, Massachusetts 01915
New York University, School of Education, 82 Washington Square East, Room 662, New York, New York 10003-6680
Penland School of Crafts, PO Box 37, Penland, North Carolina 28765
Rhode Island School of Design, Two College St., Providence, Rhode Island 02903-2787
Ringling School of Art and Design, 2700 N. Tamiami Trail, Sarasota, Florida 34234-5812
Savannah College of Art & Design, PO Box 3146, Savannah, Georgia 31402-3146
School of The Art Institute of Chicago, 37 S. Wabash, Chicago, Illinois 60603
Skidmore College, North Broadway, Saratoga Springs, New York 12866
The Bard Graduate Center for Studies in the Decorative Arts, 18 West 86th St., New York, New York 10024
Truro Center for the Arts, PO Box 756, Truro, Massachusetts 02666
University of California Extension, Santa Cruz, 740 Front St., Suite 155, Santa Cruz, California 95060
University of the Arts, 320 South Broad St., Philadelphia, Pennsylvania 19102
University of Massachusetts, Dartmouth, 285 Old Westport Rd., North Dartmouth, Massachusetts 02747
Vermont Studio Center, Box 613AN, Johnson, Vermont 05656

List 3–39 Professional Summer Development for Teachers

Art Academy of Cincinnati, 1125 St. Gregory St., Cincinnati, Ohio 45202

Art Institute of Boston, 700 Beacon St., Boston, Massachusetts 02215

Art Institute of Fort Lauderdale, 1799 Southeast Seventeenth St., Fort Lauderdale, Florida 33316

Art Institute of Houston, 1900 Yorktown, Houston, Texas 77056

Art Institute of Philadelphia, 1622 Chestnut St., Philadelphia, Pennsylvania 19103-5198

Art Institute of Phoenix, 2233 W. Dunlap Ave., Phoenix, Arizona 85021

Art Institute of Pittsburgh, 526 Penn Ave., Pittsburgh, Pennsylvania 15222

Art Institute of Seattle, 2323 Elliott Ave., Seattle, Washington 98121-1642

Art Institute of Southern California, 2222 Laguna Canyon Rd., Laguna Beach, California 92651

Bank Street College/Parson School of Design, 610 West 112th St., New York, New York 10025

Cleveland Institute of Art 11141 East Boulevard, Cleveland, Ohio 44106

Colorado Institute of Art, 200 E. 9th Ave., Denver, Colorado 80203

Columbus College of Art and Design, 107 North Ninth St., Columbus, Ohio 43215

Dauphin Island Art Center School of Photography and Creative Arts, 1406 Cadillac Ave., Dauphin Island, Alabama 36528

Fallingwater, PO Box R, Mill Run, Pennsylvania 15464

Getty Education Institute for the Arts, Los Angeles, California 90049-1683

Haystack Mountain School of Crafts, PO Box 518, Deer Isle, Maine 04627

Illinois Institute of Art at Chicago and Schaumberg, 350 North Orleans, Chicago, Illinois 60654

Lakeland Community College, 7700 Clocktower Drive, Kirtland, Ohio 44094-5198

Maine College of Art, 97 Spring St., Portland, Maine 04101

Marie Walsh Sharpe Art Foundation, 711 N. Tejon, Suite B, Colorado Springs, Colorado 80933

Marywood College, 2300 Adams Ave., Scranton, Pennsylvania 18509

Massachusetts College of Art, 621 Huntington Ave., Boston, Massachusetts 02149

Minneapolis College of Art and Design, 2501 Stevens Ave. South, Minneapolis, Minnesota 55404

Nantucket Island School of Design & Arts, Box 1848, Nantucket Island, Massachusetts 02554

National Gallery of Art, Sixth and Constitution Aves. NW, Washington, DC 20565

New York University, 25 W. 4th Street, New York, New York 10012

Philadelphia Museum of Art, Division of Education, PO Box 7646, Philadelphia, Pennsylvania 19101-7646

Phillips Academy (Andover/Pratt Visual Studies Institute for Teachers) Andover, Massachusetts 01810

Rhode Island School of Design, Two College St., Providence, Rhode Island 02903-2787

School of the Museum of Fine Arts, 230 The Fenway, Boston, Massachusetts 02115

Skidmore College, Summer Six Art Program, Saratoga Springs, New York 12866-1632

Tyler School of Art of Temple University, Beech and Penrose Aves., Elkins Park, Pennsylvania 19027

University of California Extension, Santa Cruz, 740 Front St., Suite 155, Santa Cruz, California 95060

University of Indianapolis, 1400 E. Hanna Ave., Indianapolis, Indiana 46227

List 3–40   Colleges and Universities That Offer Computer Graphics Degrees

Although Bachelor's and Master's degrees are available from many of these schools, others may offer Associate's degrees or certificates of completion. For further information, check college catalogues.

CALIFORNIA
Art Center College of Design
Chaffey Community College
Gavilan College
Ohllone College
Orange Coast College
San Francisco State University, College of Extended Learning

FLORIDA
International Fine Arts College

GEORGIA
Atlanta College of Art
Savannah College of Art and Design

ILLINOIS
Chicago Art Institute
Parkland College
Rosary College

IOWA
Teikyo Marycrest University

MARYLAND
Catonsville Community College

MASSACHUSETTS
Hampshire College

MICHIGAN
Lansing Community College

MONTANA
Miles Community College

NEBRASKA
College of Saint Mary

NEW JERSEY
Mercer County Community College

NEW MEXICO
Clovis Community College

NEW YORK
Pratt Institute
Rochester Institute of Technology
State University of New York, College of Technology at Alfred
State University of New York, Corning Community College
State University of New York, Tompkins/Cortland Community College
Syracuse University

TENNESSEE
Memphis College of Art

TEXAS
North Harris Montgomery Community College District
Tarrant County Junior College
Trinity Valley Community College

ONTARIO, CANADA
Sheridan College

List 3–41   Colleges and Universities
That Offer Art Therapy Degrees

ALABAMA
Spring Hill College

CALIFORNIA
College of Notre Dame

CONNECTICUT
Alertus Magnus College

DISTRICT OF COLUMBIA
George Washington University

FLORIDA
Florida Southern College

ILLINOIS
Adler School of Professional Psychology
Barat College
Millikin University
School of the Art Institute of Chicago
Southern Illinois University at Edwardsville
University of Illinois, Chicago

INDIANA
Marian College
University of Indianapolis

KANSAS
Emporia State University
Pittsburg State University

KENTUCKY
University of Louisville

MASSACHUSETTS
Anna Maria College
Elms College
Emmanuel College
Lesley College
Springfield College

NEW JERSEY
Burlington County College
Thomas Edison State College
Trenton State College

NEW MEXICO
College of Santa Fe

NEW YORK
College of New Rochelle
Hofstra University
Long Island University
New York University
Pratt Institute
Russell Sage College
Saint Thomas Aquinas College

OHIO
Bowling Green State University
Capital University
University of Findlay
Ursuline College

OREGON
Marylhurst College

PENNSYLVANIA
Beaver College
Indiana University of Pennsylvania
Marywood College
Mercyhurst College
Saint Vincent College
Seton Hill College

VERMONT
Norwich University

WISCONSIN
Alverno College
Edgewood College
Mount Mary College

ONTARIO, CANADA
University of Western Ontario

QUEBEC, CANADA
Concordia University

© 1998 Prentice Hall

List 3–42   Schools That Offer Master's or Bachelor's Degrees in Photography, Photojournalism, or Film

A complete listing in *The College Blue Book* (available in most libraries) includes colleges that offer certificates or Associate's degrees in photography.

ARIZONA
Arizona State University
Phoenix College
University of Arizona Center for Creative Photography

CALIFORNIA
Academy of Art College
Art Center College of Design
Brooks Institute
California College of Arts and Crafts
San Francisco Art Institute
University of Southern California

COLORADO
Colorado Mountain College, Spring Valley

CONNECTICUT
University of Connecticut
University of Hartford
Wesleyan University

DISTRICT OF COLUMBIA
George Washington University
Gallaudet University

FLORIDA
Barry University
Ringling School of Art and Design
University of Miami

GEORGIA
Atlanta College of Art
Savannah College of Art and Design

IDAHO
University of Idaho

ILLINOIS
Bradley University
Columbia College
Governors State University
School of The Art Institute of Chicago

Southern Illinois University at Carbondale
University of Illinois, Chicago
University of Illinois, Urbana-Champaign
Western Illinois University

INDIANA
Ball State University
Indiana University—Purdue University, Indianapolis
Purdue University, Lafayette

IOWA
Morningside College

KENTUCKY
Western Kentucky University

LOUISIANA
Northeast Louisiana University

MAINE
Maine College of Art

MARYLAND
Maryland Institute, College of Art
University of Maryland—Baltimore County Campus

MASSACHUSETTS
Boston University
Hampshire College
Massachusetts College of Art
Monserrat College of Art

MICHIGAN
Aquinas College
Center for Creative Studies—College of Art and Design
Cranbrook Academy of Art
Grand Valley State University
Northern Michigan University
University of Michigan

MINNESOTA
College of Associated Arts
Winona State University

List 3–42   **Continued**

MISSOURI
Kansas City Art Institute
University of Missouri, Columbia
Washington University
Webster University

NEW JERSEY
Thomas Edison State College (Trenton)

NEW MEXICO
College of Santa Fe
University of New Mexico at Albuquerque

NEW YORK
Alfred University
Bard College
Brooklyn College of the City University of New York
Cornell University
Fordham University
Ithaca College
Long Island University, C.W. Post Campus
Mercy College
Parsons School of Design
Pratt Institute
Rochester Institute of Technology
Sarah Lawrence College
School of Visual Arts
State University of New York at New Paltz
State University of New York, College at Buffalo
State University of New York, College of Ceramics at Alfred University
Syracuse University

NORTH CAROLINA
Barton College

OHIO
Antioch College
Bowling Green State University
Cleveland Institute of Art
Columbus College of Art and Design
Kent State University
Ohio University
University of Dayton

OREGON
Pacific Northwest College of Art

PENNSYLVANIA
Beaver College
Edinboro University of Pennsylvania
Marywood College
Saint Vincent College
Seton Hill College
Temple University
Tyler School of Art of Temple University
University of the Arts

RHODE ISLAND
Rhode Island School of Design

SOUTH CAROLINA
Coker College

TENNESSEE
Middle Tennessee State University

TEXAS
Abilene Christian University
East Texas State University
Sam Houston State University
Texas Southern University
Texas Woman's University
University of Houston
University of North Texas

VIRGINIA
Virginia Intermont College

WASHINGTON
Eastern Washington University
Evergreen State College

WEST VIRGINIA
Shepherd College

ONTARIO, CANADA
Ryerson Polytechnic University

QUEBEC, CANADA
Concordia University

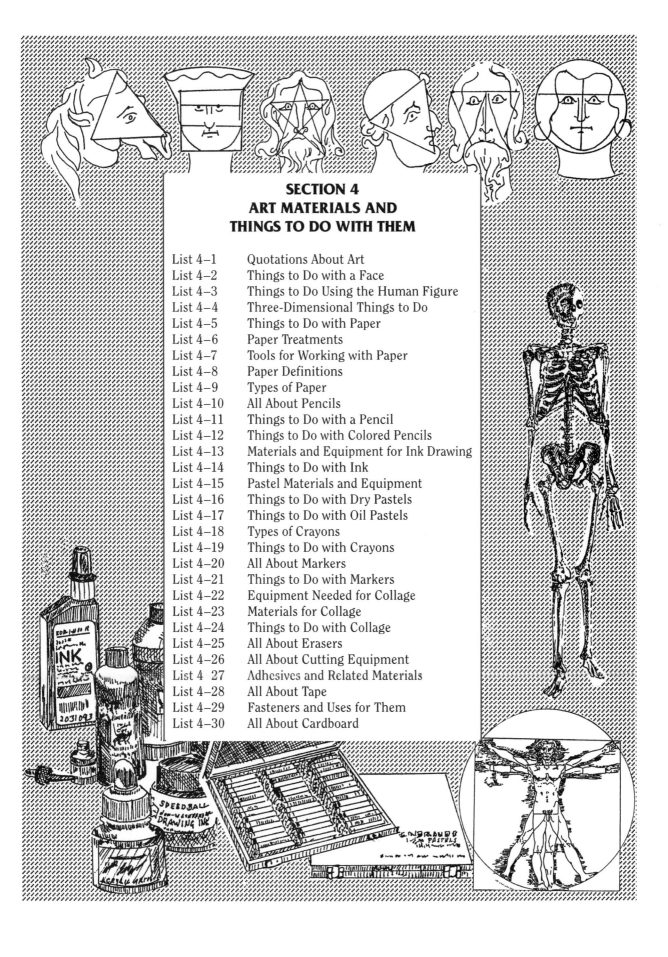

SECTION 4
ART MATERIALS AND
THINGS TO DO WITH THEM

List 4–1   Quotations About Art

"There are three forms of visual art: Painting is art to look at, sculpture is art you can walk around, and architecture is art you can walk through."

—Dan Rice

"Art is idea. It is not enough to draw, paint, and sculpt. An artist should be able to think."

—Gurdon Woods

"The final test of a painting, theirs, mine, any other, is: does the painter's emotion come across?"

—Franz Kline

"Drawing is the true test of art."

—J.A.D. Ingres

"Art flourishes where there is a sense of adventure."

—Alfred North Whitehead

"If it (painting) weren't so difficult, it wouldn't be fun."

—Edgar Degas

"All art does but consist in the removal of surplusage."

—Walter Pater

"It's like golf. The fewer strokes I can take, the better the picture."

—John Marin

"Art is like a border of flowers along the course of civilization."

—Lincoln Steffens

"Trifles make perfection and perfection is no trifle."

—Michelangelo

"Art is the most exact transcription possible of my most intimate impression of nature."

—Edward Hopper

"Art is made to disturb. Science reassures. There is only one valuable thing in art: the thing you cannot explain."

—Georges Braque

"Conception, my boy, fundamental brainwork, is what makes all the difference in art."

—Dante Gabriel Rossetti

"It is better to paint from memory, for thus your work will be your own; your sensation, your intelligence, and your soul will triumph over the eye of the amateur. . . . Do not finish your work too much."

—Paul Gauguin

"For every artist with something to say but the inability to say it well, there are two who could say something well if they had something to say."

—Paul C. Mills

List 4–2   Things to Do with a Face

- Create a mask in the style of any culture you select, using any of the following materials: screen wire, copper foil, cardboard, plaster tape, ceramic clay, or recycled aluminum drink cans.
- Carefully render a face in pencil. Then photocopy it, moving the drawing while photocopying. Then *redraw it*, reproducing the distortion.
- *Lightly* draw a grid in pencil over a face drawing, and water color each square individually. Or use colored pencil, not quite touching the lines, and varying colors slightly. Erase the pencil lines.
- Lightly draw an outline of a face. Then fill it with writing, something such as the *Constitution,* a poem, the words of a song, or as many words from the dictionary as will fit on it.
- Create a collage of a human profile "saying" a picture. For example, have an unlikely object such as a flower coming from the mouth.
- Create a face using only the first initial of your name (these could be computer-generated initials).
- Cut a portrait of a famous person into squares. Enlarge and reproduce each square separately, then reassemble to make a giant picture. Squares could be done by different people.
- Cut out and mount features cut from magazines such as eyes, mouths, and noses on several individual cards. Then draw a "Police Artist" composite photograph using various features.
- Do a self-portrait in the manner of a Post-Impressionist: Seurat, Monet, Beardsley, Gauguin, Toulouse-Lautrec, Matisse, van Gogh, Cezanne.
- Draw a face using only curvy scribble strokes; where the face is darker, use the strokes closer together.
- Draw a face with straight lines only, using a ruler and pen.
- Draw faces on old X-rays (if someone has access to some) with permanent marker or acrylic paint.

- Draw a face four or eight times the normal size. Or draw it in miniature.
- Elongate the face of a friend, in the manner of Modigliani.
- On tagboard, make a face of fabric and found materials such as buttons, foil, jewelry, etc.
- Make a face with torn pieces of construction paper.
- Notice that most magazine portraits include hands. Draw a face with the hands near or touching it.
- On a gray background, use white, black, and red conté crayons to draw a portrait of a friend.
- Paint a face on velour (velvet) paper with acrylic paint.
- Paint a portrait in the manner of Matisse's *Madame Matisse, The Green Line,* dividing the face in half, with completely different colors on the two sides.

Drawn from Villard de Honnecourt, c. 1240

- Paint a face directly on a mirror with oil or acrylic paint.
- Put a heavy piece of plastic on a mirror, and use permanent marker to draw a self-portrait on it.

List 4–2   Continued

- Photocopy a sheet of yearbook photos before they are cut apart, then color each one on the photocopy differently with colored pencil, using pattern, hats, interesting backgrounds, and accessories.
- Photocopy an 8 × 10-inch or 5 × 7-inch portrait, and cut and manipulate fadeless colored paper to make hair, lips, hat, eyelashes, or clothing before gluing onto the photocopy.
- Represent a season of the year with seasonal fruits or vegetables in place of features, hair, cheeks.
- Take two identical photos or photocopies of photos; cut one vertically and one horizontally and weave them together, gluing the ends.
- Use charcoal and a kneaded eraser to draw a portrait, making strong contrasts.
- Use only white paper to create a three-dimensional face by curling, cutting, bending, and folding.
- Paint something such as an abstract swirl or geometric design directly on someone's face with acrylic paint. The paint comes off easily by holding a damp tissue on it for a short while.
- Use water-based printing ink to quickly paint a face on glass. Then press paper on it to make a monoprint.
- Using a tagboard base, cut out a face and features, gluing everything on the base and building up layers. Varnish it with polymer medium; then use the collage as a printing plate to make a monoprint.
- With magazine cutouts, combine a face with flowers (in place of some features or hair).
- With white crayon and a ruler, make a grid. Then loosely paint a portrait with watercolor.

List 4–3   Things to Do Using the Human Figure

- After doing a charcoal drawing, go over selected areas with broad areas of ink wash.
- Use charcoal to capture movement in a series of one-minute poses.
- Cover a sheet of paper with drawings *only* of hands, or drawings *only* of feet.
- On large paper, draw three different contour drawings of the same person in three different poses with various crayon colors.
- Do a life-size paper cut-out of body parts in bright poster paper, and assemble on another color.
- Draw a larger-than-life body part (arm, torso, leg, or foot) of the human figure on 24 × 36-inch paper.
- Do a simple figure drawing on paper or plastic and transfer it to the computer screen. (If you do not have a scanner, tape the plastic in front of the screen, and draw it directly. Then change it.)
- Draw the human figure from sculpture, or from photos of sculpture.
- Encase parts of the body in plaster-impregnated gauze. Assemble into an entire human form, or draw from the various body parts that you will have lying around.
- Experiment with different drawing materials and different paper surfaces when drawing the figure.
- Fill an entire page with cartoon-like figures in a specific environment such as a circus, department store, cityscape, nightclub, or restaurant.
- From a photo, draw a life-size "action" self-portrait on foamcore®. Cut it out with a utility knife and paint with acrylic paint. ***Safety note:*** *Always keep your non-cutting hand behind the blade when cutting.*
- Go on a scavenger hunt with a camera, looking for images in manufactured materials that resemble body parts of human figures (for example, automobile-grill "faces").
- Have a model do a seated pose wrapped in a blanket. Form will emerge as you draw value differences.
- Have a model sit in front of a projector while you draw the outline on large roll paper mounted on the wall. Add a wallpaper-sample collage; draw on this with charcoal, marker, or paint.
- Have friends assume many different poses. Notice how the human figure in action seems to have many triangles (even the spaces between widespread fingers are triangles). Emphasize the triangles.
- Have the model(s) sit near food such as bread, fruit, wine (bottles only) to get the idea of a party.
- Have your model elevated (on a ladder), or you are seated on the floor, to offer a different aspect to the figure. Or you sit on a ladder and draw while looking down at a model.
- Select a magazine photo of a model or athlete. On tracing paper, make short, directional lines to indicate motion, while totally eliminating outlines and details; transfer to drawing paper, using ink.
- Select a photo with human subjects; then interpret the people in paint or pastel. Change the background.
- Make a torn-paper human form of black paper and mount it on white or gray paper. This could also be effective with two forms of different shades of gray mounted on black.
- Tear tissue paper and use polymer medium to glue it to a background on which one or more figures are drawn. Redraw the figures in ink on top of the tissue.
- Use charcoal or conté crayon to do a tonal study of the human figure, using ten value differences.
- Use found materials such as toothpicks or matchsticks to create a human form in 3-dimension.
- Use from one to three figures in a circular composition (tondo), such as a medallion design.
- Use the figure as your inspiration for a collage of found materials; 2- or 3-dimensional.
- Use the technique of foreshortening to draw a figure facing front with the enlarged feet close to the viewer.
- With marker or conté crayon, draw a rotating, standing model on one 18 × 24-inch sheet of paper. (The model should rotate every 2 minutes for five different poses.)
- With plasticine clay, create a human form to interpret a mood such as sadness, calmness, excitement, or anger.

List 4–4   Three-Dimensional Things to Do

- Build up layers of matboard, foamcore®, or balsa wood to make a wall-hung bas-relief of a group of buildings in a cityscape.
- Create a sculpture of line, such as string, wire, or thread, on an armature of dowels or plastic.
- Create a three-dimensional collage on plywood with wood scraps, nails, found metal, and wood.
- Create a tooling-foil repoussé bas-relief drawing of a Victorian house.
- Do a group environmental art project by rearranging objects found in nature (for example, arranging leaves in a circle, making a rock pattern, mud handprints, etc.); photograph it.
- Find a piece of driftwood or a rock and create an animal, making few changes.
- Make a loose interpretation of an animal in wire and wrap and fill in parts of the wire with colored tissue paper. This will hang, so it does not have to be particularly sturdy.
- Make a maquette for a monumental piece of sculpture from paper, holding it with glue and pins.
- Make a two-dimensional painting on a hard surface such as foamcore® or wood, and allow one object to project out into space from the painting.
- Make a high tower of white paper by manipulating the paper to give it strength. Hints: accordion folding, thin cylinders grouped together; square folds, flutes, or triangles grouped together.
- Origami is a Japanese method of paper-folding. Try other methods of changing the appearance of paper through folding.
- Select a favorite famous painting and interpret it three-dimensionally with cardboard, plaster tape, and paint.
- Select something from nature, such as a tree or a flower, and interpret it in wire sculpture.
- Use colored railroad board to make several geometric forms such as pyramids, cubes, and cylinders. Plan before gluing them together, and include one "foreign" object that will make it interesting or amusing.
- Use found materials to create an assemblage that explores negative space (lots of openings).
- Using plasticine clay, design your dream chair. This could be a throne, chaise lounge, etc.
- Work with a group of people to create a totem pole of any size. A base can be made from a cardboard pole used to roll carpet, large cans stacked together, or simply rolled paper.

List 4–5   Things to Do with Paper

- Create an accordion-folded book of 6 × 24-inch paper, adding a cardboard cover and string ties.
- Create fish kites from a cylinder of paper decorated and held open at the top with a tagboard strip.
- Create sculpture by making units such as cones, cubes, pyramids, and joining them with glue.
- Cut a silhouette or scene in fine black paper as the Germans do, using small scissors or a knife.
- Cut an openwork design of animals surrounded by thin lozenge shapes in construction paper. Then create a paper mola by gluing various colors underneath.
- Design a shopping bag for a specialty store, using slogan, logo, and color.
- Dip corners of folded or tied paper (block printing, white tissue, or paper towels) into dye.
- Do a paper cutting in the manner of Mexican holiday decorations by folding and cutting with a knife.
- Do paper rubbings of relief objects by using thin paper and crayon or printing ink.
- Do papier-mâché over a wire sculpture, not filling in entirely, but leaving open space.
- Dress someone in a newspaper costume, carefully using a stapler and tape to hold it together.
- Fold tissue paper, dampen in water, then draw designs with water-based felt pens, which will bleed through to the back to create repeat patterns.
- Make a bas-relief sculpture of paper by attaching a variety of shapes to a plain background.
- Make a bas-relief with corrugated paper rolled into thin tubes, then glued on a background.
- Make a fish print by coating a fish with printing ink using a brayer or brush. Then place soft paper on top and gently press.

List 4–5   Continued

- Make a full or partial mask of paper or tagboard decorated with raffia or yarn.
- Make a paper mobile (hanging) or stabile sculpture based on animal forms.
- Make a pyramid with a square bottom and triangles on each side. Score tabs, then glue.
- Make boxes in any size, adding tabs and scoring as needed for gluing together.
- Make colorful symmetrical cutouts of gummed paper and glue on a background.
- Make marbleized paper for book covers, bags, wrapping paper, or for drawing on with ink or marker.
- Make paper hats of all kinds with construction or crepe paper.
- Make stained-glass windows with colored tissue paper and black construction paper.
- Make stuffed sculpture by cutting out an animal shape from two pieces of paper at the same time; staple the edges, and stuff with newspaper.
- Paper mosaics can be made with small shapes and colors glued onto a background.
- Papier-mâché pulp can be made from soaked newspaper beaten and mixed with wheat paste.
- Papier-mâché sculpture can be created with newspaper strips on an armature.
- Scrape colored chalk on plain water and swirl with a straw. Then gently lay paper on top and carefully remove it for a marbled effect.
- Tightly roll 20 to 30 single sheets of newspapers beginning at a corner. Tie each at intervals, then assemble to create a sculpture. These can be spray painted, more string added, etc.
- Transfer pictures from comics with 1 part turpentine, 4 parts water, and a soap sliver; rub on back.
- Use a single sheet of paper to make a portrait, relying on cutting, folding, scoring, and curling techniques.
- Use a variety of papers in a collage. Then hand or machine stitch it with a variety of threads.
- Use paper straws of varying lengths to make a sculpture at least 10 inches in one direction.
- Use tissue or crepe paper to make flowers or garlands.
- Make a sculptural design of black paper mounted on white: roll, curl, cut, and assemble.

List 4–6   Paper Treatments

accordion fold	emboss	quill
batik	fingerpaint	quilt
bend	fold and dye	roll
braid	gesso	score
burn the edges	make a fan	sew
chlorine bleach	make a kite	shape
coat with oil	make flowers	snip
collage	make greeting cards	stencil
combine all kinds	make masks	tear
crumple	make mobiles	tie-dye
crumple, then iron	make mosaics	twist
curl	make pop-ups	wad
cut and expand	paint	watercolor
cut holes	papier-mâché	weave
cut it, then bend	pleat	wet and drape
dip and dye	print on	
do a crayon resist	punch holes in	

List 4–7   Tools for Working with Paper

clothespins
compass
doweling
gummed paper tape
heavy cardboard
masking tape

paper clips
pencil and eraser
protractor
ruler, metal edge
scissors, large and small
stapler

straight pins
triangle, 60°
white glue
X-acto® knife

List 4–8   Paper Definitions

acid free   pH neutral

cotton linter   sheets of pressed ground cotton; these may be torn and reground for pulp

cotton or rag paper   paper may have 100% or partial rag content mixed with paper pulp

deckle   a frame around the edges of a paper-making mold

deckle edges   the rough edges left on the paper when the deckle is removed from the screen mold

grain   fibers are aligned in one direction in machine-made paper, making it easy to tear lengthwise

laid pattern   in handmade paper, the lines left from the mold's screening

pith   the pulpy inner lining of a stalk used in paper making (such as that of the papyrus plant)

pulp   paper is created from rag or ground pulp that is floated in water, then floated onto a mold

quire   one-twentieth of a ream; 24 or 25 sheets of paper folded together

ream   480 or 500 sheets of paper of the same size and quality

sizing   a sizing solution is applied for an even surface and to prevent absorption

tooth   the texture of a paper that will hold pastels and charcoal

watermark   mark made with a metal wire on the screen of handmade paper

weight   paper has weights ranging from lightweight to heavier: 72 lb., 90 lb., 140 lb., 400 lb.

List 4–9   Types of Paper

Historically, the use of paper dates back to the Egyptians, who used the stalks of the papyrus plant to make a form of paper. Ancient scrolls date back to approximately 2200 BC. Most of these papers are available through art supply stores or art catalogues.

amate   paper made in Mexico from the inner bark of special trees

Arches®   100% cotton paper specifically for watercolor, watermarked, two deckle edges

bark paper   from the bark of fig and mulberry trees, for printing, collage, drawing, or painting

bleedproof paper   used for detailed pen-and-ink illustrations and technical pens

block printing paper   smooth printing paper, coated on one side

blotting paper   heavy, coarse paper used for blotting or fuzzy ink drawings

Printer's Marks, 1205

bogus paper   gray, coarse paper suitable for pastel, pencil, and crayon

bond   white, smooth-surfaced paper

butcher paper   white or colored roll paper, matte on one side, oiled on the other; comes in rolls

calligraphic   smooth paper for pen and ink, available in mottled parchment, white or cream

canvas paper   heavy paper that has been textured to resemble canvas

cellophane   transparent paper that comes in a variety of colors

charcoal paper   100% cotton has a laid pattern for shading with charcoal and pastels

color-aid papers   314 hues, tints, and shades available for color layouts, mock-ups, collage

construction paper   heavy, inexpensive, multi-purpose colored paper; fades quickly

contrasto paper   two-layered sheet of white over black; remove top layer with X-acto® knife

corrugated paper   brightly colored to add texture for masks, collages, signs, bulletin boards

crepe paper   slightly wrinkled stretchy paper used for a wide variety of decorating and craft uses

drawing paper   all-purpose white paper suitable for wet and dry media

embossed   paper that had a texture imprinted while it was wet

etching paper   heavy paper that must be dampened for etching

Fabriano®   light or heavy imported paper for pencil, paint, ink, or etching

fadeless paper   brilliantly colored sun-resistant paper

fadeless duet paper   paper that has a different bright color on each side and is sun-resistant

fingerpaint paper   medium-weight paper with one side very slick

graph paper   non-reproducing blue line cross-sections in grid sizes of ¼, ½, and 1 inch

graphite paper   coated with graphite on one side for use in tracing

gummed paper   gummed on the back

Ingres®   fine imported paper for charcoal, pastel, crayon, conté

kraft paper   roll paper in tan, colors, or white that has a smooth side and a rough side

manila drawing paper   buff-colored, coarse, inexpensive paper; mostly for dry media

marbleized   paper that has richly patterned color on one side; originally used in book-binding

metal foil paper   one side coated with foil; comes in a variety of colors

List 4–9   Continued

mulberry paper   translucent paper made from the inner fiber of the mulberry

neon fluorescent art paper   neon colors for drawing, charcoal, copy machine art

newsprint   rough textured wood pulp surface for pencil, pastel, or charcoal; yellows quickly

oaktag (tagboard)   many colors, smooth surface, strong, suitable for sculpture and portfolios

oatmeal paper   textured cream finish suitable for pastels, chalk, charcoal, and watercolor

onion skin   very thin unglazed tracing paper

origami paper   square of a smooth, colored, lightweight paper, normally white on one side

papyrus paper   thin strips of plant stalk from papyrus laid in horizontal and vertical layers

parchment   paper for calligraphy; originally parchment was made from sheep or goat skin

pastel paper   paper with rough or smooth surfaces that have "tooth" to hold pastel

postcard blanks   2-ply Bristol board, 4 × 6-inch

release paper   silicone-treated paper; resistant to heat; for use in laminating and dry mounting

rice paper   white, smooth, translucent paper made from the stems and branches of a plant/tree

Rives® paper   fine printmaking paper made in France

scratch paper   black coating over colors, white, silver or gold; design is scratched through the black surface to reveal the undercoat

seamless   heavy roll paper in extra-wide widths for use as photographic backdrops

silhouette paper   lightweight, tear-resistant paper with smooth, matte black finish on one side

stencil paper   heavy oiled or waxed surface that will cut easily and hold an edge

tissue   comes in many colors and surface treatments such as plain, waxed, or pearlized

tracing paper   smooth-surfaced, translucent paper

transfer paper   transfers a grease-free drawing from one surface to another

vellum   rag content, transparent, smooth and strong; originally made from calfskin

velour paper   heavy paper with one side flocked for a velvety texture

watercolor   rough textured paper used for watercolor, comes in weights from 72 to 400 (thickest)

   cold press watercolor paper   rough surface

   hot press watercolor paper   smoother surface

   rough   this surface will accept a variety of watercolor techniques

List 4–10   All About Pencils

Pencils have specific numbers that indicate hardness or softness ranging from 6B (softest), 5B, 4B, 3B, 2B, B, HB F, H, 2H, 3H, 4H, 5H, 6H, 7H, 8H, 9H (hardest).

Berol Prismacolor Art Stix®   square sticks that are the same material as Berol Prismacolor pencil®, only in stick form

carbon pencil   black charcoal that comes in five degrees of hardness: HB, B, BB, H, 2H

charcoal pencil   pencil contains willow charcoal; four degrees of hardness: HB, 2B, 4B, 6B and white

china marker   a grease pencil that will draw on china, glass, metal, plastic, photos, and film

colored pencil   thick, soft leads of light-resistant pigments; colors blend well

compass pencil   short pencil, no eraser

double color pencil   for blending; the lead is turpentine soluble; two colors per pencil

drawing pencil   wood-cased graphite pencil for professional drawing, design, and drafting

draw & iron pencil   special pencil used for drawing on paper to transfer to cloth

ebony layout pencil   thick black line, graphite lead; good for layout roughs

erasable color pencils   good for color layouts and design

flat lead sketching pencil   good for thick/thin lettering or for laying in backgrounds

graphite pencil   compressed graphite in most drawing pencils; available in powder or stick form

indelible pencil   the color will bleed through paint

layout pencil   soft pencil (6B—softest); for sketching and general layout

litho pencil   oil pencil used in printmaking to draw directly on etching stone or silk-screen

mechanical pencil   varying line widths available

multicultural pencil   these colored pencils produce a variety of skin tones

pastel pencil   the same pigment-rich pastels used in conté crayon are available in pencils

Stabilo® pencil   all-purpose wax-based pencil for any smooth surface such as glass, metal, or plastic

transfer pencil   for sign painting: design may be sketched on, then painted, and will bleed through to give a line to follow

turquoise drawing pencil   for professional design; will not reproduce in a copy machine (non-repro blue)

underglaze pencil   color pencil for sketching on ceramic bisque ware; allows for delicate shading

watercolor pencil   good for shading on dry paper, then blend with water; or work on wetted paper

woodless drawing pencil   lacquer-coated solid stick of graphite

writing pencil   standard #2 pencil for general student use

List 4–11   Things to Do with a Pencil

- A thin black ink wash applied with a brush and allowed to dry before drawing detail with a pencil is effective for a simple composition.
- Consider doing a 12-hour drawing (1 sheet of paper, worked on over several days for a total of 12 hours); values become fully developed, and enough time is allowed for complexity.
- Crush a piece of white paper, then do a perfect rendering of it.
- Distorted reflections in a window, pond, or puddle make interesting and challenging drawings.
- Do a drawing in the early morning or late afternoon, rendering shadows as realistically as possible.
- Do a mixed media drawing, incorporating pasted paper, transfers from a newspaper and photographs (see special recipes in Section 3).
- Do an atmospheric perspective drawing, with distant details faint and indistinct.
- Draw a fragment of an object, enlarging it so it is no longer recognizable as that object.
- Draw someone at his or her workplace, office, or home, giving a suggestion of the person's occupation by including tools.
- Integrate a drawing of the human figure with a still life or fantasy background.
- Interpret one of your own photos (color or black-and-white) in pencil. Develop dark areas fully.
- On a single sheet of paper, do texture rubbings in areas by placing the paper on a textured surface; develop this further by drawing on top of the textures to accentuate these areas.
- On one sheet of paper, draw two or more models or two poses by the same model in an overlapping figure or half-figure arrangement.
- Paint gesso on a piece of paper in a random manner; allow it to dry; then draw a model, buildings, or a still-life.
- Pose a model in strong lighting, and indicate value differences with charcoal pencil.
- Put in a light wash of watercolor, allow it to dry, then draw something such as a building or tree with pencil. Ink could be added for further interest.
- Render an architectural detail of a building, something such as a doorway or carved area.
- Shave sepia and sanguine conté crayons to make a small amount of conté powder; apply this dust using only your hands. Complete the composition by dipping the edge of a small folded piece of paper in the powder and "stamping" to make straight lines.
- Start with a charcoal drawing. Add any or all of the following: watercolor, turpentine, ink wash, pencil, or conté. Sometimes a media frenzy such as this gives surprisingly good results.
- Take an object and, in a series of drawings, create a metamorphosis into an entirely different type of object (example: banana/airplane, tiger/car, woman/tree).
- Use a kneaded eraser to lighten tonal areas in a pencil drawing.
- Use a paper viewfinder (hole cut in paper) as if it were a camera to isolate a scene to draw.
- Use brown or dark gray paper for a drawing with charcoal and brown and black conté.
- Use several hardnesses of pencil and charcoal pencil in the same composition for dramatic contrasts.
- Using one subject, draw it from different viewpoints (example: hand, apple, tool, appliance).

List 4–12   Things to Do with Colored Pencils

- Burnish with white pencil over areas colored with pencil. Use black pencil over dark areas, and a vinyl eraser to lift color and further enhance the light areas.
- Colored pencil is an ideal medium for a trompe l'oeil (fool the eye) composition. Make a 4 × 6-inch totally realistic drawing of one object such as a piece of fruit or a large shell.
- Do a high-key (light) drawing with mostly light colors.
- Do a low-key drawing with mostly dark pencils, using a kneaded eraser to create some highlights.
- Do a richly colored drawing of flowers. Then use an X-acto® knife to create patterns or make value differences (sgraffito technique).
- Do a small intensely colored design for a Turkish rug.
- Draw a portrait, using at least five colors to render the skin, and five colors for the hair.
- Draw a tree shape as realistically as possible, but change it with totally unrealistic colors.
- Draw on black paper with a small bar of soap; do a colored pencil (or Art Stix® drawing on top of the soap as if it were not there). Briefly put it in warm water to melt the soap; allow it to dry, then rework it if desired.
- Light a still-life from one side and reproduce the light and dark sides through the use of color only—no blacks and whites.
- Make a color wheel with colored pencil, repeatedly drawing around a small simple tagboard shape to make a circle. Color it in with analogous colors.
- Place a textured surface under drawing paper when creating a colored pencil drawing.
- To alter the appearance of a color, try one of these: use different colors in short diagonal strokes; vertical and horizontal strokes; cross-hatched; or solid color laid over solid color.
- To change texture and blend, use water with water-soluble pencils, or turpentine with wax-based pencils.
- Transform a black-and-white photograph printed on matte paper with colored pencil.
- Use a copy machine to reproduce a photo of a friend, and use colored pencil to create patterns or graffiti on the face and background.
- Use colorless blender in combination with colored pencils to change the surface or add texture.
- With pencil, *firmly* draw a design on a piece of tracing paper on *top* of drawing paper. When colored pencil is used on the drawing paper, the white lines from the tracing paper drawing will remain visible.

List 4–13   Materials and Equipment for Ink Drawing

bamboo sketching pen   bamboo section that has a carved point; used for drawing with ink

calligraphy ink   free-flowing ink with good covering power; permanent or water-soluble

China ink   permanent black ink, similar to India ink

crow quill pen   small pen with a barrel shape for drawing fine lines

dip pen   steel pen that is inserted in a pen holder and dipped into ink for writing or drawing

drawing ink   comes in a variety of colors for use with steel pens

India ink   dense black permanent ink made from carbon; free-flowing, non-clogging

ink stone   a smooth flat surfaced stone with a well/receptacle for grinding an ink stick

pearlescent ink   waterproof watercolor ink with a shimmery surface

pen cleaner   a liquid cleaner that dissolves permanent ink

stamp pad ink   for re-inking a stamp pad; extremely slow drying; can be used to transfer designs

steel brushes   flat, wide pen nibs that are suitable for lettering on posters and signs

Sumi ink   ink from vegetable oil and soot

Sumi ink stick   compressed powdered carbon and a binding agent

Suzuri grinding stone   used for grinding ink

technical pen ink   dense ink that flows freely

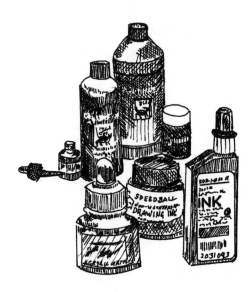

List 4–14   Things to Do with Ink

- Blot an ink wash with various items such as crumpled tissue or paper towels.
- Coat a piece of paper with ink, darker at the bottom. While it is wet, crumple plastic wrap and blot into it to make rock forms.
- Coat scratch-board with ink. Allow it to dry; then scratch a design through the ink with a sharp instrument.
- Cross hatch to make light and dark values.
- Crudely brush gesso onto heavy paper. Allow it to dry; then draw on it with ink.
- Dip a brush in ink and paint with it like watercolor.
- Dip a straw in ink, holding a finger on the end. Drip the ink on the paper and use the clean end of the straw to blow ink around to make designs. These divisions could be the start of an abstract design, or could be filled with a pattern. At the bottom of a paper, they could be plants.
- Dip a toothbrush in ink and splatter it by rubbing your thumbnail across the brush.
- Dip string into black ink, lay the string on the paper and move the string, creating curved designs. Use colored ink to create designs within the forms created.
- Do a contour figure drawing in ink. Reproduce it as nearly as possible with wire.
- Do a line drawing in ink and use marker to fill in some of the areas.
- Do a line drawing in ink. Fill in some areas with dark ink, using a brush; pour or brush on water to allow the lines to run.
- Do a watercolor painting, then draw into it with ink. Try different effects with wet or dry watercolors.
- Using India ink, draw a picture. Allow it to dry, and paint over it with watercolor.
- Draw a figure with pencil and apply colored tissue paper to it with polymer medium. Let it dry. Repeat the original drawing on top of the tissue with India ink.
- Draw on dark gray charcoal paper with white ink (or combine white ink and white pencil).
- Do a four-value drawing using the paper as one value and make the three other values with three different tools (for example, a brush, fine-line pen, bamboo pen or stick).
- Make a stamp pad by putting ink on a sponge. Make a "fingerprint" painting.
- Make an ink wash and draw into it while wet, allowing the darker ink to "bleed."
- Make an ink wash and let it dry. Draw a picture on top of it with ink.
- Make different kinds of strokes: zigzag, series of dots or dashes, "nervous" line, series of loops, short overlapping strokes, stipple marks (dots).
- Make lines of various thicknesses using different pressure and different widths of the tool.
- Try to exactly reproduce the values in a black-and-white photo by diluting India ink.
- Pour a small amount of ink into the center of a paper; fold it in half to make blots. Examine the blots to find the hidden form and make it into an organic shape such as an animal or tree.
- Put a small amount of ink in a shallow dish: put a marble in it and roll it around. Roll the marble around on paper, redip the marble, and repeat the rolling process many times.
- Use a water-based black marker to draw. Brush watercolor on it, allowing the marker to bleed. It gives a charming effect.
- Use calligraphy pens and strokes to make a bird, eagle, tiger, or other animal as Colonial calligraphers did.
- Use ink in its many varieties of color. It has a different look than watercolor.
- Use many kinds of tools for mark-making with ink: sticks, cotton swabs, long toothpicks, Asian bamboo brushes, crow-quill pens, steel lettering pens, bamboo pens, sharpened dowel stick, brushes of various sizes and weights.

List 4–15   Pastel Materials and Equipment

Pastels are ground pigment held together with a binder. They originated in Italy in the sixteenth century when painters blended pastel to resemble oil painting. Advantages are that pastels do not require water, brushes, or drying time between layers.

blender brushes   sponge heads applied to brush handles for blending colors

blending stumps   soft gray paper stumps pointed at both ends for blending pastel, charcoal, and pencil

blending Tortillon   tightly rolled, soft gray paper, pointed at one end

Caran D'Ache®   a non-flaking oil pastel with good covering property

chamois   natural chamois for blending and shading pastel, charcoal, chalk, and pencil

conté crayon   commonly used in white, black, gray, and sanguine (dark red); also available in color

Cray-pas® oil pastel sticks   work like crayons or pastels; standard, jumbo, chubbies, and square

fixative   spray for protecting pastels

Freart® art chalk   extra-large, round-tapered; ideal for use by younger students

lecturer's chalk   1 × 3-inch squares for chalkboard or paper

Nupastels®   square sticks with less dusting; cleaner handling

pastel brush   soft brush for blending and applying pastels

pastel holder   aluminum holder to keep hands clean and protect pastels from breakage

pastel paper   textured paper, often in colors, that have tooth to hold pastel

pastel pencils   soft powdery texture, with varying intensity such as full-strength, medium, and light tints

Pentel® oil pastels   permanence of oil paint; smooth

sandpaper pads   fine sandpaper mounted on a wooden handle for making points on charcoal, pastels, and crayons

Sennelier oil pastels®   iridescent and metallic pastels; smooth softness

sidewalk chalk   large, easily handled chalk for drawing outside and inside

Sketcho oil crayon®   3½ × ½-inch thick crayons with great covering power

texture plates   textured plastic plates to put underneath paper while drawing to add texture

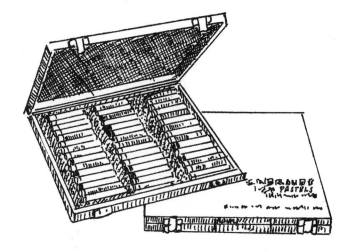

List 4–16   Things to Do with Dry Pastels

- "Dust" pastels by scraping pastel onto a paper (dusting) and pressing into place with a palette knife. Shake off excess.
- Alternate working with watercolor and soft pastels.
- Coat paper with matte polymer medium, let it dry, and draw on it. Continue to alternate layers of pastel and polymer medium.
- Combine pastel with charcoal.
- Combine primary colors with their complementary colors to make shades of gray.
- Create a color scheme of warm or cool colors, accented with a complementary color.
- Dip the pastel in water and draw with it.
- Do "scumbling" by dragging one color over another, but allowing the underneath to show through.
- Do an ink drawing and draw with pastels on top.
- Do cross hatching, building up layer after layer by having lines going in opposite directions.
- Draw with pastel, coat it with modeling paste, then draw again with pastel. Continue alternating layers.
- Cut a shape on one edge of a piece of drawing paper (something such as buildings or a mountain shape). Scribble pastel on the edge of this stencil, then place it on a piece of paper, and use a tissue to gently wipe the pastel onto the background. Move the stencil and apply a different, closely related color, once again transferring it to the background paper. This gives a soft oriental feel to the drawing.
- Make a picture using only three colors and graying with complementary colors.
- Scrape a pastel to make dust. Then apply the dust with a cotton ball or palette knife to paper. Use a stencil or kneadable eraser to create some light areas.
- Start with dark colors and put lighter colors on top.
- Use the sides of the pastel to draw, and blend with a tissue.
- Work only in line, with pastel marks all going the same direction. This is called feathering.

List 4–17   Things to Do with Oil Pastels

- Build up pastel thickly, just like oil paint.
- Combine gum solution (often used with watercolor, pastels, or ceramics) with pastel.
- Dip oil pastel into mineral spirits or turpentine and draw with it.
- Make a monotype (ink impression on paper) and enhance it with pastel.
- Make a pastel "palette" of several small areas of colored scribbles on paper, then dip a cotton swab in solvent and lift color, transferring it to pastel "painting."
- Paint a background with watercolor, let it dry, and emphasize areas with oil pastels.
- Use fluorescent markers underneath, then apply designs on top with pastels.
- Use one color on top of another, and scratch through the top color with a nail, pencil, or sharp knife, doing a form of etching.

List 4–18   Types of Crayons

anti-roll (one side flat)
chunk (large square)
extra large
gem tones
giant art crayons (hexagon shaped)
gold and silver

large
multi-colored chunk-o-crayon
multicultural skin tones
neon
Payons® watercolor crayons
plastic marker crayons

retractable crayons
square crayons
standard
unwrapped
unwrapped, large size
washable

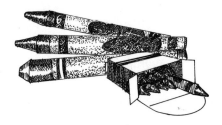

List 4–19   Things to Do with Crayons

- A combination of crayon, oil pastels, and diluted paint is an excellent choice for figure drawing.
- Color a scene firmly with crayon in "crazy" colors, then paint tempera on in "real" colors; allow to dry slightly, then gently wash tempera off.
- Color heavily on tagboard with watercolor crayons. Then place dampened white paper on top of it and use a brayer to give pressure for printing.
- Dampen watercolor crayons and rub on a sponge for stenciling through a tagboard stencil.
- Dip crayon in turpentine, then apply to paper for intense color.
- Do a crayon etching by coloring firmly with colors, then cover with black tempera or ink with liquid detergent added to make it stick. Let it dry, then scratch parallel straight vertical lines through the ink, using a ruler and a big nail.
- Do a crayon resist on white paper. Then fingerpaint over it with starch colored with tempera.
- Do a fake batik by coloring heavily, crumpling the paper, and painting with dark paint.
- Do encaustic painting on matboard, canvas board, or wood with melted crayons. Use a wax melter or muffin tins. **Safety note:** *Wax can ignite spontaneously if overheated.*
- Draw a picture with crayons, coloring heavily. Then use watercolor over it.
- Draw on sandpaper, put sandpaper on paper, then iron the back of the sandpaper to transfer drawing.
- Draw with white crayon on white construction paper. Then paint with watercolor.
- Draw firmly with crayon on tagboard. Use a sharp instrument to scratch small designs in the surface (the dye from the crayons remains underneath).
- For a sophisticated crayon drawing, work in successive layers of color, using a sharp instrument to scratch through succeeding surfaces.
- Glue several analogous colors of tissue paper on white paper with polymer medium or thinned white glue. Draw on this with black crayon or a lithographic crayon.
- Hold the end of a crayon in a candle flame to soften it, then apply it to paper. Build up colors for an encaustic effect.
- Make an outline drawing lightly in pencil, then fill in the outlines with crayon rubbings on various textures. Go over the outlines again afterwards.

List 4–19   Continued

- Melt crayons in a wax melter and paint crayon onto paper or cloth to create a batik design.
- Shave crayons into turpentine or mineral spirits, then apply with a brush to a firm background.
- Use fabric crayons to heavily color a design on paper; turn this face down on synthetic cloth, and iron the paper on the back for 30 seconds to transfer the design.
- Use the sides of crayons to make rubbings of textures in the room, netting, sink mat, leaves, bark.

List 4–20   All About Markers

art marker sets   a full range of colors; sets of 12, 36, 48, 72; fine-tip one end, broad on the other

art markers, gray   12-color sets of three different grays: cool gray, warm gray, and French gray

colorless blenders   clear marker that blends, lightens, and softens permanent markers and pencils

Blitzer Markers®   non-toxic brush markers for use with a Blitzer Air Art Gun® to give an airbrush effect

brush pens   nylon fiber brush tip, with free-flowing colors; for calligraphy and sketching

calligraphy markers   have a flat nib, come in a variety of widths

"changeable"   the color changes when a changeable marker is drawn over an original line

chart marker   non-squeaky for flip charts; will not bleed through

china marker   lead pencil/marker for writing on plastic, china, glass, film

dry-erase markers   colors erase easily from shiny surfaces with a tissue or dry cloth

fabric painters   nontoxic markers for all types of fabric; wash-fast and permanent after heat setting

fine-line markers   fine-tip markers in a variety of colors

fragrant markers   each color marker smells like a fruit of the same color (example: yellow/lemon)

highlighter   usually fluorescent colors for underlining; water-based

layout   double-nib markers used for technical work

multicultural   markers in eight skin tones

opaque marker   water-based paint markers for any surface

overwriters   similar to changeable colors; when one color is applied over another, base color remains the same, but changes the color slightly

paint   refillable marker jars contain tempera paint; blendable; any tempera may be used, large tips

paint pens   free-flowing paint in colors, metallic colors, gold, or silver; for glass, wood, paper or plastic

permanent markers   mark on most surfaces, often have odor; some are available in water-based, some odorless; *check for safety approval seal for use around children.*

poster markers   water-based paint markers for banners; 1- to 2-inch wide foam brush

projection markers   for overhead projectors; wash off plastic transparencies with damp cloth

washable   non-permanent; these colors will wash out of clothing

water-based markers   will not penetrate papers; odorless; non-toxic

white   permanent white paint marker for photos, metal, glass, plastic

List 4–21   Things to Do with Markers

- Combine Pentel® markers (add water to make them blur), gray markers, and brightly colored wide markers for an exciting cityscape.
- Draw a group of three cars in a parking lot, either from a side, back, or front view, displaying them together.
- For two different approaches to the same subject do a drawing using *only* line, or *only* shape.
- Make a drawing using only wide-line markers, allowing white space to show and simplifying detail.
- Make an interesting cityscape by using markers vertically and/or horizontally for skies and buildings.
- Make drawings of trains, or an industrial complex with machinery; to adapt this to an indoor situation, draw from equipment that has moving parts such as a clock, motor, or appliance.
- Select a famous architectural structure and re-interpret it in black marker, filling it completely with invented texture.
- With gray markers (they come in nine values), draw a cityscape or landscape, paying special attention to value.
- Work on a soft, porous paper with permanent markers, which will bleed through to the back. Leave plenty of white space around your composition. Turn the paper over and develop the design from the back. You may end up choosing either side for the finished product.

List 4–22   Equipment Needed for Collage

Naturally you won't need all of these, but this list will serve as a reminder.

Aleens® glue	hacksaw	strainer
brayer	hammer	Tacky Glue®
brushes	metal shears	toothpicks
cellulose paste	nails	tweezers
coping saw	pliers	wallpaper paste
cutting knife	polymer medium	white glue
glue gun and glue	scissors	wire cutters

List 4–23   Materials for Collage

bamboo stalks
bark and twigs
beads
bones
bottle caps
burlap
buttons
can labels
candy wrappers
catalogues
clock parts
cork
cut-outs
dried leaves
drink tabs
dryer lint
embroidery thread
feathers
felt
fine brass wire
flowers
frames

greeting cards
hair
handmade paper
jewels
keys
magazine pictures
maps
marbleized paper
matches
miniature "findings"
music pages
nails
netting
nutshells
old exams
old jeans
paper egg cartons
pebbles
picture frames
photocopies
photographs
post cards

rubbings (frottage)
sand
screen wire
seeds and pods
small wood scraps
stamps
straw
styrofoam
theater ticket stubs
toothpicks
travel brochures
wallpaper samples
watercolored paper
wine labels
wire
wire mesh
wood cut-outs from hobby shop
wood laminate
wood shavings
wrapping paper
yarn

List 4–24   Things to Do with Collage

Collage, by its very nature, is abstract and a challenge for the artist. The unexpected use of an object within a collage—and humor in interpreting a real subject—make collage exciting for the viewer.

- After creating a collage, paint some areas of it with acrylic paint, allowing texture to show.
- As a background for painting birds with acrylic paint, apply tissue paper onto matboard with polymer medium, allowing wrinkles to become part of the composition.
- Combine black-and-white photocopies with colored fadeless paper and magazine photos on a dark background.
- Create a collage within a shallow box, using both two- and three-dimensional materials.
- Create a montage of photographs or photocopies. Humor adds significantly to the composition.
- Make a collage and apply melted paraffin all over it with a brush. This gives a smooth, slightly hazy effect.
- Make a collage of textured materials and give it two coats of varnish. Then use it as a printing plate, ink it, and make collagraphs.
- Make a flat collage of grasses, leaves, etc. When finished, coat with polymer medium and apply white tissue paper on top. Give another coat of polymer medium as a varnish. Trim with fine brass wire or colored thread.
- Make a realistic human figure with pieces of crockery glued on a plywood background. Use oil pastel to fill in areas you know will show through before applying the china with a glue gun.
- Make geometric tagboard templates, then draw around them on magazine photos. Cut out the geometric magazine shapes. Experiment with positions before gluing them to a background.
- Use a straw placemat as a base for a collage, leaving the edges finished (or fray them).
- Use an open picture frame as a base, and suspend various objects *within* it, *on* it, and *hanging from* it with wire.
- Combine handmade papers with photographs and "found" paper in a collage.
- Use a map as a background for a collage/painting combination.
- Work with variations of one color from magazines, using the complementary color as accent.

List 4–25   All About Erasers

artgum eraser   pure gum rubber eraser, usually comes in 1-inch squares

cordless eraser   battery-operated eraser that accommodates varied stick erasers

electric eraser   eraser holder that accommodates varied erasers in stick style; also may be used for sharpening
lead pencils

eraser holder   holder shaped like a pencil that holds a vinyl eraser

erasing shield   steel or plastic template to protect the surface being erased

Factis Extra-Soft Eraser®   very soft eraser that picks up its own shavings and will not abrade paper

kneaded rubber eraser   soft gray eraser that kneads into any shape; for highlighting and removing chalks,
charcoal, pastels, and pencil

Magic Rub Vinyl Eraser®   nonabrasive for erasing drafting films, tracing paper, acetates, and drawing paper

Magic Rub®   sack filled with granules for erasing and cleaning large areas of film and cloth

Magic Rub®   glass-fiber eraser for removing ink and hard pencil marks

Pink Pearl® eraser   standard soft, pliable, non-smudging, self-cleaning eraser; ideal for pencil; also comes in
stick form

retractable eraser holder and refills   accommodates a vinyl eraser

soap eraser   so-called because it "washes away" pencil lines

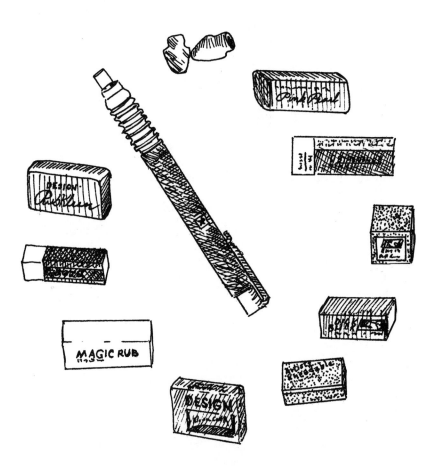

List 4–26   All About Cutting Equipment

Paper cutters are necessary to art production. *Always keep the guard in place and be conscious of safe and proper use.*

art knife   aluminum holder with sharp, angled point; multi-purpose; accepts various blade shapes

compass cutter   contains pencil leg and blade leg; cuts perfect circles from ⅞ to 26 inches

craft scissors   scissors with specially shaped blades to provide custom edges: jigsaw, ripple, wave, zipper, scallop, and pinking

craft snips   serrated blades for cutting wire, plastic, rope, leather, vinyl, dried flowers

handcrafter's knife   a plastic holder for a single-edge razor; blade changes easily

paper cutters   sizes from 12 to 36 inches square; wood or polystyrene boards; all with safety guards

plastic cutting tool   for cutting acrylic sheets up to ¼ inch thick

rotary cutter   round, rolling blade with handle; for cutting cloth, felt, leather, paper, and vinyl

rotary paper trimmer   rotary blade in a unit that clamps paper for perfect alignment

safety scissors   cutting blades are embedded in plastic for paper cutting, but will not cut fingers

scissors   all sizes and shapes for various uses, including "lefties" for left-handed people

single-edge razor blades   the standard cutting edge; *not for use by young children*

snap-off blade knives   plastic handles contain a retractable blade that allows the end to snap off for a new cutting surface; 13 new surfaces per knife, or 7 surfaces on a heavy-duty model

squizzors (snip lock or Handi-Squeeze® scissors)   handles with springs and a plastic strap to keep them from springing too far; allow disabled or young children to cut easily; round edge steel blades

stationers' shears   extra-long blades for accuracy in cutting

stencil burner   cuts through acetate, Mylar®, polyester, frisket; not for adhesive-backed items

swivel cutter   allows for easy cutting of curves and circles

teachers' shears   all-purpose; 7-inch length

utility knife   heavy-duty knife with whole-hand grip for cutting cardboard

utility snips   cuts aluminum, canvas, linoleum, fabrics, rubber, wire, tile

List 4–27   Adhesives and Related Materials

Aleene's Tacky Glue®   fast-acting craft glue; used on metal, wood, glass, ceramics, paper

art paste, Ross® or Pritt®   powdered paste dissolves in water for papier-mâché or collage

Best-Test Pik-Up®   a rubber square used for removing excess rubber cement

decorative color glue   neon and plain colors for raised, decorative painting

DryBond Adhesive Sheets®   adhesive is bonded to back of artwork for mounting

Duco cement®   all-purpose glue, used for crafts; bonds wood, metal, rubber, plastic

epoxy   two-part glue for metal, glass, plastic, ceramics

fabric   bonds fabric together; water-resistant for natural fabrics; transfers photo or print to fabric

glitter glue   glue sticks that contain glitter

glue gun   electric heater that melts glue sticks; the gun is available in regular or low-temperature or dual temperature

hot melt glue stick   sticks to *melt* with a glue gun; clear, colored sticks, or color with glitter

glue marker   may be used for temporary positioning when dry; permanent when still wet

glue stick   lipstick-style applicator for roll-on stick glue

Goop® jewelry adhesive   permanent, waterproof, washable, and clear bond

LePages® glue   animal-type hide glue; for woodworking, cloth, silk-screen

Plasti-Tak®   gum-like adhesive for displaying artwork, posters; used in place of staples or tacks

rabbit-skin glue   dried hide powder that dissolves in hot water to prepare unprimed canvas

rubber cement   pressure sensitive for temporary or permanent joining; yellows with time

rubber cement thinner   added to rubber cement when it becomes too thick

spray adhesive   for coating entire back of something for dry mounting such as a photo

Supawaxa®   waxing roller for positioning artwork; allows for lifting and repositioning

Super Glue®   permanent super-strong bond to non-porous materials

UHU®   washable glue suitable for school use

wallpaper paste   powder to be mixed with water for collage and papier-mâché

white   standard classroom glue; comes in various sizes; dries clear

white paste (library paste)   smooth white paste; applied with applicator or fingers

wood   penetrating glue for wood; available in "wood" colors; will not gum up from heat

List 4–28   All About Tape

black photographic tape   for masking clear edges on slides and reflective darkroom surfaces

colored tape   all-purpose, self-adhesive, plasticized surface

double-sided foam mounting tape   for mounting all types of artwork anywhere, heavy duty

double-sided tape   two-sided cellophane for mounting artwork on a variety of surfaces

drafting tape   for holding and positioning drawings, tracing paper, and blueprints; removable

duct tape   the inexpensive all-purpose tape that repairs almost anything

gummed paper hinging tape   good for supporting heavy paper artwork and making hinges

gummed paper tape   useful for mounting prints, sealing silk-screens, sealing packages

masking tape   flexible crepe paper tape; general purpose

removable transparent tape   repositionable; may be written on

Scotch Magic Tape®   matte surface; slightly opaque, removable and repositionable

3M White Tape®   adheres to plastic, joins foamcore® sheets; accepts marker; up to 3 inches wide

Velcro® Tape   adheres to smooth, clean surfaces

List 4–29   Fasteners and Uses for Them

brad   a small thin nail with a barrel-shaped head; can be used decoratively or to hold foamcore® pieces together

bulldog clips   steel clips with a spring for hanging prints and photographs

clothespins   plastic or wooden spring clothespins in a variety of sizes

E-Z Up Clips®   white wax-backed spring clips that will adhere to any surface to support artwork

paper clips   varied sizes, shapes, and materials such as plastic and coated or uncoated metal

pins   useful for a variety of holding purposes, or for decorative use

push pins   plastic- or metal-headed pins that are easier to use than tacks for hanging artworks, notes

T-pins   2-inch long pins with metal folded across the top to make it look like a T

Velcro® Hook and Loop Tape   adhesive-backed hook tape to stick on most surfaces or may be stapled or sewn on fabric; loop tape may be attached to whatever will be hung on it

List 4–30   All About Cardboard

Cardboard comes with a variety of surfaces and weights. It is normally ordered according to ply, which is the number of layers in cardboard ranging from single-ply (almost like paper) to 24 ply. The higher the number, the thicker the board.

archival mount board   acid-free, neutral pH mount board for protection of fine art work and photographs

Bristol board   100% cotton fiber, acid-free; for pencil, charcoal, pastel, washes, gouache

chipboard   rough, uncoated gray to black board ranging from medium to heavy weight

cold press   illustration board with a toothy surface

corrugated board   light, varicolored, corrugated on one side, mounted on white

display boards   heavy-duty posterboard with a laminated middle for extra strength and rigidity

fadeless art board   fade-resistant board for sculpture, posters, and other uses

foamcore®   polystyrene foamcore laminated on both sides with white or color

hot press   smooth surface illustration board

illustration board   heavy-quality board for commercial art, for pen and ink, and mounting

mounting board   heavy 14-ply board suitable for photographs

posterboard   varicolored 5- to 14-ply; suitable for all media

railroad board   smooth, bristol-type board, brightly colored or white; 2-, 4-, and 6-ply

scratchboard   board coated with white china clay, then coated with black ink

stipple board   white drawing board with a stippled texture

tagboard   cream-colored cardboard that is used for tags, also file folders; comes in many sizes

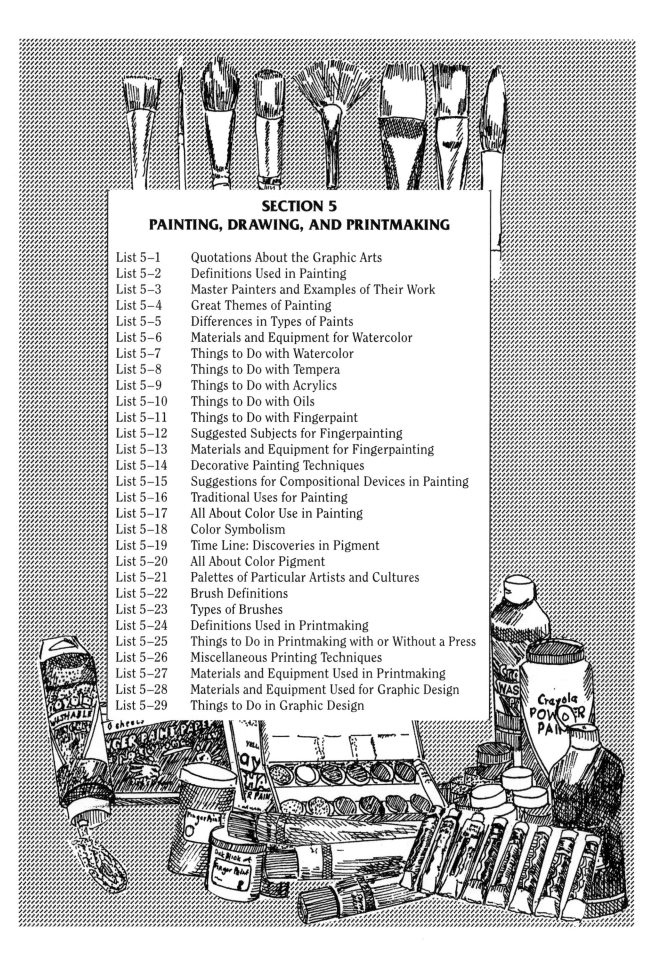

SECTION 5
PAINTING, DRAWING, AND PRINTMAKING

List 5–1   Quotations About the Graphic Arts

"A painter paints a picture with the same feeling as that with which a criminal commits a crime."

—EDGAR DEGAS

"There is nothing more difficult for a truly creative painter than to paint a rose, because before he can do so, he must first forget all the roses that were ever painted."

—HENRI MATISSE

"Mixing verdigris with an amount of Caballine aloe bestows a great measure of beauty; still more from saffron, but saffron tends to fade. The quality of this aloe, however, is proved when you dissolve it in *warm brandy;* then having already used the verdigris and finished the detail, you might glaze it over thinly with the dissolved aloe and produce a very fine color. You can also grind it into the oil itself."

—LEONARDO DA VINCI

"Any color is more distinctly seen when opposed to its contrary: thus, black on white, blue near yellow, green near red, and so on."

—LEONARDO DA VINCI

"Every time I paint, I throw myself into the water in order to learn how to swim."

—EDOUARD MANET

"Painting is concerned with the ten things you can see; these are: darkness and brightness, substance and color, form and place, remoteness and nearness, movement and rest."

—LEONARDO DA VINCI

"Flesh was the reason why oil painting was invented."

—WILLEM DE KOONING

"How beautiful an old woman's skin is! All those wrinkles!"

—THOMAS EAKINS

"I can always paint very well with my eyes, but with my hands it doesn't always work out."

—KÄTHE KOLLWITZ

"When you first commence painting everything is a muddle. Even the commonest colors seem to have the devil in them."

—THOMAS EAKINS

"My brushwork is quite unsystematic. I slam the paint on in all sorts of ways and leave each result to take care of itself."

—VINCENT VAN GOGH

"To draw, you must close your eyes and sing."

—PABLO PICASSO

"Drawing and color are by no means two different things. As you paint, you draw. . . . When color is at its richest, form is at its fullest."

—PAUL CEZANNE

"So I said to myself—I'll paint what I see—what the flower is to me but I'll paint it big and they will be surprised into taking time to look at it—I will make even busy New Yorkers take time to see what I see of flowers."

—GEORGIA O'KEEFFE

List 5–2 Definitions Used in Painting

acrylic   water-soluble polymer-based paint that may be used as "watercolor" or "oil"

acrylic retarder   added to color, it slows drying time

aerial perspective   sense of depth created through using subdued colors to indicate distance

alkyd   alkyd resin binder modified with oil; rapid drying, similar to oil in texture

alla prima   the application of paint "all at once," which in oil paint means that it is not allowed to dry between coats

beeswax   a natural white or yellow wax mixed with dry pigment to produce a matte look

Drawn from *Eight Water Glasses Under Fluorescent Light,* Janet Fish, 1974, Private collection, New York City

bleeding   the tendency for some colors to show through a second layer of paint

blending   the transition of color from one tone to another; for example, in a sky

buon (true) fresco   the application of pigment into a freshly plastered still-damp surface

canvas   heavy fabric that is "stretched" on a wooden frame as a support for painting

carbon compounds   very strong dye colors: alizarin crimson, thalo blue, thalo green

casein   a milk-based opaque paint that may be diluted with water; intermixable

chiaroscuro   the contrast of light and dark areas in a painting

complementary colors   colors opposite each other on the color wheel: red/green, blue/orange, yellow/violet

cool colors   colors that recede, such as blue, green, violet

designer colors   opaque watercolors used mostly in commercial art

drybrush painting   making the brush almost free of pigment before applying

earth colors   pigments that occur naturally in earth or ore; for example, raw sienna, burnt sienna, burnt umber, yellow ochre

egg tempera   pigment mixed with egg yolk and linseed oil for use in painting frescoes, canvases, or panels

encaustic wax   pigment already available in wax molds that become molten when heated

figure/ground relationship   the contrast between a subject and its background

fingerpaint   washable paint with a buttery smooth consistency

fluorescent tempera   brilliant colors (powder or liquid)

fresco secco   the application of pigment into a dried plastered surface

gel medium   add to acrylic paint as an extender for thick, transparent glazes; increases gloss and handling time

gesso   mixture of glue, whiting, and water used as an undercoat for a painting

glair   egg-white binding agent for pigment; used in illuminated manuscripts or for gilding with gold dust

glaze   a transparent coat of paint that allows the underneath to show through, or the building up of an area through separate applications of color

gloss medium   when added to acrylic paint gives a glossy finish; also acts as varnish or glue

gouache   opaque watercolor paint with a high concentration of pigment, or paint to which white pigment has been added; sometimes called poster paint

grisaille   a term for paintings done all in gray, black, and white

ground   the underpainted surface that gives tonal qualities to paintings; for example, white, umber, or ochre

heavy gel medium   when mixed with acrylic paint, produces textures similar to oils

high key   color applied in its purest intensity; a very light composition

highlight   white or a light tone that has reflective qualities

hue   color at its purest intensity

illuminated manuscript   an illustrated text of the middle ages, often highlighted with gold

List 5–2   Continued

impasto   the thick building up of pigment to give a visible texture

intensity   color used in its purest hue without mixing can be said to have its purest intensity

linear perspective   the use of lines and diminishing size to create a feeling of depth; based on a geometric system of measurement

low key   subdued, grayed color, or a very dark composition

magna   a trade name for a line of straight acrylic colors

Masonite®   fiberboard made from wood fiber; used as a support for painting

matte gel   when added to acrylic paint, increases working time and transparency; also acts as an adhesive

medium   a painting *method* such as oil, watercolor, or gouache; or a *liquid* such as copal varnish or linseed oil that is mixed with oil paints

minerals   cadmium red, ultramarine blue, cobalt, cadmium yellow

modeling paste   produces lightweight thick textures for use with acrylics

multicultural tempera   these colors feature the skin tones of various populations

neutral colors   complementary colors mixed to produce a dull, subdued color (variations of gray); the noncolors of black and white

oil paint   traditional painting medium; slow drying; pure pigment mixed with oil; permanent

opaque   pigment that does not allow underneath colors to show through

oriental papers   rice, mulberry, etc.; range from heavy to quite delicate

ox gall   a wetting agent that causes pigment to separate; used in marbleizing

palette   the wooden, metal, plastic, or paper surface on which paint is placed and mixed

panel   a painting surface of prepared wood, Masonite®, or canvas-covered cardboard

paper weight   a rating system for thickness of paper, ranging from 40- to 400-pound (heaviest)

pigment   earth, minerals, or chemicals finely ground and evenly suspended in a wet or dry medium

polychrome   multicolored

poster tempera   paint that has better-than-average covering power

powdered pigments   ground pure color powder, to be mixed with a medium such as oil or water

powdered tempera   pigment makes creamy opaque paint when water is added

primary colors   the colors that cannot be produced by mixing; red, blue, yellow

scumbling   adding a thin layer of color over a dry underlayer, allowing the underlayer to show through

secondary colors   the colors achieved when two primaries are mixed; orange, violet, green

sfumato   a smoky, hazy effect with soft edges

shade   any color mixed with black

stretchers   wooden strips of varying lengths fitted together to make a support frame for canvas

tempera (dry cakes)   thick squares of dry tempera that do not have the covering power of most temperas

tempera (liquid)   creamy, opaque, water-based paint in a variety of grades, colors, and sizes

Tempra-marker®   self-dispensing, refillable markers for any brand of tempera paint

tertiary colors   the colors achieved by mixing a primary with its adjacent secondary color; for example, red mixed with orange to make red-orange

tint   any color mixed with white

transparent colors   those that allow a strong underneath color to show through

warm colors   colors that advance such as red, red-orange, orange, yellow

wash   a thin application of paint

watercolor   pigments in a gum solution, to be applied with a wet brush; comes in tubes or cakes

watercolor paper   hot press (smooth), cold press (textured), rough (unfinished surface)

wet-in-wet   the action of spreading paint when new pigment is added to a wet paper

whiting   powdered calcium carbonate used in gesso, or added to rabbit-skin glue for gesso

List 5–3   Master Painters and Examples of Their Work

ALBERS, JOSEF, 1888–1976, AMERICA, b. GERMANY

Study for Homage to the Square, 1963, Tate Gallery, London

AUDUBON, JOHN JAMES, 1785–1851, AMERICA, b. HAITI

The Birds of America, 1826, New York Historical Society, New York City

Brown Thrasher, 1829, New York Historical Society, New York City

Great Blue Heron, 1821, New York Historical Society, New York City

BEARDEN, ROMARE, 1914–1988, AMERICA

The Falling Star, 1980, Estate of Romare Bearden, ACA Galleries, New York City

The Piano Lesson, 1983, Estate of Romare Bearden, ACA Galleries, New York City

House in Cotton Field, 1968, Estate of Romare Bearden, ACA Galleries, New York City

BENTON, THOMAS HART, 1899–1975, AMERICA

Independence and the Opening of the West, 1959–1962, Mural, Harry S. Truman Library, Independence, Missouri

Arts of the West, 1932, New Britain Museum of American Art, New Britain, Connecticut

The American Historical Epic, 1924–1927, Nelson-Atkins Museum of Art, Kansas City, Missouri

Cotton Pickers (Georgia), 1928–1929, Metropolitan Museum of Art, New York City

Hollywood, 1937, Nelson-Atkins Museum of Art, Kansas City, Missouri

BIERSTADT, ALBERT, 1830–1902, AMERICA

The Rocky Mountains, Lander's Peak, 1863, Metropolitan Museum of Art, New York City

The Buffalo Trail, the Impending Storm, 1869, Corcoran Gallery, Washington, DC

Thunderstorm in the Rockies, 1859, Museum of Fine Arts, Boston, Massachusetts

Storm in the Rocky Mountains, 1866, Brooklyn Museum, New York

BINGHAM, GEORGE CALEB, 1811–1879, AMERICA

Raftsmen Playing Cards, 1847, St. Louis Art Museum, Missouri

The Jolly Flatboatmen in Port, 1857, St. Louis Art Museum, Missouri

The County Election, 1851–1852, St. Louis Art Museum, Missouri

Fur Traders Descending the Missouri, 1845, Metropolitan Museum of Art, New York City

BOTTICELLI, SANDRO, 1444–1510, ITALY

Madonna of the Magnificat, c. 1483, Uffizi Gallery, Florence

Birth of Venus, c. 1480, Uffizi Gallery, Florence

Primavera, c. 1478, Uffizi Gallery, Florence

Mystic Nativity, 1500, National Gallery, London

BRUEGHEL, PIETER, 1568–1625, FLEMISH

Landscape with the Fall of Icarus, 1555, Musées Royaux des Beaux-Arts de Belgique, Brussels

Netherlandish Proverbs (The Blue Cloak), 1559, Kaiser Friedrich Museum, Berlin

Dulle Griet (Mad Meg), 1562, Musée Meyer Van den Bergh, Antwerp, Belgium

Peasant Wedding, 1567, Kunsthistorisches Museum, Vienna

Hunters in the Snow, 1565, Kunsthistorisches Museum, Vienna

CARAVAGGIO, MICHELANGELO MERISI DA, 1571–1610, ITALY

Calling of Saint Matthew, c. 1599–1600, S. Luigi dei Francesi, Rome

Crucifixion of St. Peter and Conversion of St. Paul, 1600–1601, Sta. Maria del Popolo, Rome

Entombment, 1602–1604, Vatican, Rome

The Death of the Virgin, 1605–1606, Louvre, Paris

CASSATT, MARY, 1845–1926, AMERICA

The Bath, 1891, Mary Cassatt, Art Institute of Chicago, Illinois

At the Opera, 1879, Museum of Fine Arts, Boston, Massachusetts

Mother and Child, 1900, Brooklyn Museum, New York

The Caress, 1902, National Museum of American Art, Washington, DC

Maternal Kiss, 1897, Philadelphia Museum of Art, Pennsylvania

CATLIN, GEORGE, 1796–1872, AMERICA

Buffalo Bull's Back Fat, Head Chief, Blood Tribe, 1832, American Museum, Washington, DC

Tal-lee, a Warrior of Distinction, 1834, American Museum, Washington, DC.

CEZANNE, PAUL, 1839–1906, FRANCE

Card Players, c. 1893, Courtauld Institute Galleries, London

Self-Portrait, 1877, Bayerische Staatsgemalde Collection, Munich

Mont Ste. Victoire, 1885–1887, Courtauld Institute Galleries, London

Mont Ste. Victoire, 1885–1887, Stedelijk Museum, Amsterdam

CLOSE, CHUCK, 1940, AMERICA

Fanny, Fingerpainting, 1985, National Gallery of Art, Washington, DC

Keith, 1970, St. Louis Art Museum, Missouri

Self-Portrait, 1968, Walker Art Center, Minneapolis, Minnesota

Stanley (large version), 1980–1981, Solomon R. Guggenheim Museum, New York City

List 5–3   Continued

COLE, THOMAS, 1801–1848, AMERICA

View from Mount Holyoke, Massachusetts, after a Thunderstorm—The Oxbow, 1836, Metropolitan Museum of Art, New York City

The Voyage of Life, 1840, Williams-Proctor Institute, Utica, New York

The Course of Empire, 1836, New York Historical Society, New York City

COPLEY, JOHN SINGLETON, 1738–1815, AMERICA

Paul Revere, 1768–1770, Museum of Fine Arts, Boston, Massachusetts

Brook Watson and the Shark, 1782, Detroit Institute of Arts, Michigan

DAVID, JACQUES LOUIS, 1748–1825, FRANCE

Coronation of Napoleon and Josephine, 1805–1807, Louvre, Paris

Oath of the Horatii, 1784–1785, Louvre, Paris

The Death of Socrates, 1787, Metropolitan Museum of Art, New York City

Death of Marat, 1793, Modern Art Museum of Belgium, Brussels

Mme Recamier, 1800, Louvre, Paris

DALI, SALVADOR, 1904–1989, SPAIN

The Persistence of Memory, 1931, Museum of Modern Art, New York City

Crucifixion of St. John of the Cross, 1951, Glasgow Art Gallery, Scotland

Illumined Pleasures, 1929, Museum of Modern Art, New York City

DAVIS, STUART, 1894–1964, AMERICA

Colonial Cubism, 1954, Walker Art Center, Minneapolis, Minnesota

Egg Beater, Number 2, 1927, Whitney Museum of American Art, New York City

Blips and Ifs, 1963–1964, Amon Carter Museum, Fort Worth, Texas

The Paris Bit, 1959, Whitney Museum of American Art, New York City

Visa, 1951, Museum of Modern Art, New York City

DEGAS, EDGAR, 1834–1917, FRANCE

Singer with Glove, 1878, Fogg Art Museum, Harvard University, Boston, Massachusetts

Little Fourteen-Year-Old Dancer, 1881, St. Louis Art Museum, Missouri

Portrait of Mlle Hortense Valpincon, c. 1871, Minneapolis Institute of Arts, Minnesota

Ballet Dancers in the Wings, 1900, St. Louis Art Museum, Missouri

DE KOONING, WILLEM, 1904–1997, AMERICA, b. NETHERLANDS

Woman and Bicycle, 1952–1953, Whitney Museum of American Art, New York City

Queen of Hearts, 1943–1946, Hirshhorn Museum and Sculpture Garden, Washington, DC

DELACROIX, EUGENE, 1798–1863, FRANCE

Greece on the Ruins of Missolonghi, 1826, Musée des Beaux-Arts, Bordeaux

Tiger Hunt, 1854, Louvre, Paris

The Barque of Dante, 1822, Louvre, Paris

The Massacre at Chios, c. 1824, Louvre, Paris

Jacob and the Angel, 1853–1861, Luxembourg Palace, Paris

DEMUTH, CHARLES, 1883–1935, AMERICA

Acrobats, 1919, Museum of Modern Art, New York City

I Saw the Figure 5 in Gold, 1928, Metropolitan Museum of Art, New York City

DOVE, ARTHUR, 1880–1946, AMERICA

Sand Barge, 1930, Phillips Collection, Washington, DC

The Red One, 1944, William H. Lane Foundation, Leominster, Massachusetts

DUCHAMP, MARCEL, 1887–1968, AMERICA, b. FRANCE

Nude Descending a Staircase, No. 2, 1912, Philadelphia Museum of Art, Pennsylvania

Chocolate Grinder, No. 1, 1913, Philadelphia Museum of Art, Pennsylvania

The Bride Stripped Bare by Her Bachelors, Even (The Large Glass), 1915–1923, Philadelphia Museum of Art, Pennsylvania

Fountain, 1917, Louise and Walter Arensberg Collection, Philadelphia Museum of Art, Pennsylvania

DURER, ALBRECHT, 1471–1528, GERMANY

Knight, Death, and the Devil, 1513, Museum of Fine Arts, Boston, Massachusetts

Self Portrait, 1500, Alte Pinakothek, Munich

Self Portrait, 1498, Prado, Madrid

Four Horsemen of the Apocalypse, c. 1497–1498, British Museum, London

Melencolia I, 1514, Metropolitan Museum of Art, New York City

DYCK, ANTHONY VAN, 1599–1641, BELGIUM

Portrait of King Charles I, 1635, Louvre, Paris

Madonna of the Rosary, 1624–1627, Oratorio della Compagnia del Rosario di S. Domenico, Palermo, Italy

List 5–3   Continued

EAKINS, THOMAS, 1844–1916, AMERICA

The Gross Clinic, 1875, Thomas Eakins, Jefferson Medical College, Philadelphia, Pennsylvania

The Agnew Clinic, 1889, Jefferson Medical College, Philadelphia, Pennsylvania

Fairman Rogers Four-in-Hand, 1879, Philadelphia Museum of Art, Pennsylvania

Max Schmitt in a Single Scull, c. 1871, Metropolitan Museum of Art, New York City

ESCHER, MAURITS CORNELIS, (M. C.), 1898–1972, NETHERLANDS

Day and Night, 1938, National Gallery of Art, Washington, DC

Metamorphose, 1939–1940, Vorpal Galleries, San Francisco, California, and Chicago, Illinois

Concave and Convex, 1955, National Gallery of Art, Washington, DC

Drawing Hands, 1948, Vorpal Galleries, San Francisco, California, and Chicago, Illinois

House of Stairs, 1951, National Gallery of Art, Washington, DC

EYCK, JAN VAN, 1390–1441, BELGIUM

Ghent Altarpiece, (with brother Hubert), 1432, Church of St. Bavo, Ghent, Belgium

Madonna of Chancellor Rolin, c. 1433–1434, Louvre, Paris

Man in a Red Turban (Self-portrait?), 1433, National Gallery, London

FISH, JANET, 1938, AMERICA

Hunt's Vase, 1984, collection, the artist

Chinoiserie, 1984, collection of Paine Webber Group, Inc., New York City

Painted Water Glasses, 1974, Whitney Museum of American Art, New York City

Raspberries and Goldfish, 1981, Metropolitan Museum of Art, New York City

Kara, 1983, Museum of Fine Arts, Houston, Texas

FLACK, AUDREY, 1931, AMERICA

Jolie Madame, 1972, Australian National Gallery, Canberra, Australia

Leonardo's Lady, 1975, Museum of Modern Art, New York City

Marilyn (Monroe), 1977, University of Arizona Museum of Art, Tucson

Buddha, 1975, Audrey Flack, St. Louis Art Museum, Missouri

GAUGUIN, PAUL, 1848–1903, FRANCE

Girl with Mango, 1892, Baltimore Museum of Art, Maryland

Vision After the Sermon, 1888, National Gallery of Scotland, Edinburgh

The Day of the God, 1894, Art Institute of Chicago, Illinois

La Orana Maria, 1819, Metropolitan Museum of Art, New York City

Fatata te Miti (By the Sea), 1892, National Gallery of Art, Washington, DC

GOGH, VINCENT VAN, 1853–1890, NETHERLANDS

The Starry Night, 1889, Museum of Modern Art, New York City

The Potato Eaters, 1885, Vincent van Gogh Foundation, Amsterdam

Bedroom at Arles, 1888, Art Institute of Chicago, Illinois

The Night Cafe, 1888, Yale University Art Gallery, New Haven, Connecticut

GRECO, EL (DOMENIKOS THEOTOKOPOULOS), 1541–1614, SPAIN, b. GREECE

The Burial of Count Orgaz, 1586, Toledo, Spain

Resurrection, c. 1597–1604, Prado, Madrid

Grand Inquisitor Don Fernando Nino de Guevara, c. 1600, Metropolitan Museum of Art, New York City

GOYA, FRANCISCO, 1746–1828, SPAIN

The Third of May, 1814–1815, Francisco Goya, Prado, Madrid

Family of Charles IV, 1799, Prado, Madrid

Clothed Maja, and *Naked Maja,* c. 1799, Prado, Madrid

The Second of May, 1808, and *The Third of May,* c. 1808, Prado, Madrid

The Disasters of War, 1810–1814, Prado, Madrid

HALS, FRANS, 1582–1666, NETHERLANDS

Banquet of the Officers of the Saint George Guard Company, 1616, Frans Hals Museum, Haarlem

The Women Regents of the Old Men's Almshouse, c. 1664, Frans Hals Museum, Haarlem

Regents of the St. Elizabeth Hospital, 1641, Frans Hals Museum, Haarlem

The Laughing Cavalier, 1624, Wallace Collection, London

HARING, KEITH, 1958–1990, AMERICA

Mural, 1987, Exterior Stairwell, Necker Children's Hospital, Paris

New York City Subway Panels, 1984, Fifth Avenue, New York City

Mural, 1989, Church of Sant'Antonio, Pisa, Italy

Mural, 1984, Collingwood Technical School, Melbourne, Australia

The Ten Commandments, 1985, Contemporary Art Museum, Bordeaux, France

HARNETT, WILLIAM MICHAEL, 1848–1892, AMERICA

Just Dessert, 1891, Art Institute of Chicago, Illinois

After the Hunt, 1885, California Palace of the Legion of Honor, San Francisco

Still Life—Violin and Music, 1888, Metropolitan Museum of Art, New York City

List 5–3 Continued

HARNETT, WILLIAM MICHAEL, 1848–1892, AMERICA (cont.)

The Artist's Letter Rack, 1879, Metropolitan Museum of Art, New York City

My Gems, 1888, National Gallery of Art, Washington, DC

HARTLEY, MARSDEN, 1877–1943, AMERICA

Portrait of a German Officer, 1914, Metropolitan Museum of Art, New York City

Painting, Number 5, 1914–1915, Whitney Museum of American Art, New York City

Berlin Abstraction, 1914–1915, Corcoran Gallery of Art, Washington, DC

Berlin Ante-War, 1915, Columbus Gallery of Fine Arts, Columbus, Ohio

The Window, 1928, Columbus Gallery of Fine Arts, Columbus, Ohio

HENRI, ROBERT, 1865–1929, AMERICA

The Masquerade Dress, 1911, Metropolitan Museum of Art, New York City

New York Street in Winter, 1902, National Gallery of Art, Washington, DC

HICKS, EDWARD, 1780–1849, AMERICA

The Peaceable Kingdom, c. 1830–1840, Brooklyn Museum, New York

Peaceable Kingdom, 1845, Albright-Knox Art Gallery, Buffalo, New York

The Peaceable Kingdom, date unknown, Abby Aldrich Rockefeller Folk Art Center, Williamsburg, Virginia

The Cornell Farm, 1848, National Gallery of Art, Washington, DC

HOLBEIN, HANS, THE YOUNGER, 1497/98–1543, GERMANY

Bonifacius Amerbach, 1519, Offentliche Kunstsammlung, Basle, Switzerland

Madonna of Burgomaster Meyer, 1526, Schlossmuseum, Darmstadt, Germany

The Ambassadors, 1533, National Gallery, London

Erasmus, 1523–1526, Louvre, Paris

Anne of Cleves, 1539, Louvre, Paris

HOMER, WINSLOW, 1836–1910, AMERICA

Country School, 1871, St. Louis Art Museum, Missouri

The Croquet Game, 1866, Art Institute of Chicago, Illinois

Breezing Up (A Fair Wind), 1876, National Gallery of Art, Washington, DC

Taking on Wet Provisions, Key West, 1903, Metropolitan Museum of Art, New York City

HOPPER, EDWARD, 1882–1967, AMERICA

Early Sunday Morning, 1930, Whitney Museum of American Art, New York City

Nighthawks, 1942, Art Institute of Chicago, Illinois

Bow of Beam Trawler Osprey, 1926, St. Louis Art Museum, Missouri

INDIANA, ROBERT, 1928, AMERICA

The Demuth American Dream No. 5, 1963, Art Gallery of Ontario, Toronto

Triumph of Tira, 1961, Sheldon Memorial Art Gallery, Lincoln, Nebraska

Louisiana, 1966, Krannert Art Gallery, University of Illinois, Champaign, Illinois

The Calumet, 1961, Rose Art Museum, Brandeis University, Waltham, Massachusetts

LOVE, 1966, Indianapolis Museum of Art, Indianapolis, Indiana

JOHNS, JASPER, b. 1930, AMERICA

Target with Four Faces, 1955, Museum of Modern Art, New York City

Flag, 1954–1955, Museum of Modern Art, New York City

Numbers 0 Through 9, 1961, Hirshhorn Museum and Sculpture Garden, Washington, DC

Painted Bronze, (Ballantine Ale Cans), 1960, Museum Ludwig, Cologne

KAHLO, FRIDA, 1907–1954, MEXICO

Self Portrait with Cropped Hair, 1940, Museum of Modern Art, New York City

Fulang-Chang and I, 1937, Museum of Modern Art, New York City

Self Portrait with Monkey and Parrot, 1942, Collection of IBM Corp., Armonk, New York

KLIMT, GUSTAVE, 1862–1918, AUSTRIA

Judith I, 1901, Osterreichische Galerie, Vienna

The Kiss, 1907–1908, Osterreichische Galerie, Vienna

Baby, 1917–1918, Private Collection, New York

LAWRENCE, JACOB, b. 1917, AMERICA

Cabinet Makers, 1946, Hirshhorn Museum and Sculpture Garden, Washington, DC

John Brown, 1941, Detroit Institute of Arts, Michigan

The Studio, 1977, Brooklyn Museum, New York

Study for the Munich Olympic Games, Poster, 1972, Seattle Art Museum, Washington

Dreams # 2, 1965, National Museum of American Art, Washington, DC

LEONARDO DA VINCI, 1452–1519, ITALY

Last Supper, c. 1495–1498, Sta. Maria delle Grazie, Milan

Mona Lisa, 1503–1506, Louvre, Paris

Madonna of the Rocks, c. 1483, Louvre, Paris

Madonna and Saint Anne, c. 1501, Louvre, Paris

List 5-3   Continued

LEUTZ, EMANUEL GOTTLIEB, 1816–1868, AMERICA, B. GERMANY

Nathaniel Hawthorne, 1862, National Portrait Gallery, Washington, DC

On the Banks of a Stream, c. 1860, Corcoran Gallery, Washington, DC

Washington Crossing the Delaware, 1851, Metropolitan Museum of Art, New York City

Westward the Course of Empire Takes its Way, 1861–1862, mural, Capitol Building, Washington, DC

LICHTENSTEIN, ROY, b. 1923, AMERICA

Mural with Blue Brushstroke, 1986, Equitable Life Assurance Society building, New York City

Blam, 1962, Yale University Art Gallery, New Haven, Connecticut

Popeye, 1961, collection of David Lichtenstein, New York City

Goldfish Bowl II, 1978, St. Louis Art Museum, Missouri

MAGRITTE, RENE, 1898–1967, FRANCE

The Promenades of Euclid, 1955, Minneapolis Institute of Arts, Minnesota

The False Mirror, 1928, Museum of Modern Art, New York City

The Menaced Assassin, 1926, Museum of Modern Art, New York City

MANET, EDOUARD, 1832–1883, FRANCE

The Fifer, 1866, Musée d'Orsay, Paris

The Reading, 1868, Musée d'Orsay, Paris

Le Dejeuner sur l'Herbe (Luncheon on the grass) 1863, Musée d'Orsay, Paris

MARIN, JOHN, 1870–1953, AMERICA

Singer Building, 1921, Philadelphia Museum of Art, Pennsylvania

Maine Islands, 1922, Phillips Collection, Washington, DC

Brooklyn Bridge, 1910, Metropolitan Museum of Art, New York City

Lower Manhattan, 1922, Museum of Modern Art, New York City

MATISSE, HENRI, 1869–1954, FRANCE

Lady in Blue, 1937, collection Mrs. John Wintersteen, Philadelphia, Pennsylvania

Luxe, Calme et Volupte, 1904–1905, Musée d'Orsay, Paris

The Back, I–IV, 1900–c. 1929, Hirshhorn Museum and Sculpture Garden, Washington, DC

Bathers by a River, 1916–1917, Art Institute of Chicago, Illinois

MICHELANGELO BUONARROTI, 1475–1564, ITALY

Sistine Chapel, 1508–1512, Vatican, Rome

Holy Family, 1506, Uffizi Gallery, Florence

Pietà, 1498–1499, St. Peter's, Rome

David, 1504, Accademia, Florence

MIRÓ, JOAN, 1893–1983, SPAIN

Painting, 1933, Museum of Modern Art, New York City

Dutch Interior, 1928, collection of Peggy Guggenheim, Venice

Dog Barking at the Moon, 1926, Philadelphia Museum of Art, Pennsylvania

The Harlequin's Carnival, 1924–1925, Albright-Knox Art Gallery, Buffalo, New York

MONET, CLAUDE, 1840–1926, FRANCE

Madame Gaudibert, 1868, Musée d'Orsay, Paris

The River, 1868, Art Institute of Chicago, Illinois

Impression Sunrise—Le Havre, 1872, Musée Marmottan, Paris

Rouen Cathedral: Early Morning, 1894, Museum of Fine Arts, Boston, Massachusetts

Water Lilies, c. 1920, Carnegie Institute, Pittsburg, Pennsylvania

MOSES, ANNA MARY (GRANDMA), 1860–1961, AMERICA

The Eisenhower Farm, 1956, Dwight D. Eisenhower Library, Abilene, Kansas

Home of Hezekiah King, 1942, Phoenix Art Museum, Phoenix, Arizona

Battle of Bennington, 1953, Daughters of the American Revolution, Washington, DC

First Snow, 1957, Bennington Museum, Bennington, Vermont

MUNCH, EDVARD, 1863–1944, NORWAY

The Scream, 1893, National Gallery, Oslo, Norway

Between the Clock and the Bed, 1940–1942, Munch Museum, Oslo

O'KEEFFE, GEORGIA, 1887–1986, AMERICA

Cow's Skull—Red, White and Blue, 1931, Metropolitan Museum of Art, New York City

Black Iris III, 1926, Metropolitan Museum of Art, New York City

Red Hills and Bones, 1941, Philadelphia Museum of Art, Pennsylvania

Sky Above Clouds IV, 1965, Art Institute of Chicago, Illinois

PEALE, CHARLES WILLSON, 1741–1827, AMERICA

Exhuming the Mastodon, 1806–1808, Peale Museum, Baltimore, Maryland

Washington After Trenton, 1767, Metropolitan Museum of Art, New York City

George Washington at the Battle of Princeton, 1780–1781, Yale University Art Gallery, New Haven, Connecticut

The Staircase Group, (1795), Philadelphia Museum of Art, Pennsylvania

List 5–3   Continued

PEALE, REMBRANDT, 1778–1860, AMERICA

George Washington, Patriae Pater, c. 1824, Pennsylvania Academy of Fine Arts, Philadelphia

The Court of Death, 1821, Detroit Institute of Arts, Michigan

PETO, JOHN F., 1854–1907, AMERICA

Reminiscences of 1865, after 1890, Minneapolis Institute of the Arts, Minnesota

Poor Man's Store, 1885, Museum of Fine Arts, Boston, Massachusetts

Still Life With Lanterns, 1889, Brooklyn Museum, New York

PICASSO, PABLO, 1881–1973, SPAIN

Les Demoiselles d'Avignon, 1907, Museum of Modern Art, New York City

Woman's Head, (sculpture), 1909, Museum of Modern Art, New York City

Three Musicians, 1921, Philadelphia Museum of Art, Pennsylvania

Guernica, 1937, Prado, Madrid

POLLOCK, JACKSON, 1912–1956, AMERICA

Number 27, 1950, Whitney Museum of American Art, New York City

Number 1, 1948, Museum of Modern Art, New York City

The She-Wolf, 1943, Museum of Modern Art, New York City

Portrait and a Dream, 1953, Dallas Museum of Art, Texas

PRENDERGAST, MAURICE, 1859–1924, AMERICA

Central Park, 1908–1910, Metropolitan Museum of Art, New York City

The Promenade, 1913, Whitney Museum of American Art, New York City

On the Beach No. 3, 1918, Cleveland Museum of Art, Ohio

Seashore, c. 1910, St. Louis Art Museum, Missouri

RAPHAEL (RAFAELLO SANZIO), 1483–1520, ITALY

Madonna of the Chair, 1515–1516, Pitti Palace, Florence

The School of Athens, c. 1511, Vatican, Rome

Galatea, 1511–1512, Villa Farnesina, Rome

Baldassare Castiglione, c. 1515, Louvre, Paris

Sistine Madonna, c. 1512–1514, Gemaldegalerie, Dresden

RAUSCHENBERG, ROBERT, b. 1925, AMERICA

Doric Circus, 1979, National Gallery of Art, Washington, DC

Tracer, 1964, Nelson-Atkins Museum of Art, Kansas City, Missouri

Odalisk, 1955–1956, collection of Peter Ludwig, Wallraf-Richartz Museum, Cologne, Germany

Bed, 1959, collection of Mr. and Mrs. Leo Castelli, New York

Monogram, 1955–1959, Robert Rauschenberg, Moderna Museet, Stockholm

REDON, ODILON, 1840–1916, FRANCE

The Birth of Venus, 1912, Kimbell Art Foundation, Fort Worth, Texas

Woman Amidst Flowers, 1909–1910, Jonas Collection, New York

Portrait of Mademoiselle Violette Heymann, 1909, Cleveland Museum of Art, Ohio

Orpheus, 1903, Cleveland Museum of Art, Ohio

Roger and Angelica, 1910, Museum of Modern Art, New York City

Profile and Flowers, 1912, McNay Art Institute, San Antonio, Texas

REMBRANDT HARMENSZ VAN RIJN, 1606–1669, NETHERLANDS

Anatomy Lesson of Dr. Tulp, 1632, Mauritshuis, The Hague

The Night Watch, 1642, Rijksmuseum, Amsterdam

The Three Crosses, 1660–1661, Metropolitan Museum of Art, New York City

The Polish Rider, c. 1655, Frick Collection, New York City

The Conspiracy of Claudius Civilis, 1661–1662, Nationalmuseum, Stockholm

REMINGTON, FREDERIC, 1861–1909, AMERICA

The Fight for the Waterhole, c. 1895–1900, Houston Museum, Texas

The Bronco Buster, 1895, St. Louis Art Museum, Missouri

His First Lesson, 1903, Amon Carter Museum, Fort Worth, Texas

Calvary Charge on the Southern Plains, 1907, Metropolitan Museum of Art, New York City

RENOIR, PIERRE-AUGUSTE, 1841–1919, FRANCE

Venus Victorious, 1914, Tate Gallery, London

Gabrielle with a Rose, c. 1911, Musée d'Orsay, Paris

The Ball at the Moulin de la Galette, Monmartre, 1876, Musée d'Orsay, Paris

RINGGOLD, FAITH, b. 1930, AMERICA

Jo Baker's Birthday, 1994, St. Louis Art Museum, Missouri

The Church Picnic, 1987, High Museum, Atlanta, Georgia

Tar Beach, 1988, Solomon R. Guggenheim Museum, New York City

The French Collection, Part I #4 *Sunflowers Quilting Bee at Arles,* 1991, collection, Oprah Winfrey, Chicago, Illinois

RIVERS, LARRY, b. 1923, AMERICA

The History of the Russian Revolution: From Marx to Mayakovski, 1965, Hirshhorn Museum and Sculpture Garden, Washington, DC

First New York Film Festival Billboard, 1963, Hirshhorn Museum and Sculpture Garden, Washington, DC.

Berdie with the American Flag, 1955, Nelson-Atkins Museum of Art, Kansas City, Missouri

Last Civil War Veteran, 1961, collection of Martha Jackson, New York City

The Studio, 1956, Minneapolis Institute of Arts, Minnesota

List 5–3   Continued

RUBENS, PETER PAUL, 1577–1640, BELGIUM

Henry the IV Receiving the Portrait of Maria de Medici, 1621–1625, Louvre, Paris

Wedding Portrait, 1609, Alte Pinakothek, Munich

Descent from the Cross, 1611–1614, Antwerp Cathedral, Belgium

Helene Fourment with Two of Her Children, c. 1637, Louvre, Paris

SARGENT, JOHN SINGER, 1856–1925, AMERICA

Portrait of Lady Agnew, c. 1892–1893, National Galleries of Scotland, Edinburgh

Lady X, 1884, Metropolitan Museum of Art, New York City

Mrs. George Swinton, 1896, Art Institute of Chicago, Illinois

Gassed, 1918, Imperial War Museum, London

SEURAT, GEORGES, 1859–1891, FRANCE

Woman with Parasol, 1884, Emil G. Buehrle Collection, Zurich

Bathers at Asnieres, 1883–1884, National Gallery, London

Sunday Afternoon on the Island of La Grande Jatte, 1884–1886, Art Institute of Chicago, Illinois

Woman Powdering Herself, 1890, Courtauld Institute, London

SHAPIRO, MIRIAM, b. 1923, AMERICA

Murmur of the Heart, 1980, collection of the artist

The Azerbajani Fan, 1980, collection of the artist

Conservatory, 1988, collection of the artist

I'm Dancin' as Fast as I Can, 1980s, collection of the artist

SHEELER, CHARLES, 1883–1965, AMERICA

Barn Abstraction, 1918, Philadelphia Museum of Art, Pennsylvania

River Rouge Plant, 1932, Whitney Museum of American Art, New York City

Upper Deck, 1929, Fogg Art Museum, Cambridge, Massachusetts

Classic Landscape, 1931, St. Louis Art Museum, Missouri

STUART, GILBERT, 1755–1828, AMERICA

The Skater, 1782, National Gallery of Art, Washington, DC

George Washington (the "Athenaeum" Portrait), 1796, Museum of Fine Arts, Boston, Massachusetts

George Washington (The "Lansdowne" Portrait), 1796, Pennsylvania Academy of Fine Arts

TURNER, JOSEPH MALLORD WILLIAM, 1775–1851, ENGLAND

The Fighting Temeraire, 1838, National Gallery, London

Rain, Steam, and Speed, 1844, National Gallery, London

Yacht Approaching the Coast, 1840–1845, Tate Gallery, London

Venice: *The Piazzetta from the Water,* c. 1835, Tate Gallery, London

VELAZQUEZ, DIEGO, 1599–1660, SPAIN

Las Meninas, 1656, Prado, Madrid

Triumph of Bacchus, c. 1628, Prado, Madrid

Surrender of Breda, 1634–1635, Prado, Madrid

Juan de Pareja, 1650, Metropolitan Museum of Art, New York City

King Philip IV of Spain, 1644, Metropolitan Museum of Art, New York City

Portrait of Queen Mariana, 1632–1633, Louvre, Paris

VERMEER, JAN, 1632–1635, NETHERLANDS

View of Delft, c. 1662, Mauritshuis, The Hague

Street in Delft, c. 1660, Rijksmuseum, Amsterdam

Allegory of the Art of Painting, c. 1670–1675, Kunsthistorisches Museum, Vienna

Kitchen Maid, c. 1658, Rijksmuseum, Amsterdam

WARHOL, ANDY, 1930–1988, AMERICA

Green Coca-Cola Bottles, 1962, private collection, New York

Dollar Bills, 1962, collection of Mr. and Mrs. Robert C. Scull, New York

Campbell's Soup Can, 1965, Museum of Modern Art, New York City

Marilyn Monroe's Lips, 1962, Hirshhorn Museum and Sculpture Garden, Washington, DC

WATTEAU, JEAN-ANTOINE, 1684–1721, FRANCE

A Pilgrimage to Cythera, 1717, Louvre, Paris

Signboard of Gersaint, c. 1721, Staatliche Museen, Berlin

WEST, BENJAMIN, 1738–1820, AMERICA

Penn's Treaty with the Indians, 1772, Pennsylvania Academy of the Fine Arts, Philadelphia

The Death of General Wolfe, 1770, National Gallery of Canada, Ottawa

WHISTLER, JAMES ABBOTT MCNEILL, 1834–1903, AMERICA

Arrangement in Gray and Black, No. 1: The Artist's Mother, 1871, Musée d'Orsay, Paris

Portrait of Thomas Carlyle: Arrangement in Grey and Black, No. 2, 1872, Glasgow Art Gallery and Museum

The White Girl: Symphony in White No. 1, 1862, National Gallery of Art, Washington, DC

Nocturne in Black and Gold: Falling Rocket, c. 1874, Detroit Institute of Arts, Michigan

WOOD, GRANT, 1892–1942, AMERICA

Midnight Ride of Paul Revere, 1931, Metropolitan Museum of Art, New York City

The Birthplace of Herbert Hoover, 1931, New York Historical Society, New York City

Daughters of Revolution, 1932, Cincinnati Art Museum, Ohio

Parson Weems' Fable, 1938–1939, private collection

List 5-4   Great Themes of Painting

UNIVERSAL PAINTING THEMES

adoration
allegorical
animals
artists' families
carnivals
children
circus
cities
the elements: earth, air, fire, water
families
farming
festivals
figural
flowers
gardens
genre
grief
historical events
hunting
interiors
landscape
love
music
musicians
mythology
narrative
nighttime
other artists at work
outdoors
people
portraiture
processions
religious subjects
seascape
self-portraits
sports
still life
storytelling
theater
transportation
trees
war
water

ASIAN THEMES

animals
birds
Buddha
fans
flowers
mountains
nature

Drawn from *Snow in New York,*
1902, Robert Henri, National
Gallery of Art, Washington, DC

trees
water

INDIAN THEMES

adventure scenes
animals
hunting scenes
illustrations of love poetry
legends
life of Buddha
lives of the gods
manuscript illumination
portraits of court officials
romantic scenes
scenes at court
story illustration

NATIVE AMERICAN THEMES

animal totems
dances
exploits on horseback
nature
symbols for nature

CHRISTIAN RELIGIOUS THEMES

adoration of the Golden Calf
adoration of the Magi
adoration of the shepherds
annunciation
assumption
Bathsheba
beheading of St. Paul
Biblical stories
birth of the Virgin
carrying of the cross
Christ before Pilate
Christ in Majesty

circumcision
coronation of the Virgin
crucifixion
David and Goliath
death of the Virgin
descent from the cross
dormition of the Virgin
doubting Thomas
entombment
entry into Jerusalem
flight into Egypt
flood
Garden of Eden
holy family
immaculate conception
in the garden
John the Baptist in the wilderness
last judgment
life of St. Stephen
lives of the saints
Madonna in the clouds
martyrdom of Saint Paul
martyrdom of the saints
Moses striking the rock
nativity
pietà
portraits of popes and cardinals
presentation in the temple
presentation of the Virgin in the
    temple
raising of Lazarus
rest on the flight into Egypt
sacrifice of Abraham
supper at Emaus
the Last Supper
the trial of Moses
tree of Jesse
Virgin among Virgins
Virgin and Child
visitation

Madonna of the Magnificat, c. 1483
Sandro Botticelli, Uffizi Gallery, Florence

List 5–5   Differences in Types of Paints

ACRYLICS

Advantages

all colors dry at the same rate

brilliant colors may be purchased premixed

can be used as an underpainting for oil

colors are permanent

comes pre-mixed in jars or tubes, various qualities

easy to put one layer on top of another

fast-drying

flexible; canvases may be rolled when dry

may be used thinly like watercolor

paint can be thinned with water

relatively odorless

sticks to almost any surface

textures can be built up with the addition of gel medium or marble powder

Disadvantages

brushes must be kept in water or cleaned immediately

impasto textures are more difficult to achieve

quick drying means palette dries out rapidly

smooth blending almost impossible

surface often lacks the richness of oil texture

OILS

Advantages

allows blending techniques

can be worked into while it is wet

impasto textures

permanent

proven durability and light-fastness

rich colors

slow drying

Disadvantages

brushes must be cleaned with mineral spirits or turpentine

cracks develop over time unless care is taken

expensive

leaves an oily residue on paper

paint is usually mixed with a painting medium

slow drying; at times you must wait until it dries to work on a specific area

some colors may be toxic

strong odor

TEMPERA

Advantages

easy clean-up

fast drying

inexpensive

may be mixed with egg yolk or polymer medium for permanence

may be overpainted

opaque; covers well

works on paper

Disadvantages

cracks when built up in layers

may flake off

WATERCOLOR

Advantages

fast-drying

loose effect

paints come in tube or cake form

quick clean-up

transparent

Disadvantages

may fade over time

paper support requires humidity control

List 5–6   Materials and Equipment for Watercolor

bamboo pen

bar of soap

small glass beads (to put into wet surface)

brayer

brushes: flat, round, fan, striping, utility

candles, paraffin or crayons

chalk and pastels

colored pencils

cotton swabs

drafting tape

drinking straws

eraser

hair dryer

India ink

liquid frisket

masking tape

oil pastels

opaque white

ox-gall

palette knife

plastic wrap

polymer medium

razor blades (single-edge)

rice paper

rock salt or regular salt

rubber cement

sand

sponges

spray bottles: water and alcohol

squeeze bottles

sticks

thread

thumb tacks

tissue paper

tissues

toothbrush

tray or palette for paints

turpentine

water-soluble felt-tip pens

white glue

wide-blades of grass

X-acto® knife

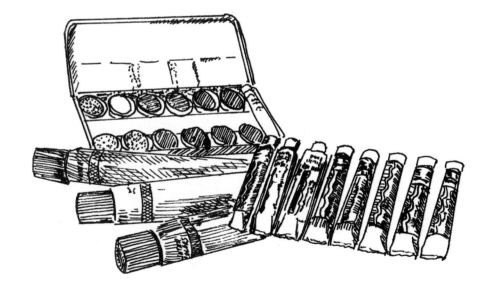

List 5–7   Things to Do with Watercolor

- Add rock (or Kosher) salt to it when it is wet to make textural differences. Rub off when dry.
- Apply in even strokes across the page to make an even wash for skies and water.
- Apply watercolor with a sponge.
- Brush turpentine onto paper before painting to give a wonderfully oily, somewhat uncontrollable resist; interesting for skies and water.
- Coat a brush with soap before dipping in pigment to cause separation of strokes; good for grass.
- Cut up a credit card and use the stiff plastic to make marks in a wet surface.
- Do a watercolor painting and allow it to dry. Then go over it with oil or dry pastels.
- Draw with felt-tipped black marker before painting it with watercolor. The black line will run and bleed through. This is especially effective when drawing architecture.
- Draw with white crayon on a white background; then paint over it.
- For a textured surface, crumple tissue, place it on *dry* paper with polymer medium underneath before beginning to paint in watercolor.
- Glaze with watercolor—put on light colors and build them up in intensity.
- Glue a few large torn pieces of rice paper on watercolor paper before painting.
- Lay waxed paper onto wet pigment and allowed it to almost dry before removing for varying textures.
- Place colored tissue into wet pigment and paint on top of it.
- Let a watercolor dry; then outline with black fine-line marker.
- Lift off areas of color with a damp tissue or cotton ball.
- Liquid frisket can be dripped or spattered onto paper before painting or even into wet paint for entirely different effects.
- Make a design by squeezing white glue from a bottle onto white paper. Allow it to dry overnight, then paint.
- Make a graduated wash by diluting pigment as you go down the page.
- Make a paper batik by using melted wax as part of the design; apply on white paper or to preserve certain areas of color after they have dried.
- Make paper stencils and spatter paint on top to make interesting lines.
- Make rocks by crumpling plastic wrap, and blotting it against a still-wet painted area.
- Make rocks by spattering with water, then blotting.
- Make texture in already wet areas by blotting with a sponge.
- Paint watercolor paper with a mix of gesso and polymer medium. When dry, paint on it with watercolor.
- Paint with sticks, cotton swabs, cotton balls, broken popsicle sticks, or fingers.
- Put torn masking tape on paper to act as a resist; when dry, remove.
- Rocks, beads, and sand can be added to wet pigment and the paint allowed to dry, then brushed off.
- Scratch into a *dry* watercolor surface with a knife for interesting textural effects.
- Scratch lines into a *wet* painting with a sharp instrument.
- Spatter white or dark pigment on the painting with a toothbrush or paint brush.
- Spray, drip, or use a brush to draw with *alcohol* into wet or dry pigment.
- Stipple by applying small strokes with a stiff brush.
- To paint wet-in-wet, apply pigment into an already wet area, allowing it to spread.
- Use a brayer to spread pigment over large wet areas.
- Use a cotton swab to lift paint from a wet surface or to create texture.
- Use a dry-brush technique to make stripes. Or dry brush on top of a painted area.

List 5–7   Continued

- Use a small rectangle of cardboard as a brush to apply broad areas of watercolor.
- Use cardboard (corrugated or matboard) edges to stamp details.
- Use colored inks such as sepia, red, blue, and green for a spreading effect in wet pigment.
- Use India ink instead of marker for drawing, before or after (or before *and* after) applying watercolor.
- Use rubber cement as a resist to make areas stay white.
- Use textures, such as bubble wrap, string, fabric, mesh, to press into wet surface for variety.
- Use various other materials with a finished watercolor such as pastels, watercolor pencils, colored pencils, ballpoint pen, charcoal pencil. Go over a finished painting with water-soluble colored pencils to add detail.
- Use watercolor in an insect spray gun to outline large stencils on butcher roll paper.
- Take advantage of the "happy accident" when color runs, tilting the paper to use it advantageously.
- Make a portrait with only a partially-lit face and a dark background.
- Emphasize clouds and skies by creating a low horizon line.
- Try not to have extreme value contrasts at the edges of the paper.
- If you are working with warm colors in one area, add a cool color as a contrast, and vice versa.
- For delicate texture, apply ArtistColor® Transparent Liquid Acrylic color on top of a dried watercolor painting.

List 5–8   Things to Do with Tempera

Tempera is powdered pigment mixed with water, egg yolk, or acrylic gel medium. It was used in ancient Greece and Egypt.

SUGGESTIONS FOR USE

Pour tempera on a folded paper towel or sponge to make a stamp pad.

Pour a small amount of each color into an egg carton; mix colors in the lid.

Add polymer medium to tempera for the shiny effect of acrylic.

Make a painting palette of a double-page fold of a slick news magazine or wax paper.

While it is wet, "spritz" it with water or alcohol from a spray bottle.

Mix tempera with starch for fingerpainting.

Thin tempera to make it somewhat transparent.

Dip a piece of sponge in tempera and use it as your painting tool.

PROJECT IDEAS

- Draw heavily with white or black crayon, then paint over with tempera.
- Cover paper with Pritt® paste and use a brayer to "paint" with tempera while the paper is wet.
- Color firmly with crayons in "strange" colors. Paint over it with "regular colors." Allow to dry slightly, then wash off most of the tempera.
- To learn color mixing, cut 12 identical tagboard shapes approximately 3 × 5 inches. Begin with only red, blue, and yellow, and mix these colors (R, RO, O, YO, Y, YG, G, BG, B, BV, V, RV), painting a different one on each piece of tagboard. Make a complete color wheel by gluing the shapes onto a white or black background.
- Do a tempera mural on a painter's heavy rubberized drop cloth.
- Do a tempera mural on butcher paper.
- Draw a pizza-sized circle and paint a circular motif within it, distorting the subject if necessary to make it fit.
- Draw three circles of different sizes on drawing paper. Do a still-life drawing, but use the circles like magnifying glasses, enlarging what is "seen" through the glass.
- Make a monochromatic painting of one hue, adding white or black to change it.
- Make a stencil of a leaf and spatter-paint it with tempera rubbed across a screen with a toothbrush; remove the leaf.
- Paint an entire "dark" composition. Then use a fine brush to enliven it by making numerous details with white paint.
- Paint with tempera mixed with starch, then scratch a design with a sharp instrument.
- *Tempera batik:* Paint with it, let it dry, go over it with black ink, and wash off the ink.
- Use three warm or cool colors of equal intensity, and one "opposite" color; for example, blue/green/violet, red.
- Use undiluted paint to paint on black paper, leaving areas such as lines and shapes unpainted.
- Work on a gessoed background on any surface with tempera mixed with polymer medium.

List 5–9   Things to Do with Acrylics

- Acrylic is the perfect paint for large murals because it dries quickly and clean-up is easy. Photocopy photos on overhead transparencies and project them onto the wall, outline with pencil, then fill in with acrylic paint.
- Apply photographs to heavy posterboard. Then use acrylic paint to "extend" the photo out to the edges, leaving the photograph unpainted.
- Create a painting overlapping many figures such as a crowd in the theater or at a parade.
- Do a huge reproduction on cardboard of an "old master" that includes more than one figure. Then cut out ovals where the faces would be for people to put their faces through for a group photo.
- Do a photo silk-screen on paper or a T-shirt.
- Do a portrait from a photo of yourself or a friend making a "funny face," rather than in a normal portrait expression.
- Do a reproduction of an "old master" painting as perfectly as possible, but substitute your own face for that of the person in the painting.
- Do a figure painting on a three-dimensional surface such as a heavy cardboard tube or a section of 4 × 4-inch or 6 × 6-inch fence post.
- Draw an outline in permanent marker on an overhead projector transparency. Project it onto a wall or large canvas to enlarge it in acrylic paint.
- Have only one realistic subject such as a barn, rock, or house, and paint the landscape with an overall pattern.
- Paint a portrait with a deliberately elongated face.
- Paint a self-portrait directly onto a mirror (or on plastic taped onto the mirror).
- Staple black-and-white photographs to canvasboard. Paint, allowing the staples to remain, and adding many more staples where they will enhance the design.
- Use masking tape to make a straight line design on canvas. Paint with acrylic; allow to dry and remove tape. Retape and add different colors.
- Do a Victorian-style "glass painting" on a plastic panel. This will be seen from the unpainted side, so highlights go on first, with the background done last.
- Make a layered painting by doing a dark scene first, placing cut-out animals, people or buildings on top. Cover with plastic, then paint accents on top of the plastic to create a very "full" composition.
- Use vegetables such as the ends of celery, carrots, broccoli, green pepper, and potatoes to stamp designs on T-shirts. These designs may be flowers, abstractions, or geometric figures.

List 5–10 Things to Do with Oils

- Abstract the ordinary. Take a subject, and distort, fracture, change color, hide, or otherwise make changes that still allow the viewer to know what the original subject was.
- Do a composition of two figures. They may face each other, be side-by-side, or overlap.
- Do a painting of the view out your window, showing the frame, curtains, and window sill.
- Do a perspective painting, using one-, two-, or three-point perspective. Allow space to dominate.
- Do an underpainting on the entire canvas with a thin wash of burnt umber mixed with turpentine; work out value differences in advance before adding any color.
- Make a giant still-life. Use a viewfinder to isolate one area to paint.
- Make a painting in neutral colors only (grayed complements, black, white, tan). If you must, add one or two accents of pure color, but use it sparingly.
- Make an "at the table" painting showing something that would be found on *any* kind of table.
- Make the small *monumental,* taking something such as a shell, flower, or cup and saucer, and causing it to dominate the canvas.
- Paint a still life of a bowl of eggs on white, using strong directional light from a photo flood lamp. Do this realistically or abstractly.
- Paint to music. Listen first, allowing colors and shapes to go through your mind; then begin painting.
- Paint with a palette knife, mixing colors on a palette before applying them to a canvas.
- Use dots to create form, allowing the eye to mix the color, as Georges Seurat did.

List 5–11   Things to Do with Fingerpaint

Fingerpaint is not only for young children; adults also find it a challenging medium. Fingers, hands, and arms are simply tools like a brush or computer.

- Cut design(s) into a piece of fingerpaint paper, paint it, then lay it paint-side down on a clean sheet of paper. Fingerpaint over both layers (including the hole[s]); lift off the top sheet.
- Dip a toothbrush in water to do a spatter painting by holding it above the fingerpainting and rubbing it with your finger.
- Fold a wet painting; after opening, experiment with further changes along the folds.
- If using powder fingerpaint, sprinkle into a wet surface.
- Make a collage by cutting out areas of a dried fingerpainting and combining them with other materials.
- Make a monochromatic scheme with values of one hue, adding white or a dark color to change.
- Make a monoprint by covering a paper with fingerpaint. Then, while it is still wet, place a clean sheet on the surface and press on the back with a brayer, squeegee, or your hand.
- Make a monoprint drawing by placing a clean sheet of paper on a wet fingerpainting. Then draw with pencil on the back of the clean paper to "lift" color.
- Make a plaid pattern by painting first in one direction, then in the other.
- Make a tagboard stencil and scribble around the edges with crayon several places on the fingerpaint paper; then fingerpaint on top of the crayon.
- Materials to change the surface of a fingerpaint monoprint are: confetti, leaves, grass, lace, paper, and tape.
- Paint a place in your memory such as a waterfall, ocean, mountain scene, park, home.
- Paint to music, allowing the hands to "dance" in the painting.
- Press a long piece of string loosely into a still-wet painted surface, then make a monoprint.
- Put paint on paper and create a design using first the forearm, then the bottom of a fist, the fingers, the fingernails.
- Sponge-paint with small pieces to create designs such as trees and grasses.
- Take a long piece of string, grasp it in both hands, and drag the loop through painted paper.
- Think about a specific season of the year or kind of day (rainy, sunshiny, cloudy, windy).
- Use both hands and arms at the same time, trying reverse motions.
- Use man-made tools such as a comb, can top, toothbrush, pastry brush, cardboard, hair curler, paint roller, cork, toothpick, dowel, clothespin, or cardboard to create a design.
- Use two or three fingers together to make pattern designs such as scallops, circles, zigzag, curves, spirals, squares, and triangles.
- Work with two or three analogous colors on the color wheel.

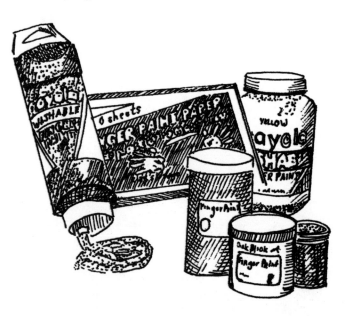

List 5–12   Suggested Subjects for Fingerpainting

animals

birds

circus figures

decorative repeat pattern

dinosaurs

figures at the beach

fish

flower garden

groups of figures

jungle print

pets

portrait

prehistoric scene

rainy day

space station

tornado

undersea scene

windstorm

List 5–13   Materials and Equipment for Fingerpainting

buckets for washing hands

drying areas

fingerpaint (powder or moist)

flat surface, easily cleaned

iron or weights (for pressing out wrinkles)

newsprint (for pressing wrinkles from paper)

paint storage

paper

   butcher

   fadeless

fingerpaint

freezer

metallic

shelf

textured

pencil (for identifying work on dull side of paper)

smocks or large plastic bags to protect clothing

sponges for clean-up

sponges for wetting paper

spoon or spatula for dipping out paint

List 5–14   Decorative Painting Techniques

These techniques are mostly used on walls, furniture, and frames, although some terms are also used in traditional painting.

antique   to paint a thin glaze of burnt sienna or burnt umber over a base coat and wipe most of it off with a soft rag

color wash   to apply a thin second color on top of a first, allowing the undercoat to show

comb   to make designs with professional rubber or steel combs or one made of cardboard or a squeegee by cutting the edges

decoupage   to cut out designs, glue them on a surface, and varnish to protect the cutouts

drag   to apply a second color of paint on top of a first, allowing the brushstrokes to show

faux (false) bamboo   to paint round legs on furniture to look as if they are bamboo

faux stone   to paint blocks on a wall to resemble stone

flog   to apply glaze, then while it is wet, to hit with the flat brush to create texture

gild   to add gold or silver leaf to something through using a size and thin gold or silver sheets (modern substitutes for genuine gold and silver sheets are available in craft shops)

glaze   to apply one transparent color over another, changing the color of each as it is built up

grain   to make designs with rubber rollers or rubber squeegees that have had lines carved in them

lapis lazuli   to create the effect of lapis lazuli with a Prussian blue glaze

lime   to apply white latex mixed with plaster of Paris, allowing it to remain in the grain of the wood, then to wipe it off before applying a pale varnish

malachite   to make a malachite effect, use a green underglaze, then add different green values and greenish-black in patterns

marble   to paint designs on a wall to resemble marble; this can be done with a combination of brushes, a sponge, and a feather

moiré   to use a fine comb to make designs resembling moiré silk

pickle   to wipe a whitish paint onto a surface and wipe off (same as *lime*)

porphyry   to create the effect of this granite-like rock, apply glaze, smooth the glaze with a sponge, then spatter two or three values on top, including gold, if you wish

rag   to roll a rag in wet paint, removing paint in an abstract pattern

spatter   to flick paint from a brush that has been dipped in contrasting paint (or use denatured alcohol on an oil-based glaze)

sponge   to dip a sponge in paint of a different color than the base coat, and apply to give a regular or irregular pattern

stencil   to apply paints to a surface by stippling through openwork designs cut in oiled sheets or plastic stencils

stipple   to make individual small dots with a stiff brush in a slightly darker color(s)

trompe l'oeil   to paint a subject on a wall or furniture so realistically that it "fools the eye"

verdigris   to apply turquoise and green paints to make something appear like oxidized copper

wood grain   to use brushes to make the "grain" of the wood, then use a "mottler" to create grains

List 5–15   Suggestions for Compositional Devices in Painting

These are not specific projects, themes, or colors . . . simply ways to use proven compositional devices.

- Arrange figures in triangular groups as the great Renaissance masters often did.
- Consciously create a painting without a single straight line.
- Create a "golden section" (roughly 8 × 13) as the perfect proportion for a painting.
- Create a formally balanced painting with a central subject.
- Create an all-white or all-ochre painting, varying values through the addition of various hues.
- Create shallow space by making all figures approximately the same size.
- Depict one area of the canvas realistically, while allowing the rest of the composition to be very loosely interpreted.
- Divide the background by several lightly drawn lines in any direction. Vary the color slightly at the dividing lines.
- Divide the surface with a tic-tac-toe grid and place the main subject on an intersection.
- Draw a circle within a rectangular format and concentrate the subject within the circle.
- Employ side lighting to call attention to your subject.
- Frame the composition by looking through a doorway, window, or arch.
- If painting on paper, draw a 1-inch border around the edge for easier handling and framing.
- Make a central vanishing point with everything leading to it.
- Make a round painting (tondo). *Caution:* It appears to roll unless weight is kept at the bottom.
- Paint within an uncommon format such as an oval, triangle, or square.
- Paint the part of the figure closest to the viewer dramatically larger to create depth (foreshorten).
- Use advancing (red, yellow) colors or retreating (blue, violet, green) colors in the composition.
- Use diagonal lines as part of the composition to make it more dynamic.
- Use either a high or low horizon line.
- Use geometric forms as part of a composition on nature.
- Use only straight lines in a painting.
- Use short brush strokes of pure color.
- Work with light or dark gray values to create a tranquil or menacing mood.

List 5–16   Traditional Uses for Painting

animal studies
architectural renderings
book illustrations
books of hours (prayer books)
botanical illustrations
calendars
caricatures
cartoons
clothing designs and illustrations
costume designs
decoration

fans
illuminated manuscripts
illustrating travel journals
interior decorations
manuscripts
maps
miniature paintings
murals
portraits of rulers
preparatory cartoons for ceiling
   paintings

religious illustrations
studies of armor
studies of people
studies of places
tapestry designs
tomb paintings
travel posters
travel studies
wallpaper design

List 5–17   All About Color Use in Painting

The color wheel is an artificial arrangement of the colors of the spectrum. It is useful, however, when thinking about colors that are effective together.

- A high-key painting shows dramatic differences in colors because of bright, reflected light; color is used in its purest intensity.
- A low-key painting shows subdued changes, hazy effects. Color is subdued and neutralized, often with the addition of its complement.
- Complementary color scheme: colors opposite each other on the color wheel; for example, red/green, yellow/violet, and blue/orange.
- Neutral colors are black, white, brown, and grays made by mixing complements together, sometimes with the addition of white.
- Almost any painting needs both light and dark areas to be effective.
- The light in seasonal changes such as summer or autumn can be controlled by how light or dark a painting is.
- A monochromatic color scheme may be used, with a single complement to heighten intensity.
- A complementary color scheme may be used, with hues of equal or unequal intensity.
- Because of differing color intensities, if using complements in a color scheme, it is effective to use: red 50%/green 50%; blue 66%/orange 33%; violet 75%/yellow 25%.
- Figure/ground relationships are especially important in using color, with choices of color calling attention to or minimizing a specific area.

List 5–18   Color Symbolism

Colors may mean different things to different cultures. An example is the use of black for mourning in Western cultures, while white is the color for mourning in some Eastern traditions. Some generally accepted meanings are listed here.

black   associated with bad luck; mournful, stark, dramatic; traditional symbol for evil

blue   a calm, soothing, and tranquil color, sometimes associated with sadness or depression; usually was the color for the Virgin Mary

green   signifies life or hope; poison, envy; was "traditionally worn as a symbol for fertility at European weddings"

orange   Buddhist monks traditionally wear this color; striking, sharp

purple   a symbol for royalty or wealth; also used for the passion of Christ in Christian symbolism

red   often associated with evil or danger; symbolizes love; a lucky color for the Chinese; dynamic in design

white   symbolizes purity, truth, innocence, and light; also cold or unemotional

yellow   a cheery color that embodies warmth and light; symbolizes joy and youth; sickness or cowardice

List 5–19   Time Line: Discoveries in Pigment

Pigments are ground animal, vegetable, or mineral sources combined with a binder—such as gum arabic for watercolor pigments, and oil for oil painting pigments.

30,000 BC	colors used in cave paintings: black and yellow manganese, red and yellow ochre, violet; mixed with water, egg white, or blood
5000 BC	Egyptian palette found in ancient scrolls and tomb paintings: black, blue, brown, green, red, white, yellow tempera
850–700 BC	(Greek palette) black overall geometric designs on vases
700–600 BC	(Greek palette) black figures on red clay vases
650–480 BC	(Greek palette) black figures with incised details on red clay vases
530 BC	(Greek palette) red figures on vase with background painted black
480–323 BC	(Greek palette) colors such as violet and yellow painted on white background vases
100–44 BC	realistic colors used by Romans on fresco in public and private decorations
200 BC–AD 200	encaustic panel portraits painted in Egypt
c. 700–1400 AD	rich colors and gold leaf used to illuminate manuscripts on vellum or parchment
c. 900	encaustic seldom used
1000–1520	fresco painting on walls
1300–1600	egg tempera painting on wood panels
1380–1600	manuscript illumination on paper
1450	painted leather
1498–1520	oil on canvas or wood panel
1500	watercolor
1533	oil and tempera pigment combined on canvas
1600–present	oil on canvas
1829	introduction of cadmium colors into oil painting
1840s	aniline dyes from coal tars: emerald greens, magenta
1856	first coal-tar dye: Perkin's violet
c. 1900	silk-screen enamel used for textile printing
1930s	silk-screen as an artistic medium
1940s	acrylic paint (magna)
1950s	encaustic revival led by artist Jasper Johns

List 5–20   All About Color Pigment

This list includes sources of pigments used in different times and cultures. Many of these are no longer available, with modern synthetic pigments derived from coal-tar replacing them.

artificial mineral colors   cadmium yellow, zinc oxide

bistre   transparent brown pigment made from the soot of burned beechwood; formerly used as a wash in watercolor

bole   colored clay used decoratively and for gilding (often red)

cadmium red   cadmium sulfide and cadmium selenide combination

cadmium yellow   cadmium sulfide

calcined earths (fired at a high temperature)   burnt umber (iron oxide), burnt sienna

carmine red   female cochineal beetles from Peru and the Canary Islands were dried and crushed

cinnabar   red mercuric sulfide used as a pigment

cobalt yellow (aureolin)   precipitate of potassium cobaltinitrite

earths   naturally colored clays and mineral pigments; include terra verde (green earth), ochre (iron oxide), raw umber (iron oxide), raw sienna

Egyptian blue   copper silicate mixture; used in ancient Egyptian wall paintings

gamboge   orange to brown gum resin from Asian trees; strong yellow pigment

green   ground malachite mixed with gum arabic

Indian (India) yellow   derived from the urine of cows who were denied water and fed only mango leaves

indigo (blue)   a plant that yields a dark grayish blue

iron oxide reds   Indian red, light red, and Mars red

lakes   colors made from synthetic dyes

madder red   a transparent ruby-red color from the root of the madder plant; mostly replaced today by alizarin crimson

organic pigments   synthetically made from coal-tar derivatives; examples are hansa yellow or phthalocyanine green or blue

orpiment   native arsenic trisulfide, bright golden yellow to orange; rarely used today

oxidized copper   (green or red)

oxidized iron   (green or brown)

purple   ground mollusk shell

raw sienna   clay, rich in iron, found near Sienna, Italy

red lead (oxide)   one of the earliest pigments, mentioned by Pliny the Elder in the first century

red ochre   impure iron ore used as a pigment

rose madder and alizarin crimson   dye from the madder plant

sanguine   chalk with a reddish-brown tinge

sinopia   red iron oxide

smalt   a deep blue pigment primarily used in ceramics; contains silica, cobalt, and potash synthetic organic pigments

terra verde (green earth)   natural earth pigment dyes made from the distillation of coal tar; a green clay, primarily from Cyprus; contains celadonite and glauconite (used for underpainting flesh in medieval times)

turquoise   ground turquoise stone

ultramarine   ground lapis lazuli mainly from Persia and China; today it is made artificially

verditer (Bremen blue or Bremen green)   hydrated copper carbonate

white lead (flake white)   basic lead carbonate; has basically been replaced by zinc white or titanium white

yellow   saffron (a type of crocus)

zinc oxide (Chinese white)   a by-product of brass production was used to replace lead white

List 5–21   Palettes of Particular Artists and Cultures

A palette was not only the surface on which paint was arranged, but also referred to the colors used by various artists. For example, Monet was said to have a bright palette, while that of Manet was more somber. A full range of colors on a palette would normally be 12 to 14 hues.

EGYPTIAN MURAL PALETTE

black: carbon (lampblack)
blue: azurite and Egyptian blue frit
brown: native earths
green: malachite and crysocolla

red: native red oxides
white: chalk and gypsum
yellow: ochre and native orpiment

(From *The Artist's Handbook* by Ralph Mayer, Macmillan, New York, 1970)

TEMPERA PALETTE USED IN FRESCO

Pigments were mixed with egg yolk and added into wet (buon fresco) or dry (fresco secco) plaster.

black: lampblack or burnt almond shells
blue: Egyptian blue, copper ores
brown: native earths
cinabrese red: a mixture of sinopia and lime white
flesh tint: three shades of cinabrese red with lime white
gold leaf applied over red clay (bole)
green, Egyptian green, green earth
lime white
red ochre (sinopia)
red, native oxides, Pozzuoli red, etc.
ultramarine blue (lapis lazuli)

vermilion red (cinnabar ore)
white, lime
yellow, ochres

NATIVE AMERICANS' PALETTE

Native Americans combined pigment with animal fat or oil of pinon seeds; or with water, yucca syrup, and egg (sometimes eagles' eggs), and melon or ground seeds. Contemporary artists use a wide variety of colors, though selected colors frequently reflect their habitat and traditions. Favored colors were:

black
blue or green

brown
gold

reddish brown
white

ABORIGINALS' PALETTE

Aboriginal paintings were originally made with natural minerals and earth. Contemporary Australian aboriginal people mostly rely on acrylic paints, although many continue to use traditional colors. Traditional colors are:

black (charcoal)
brown

red
white

yellow

J.M.W. TURNER'S PALETTE (ON *YACHT APPROACHING THE COAST*)

barium yellow
blue verditer

chrome scarlet
cobalt blue

viridian green

GEORGE SEURAT'S PALETTE (ON *BATHERS, ASNIERES*)

alizarin crimson
cadmium yellow
cerulean blue
cobalt blue

emerald green
mixed orange and raw sienna
ultramarine blue
vermilion

violet
yellow ochre

List 5–21   Continued

VINCENT VAN GOGH'S PALETTE (ON *CHAIR WITH PIPE*)

cadmium yellow	emerald green	ultramarine blue
cobalt violet	lead white	vermilion
cobalt blue	other earth colors	viridian green

GUSTAVE COURBET'S PALETTE (FOR *THE MEETING*)

black	lead white	viridian
cobalt blue	mixed greens	
iron oxides	red	

AUGUSTE RENOIR'S PALETTE (FOR *WOMAN'S TORSO IN SUNLIGHT*)

alizarin crimson	emerald green	ultramarine blue
chrome yellow	flake white	vermilion
cobalt blue	Naples yellow	viridian green

REMBRANDT'S PALETTE (FOR THE *FEAST OF BALTHAZZAR, THE WRITING ON THE WALL*)

azurite	greens made by mixing lead-	organic red lake
bistre	tin yellow with azurite or	red ochre
black	smalt	smalt
brown	lead white	vermilion
Cologne earth	lead-tin yellow	

WILLIAM BLAKE'S PALETTE (FOR THE *BODY OF ABEL FOUND BY ADAM AND EVE*)

black	madder red	vermilion
gamboge	ochres	
gold	Prussian blue	

JEAN MILLET'S PALETTE (FOR *LE DEPART POUR LE TRAVAIL*)

black	green	vermilion
blue	iron oxide red	white

© 1998 Prentice Hall

List 5–22   Brush Definitions

A vast number of brushes exist, designed for specific purposes, in qualities ranging from fine to student grade, and in sizes ranging from 3–0 to 14 (used for round brushes), and ¼ to 2-inch (for flat brushes).

ferrule   the metal piece that attaches hairs to a brush handle

filaments   individual hairs in a brush

flagged tips   V-shaped split at the end of the hair; softer tips that will hold more paint

hair   animal hair used in brushes includes sable, goat, mongoose, badger, hog, ox, squirrel, pony

sabeline   ox hair dyed to resemble red sable

synthetic   man-made nylon or polyester filaments

taklon brushes   man-made filaments dyed and baked to make them softer and more absorbent

List 5–23   Types of Brushes

acid swab paste brush   for use in pasting, acids, solvents, etching, soldering

acrylic   usually nylon brushes that wash easily

air brushes   not actually a brush, but a spray attached to a generator that applies pigment evenly

bamboo   bristle brush in bamboo handle; used for calligraphy, watercolor, oriental-style painting

bright   flat ferrule brush with short filaments

bristle   firm hog bristle, cut straight across or slightly rounded; normally with flat ferrule

calligraphic   bamboo-handled brush used for calligraphy

camel hair   usually made of squirrel, goat, ox, pony, or a blend; not from camels

ceramic brushes   a variety of brushes to allow for painting specific details

duster   handled brush for removing dust and erasures

easel   long-handled, long-filament brush for use in the classroom

fan   flat ferrule with spread filaments; good for special effects in watercolor

faux finishing   specialty brushes for graining, glazing, blending, stippling, combing, and faux lines

filbert   flat ferrule, thick filaments, medium to long, with an oval end

fitch   long-handled brush with a round ferrule and chiseled sides

flat   square ended, medium to long bristles, in a flat ferrule

foam   flexible foam brush for wetting paper or applying acrylic finishes; sizes 1 to 4 inches

funny brush   rubber filaments in a plastic holder; for effects on trees, grass, hair, fur, or stippling

gilder's tip   soft camel hair brush for applying gold leaf; 4 inches wide × 2⅛-inches long

hake   an oriental-style wash brush on a long handle, cut straight across

lettering   long-haired brush that holds enough pigment to allow one-stroke lettering

ox hair   strong-bodied hair, often blended with other hairs for a finer tip

paste   short-handled nylon flat brush for applying school paste

pastel   short, fluffy pony-hair brushes for blending and applying pastels

sable   not necessarily from sable, but from any member of the weasel family

sabeline   ox hair dyed to resemble "sable" and sometimes blended with it

script   long, tapered, or flat brush for ornate script lettering

shader   short filament, full-bodied brush for blending

spotter   a brush for fine detail work such as spotting photographs

steel   actually a flexible wide pen nib for applying lines with ink

stencil   short-handled round brush with flat stiff bristles for stippling or stenciling

striping   a short-handled brush with *very* long bristles; "stripers" are flat, tapered, and pointed

Sumi   pointed brush of soft, dyed hair; set in bamboo or wooden handle

utility   natural bristle brushes ranging from 1 to 2 inches

varnish   extra-long hog bristle used for special effects in finishing

wash/mop   flat oval shape, full-bodied, camel hair; good for large areas in watercolor

watercolor   brushes range in size from smallest, 00, to largest, 14

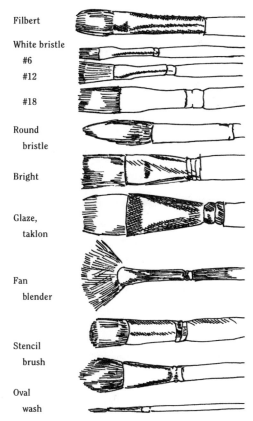

Filbert

White bristle

#6

#12

#18

Round
bristle

Bright

Glaze,
taklon

Fan
blender

Stencil
brush

Oval
wash

Spotter

List 5–24   Definitions Used in Printmaking

additive drawing   a direct painting onto glass or plastic that is then printed on paper

aquatint   a method of etching that relies on flecks of material such as sprinkled powdered resin or spray paint; used to prevent acid from eating away certain areas of a metal plate

artist's proof   proofs of work in progress, or a few finished proofs reserved for the use of the artist

baren   4½-inch circular tool used for pressing paper onto a plate for hand printing

bench hook   a metal or wooden plate with a raised edge to hold a woodcut or linocut in place on a table while cutting

block print   print made from wood, linoleum, or vinyl

brayer   a roller for transferring ink to the plate for printing

burin (graver)   an engraving tool with a wooden knob to fit the palm of the hand on one end and, on the other end, a point of a variety of shapes on the short steel rod

burnisher   a steel engraving tool with a curved end used for polishing the plate

burr   the metal fuzz left after a scratch is made into a metal plate; this may be left untouched and inked for richer blacks, or scraped off and the area burnished

collagraph   a collage-like assemblage built up on a surface such as masonite, wood, or matboard; it is then varnished, inked, and printed

drypoint   a technique of scratching directly into the plate with a needle; may be added after a plate is completely etched

embossing   damp paper is run through a press on an uninked plate, creating impressions in the paper, but no color

engraving   lines are cut into a metal plate with a V-shaped tool called a burin; ink is then forced into these lines and wiped from the surface of the plate, which is then printed

etching   a drawing is scratched through a wax-covered metal plate which is then placed in acid that eats into the scratched area

gouge   a tool for cutting a wood or linoleum block; V-shaped, U-shaped

hard ground   a waxy acid-resistant substance painted or rubbed and melted onto the etching plate; a design is scratched through it

inks   oil-based or water-based inks

intaglio printing   (an Italian term) the ink is deposited below the surface of the plate which has been corroded, scratched, or incised, and the surface wiped clean; a damp paper forced into the surface is printed

linocut   a relief print made when lines are cut into linoleum; the removed area remains white

mezzotint   very dark etching made with a tool that has many tiny points, sometimes called a rocker tool, or a roulette

mineral spirits   distillate from petroleum used for cleaning oil-based ink

monotransfer   turpentine put directly on fresh newspaper or magazine prints and placed on fresh paper, then burnished on the back with a pencil to transfer the prints to the clean paper

mordant   acid used in etching: nitric acid, hydrochloric acid, and ferric chloride

plate   the basis for a print—can be a wooden or linoleum block, cardboard collagraph, or metal

proofing   after a change is made on a plate, it is necessary to see what has been done before going to the next step

rainbow roll   placing three inks next to each other, then using a brayer to transfer them to a printing plate

reduction block print   one plate is printed several times, removing a portion and changing color each time (working from lightest to darkest)

registration   correctly aligning a printing plate when printing successive colors

slab of glass   used for mixing inks (usually has white paper kept under it)

soft ground   a waxy acid-resistant substance that is rubbed onto a warmed metal plate; it is sensitive to pressure, and materials may be pressed into the surface or a design drawn into it

stopping out   applying varnish to areas of a metal plate to prevent acid from etching; usually combined with aquatint

sugar-lift   a sugar-water solution painted onto a metal plate will crawl; when the solution is dry, a wax resist is painted on top and the sugar water removed; the plate is then immersed in acid to etch the open areas

wood engraving   a relief printing cut with engraving tools into end-blocks of wood, which are more dense than regular woodcut plates

woodcut   a relief print made by cutting away the surface of a wooden plate and printing the surface; the cutaway areas remain white

List 5–25   Things to Do in Printmaking with or Without a Press

Many of these projects can be done either with or without a printing press. Rubbing on the back of the paper with a baren or the back of a spoon or the flat of the hand gives a satisfactory effect.

COLLAGRAPHS

- Create a cityscape on a heavy cardboard base using various widths and textures of tape.
- Create a line design with string of various textures and sizes glued onto tagboard.
- Create a line design with white glue; let dry before inking.
- Cut up corrugated cardboard and glue to a plain corrugated background; varnish with polymer medium before printing.
- Glue a variety of textured cloths onto a masonite or matboard background to create an abstract design.
- Make a design of layers of tagboard, varnish with polymer medium, and then ink and print.
- Use string, modeling paste, leaves, and twigs to make an outdoor country scene.

FROTTAGE

- Stencil print with purchased stencils using sponges and tempera. Even using one stencil letter has great potential.
- Tape silk on the inside bottom of a hole cut in a small box lid. Block out part of the silk underneath, either with torn newsprint or lines formed with glue. Print it like silk-screen using a piece of matboard as a squeegee.
- Use crayon to rub textures (like you used to put paper on a coin and rub it with a pencil). Cut up the rubbing and combine with collage materials.

MONOTYPE (MONOPRINT)

- Change the surface of a plain, inked plate by drawing into it with stiff cardboard or a roller.
- Ink over tape or grasses on a plate. Remove these; then print the resulting linear design.
- Ink sheet glass or plastic, place paper on it, and draw the design on the back of the paper. Rub the paper in some places for more ink. This is basically a line design.
- Paint a design with black or colored ink on sheet plastic. Then place paper on it, rub on the back of the paper, and lift off the design.
- Spritz water, alcohol, or mineral spirits onto an inked or painted surface before printing on paper.
- Use a brayer to spread ink over a paper. Use the flat part or end of the brayer. Interrupt the line sometimes, or make a plaid by using different colors. Make circular designs by holding one end of a brayer in place while you swirl the other end.
- Use a dull pencil to draw on an inked brayer. You will get an unexpected pattern when it is rolled.

RELIEF PRINT

- Draw a design on a Styrofoam butcher's tray (with edges removed) with pencil. Ink the tray and print from it.
- Carve a design in sheet linoleum. What is cut away will remain white.
- Do a reduction print in linoleum by removing part of the plate each time you change color. Each time you have printed, cut away more of the plate; then print over the original print.
- Make an embossed surface by cutting a design in a linoleum block. Without inking, run dampened paper through a printing press on top of the plate.
- Pour plaster into a paper drinking cup. Let it set up and tear off the paper. Scratch designs into the top, bottom, and sides, and use it as a roller or stamp to print with it.

List 5–25   Continued

- Use a nail or carving tool to cut a design in wood for printing.
- Waterprinting is done by floating diluted oil-based ink on water, and floating paper on the surface. Block out areas of the paper with wax or rubber cement before printing.
- Grain printing is done by drawing on glass or fine sandpaper with a wax crayon; paper dampened with turpentine and blotted, is laid on top of the drawing, then the back of the paper is burnished to bring out the print.

STAMPING
- Carve a design into an eraser and stamp designs with it.
- Make a Chinese stamp by carving calligraphy characters into an eraser. Print it with red ink.
- Stamp with kitchen objects such as fork, potato masher, tin can, cookie cutters.
- Stamp with vegetables: onions, carrots, potatoes, green pepper.
- Use plasticine clay to form a stamp. Draw a calligraphy design with a toothpick. Print it with red ink.
- Use small pieces of shaped sponge to stamp designs. Change colors as you change shapes.
- Use your thumb and fingerprints on a stamp pad or paper towel soaked with tempera.

The following are specific projects you can do with a printing press.

INTAGLIO PRINT
- Change a plate by etching in acid: hard-ground, soft-ground, aquatint, needle-etching.
- Use a sharp needle to scratch a design into plastic or metal. Ink, then wipe the surface before printing, leaving ink in the incised lines.

MONOPRINT
- Paint a design directly on plastic with oil paint or ink. Then run it through the press with damp paper.
- Do a chine collé print by cutting or tearing fadeless, colored paper, putting library paste on the back, and placing the glued pieces face-side down on the inked plate under the white paper before running it through the press.

List 5–26   Miscellaneous Printing Techniques

- Print twice over the same print.
- Transform a print by accenting with ink, colored pencil, oil pastels, pencils, or paint.
- Try a rainbow roll by inking with two or three colors of ink. Transfer with the brayer to the plate.
- Overprint by printing a different design on top of a dry print.
- Before printing, change the surface of paper with a resist of candle wax.
- Do a ghost print by printing over a plate a second time without re-inking. Draw on it with colored pencil.

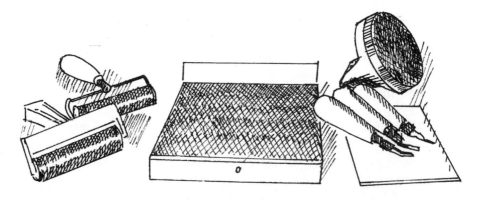

List 5–27   Materials and Equipment Used in Printmaking

COLLAGRAPHS

acrylic gel   a thicker, tackier glue than polymer medium used in collagraphs

acrylic medium   used as both a glue to hold things in place and a varnish

aluminum foil   glued to a collagraphic plate to give a texture

battleship gray linoleum   easy-to-carve linoleum, ⅛-inch thick

Flextex®   a textured material of marble dust and opaque white acrylic

gesso   can be applied with a palette knife to offer different textures

materials suitable are   cloth, organza, mylar® tape, aluminum foil, dried flower leaves, weeds, matchsticks, wires, raffia, seeds, beans, string, bark, feathers, rice paper, tissues, coffee, twigs

modeling paste   a stiff paste, sometimes made of marble dust; similar to gesso, but thicker

mylar   a very smooth metallic sheet that wipes clean for use in collagraphs

organza   a fine, thin material that holds ink well on a collagraphic plate

sandpaper of various grits   these offer different textures in a plate

tapes   bookbinding tapes, smooth tapes, and masking tape all hold ink differently

Drawn from *Black and White Numerals: Figure 7,* 1968, Jasper Johns, The St. Louis Art Museum

ETCHING

blankets   these felts, some hard, some softer, are used on top of the paper and plate to force the paper into textural differences on a printing plate

blotters   heavy, coarse white blotters to absorb excess water from etching paper

burin   a diamond-shaped steel blade in a wood holder used for engraving lines in a metal plate

burnisher   a smooth, slightly curved metal surface in a wooden handle for smoothing metal

burnishing roller   a brayer-type roller for applying pressure to the back of a monoprint

burnt plate oil   an oil used for thinning etching ink

etching ink   comes in tubes or cans in black and a variety of colors

etching needle   a fine, round steel point in a wooden holder

etching press   a mechanical flat bed with a steel roller through which printing plates and paper are forced under pressure to make a print

feather   used to gently remove bubbles formed by the biting action of the acid

gelatin or rubber brayer   a soft or hard circular roller for picking up ink and transferring it to a plate

ink daubers   felt compressed into a 1 × 3-inch roll held together with rubber bands to thoroughly apply ink

metal ruler   a 36-inch long ruler to assist in tearing etching paper into a desired size or shape

rolling pin   used to remove excess water from etching paper by rolling on top of blotters

scraper   a triangular metal blade in a wooden handle for shaving metal to bevel the edge or remove unwanted details from the surface

tarlatan   a heavily-starched cheesecloth-like material that is used for evenly distributing ink

LINOLEUM AND WOODCUT RELIEF PRINTS

baren   a round tool for applying pressure on the back of the paper for printing

block printing foam   soft material similar to meat trays; designs can be impressed with a pencil

brayers   rubber rollers for rolling in ink and applying ink to the plate

flexible printing plates   vinyl material that is soft, flexible, and easy to carve; both sides may be used; any shape can be cut; for use with water-based ink only

inking plate/bench hook   combination 7 × 9-inch metal plate to hook on edge of table for safely holding linoleum block in place while cutting; also may be used for inking

linoleum cutters and handles   special shapes for cutting various types of lines: liner, V-gouge, large line, U-gouge, knife; blades sold separately to be fitted into handles

plywood blocks   in various sizes used for woodcuts

wood-cutting tools   short-handled tools similar to those used in linoleum cutting

List 5–28 Materials and Equipment Used for Graphic Design

cutting knife   a necessity for cutting and paste-up

drafting brush   horse-hair brush for cleaning off excess erasure residue and dust

drafting tape   low-tack, easy-release adhesive masking tape for holding work in place

drawing templates   circles, ellipses, isometric ellipses, varied shapes, human figure, squares, lines at specific angles, lettering guides

erasers   electric eraser with removers for graphite and ink

flexible curve   vinyl plastic adjustable strip to aid in ink ruling

French curves   transparent plastic curves to aid in technical drawing

illustration supplies   paint, pastels, oil pastels, charcoal

light box   fluorescent light box for tracing and slide viewing

pencils   black lead, china marker, turquoise drawing (non-repro blue), charcoal, graphite, drawing, colored, watercolor

proportional scale   used to calculate proportional enlargements and reductions

protractor   plastic protractor in ½-degree graduation

spray adhesive   used for positioning elements for layout

T-square   wooden, metal, or plastic square from 18 to 36 inches long for making accurate lines

taboret   rolling set of drawers to hold drafting and graphic art supplies

technical pens   pens with permanent ink cartridges that come in a variety of widths and points

triangles   transparent triangle with double-bevel edge; used for accurate drawing 30/60° and 45/90°

tweezers   special tweezers for handling pieces of paper for paste-up

List 5–29   Things to Do in Graphic Design

- Combine a photograph with an appropriate typeface to create a magazine ad for something in the photo.
- Create a black-and-white advertisement for an artist or event (premier or opening) that uses only space and type, yet still effectively catches the eye.
- Create a complete department or specialty store packaging line, including gift boxes, a shopping bag, and small sacks. Unify with the name, logo, and color.
- Design a CD cover using plasticine clay. This can then be photographed and enlarged through color laser-printing to fit within the box cover.
- Design a contemporary postage stamp. As an alternative, design a 4-block stamp in which each part contributes to the whole.
- Design a logo for a business, and make necessary changes to apply it to a business card, stationery, building sign, and parking sticker.
- Design a new format for a magazine or newspaper. Decide how wide columns will be, whether you will use color, what the new typeface will be.
- Design a paperback bookcover for a classic piece of literature—from taste to trash in one step!
- Design a public service poster to promote your favorite cause (environment, antiwar, save the whales, etc.).
- Design a textured one-color advertising brochure for a business, such as a ranch, pet shop, or fast-food restaurant. Use an X-acto® knife to cut designs, curling, folding, and making surface differences that would be visible when photographed.
- Design an artwork to advertise a local business to be photographed on a slide for projection at a local movie theater.
- Do a portrait illustration of a famous person for a national news magazine cover using clay, wire, collage, cut paper, or other sculpture material. Then photograph it.
- Do an advertisement for a piece of sports equipment such as a tennis racquet or special shoes where the equipment dominates the page.
- Utilize a reproduction of an existing artwork from a catalogue and incorporate it into a magazine or TV advertisement.
- Use acrylic paint to design a reusable bookcover on plastic to hide trashy book covers.

SECTION 6
SCULPTURE

List 6–1   Quotations About Sculpture

"There is a right physical size for every idea."

—HENRY MOORE

"Simplicity is not a goal, but one arrives at simplicity in spite of oneself, as one approaches the real meaning of things."

—CONSTANTIN BRANCUSI

"Brancusi, like the Japanese, would take the quintessence of nature and distill it. Brancusi showed me the truth of materials."

—ISAMU NOGUCHI

"The Human Body is the mirror of the soul, and it is from this fact that it derives its greatest beauty."

—AUGUSTE RODIN

"Above all, sculpture is a conquest of space, a space that is delineated by forms."

—HENRI LAURENS

"My work is a very specific fight against specific fears, one at a time. It comes close to a defining, an understanding and accepting, of fear."

—LOUISE BOURGEOIS

"I have made my world and it is a much better world than I ever saw outside."

—LOUISE NEVELSON

"Whatever the artist makes is always some kind of self-portrait."

—MARISOL

"It is easy. You just chip away the stone that doesn't look like David." (Michelangelo in explaining how he made his statue of David.)

—MICHELANGELO

"One must work, nothing but work, and one must have patience."

—AUGUSTE RODIN

"In modern work, the spectator has to bring with him more than half the emotion."

—ALEXANDER CALDER

"True strength is delicate."

—LOUISE NEVELSON

"A good statue can be rolled down hill without damage."

—MICHELANGELO

List 6–2   Things to Do in Sculpture

Sculpture techniques are listed below. The techniques and tools vary considerably depending on the material used.

ASSEMBLAGE

- Buy plastic scraps of various thicknesses, sawing and sanding the edges. Use colored light below to allow the color to reflect on the edges.
- Collect natural materials such as bones, (pine) cones, and stones, and use wire or a glue gun to attach them to each other. Or assemble them within a frame to unify them.
- Create a bas-relief design using one sheet of foamboard, cutting out and reassembling the design. Add sand to acrylic paint and paint in one color.
- Create a wire figure in action; tack it to a board, then wrap the figure in sculpt-tape®; paint or stain.
- Interpret a painting three-dimensionally. Use cardboard, sculpt-tape®, and other found materials.
- Make a sculpture of *units* of manufactured materials for sculpture: items such as cotton balls, cotton swabs, foam cups, foam balls, toothpicks, or straws.
- Make units such as cubes, triangles, or pyramids from paper. Group and glue these units together.
- Use sheet plastic and plastic dowels to create a sculpture, cutting pieces with a saw, and joining with plastic cement or epoxy glue.
- Use the inside of a shallow box (preferably wood) as the base for a box-sculpture, using maps, paper, and found objects. Attach with a glue gun; cover with plexiglass before hanging.
- With sculpt-tape®, cover an armature made of taped newspaper or tagboard to create an animal or human form.
- Wood scraps may be purchased (or donated) from a carpentry shop. Assemble these with glue, painting if desired with acrylic paint.

CARVING TECHNIQUES

- Carve a design in a paraffin block.
- Carve a sculpture from firebrick with rasps, knives, and coarse sandpaper.
- Carve large pieces of Styrofoam® packing material with a heated blade; finish with rasps; paint.
- Carve or incise designs on shells and bones.
- Create a carved "shop sign" for yourself or a friend, combining the name with a symbol such as glasses or a shoe.
- Create three variations of a simple geometric form in three different materials such as wax, plaster, and wood. Combine them.
- Find a piece of wood in nature and change it by sawing, weaving, removing, or adding something to it to create an entirely new form.
- Fragment and reassemble an object by sawing it in slices, then gluing it slightly "off."
- Get a 2- to 3-inch thick candle and carve a design-in-the round on it with a knife. Antique with acrylic burnt umber; wipe off the excess.
- If you have access to electrical tools, create a sculpture only by sawing a piece of wood or only by drilling; or only by working on the lathe.
- Interpret a tree or another natural object in a bas-relief sculpture. If a carving "mistake" is made, natural objects are "forgiving," where something such as a realistic portrait is not.
- Mix plaster with vermiculite and pour into a milk carton; carve with a knife or plaster rasps.
- Soap-carving is age-old, but continues to be a good introduction to carving, as it demonstrates the technique of removing only small amounts of material at a time.
- Use slate for a bas-relief sculpture, carving with stone tools, rasps, and sandpaper.

CASTING TECHNIQUES

- Create a clay model, make a plaster mold from it, and then cover the mold with paper pulp.
- Do a sand-casting in a box (or at the beach). Make a pattern in damp sand, pour plaster, and allow it to harden. Put a large paper clip in the back while not completely set to hang this on the wall.
- Grind cotton linters (for papermaking) in a blender; drain through a sieve; pat the pulp into a plaster or plastic mold.

List 6–2   Continued

- Make a bas-relief by creating a design in oil-based or ceramic clay, building up the sides to make a shallow tray, and pouring plaster into it.
- Make a plaster model of your hand in a greased shoebox by pouring in a 2-inch layer of plaster and doing half your hand one day and the other half the next day. Grease the first mold before reinserting your hand. Join the two greased hardened halves together and pour plaster inside the mold. After it hardens, open the mold.
- Mix and pour plaster into a plastic bag, holding the bag against your body until it sets (remember you have to be able to remove it from your body after it hardens). Smooth and shape with rasps and sandpaper.

MODELING TECHNIQUES

- Assemble several pieces of Styrofoam® with dowels to hold them together, then shape. Cover with plaster. Use rasps and sandpaper to smooth plaster if desired.
- Create a clay portrait head by making an egg shape and putting it on a neck. After it is carved, hollow it out to a 1-inch thickness, leaving an opening in the bottom.
- With ½ pound of oil clay, interpret a *word* such as "calm," "angry," "sad," or a word of your choice such as "love." Avoid the trite or obvious, and think of the mood you are showing in sculpture.
- With ceramic or oil clay, create a human form in a seated position, with arms held close to the body or head.

List 6–3   Sculpture Definitions

academic sculptors   sculptors who interpret forms in the classical tradition

annealed wire   wire that has already been heated for easy bending

armature   a base made of wire, iron, cardboard, or sticks for supporting modeling clay

assemblage   a sculpture created of related or unrelated materials

bas-relief   literally low-relief; a three-dimensional sculpture to be seen only from the front

bruise   if a stone is hit incorrectly, it may rearrange molecules deep inside that will cause it to break

Carrara   a quarry in Italy that is used today for fine marble, even as it was in Michelangelo's time

carving   removing material from a surface such as wood, stone, or plaster

casting   pouring liquid such as molten metal, plaster, polyester resin, or clay into a mold

form   a three-dimensional shape, such as the human form or an abstract form

hardwood   woods that drop their leaves, such as maple, walnut, ash

maquette   a small preliminary model for a sculpture

modeling stand   a revolving chest- or eye-level stand for supporting clay while modeling

monumental   literally a monument to someone; a large sculpture; or the *idea* of a large sculpture

moulage   a rubberized material to place on face or hands for making a reusable mold for plaster

negative space   the interior space or space that surrounds a piece of sculpture; lets air into it

polyester casting resin   liquid material that is mixed and, when cast into a mold, hardens clear

quarry   a place where sculpture materials are mined

roughing out   removing the extraneous material from a carving surface prior to refining

softwood   wood with needles, such as pine, fir; easier to carve, but splinters easily

Twisteeze wire®   plastic-coated copper wire for jewelry and sculpture

wire bending jig   small metal or wooden form that holds wire while it is being bent

List 6–4   Materials for Sculpture: Assemblage, Carving, Casting, Modeling

ASSEMBLAGE

found materials   metal, twigs, cardboard, electrical parts, clock parts, cloth, wood scraps, bones, frames

plaster gauze   plaster-impregnated strips that may be further cut, dipped in water, and used to make sculpture; originally developed for use in casts for broken limbs

CARVING

alabaster   soft material usually white or veined with gray; takes a fine polish, translucent

Balsa Foam®   soft plastic foam easily carved with ceramic loop tools or knife

carving wax   this wax may be carved for jewelry or small investment casting

clay   Indian red, white sculpture, raku, clay with grog, white talc, stoneware clay

firebrick   inexpensive beige porous brick, quite soft, may be finished with rasps or knives

limestone   porous gray or beige stone that is relatively easy to carve and finish

marble   more difficult to carve, takes a high polish

plaster of Paris (gypsum)   a quick-setting white powder that is mixed with water; the addition of vermiculite makes carving much easier

soapstone   easy-to-carve stone that finishes to a high polish; gray, green, or off-white

Styrofoam® blocks   these blocks may be carved

Styrofoam® cutter   heated-wire cutters for Styrofoam®; electrical or battery operated

vermiculite   available at garden supply shops; lightweight filler; mix with plaster for easier carving

CASTING

Crea-Stone®   a refined form of plaster of Paris; may be carved or cast

hand-made paper pulp   created by grinding paper and/or cotton linters in a blender

hydrocal   slower setting than plaster of Paris, and has a less porous surface; can be carved

hydrostone   hardest of the gypsum plasters; five times the strength of plaster of Paris; not for carving

plaster of Paris   gypsum in powder form; when mixed with water it quickly hardens

MODELING

Celluclay®   instant papier-mâché powder

microcrystalline wax   soft brown wax that softens in warm water or with handling, for building on an armature; may be cast, or simply left in the wax form

Model Magic®   a soft white dough compound that is clean, easily molded, and may be painted

modeling dough   reusable dough similar to Play-doh®; hardens when exposed to air

Ovencraft clay®   may be fired in a 350° oven for one hour; may be painted or stained

paperclay   pulp-based white modeling clay; paint may be added prior to modeling

plasticine modeling clay   an oil-based clay that never hardens; comes in colors; reusable

Sculp-metal®   looks and handles like clay, but air hardens into metal that can be burnished to give an aluminum-like finish; the surface can be enhanced through metallic sprays

Sculpey®   modeling compound that remains pliable until it is baked

self-hardening clays   air-dried projects resemble kiln-fired ceramics and may be painted or stained

List 6–5   Hardwoods, Leaf-Bearing Trees

Hardwoods are from broadleaf trees such as ash, oak, or walnut, and have greater density than the "softwoods," making them a little more difficult to work with. Their beautiful close grain and patterns make them the ideal choice for sculpture.

apple	cherry	lignum vitae	oak, white
ash, brown	cherry, black	lime	pear
ash, white	chestnut	magnolia	poplar
balsa	cottonwood	mahogany, Honduras	rosewood
basswood	ebony	mahogany, Philippine	sycamore
beech	elm	mahogany, West African	walnut, English
birch	gum, red	maple, hard	willow
black walnut, American	hickory	maple, soft	zebrawood
butternut	holly	oak, red	

Drawing from *The Three Trees*, Rembrandt, 1643

List 6–6   Softwoods, Cone-Bearing Trees

Softwoods are coniferous trees that have a simpler cell structure, and are more porous than hardwoods. They are slightly easier to carve, but the grain is not so appealing as that of hardwoods.

balsam	cypress	pine, yellow longleaf	pine, sugar
cedar	fir, Douglas	pine, northern white	redwood
cedar, Tennessee red	fir, white	pine, ponderosa	spruce

List 6–7   Tools and Equipment for Sculpture

GENERAL PURPOSE TOOLS

bastard file   flat file used for straight or curved edge and surface filing

C-clamps   clamps shaped like a C that greatly vary in size; used for holding material for carving

center punch   used for beginning a hole to be drilled

compass saw   used for cutouts of curved shapes in wood or plywood

drawknife   a two-handled blade that allows you to shape wood quickly

drill (electric or hand)   used to create openings when carving

file cleaner   stiff wire brush for cleaning dust from files

finishing files   all-purpose files with various shapes for finishing wood, stone, plaster, and metal

hacksaw   a handsaw used primarily for cutting metal

miter box   a guide for using a saw to cut angles accurately in wood or metal; used in framing

perforated rasps   "open" rasps, used for plaster and soft stone such as alabaster or soapstone

rasps   round, flat, half-round, plane-type, or perforated textured tools with handles

rifflers   finishing tools for carving; varied angles and shapes on both ends of a steel shaft for reaching and finishing hard-to-reach areas

saber saw   cutting tool for Styrofoam®, wood, brass, wire and nails

scriber   tempered steel marker with fine points

sharpening stone   used with oil for honing the edges of chisels

vise   adjustable piece of equipment that holds work firmly while it is worked on; fits on a table

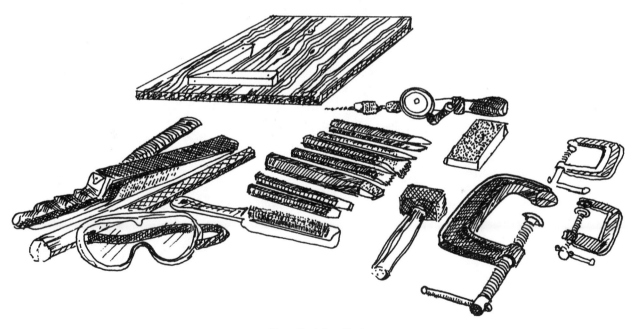

Stone Sculpture Tools

CASTING EQUIPMENT

mixing bowls and scraper   pliable bowls for mixing plaster; quick cleaning

rubber mold-making kit (for casting rubber molds)   molds that are easily removed and reusable

EQUIPMENT FOR CLAY MODELING

clay extrusion tool   tube with interchangeable tips for making unusual decorative details with clay

fettling knife   long-bladed knife especially for carving clay

List 6–7   Continued

EQUIPMENT FOR CLAY MODELING (cont.)

greenware files   flexible files for cleaning greenware before firing; also for low-fire clay

loop tools   these have loops made of heavy stainless steel ribbon in various shapes

modeling tools   plastic or boxwood tools for creating detail in clay sculpture

sgraffito and clean-up tool set   tools of varied shapes for cleaning hard-to-reach places

straight needle   needle in handle for throwing, decorating, or leveling a thrown pot

STONE-CARVING TOOLS AND EQUIPMENT

bush hammer   textured-face hammer for rounding stone and giving a texture to surface

flat chisel   metal chisel with a straight-across broad head for a fine finish

point chisel   metal chisel that comes to a point; different sizes from ¼ to ½ inch

powdered pumice   a fine powder used with cloth and water for final polishing

sand bags   canvas bags filled with sand for supporting sculpture while carving

stone hammer   short-handled iron hammer for use with iron stone-carving tools

stone rasps   flat rasps with curved surface lines for smoothing stone

tooth chisel   metal chisel with a broad head with numerous points; many sizes available

wet and dry sandpaper   paper that comes in different grit densities; used wet for polishing stone or metal

WOOD-CARVING TOOLS AND MATERIALS

bent gouge (sometimes called spoon gouge)   has a spoon-like end; available in deep and shallow

bent knife   the blade is bent almost at a right angle

chisel   flat-bladed tool for carving, used with a mallet

coping saw   a saw with a deep neck and fine blade; may be used for interior cuts after a hole is drilled

dividers   tool similar to calipers for checking on symmetry

gouge   a carving tool with a rounded blade; gouges come with ⅛- to 1-inch tips

mallet   a specially shaped tool for pounding on chisels to remove wood; often made of lignum vitae, the hardest wood

palm-grip carvers   handles are rounded and the blade is short; suitable for wood relief

parting tool   a V-shaped tool used for cutting lines and corners

rasps   round, flat, half-round tools with handles; used for finishing prior to sanding

salmon bend gouge   the entire blade is like a scoop, sizes from 1/16 to ¾ inches

sharpening slips   stones of various sizes and shapes to use with oil for sharpening chisels and gouges

Wood Sculpture Tools

skew chisel   the end of a skew chisel is angled; a bent skew chisel has a spoon-like curve at the end

vise   an adjustable clamp for a workbench that will hold wood for carving in place

whittling knife   a knife with a short blade, sometimes at a right angle for whittling

wood carver's adz   long-handled double-edged for roughing out a log

wood chisels   wood- or plastic-handled steel tools for carving

List 6–8   Safety Reminders for Sculpture

- Always find a way to secure an object for carving: a vise, sandbag, C-clamps, a wood-carver's bench screw, or a V-board (made by screwing two 2 × 4-inch boards at right angles on a large base of plywood that you could either sit upon or clamp to a table).
- Never hold something between your legs for carving; chisels can slip!
- Don't use solvents or chemicals where there are flames.
- Lock chemicals and solvents in a metal cabinet.
- Never work by yourself in a room. Have a buddy system in case you need help.
- When carving with sharp tools, always wear goggles or a mask.
- When using electrical equipment such as a drill, band-saw, sander, table saw or torch, wear goggles or a mask, push sleeves above elbows, tie back long hair, and remove all jewelry.
- When working with materials such as foam, poured urethane, or other material with a strong odor, wear a mask and pour in the evening so fumes can dissipate.

List 6–9   Survey of Sculpture: Important Works of Art

AFRICAN

Head of Queen Olokun, Ife, c. 11th–15th century AD, Nigeria, British Museum, London

Leopard, c. 16th–17th century AD, British Museum, London

Portrait of a Yoruba of Ancient Ife, c. 15th century, British Museum, London

Princess, Benin c. 14th–16th century AD, Nigeria, British Museum, London

AMERICAN

American Colonial Sculpture

Grasshopper Weathervane, 1749, Shem Drowne, Faneuil Hall, Boston, Massachusetts

Gravestone of John Foster, 1681, unknown artist, Dorchester, Massachusetts

Indian Weathervane, 1716, Shem Drowne, Province House, Boston, Massachusetts

Little Admiral, c. 1750, unknown sculptor (possibly Shem Drowne), Old State House, Boston, Massachusetts

American Revolutionary Period

Agriculture, Liberty, and Plenty, 1791, John and Simeon Skillin, Jr., Yale University Art Gallery, New Haven, Connecticut

Andrew Jackson, 1834, John Frazee, Art Museum, Princeton University, Princeton, New Jersey

Benjamin Franklin, 1778, Jean-Antoine Houdon, St. Louis Art Museum, Missouri

Benjamin Franklin, 1785–1790, William Rush (attributed), Historical Society of Delaware, Wilmington

Benjamin Franklin and *George Washington,* (wax busts), c. 1725, Patience Lovell Wright, Maryland Historical Society, Baltimore

Governor John Winthrop, 1798, Samuel McIntire, American Antiquarian Society, Worcester, Massachusetts

Hope, c. 1790, attributed to John and Simeon Skillin, Jr., Henry Francis du Pont Winterthur Museum, Winterthur, Delaware

Sacred Cod, date unknown, John Welch, Boston State House, Boston, Massachusetts

Thomas Jefferson, 1785, J. A. Houdon, New York Historical Society, New York City

The American Period of Expansion

Andrew Jackson, 1835, Hiram Powers, Metropolitan Museum of Art, New York City

Baltimore Washington Monument, 1814–1842, Robert Mills, Baltimore, Maryland

Daniel Webster, 1858, Hiram Powers, State House, Boston, Massachusetts

George Washington, 1814, William Rush, Philadelphia Museum of Art, Pennsylvania

George Washington, 1832–1841, Horatio Greenough, Smithsonian Institution, Washington, DC

The Greek Slave, 1843, Hiram Powers, Yale University Art Gallery, New Haven, Connecticut

John Trumbull, 1834, Robert Ball Hughes, Yale University Art Gallery, New Haven, Connecticut

Schuylkill Freed, c. 1828, William Rush, Philadelphia Museum of Art, Pennsylvania

Water Nymph and Bittern, c. 1828, William Rush, Philadelphia Museum of Art, Pennsylvania

American Victorian Sculpture

Bacchante and Infant Faun, 1894, Frederick MacMonnies, Philadelphia Museum of Art, Pennsylvania

List 6–9   Continued

AMERICAN (cont.)

American Victorian Sculpture (cont.)

Daphne, 1854, Harriet Hosmer, Washington University Gallery of Art, St. Louis, Missouri

George Washington, 1883, John Quincy Adams Ward, Federal Hall National Memorial, New York City

Minute Man, 1889, Daniel Chester French, Concord, Massachusetts

Nydia, the Blind Girl of Pompeii, 1895, Randolph Rogers, Pennsylvania Academy of Fine Arts, Philadelphia

Roma, 1869, Anne Whitney, Wellesley College Museum, Wellesley, Massachusetts

The White Captive, 1859, Erastus Dow Palmer, Metropolitan Museum of Art, New York City

Zenobia, 1858, Harriet Hosmer, Metropolitan Museum of Art, New York City

American Modern Sculpture

Dancer and Gazelles, 1916, Paul Manship, Corcoran Gallery of Art, Washington, DC

End of the Trail, 1915, James Earle Fraser, Brookgreen Gardens, South Carolina

Hostess, 1918, Elie Nadelman, Hirshhorn Museum and Sculpture Garden, Washington, DC

In Advance of a Broken Arm, 1915, Marcel Duchamp, Yale University Art Gallery, New Haven, Connecticut

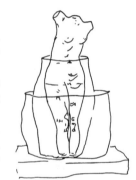

Study for *Delusions of Grandeur,* 1967, René Magritte

Lincoln, 1908, John Gutzon Borglum, Washington, DC

Lincoln, 1922, Daniel Chester French, Lincoln Memorial, Washington, DC

Man in the Open Air, 1915, Elie Nadelman, Museum of Modern Art, New York City

Woman Combing Her Hair, 1915, Alexander Archipenko, Museum of Modern Art, New York City

Young Lincoln, 1927, Lorado Taft, Urbana, Illinois

American Sculpture Between the Wars

Cloud, 1939, José de Creeft, Whitney Museum of American Art, New York City

Figure, 1926–1930, Jacques Lipchitz, Museum of Modern Art, New York City

Floating Figure, 1935, Gaston Lachaise, Museum of Modern Art, New York City

Gertrude Stein, 1920, Jo Davidson, Whitney Museum of American Art, New York City

Handlebar Riders, 1935, Chaim Gross, Museum of Modern Art, New York City

Indian Hunter with Dog, 1926, Paul Manship, Metropolitan Museum of Art, New York City

Kneeling Figure, 1935, Robert Laurent, Whitney Museum of American Art, New York City

Lobster Trap and Fish Tails, 1939, Alexander Calder, Museum of Modern Art, New York City

American Mid-Twentieth-Century Sculpture

An American Tribute to the British People, 1960–1965, Louise Nevelson, Tate Gallery, London

One and Others, 1955, Louise Bourgeois, Whitney Museum of American Art, New York City

Sacrifice II, 1948, Jacques Lipchitz, Whitney Museum of American Art, New York City

Pop Art Sculpture

Ale Cans, 1960, Jasper Johns, collection of Dr. Peter Ludwig, New York City

Cinema, 1963, George Segal, Albright-Knox Gallery, Buffalo, New York

Corridor, 1967, Lucas Samaras, Los Angeles County Museum of Art, California

Clothespin, 1976, Claes Oldenburg, Philadelphia, Pennsylvania

Cubi XIX, 1964, David Smith, Tate Gallery, London

Fur-Lined Teacup, 1936, Meret Oppenheim, Museum of Modern Art, New York City

Pony, 1959, Ellsworth Kelly, Dayton's Gallery 12, Minneapolis, Minnesota

Soft Giant Drum Set, 1967, Claes Oldenburg, collection of Kimiko and John G. Powers, New York City

Target with Four Faces, 1955, Jasper Johns, Museum of Modern Art, New York City

Three Way Plug, Scale A, Prototype in Blue, 1971, Claes Oldenburg, Des Moines Art Center, Iowa

Two Cheeseburgers with Everything, 1962, Claes Oldenburg, Museum of Modern Art, New York City

American Expressionist Sculpture

Bird E-Square Bird, 1958–1966, Isamu Noguchi, collection of Mr. Carl E. Solway, Cincinnati, Ohio

Camel VII, Camel VI, Camel VIII, 1968–1969, Nancy Graves, National Gallery of Canada, Ottawa

Depression Bread Line, 1991, George Segal, Sidney Janis Gallery, New York City

Labyrinth, 1974, Robert Morris, Institute of Contemporary Art, Philadelphia, Pennsylvania

Medici Slot Machine, 1942, Joseph Cornell, Solomon R. Guggenheim Museum, New York City

Object to Be Destroyed, 1958, Man Ray, metronome and photograph, collection of Morton G. Neumann, Chicago, Illinois

Praise for Elohim Adonai, 1966, Mark De Suvero, St. Louis Art Museum, Missouri

Reclining Figure: Angles, 1979, Henry Moore, collection of Patsy and Raymond Nasher, Dallas, Texas

List 6–9   Continued

American Expressionist Sculpture (cont.)

Rush Hour, 1983, George Segal, Sidney Janis Gallery, New York City

Sitting Bull, 1959, Peter Voulkos, Santa Barbara Museum of Art, California

The State Hospital, 1966, Edward Keinholz, Moderna Museet, Stockholm

The Wait, 1964–1965, Edward Keinholz, Whitney Museum of American Art, New York City

Times Square Sky, 1962, Chryssa, Walker Art Center, Minneapolis, Minnesota

Torso, 1930, Gaston Lachaise, Whitney Museum of American Art, New York City

Untitled, 1969, Donald Judd, Hirshhorn Museum and Sculpture Garden, Washington, DC

American Environmental Art

Double Negative, 1969–1971, Michael Heizer, Virgin River Mesa, Nevada

Hart Plaza, 1980, Isamu Noguchi, Detroit, Michigan

Isla de Umunnum, The Mound, 1986–1990, Heather McGill and John Roloff, Estuarine Research Reserve, California

Mill Creek Canyon Earthworks, 1982, Herbert Bayer, Kent, Washington

Revival Field, 1990–present, Mel Chin, St. Paul, Minnesota

Spiral Jetty, 1970, Robert Smithson, Great Salt Lake, Utah

The City, Complex One, 1972–1974, Michael Heizer, Central Eastern Nevada

American Sculpture with Light

Head with Blue Shadow, 1965, Roy Lichtenstein, collection of Patsy and Raymond Nasher, Dallas, Texas

Ohayo, 1986, Judy Pfaff, Holly Solomon Gallery and Max Protetch Gallery, New York City

Pergusa, 1981, Frank Stella, collection of Holly Hunt Thackberry, Winnetka, Illinois

Pink and Gold, 1968, Dan Flavin, Museum of Contemporary Art, Chicago, Illinois

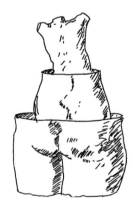

René Magritte, study for the sculpture *Delusions of Grandeur,* 1967

American Post Modern

Extravaganza Televisione, 1984, Kenny Scharf, Tony Shafrazi Gallery, New York City

Self Portrait with Sculpture, 1980, John De Andrea, collection of Foster Goldstrom, San Francisco, California

Women, 1985, Magdalena Abakanowicz, Xavier Fourcade, Inc., New York City

AUSTRIA
Prehistoric

Venus of Willendorf, c. 25,000–20,000 BC, Museum of Natural History, Vienna

BELGIUM

Baptismal Font, 1107–1118, Rene de Huy, St. Barthlemy, Liege, Belgium

CHINA

Bactrian Camel with Packsaddle, c. 700–755 AD, Nelson-Atkins Museum of Art, Kansas City, Missouri

Divine Winged Animal, 220–420 AD, Hebei Research Institute of Cultural Relics, China

Elephant, c. 1122–249 BC, Freer Gallery of Art, Washington, DC

Four Ladies of the Court Playing Polo, 650–700 AD, Nelson-Atkins Museum of Art, Kansas City, Missouri

Musicians, 618–906 AD, T'ang Dynasty, Rietberg Museum, Zurich

Stone Mythical Creatures (18 pairs), 1368–1644 AD, Ming tombs, near Beijing, China

Tomb effigies (men and horses), c. 246–210 BC, Xian, China

EGYPT

Chefren, c. 2530 BC, Egyptian Museum, Cairo

Colossal Statues of Ramesses II, 1275 BC, Abu Simbel, Egypt

Gold Coffin Cover of Tutankhamen, c. 1340 BC, Egyptian Museum, Cairo

Mycerinus and Queen, c. 2470 BC, Museum of Fine Arts, Boston, Massachusetts

Narmer's Palette, c. 3000 BC, Egyptian Museum, Cairo

Nefertiti, c. 1375–1357 BC, Dahlem Museum, Berlin

Prince Rahotep and His Wife, Nofret, c. 2580 BC, Egyptian Museum, Cairo

Rosetta Stone, 196 BC, British Museum, London

Seated Scribe, c. 2400 BC, Louvre, Paris

Great Sphinx, c. 2500 BC, Giza, Egypt

ENGLAND

Family Group, 1947, Henry Moore, The British Council, London

Head (Elegy), 1952, Barbara Hepworth, University of Nebraska Art Gallery, Lincoln

Internal and External Forms, 1953–1954, Henry Moore, Elm Wood, Albright-Knox Art Gallery, Buffalo, New York

FRANCE
Prehistoric

Bison, c. 15,000–10,000 BC, Les Eyzies

Venus of Laussel, 25,000–20,000 BC, Dordogne

List 6–9 Continued

FRANCE (cont.)
Romanesque

Four Figures (the ancestors of Christ?), c. 1150, Chartres Cathedral, West front, Chartres

Northern Renaissance Sculpture

Portal of the Chartreuse de Champmol, 1391–1397, Claus Sluter, Dijon

Virgin and Child, 14th century, artist unknown, Victoria and Albert Museum, London

Well of Moses, 1395–1403, Claus Sluter, Dijon

Neo-Classical Sculpture

George Washington, 1788–1792, Jean Antoine Houdon, State Capitol, Richmond, Virginia

La Marseillaise, 1833–1836, François Rude, Arc de Triomphe de l'Etoile, Paris

"Impressionist" Sculpture

Balzac, 1897, Auguste Rodin, Hirshhorn Museum and Sculpture Garden, Washington, DC

Burghers of Calais, 1884–1886, Auguste Rodin, Hirshhorn Museum and Sculpture Garden, Washington, DC

Jeanette III, 1910–1913, Henri Matisse, Museum of Modern Art, New York City

Little Dancer of Fourteen Years, 1840–1845, Edgar Degas, St. Louis Art Museum, Missouri

The Gates of Hell, 1840–1845, Auguste Rodin, Musée Rodin, Paris

The Three Shades, 1880, Auguste Rodin, Musée Rodin, Paris

The Walking Man, 1877, Auguste Rodin, National Gallery of Art, Washington, DC

Modern Sculpture

Be in Love, You Will Be Happy, 1901, Paul Gauguin, Museum of Fine Arts, Boston, Massachusetts

Bell and Navels, 1931, Jean Arp, the Museum of Modern Art, New York City

Bottle Rack (ready-made), 1914, Marcel Duchamp, (original lost), Galeria Schwarz, Milan

Cock, c. 1932, Pablo Picasso, Tate Gallery, London

Horse, 1914, Raymond Duchamp-Villon, Art Institute of Chicago, Illinois

La Riante Contre, Theatres de Memoirs, Jean Dubuffet, 1975–1978, collection of Arne and Milly Glimcher, New York City

The Serpentine, 1909, Henri Matisse, Museum of Modern Art, New York

GERMANY

Ekkehard and Uta, c. 1245–1260, Naumburg Cathedral, Naumberg

Pieta, early 14th century, Provinzialmuseum, Bonn

The Gero Crucifix, c. 975–1000 AD, Cathedral, Cologne

GREECE OR MYCENAE

"Agamemnon" Gold Mask, c. 1500 BC, National Museum, Athens

Alexander the Great, 2nd century BC, Acropolis Museum, Athens

Apollo Belvedere, 4th or 1st century BC, Vatican Museums, Rome

Calf Bearer, c. 570 BC, Acropolis Museum, Athens

Study for Sculpture, *Delusions of Grandeur,* 1967

Caryatid Figures, 421–409 BC, Acropolis Museum, Athens

Charioteer of Delphi, c. 470 BC, Delphi

Cyclades Statuettes, c. 3000 BC, National Museum, Athens

Discus Thrower (Discobolus), c. 450 BC, National Museum, Rome

Dying Gaul, c. 230–220 BC, Capitoline Museums, Rome

Dying Warrior, c. 490 BC, Staatliche Museum, Munich, Germany

Elgin Marbles (from the Parthenon), 432 BC, British Museum, London

Hera of Samos, c. 565 BC, Louvre, Paris

Kore from Chios, c. 520 BC, Acropolis Museum, Athens

Kouros of Sounion, c. 600 BC, National Archaeological Museum, Athens

Kritios Boy, c. 480 BC, Acropolis Museum, Athens

Lion Gate, c. 1250 BC, Mycenae, Greece

Medusa, c. 600–580 BC, Archaeological Museum, Corfu

Nike of Samothrace (Winged Victory), c. 200 BC, Louvre, Paris

Poseidon, c. 460–450 BC, National Museum, Athens

Rosetta Stone, 196 BC, British Museum, London

Snake Goddess, c. 1600 BC, Museum, Heraklion, Crete

Spear Bearer, c. 450–440 BC, Polykleitos, National Museum, Naples

The Rampin Head, c. 560 BC, Louvre, Paris

Three Goddesses, c. 438–432 BC, British Museum, London

Vaphio Cups, c. 1500 BC, National Museum, Athens

Venus de Milo, c. 150 BC, Louvre, Paris

ITALY
Etruscan

Apollo of Veii, c. 515–490 BC, Villa Giulia, Rome

Belvedere Torso, 1st century BC, Vatican Museums, Rome

Boy Removing a Thorn, c. 200 BC–AD 27, Capitoline Museums, Rome

Bronze Boxer, 1st century BC, National Museum, Rome

Romulus and Remus, 15th century, Capitoline Museums, Rome

List 6–9   Continued

Etruscan (cont.)

Sarcophagus from Ceveteri, c. 520 BC, Villa Giulia, Rome
She-Wolf, c. 500–480 BC, Capitoline Museums, Rome

Early Italian Sculpture

Ara Pacis, 13–9 BC, Rome
Augustus of Prima Porta, c. 20 BC, Vatican Museums, Rome
Aulus Metellus (L'Arringatore), early 1st century BC, Archaeological Museum, Florence
Constantine the Great (bust), 325–326 AD, Palazzo dei Conservatori, Rome
Equestrian Statue of Marcus Aurelius, 161–180 AD, Piazza del Campidoglio, Rome
Laocoön, 1st century AD, Vatican Museums, Rome (copy of Greek original)
Philippus the Arab, c. 244–249 AD, Vatican Museums, Rome
Portrait of a Lady, c. AD 90, Capitoline Museums, Rome

Italian Romanesque Sculpture

Crucifixion, c. 1087, nave fresco, Sant' Angelo in Foris, near Capua

Italian Renaissance Sculpture

David, c. 1430–1432, Donatello, National Museum, Florence
David, 1501–1504, Michelangelo, Galleria dell'Accademia, Florence
Equestrian Monument of Bartolomeo Colleoni, c. 1483–1488, Andrea del Verrocchio, Venice
Gates of Paradise, c. 1435, Lorenzo Ghiberti, Baptistery, Florence
Gattemelata (Equestrian Statue of Erasmo da Narni), c. 1445–1450, Donatello, Padua
Hercules and Antaeus, c. 1475, Antonio Pollaiuolo, Museo Nazionale, Florence
Madonna and Child, c. 1455–1460, Luca della Robbia, Florence
Moses, Michelangelo, c. 1513–1515, St. Peter in Chains, Rome
Pieta, Michelangelo, 1499–1500, St. Peter's, Vatican, Rome
Saltcellar of Francis I, 1539–1543, Benvenuto Cellini, Kunsthistorisches Museum, Vienna

Delusions of Grandeur, René Magritte, 1967, bronze sculpture

Tomb of Lorenzo and Giuliano de Medici, 1524–1534, Michelangelo, Florence

Italian Baroque Sculpture

Apollo and Daphne, 1622–1624, Gianlorenzo Bernini, Galleria Borghese, Rome

David, 1623, Gianlorenzo Bernini, Galleria Borghese, Rome
Ecstasy of Saint Theresa, 1645–1652, Gianlorenzo Bernini, Sta. Maria della Vittoria, Rome
Rape of Proserpina, 1621–1622, Gianlorenzo Bernini, Galleria Borghese, Rome

Italian Neo-Classical Sculpture

Pauline Borghese as Venus, 1788–1792, Antonio Canova, Borghese Gallery, Rome
The Three Graces, 1813, Antonio Canova, Hermitage, St. Petersburg, Russia

Italian Modern Sculpture

Caught Hand, 1932, Alberto Giacometti, The Alberto Giacometti Foundation, Kunsthaus, Zurich
Development of a Bottle in Space, 1912, Umberto Boccioni, collection of Harry L. Winston, New York City
Head, c. 1913, Amedeo Modigliani, Tate Gallery, London
Horseman, 1947, Marino Marini, Tate Gallery, London
The City Rises, 1910–1911, Umberto Boccioni, Museum of Modern Art, New York City
The Table, 1932, Alberto Giacometti, Musée National d'Art Moderne, Paris

JAPAN

Amida Buddha, c. 1053, Jocho, Byodo-in, near Kyoto
Haniwa (figure), 6th century AD, Tokyo National Museum
Kuya Preaching, c. 1207, Kosho, Rokuhara Mitsu-ji, Kyoto

MEXICO

Chac Mool, the Rain Spirit, 948–1697 AD, Museo Nacional de Antropologia, Mexico City
Colossal Head, c. 900–500 BC, Olmec, La Venta Park, Tabasco
Colossi at Tula, 12th–13th centuries, Toltec, near Mexico City
Dog, 500 BC–AD 1521, from Colima, Museo Nacional de Antropologia, Mexico City
Mask of Green Serpentine, c. 800–1200 AD, Toltec, National Gallery of Art, Washington, DC
Rock Crystal Carved Skull, c. 1324–1521, Aztec, British Museum, London

ANCIENT NEAR-EASTERN ART

Assyrian Human-Headed Winged Lion, 883–859 BC, Metropolitan Museum of Art, New York City
Billy Goat and Tree (Ur), c. 2600 BC, University Museum, Philadelphia, Pennsylvania
Darius and Xerxes Giving Audience, c. 490 BC, Treasury, Persepolis, Iran
Gold Rhyton (cup), 5th–3rd century BC, Archaeological Museum, Teheran

List 6–9   Continued

ANCIENT NEAR-EASTERN ART (cont.)

Head of Gudea, 2150 BC, Neo-Sumerian, Museum of Fine Arts, Boston, Massachusetts

Lion Gate, 1400 BC, Boghazkoy, Turkey

Stele of Hammurabi, c. 1760 BC, Louvre, Paris

NORWAY

Animal Head from the *Oseberg* Ship-Burial, c. AD 825, University of Antiquities, Oslo

ROMANIA

Bird, 1912, Constantin Brancusi, Philadelphia Museum of Art, Pennsylvania

Mlle. Pogany, 1913, Constantin Brancusi, Museum of Modern Art, New York City

Mlle. Pogany (Version II), 1919, Constantin Brancusi, Solomon R. Guggenheim Museum, New York City

Mlle. Pogany, 1920, Constantin Brancusi, Albright Art Gallery, Buffalo, New York

Sleeping Muse, 1910, Constantin Brancusi, Musée National d'Art Moderne, Paris

Torso of a Young Man, 1925, Constantin Brancusi, Hirshhorn Museum and Sculpture Garden, Washington, DC

RUSSIA

Construction Suspended in Space, 1952, Naum Gabo, Baltimore Museum of Art, Maryland

Construction in an Egg, 1948, Antoine Pevsner, Albright-Knox Art Gallery, Buffalo, New York

Head of a Woman, 1916–1917, Naum Gabo, Museum of Modern Art, New York City

SPAIN

Venus de Milo with Drawers, 1936, Salvador Dali, Gallerie du Dragon, Paris

Head of Fernande Olivier, 1909, Pablo Picasso, Hirshhorn Museum and Sculpture Garden, Washington, DC

SWITZERLAND

Endless Loop I, 1947–1949, Max Bill, Hirshhorn Museum and Sculpture Garden, Washington, DC

Homage to New York, 1960, Jean Tinguely, Museum of Modern Art, New York City

OTHER

Stone Images, c. 17th century, Easter Island

List 6–10 Master Sculptors and Examples of Their Work

BERNINI, GIANLORENZO, 1598–1680, ITALY

Costanza Buonarelli, c. 1645, Bargello, Florence

Ecstasy of St. Theresa, 1645–1652, Sta. Maria della Vittoria, Rome

Fountain of the Four Rivers, 1648–1651, Piazza Navona, Rome

BOURGEOIS, LOUISE, 1911, AMERICA (b. FRANCE)

Cell (Eyes and Mirrors), 1989–1993, Tate Gallery, London

Cell II, 1991, Carnegie Museum of Art, Pittsburgh, Pennsylvania

Femme Voltage, 1951, Solomon R. Guggenheim Museum, New York City

Le Defi, 1992, Solomon R. Guggenheim Museum, New York City

Mortise, 1950, National Gallery of Art, Washington, DC

Nature Study, 1984, Whitney Museum of American Art, New York City

Sleeping Figure, 1950, Museum of Fine Arts, Boston, Massachusetts

Spiral Woman, 1951–1952, Miller Gallery, New York City

BRANCUSI, CONSTANTIN, 1876–1957, ROMANIA

Bird in Space, 1928, Museum of Modern Art, New York City

Bird in Space, 1940, Peggy Guggenheim Collection, Venice, Italy

Mlle. Pogany, 1913, Philadelphia Museum of Art, Pennsylvania

The Kiss, 1909, Montparnasse Cemetery, Paris

Torso of a Young Man, 1924, Hirshhorn Museum and Sculpture Garden, Washington, DC

BUTTERFIELD, DEBORAH, 1949, AMERICA

Horse # 6–82, 1982, Dallas Museum of Art, Texas

Horse # 9–82, 1982, collection of Ethan and Sherry Wagner

Resting Horse, 1977, Whitney Museum of American Art, New York City

Small Horse, 1977, private collection

CALDER, ALEXANDER, 1898–1976, AMERICA

Circus, mixed media, 1932, Whitney Museum of American Art, New York City

The Crab, stabile, 1962, Museum of Fine Arts, Houston, Texas

Flamingo, stabile, 1974, Federal Center Plaza, Chicago, Illinois

Lobster Trap and Fish Tails, 1939, Museum of Modern Art, New York City

Red, Black and Blue, 1967, Dallas-Fort Worth Airport, Dallas, Texas

David, Verrocchio, c. 1476, Bargello, Florence

CHRISTO (JAVACHEFF), 1935, AMERICA (b. BULGARIA)

Package on Wheelbarrow, 1963, Museum of Modern Art, New York City

Strip-tease (empaquetage), 1963, private collection

Surrounded Islands, Biscayne Bay, drawing, 1983, private collection, New York City

CORNELL, JOSEPH, 1903–1972, AMERICA

Isabelle (Dien Bien Phu), 1954, St. Louis Art Museum, Missouri

Medici Slot Machine, 1942, collection of Mr. and Mrs. Bernard J. Reis, New York City

Soap Bubble Set, 1950, Art Institute of Chicago, Illinois

Space Object Box, 1959, Allan Stone Gallery, New York City

DEGAS, EDGAR, 1834–1917, FRANCE

Dressed Ballerina, 1920, Metropolitan Museum of Art, New York City

The Masseuse, c. 1896–1911, Hirshhorn Museum and Sculpture Garden, Washington, DC

Prancing Horse, 1865–1881, Hirshhorn Museum and Sculpture Garden, Washington, DC

DONATELLO, 1386?–1466, ITALY

David, c. 1430–1432, Bargello, Florence

Mary Magdalene, c. 1454–1455, San Lorenzo Baptistery, Florence

St. George, c. 1415–1417, Bargello, Florence

Zuccone, 1423–1425, Campanile, Florence Cathedral, Florence

List 6–10 Continued

GIACOMETTI, ALBERTO, 1901–1966, SWITZERLAND

Hands Holding the Void, 1934–1935, St. Louis Art Museum, Missouri

Man Pointing, 1947, Museum of Modern Art, New York City

GRAVES, NANCY, 1940–1995, AMERICA

Fayum, 1982, Knoedler Gallery, New York City

Fought Cight Cockfight, 1984, St. Louis Art Museum, Missouri

Zaga, 1983, Nelson-Atkins Museum of Art, Kansas City, Missouri

GROOMS, RED, 1937, AMERICA

City of Chicago, 1967, Art Institute of Chicago, Illinois

Discount Store, 1970, collection of Norman Braman, Miami, Florida

Loft on 26th Street, 1965–1966, Hirshhorn Museum and Sculpture Garden, Washington, DC

Mr. and Mrs. Rembrandt, 1971, Cheekwood Art Museum, Nashville, Tennessee

Ruckus Manhattan: A Sculptural Novel, 1976, collection of the artist, New York City

HANSON, DUANE, 1925–1996, AMERICA

Motorcycle Accident, 1969, Gallery of Contemporary Art, Portland, Oregon

Museum Guard, 1976, Nelson-Atkins Museum of Art, Kansas City, Missouri

The Seated Artist, 1972, collection of Byron and Eileen Cohen, Mission Hills, Kansas

Tourists, 1970, National Gallery of Modern Art, Edinburgh

Woman with Dog, 1977, Whitney Museum of American Art, New York City

HEPWORTH, BARBARA, 1903–1975, ENGLAND

Assemblage of Sea Forms, 1972, Norton Simon Inc. Foundation, Los Angeles, California

Doves, 1927, Manchester City Art Gallery, England

Pelagos, 1946, Tate Gallery, London

Single Form (Memorial to Dag Hammerskjould), 1962–1963, United Nations Bldg., New York City

LIPCHITZ, JACQUES, 1891–1973, AMERICA (b. LITHUANIA)

Figure, 1926–1930, Norton Simon Inc. Foundation, Los Angeles, California

Man With Guitar, 1916, Museum of Modern Art, New York City

Prometheus Strangling the Vulture, 1944–1953, Walker Art Center, Minneapolis, Minnesota

Still Life With Musical Instruments, 1918, estate of the artist

MAILLOL, ARISTIDE, 1861–1944, FRANCE

The River, 1939–1943, Norton Simon Inc. Foundation, Los Angeles, California

Summer, 1910, National Gallery of Art, Washington, DC

Venus With the Necklace, 1928–1929, St. Louis Art Museum, Missouri

MARISOL (ESCOBAR), 1930, AMERICA (b. COLOMBIA)

The Bicycle Race, 1962–1963, The Harry N. Abrams Family Collection, New York City

The Family, 1962, Museum of Modern Art, New York City

The Generals, 1961–1962, Albright-Knox Art Gallery, Buffalo, New York

John Wayne, 1907–1979, 1963, Colorado Springs Fine Arts Center, Colorado

The Party, 1965–1966, collection of Mrs. Robert Mayer, Winnetka, Illinois

MATISSE, HENRI, 1869–1954, FRANCE

The Back, I–IV, 1909–c. 1929, Hirshhorn Museum and Sculpture Garden, Washington, DC

Luxe, Calme et Volupte, 1904–1905, Musée d'Orsay, Paris

Seated Nude, 1925, Art Institute of Chicago, Illinois

MICHELANGELO (BUONARROTI), 1475–1564, ITALY

David, 1501–1504, Galleria dell'Accademia, Florence

Medici Tombs, 1519–1534, San Lorenzo, Florence

Moses, c. 1513–1515, St. Peter in Chains, Rome

Pieta, 1498–1499, St. Peter's, Rome

The Rebellious Slave, 1513–1516, Louvre, Paris

MOORE, HENRY, 1898–1986, ENGLAND

Draped Seated Woman, 1957–1958, Hebrew University, Jerusalem

Fallen Warrior, 1956–1957, Hirshhorn Museum and Sculpture Garden, Washington, DC

Reclining Figure, 1929, Leeds City Art Galleries, England

Reclining Mother and Child, 1960–1961, Walker Art Center, Minneapolis, Minnesota

Recumbent Figure, 1938, Tate Gallery, London

The King and Queen, 1952–1953, Hirshhorn Museum and Sculpture Garden, Washington, DC

List 6–10 Continued

Drawn from *Flying Dragon*, 1975, Alexander Calder, The Art Institute of Chicago

NEVELSON, LOUISE, 1899–1988, AMERICA (b. RUSSIA)

An American Tribute to the British People, 1960–1965, Tate Gallery, London

Black Chord, 1964, collection of Joel Ehrenkranz, New York City

New Continent, 1962, St. Louis Art Museum, Missouri

Sun Garden, No. 1, 1964, collection of Mr. and Mrs. Charles M. Diker, New York City

Transparent Sculpture VI, 1967–1968, Whitney Museum of American Art, New York City

OLDENBURG, CLAES, 1929, AMERICA

Giant Ice Bag, 1969–1970, Thomas Segal Gallery, Boston, Massachusetts

Lipstick Ascending on Caterpillar Tracks, 1969, Yale University Art Gallery, New Haven, Connecticut

Soft Giant Drum Set, 1967, collection of Kimiko and John G. Powers, New York City

Soft Pay Telephone, 1963, collection of William Zierler, New York City

Soft Toilet, 1966, collection of Mr. and Mrs. Victor W. Ganz, New York City

The Stove, 1962, private collection

PICASSO, PABLO, 1881–1973, SPAIN

Baboon and Young, 1951, Museum of Modern Art, New York City

Head of a Woman, 1909, Art Institute of Chicago, Illinois

Horse, 1967, Art Institute of Chicago, Illinois

The Goat, 1950, Musée Picasso, Paris

Woman With a Baby Carriage, 1950, Hirshhorn Museum and Sculpture Garden, Washington, DC

REMINGTON, FREDERIC, 1861–1909, AMERICA

Coming Through the Rye, 1902, Art Museum, Princeton University, Princeton, New Jersey

The Bronco Buster, 1895, St. Louis Art Museum, Missouri

The Cheyenne, 1901, Denver Art Museum, Colorado

Trooper of the Plains, 1909, National Cowboy Hall of Fame and Western Heritage Center, Oklahoma City, Oklahoma

RODIN, AUGUSTE, 1840–1917, FRANCE

Balzac, 1840–1845, Hirshhorn Museum and Sculpture Garden, Washington, DC

Burghers of Calais, 1884–1886, Hirshhorn Museum and Sculpture Garden, Washington, DC

Eve, 1881, Musée Rodin, Paris

The Gates of Hell, 1840–1845, Musée Rodin, Paris

She Who Was Once the Helmet Maker's Beautiful Wife, 1888, Musée Rodin, Paris

SAAR, BETYE, 1926, AMERICA

Bessie Smith Box, 1974, collection of Monique Knowlton, New York City

Imitation of Life, 1975, collection of the artist

Indigo Mercy, 1975, Studio Museum in Harlem, New York City

Veil of Tears, 1976, collection of Mr. and Mrs. Alvin P. Johnson

SEGAL, GEORGE, 1924, AMERICA

The Bus Driver, 1962, Museum of Modern Art, New York City

Cinema, 1963, Albright-Knox Art Gallery, Buffalo, New York

The Dancers, 1971, National Gallery of Art, Washington, DC

The Gas Station, 1963–1964, National Gallery of Canada, Ottawa

SMITH, DAVID, 1906–1965, AMERICA

Agricola, 1951, Hirshhorn Museum and Sculpture Garden, Washington, DC

Cockfight, 1945, St. Louis Art Museum, Missouri

Cubi I, 1963, Detroit Institute of Arts, Michigan

Medals for Dishonor, 1937–1940, Hirshhorn Museum and Sculpture Garden, Washington, DC

Voltri-Bolton, 1962, Museum of Fine Arts, Boston, Massachusetts

Zig, 1960, Lincoln Center, New York City

List 6–11   Famous Sculptors, Listed by Country

Some American sculptors may also be listed in the countries from which they immigrated.

AMERICA

Adams, Herbert, 1858–1945
Africano, Nicholas, 1948
Akers, B. Paul, 1825–1861
Andre, Carl, 1935
Archipenko, Alexander, 1887–1964, b. Russia
Arneson, Robert, 1930–1993
Artschwager, Richard, 1924
Augur, Hezekiah, 1791–1858
Aycock, Alice, 1946
Baizerman, Saul, 1889–1957, b. Russia
Ball, Thomas, 1819–1911
Barnard, George Grey, 1863–1938
Bartholomew, Edward Sheffield, 1822–1858
Bartlett, Paul Wayland, 1865–1925
Baskin, Leonard, 1922
Bell, Larry, 1939
Benglis, Lynda, 1941
Bertoia, Harry, 1915–1978
Bitter, Karl, 1867–1915
Bladen, Ronald, 1918–1988, b. Canada
Bochner, Mel, 1940
Borglum, Gutzon, 1867–1941
Borglum, Solon H., 1868–1922
Borofsky, Jonathan, 1942
Bourgeois, Louise, 1911, b. France
Brenner, Michael, 1885–1969, b. Lithuania
Brenner, Victor D., 1871–1924
Browere, John H.I., 1790–1834
Brown, Henry Kirke, 1814–1886
Burton, Scott, 1939
Butterfield, Deborah, 1949
Calder, A. Stirling, 1870–1945
Calder, Alexander Milne, 1846–1923
Calder, Alexander, 1898–1976
Callery, Mary, 1903–1977
Ceracchi, Giuseppi, 1751–1802
Chamberlain, John, 1927
Christo (Javacheff), 1935, b. Bulgaria
Chryssa, 1933
Clevenger, Shobal Vail, 1812–1843
Coffee, William John, 1744–c.1846
Cogdell, John, 1778–1847
Conner, Bruce, 1933
Cornell, Joseph, 1903–1972
Crawford, Thomas, 1813?–1857
Creeft, José de, 1884–1982, b. Spain
Dallin, Cyrus, 1861–1944
Davidson, Jo, 1883–1952
De Maria, Walter, 1935
Dexter, Henry, 1806–1876
di Suvero, Mark, 1933

Dodge, Charles J., 1806–1886
Duchamp, Marcel, 1887–1968, b. France
Duff, John, 1943
Eberle, Abastenia St. Leger, 1878–1942
Epstein, Jacob, 1880–1959
Faggi, Alfeo, 1885–1966, b. Italy
Ferber, Herbert, 1906–1991
Fiene, Paul, 1899–1949
Flavin, Dan, 1933
Foley, Margaret, 1820–1877
Frank, Mary, 1933
Fraser, James Earl, 1876–1953
Frazee, John, 1790–1852
French, Daniel Chester, 1850–1931
Gabo, Naum, 1890–1977, b. Russia
Gallo, Frank B., 1933
Gilhooly, David, 1943
Goodnough, Robert, 1917
Grafly, Charles, 1862–1929
Graham, Robert, 1938
Graves, Nancy, 1940–1995
Greene, Gertrude, 1911–1956
Greenough, Horatio, 1805–1852
Greenough, Richard, 1819–1904
Grooms, Red, 1937
Gross, Chaim, 1904–1991, b. Austria
Grosvenor, Robert, 1937
Hamilton, Ann, 1956
Hampton, James, 1909–1964
Hanson, Duane, 1925–1996
Hare, David, 1917–1992
Hart, Joel Tanner, 1810–1877
Harvey, Eli, 1860–1957
Haseltine, Herbert, 1877–1962
Heizer, Michael, 1944
Hesse, Eva, 1936–1970, b. Germany
Hoffman, Malvina, 1887–1966
Holland, Tom, 1936
Holzer, Jenny, 1950
Hosmer, Harriet, 1830–1908
Hudson, Robert, 1938
Hughes, Robert Ball, 1806–1868
Hunt, Bryan, 1947
Hunt, Richard, 1935
Huntington, Anna Hyatt, 1876–1973
Indiana, Robert, 1928
Irwin, Robert, 1928
Ives, Chauncey, 1810–1894
Jennewein, Carl Paul, 1890–1978
Johns, Jasper, 1930
Jones, Thomas Dow, 1811–1891

Drawing after *Fought Cight Cockfight,* Nancy Graves, 1984, St. Louis Art Museum

List 6–11   Continued

Judd, Donald, 1928–1994
Kelly, Ellsworth, 1923
Kemeys, Edward, 1843–1907
Kienholz, Edward, 1927–1994
Kiesler, Frederick, 1896–1965, b. Austria
Kiester, Steve, 1949
Konti, Isidore, 1862–1938
Koons, Jeff, 1925
Lachaise, Gaston, 1882–1935, b. France
Laessle, Albert, 1877–1954
Lassaw, Ibram, 1913, b. Egypt
Laurent, Robert, 1890–1970, b. France
LeVa, Barry, 1941
Lee, Arthur, 1881–1961
Lewis, Edmonia, 1845–c. 1909
LeWitt, Sol, 1928
Lichtenstein, Roy, 1923
Lipchitz, Jacques, 1891–1973, b. Lithuania
Lippold, Richard, 1915
Lipton, Seymour, 1903–1986
Lombard, James, 1865–1920
MacMonnies, Frederick, 1863–1937
MacNeil, Hermon Atkins, 1866–1947
Manship, Paul, 1885–1966
Marisol (Escobar), 1930, b. Colombia
Mason, John, 1927
McIntire, Samuel, 1757–1811
McKillop, Edgar Alexander, 1878–1950
Mills, Clark, 1815–1883
Moore, Bruce, 1905–1980
Moore, Henry, 1898–1986
Morris, George L.K., 1905–1975
Morris, Robert, 1931
Moses, Thomas, 1844–1917
Nadelman, Elie, 1882–1946, b. Poland
Nakian, Reuben, 1897–1986
Nauman, Bruce, 1941
Nevelson, Louise, 1899–1988, b. Russia
Niehaus, Charles, 1855–1935
Noguchi, Isamu, 1904–1988
Oldenburg, Claes, 1929, b. Sweden
Olitski, Jules, 1922
Oppenheim, Dennis, 1938
Paik, Nam June, 1932, b. Korea
Palmer, Erastus Dow, 1817–1904
Partridge, William Ordway, 1861–1930
Pepper, Beverly, 1924
Pfaff, Judy, 1946
Piccirilli Attilio, 1866–1945
Potter, Edward, 1857–1923
Powers, Hiram, 1805–1873
Pratt, Bela, 1867–1917
Price, Kenneth, 1935
Proctor, A. Phimister, 1860–1950
Puryear, Martin, 1941

Rauschenberg, Robert, 1925
Ray, Man, 1890–1977
Remington, Frederic, 1861–1909
Rhind, John Massey, 1860–1936
Rickey, George, 1907
Rimmer, William, 1816–1879, b. England
Rinehart, William, 1825–1874
Rivera, José de, 1904
Rivers, Larry, 1923
Robb, Samuel Anderson, 1851–1928
Robus, Hugo, 1885–1964
Rogers, John, 1829–1904
Rogers, Randolph, 1825–1892
Roszak, Theodore, 1907–1981, b. Poland
Ruckstull, Frederic Wellington, 1853–1942
Rush, William, 1756–1833
Russell, Charles M., 1864–1926
Saar, Betye, 1926
Saint-Gaudens, Augustus, 1848–1907, b. Ireland
Samaras, Lucas, 1936, b. Greece
Sampson, Charles A. L., 1825–1881
Savage, Augusta, 1892–1962
Schamberg, Morton L., 1881–1918
Scott, Tim, 1937
Segal, George, 1924
Serra, Richard, 1939
Shapiro, Joel, 1941
Shaw, Richard, 1941
Simmons, Franklin, 1839–1913
Simonds, Charles, 1945
Skillin, John, 1746–1800
Skillin, Simeon Jr., c. 1756–1806
Skillin, Simeon Sr., 1716–1778
Smith, David, 1906–1965
Smith, Tony, 1912–1980
Smithson, Robert, 1938–1973
Sonnier, Keith, 1941
Stankiewicz, Richard, 1922–1983
Steinberg, Saul, 1914
Stella, Frank, 1936
Stone, Sylvia, 1928
Storrs, John, 1885–1956
Story, William Wetmore, 1819–1895
Sugarman, George, 1912
Surls, James, 1943
Taft, Lorado, 1860–1931
Therrien, Robert, 1947
Thiebaud, Wayne, 1920
Thorwaldsen, Bertel, 1768–1844
Trova, Ernest, 1927
Truitt, Anne, 1921
Tucker, William, 1935
Turrell, James, 1943
Tuttle, Richard, 1941

Two Circle Sentinel,
1961, David Smith,
Museum of Fine Arts,
Houston

List 6–11   Continued

AMERICA (cont.)

Volk, Leonard, 1828–1895
Vonnoh, Bessie Potter, 1872–1955
Voulkos, Peter, 1924
Ward, John Quincy Adams, 1830–1910
Warner, Olin Levi, 1844–1896
Weber, Max, 1881–1961, b. Russia
Weinman, Adolph A., 1870–1952, b. Germany
Westermann, H.C., 1922
Wharton, Margaret, 1943
Whitney, Anne, 1821–1915
Whitney, Gertrude Vanderbilt, 1877–1942
Wickey, Harry, 1892–1968
Wiley, William T., 1937
Wilmarth, Christopher, 1943
Winsor, Jackie, 1941
Wolfe, James, 1944
Wright, Patience Lovell, 1725–1786
Young, Mahonri, 1877–1957
Yunkers, Adja, 1900–1943
Zorach, William, 1889–1966, b. Lithuania

BELGIUM

Bury, Pol, 1922
Magritte, René, 1898–1967

DENMARK

Thorwaldsen, Bertel, 1768–1844

ENGLAND

Annesley, David, 1936
Armitage, Kenneth, 1916
Butler, Reg, 1913–1981
Caro, Anthony, 1924
Chadwick, Lynn, 1914
Deacon, Richard, 1949
Epstein, Jacob, 1880–1959
Goldsworthy, Andrew, 1956
Gormley, Antony, 1950
Hepworth, Barbara, 1903–1975
King, Philip, 1934
Long, Richard, 1945
Moore, Henry, 1898–1986
Scott, Tim, 1937
Tucker, William, 1935

FRANCE

Arp, Jean, 1887–1966
Bourdelle, Emile-Antoine, 1861–1929
Brancusi, Constantin, 1876–1957, b. Romania
Degas, Edgar, 1834–1917
Dubuffet, Jean, 1901–1985
Duchamp, Marcel, 1887–1968
Duchamp-Villon, R., 1876–1918
Ernst, Max, 1891–1976

Gauguin, Paul, 1848–1903
Guimard, Hector, 1867–1942
Houdon, Jean Antoine, 1741–1828
Lachaise, Gaston, 1882–1935
Laurens, Henri, 1885–1954
Maillol, Aristide, 1861–1944
Matisse, Henri, 1869–1954
Pevsner, Antoine, 1884–1962, b. Russia
Picabia, Francis, 1879–1953
Rodin, Auguste, 1840–1917
Rude, François, 1784–1855
Saint-Phalle, Niki de, 1930

GERMANY

Barlach, Ernst, 1870–1938
Beuys, Joseph, 1921–1986
Ernst, Max, 1891–1976
Horn, Rebecca, 1944
Moholy-Nagy, Lázló, 1895–1946, b. Hungary
Schwitters, Kurt, 1887–1948
von Hildebrand, Adolph, 1847–1921

ITALY

Bernini, Gianlorenzo, 1598–1680
Boccioni, Umberto, 1882–1916
Canova, Antonio, 1757–1822
Donatello, (Donato di Niccolo), 1386?–1466
Marini, Marino, 1901–1980
Michelangelo, (Buonarroti), 1475–1564
Modigliani, Amedeo, 1884–1920
Pollaiuolo, Antonio, 1429?–1498
Rosso, Medardo, 1858–1928
Verrocchio, Andrea del, 1435–1488

LITHUANIA

Lipchitz, Jacques, 1891–1973

NORWAY

Vigeland, Gustave, 1869–1943

RUSSIA

Gabo, Naum, 1890–1977
Pevsner, Antoine, 1886–1962
Tatlin, Vladimir, 1885–1953

SPAIN

Gonzales, Julio, 1876–1942
Miró, Joan, 1893–1983
Picasso, Pablo, 1881–1973

SWITZERLAND

Bill, Max, 1908–1995
Giacometti, Alberto, 1901–1966
Oppenheim, Meret, 1913–1985, b. Germany

List 6-12 American Sculpture Parks

Some of these parks are devoted only to sculpture, and include permanent and temporary installations. Many are affiliated with and adjacent to museums. Only a few large commercial sculpture parks have been included.

ALABAMA

Charles Ireland Sculpture Garden, Birmingham Museum of Art, 2000 Eighth Avenue N., Birmingham

ARIZONA

Arlene Dunlop Smith Garden, 312 N. Granada, Tucson

Tempe Arts Center and Sculpture Park, Tempe

CALIFORNIA

Art Center College of Design Sculpture Garden, 1700 Lida St., Pasadena

B. Gerald Cantor Rodin Sculpture Garden, Stanford Museum, Stanford

B. Gerald Cantor Sculpture Gardens, Los Angeles County Museum of Art, 5905 Wilshire Blvd., Los Angeles

California Scenario and South Coast Plaza, San Diego Freeway at Bristol St., Costa Mesa

Clos Pegase Sculpture Garden, 106 Dunaweal Lane, Calistoga

Djerassi Sculpture Garden, 2325 Bear Gulch Rd., Woodside

Edwards Garden, Museum of Contemporary Art, San Diego, 700 Prospect St., La Jolla

Franklin D. Murphy Sculpture Garden, University of California, 10899 Wilshire Blvd., Los Angeles

Living Memorial Sculpture Garden, Weed

Napa/De Rosa/Preserve, 5200 Carneros Hwy., Napa

Norton Simon Museum Sculpture Garden, Colorado and Orange Grove Blvds., Pasadena

Oakland Museum Sculpture Garden, 1000 Oak St., Oakland

Stuart Collection, University of California, San Diego Campus, La Jolla

COLORADO

Benson Park Sculpture Garden, 29th and Aspen Dr., Loveland

Colorado Springs Fine Art Center Sculpture Courtyard and Sculpture Garden, 30 West Dale, Colorado Springs

Museum of Outdoor Arts, Greenwood Plaza, 7600 E. Orchard Rd., Englewood

CONNECTICUT

Aldrich Museum of Contemporary Art, 258 Main St., Ridgefield

DISTRICT OF COLUMBIA

Hirshhorn Museum and Sculpture Garden, Independence Ave. at 8th St., SW, Washington, DC

FLORIDA

Ann Norton Sculpture Gardens, Inc., 253 Barcelona Rd., West Palm Beach

Artpark, The Art Museum at Florida International University, 107th Ave. and SW 8th, Miami

HAWAII

The Contemporary Museum Sculpture Garden, 2411 Makiki Heights Dr., Honolulu

IDAHO

Kagan Sculpture Garden, 206 Chocolate Gulch, Ketchum

ILLINOIS

Cedarhurst Sculpture Park, Richview Rd., Mount Vernon

Nathan Manilow Sculpture Park, Governors State University, University Park

Skokie Northshore Sculpture Park, McCormick Blvd. between Main and Dempster, Skokie

IOWA

Des Moines Art Center, 4700 Grand Ave., Des Moines

KANSAS

Edwin A. Ulrich Museum of Art, Wichita State University, Wichita

Johnson County Community College Sculpture Collection, Gallery of Art, 12345 College Blvd., Overland Park

MARYLAND

Janet and Allen Wurtzburger and Ryda and Robert H. Levi Sculpture Gardens, Baltimore Museum of Art, Art Museum Dr., Baltimore

Sculpture at Quiet Waters, Anne Arundel County Department of Recreation and Parks, 600 Quiet Waters Rd., Annapolis

MASSACHUSETTS

Butler Sculpture Park, 481 Shunpike Rd., Sheffield

Decordova and Dana Museum and Park, Sandy Pond Rd., Lincoln

MICHIGAN

Cranbrook Educational Community, 1221 N. Woodward Ave., Box 801, Bloomfield Hills

Frederick Meijer Gardens, 3411 Bradford NE, Grand Rapids

Sculpture, February, 1996. This list was compiled by the International Sculpture Center and used with permission. For more information, contact the I.S.C. at 1050 17th St., Suite 250, Washington, DC 20036.

List 6–12   Continued

MINNESOTA

General Mills Art Collection Sculpture Program, 1 General Mills Blvd., Minneapolis

Minneapolis Sculpture Garden, Hennepin and Lyndale Aves., Minneapolis

St. Paul Cultural Garden, 1120 Norwest Center, St. Paul

MISSOURI

The E.F. Pierson Sculpture Garden and the Kansas City Sculpture Park, Nelson-Atkins Museum of Art, 4525 Oak Street, Kansas City

Laumeier Sculpture Park, 12580 Rott Rd., St. Louis

NEBRASKA

Prairie Peace Park, Dale/Crete Exit, Lincoln

Sheldon Sculpture Garden, Sheldon Art Center, University of Nebraska, 451 North 12th St., Lincoln

NEW JERSEY

Burlington County College, County Route 530, Pemberton

Grounds for Sculpture, 18 Fairground Rd., Hamilton

John B. Putman, Jr. Memorial Collection, The Art Museum, Princeton University, Princeton

Newark Museum Sculpture Garden, 49 Washington St., Newark

NEW MEXICO

Lightning Field (Walter De Maria's 400 stainless steel poles), Dia Center for the Arts, Corales

Nedra Matteucci's Fenn Galleries, 107 Paseo de Peralta, Santa Fe (commercial)

Shidoni Gallery and Sculpture Garden, Tesuque (commercial)

NEW YORK

Abby Aldrich Rockefeller Sculpture Garden, Museum of Modern Art, 11 West 53rd St., New York City

Donald N. Kendall Sculpture Garden, PepsiCo World Headquarters, Purchase

Griffis Sculpture Park, 6902 Mill Valley Rd., East Otto

Iris and B. Gerald Cantor Roof Garden, Metropolitan Museum of Art, 5th Avenue at 82nd St., New York City

Kykuit Gardens, Kykuit Visitor Center at Philipsburg Manor, North Tarrytown

Nassau County Museum of Art, 1 Museum Dr., Rosslyn Harbor

The Noguchi Garden Museum, 32–37 Vernon Blvd., Long Island City

Socrates Sculpture Park, Broadway and Vernon Blvd., Long Island

Stone Quarry Hill Art Park, 3883 Stone Quarry Rd., Cazenovia

Storm King Art Center, Old Pleasant Hill Rd., Mountainville

NORTH CAROLINA

Southern Center for Contemporary Art, 750 Marguerite Dr., Winston-Salem

OHIO

Columbus Museum of Art Sculpture Park, 480 East Broad St., Columbus

OREGON

Evan H. Roberts Memorial Sculpture Garden, Portland Art Museum, 1219 SW Park Ave., Portland

PENNSYLVANIA

Abington Art Center Sculpture Garden, 515 Meeting House Rd., Jenkintown

Drexel University, 3141 Chestnut St., Philadelphia

James Wolf Sculpture Trail, Johnstown

Lookout Sculpture Park, RD 1, Damascus

Madeline K. Butcher Sculpture Garden and the Morris Arboretum, University of Pennsylvania, 34th and Walnut Sts., Philadelphia

Phillip and Muriel Berman Sculpture Park, LeHigh Valley Hospital, 1243 South Cedar Crest Blvd., Allentown

SOUTH CAROLINA

Brookgreen Gardens, U.S. Highway 17 South, Murrells Inlet

TEXAS

Chianti Foundation, 1 Calvary Row, Marfa

Dallas Museum of Art Sculpture Garden, 1717 North Harwood St., Dallas

Lillie and Hugh Roy Cullen Sculpture Garden, Museum of Fine Arts, 1001 Bissonnet St., Houston

San Antonio Museum of Art Sculpture Garden, 200 West Jones Ave., San Antonio

Umlauf Sculpture Garden and Museum, 605 Robert E. Lee Rd., Austin

VERMONT

Marble Street Sculpture Park, Marble Street Extension, West Rutland

VIRGINIA

Virginia Museum of Fine Arts, 2800 Grove Ave., Richmond

WASHINGTON

Chapman University, 333 N. Glassell St., Orange

Gardens of Art, 2900 Sylvan St., Bellingham

Western Washington University Sculpture Collection, Bellingham

WISCONSIN

Bradley Family Foundation Sculpture Park, 2145 West Brown Deer Rd., Milwaukee

Woodlot Outdoor Sculpture Gallery, 5215 Evergreen Dr., Sheboygan (commercial)

List 6-13   International Sculpture Parks

ARGENTINA

Museo de Bellas Artes de la Voca, Pedro de Mendoza, 1835-43, Buenos Aires

AUSTRALIA

Museum of Modern Art at Heide, 7 Templestowe Rd., Bulleen, Melbourne, Victoria

AUSTRIA

Museum Moderner Kunst Stiftung Ludwig Wien Sculpture Garden, Furstengasse 1, A-1030, Vienna

BELGIUM

Middelheim-Openluchtmuseum Voor Beeldhouwkunst, Middelheimlaan 61, Antwerp

BRAZIL

Museo de Arte Moderna, Avenida Beira Mar 20021, Rio de Janeiro

CANADA

Canadian Centre for Architecture Sculpture Garden, Canadian Centre for Architecture, 1920 Baile St., Montreal, Quebec

Geert Maas Sculpture Gardens, RR 1, 250 Reynolds Rd., Kelowna, British Columbia

Toronto Sculpture Garden, 115 King St. East, Toronto

CZECH REPUBLIC

Klenova Castle, Namesti 149, 339 01 Klatovy

DENMARK

Forest Art, Lars Kruses Gade 4, DK 8000, Arhus

Krakamarken Nature Art Park, Brusgard Production School, Brusgardsvej 25, DK 8900, Randers

Louisiana Museum of Modern Art Sculpture Garden, Gl. Strandvej 13, DK-3050, Humlebaek

Tørskind Gammel Grusgrav Sculpture Park, near Egtved, 25 km from Vejle

Tranekaer International Center for Art and Nature (Tickon), Ostergade 10, Rudkøbing

ENGLAND

Barbara Hepworth Museum and Sculpture Garden, Barnoon Hill, St. Ives, Cornwall

Grizedale Forest Project, Hawkshead, near Ambleside, Cumbria

Henry Moore Foundation, Dane Tree House, Much Hadham, Hertfordshire

Roche Court Sculpture Garden, New Arts Center, Roche Court, East Winterslow, near Salisbury, Wiltshire

Yorkshire Sculpture Park, Bretton Hall College, West Bretton, near Wakefield, West Yorkshire

FRANCE

Centre D'Art Contemporain de Vassiviere en Limousin, Ile de Vassiviere, 87120 Beaumont-du-lac

Chateau de Kerguehennec, Bignan, 56500 Locmine, Morbihan

Chateau de Pourtales, Schiller University, 161 rue Melanie, 67000 Strasbourg

Essaim-Art, 16 Blvd. Marechal-Joffre, 06310 Beaulieu-sur-Mer

Fondation Cartier Pour L'Art Contemporain, 261, Boulevard Raspail, 75014, Paris

The Galerie Beaubourg Sculpture Garden, Chateau Notre-Dame-des-Fleurs, Vence

Jardin de Sculptures Musée D'Art Contemporain, Avenue des Bains, 59140 Dunkerque, Nord

Maeght Foundation, Route de Passe-Prest, Saint-Paul-de-Vence, 06470

Musée de Sculpture de Plein Air de la Ville de Paris, Quai Saint-Bernard, 75005 Paris

Musée National d'Art Moderne, Centre de'Art et de Culture, George Pompidou, Rue Saint-Merrii, 75191 Paris

Musée Rodin, Hotel Biron 77, rue de Varenne, 75007 Paris

Musée Zadkine, 100 bis, rue d'Assas, 75006 Paris

GERMANY

Skulpturenpark, E. v. 17509 Katzow Unterreihe 11

Skulpturenpark AM Seestern, Dusseldorf

Stadelsches Kunstinstitut Und Stadtische Galerie, Dürerstrasse 2, D-60596, Frankfurt am Main

Stiftung Europaischer Skulpturenpark, Schloss, D-3533 Willebadessen

Wilhelm Lehmbruck Museum, Friedrich-Wilhelm-Strasse 40, D-47049 Duisberg

HUNGARY

Szoborparkban, Müvelödési Has Nagyatád, Baross Gábor utca 2. H-7501

Sculpture, February, 1996. This list was compiled by the International Sculpture Center and used with permission. For more information, contact the I.S.C. at 1050 17th St., Suite 250, Washington, DC 20036.

List 6–13   Continued

ISRAEL

Billy Rose Sculpture Garden, Israel Museum, Ruppin Blvd., 91012 Jerusalem

Tefen/The Open Museum, Tefen Industrial Park, Kfar Vradim

Yad Vashem, Jerusalem

ITALY

Fattoria Di Celle, Villa Celle, 51030 Santomato, Pistoia, near Florence

Giardino Dei Tarochi, (Niki de Saint Phalle) Pesche di Capalvia, near Garavicchio, Tuscany

The Nasher Sculpture Garden, The Peggy Guggenheim Collection, Palazzo Venier dei Leoni, Grand Canal, Dorsoduro, Venice

JAPAN

The Hakone Open-Air Museum, Ninotaira Hakone-machi, Kanagawa 250–04

Hara Museum Arc, 2844 Kanai, Shibukawashi, Gun-maken

Hara Museum of Contemporary Art, 4–7-25 Ki-tashinawaga, Shinagawa-ku, Tokyo 140

Sapporo Art Park Sculpture Garden, 2–75 Geijutsu-no-mori, Minami-ku, Sapporo

The Utsukushi-Ga-Hara Open Air Museum, Ut-sukushi-ga-hara Kogen Dai Ue, Takeshimura, Chi-isagata-gun-gun, Nagano-Ken (located in the Yatsugatake-chushin-Kogen-Quasi National Park)

LATVIA

The Pedvale Open-Air Art Museum, Pedvale, Abavas pa-gasts, Talsu Rajons LV 3295

LITHUANIA

Central Europe Open-Air Sculpture Museum, Europos Parkas, Joneikiskiu k., 4013 Vilniaus raj

MEXICO

Museo de Arte Moderno, Paseo de la Reforma y Gandhi, Bosque de Chapultepec, Mexico

THE NETHERLANDS

Haags Gemeentemuseum, Stadhouders Laan 41, 2517 HV The Hague

Kröller-Müller Museum, National Park De Hoge Veluwe, Otterlo

NORWAY

Vigeland Sculpture Park, Viegland Museum, Nobelsgt 32, Oslo

POLAND

Center of Polish Sculpture, 26–681 Orónsko, Ul. Topolowa

SOUTH KOREA

Olympic Park, Left bank of the Han River, Seoul

SPAIN

Barcelona Open Air Sculpture Gallery

SWEDEN

Millesgarden, Carl Milles Vag # 2, Lidingö, S18134 Stockholm

Moderna Museet, 10327 Stockholm

List 6–14   Earthworks, Past and Present

Many ancient earthworks such as the *Great Serpent Mound* at Chillicothe, Ohio, or the *Pyramids* in Egypt may still be seen today. Contemporary earthworks may or may not have been intended as permanent installations, but were artistic statements about that particular environment at the time they were created. Some have already disappeared.

Acconici, Vito, *Face of the Earth #3,* 1988, Laumeier Sculpture Park, St. Louis, Missouri

Aycock, Alice, *A Simple Network of Underground Wells and Tunnels,* 1975, Merriewold West, Far Hills, New Jersey

Bayer, Herbert, *Mill Creek Canyon Earthworks,* 1979–1982, a reconstruction of the earth that allowed a stream to be dammed in a natural, beautiful way, Kent, Washington

Brancusi, Constantin, *Table of Silence,* 1935–1938, circular stone surrounded by "seats" consisting of two half-circles balanced on the rounded sides, Tirgu-Jiu, Romania

Christo (Javacheff), *Running Fence,* 1972–1976, 24-½ miles of 18-ft. high woven nylon held in place by poles and cables, running along the top of a ridge to the water, Sonoma and Marin counties, California (dismantled)

Christo (Javacheff), *Surrounded Islands,* 1983, 6-½ million square feet of pink polypropylene made into pink "skirts" and placed temporarily around the bay islands, Biscayne Bay, Miami, Florida

Finlay, Ian Hamilton, *Five Columns for the Kröller Müeller,* 1982, five trees with column bases, Otterlo, Netherlands

Fleischner, Richard, *Sod Maze,* 1974, concentric circles in mounded turf, 142 ft. in diameter, 18 inches high, Newport, Rhode Island

Goldsworthy, Andy, *Heron Feathers,* 1982, photograph, Goldsworthy moves things in nature such as stones, sticks, leaves, pebbles, then makes beautiful color photos of his transformations

Heizer, Michael, *Double Negative,* 1969–1970, vertical slits in two facing buttes, near Overton, Nevada

Heizer, Michael, *Isolated Mass/Circumflex,* 1968, 120 × 12 × 1 ft. hole, Massacre Dry Lake, Nevada (deteriorated)

Heizer, Michael, *Rift,* 1968, geometric zigzags cut into a dry lake bed, Jean Dry Lake, Nevada

Holt, Nancy, *Sun Tunnels,* 1973–1976, four large concrete pipes aligned to the rising and setting of the sun on the summer and winter solstices, Lucin, Utah

Lin, Maya, *Vietnam War Memorial,* 1982, 250-ft. black granite wall covered with the names of the Vietnam dead; it appears to be carved into the ground, Washington, DC

Lin, Maya, *The Wave Field,* 1995, 90-ft. plot of mounds covered with grass, Ann Arbor, Michigan

Long, Richard, *Walking a Line in Peru,* 1972, Long specializes in simply walking a straight line, sometimes slightly altering the landscape when he does; he records the lines photographically

Lord, Chip, *Cadillac Ranch,* 1974, Hudson Marquez, Doug Michels, 10 half-buried Cadillacs, Amarillo, Texas

Maria, Walter de, *Las Vegas Piece,* 1969, a square made in the desert with a 6-foot bulldozer blade, Las Vegas, Nevada

Maria, Walter de, *The Lightning Field,* 1974–1977, 20-½ ft. high stainless steel poles in a field to attract lightning, near Quemado, New Mexico

Morris, Robert, *Untitled Reclamation Project,* 1979, a grass-covered concentric circle earthwork to reclaim an unused gravel pit, King County, Washington

Morris, Robert, *Grand Rapids Project,* 1973–1974, circular earthwork in an on–off ramp of a highway, Grand Rapids, Michigan

Nash, David, *Running Table,* 1978, photo taken in Grizedale forest; Nash takes found wood and sometimes simply moves it or alters it, finding art in nature, Cumbria, England

Neville, Jack, *Pebble Beach Golf Course,* 1919, the course takes advantage of the natural beauty of rocks, trees, and seashore, near Monterey, California

Pierce, James, *Earthwoman,* 1976–1977, 5 × 30 × 15 ft. mound of dirt that appears to be a woman on her stomach, Pratt Farm, near Clinton, Maine

Pepper, Beverly, *Cromlech Glen,* 1985–1990, Laumeier Sculpture Park, St. Louis, Missouri

List 6–14   **Continued**

Serra, Richard, *Twain,* 1982, vertical weathering steel plates enclose a space that occupies an entire square block, St. Louis, Missouri

Simonds, Charles, *Dwelling, Chicago,* 1981, 44-ft. long clay and wood models of dwellings, Museum of Contemporary Art, Chicago, Illinois

Smithson, Robert, *Amarillo Ramp,* 1973, 150-ft. diameter, ¾ circle partially submerged in a lake, Amarillo, Texas

Smithson, Robert, *Spiral Jetty,* 1970, 1,500-ft. spiral made of rock and earth into the Great Salt Lake and now covered with water, Great Salt Lake, Utah

Turrell, James, *Roden Crater,* 1980, natural-appearing crater, near Flagstaff, Arizona

Unknown workers, *Great Pyramids,* 2470–2530 BC, Giza, Egypt

Unknown workers, *Stonehenge,* c. 2000 BC, a circular grouping of gigantic monoliths, Wiltshire, Salisbury Plains, England

Unknown workers, *Teotihuacan,* 300–900 AD, pyramid of the Sun dominates this ancient city, Teotihuacan, Mexico

Unknown workers, *Terrace of One Hundred Fountains,* 16th century, Villa d'Este, Tivoli, Italy

Unknown workers, *Great Serpent Mound,* c. 300 BC–AD 400, Chillicothe, Ohio

Unknown workers, *Great Wall of China,* unified c. 210 BC, the only earthwork that can be seen from the moon may be seen at Beijing

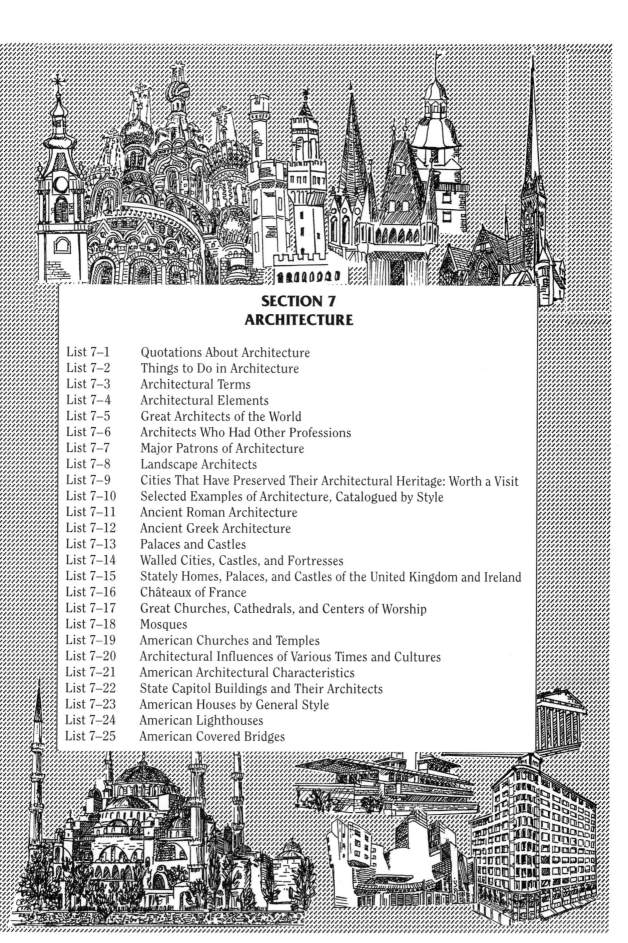

SECTION 7
ARCHITECTURE

List 7–1   Quotations About Architecture

"Early in life I had to choose between arrogance and hypocritical humility. I chose honest arrogance and have seen no occasion to change."

—FRANK LLOYD WRIGHT

"You have to give this much to the Luftwaffe (German bombers)—when it knocked down our buildings it did not replace them with anything more offensive than rubble. We did that."

—CHARLES, PRINCE OF WALES

"Buildings should be good neighbors."

—PAUL THIRY

"The materials of city planning are sky, space, trees, steel and cement in that order and in that hierarchy."

—LE CORBUSIER

"Light, God's eldest daughter, is a principal beauty in a building."

—THOMAS FULLER

"We shape our buildings; thereafter they shape us."

—SIR WINSTON CHURCHILL

"No architecture can be truly noble which is not imperfect."

—JOHN RUSKIN

"Architecture is inhabited sculpture."

—CONSTANTIN BRANCUSI

"Architecture should be dedicated to keeping the outside out and the inside in."

—LEONARD BASKIN

"Always design a thing by considering it in its next larger context—a chair in a room, a room in a house, a house in an environment, an environment in a city plan."

—EERO SAARINEN

"A house is a machine for living."

—BUCKMINSTER FULLER

"A doctor can bury his mistakes, but an architect can only advise his clients to plant vines."

—FRANK LLOYD WRIGHT

"Form ever follows function."

—LOUIS H. SULLIVAN

"Architecture is space structured to serve man and to move him."

—ETIENNE GABOURY

"Less is more."

—LUDWIG MIES VAN DER ROHE

"Have nothing in your houses that you do not know to be useful, or believe to be beautiful."

—WILLIAM MORRIS

List 7–2   Things to Do in Architecture

- Design a museum or hall of fame to display a collection that is of personal interest (history, stamps, bowling, golf, dogs, art, hall-of-fame, the life of one person, quilt, or folk art).
- Design a new capitol building for a desert country or state.
- Design a stained-glass window by cutting out shapes in black construction paper and filling in behind with various colors of tissue paper or colored plastic.
- Design a stained-glass window to go in a modern or historical building. Examples are Chagall's windows in the United Nations, Matisse's windows in a chapel, Frank Lloyd Wright's windows in private homes, or Medieval rose windows in churches.
- Make a "stained glass" window on an overhead transparency using black glue for outlining (allow it to dry) and permanent markers.
- Do a drawing of your room including an open closet door.
- Draw a plan for organizing your closet or office for maximum efficiency.
- Draw a city street plan for a capital city in a country of your choice. Consider the country's location, weather, and historical building traditions.
- Make an architectural photo record of your town (homes, historic landmarks, parks, public buildings). This can be done with slides, video, or photos arranged in a notebook or album.
- Select a local architect who has done notable work in your region, and make a photographic essay of all the buildings designed by that person.
- If one building or area in your town could be preserved, which should it be in your opinion? Discuss this with friends and arrive at a consensus. Then decide how you would go about raising money and gaining support to save it.
- Make a cardboard (tagboard, chipboard) façade of your own home, building up layers of cardboard to make architectural details. Hold pieces together with glue, then mount on thin plywood cut to size. Paint it realistically.
- Work with others to make an architectural timeline on white construction paper or posterboard. Cut out shapes of buildings on black construction paper, then arrange on the background (join pieces together if necessary). Write in dates and names of the buildings.
- Make a timeline of the major buildings where you live, using photographs, drawings, or cut-paper outlines.
- Interview people from an older generation about how houses of their time differed from those of today, and get their opinions about why some of the changes might have been made.
- Make an architectural model of your ideal home, using two pieces of 3 × 4-foot chipboard. Detailed drawings must be worked out in advance before cutting. This is effective unpainted. This can also be interesting done in unpainted corrugated cardboard.
- Select one style of ethnic housing from a foreign culture. Design a new house using the "influence" of that type of building.
- Design tiles based on nature for use in your building, as architect Louis Sullivan did.

List 7–3 Architectural Terms

abacus   a rounded slab of stone at the top of a capital

abbey   a religious center for monks or nuns; an abbey church and surrounding buildings

acropolis   the center of culture and religion in ancient Greek cities; usually located on a hill

adobe   sun-dried brick made from mud and straw; used to construct homes

agora   the center of commerce and government in Greek cities; the equivalent of a Roman forum

aisle   in a church, the space between the nave and supporting columns and the outside wall

altar   a location where offerings are made to a spirit; in Christian churches, a table-like structure

altarpiece   a decorative screen behind an altar, often with many scenes and movable wings

ambulatory   a walking space behind the high altar in a Gothic cathedral; covered walkway

amphitheater   an oval or circular structure with tiers of seats

apse   a round or polygonal vaulted space behind an altar at the eastern end of a cathedral

aqueduct   a conduit for water transported from a distant source

arcade   a series of columns combined with arches to support a roof

arch   a (usually) curved structural element that spans an opening and supports the weight above

archaic art   Greek art c. 620–c. 500 BC

architrave   in classical architecture, the part between the column and the pediment

archivolt   the continuous band of stone or brick that frames an arch

arena   an enclosed area for competitions or entertainment

Art Deco   architecture of the 1930s featuring flat roofs, geometric design, and simplified shapes

ashlar   stones that have been shaped and smoothed for building use, rather than left rough

atrium   an open court in the center of a building; or an entry court

baldachin   an architectural canopy above a throne or high altar

balusters   short, rounded, pillar-like columns that support a railing on a balcony or balustrade

balustrade   a porchlike parapet or balcony that has a railing with short balusters

baptistery   a portion of a church that is used specifically for baptism; often octagonal or round

Baroque   type of architecture characterized by curved lines, movement, and excessive decoration

basilica   a long colonnaded hall used in Roman times for commerce; later used for church design

Bauhaus   a German school that brought together all the arts and united them through architecture

bay   an opening in a building that is created by walls or columns; a projecting window unit

beam   a support for a roof or floor, usually going from wall to wall

blind arcade   a series of decorative columns attached to a wall

boiserie   wooden paneling often found in French interiors of the 17th and 18th centuries

bracket   a weight-bearing support that projects outward from a wall

brickwork   decorative arrangement of bricks; particularly popular in Victorian architecture

broken pediment   a triangular pediment separated by a half-circle at its apex

bungalow   an early 1900s house style with brick and a hipped roof

buttresses   projecting supports that allow exterior walls to be built higher

campanile   a bell tower, sometimes free-standing, or sometimes an integral part of a church

cantilever   a projecting structure such as a balcony, supported by a downward force behind a fulcrum, appearing to be unsupported

capital   the top of a column; a variety of styles from various cultures

caryatid   a carved female figure that takes the place of a column to support a roof

catacomb   an underground cemetery with wall niches used for burial

cathedral   a church that contains the throne of a bishop (cathedra)

cella   the central part of a classical Greek temple

chancel   the part of a church reserved for the clergy

choir   the part of a church behind the altar for singers and the clergy

classical temple   design canon from ancient Greece and Rome

clerestory   the window-filled upper portion of a wall

cloister   an open courtyard surrounded by a covered colonnade

coffer   a boxlike ceiling, often octagonal or rectangular

colonnade   a series of columns that support a roof

colossal order   columns or pilasters that are used to decorate or extend through more than one story

column   a usually round or fluted post to support beams or a roof

composite order   a capital that consists of the acanthus leaf combined with a volute (Roman)

List 7–3   Continued

corbel   a projecting support usually of carved blocks of stone or wood

cornice   a horizontal roof overhang; a raking cornice is a diagonal overhang found in a pediment

crenellation   battlements, a notched parapet for defense, usually found in a castle

cromlech   standing stone circles from ancient religions

crossing   the central area of a church where a transept intersects a nave

cupola   a small dome atop a roof

curtain wall   curving brick walls; non-load-bearing outer walls

dome   an evenly curved vault on a base

dormer   an attic window usually with a gable and roof

eaves   the lower portion of a roof that projects beyond the wall

elevation   a straight-on drawing of one side of a building without using perspective

engaged column   a column attached to the wall directly behind it

entablature   the horizontal support beam (lintel) between columns and a roof

entasis   the gentle convex swelling of a column that makes it appear straight rather than concave

façade   the front view (elevation) of a building

fascia   a plain horizontal board above a window, or in an architrave in Greek architecture

Federal style   style of building in the United States from 1789 to c. 1830; neo-Classicism

fenestration   the use of windows in a building

finial   an ornament that caps something such as a newel post, buttress, roof apex, or canopy

fluting   ornamental grooves carved into a vertical column

flying buttress   a support for a wall with an arched opening to give it strength

folly   an apparently useless building that enhanced the view, for example, a fake "ruin"

formal balance   symmetrical arrangement of architectural elements on each side of a center axis

forum   a place of assembly for markets, religion, commerce, and justice

fresco   decorative painting done on wet lime or gypsum plaster

frieze   decorative ornamentation that is part of the entablature; a decorative strip on upper walls

gable   the upper, pointed part of a wall underneath a pitched roof

gallery   an open second story above the aisle of a church and below the clerestory

gambrel roof   barn-like roof imported to the United States from The Netherlands

gargoyle   a water spout of lead or carved stone that resembled a beast or monster

gazebo   a small open-air summer house with a view

geodesic dome   a geometric dome created with light metal bars, connectors, and glass

Georgian style   architecture associated with King Georges I, II, III, and IV (1714–1820)

girder   a beam, usually steel

Gothic cathedral   a church with flying buttresses and pointed-arch windows (c. 1250 to c. 1500)

Greek Orthodox church   a cross-shaped church with all four wings of the same length

groin   an angle formed by two intersecting vaults

half-timbering   exterior decorative timber allowed to show, contrasting with white walls

Hall church   a church with nave and aisles of the same height

hipped   a traditional gabled roof, but with the ends slanted and enclosed

hippodrome   an enclosed racecourse or theater that featured animal acts

hypostyle hall   a large hall with the roof supported by a vast number of columns (Egyptian origin)

impost   the widened space at the top of a column or pier that joins an arch or vault to the pier

insula   the first "apartment building"; Roman tenement blocks

international style   box-like buildings often with walls of glass

jambs   the vertical sides of an opening such as a church entrance; frequently carved

keystone   the stone that goes at the very top of an arch to complete its load-bearing quality

lantern   a round turret with side openings that extends above a dome to let in light

lintel   the horizontal beam at the top of two vertical supports to support the wall above it

loggia   an attached gallery that is open on one side with an arcade or columns

lunette   a semicircular space above a door or window (similar to a tympanum)

machicolation   the opening behind battlements in a castle that allows oil or pitch to be poured

mansard roof   a roof with two slopes, the first quite steep, the second less steep

mausoleum   an imposing tomb, usually for an important person; example, the Taj Mahal

mihrab   a Mecca-facing hollow niche in a mosque

minaret   slender tower(s) attached to a mosque from which prayers are sung

List 7–3   Continued

molding   a decoratively carved ornamental strip mostly used in classical architecture

mosaic   a decorative floor or wall mural made of pieces of stone or colored glass

narthex   a porch in the front of a church or a vestibule just outside the nave of the church

nave   the long space in a Christian church reserved for worshippers

niche   a rounded, concave opening in a wall for sculpture

obelisk   a monumental block of stone tapered toward the top, originated in Egypt

oculus   literally an eye (round window) to let in light, such as that in the *Pantheon*

orders of architecture   a system of categorizing columns and the entablature

pagoda   a Chinese or Indian temple built of many stories, each smaller than the one below

Palladian   an architectural movement based on the work of Andrea Palladio

parapet   a low wall at the edge of a balcony or terrace

pedestal   the lowest part of a support for a column, often square

pediment   the triangular decoration above a door or temple, often decoratively carved

pendentive   a curved triangular piece of masonry placed at each corner of a square pillar or drum for attaching a rounded dome

peristyle court   a many-columned court (colonnade) around an open courtyard

pier   a massive support, sometimes square, but often formed of several columns (compound pier)

pilaster   a rectangular attached (engaged) column with capital and base

pillar   a vertical structural support; includes columns, piers, and pilasters

porte-cochère   a covered area that allows passengers to be sheltered while leaving a vehicle

post and lintel   a support system that consists of vertical uprights and a horizontal beam

post-modernism   a 1970s style that is based on traditional classical or decorative architecture

propylaeum   the monumental entrance to a temple

proscenium   a Roman or Greek stage; the space between the curtain and an orchestra

pylon   sloping walls (as in Egyptian temples); or flanking structures at an entrance or bridge

pyramid   a structure with a square base with sides that slope upward to a point

qibla   the wall in a mosque that faces Mecca which contains the mihrab niche

rose window   a stained-glass circular window with tracery, often found in Gothic churches

rotunda   a circular interior space, usually surmounted by a dome

rustication   the deliberate roughness left on stone; also indented edges where stones were joined

sacristy   a room near the altar where clothing and vessels for a church service are kept

sanctuary   the inner part of a church where the altar and worshippers are

shaft   the vertical portion of a column or pilaster

spandrel   the triangular area formed between the tops of two adjacent arches

spire   the pointed top portion of a tower

squinch   a triangular arch placed diagonally on corners of a square base to link a rounded dome

steeple   a spire and its supporting structure

stereobate   the underlayer of a building (Greek Temple); the stylobate is the top layer

stoa   a long narrow building used for a market in Greek and Roman cities

stringcourse   a decorative horizontal band on a building, often in a contrasting color

terrazzo   marble chips and cement combined and poured, then highly polished

tholos   a circular building used as a temple, or in Mycenae as a tomb

tokonoma   a niche in a Japanese home or tea-ceremony room to display artwork

tracery   stone or wood carving used decoratively in stained-glass windows, panels, and screens

transept   the arm of a church that forms a right angle "crossing" in a basilican-style church

turret   a small tower attached to the top of a castle

tympanum   a rounded space above doors usually filled with sculpture

vault   an arched ceiling usually of brick, stone, or concrete

veranda   an attached open porch supported by columns

volute   a scroll ornament used in Ionic and (often) Corinthian capitals

voussoir   wedge-shaped stones used in an arch

wattle and daub   a wall composed of woven branches filled with mud or plaster

westwork   the west end of a church that contains the main doorway, towers, and narthex

ziggurat   a flat-topped pyramid formed of a series of platforms on which a temple was built

List 7–4   Architectural Elements

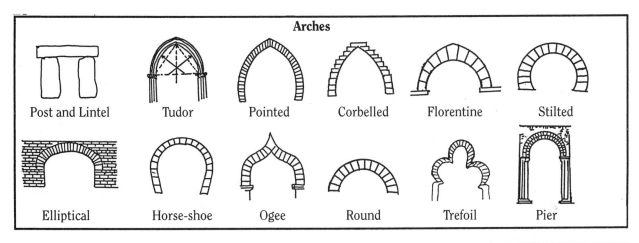

Arches

Post and Lintel   Tudor   Pointed   Corbelled   Florentine   Stilted

Elliptical   Horse-shoe   Ogee   Round   Trefoil   Pier

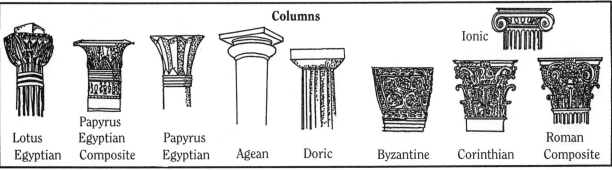

Columns

Lotus Egyptian   Papyrus Egyptian Composite   Papyrus Egyptian   Agean   Doric   Byzantine   Ionic   Corinthian   Roman Composite

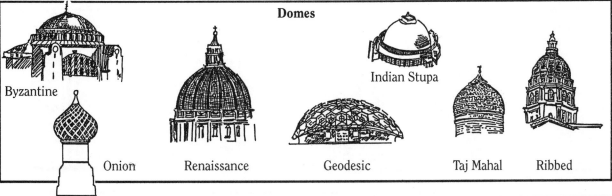

Domes

Byzantine   Onion   Renaissance   Indian Stupa   Geodesic   Taj Mahal   Ribbed

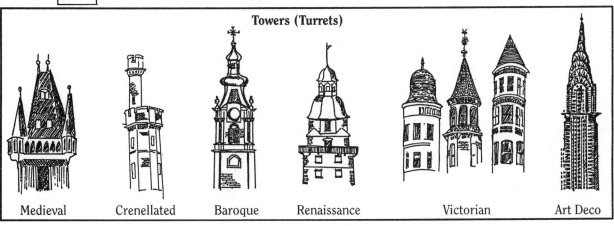

Towers (Turrets)

Medieval   Crenellated   Baroque   Renaissance   Victorian   Art Deco

List 7–4 Continued

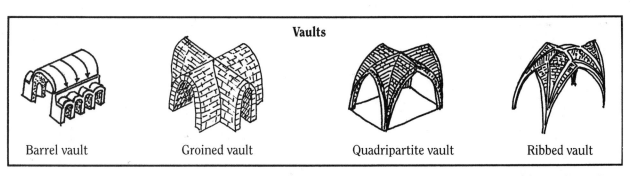

Vaults

Barrel vault · Groined vault · Quadripartite vault · Ribbed vault

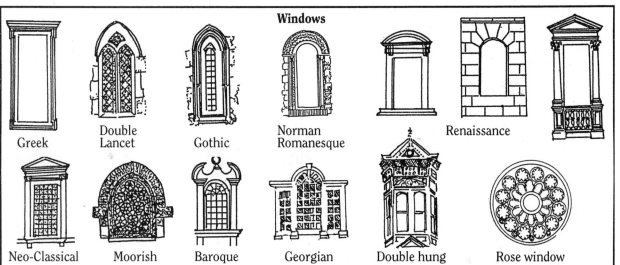

Windows

Greek · Double Lancet · Gothic · Norman Romanesque · Renaissance

Neo-Classical · Moorish · Baroque · Georgian · Double hung · Rose window

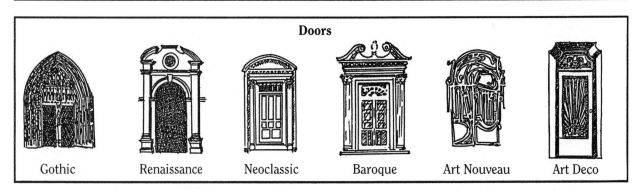

Doors

Gothic · Renaissance · Neoclassic · Baroque · Art Nouveau · Art Deco

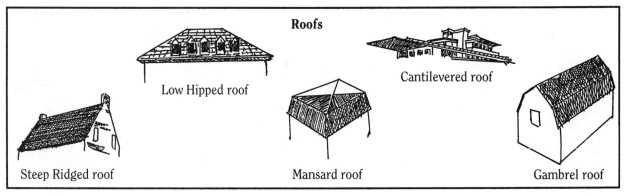

Roofs

Low Hipped roof · Cantilevered roof

Steep Ridged roof · Mansard roof · Gambrel roof

List 7–5   Great Architects of the World

One example of the work of each of these outstanding architects is listed.

AMERICA

Adler, Dankmar, 1844–1900 (b. Germany), *Auditorium,* 1886–1890, Chicago, Illinois

Breuer, Marcel, 1902–1981 (b. Hungary), *Whitney Museum of American Art,* 1963–1966, New York City

Buckland, William, 1734–1774, *Hammond-Harwood House,* 1774, Annapolis, Maryland

Bulfinch, Charles, 1763–1844, *Beacon Monument,* 1791, and *State House,* 1795–1798, Boston, Massachusetts

Burgee, John, 1933, (with Philip Johnson), *Pennzoil Place,* 1976, Houston, Texas

Burnham, Daniel Hudson, 1846–1912, *Flatiron Building,* 1902, New York City

Fowler, Orson Squire, 1809–1887, *Longwood* (Octagon House), 1860–1862, Natchez, Mississippi

Fuller, Buckminster, 1895–1983, *Geodesic dome,* 1967, Pavilion at Montreal

Furness, Frank, 1839–1912, *Pennsylvania Academy of Fine Arts,* 1872–1876, Philadelphia, Pennsylvania

Gilbert, Cass, 1859–1934, *Woolworth Building,* 1913, New York City

Gill, Irving J., 1870–1936, *Bentham Hall and Tower,* 1909, La Jolla, California

Graves, Michael, 1934, *Humana Tower,* 1982–1986, Louisville, Kentucky

Greene, Charles Sumner, 1868–1957, *Gamble House,* 1908–1909, Pasadena, California

Greene, Henry Mather, 1870–1954, *J.H. Cuthbertson House,* 1902, Pasadena, California

Gropius, Walter, 1883–1969 (b. Germany), *Pan Am Building,* 1958–1963, New York City

Haviland, John, 1792–1852, *Franklin Institute,* 1825–1826, Philadelphia, Pennsylvania

Holl, Steven, 1947, *Helsinki Museum of Contemporary Art,* 1998, Finland

Hood, Raymond, 1881–1934, (with John Mead Howells), *Tribune Tower,* 1923–1925, Chicago, Illinois

Hunt, Richard Morris, 1827–1895, *Biltmore House,* 1895, Asheville, North Carolina

Jefferson, Thomas, 1743–1826, *Virginia State Capitol,* 1785–1798, Richmond

Jenney, William Le Baron, 1832–1907, *Home Insurance Building,* 1884–1885, Chicago, Illinois

Johnson, Philip, 1906, *PPG Place,* 1984, Pittsburgh, Pennsylvania

Kahn, Louis I., 1901–1974, *Kimbell Art Museum,* 1972, Fort Worth, Texas

Latrobe, Benjamin, 1764–1820, *Bank of Pennsylvania,* 1798–1800, Philadelphia

Maybeck, Bernard, 1862–1957, *First Church of Christ, Scientist,* 1909–1911, Berkeley, California

McKim, Charles, 1847–1909, *Public Library,* 1887–1895, Boston, Massachusetts

Mead, Rutherford, 1846–1928, *William G. Low House,* 1886–1887, Bristol, Rhode Island

Meier, Richard, 1934, *High Museum of Art,* 1980–1983, Atlanta, Georgia; *Getty Museum,* 1997, Los Angeles, California

Mendelsohn, Erich, 1887–1953 (b. Germany), *B'nai Amoona Temple,* 1950, St. Louis, Missouri

Mills, Robert, 1781–1855, *Washington Monument,* 1848–1884, Washington, DC

Mizner, Addison, 1872–1933, *Everglades Club,* 1918–1919, Palm Beach, California

Morgan, Julia, 1872–1957, *First Baptist Church,* 1906, Oakland, California

Neutra, Richard, 1892–1970, *Garden Grove Community Church,* 1962, Garden Grove, California

Pei, Ioeh Ming, 1917, *East Building, National Gallery of Art,* 1968–1978, Washington, DC

Renwick, James, 1818–1895, *Grace Church,* 1843–1846, New York City

Richardson, Henry Hobson, 1838–1886, *Sever Hall,* 1878–1880, Harvard, Cambridge, Massachusetts

Root, John Wellborn, 1850–1891, (Burnham & Root), *Reliance Building,* 1891–1894, Chicago, Illinois

Saarinen, Eero, 1910–1961 (b. Finland), *Jefferson Arch,* completed 1965, St. Louis, Missouri

Saarinen, Eliel, 1873–1950 (b. Finland), *Cranbrook Foundation Buildings,* 1926–1943, Bloomfield Hills, Michigan

Safdie, Moshe, 1938 (b. Israel), *National Gallery of Canada,* 1988, Ottawa

Scott Brown, Denise, 1931, (with Venturi-Rauch-Brown), *Trubek-Wislocki Houses,* 1970, Nantucket, Massachusetts

Skidmore, Louis, 1897–1962, (Skidmore, Owings, and Merrill), *Lever House,* 1950–1952, New York City

Smibert, John, 1688–1751, *Fanueuil Hall,* 1740–1742, Boston, Massachusetts

Smith, Robert, c. 1722–1777, *Carpenters' Hall,* 1770, Philadelphia, Pennsylvania

Stern, Robert, 1939, *Observatory Hill Dining Hall,* 1982–1984, University of Virginia, Charlottesville

Stone, Edward Durrell, 1902–1978, *Kennedy Center for the Performing Arts,* 1971, Washington, DC

Strickland, William, 1788–1854, *U.S. Mint,* 1829–1833, Philadelphia, Pennsylvania

List 7–5 Continued

AMERICA (cont.)

Sullivan, Louis, 1856–1924, *Carson, Pirie and Scott Building,* 1898–1904, Chicago, Illinois

Thornton, Dr. William, 1759–1828, *U.S. Capitol Building Design,* 1793–1827, Washington, DC

Tsien, Billie and Tod Williams, *Phoenix Art Museum Sculpture Pavilion,* Arizona

Upjohn, Richard, 1802–1878, *Trinity Church,* 1839–1846, New York City

Van Alen, William, 1883–1954, *Chrysler Building,* 1930, New York City

Van Der Rohe, Ludwig Mies, 1886–1969, *Lake Shore Drive Apts.,* 1948–1951, Chicago, Illinois

Lake Shore Drive Apartments, 1948–1951, Chicago, Illinois, Mies Van der Rohe

Venturi, Robert, 1925, *Seattle Art Museum,* c. 1991, Washington

Walter, Thomas U., 1804–1887, *Matthew Newkirk House,* 1835, Philadelphia, Pennsylvania

White, Stanford, 1853–1906, (McKim, Mead, and White), *Villard Houses,* 1882–1885, New York City

Wright, Frank Lloyd, 1867–1959, *Unity Temple,* 1906, Oak Park, Illinois

AUSTRIA

Fischer von Erlach, Johann, 1656–1723, *Hofbibliothek,* begun 1723, Hofburg, Vienna

Hoffman, Joseph, 1870–1956, *Palais Stocklet,* 1904–1915, Brussels

Loos, Adolf, 1870–1933, *Steiner House,* 1910, Vienna

Prandtauer, Jakob, 1660–1726, *Monastery,* 1702–1738, Melk

Von Hildebrandt, L., 1668–1745, *Upper Belvedere Palace,* 1714–1715, Vienna

Wagner, Otto, 1841–1918, *Postal Savings Bank Office,* 1904–1912, Vienna

BELGIUM

Horta, Victor, 1861–1947, *House,* #4 Avenue Palmerson, 1894, Brussels

van de Velde, Henri, 1863–1957, *Kröller-Müller Museum,* 1938, Otterlo, The Netherlands

BRAZIL

Niemeyer, Oscar, 1907, *St. Francis at Pampulha,* 1942–1943, near Belo Horizonte

CANADA

Baillairgé, Thomas, 1791–1859, *St. Joseph Lauzon,* 1830–1832, Quebec

Bourgeau, Victor, 1809–1888, *Cathedral of St. James,* 1875–1885, Montreal

Cumberland, W.C., 1821–1881, *University College,* 1856–1858, Toronto

Michaud, Joseph, 1822–1902 (with Bourgeau), *Cathedral of St. James,* 1875–1885, Montreal

O'Donnel, James, 1774–1830, *Notre Dame,* 1824–1829, Montreal

Revell, Viljo, 1910–1964, *City Hall,* 1958–1965, Toronto

EGYPT

Imhotep, active 2650–2600 BC, *King Zoser's Step Pyramid,* c. 2630 BC, Sakkara

ENGLAND

Barry, Sir Charles, 1795–1860, *Travellers' Club,* 1829–1831, London

Butterfield, William, 1814–1900, *All Saints,* 1849–1859, London

Chambers, Sir William, 1723–1796, *Somerset House,* begun 1776, London

Fry, Maxwell, 1899–1987, *Impington Village College,* 1936, Impington

Inwood, Henry W., 1794–1843, *St. Pancras Church,* 1819–1822, London

Jones, Inigo, 1573–1652, *Queen's House, Greenwich Palace,* 1616–1635, Kent

Kent, William, 1685–1748, *Holkham Hall,* begun 1734, near Blakeney

Luytens, Sir Edwin L., 1869–1944, *British Embassy,* 1927–1928, Washington, DC

Nash, John, 1752–1835, *Royal Pavilion,* 1815–1818, Brighton

Paxton, Sir Joseph, 1801–1865, *Crystal Palace,* 1851, London

Pugin, Augustus Welby, 1812–1852, *decoration of the Houses of Parliament,* 1836–1860, London

Scott, Sir George Gilbert, 1811–1878, *Foreign Office, Whitehall,* 1862–1873, London

Shaw, Richard Norman, 1831–1912, *New Zealand Chambers,* 1872, London

Smirke, Sir Robert, 1781–1867, *main facade, British Museum,* 1823–1847, London

Soane, Sir John, 1753–1837, *Bank of England; Soane Museum; Art Gallery,* 1811–1814, Dulwich

Vanbrugh, Sir John, 1664–1726, *Blenheim Palace,* 1705–1724, *Castle Howard,* 1699–1726, Malton

List 7–5 Continued

ENGLAND (cont.)

Walpole, Horace, 1717–1797, *Strawberry Hill,* 1748–1777, Twickenham

Webb, Phillip, 1831–1915, *William Morris home,* 1859, Bexley Heath

Wren, Sir Christopher, 1632–1723, *St. Paul's Cathedral,* 1675–1710, London

Church of The Madeleine, Paris, 1806–1843, Alexandre-Pierre Vignon

FINLAND

Aalto, Alvar, 1898–1976, *Baker House,* M.I.T., 1949, village center, Saynatsalo, 1951, Finland

Saarinen, Eliel, 1873–1950, *Railroad Station,* 1905–1914, Helsinki

FRANCE

Delorme, Philibert, 1512–1570, *Tomb of Francis I,* begun c. 1547, St. Denis, near Paris

Eiffel, Gustave, 1832–1923, *Eiffel Tower,* 1887–1889, Paris

Garnier, Charles, 1825–1898, *Opera,* 1861–1875, Paris; *Casino,* 1879–1885, Monte Carlo

Garnier, Tony, 1869–1948, *Stadium,* 1913–1916, Lyon

Guimard, Hector, 1867–1942, *designs for the Metro,* 1899–1904, Paris

Hardouin-Mansart, Jules, 1646–1708, *Church of the Invalides,* 1679–1691, Paris

Labrouste, Henri, 1801–1875, *Bibliothèque Nationale,* 1843–1850, Paris

Ledoux, Claude Nicolas, 1736–1806, *Pavilion de Louveciennes and Theater,* 1771–1773, Besançon

L'Enfant, Pierre, 1754–1825, *City Plans for Washington, DC,* 1791; *Federal Hall,* 1788–1789, New York City

Le Vau, Louis, 1612–1670, *Institute de France,* begun 1661; Paris, *Louvre,* 1661–1670, Paris

Mansart, François, 1598–1666, *Maison Lafitte,* 1642–1651, near Paris

Perrault, Claude, 1613–1688, *East Front of the Louvre,* 1667–1670, Paris

Soufflot, Jacques Germain, 1713–1780, *Ste. Genevieve,* begun 1756 (called the Pantheon), Paris

GERMANY

Behrens, Peter, 1868–1940, *A.E.G. Turbine Factory,* 1908–1909, Berlin

Gropius, Walter, 1883–1969, *Bauhaus Building,* 1925–1926, Dessau

Mendelsohn, Erich, 1887–1953, *Einstein Tower,* 1919–1921, Potsdam

Neumann, Johann Balthasar, 1687–1753, *Bishop's Residenz,* c. 1719–1750, Wurzburg

Scharoun, Hans, 1893–1972, *Berlin Philharmonic,* 1963; *Juliet Apartments,* 1955, Stuttgart

Schinkel, Karl Friedrich, 1781–1841, *Old Museum,* 1830, Berlin

Speer, Albert, 1905–1981, *Reichschancellery,* 1938–1939, Berlin

Zimmerman, Dominikus, 1685–1766, *Die Wies Pilgrimage Church,* c. 1745, Bavaria

GREECE

Hippodamus of Miletus, c. 542–468 BC: the man given credit for founding town planning

Ictinus, together with Callicrates, designed the *Parthenon,* 442–437 BC, Athens

Callicrates, worked on *Parthenon,* 442–437 BC, Athens

ITALY

Alberti, Leon Battista, 1404–1472, *exterior of Church of San Francesco,* c. 1450–1461, Rimini

Bernini, Gian Lorenzo, 1598–1680, *interior and colonnade of St. Peter's,* 1656–1657, Rome

Borromini, Francesco, 1599–1667, *San Carlo alle Quattro Fontana,* 1638–1667, Rome

Bramante, Donato, 1444–1514, *Santa Maria delle Grazie,* c. 1492, Milan

Brunelleschi, Filippo, 1377–1446, *Cathedral dome,* 1420–1436, Florence

Cortona, Pietro da, 1596–1669, *S.S. Martina e Luca,* 1634–1639, Rome

Guarini, Guarino, 1624–1683, *San Lorenzo,* 1668–1687, Turin

Giotto (di Bondone), c. 1266–1337, *Campanile, Cathedral,* 1334–1337, Florence

Maderno, Carlo, 1556–1629, *St. Peter's,* 1607–1615; *Palazzo Barberini,* 1628, Rome

Michelangelo (Buonarroti), 1475–1564, *Medici Chapel,* 1520–1534, Florence

Nervi, Pier Luigi, 1891–1979, *Stadium,* 1930–1932, Florence

List 7–5   Continued

ITALY (cont.)

Palladio, Andrea, 1508–1580, *Villa Rotunda,* 1567–1570, Vicenza

Pisano, Giovanni, 1245–1315, *Cathedral,* 1290; *Sienna Cathedral,* 1296, Pisa

Primaticcio, Francesco, 1505–1570, *theatre wing of the Palace at Fontainbleu,* 1528, near Paris

Sangallo, Antonio da, 1483–1546, *Palazzo Farnese,* begun c. 1519, Rome

Vignola, Giacomo da, 1507–1573, *Villa Giulia,* 1551–1555, Rome

JAPAN

Ando, Tadao, 1941, *Matsumoto Residence,* 1980, Wakayama; *Rokko Housing,* 1983, Hyogo

Isozaki, Arata, 1931, *Museum of Contemporary Art,* 1984, Los Angeles, California; *Civic Centre,* 1979–1983, Tsukuba

Mayekawa, Kunio, 1905–1986, *Festival Halls,* 1961, Tokyo and Kyoto

Otani, Sachio, 1924, *International Conference Building,* 1963–1966, Kyoto

Raymond, Antonin, 1889–1976, *Readers' Digest Offices,* 1949, Tokyo

Sakakura, Junzo, 1904–1969, *Town Hall,* 1919, Hajima

Tange, Kenzo, 1913, *Olympia Sports Stadium,* 1963–1964, Tokyo; *Akasaka Prince Hotel,* 1983, Tokyo

Watanabe, Hiroshi, 1905, *Imperial Museum,* 1938, Tokyo

NETHERLANDS

Berlage, Hendrik P., 1856–1934, *Diamond Workers' Union Building,* 1899–1901, Amsterdam

Koolhaas, Rem, 1944, *Kunsthal,* 1997, Rotterdam; *Congrexpo,* 1997, Lille, France

Oud, J.J.P., 1890–1963, *Shell Building,* 1938–1942, The Hague

Rietveld, Gerrit, 1888–1964, *Rietvelt chair; Schroder House,* 1924, Utrecht

van de Velde, Henri, 1863–1957, *Art School at Weimar,* 1906, Germany

SCOTLAND

Adam, Robert, 1728–1792, *Syon House,* 1762–1769, Middlesex

Gibbs, James, 1682–1754, *King's College Fellows' Building,* 1724–1749, Cambridge

Macintosh, Charles Rennie, 1868–1928, *School of Art,* begun 1896, Glasgow

Telford, Thomas, 1757–1834, *St. Katherine's Docks,* 1827, London

SWEDEN

Ostberg, Ragnar III, 1866–1945, *City Hall,* 1909–1923, Stockholm

Tessin, Nicodemus II, 1615–1681, *Drottningholm Palace,* 1662, Stockholm

SPAIN

Gaudi, Antoni, 1852–1926, *Church of the Sagrada Familia,* 1883–1926, Barcelona

de Toledo, Juan Bautista, d. 1567, (with Juan de Herrera, 1530–1597) *Escorial,* begun 1559–1584, Madrid

SWITZERLAND

Botta, Mario, 1943, *San Francisco Museum of Art,* 1995, San Francisco, California

Herzog, Jacques, 1950, and Pierre de Meuron, 1950, *Goetz Collection,* c. 1997, Munich; renovation of *Bankside Power Station* into Tate Gallery Branch, 1997

LeCorbusier (Charles-Edouard Jeanneret), 1887–1966, Swiss-French, *United Nations Buildings,* 1947–1953, New York City

Dulles International Airport, 1958–1962, Chantilly, Virginia, Eero Saarinen

List 7–6   Architects Who Had Other Professions

ATTORNEY

Abrams, Charles, Polish American, 1901–1970, city planner

DESIGNER

Eames, Charles, American, 1907–1978, designer of furniture industrial materials

Endell, August, German, 1871–1925, stucco design on the *Elvira Photo Studio,* c. 1897, Munich

Hoffman, Joseph, Austria, 1870–1856, book illustrator and furniture designer

Jacobsen, Arne, Danish, 1902–1971, furniture designer, *S.A.S. Hotel,* 1960, Copenhagen

Kent, William, English, 1685–1748, painter and designer of furniture and gardens

Loewy, Raymond, French American, 1893–1986, industrial design; *1947 Studebaker*

Mackmurdo, Arthur H., English, 1851–1942, his drawings were the basis for Art Nouveau

Urban, Joseph, Austrian American, 1872–1933, *New School for Social Research,* 1930, New York City

ENGINEER

Adler, Dankmar, German American, 1844–1900, *Carson Pirie Scott,* 1899, Chicago, Illinois

Coates, Wells, English, 1895–1958, Mass housing, worked on *Metropolitan Cathedral,* Liverpool

Eiffel, Gustave, French, 1832–1923, *Eiffel Tower,* 1887–1889, Paris; *Statue of Liberty* (with Bartholdi), New York City

Freyssinet, Eugene, French, 1879–1962, concrete engineer, *Bridge,* 1926, Elorn

Hildebrandt, Johann Lukas von, Austrian, 1668–1745, *Upper and Lower Belvederes,* c. 1714–1724, Vienna

Jenney, William Le Baron, American, 1832–1907, *Home Insurance Building,* 1885, Chicago, Illinois

Latrobe, Benjamin, English American, 1764–1820, *Capitol Building,* Washington, DC

Nervi, Pier Luigi, Italian, 1891–1979, *Olympic architecture,* 1960, Rome

Neumann, Johann Balthasar, German, 1687–1753, *Bishop's Residenz,* 1719–1750, Wurzburg

Telford, Thomas, Scottish, 1757–1834, *London Bridge; St. Katherine's Docks,* London

Vitruvius, Roman, active 46–30 BC, wrote treatise on architecture, *Basilica at Fano* (destroyed)

Wachsmann, Konrad, German American, 1901–1980, pre-fabricated buildings, 1925

ENGRAVER

Du Cerceau, Jacques A., French, 1515–1590, known for books and engravings on architecture

GOLDSMITH

Brunelleschi, Filippo, Italian, 1377–1446, *Pazzi Chapel,* c. 1429, *Dome of Cathedral of Florence*

ILLUSTRATOR

Ferriss, Hugh, American, 1889–1962, illustrated for *Rockefeller Center* team and Raymond Hood

INVENTOR

Bell, Alexander Graham, American, 1847–1922, built tetrahedron space frames and the telephone

Bogardus, James, American, 1800–1874, invented pre-fabricated cast-iron façades, 1840s

Fuller, Buckminster, American, 1895–1983, *Geodesic Dome,* Montreal

MATHEMATICIAN

Anthemius of Tralles, Lydian, d. AD 534, *Hagia Sofia,* 532–537 AD, Istanbul

Guarini, Guarino, Italian, 1624–1683, *Collegio dei Nobili,* 1678, Turin, Italy

Isidore of Miletus, Turkish, *Hagia Sofia,* 532–537 AD, Istanbul

PAINTER

Bill, Max, German, b. Switzerland, 1908–1995, painter and sculptor, and director of Art and Architecture at Ulm

da Cortona, Pietro, Italian, 1596–1669, *S. Maria della Pace,* Rome

Giotto, Italian, c. 1266–1337, painter and sculptor; designed *Campanile of Florence Duomo*

Laurana, Luciano, Italian, c. 1420–1479, *Duke's Palace at Urbino*

Leonardo da Vinci, Italian, 1452–1519, *Last Supper,* c. 1495–1498, Milan

Primaticcio Francesco, Italian, 1505–1570, *Theater wing of Palace of Fontainebleau,* near Paris

Raphael Sanzio, Italian, 1483–1520, *School of Athens; St. Peter's, Stanza della Signatura*

Romano, Giulio, Italian, 1492–1546, *Palazzo de Te,* Mantua, 1526; *Garden, Versailles*

PHYSICIAN

Thornton, Dr. William, English American, 1759–1828, *U.S. Capitol Building,* 1793, Washington, DC

List 7-6   Continued

POLITICAL LEADER

Jefferson, Thomas, American, 1743–1826, U.S. President; *Monticello,* 1770–1809, *University of Virginia,* c. 1817

Speer, Albert, German, 1905–1981, Minister of Armaments, *Reichschancellery,* 1938–1939, Berlin

PRIEST

Bohm, Dominikus, German, 1880–1955, *St. Maria Konigen,* 1954, Cologne

Suger, Abbot, French, 1081–1151, *Church of St. Denis,* c. 1135–1144, near Paris

SCIENTIST

Wren, Christopher, English, 1632–1723, *St. Paul's Cathedral,* London, 1675–1710, anatomy and geometry professor, then an architect

SCULPTOR

Ammanati, Bartolommeo, Italian, 1511–1592, *Pitti Palace,* garden and façade, 1558–1570, Florence

Bernini, Giancarlo, Italian, 1598–1680, sculpture; *Colonnade of St. Peter's,* 1656–1657

da Maiano, Giuliano, Italian, 1432–1490, rustication, *Palazzo Spannocchi,* c. 1473, Sienna

da Sangallo, Guiliano, Italian, 1445–1516, *Palazzo Gondi,* 1494, Florence

Ghiberti, Lorenzo, Italian, 1378–1455, Baptistry Doors, *Gates of Paradise,* c. 1435, Florence

Michelangelo Buonarroti, Italian, 1475–1564, *St. Peter's Dome, Medici Chapel, Capitoline Hill,* 1513–1516

Pisano, Giovanni, Italian, 1245–1315, master mason of *Cathedral of Sienna,* 1290

SOLDIER

L'Enfant, Pierre, French, 1754–1825, boulevard system of Washington, DC; *Federal Building,* 1789, New York City

TEACHER

Cret, Paul, French American, 1876–1945, *Pan-American Union,* c. 1908, Washington, DC

Kallmann, Gerhard, German American, 1915, *Boston City Hall,* 1964–1969

Rapson, Ralph, American, 1914, *University of Chicago International Studies Building,* 1971; *Arts Center,* 1972, Minneapolis

WRITER

Campbell, Colen, English, 1676–1729, *Villa Rotondo at Mereworth Castle,* 1722–1725, England

Condit, Carl, American, 1914, Historical writer of architectural textbooks

Cram, Ralph Adams, American, 1863–1942, *Princeton Chapel,* c. 1911; *St. John the Divine,* 1911–1926, New York City

Downing, Andrew, American, 1815–1852, writer about landscape gardening

Halfpenny, William M. H., English, 1687–1755, 20 volumes of illustrations, plans, and elevations

Vanbrugh, Sir John, English, 1664–1726, spy, playwright; *Castle Howard,* 1699–1726; *Blenheim Palace,* 1705

Vasari, Giorgio, Italian, 1511–1574, *Lives of Architects, Painters, and Sculptors,* Uffizi Gallery, 1560–1580

List 7–7   Major Patrons of Architecture

A patron of architecture was one who had a personal interest in seeing something built. Patrons, whether they were royal or simply someone of wealth, had a vision and selected an architect who could carry out that vision. This list includes one or two examples of architecture done under the leadership of these major patron(s).

Abbot Suger, *Church of St. Denis,* c. 1135–1144, near Paris

Akbar the Great, Moghul Dynasty, *Fatehpur Sikri Palace,* c. 1568–1585, near Agra

Baron Georges-Eugene Haussmann, 1809–1891, French, city planner of Paris

Charlemagne, *Palace Chapel at Aachen,* 792–805, Germany

Charles I of England, *Banqueting Hall in Whitehall,* 1619–1622, London

Constantine the Great, *Arch of Constantine,* 312–315, Rome

Diocletian, *Palace at Split,* 284–316, Croatia

Duke Federigo Montefeltro, *Ducal Palace,* c. 1465–1479, Urbino

Elizabeth I of England, *Longleat House,* begun 1546, England

Emperor Hadrian, *Palace at Tivoli,* early 1st century, near Rome

Emperor Justinian, *Hagia Sophia,* 532–537, Istanbul

Ferdinand and Isabella of Spain, *Tempietto,* 1502, Rome

Francis I of France, 1515–1547, *Fontainebleu,* 1528, near Paris

Hans of Cologne, *Burgos Cathedral,* 1466, Cologne

Henry II of France, 1547–1559, *continued work on Fontainebleau,* near Paris

Henry VI of England, *King's College Chapel,* 1446, Cambridge

Henry VII of England, *Chapel, Westminster Abbey,* 1503–1519, London

Hugh, Abbot of Cluny, *St. Sernin,* c. 1080–1120, Toulouse, France

King João V of Portugal, *Queluz Palace,* 1747–1768, near Lisbon, Portugal

King Suleiman II, *Suleimaniye Mosque,* 16th century, Istanbul, Turkey

Louis XIII, *Versailles Hunting Lodge* and *first Versailles Chateau,* 1624–1641, Paris region

Louis XIV of France, *Louvre,* 1667–1670; *Versailles renovation,* 1669–1685

Louis XV, *Petit Trianon,* 1768; *Versailles,* near Paris

Ludwig II of Bavaria, *Neuschwanstein Castle,* 1868; and *Linderhof,* 19th century, near Munich, Germany

Maximian, Villa of Maximian, *Piazza Amerina,* c. AD 300, Sicily, Italy

Moghul Dynasty, *Red Fort, Pearl Mosque,* 1646–1653, Agra, India

Nayak Dynasty (India), *Great Temple Complex,* 17th century, Madurai, India

Ottoman Dynasty, Sultan Mehmed II the Conqueror, *Topkapi Palace,* 15th century, Istanbul

Ottonian Dynasty, *Benedictine Abbey Church of St. Michaels,* c. 1015, Hildesheim, Germany

Philip II of Spain, *Escorial,* 1559–1584, Madrid

Pope Julius II, *Sistine Chapel,* 1508–1512, Rome; *Medici Tomb Design,* 1513–1516, Florence

Prince Eugen of Savoy, *Upper Belvedere Palace,* 1714–1715, Vienna

Shah Jahan, *Taj Mahal,* 1632–1654, Agra, India

Tsar Ivan III, *Church of the Deposition,* c. 1485, Kremlin, Moscow

List 7–8   Landscape Architects

Abbott, Stanley William, 1908–1975, American, *Blue Ridge Parkway,* Virginia

Alphand, Jean-Charles-Adolphe, 1817–1891, French, *Bois de Boulogne,* Paris

Andre, Edouard François, 1840–1922, French, *Gardens of Villa Borghese,* Rome

Bac, Ferdinand, 1859–1952, French, interior design, hotels, Paris

Barragan, Luis, 1902–1989, Mexican, *San Cristobal Estate,* near Mexico City

Bottomly, William Lawrence, 1883–1951, American, *Williamsburg Restoration,* Virginia

Bridgeman, Charles, d. 1738, English, *Chicheley Hall, Bower House, Wimbleton House, Warwick Castle, Longleat, Hampton Court,* England

Brown, Lancelot "Capability," 1716–1783, English, *Blenheim Palace,* Woodstock, England

Burle-Marx, Roberto, 1909–1994, Brazilian, *Ministry of Health and Education,* Rio de Janeiro

Chambers, Sir William, 1726–1796, English, *Kew Gardens,* London

Child, Susan, Mary Miss, Stanton Ekstut, Americans, *South Cove, Battery Park,* New York City

Cleveland, Horace William Shafer, 1814–1900, American, *Jeckyll Island Club,* Georgia

Downing, Andrew Jackson, 1815–1852, American, *Lyndhurst,* wrote copybooks on gardening

Duchene, Achille, 1866?–1947, nationality unknown, *East front gardens of Blenheim Palace,* England

DuPont, Pierre, 1870–1954, American, *Longwood Garden,* Pennsylvania

Farrand, Beatrix, 1872–1959, English, *Dartington Hall,* Devonshire

Hall, William Hammond, 1846–1934, American, *Golden Gate Park,* San Francisco, California

Halfprin, Lawrence, 1916, American, *McIntyre Watergardens,* Hillsborough, California

Jefferson, Thomas, 1743–1826, American, *University of Virginia* and *Monticello Gardens,* Virginia

Jekyll, Gertrude, 1843–1932, English, *Sissinghurst Castle Gardens,* Kent, England

Jellicoe, Geoffrey, 1900–1996, English, *Shute House,* Wiltshire; *Sandringham House,* Huntstanton, England

Jensen, Jens, 1860–1951, Danish American, *Lincoln Memorial Garden,* Springfield, Illinois

Johnson, Philip, 1906, American, *Sculpture Garden,* Museum of Modern Art, New York City

Kent, William, 1685–1748, English, *Chatsworth, Chinese House,* Stowe, garden houses, England

LeNotre, Andre, 1613–1700, French, *Vaux-le-Vicompte,* gardens near Fontainebleau, France

Lin, Maya, 1959, American, *Vietnam Veterans' Memorial,* Washington, DC

Olmsted, Frederick Law, 1822–1903, American, *Biltmore, Central Park,* New York City; *Fairmont Park,* Philadelphia, Pennsylvania

Paxton, Sir Joseph, 1801–1865, English, *Chatsworth, Crystal Palace,* London

Repton, Humphry, 1752–1818, English, invented French doors

Romano, Giulio, 1492–1546, Italian, *Palace-garden design,* Versailles, France

Steele, Fletcher, 1885–1971, American, *Choate Garden,* Stockbridge, Massachusetts

Verdure, Mordant, 1899–1934, French American, *Barrymore's Summer Castle,* Palm Beach, Florida

Wirtz, Jacques, 1925, Belgian, *Tuilerie Gardens,* Paris

List 7–9   Cities That Have Preserved Their Architectural Heritage: Worth a Visit

Throughout the world are places that are worth a visit because of a unique set of circumstances that have caused them to maintain at least a portion of their architectural heritage. These are some that have special appeal.

AMERICA

Annapolis, Maryland: charming colonial city with many ancient houses

Boston, Massachusetts: colonial area well maintained

Chicago, Illinois: architectural heritage in downtown area is maintained

Economy, Pennsylvania: 1824, settled by the Bavarian Pietists (Harmonie sect)

Harmony (near Pittsburgh), Pennsylvania: 1804, settled by the Bavarian Pietists (Harmonie sect)

Mackinac Island, Michigan: a place that treasures its quiet past

New Harmony, Indiana: settled by the Bavarian Pietists (Harmonie sect), many restored homes

Newport, Rhode Island: "cottages" (mansions) built by the wealthy for summer residence

Oak Park, Illinois: numerous Frank Lloyd Wright homes

Old Deerfield Village, Massachusetts: colonial New England homes

Old Mystic Seaport, Connecticut: harbor, old wharf and buildings

Salem, Massachusetts: colonial houses and harbor remain much as they did in early days

San Francisco, California: "painted ladies"—beautifully painted Victorian homes on hillsides

Santa Fe, New Mexico: traditional Southwest building styles using mostly adobe

Savannah, Georgia: established in 1710, has retained its colonial charm

Springfield, Illinois: Lincoln's home, and 27 existing homes in the neighborhood maintained

St. Augustine, Florida: oldest city in the U.S. has maintained 31 original buildings

St. Genevieve, Missouri: French heritage homes open for viewing

St. Louis, Missouri: brick housing stock maintained in parts of town

Taos, New Mexico: a Pueblo that retains traditional adobe building style

Williamsburg, Virginia: colonial housing renovated and reconstructed

Zoar, Ohio: 1804, another "branch" of Bavarian Pietists

AUSTRIA

Melk: beautiful Baroque monastery, charming small town

Salzburg: castles, churches, charming city center, good walking

Vienna: palaces, Baroque architecture everywhere you look

BELGIUM

Antwerp: guild houses, medieval castle, home of Rubens

Bruges: city of canals and medieval buildings; even new buildings look old

Brussels: guild houses on the Grande Place

Ghent: oldest house in Europe (1066) is in Ghent; medieval castle, canals

CANADA

Duncan, B.C.: the home of totem poles and a Native American enclave

Montreal: cosmopolitan city with lovely old homes

Quebec City: city high on a bluff with very old homes

Victoria: island city that has preserved many homes and the old town

CROATIA

Dubrovnik: walled port city on the Adriatic Sea

Split: port city with *Diocletian's Palace*

FRANCE

Honfleur: charming preserved port city

Mont-Saint-Michel: c. 11th century, small island in Gulf of St. Malo

Paris: Paris truly deserves to be called the "City of Light," and proudly maintains its neighborhoods and architectural heritage

GERMANY

Dinklesbuhl: a charming stop on the Romantic Road

Heidelburg: this old town by the Neckar river has town gates and a grand castle

Meissen: a town that retains its heritage; visit the porcelain factory, palace, and museum

Rothenburg: a walled city, it has been preserved in most details

List 7–9   Continued

GREAT BRITAIN

Bath: Georgian architecture (crescent circles), ancient Roman baths restored

Broadway: charming Cotswold village, wide main street, beautiful old stone buildings

Cambridge: many colleges, a vibrant new/old city

Canterbury: this ancient city is wonderful for walking about; historic cathedral

Edinburgh, Scotland: *Edinburgh Castle,* a city in gray stone

London: many neighborhoods as they have been for hundreds of years

Lower Slaughter: golden cottages beside small streams; roses growing to the rooftops

Oxford: *Bodleian Library,* many colleges

Stratford-upon-Avon: the home of Shakespeare; many half-timbered houses

Stowe-on-the-Wold: Cotswold architecture, golden stone, town square, very Shakespearean

York: walk the Roman city walls; see half-timbered houses

ITALY

Florence: golden city with Medieval and Renaissance structures

Herculaneum: ancient city destroyed at the same time as Pompeii; excavation continues

Pompeii: excavation continues in this city buried in ashes in AD 79

Rome: ancient structures incorporated into modern city

Sienna: medieval city with very well-preserved center city and structures

SOUTH AMERICA

Bahia, Brazil: very old city built on two levels, preserving the heritage in both

Brazilia: new city that embodies modern city planning

Cuzco, Peru: this city high in the Andes seems as it must have for hundreds of years

Embu, Brazil: colonial city of small, charming buildings

Manaus, Brazil: city on the Amazon with an opulent opera house and other colonial buildings

Ouro Prato, Brazil: World Heritage city from colonial times; beautiful Baroque churches

OTHER

Prague, Czech Republic: Medieval city untouched by the ravages of war; beautiful Baroque buildings also

Venice

List 7–10   Selected Examples of Architecture, Catalogued by Style

Names of architects and dates of construction are listed if they are known.

AFRICA

Buildings at *University of Lagos,* (date unknown), Alan Vaughan-Richards, Lagos, Nigeria

Nigerian Railway Corporation Hospital, (date unknown), A. Ifeanyi Ekwueme, Lagos, Nigeria

Regional Tribunal and Palace of Justice, 1964, Jean-François Zevaco, Mohammedia, Morocco

School of Architecture, Kumasi University, 1960, Charles I. Hobbis, Ghana

Tourist Center and Hotel "Petit Merou," 1968, Elie Azagury, Cabo Negro, Morocco

Western Enclosure, c. 1000–1500 AD, Zimbabwe

AMERICA

Colonial Architecture, c. 1600–1820

Bank of Pennsylvania, 1798–1800, Benjamin Henry Latrobe, Philadelphia, Pennsylvania

Cahokia Courthouse, 1737, Cahokia, Illinois

Carpenters' Hall, 1770–1775, Robert Smith, Philadelphia, Pennsylvania

Castillo de San Marcos, 1672–1754, St. Augustine, Florida

Colony House, 1739, Richard Munday, Newport, Rhode Island

Drayton Hall, 1738–1742, Charleston County, South Carolina

Fanueuil Hall, 1740–1742, John Smibert, Boston, Massachusetts

First Baptist Meeting House, 1774–1775, Providence, Rhode Island

Governor's Palace, 1609–1614, Santa Fe, New Mexico

Hammond-Harwood House, 1773–1774, William Buckland, Annapolis, Maryland

Hancock House, 1735, Boston, Massachusetts

Independence Hall, 1731, Philadelphia, Pennsylvania

Miles Brewton House, 1765–1769, Charleston, South Carolina

Monticello, 1770–1809, Thomas Jefferson, Charlottesville, Virginia

Palace of the Governors, 1749–1751, Henry Cary, Williamsburg, Virginia

San Esteban, pre-1644, Acoma, New Mexico

Stanley-Whitman House, c. 1660, Farmington, Connecticut

The *"Saron" or Sister's House,* 1743, Ephrata, Pennsylvania

University of Virginia, 1804–1817, Thomas Jefferson, Charlottesville, Virginia

Virginia State Capitol, 1785–1798, Thomas Jefferson, Richmond, Virginia

Romantic Architecture, c. 1820–1880

Adams Memorial, 1886–1891, August Saint-Gaudens, Rock Creek Cemetery, Washington, DC

Baltimore Cathedral, 1804–1821, Benjamin Henry Latrobe, Baltimore, Maryland

New York University, 1832–1837, Alexander Jackson Davis, New York City

Pennsylvania Academy of Fine Arts, 1871–1876, Frank Furness, Philadelphia

Quincy Market, 1825–1826, Alexander Paris, Boston, Massachusetts

Renwick Gallery, 1859–1861, James Renwick, Washington, DC

Tennessee State Capitol, 1845–1859, William Strickland, Nashville

The Smithsonian Institution, 1846–1855, James Renwick, Washington, DC

The Treasury Building, 1836–1869, Robert Mills, Washington, DC

Trinity Church, 1839–1846, Richard Upjohn, New York City

U.S. Mint, 1829–1833, William Strickland, Philadelphia, Pennsylvania

United States Capitol, 1855–1864, Thomas Ustick Walter, Washington, DC

Victorian Architecture, c. 1860–1900

Biltmore House, 1895, Richard Morris Hunt, Asheville, North Carolina

The Breakers, 1892–1895, Richard Morris Hunt, Newport, Rhode Island

Carson Pirie Scott, 1898–1904, Louis Sullivan, Chicago, Illinois

Col. Walter Gresham House, 1887–1893, Nicholas J. Clayton, Galveston, Texas

The Griswold House, 1863, Stick style, Richard Morris Hunt, Newport, Rhode Island

The Long-Waterman House, 1889, Queen Anne style, B.B. Benson, San Diego, California

Marshall Field Wholesale Store, 1887, Henry Hobson Richardson, Chicago, Illinois

State, War and Navy Building, 1888, Alfred B. Mullett, Washington, DC

Terrace Hill, 1869, Second Empire style, W. W. Boyington, Des Moines, Iowa

Wainwright Building, 1891, Louis Sullivan, St. Louis, Missouri

William G. Low House, 1887, McKim, Mead and White, Bristol, Rhode Island

Early Twentieth Century Architecture

Ayer Building, 1900, Holabird and Roche, Chicago, Illinois

Cannon House, Office Building, 1908, Carrere and Hastings, Washington, DC

First Church of Christ Scientist, 1909–1911, Bernard Maybeck, Berkeley, California

List 7–10 Continued

AMERICA (cont.)

Early Twentieth Century Architecture (cont.)

Flatiron Building, 1902, D.H. Burnham and Company, New York City

Frederick C. Robie House, 1908–1909, Frank Lloyd Wright, Chicago, Illinois

Frick Gallery, 1914, Carrere and Hastings, New York City

Pennsylvania Station (demolished), 1906–1910, McKim, Mead and White, New York City

Singer Tower, 1907, Ernest Flagg, New York City

St. Louis Art Museum, 1904, Cass Gilbert, St. Louis, Missouri

Unity Church, 1906, Frank Lloyd Wright, Oak Park, Illinois

Ward Willits House, 1900–1902, Frank Lloyd Wright, Highland Park, Illinois

Woolworth Building, 1910–1913, Cass Gilbert, New York City

Art Deco Style

Chrysler Building, 1928–1930, William Van Alen, New York City

Empire State Building, 1932, Shreve, Lamb, and Harmon, New York City

Gulfstream Golf Club, 1923, Addison Mizner, Palm Beach, Florida

McGraw-Hill Building, 1931, Raymond Hood, New York City

Rockefeller Center, 1931–1939, Raymond M. Hood, Wallace K. Harrison, others, New York City

Tribune Tower, 1925, Hood and Howells, Chicago, Illinois

Architecture Between the Two World Wars

Falling Water, Kaufmann House, 1936–1937, Frank Lloyd Wright, Bear Run, Pennsylvania

House for Dr. Phillip Lovell, 1927–1929, Richard Neutra, Los Angeles, California

Johnson Wax Building, 1936, Frank Lloyd Wright, Racine, Wisconsin

La Casa Grande, 1919–1939, Julia Morgan, San Simeon, California

Taliesin West, 1938–1959, Frank Lloyd Wright, Phoenix, Arizona

William L. Clements Library, 1920–1921, Albert Kahn, University of Michigan, Ann Arbor

Post World War II Architecture

Boston City Hall, 1964–1969, Kallman, McKinnell and Knowles, Boston, Massachusetts

City Corp Center, 1974–1977, Hugh Stubbins Associates, New York City

C.B.S. Building, 1960–1964, Eero Saarinen, New York City

Dr. Edith Farnsworth House, 1945–1951, Ludwig Mies van der Rohe, Plano, Illinois

General Motors Technical Center, 1948–1952, Eliel and Eero Saarinen, Warren, Michigan

Guggenheim Museum, 1946–1959, Frank Lloyd Wright, New York City

John Hancock Tower, 1977, I.M. Pei and Henry N. Cobb, Boston, Massachusetts

Johnson House (Glass House), 1945–1949, Philip Johnson, New Canaan, Connecticut

Kresge Auditorium, 1955, Eero Saarinen, M.I.T., Cambridge, Massachusetts

Lake Shore Apartment Houses, 1949–1951, Ludwig Mies van der Rohe, Chicago, Illinois

Lever House, 1950–1952, Skidmore, Owings, Merrill, New York City

Marina City, 1959–1967, Bertram Goldberg Associates, Chicago, Illinois

Richards Medical Research Building, 1957–1961, Louis I. Kahn, University of Pennsylvania, Philadelphia

Seagram Building, 1954–1958, Ludwig Mies van der Rohe and Philip Johnson, New York City

T.W.A. Terminal, 1956–1962, Eero Saarinen, Kennedy Airport, New York City

Union Carbide Building, 1957–1960, Skidmore, Owings, Merrill, New York City

United Nations Secretariat, 1947–1950, Wallace K. Harrison, New York City

United States Air Force Academy, 1955–1958, Skidmore, Owings, and Merrill, Colorado Springs, Colorado

United States Embassy, 1957–1959, Edward Stone, New Delhi, India

Yale Center for British Art, 1969–1972, Louis I. Kahn, New Haven, Connecticut

Post-Modern Architecture

AT&T Corporate Headquarters, 1979–1984, John Burgee Architects, New York City

Crystal Cathedral, 1980, Philip Johnson, Garden Grove, California

East Building, National Gallery of Art, 1968–1978, I.M. Pei and Partners, Washington, DC

Entrance Pyramid, Le Grand *Louvre,* 1989, I.M. Pei, Paris

Euro Disney Complex, 1991–1992, Robert A.M. Stern, Arata Isozaki, Frank Gehry, Charles Gwathmey, Robert Siegel, and Michael Graves, Orlando, Florida

Getty Center, 1997, Richard Meier, Los Angeles, California

High Museum of Art, 1980–1983, Richard Meier, Atlanta, Georgia

Hirshhorn Museum, 1973, Skidmore, Owings, Merrill, Washington, DC

Jefferson Arch, 1965, Eero Saarinen, St. Louis, Missouri

John Hancock Center, 1970, Skidmore, Owings, Merrill, Chicago, Illinois

Kimbell Art Museum, 1972, Louis I. Kahn, Fort Worth, Texas

Pennzoil Place, 1976, John Burgee (with Philip Johnson), Houston, Texas

Portland Public Services Building, 1980, Michael Graves, Portland, Oregon

List 7–10   Continue

Post-Modern Architecture (cont.)

Republic Bank, 1981–1984, Philip Johnson and John Burgee, Houston, Texas

San Francisco Museum of Modern Art, 1995, Mario Botta, San Francisco, California

Sea Ranch Condominiums, 1965, Charles, Moore, Gualala, California

Sears Roebuck Tower, 1973, Skidmore, Owings, Merrill, Chicago, Illinois

Seattle Art Museum, c. 1991, Venturi, Scott Brown, Seattle, Washington

The Humana Building, 1982, Michael Graves, Louisville, Kentucky

Town of Seaside, 1978–1983, Andres Duaney and Elizabeth Plater-Zybert, Florida

Transamerica Pyramid, 1972, William Pereira, San Francisco

Vanna Venturi House, 1963–1965, Robert Venturi, Chestnut Hill, Pennsylvania

Whitney Museum of American Art, 1981, Michael Graves, New York City

World Trade Center, 1972, Minoru Yamasaki, New York City

First Interstate Bank World Center, 1989, Pei, Cobb, and Freed, Los Angeles, California

AUSTRALIA

Darling Harbor Redevelopment, 1988, Philip Cox, Richardson and Taylor, Sydney

New Parliamentary Buildings, 1988, Michell/Giurgola and Thorp, Canberra

Opera House, 1959–1973, John Utzon, Sydney

Rialto Center, 1985, Gerard de Preu, Melbourne

AUSTRIA

Baroque

Benedictine Abbey, 1702–1738, Jakob Prandtauer, Melk

Burgtheater, 1880–1886, G. Semper and Karl von Hasenauer, Vienna

Karlskirche, 1716–1737, Johann Bernhard Fischer von Erlach, Vienna

Modern

Steiner House, 1910, Adolf Loos, Vienna

BELGIUM

Cathedral, 1352–1521, Antwerp

House, #4 Avenue Palmerson, 1894, Victor Horta, Brussels

Palais Stoclet, 1905–1911, J. Hoffmann, Brussels

Salon, Van Eetvelde House, 1895, Victor Horta, Brussels

CANADA

Canadian Museum of Civilization, 1989, Hull, Douglas Cardinal and Associates, Quebec

Civic Buildings, 1961–1965, Viljo Revell, Toronto

Geodesic Dome, 1967, Buckminster Fuller, American Pavilion, Montreal, Quebec

Habitat, 1964–1967, Moshe Safdie (b. Israel), David Barott and Boulva, Montreal

Parliamentary Library, 1859–1867, Thomas Fuller and C. Jones, Ottawa

U.S. Pavilion, 1967, R. Buckminster Fuller, Montreal

CHINA

Big Goose Pagoda, AD 645, Ch'ang-an, Xian

Central Plaza, 1992, Ng Chun Man & Associates, Hong Kong

Fo Kuang Temple Hall, 857, Beijing

Sung Yueh Pagoda, 523, Mount Sung, Shanghai

T'ai-ho Tien, Forbidden City, 1406–1420, Beijing

Temple of Heaven Group, begun 14th century, Beijing

Tien, I-ho Yuan, Summer Palace, 1750, 1888, 1903, Beijing

EGYPT

Funerary Temple of Queen Hatshepsut, 1480 BC, Deir el Bahari (near Thebes)

Great Pyramids, 2470–2530 BC, Giza

Great Sphinx, c. 2500 BC, Giza

Pyramid of Chefren, 2530 BC, Giza

Pyramid of Cheops, 2528 BC, Giza

Pyramid of Mycerinus, 2500 BC Giza

King Zoser's Step Pyramid at Sakkara, Imhotep, c. 2630 BC, Giza

Temple of Amon, c. 1570–1085 BC, Karnak

Temple of Horus, begun 327 BC, Edfu

Temple of Ramesses II, c. 1257 BC, Abu Simbel

St. Basil's Cathedral, Moscow

List 7–10   Continued

ENGLAND

Stonehenge, c. 2000 BC, near Salisbury

Gothic

Salisbury Cathedral, 1220–1270, Salisbury
Winchester Cathedral, c. 1394–1450

Baroque

Banqueting Hall, 1619–1622, Inigo Jones, London
New St. Paul's, 1675–1710, Christopher Wren, London
Queen's House, 1616–1635, Inigo Jones, Greenwich

Later Periods

Chiswick House, 1725–1729, Lord Burlington and William
    Kent, London
Crystal Palace, 1851, John Paxton, London
Holkham Hall, 1734, William Kent and Lord Burlington,
    Norfolk
Houses of Parliament, 1836–c. 1860, Sir Charles Barry and
    A. Welby Pugin, London
Museum of Science, 1855–1858, Benjamin Woodward, Oxford
One Canada Square, 1991, Cesar Pelli, London
Royal Crescent, 1767, John Wood the Elder, John Wood the
    Younger, Bath
Royal Pavilion, 1815–1818, John Nash, Brighton
Strawberry Hill, 1748–1777, Horace Walpole, Robert Adam,
    others, Twickenham
Syon House, 1762–1763, Robert Adam, Middlesex

FRANCE
Romanesque

Cathedral, 1067, St. Etienne
St. Sernin Cathedral, 1080–1120, Toulouse

Gothic

Abby Church of St. Denis, c. 1135–1144, St. Denis
Cathedral, 1220–1236, Amiens
Chartres Cathedral, 1140–1220, Chartres
Notre Dame, 1163–1250, Paris
Sainte Chappelle, 1243–1248, Paris

Renaissance and Post-Renaissance

Louvre east front, 1667–1670, Louis LeVau, Charles Le
    Brun, and Claude Perrault, Paris

Baroque and Neo Classical

Arc de Triomphe de l'Etoile, 1806–1835, Jean-Francois-
    Therese Chalgrin, Paris
Bibliothèque Nationale, 1843–1850, H. Labrouste, Paris
Church of the Invalides, 1679–1691, Jules Hardouin
    Mansart, Paris
Church of the Madeleine, 1806–1843, Pierre Vignon, Paris
City Plan of Washington, DC, 1791, Pierre Charles L'Enfant,
    Washington, DC

L'Opera, 1861–1875, Charles Garnier, Paris
Versailles, 1669–1685, Louis LeVau, Jules Hardouin Mansart,
    near Paris

Modern

Centre Georges Pompidou for Arts and Culture, 1977, Renzo
    Plano and Richard Rogers, Paris
Eiffel Tower, 1887–1889, Gustave Eiffel, Paris
Galerie des Machines, 1889, International exposition, Ferdi-
    nand Dutert, Paris
Gare d'Orsay, 1898–1900, Victor Laloux, Paris
Metro Stations, 1899–1904, Hector Guimard, Paris
New Opera House, 1989, Carlos Ott, Paris
Notre Dame de Haute, 1950, Le Corbusier, Ronchamp
Ozenfant House, 1922, Le Corbusier, Paris
Unite d'Habitation, 1947–1952, Le Corbusier, Marseilles
Villa Savoye, 1929, Le Corbusier, Poissy

GERMANY
Pre-Romanesque–19th century

The Carolingian Palatine Chapel, 792–805, Aachen
St. Michael's, 1001, Hildesheim

Baroque and Neo-Classical

Altes Museum, 1824–1828, Karl Friedrich Schinkel, Berlin
Schauspielhaus, 1819–1821, Karl Friedrich Schinkel, Berlin
Zwinger, 1709, Dresden

Modern

A.E.G. Turbine Factory, 1908–1909, Peter Behrens, Berlin
Art School and School of Arts and Crafts, 1904–1907, Henri
    van de Velde, Weimar, Germany
Bauhaus Building, 1925–1926, Walter Gropius, Dessau
Einstein Tower, 1919–1921, Erich Mendelsohn, near Pots-
    dam
Fagus Factory, 1910–1914, Walter Gropius and Hannes
    Meyer, Alfeld-an-der-Leine
German Pavilion, International Exposition, 1929, Ludwig
    Mies van der Rohe, Barcelona
Messeturm, 1990, Helmut Jahn, Frankfurt
Neue Staatsgalerie, 1977–1984, James Stirling and Michael
    Wilford, Stuttgart
Philharmonie Concert Hall, 1960–1963, H. Scharoun, Berlin
Pilgrimage Church, c. 1960, Gottfried Bohm, Neviges
Theater, Werkbund Exhibition of 1914, Henry van de Velde,
    Cologne

GREECE AND GREEK ISLANDS (SPREAD FAR
BEYOND GREECE)

Altar of Zeus, Pergamon, c. 180 BC (now on view in Berlin)
Church of the Dormition, c. 1100, Daphni
Parthenon, Acropolis, 437–442 BC, architects Ictinos and
    Phidias, Athens
Erechtheum, Acropolis, 421–405 BC, Athens

List 7–10   Continued

GREECE AND GREEK ISLANDS (SPREAD FAR BEYOND GREECE) (cont.)

Propylaea, Acropolis, 437–432 BC, Athens
Temple of Athena Nike, Acropolis, 427–424 BC, Athens
Palace of King Minos, c. 2000 BC, Knossos
Temple of Apollo, 513–505 BC, Delphi
Temple of Artemis, c. 580 BC, Corfu
Temple of Hephaestus, 449–c. 430 BC, Athens
Tholos Tomb, Lion Gate, c. 1250 BC, Mycenae
Treasury of Atreus, c. 1300–1250 BC, Mycenae
Treasury of the Athenians, c. 489 BC, Delphi

Byzantine

Church of Gorgeopekos, c. 1190–1195, Athens
Church of Our Lady of the Coppersmiths, 1028, Thessaloniki
Church of the Holy Apostles, 1310–1314, Thessaloniki

INDIA

Ajanta Cave #1, late 5th century, Ajanta
Capitol Buildings, 1951–1957, Le Corbusier, Chandigarh
Great Stupa, 3rd century BC–early 1st century AD, Sanchi
Great Temple Complex, 17th century, Madurai
Kailasanatha Temple, c. 757–790, Elura
Kandariya Mahadeo Temple, c. 1025–1050, Chandella
Mukteshvara Temple, c. 950, Bhuvaneshvar
Surya Temple, c. 1240, Konarak, Eastern Ganga
Taj Mahal, 1632–1654, Agra

IRAN

Blue Mosque, 1467, Tabriz
Darius' Palace, c. 520 BC, Persepolis
Legislature Buildings, 1964, Teheran
Tarik Khana Mosque, early 8th century, Damghan

IRAQ

Babylon Ruins, 6th century BC, near al-Hillah
Maliwa (spiral brick minaret), c. AD 1000, Samarra

ITALY

Basilica, (Temple of Hera I), 530 BC (Doric), Paestum
Basilica, (Temple of Hera II), 448–430 BC (Doric), Paestum

Etruscan

Tomb of Hunting and Fishing, c. 510–500 BC, Tarquinia
Tomb of the Reliefs, 6th to 4th century BC, Ceveteri

Early Christian

Church of S. Sabina, 422–432 AD, Rome
Hadrian's Villa, 125–138 AD, near Rome
Old St. Peter's Cathetral, AD 330, Rome
The Orthodox Baptistry, c. 400–450 AD, Rome
Santa Costanza, c. AD 350, Rome
S. Maria Maggiore, c. AD 432, Rome
S. Paolo Outside the Walls, begun AD 385, Rome

Roman Architecture

Ara Pacis, 13–9 BC, Rome
Baths of Caracalla, 212–216 AD, Rome
Forum Romanum, 46 BC, Rome
Khazna Temple, c. AD 120, Petra, Jordan
Palace of Diocletian, 284–316 AD, Split, Croatia
Pantheon, c. 118–128 AD, Rome
Pont Du Gard (aqueduct), AD 14, Nimes, France
Porta Nigra, c. AD 320, Trier, Germany
Temple of Castor and Pollux, 484 BC, The Forum, Rome
Temple of Vesta, c. 27 BC, Tivoli, Rome
The Colosseum, AD 80, Rome

Byzantine

Mausoleum of Galla Placida, c. AD 425, Ravenna
Mausoleum of King Theodoric, c. AD 526, Ravenna
San Apollinare in Classe, 432–449 AD, Classe (near Ravenna)
San Vitale, 526–548 AD, Ravenna
St. Mark's Cathedral, c. 1063, Venice

Medieval

Cathedral Group, 1153–1283, Pisa, Italy

Renaissance

Campidoglio Plaza (Capitoline Hill), 1538–1561, Michelangelo Buonarroti, Rome
Dome of St Peter's, 1546–1564, Michelangelo Buonarroti, Rome
Palazzo Uffizi, Giorgio Vasari, 1560–1580, Florence
Tempietto, 1500–1502, Donato Bramante, Rome
Villa Rotonda, Vicenza, 1567–1570, Andrea Palladio, Vicenza

Baroque

Castello Nuovo, 1260, Naples
Cathedral, 1380, Milan
Doges Palace, 1345, Venice
Farnese Palace, 1535, Rome
New St. Peter's façade, 1607–1615, Carlo Maderno, Rome
S. Andrea al Quirinale, c. 1650, Rome
San Carlo alle Quattro Fontana, 1638–1667, Rome
San Giorgio Maggiore, 1565, Venice
Sant' Agnese, Piazza Navone, 1653–1666, Francesco Borromini, Rome
St. Peter's Colonnade, 1656–1657, Gian Lorenzo Bernini, Rome

Post Renaissance

Vittorio Emanuele Monument, 1865–1867, Giuseppe Mengoni, Milan

List 7–10   Continued

JAPAN

Castle, 1550, Osaka
City Hall, 1952–1957, Kenzo Tange, Tokyo
Edo Castle, c. 16th century, Tokyo
Great Buddha Hall, begun AD 738, Nara
Hoodo (Phoenix Hall), 1052, Uji, near Kyoto
Ishiyamadera Temple, 1194, Lake Biwa
Kinkakuji (Golden Pavilion), 1397, Kyoto
Landmark Tower, 1993, Yokohama
Museum of Contemporary Art, 1988, Kisho Kurokawa, Hiroshima
Nijo Castle, 1602, Kyoto
Pagoda of the Yakushiji, c. 8th century, Nara,
Palace, AD 1607, Nara
Shrine, AD 300, (shrine rebuilt every 20 years since 478), Ise

MEXICO

Church of San Francisco, 1521, Tlaxcala
El Castillo, AD 800, Chichen Itza, Yucatan
House of the Virgins, c. 530, Chichen Itza, Yucatan
Metropolitan Cathedral, 1570–c. 1810, Mexico City
Monte Alban, 1st century to c. 950 AD, Oaxaca
Pyramid of the Sun, AD 25, Teotihuacan
Temple of Tlahuizcalpantecuhtli, c. AD 1000, Tula
Terraced city, c. AD 900, Uxmal

NETHERLANDS

Café de Unie, 1925, J.J.P. Oud, Rotterdam
NMB Bank, 1988, Ton Alberts, Amsterdam
Schroder House, 1924–25, Gerrit Rietveld, Utrecht
Town Hall, 1926–1930, Willem Marinus Dudok, Hilversum

PORTUGAL

Palacio Nacional de Queluz, 1747–1768, near Lisbon

SCOTLAND

School of Art, 1896–1910, Charles Rennie Macintosh, Glasgow

SPAIN
Islamic

The Alhambra, 1354–1391, Granada
Mosque, begun 785, Cordoba

Medieval

Santiago de Compostela, 1060–1130, Spain

Baroque

Hospice of San Fernando (Municipal Museum), 1722, Pedro de Ribera, Madrid
Sacristy of the Cartuja, 1732–1743, Francisco Hurtado Izquierdo, Granada

Art Nouveau

Casa Batlo, 1905–1907, Antoni Gaudi, Barcelona
Casa Mila Apartment House, 1905–1907, Antoni Gaudi, Barcelona
Church of the Sagrada Familia, 1883–1926, Antoni Gaudi, Barcelona

Contemporary

Guggenheim Museum, 1998, Frank Gehry, Bilbao

SWEDEN

The Globe Arena, 1989, Berg Arkitekkontor, AB, Stockholm

TURKEY

Binbirdirek Cistern (the Cistern of the Thousand and One Columns), 6th century, Istanbul
Hagia Sophia, (formerly a Christian Church), 532–537, Istanbul
Mosque of Ahmed I, 1609–1616, Istanbul
Mosque of Selim II, 1570–1574, Edirne
Mosque of Sultan Suleyman, 1150, Istanbul
St. Saviour, rebuilt early 14th century, Khora
Temple of Artemis, c. 356 BC, Epidaurus
Theater, c. 350 BC, Polycleitos the younger, Epidaurus
Tholos, c. 350 BC, Epidaurus

OTHER

Angkor Wat, 12th century, Cambodia
Brazilian Civic Center, 1955, Brasilia, Oscar Niemeier, Brazil
Byzantine Church, 1318–1321, Gracanica, Bosnia Herzegovina
Cathedral of the Assumption, 12th century, Vladmir, Russia
Civic Center, 1950–1951, Aalto, Saynatsalo, Finland
Diocletian's Palace, 284–316 AD, Split, Croatia
El Deir Temple, 2nd century BC, Petra, Jordan
Great Mosque of Samarra, AD 800, Arabia
Ishtar Gate, Babylon, c. 575 BC, on view at State Museum, Berlin
Stupa of Borobudur, 9th century, Java
Terraces of Machu Picchu, c. AD 1450, Peru
Ziggurat at Ur, 2100 BC, Arabia

List 7–11 Ancient Roman Architecture

Many cities within the ancient Roman empire have portions of ruins that may be explored. There were 952 baths in the city of Rome at its peak, so one would expect continued discoveries and excavations of ruins. Modern geographical names and locations are listed. A (mostly) complete listing of excavations is in the *Princeton Encyclopedia of Classical Sites.*

AMPHITHEATERS

Amphitheater, 1st–3rd centuries AD, Catania, Sicily

Amphitheater, Nimes, c. 30 BC, Nimes, France

Amphitheater, 80–70 BC, Pompeii

Amphitheater, AD 50, Orange, France

Amphitheater, AD 56, Lepcis, Libya

Amphitheater, 1st to 2nd centuries AD, Newport, South Wales

Arena, 1st century AD, Pula, Croatia

Arena, c. 100–50 BC, Verona, Italy

Colosseum, c. 45 BC, El Djem, Tunisia

Colosseum, AD 80, Rome

Colosseum, before 55 BC, Arles, France

Colosseum, Rome, 80 AD

AQUEDUCTS

Albarregas Aqueduct, 3rd century, Badajoz, Spain

Aqueduct, 122 BC, Carthage, Tunisia

Aqueduct, 1st century BC, Merida, Spain

Aqueduct, 1st to 3rd century AD, Cherchel, Algeria

Aqueduct, c. AD 10, Segovia, Spain

Aqueduct, 2nd century AD, Moria, Lesbos

Las Perreras Aqueduct, 1st or early 2nd century AD, Tarragona, Spain

Marcian Aqueduct, 144 BC, near Rome

Pont du Gard, c. AD 14, near Nimes, France

TRIUMPHAL ARCHES

Arch of Argentarii, AD 204, Rome

Arch of Augustus, 27 BC, Rimini, Italy

Arch of Augustus, 8 BC, Susa, Italy

Arch of Augustus, c. 20 BC, Forum, Rome

Arch of Caracalla, AD 217, Meknes, Morocco

Arch of Constantine, 312–315 AD, Rome

Arch of Galerius, c. AD 300, Salonica, Greece

Arch of Hadrian, AD 138, Athens

Arch of Janus, AD 315, Rome

Arch of the Julii, c. 40 BC, St. Remy, France

Arch of Marcus Aurelius, AD 163, Oea, Tripoli, Libya

Arch of Septimius Severus, c. AD 203, Forum, Rome

Arch of Septimius Severus, c. AD 200, Lepcis, Libya

Arch of Septimus Severus, AD 235, Dougga, Tunisia

Arch of Tiberius, c. AD 26, Orange, France

Arch of Trajan, c. AD 114, Timgad, Algeria

Arch of Titus, AD 81, Rome

Archway, 1st century AD, Palmyra

BASILICAS

Basilica of Maxentius and Constantine, c. 307–312 AD, Forum, Rome

Basilica Nova, AD 313, Forum, Rome

Basilica of Porcia, 184 BC, Forum, Rome

Basilica, 98–117 AD, Cyrene, Libya

Basilica, 2nd century BC, Tuscany, Italy

Basilica, c. 125 BC, Pompeii

Basilica, c. AD 310, Trier, Germany

Basilica Vetus, AD 216, Lepcis, Libya

BATHS

Achellian Baths, (no date available), Catania, Sicily

Bath, 1st century, Bath, England

Baths at Trier, c. AD 300, Germany

Baths of Caracalla, AD 216, Rome

Baths of Diocletian, AD 305, Rome (now church of S. Maria degli Angeli)

Baths of Diocletian, c. 298–306 AD, Split, Croatia

Baths of Titus, c. AD 80, Rome

Baths of Trajan, AD 109, Rome

Forum Baths, 1st century BC, Pompeii

Forum Baths, AD 160, Ostia, Italy

Hadrianic Baths, AD 127, Lepcis, Libya

Harbor Baths, late 2nd century AD, Ephesus, Turkey

North Baths, 4th century AD, Timgad, Algeria

List 7–11 Continued

BATHS (cont.)

Stabian Baths, 2nd century BC, Pompeii

Winter Baths, 2nd century AD, Henchir Kasbat, Tunisia

BRIDGES

Alcantara Bridge, 105–106 AD, River Tagus, Spain

Bridge at Narni, c. 27 BC, Narni, Italy

Bridge at Merida, c. 3rd century AD, Merida, Spain

Pons Aelius, AD 135, Rome

Pons Cestius, 46 BC, Rimini, Italy

Pons Fabricius, 62 BC, River Tiber, Rome

Ponte Molle, 109 BC, Rome

Salamanca, c. 1st century AD, Spain

FORUMS

Forum of Augustus, 31–2 BC, Rome

Forum of Nerva, AD 97, Rome

Forum Romanum, 46 BC, Rome

Forum of Trajan, AD 113, Rome

Forum of Vespasian, 71–75 AD, Rome

Forum Vetus, c. 30–20 BC, Lepcis, Libya

Forum, 1st century BC, Annaba, Algeria

Forum, 2nd century AD, Henchir Kasbat, Tunisia

Forum, c. 1st century BC, Pompeii

Forum, 2nd century AD, Dougga, Tunisia,

Hadrian's Forum, 125–128 AD, Rome

Severan Forum, AD 216, Lepcis, Libya

FORTRESSES

Carnuntum, AD 73, near Vienna, Austria

Carvoran, c. 120–132 AD, near Greenhead, England

Chesters Roman Fort, c. 120–125 AD, near Chollerford, England

Housesteads Roman Fort, 2nd century AD, near Bardon Mill, England

Vindolanda, c. AD 80, near Bardon Mill, England

LIBRARIES

Library, 4th century AD, Timgad, Algeria

Library of Celsus, AD 115, Ephesus, Turkey

MONUMENTS

Ara Pacis, 13–9 BC, Rome

Column of Marcus Aurelius, 176–193 AD, Rome

Mausoleaum, 40 BC, St. Remy, France

Mausoleum of Augustus, c. 25 BC, Rome

Tomb of Caecilia Metella, c. 20 BC, Rome

Trajan's Column, AD 113, Rome

PALACES

Domus Aurea, 1st century AD, Rome

Domitian's Palace, c. AD 75, Palatine, Rome

Fishbourne, c. AD 80, Chichester, England

Palace of Diocletian, 284–316 AD, Split, Croatia

TEMPLES

Bacchus, c. 150–200 AD, Baalbek, Lebanon

Apollo, 431 BC, Rome

Apollo, 1st century AD, Pompeii

Artemis, 6th century BC, Ephesus, Turkey

Artemis, 2nd century AD, Jerash, Jordan

Bel, AD 32, Palmyra, Tadmor, Sicily

Capitoline Jupiter, 509 BC, Rome

Castor and Pollux, 484 BC, The Forum, Rome

*Concor*d, AD 10, Rome

Deified Claudius, AD 70, Rome

Deified Hadrian, AD 145, Rome

Fortuna Virilis, c. 120 BC, Rome

Hadrian, c. 2nd century AD, Ephesus, Turkey

Hercules Victor, c. 120 BC, Rome

Hercules, c. 100 BC, Latium, Italy

Jupiter, 1st century AD, Baalbek, Lebanon

Maison Carré, 16 BC, Nimes, France

Pantheon, c. 118–128 AD, Rome

Pergamon, 180 BC, Mysia, Turkey

Portumnus, 31 BC, Rome

Rome and Augustus, c. 1st century AD, Lepcis, Libya

Sanctuary of Fortuna Primigenia, 1st century BC, Praeneste (near Rome), Italy

Septimus Severus, c, 1st century AD, Djemila, Algeria

The Sybils, early 1st century BC, Tivoli

Venus and Rome, 123–135 AD, Rome

Venus, c. 118–135 AD, Hadrian's Villa, Tivoli

Venus, c. 2nd–3rd century AD, Baalbek, Lebanon

Vespasian, c. 62–79 AD, Pompeii

Vesta (now S. Maria del Sole), c. 27 BC, Tivoli

THEATERS

Theater, c. 1st century BC, Annaba, Algeria

Theater, c. 46 BC, Arles, France

Theater at Aspendos, 161–180 AD, Pamphylia, Turkey

Theater, 8 BC, Badajoz, Spain

Theater, c. 2nd century BC, Ephesus, Turkey

Theater, 1–2 AD, Lepcis, Libya

Theater, 1st century BC, Lyon, France

List 7–11 Continued

THEATERS (cont.)

Theater, c. 30 BC, Nimes, France

Theater, 1st century AD, Orange, France

Theater, 2nd century AD, Petra, Jordan

Theater Marcello, 13–11 BC, Rome

Theater at Sabratha, AD 180, Tripolis, Libya

Theater at St. Albans, 43–44 AD, Hertfordshire, England

Theater, 2nd century AD, Taormina, Sicily

Theater, c. 100–54 BC, Veneto, Italy

TOMBS

Catacombs, c. 100–300 AD, Rome

Mausoleum of Hadrian, AD 140, Tivoli, Italy

Pyramid of Caius Cestius, c. 18–12 BC, Rome

Rock-cut tomb of ed-Deir, Petra, 2nd century AD, Jordan

TOWN GATEWAYS

Colcester Town Gateway, c. AD 120, England

Gate of Augustus, 16 to 15 BC, Nimes, France

Market Gate, c. AD 160, Miletus (now in State Museums, Berlin)

Porta Appia, 275–280 AD, Rome

Porta Augusta, 2nd century BC, Perugia, Italy

Porta Aurea, c. AD 300, Split, Croatia

Porta Borsari, 1st century AD, Verona, Italy

Porta Maggiore, AD 52, Rome

Porta Nigra, c. AD 320, Trier, Germany

Porta Sanguinaria, 2nd century BC, Ferentino

Porta San Sebastiano, c. 3rd century AD, Rome

Two *Town Gateways,* c. 20 BC, Autun, France

VILLAS

Amor and Psyche, AD 4th century, Ostia, Italy

Brading Roman Villa, 3rd century, Brading, England

Diana, 2nd century AD, Ostia, Italy

Golden House of Nero, c. AD 64, Rome

Hadrian's Villa, c. 125–138 AD, Tivoli

House of the Faun, 180 BC, Pompeii

House of the Red Walls, pre AD 79, Pompeii

House of the Silver Wedding, 1st century AD, Pompeii

House of the Surgeon, 3rd century BC, Pompeii

House of Vettii, 63–79 AD, Pompeii

Lucretius Fronto, c. AD 30, Pompeii

Tiberius' Villa, c. AD 27, Capri

Villa at Boscoreale, 1st century BC, near Pompeii

Villa of the Mysteries, c. 50 BC, Pompeii

Villa, c. AD 200, Tripolis, Lebanon

Villa Jovis, 14–37 AD, Capri, Italy

WALLS

Augustan Walls, 6th–3rd centuries BC, Tarragona, Spain

Aurelian's Wall, c. AD 270, Rome

Hadrian's Wall, AD 136, England

List 7–12 Ancient Greek Architecture

Many of these ruins have been restored, but many have only a few columns intact and the rest is left to your imagination. However, the grandeur that was ancient Greece is evident even in its ruins.

GREECE

Athens

Erechtheum, 421–405 BC, Athens
Monument of Lysicrates, c. 334 BC, Athens
Olympieion, c. 170 BC, Athens
Parthenon, 437–442 BC, Athens
Propylaea, 437–432 BC, Athens
Stadium, begun 331 BC, Athens
Stoa of Attalos, c. 150 BC, Athens
Temple of Athena Nike, 427–424 BC, Athens
Temple of Zeus, AD 131–132, Athens
Theater of Dionysus, c. 330 BC, Athens

Corinth

Temple of Athena Nike, c. 1st century BC, Corinth
Temple of Apollo, c. 540 BC, Corinth

Delphi

Temple of Apollo, 513–505 BC, Delphi
Treasure of the Athenians, c. 489 BC, Delphi
Treasury of the Siphnians, c. 530 BC, Delphi
Theater, 2nd century BC, Delphi

Delos

Athenian Temple, 425–420 BC, Delos
Basilica of St. Ciriacus, 3rd to 2nd centuries BC, Delos
House of Dionysos, 2nd century BC, Delos
House of the Masks, 2nd century BC, Delos
Poseidoniastes, 2nd century BC, Delos
Temple to Apollo, 7th century BC, Delos

Epidaurus

Temple of Aphrodite, 4th to 3rd centuries BC, Epidaurus
Temple of Apollo, c. 510 BC, Epidaurus
Theater, c. 350 BC, Epidaurus

Other

Lion Gate to the Palace, 1250 BC, Mycenae
Sanctuary of the Great Gods, 340 BC, Samothrace
Temple of Aphaia, 490 BC, Aegina
Temple of Apollo, 5th century BC, Arkadia
Temple of Poseidon, 444–440 BC, Sounion
Theater, 2nd century BC, Priene
Treasury of Atreus, c. 1300–1250 BC, Mycenae

ITALY

Basilica, c. 530, Paestum
Greek Theater, 2nd century BC, Pompeii
Greek Theatre, 3rd century BC, Taormina, Sicily
Greek Theatre, begun 3rd century BC, Syracuse
Temple of Apollo, c. 565 BC, Syracuse
Temple of Concord, c. 430 BC, Agrigento, Sicily
Temple of Demeter, c. 510 BC, Paestum
Temple of Hera Argiva, 448–430 BC, Paestum
Temple of Poseidon, c. 460 BC, Paestum
Temple of Zeus Olympus, c. 510–409 BC, Agrigento

LIBYA

Temple of Zeus, 6th century BC, Cyrene, Libya

TURKEY

Carea Hellenistic Theater, 3rd century BC, Mysia, Turkey
Temple of Artemis, c. 350 BC, Ephesus
Temple of Artemis, c. 334 BC, Sardis, Turkey
Temple of Pergamon, (now in Berlin), c. 180 BC, Mysia, Turkey

OTHER

Temple of Artemis, c. 580 BC, Corfu

Parthenon

List 7–13   Palaces and Castles

While these may vary from relatively modest "palaces" such as the American *White House* to grandiose complexes such as the *Summer Palace* in Beijing, still these were considered the finest that could be built in their time.

AMERICA

Biltmore, 1890–1895, Asheville, North Carolina

Governor's Palace, 1706–1720, Williamsburg, Virginia

San Simeon, 1919–1939, San Luis Obispo, California

Vizcaya, 1914–1916, Miami, Florida

The White House, 1792–1829, Washington, DC

Winterthur, 1839, Wilmington, Delaware

AUSTRIA

Hofburg Palace, 1279, Vienna

Hochosterwitz, 1570–1586, Carinthia

Schonbrunn Palace, 1696, Vienna

Schwarzenburg, 1697–1723, Vienna

Upper Belvedere Palace, 1714–1715, Vienna

BRAZIL

Itamarati Palace, 1851–1854, Rio de Janeiro

CHINA

Forbidden City, 1406–1420, Beijing

Summer Palace, 1750, 1888, Beijing

CROATIA

Diocletian's Palace, 284–316 AD, Split

DENMARK

Borreby, c. 1550, Zealand

ENGLAND AND WALES

Arundel, 11th century, Arundel

Beaumaris Castle, 1283–1323, Anglesey

Blenheim Palace, 1705–1724, Oxfordshire

Bodiam Castle, 1385, Hawkhurst

Buckingham Palace, 1825–1913, London

Carisbrooke Castle, 1150–1200, Isle of Wight

Inverness, Scotland

Caernarfon, 1283–1323, Caernarfon, Wales

Castle Drogo, 1910–1930, Devonshire

Castle Howard, 1699–1726, Yorkshire

Chatsworth House, 1686, Derbyshire

Chiswick House, 1725–1729, Middlesex

Conway Castle, 1283–1289, Conway

Corfe Castle, 1105, Wareham

Deal Castle, 1540, Deal

Dover, 1180–1240, Kent

Dunster, 13th century, Somerset

Durham Castle, 1284, Durham

Easton Neston, 1696–1702, Northhamptonshire

Hampton Court Palace, 1514–c. 1700, near London

Harlech Castle, 1283–1290, Porthmadog, Wales

Hastings, 1069, Hastings

Hever Castle and Gardens, 13th century, Royal Tunbridge, Wells

Kenilworth, 1120, Baddesly Clinton

Knole, 15th century, Chartwell

Leeds Castle, c. 10th century, Maidstone, Kent

Lincoln, 1068, Lincoln, East Anglia

Norwich, 11th century, Norwich

Penshurst Place, c. 1340–1607, Kent

Penzance, 14th century, Penzance

Portchester Castle, AD 400, Portsmouth

Powis Castle, 11th century, Abergavenny, Wales

Richborough Castle, 4th century, Sandwich

Royal Pavilion, 1815–1818, Brighton

Sherborne, 1655, Dorset

Sissinghurst Castle, 13th century, near Cranbrook

Stokesay Castle, 1285–1305, Shropshire

Strawberry Hill, 1748–1777, Twickenham

Tattershall Castle, 1436–1446, Lincolnshire

Thornbury, 16th century, Bristol

Tintagel, c. 1150, Tintagel

Walmer Castle, c. 1540, Deal

Wardour, 1760–1766, Wiltshire

Warwick, c. 14th century, Warwickshire

Windsor Castle, 11th century, Windsor

FRANCE

Azay-le-Rideau, 1518–1527, Indre-et-Loire

Chateau d'Anet, 1547–1550, Eure-et-Loire

Fontainebleau, 1528, near Paris

List 7–13   Continued

FRANCE (cont.)

Louvre, 1667–1670, Paris

Luxembourg Palace, 1614–1624, Paris

Palace of the Popes, 1316–1370, Avignon

Palais Jacques Coeur, 1443–1451, Bourges

Petit Trianon, 1768, Versailles

Vaux-le-Vicomte, 1656–1661, Melun, Seine-et-Marne

Versailles, 1669–1685, near Paris

GERMANY

Aachen, 792–805, Aachen

Charlottenburg Palace, 1695, Berlin

Der Zwinger, 1711–1722, Dresden

Hohenschwangau, 19th century, Bavaria

Linderhof, 19th century, Bavaria

Meissen Castle, 1471–1485, Meissen

Neuschwanstein, begun 1868, Bavaria

Nymphenburg Palace, 1664–c. 1728, Munich

Residenz, 1719–1750, Wurzburg

GREECE

Palace of King Minos, c. 2000 BC, Hosios Loukas, Crete

HUNGARY

Sarospatak, c. 1540–1610, Miskolc

INDIA

Fatehpur Sikri Palace, c. 1568–1585, Agra

Viceroy's Palace, 1920–1931, New Delhi

IRAQ

Palace, 1764–1778, Ukhaydir

Palace, 849–859, Samarra

ITALY

Ca' d'Oro, 1422–c. 1440, Venice

Caserta, 1751, near Naples

Doge's Palace, 1309–1340, Venice

Hadrian's Villa, 1st century, BC, Rome

Palazzo Barberini, 1626, Rome

Palazzo Chiericata, 1550s, Vicenza

Palazzo dei Diamanti, 15th century, Ferrara

Palazzo Ducale, 1465–1479, Urbino

Palazzo Farnese, begun c. 1519, Rome

Palazzo Medici-Riccardi, 1444, Florence

Palazzo Pitti, 1458–1466, Florence

Palazzo Pubblico, 1298–1348, Sienna

Palazzo Uffizi, 1560–1580, Florence

Royal Hunting Palace, 1719–1733, Stupinigi

Vatican Palace, begun c. 1503, Rome

Villa d'Este, 1550, Tivoli

Villa Foscari, c. 1558, Malcontenta

Villa Farnesina, 1509–1511, Rome

Villa Lante, 1556–1589, Bagnia

Villa Rotonda, 1567–1570, Vicenza

JAPAN

Himeji Castle, 1601–1614, Himeji City

Katsura Palace, c. 1600, Kyoto

Nijo Castle, 1603, Kyoto

Tosanjo Palace, 1043–1166, Kyoto

JORDAN

Palace, c. 743, Mshatta

PORTUGAL

Summer Palace, 1747–1768, Queluz

SCOTLAND

Holyrood Palace, c. 1128, Edinburgh

Sandringham, 1787–1827, Balmoral

SPAIN

Alcazar, c. 1455, Segovia

The Alhambra, 1354–1391, Granada

Escorial, 1559–1584, Madrid

Santa Maria de Naranco, 9th century, northern Spain

SYRIA

Krak des Chevaliers, 13th–14th centuries, Syria

TANZANIA

Husuni Palace, 13th–14th centuries, Kilwa Kisiwani

TURKEY

Tekfur Serai, late 13th century, Istanbul

Topkapi Palace, 15th century, Istanbul

OTHER

Aleppo, 13th century, Syria

Clam-Gallas Palace, 1701, Prague

Esterhazy Palace, 1720, Fertod, Hungary

Vladislav Hall, 1493–1502, Prague

List 7–14 Walled Cities, Castles, and Fortresses

Castles were built primarily for war, with provisions always ready for a siege. Many castles in England later became fortresses, with the addition of cannons and firearms. Most that are listed below are in various states of repair, and may still be visited

AMERICA

Mesa Verde, begun c. 600–1100, Colorado

BELGIUM

Gravensteen, 9th century, Ghent

CHINA

Great Wall of China, 214 BC
Imperial City, pre-1403, Beijing
Xian City Wall, begun c. 14th century

CZECH REPUBLIC

Hradcany Castle, 1485–1502, Prague
Hrezda Castle, 1555–1556, Prague

ENGLAND

Barnard Castle, 14th century, Barnard
Beaumaris Castle, c. 1283–1323, Anglesey
Berkeley Castle, 1327, Berkeley
Bodiam Castle, 1385, Sussex
Canterbury, c. 12th century, Canterbury
Deal Castle, c. 1540, Kent
Dover Castle, c. 1180–1240, Dover
Niort, 1155, Niort
Rochester, 11th–12th centuries, Kent
Tower of London, c. 1077, London
Warwick Castle, c. 14th century, Warwickshire
Windsor Castle, 11th century, Windsor
York City Walls and Minster, 15th century, York

FRANCE

Chateau D'Angers, 1228, Angers
Chateau des Ducs de Bretagne, 1466, Nantes
Chateau Gaillard, begun 1196, Les Andeleys
Chateau de Chinon, begun 10th century, Chinon
Cité at Carcassonne, 13th century, Carcassonne

GERMANY

Dinkelsbuhl, 10th century, walled city
Ehrenbreitstein Fortress, 10th century, Koblenz
Heidelberg Castle, 1531–1615, Heidelberg
Landgrafenschloss, 14th century, Marburg
Marksburg Castle, pre 1400, Braubach
Kaiserburg, 1050, Nuremberg
Reichenstein Castle, 13th century, Trechtingshausen
Rothenburg ob der Tauber, c. 1240, walled city
Stahleck Castle, 1135, Bacharach
Stolzenfels Castle, c. 1816–1830, Kapellen
The Wartburg, 1067, Eisenach
Wurtzburg, 8th century, Wurtzburg

IRELAND

Bunratty Castle, 1251, Limerick
Dublin Castle, c. 1300, Dublin
Kilkenny Castle, 1172, Kilkenny

ITALY

Assisi Castle on Rocca Maggiore, 14th century, Assisi
Castel Bari, c. 1220, Bari
Castel Del Monte, c. 1240–1250, Apulia
Castel Sant' Angelo, 11th century, Rome
Castel Ursino, c. 1220
Castle Nuovo, 13th century, Naples
Castello Sforzesco, 1450–1477, Milan
Palazzo Vecchio, early 14th century, Florence
Trani, c. 1233–1249, Apulia

SCOTLAND

Bothwell Castle, 13th century, near Glasgow
Edinburgh Castle, 11th century, Edinburgh
Stirling Castle, 15th and 16th centuries, near Glasgow

SPAIN

Alcazaba, c. 1236–1391, Malaga
Alcazar, begun c. 1083, Segovia
The Alhambra, c. 1354–1391, Granada
Avila Fortifications, c. 1050–1350, Avila
Casa de Pilatos, c. 1510, Seville
Castel Coca, c. 15th century, near Segovia
Castilo de la Mota, c. 15th century, Medina
Penafiel, 11th–15th centuries, Valadolid

SWITZERLAND

Chateau de Chillon, 10th century, Montreux

WALES

Caernarfon, c. 1283–1323, Wales
Cardiff, c. 11th century, Wales
Conway Castle, 1283–1289, Wales
Harlech Castle, 1283–1290, Wales

OTHER

Aleppo, 13th century, Syria
City Walls, 5th century, Istanbul, Turkey
Great Zimbabwe, 13th–15th centuries, Africa
Himeji Castle, 16th–17th centuries, Himeji, Japan
Hradcany Castle, 1485–1502, Prague, Czech Republic
Krak des Chevaliers, c. 1100, Syria
Luxembourg Castle and Fortifications, AD 963, Luxembourg City
Masada, AD 73, Israel
Mohenjo-Daro, c. 2000 BC, Pakistan
Old City, c. AD 1000, Dubrovnik, Croatia
Teotihuacan, 300–750 AD, Mexico

List 7–15   Stately Homes, Palaces, and Castles of the United Kingdom and Ireland

The present state of these "Stately" homes and castles usually bears little resemblance to the original buildings, which were added to and refined over the years. Generations added wings and remodeled completely in many instances. Several of these are also included in other lists. Many are open to the public.

ENGLAND

Avon

Badminton House
Clevedon Court
Doddington House
Dyrham Park

Bedfordshire

Lutton Hoo
Woburn Abbey

Berkshire

Basildon Park
Clivedon

Borders

Abbotsford House

Buckinghamshire

Ascott
Chichely Hall
Claydon House
Hughenden Manor
Stowe
Waddesdon Manor
West Wycombe Park

Cambridgeshire

Abbots Ripton Hall
Anglesey Abbey
Wimpole Hall

Cheshire

Arley Hall
Berkeley Castle
Capesthorne
Dunham Massey
Peover Hall
Tatton Park

Cornwall

Antony House
Caerhays Castle
Cotehele House
Lanhydrock
Mount Edgcumbe
St. Michael's Mount
Treice
Trewithen

Cumbria

Holker Hall
Levens Hall
Muncaster Castle
Sizergh Castle

Derbyshire

Chatsworth
Haddon Hall
Hardwick Hall
Kedleston Hall
Melbourne Hall
Renishaw Hall
Sudbury Hall

Devon

Bradley Manor
Castle Drogo
Compton Castle
Knightshayes Court
Powderham Castle
Saltram House
Ugbrooke

Dorset

Athelhampton House
Clouds Hill
Forde Abbey
Lulworth Castle
Mapperton House
Sherborne Castle

East Sussex

Bateman's Firle Place
Glynde Place
Great Dixter
Sheffield Park

Essex

Audley End
Saling Hall

Gloucestershire

Hidcote Manor
Kiftsgate Court
Misarden Park
Painswick
Sudeley Castle
Westbury-on-Severn

Hampshire

Beaulieu Abbey and Palace House
Bramdean House
Broadlands
Exbury House
Highclere Castle
The Manor House, Upton Grey
Mottisfont Abbey
Stratfield Saye House
The Vyne

Hereford and Worcester

Croft Castle
Eastnor Castle

Hertfordshire

Gorhambury House
Hatfield House
Knebworth House
Shaw's Corner

Humberside

Burton Agnes Hall
Burton Constable
Sledmere House

Kent

Cobham Hall
Deal Castle
Hever Castle
Ightham Mote
Knole

List 7–15 Continued

Kent (cont.)

Leeds Castle
Penshurst Place
Quebec House
Richborough Castle
Scotney Castle
Sissinghurst Castle
Squerryes Court
Walmer Castle

Lancashire

Hoghton Tower

Leicestershire

Belvoir Castle
Quenby Hall
Stanford Hall

Lincolnshire

Belton House
Doddington Hall
Gunby Hall

Greater London

Apsley House
Avery Row
The Belgravia House
Chiswick House
Fenton House
Ham House
Hampton Court Palace
Kenwood
Little Venice
Marble Hill House
Osterley Park House
Whitehall Palace

Middlesex

Syon House

Norfolk

Blickling Hall
Felbrigg Hall
Holkham Hall
Houghton Hall
Mannington Hall
Oxburgh Hall
Sandringham House

Northamptonshire

Althorp
Boughton House
Burghley House
Cottesbrooke Hall
Hinwick House
Holdenby House
Lamport Hall
Rockingham Castle
Weston Hall

Northumberland

Alnwick Castle
Bamburgh Castle
Belsay Hall
Callaly Castle
Cragside House
Howick Hall
Seaton Delaval Hall
Wallington Hall

North Yorkshire

Beningbrough Hall
Castle Howard
Newby Hall
Studley Royal

Nottinghamshire

Flintham Hall

Oxfordshire

Blenheim Palace
Broughton Castle
Buscot Park
Mapledurham House
Milton Manor House
Rousham Park
Stonor Park

Perthshire

Blair Castle

Shropshire

Attingham Park
Benthall Hall
Hawkstone Park
Weston Park

Somerset

Brympton d'Evercy
Dunster Castle

Hatch Court
Hestercombe House
Lytes Cary Manor
Montacute House
Tintinhull House

South Yorkshire

Wentworth Castle

Staffordshire

Barlaston Hall
Shugborough

Suffolk

Elveden Hall
Helmingham Hall
Ickworth
Melford Hall
Somerleyton Hall

Surrey

Clandon Park
Hampton Court
The Homewood
Loseley House
Painshill Park
Polesden Lacey

Sussex

Charleston Manor
Horsted Place
Nymans

Warwickshire

Arbury Hall
Charlecote Park
Coughton Court
Honington Hall
Packwood House
Ragley Hall
Upton House
Warwick Castle

West Midlands

Hagley Hall
Wightwick Manor

Wiltshire

Bowood House
Corsham Court
Iford Manor

List 7–15   Continued

Wiltshire (cont.)

Lacock Abbey
Longleat House
Stourhead
Wilton House

West Sussex

Arundel Castle
Borde Hill
Goodwood House
Parham
Petworth House
Uppark

West Yorkshire

Bramham Park
Harewood House
Lotherton Hall
Nostell Priory
Oakwell Hall
Temple Newsam

Worcestershire

Madresfield Court

Yorkshire

Burton Constable
Carlton Towers
Castle Howard
Newby Hall
Nostell Priory
Thorp Perrow

HOMES AND CASTLES OF IRELAND

Aras an Uachtarain, Dublin
Ardress House, County Armagh
The Argory, County Armagh
Bantry House, Bantry
Beaulieu, Drogheda

Ballinlough Castle, Clonmellon
Bellamont Forest, Cootehille
Birr Castle, Birr, County Offaly
Carton, Maynooth
Castle Coole, Enniskillen
Castle Leslie, Glaslough
Castletown, Cellbridge
Castle Ward, Strangford
Clonalis House, Castlerea
Dunsany Castle, Dunsany
Emo Court, Coolbanagher
Florence Court, Fermanagh
Fota, Carrigtohill
Glin Castle, Glin
Kilshannig, Rathcormack
Kylemore Abbey, Letterfrack
Lismore Castle, Waterford
Lissadell House, Drumcliff
Lucan House, Dublin
Malahide Castle, Dublin
Muckross House, Killarney
Russborough, Blessington
Slane Castle, Slane
Tullynally Castle, Castlepollard
Westport House, Westport

HOMES AND CASTLES OF SCOTLAND

Aberdeenshire

Abbotsford House
Bowhill
Floors Castle
Haddo House
Manderston
Mellerstain
Traquair House

Dumfries and Galloway Region

Drumlanrig Castle

Grampian Region

Braemar Castle
Brodie Castle
Castle Fraser
Craigievar Castle
Drum Castle

Highland Region

Cawdor Castle
Dunvegan Castle

Lothian Region

Hopetown House
The House of Bins
Lennoxlove
Palace of Holyrood

Strathclyde

Culzean Castle
Inveraray Castle
Torosay Castle

Tayside Region

Glamis Castle
Scone Palace

CASTLES OF WALES

Caernarfon
Cardiff

Clwyd

Bodrhyddan Hall
Chirk Castle
Erddig

Gwynedd

Plas Newydd
Penrhyn Castle

Powys

Powis Castle

List 7–16   Châteaux of France

There are hundreds of châteaux throughout France, some of which are open to the public as museums, many that are in private hands, and some that have been converted to other uses. Some of these châteaux were built on top of ruins or fortresses from much earlier times, or were additions to towers or churches that were already in existence. The dates given are when the major construction began.

Abondant, c. 1620
Alincourt, 15th century
Ambleny, 13th century
Ambleville, 16th century
Amboise, begun 15th century
Ancy-le-Franc, c. 1546
Anet, 1547–1555
Angers, 13th century
Anjony, 1439–1540
Azay-le-Rideau, 1518–1527
Bagatelle, 1751–1754
Bailleul, after 1550
Balleroy, 1626–1636
Benouville, 14th–18th centuries
Beychevelle, after 1661
Beynes, 14th century
Blandy, 13th century
Blerancourt, 1612
Blois, 13th century
Bois Preau, 18th century
Bois-Ruffin, 18th century
Broglie, 17th century
Bussy-Rabutin, early 16th century
Caradeuc, 18th century
Castries, 1560–1570
Celle Les Bordes, c. 1413
Chambord, begun 1519
Champlatreux, 1757
Champs, 1699–1799
Château d'O, 11th–15th centuries
Château Lafite, 15th–18th centuries
Château-Thierry, 15th century
Châteaudun, 12th century
Chaumont, 1470–1510
Chenonceaux, begun c. 1512
Cheverny, 1604–1634
Chevreuse, c. 1550
Chinon, 10th–15th centuries
Cleres, 13th–16th centuries
Combourg, 11th–15th centuries
Coucy-Le-Chateau, 13th century
Coudray-Montpensier, 15th century
Courances, begun c. 1550
Craon, c. 17th century
Dampierre, begun c. 1550
Epinay, 1760
Ferrieres, 19th century

Fontaine-Henry, 13th–16th centuries
Fontevrault, 1098–16th century
Fougeres, 12th–15th centuries
Frazé, 15th century
Gordes, 1525–1541
Grosbois, 1226–1616
Groussay, 1803
Guermants, begun c. 1610
Josselin, 1008–1505
Jossigny, 18th century
Kergrist, 14th–18th centuries
Kerjean, begun 1545
La Baume, 1708–1710
La Brede, 1300–1309
La Dame Blanche, mid-18th century
La Lorie, mid-17th century
La Malmaison, 17th century
La Rochepot, 11th–13th centuries
Langeais, begun 1465
Lauzun, 13th–17th centuries
Le Bouilh, begun 1789
Le Champ-de-Bataille, 1686–1701
Le Chateau des Rohan, 1727–1731
Le Lude, 13th–19th centuries
Le Marais, after 1770
Le Moulin-a-Lassay, begun 1480
Le Plessis Mornay, 16th century
Le Rocher-Portail, begun 1617
Loches, 14th–15th centuries
Louveciennes, 1681
Luneville, 1703–1720
Luynes, 15th century
Maintenon, 13th–17th centuries
Maisons-Laffitte, 16th century

Manoir d'Ango, 1530–1545
Montal, 1523–1534
Montceaux, 1549–1560
Montgeoffroy, 16th–18th centuries
Montresor, 10th–15th centuries
Montreuil-Bellay, 13th–15th centuries
Nantouillet, mid-16th century
Nohant, c. 17th century
Pierrefonds, 14th–19th centuries
Ponchartrain, begun 1614
Raray, begun c. 1600
Royaumont, 1783
Saint-Fargeau, 10th–17th centuries
Saint-Germain-de-Livet, 15th–16th
   centuries
Saumur, 10th–14th centuries
Sceaux, 15th–17th centuries
Senlis, 1204
Serrant, begun 1546
Sully-sur-Loire, 13th–16th centuries
Talcy, renovated in 1520
Tanlay, 1559–1648
Tarascon, early 15th century
Tavant, c. late 11th century
Tonnere, 10th century
Tours, 4th–19th century
Trecesson, after 1575
Usse, 15th–17th centuries
Valençay, begun c. 1540
Vaux-le-Vicomte, 1657–1661
Vayres, 11th–17th centuries
Villandry, 1532–1754
Vitre, 11th–15th centuries

Chantilly, France

List 7–17 Great Churches, Cathedrals, and Centers of Worship

Often great cathedrals were built on the sites of very early churches or temples. Many of them were transformed from the original religion to another (such as cathedral to mosque or vice versa). The building of a great cathedral often covered a span of several hundred years, as chapels, façades, steeples, and carvings were added.

AMERICA

Cathedral, begun 1805, Baltimore, Maryland
National Cathedral, begun 1907, Washington, DC
St. John the Divine, 1915–1941, New York City
St. Patrick's Cathedral, 1858–1888, New York City
Trinity Church, 1839–1846, New York City

Mexico City Cathedral, 1563

AUSTRIA

Karleskirche, 1716–1737, Vienna
Melk Monastery, 1702–1738, Melk

BELGIUM

Antwerp Cathedral, 1352–1521, Antwerp

ENGLAND

Cathedral, 1074–1503, Canterbury
Cathedral, 1083–1348. Ely
Cathedral, 1085–1108, Chichester
Cathedral, 1089–1540, Gloucester
Cathedral, 1135–c. 1350, Wells
Cathedral, 11th century, Worcester
Cathedral, 1200–c. 1350, Litchfield
Cathedral, 1220–1270, Salisbury
Cathedral, 627–c. 1310, York
Cathedral, 8th–11th centuries, Oxford
Cathedral, c. 1093–1130, Durham
Cathedral, c. 1394–1450, Winchester
Glastonbury Abbey, c. 1090, Glastonbury
St. Mary's Cathedral, 1072, Lincoln

St. Paul's, 1675–1710, London
Westminster Abbey, c. 1503–1519, London

FRANCE

The Abbey, 1022–1135, Mont St. Michel
Abbey Church, begun 1122, St. Denis
Albi Cathedral, 1220–1236, Amiens
Cathedral, 1077–c. 15th century, Bayeux
Cathedral, 1140–1220, Chartres
Cathedral, 1160–1225, Laon
Cathedral, 1165–c. 1393, Lyons
Cathedral, 1176–c. 1505, Strasbourg
Cathedral, 1195–1255, Bourges
Cathedral, 1202–1509, Rouen
Cathedral, 1211–1299, Rheims
Cathedral, 1218–1291, Coutances
Cathedral, 1225–1569, Beauvais
Cathedral, 1287–1568, rebuilt 1759, Orleans
Cathedral, c. 11–13th centuries, Aix-en-Provence
Cathedral, c. 1273–16th century, Limoges
Cathedral, completed 1547, Tours
Church of St. Pierre, 1085–1130, Cluny
Church of the Invalides, c. 1679–1691, Paris
Church of the Madeleine, 1806–1843, Paris
Notre Dame, 1163–1250, Paris
St. Etienne, c. 1066–1100, Caen
St. Lazare, 1121–1146, Autun
St. Sernin, c. 1080–1120, Toulouse
Ste. Chapelle, c. 1243–1248, Paris
Ste. Genevieve (Pantheon), begun 1756, Paris
Ste. Madeleine, c. 1104–1132, Vezelay

GERMANY

Cathedral of St. Martin, 1009, Mainz
Cathedral, 1122–1252, Freiburg
Cathedral, 1248–1322, Cologne
Cathedral, begun 1030, Spier
Cathedral, c. 1000–13th century, Worms
Palatine Chapel, 792–805, Aachen
Sankt Johannes Nepomuk, 1733–1746, Munich
Ulm Minster, 1377–1417, Ulm

List 7–17   Continued

INDIA

Kailasa Temple, AD 8th century, Ellora, Maharashtra
Seven Pagodas, AD 8th century, Mahabalipuram
Stupa, 2nd century BC–3rd century AD, Sanchi

Notre Dame, 1163, Gothic

ITALY

Cathedral Group, 1063–1283, Pisa
Cathedral, 1290–c. 1500, Orvieto
Cathedral, begun 1386, Milan
Duomo, begun, 1368–1436, Florence
Holy Virgin Cathedral, 1226–1380, Sienna
Mausoleum of Galla Placida, c. 425, Ravenna
Mausoleum of King Theodoric, c. AD 526, Ravenna
S. Andrea al Quirinale, c. 1650, Rome
San Apollinare in Classe, 432–449 AD, Classe
San Carlo alle Quattro Fontana, 1638–1667, Rome
S. Paolo Outside the Walls, begun AD 385, Rome
San Giorgio Maggiore, begun 1566, Venice
San Lorenzo, 1421–1469, Florence
San Marco, begun 1063, Venice

San Vitale, 525–547, Ravenna
Sant' Agnese, 1653–1666, Piazza Navone, Rome
Santa Costanza, c. AD 350, Rome
Santa Croce, 1294–1440, Florence
Santa Maria Assunta, 1058–1284, Parma
Santa Maria Maggiore, 432–440, Rome
Santa Maria Novella, 1278–1456, Florence
St. Mark's Cathedral, c. 1063, Venice
St. Peter's, 1607–1615, Vatican City, Rome

JAPAN

Golden Pavilion Temple, 1347, Kyoto
Horyu-ji Temple, 7th century, Nara
Todaiji Temple, 8th century, Todaiji
Yakushiji Temple, AD 680, Yakushiji

RUSSIA

Basil the Blessed, 1554–1560, Moscow
Cathedral of the Assumption, 1475, Moscow
Peter and Paul, 18th century, St. Petersburg
St. Demetrius, 1193–1197, Vladimir
St. Sophia, 1037, Kiev

SPAIN

Cathedral, 1248–1511, Seville
Cathedral, begun 1522, Segovia
Cathedral, c. 700–1526, Cordoba
Our Lady of Toledo, begun 1227, Toledo
Sagrada Familia, 1883–1926, Barcelona
Santa Maria, 1075–1568, Burgos
Santiago de Compostela, 1060–1130, Compostela

THAILAND

Wat Po (Wat Phra Chetupon), 16th century, Bangkok

List 7–18   Mosques

AMERICA

Islamic Cultural Center Mosque, 1991, New York City
The Mosque, 1981, Plainfield, Indiana

EGYPT

Ahmad ibn Tulun, 876–879, Cairo
Madrasah of Sultan Hasan al-Nasir, 1362, Cairo
Mosque of Ibn Tulun, begun 876, Cairo
Mosque of Al-Hakim, 990–1013, Cairo
Mosque of Sultan Barquq, 1384, Cairo

IRAN

Blue Mosque, 1465, Tabriz
Masjid-i-Shah, 1612–1637, Isfahan
Mosque of Gauhar Shad, 1419, Mashad
Mosque of Luftullah, 17th–18th centuries, Isfahan
Masjid-I-Jami, early 10th century, Nayin
Masjid-i-Jami (Friday Mosque), 8th century, Isfahan
Shrine of Hadrat-e Masumeh, 816, Qom
Tarikk Khana Mosque, early 8th century, Damghan

IRAQ

Mosque of Mutawakkil, 848–852, Samarra
Mosque, c. 1204, Tabriz

INDIA

Pearl Mosque, 1662, Delhi
Taj Mahal, 1632–1654, Agra

ISRAEL

Dome of the Rock, 691–692, Jerusalem
El-Aqsa Mosque, c. 1000, Jerusalem
Shrine of the Book, 1965, Jerusalem

MALI

Great Friday Mosque, 13th century, rebuilt 1907, Djenne
Great Mosque, 1935, Mopti
Sakore Mosque, 1840s, Timbuktu

MOROCCO

Kairouan Mosque, c. 850, Fez
Mosque of Al-Mansur, 12th century, Rabat
Qarawiyyin Mosque, 859

PAKISTAN

Badshahi Mosque, 1673–1674, Lahore Fort
Pearl Mosque, c. 1645, Lahore
Wazir Khan Mosque, 1634–1635, Lahore

SPAIN

The Alhambra, 1354–1391, Granada
Mosque, begun 785, Cordoba

SOMALI REPUBLIC

The Great Mosque, 1269, Mogadishu

SYRIA

The Great Mosque, 705–715, Damascus

TUNISIA

The Great Mosque, c. 670, Kairouan
The Great Mosque, begun 850, Sousse

TURKEY

Ahmet Pasha Mosque, n.d., Kaysarij
Beyazit Mosque, 1497–1505, Istanbul
Blue Mosque (Sultan Ahmet Mosque), 11th century, Istanbul
Hagia Sophia, 532–537, Istanbul
Kariye Mosque, 14th century, Istanbul
Kulliye of Beyazit II, 15th century, Edirne
Mosque of Ahmed I, 1609–1616, Istanbul
Mosque of the Conqueror, 1463–1470, Istanbul
Mosque of Ilyas Bey, 15th century, Miletus
Mosque of Isa Bey, 1375, Ephesus
Mosque of the Prince, 1544–1548, Istanbul
Mosque of Selim I, 1520–1522, Istanbul
Mosque of Selim II, 1569–1575, Edirne
Mosque of Sultan Suleyman, 1550–1557, Istanbul
Orhan Jami, 1417, Bursa
Ulu Jami, 12th century, Ezurum

OTHER

Aba Khuvaja Mosque, 18th century, Xinjiang Province, China
Amin Mosque, 1778, Turfan, China
Bright Moon Pavilion, c. 1275, Yangzhou, China
Chor-Minar, 1807, Bukhara, Uzbekistan
Friday Mosque, 10th century, Nain
Great Mosque, 1136, Tlemcen, Algeria
Great Mosque, 1392, Xian, China
Islamic Centre Mosque, 1977, Rome
Jami Masjid, 1830–1855, Singapore
Jami Masjid, 1897, Kuala Lumpur, Malaysia
Niu Jie (Ox St.) Mosque, 1362, Beijing, China
Qubba al-Ba'adiyyin, c. 1120, Marrakesh
Riadha Mosque, 1902–1903, Lamu Island, Kenya
Sultan Mosque, 1924–1928, Singapore

Blue Mosque, Istanbul, 11th century

List 7–19   American Churches and Temples

These places of worship are noteworthy either because of unusual architecture, historical significance, or because of the architect who designed them.

ALABAMA

Government Street Presbyterian Church, 1835–1837, Charles Dakin, Mobile

Tuskegee Chapel, Tuskegee Institute, 1969, Paul Rudolph, Tuskegee

ARIZONA

Mission San Xavier Del Bac, 1783–1797, Tucson

ARKANSAS

Thorncrown Chapel, 1980, Fay Jones, Eureka Springs

CALIFORNIA

Crystal Cathedral (Garden Grove Community Church), 1980, Philip Johnson, Garden Grove

First Church of Christ Scientist, 1909–1911, Bernard Maybeck, Berkeley

COLORADO

Air Force Academy Cadet Chapel, 1956–1962, Walter A. Netsch, Jr., Colorado Springs

CONNECTICUT

First Church of Christ, 1814, based on Asher Benjamin design, New Haven

First Congregational Church, 1817, Samuel Belcher, Old Lyme

DELAWARE

Holy Trinity Church (Old Swedes Church), 1699, belfry designed in 1802 by Thomas Cole, Wilmington

DISTRICT OF COLUMBIA

Cathedral Church of St. Peter and St. Paul, begun 1907, George F. Bodley, Washington, DC

FLORIDA

Annie Pfeiffer Memorial Chapel, 1941, Florida Southern University, Frank Lloyd Wright, Lakeland

ILLINOIS

Holy Trinity Orthodox Cathedral, 1900–1903, Louis Sullivan, Chicago

Kehileth Anshe M'Ariv Synagogue (now *Pilgrim Baptist Church*), 1890–1891, Louis Sullivan, Chicago

St. Gabriel's Church, 1887, Burnham and Root, Chicago

St. Saviour's Chapel, Illinois Institute of Technology, 1952, Ludwig Mies van der Rohe, Chicago

Unity Temple (Unitarian Universalist Church), 1904–1906, Frank Lloyd Wright, Oak Park

INDIANA

First Christian Church, 1942, Eliel and Eero Saarinen, Columbus

North Christian Church, 1964, Eero Saarinen, Columbus

The Roofless Church, 1960, Philip Johnson, New Harmony

IOWA

First Church of Christ Scientist (now *Christ First Dayspring Tabernacle*), 1902–1903, Hugh M.G. Garden, Marshalltown

St. Paul's United Methodist Church, 1910–1914, Louis Sullivan, Cedar Rapids

LOUISIANA

Cathedral of St. Louis the King, 1850, J.N.B. DePouilly (other architects Benjamin Latrobe and Alexander Sampson), New Orleans

MAINE

United Church of Christ, 1843, architect unknown, Bath

MARYLAND

The Basilica of the Assumption (Baltimore Cathedral), 1804–1818, Benjamin Latrobe, Baltimore

MASSACHUSETTS

First Church of Christ, 1816, Charles Bulfinch, Lancaster

King's Chapel, 1749–1754, Peter Harrison, Boston, Massachusetts

Massachusetts Institute Chapel, 1955, Eero Saarinen, Cambridge

Old Ship Meetinghouse (church), 1681, Hingham

Trinity Church, 1872–1877, Henry Hobson Richardson, Boston

MICHIGAN

St. James Episcopal Chapel, 1867–1868, Gordon Lloyd, Grosse Ille

MINNESOTA

Abbey Church of St. John the Evangelist, 1961, Marcel Breuer, Collegeville

MISSOURI

Basilica of St. Louis the King (Old Cathedral), 1831–1834, St. Louis

St. Louis Priory Church, 1962, Gyo Obata, Hellmuth, Obata, and Kassabaum, St. Louis

Many of these churches are listed in *American Churches,* Roger G. Kennedy, Stewart, Tabori & Chang, 1982, New York, 10012.

List 7–19 Continued

NEW HAMPSHIRE

First Congregational Church, 1820, Elias Carter, Hancock
South Congregational Church, 1823, Elias Carter, Newport
United Church, 1820, Elias Carter, Acworth

NEW JERSEY

Russian Orthodox Church, 1964, Sergi Padukow, New Kuban
St. Mary's Episcopal Church, 1846–1848, Richard Upjohn, Burlington

NEW MEXICO

San Estevan Del Rey Mission Church, 1629–1642, Acoma
San Francisco de Asis, 1805, Ranchos de Taos, Taos

NEW YORK

The Cathedral Church of St. John the Divine, begun 1893, Ralph Adams Cram, New York City
The Church of St. Vincent Ferrer, 1916–1918, Bertram Goodhue, New York City
First Presbyterian Church (Old Whalers'), 1843–1844, Minard Lafever, Sag Harbor
Hamilton College Chapel, 1827, Philip Hooker, Clinton
Riverside Church, 1927, Charles Collens and Henry C. Pelton, New York City
St. Mary's-in-Tuxedo, 1888, William A. Potter, Tuxedo Park
St. Patrick's Cathedral, 1858–1888, James Renwick, New York City
St. Paul's Chapel of Trinity Church, 1766, Thomas MacBean, New York City
Temple Emanu-el, 1919, Robert D. Kohn, Charles Butler and Clarence S. Stein, New York City
Unitarian Church of Rochester, 1962, Louis Kahn, Rochester

OKLAHOMA

Christ the King Catholic Church, 1926, Barry Byrne, Tulsa

OREGON

Tualatin Plains Presbyterian Church (Old Scotch Church), 1878, Mr. Balantyne, Hillsboro

PENNSYLVANIA

Cathedral Church of Bryn Athyn, 1913–1929, Cram & Ferguson, Raymond Pitcairn, Bryn Athyn
Christ Church, 1727–1744, Dr. John Kearsley, Philadelphia
Church of St. James the Less, 1846–1848, builder, Robert Ralston, Philadelphia
Emmanuel Episcopal Church, 1883–1886, Henry Hobson Richardson, Pittsburgh
Episcopal Cathedral, begun 1932–1970s, Edward R. Watson (of Mirick Pearson Batchelor), Philadelphia
First Unitarian Church, 1883–1886, Frank Furness, Philadelphia

RHODE ISLAND

Manning Hall, Brown University, 1833, Russell Warren/ James C. Bucklin, Providence
St. Paul's Church (Old Narragansett Church), 1707, Wickford
Touro Synagogue of Congregation Jeshuat Israel, 1759–1763, Peter Harrison, Newport

SOUTH CAROLINA

Centenary Methodist Episcopal Church, 1842, E.B. White, Charleston
New Tabernacle Fourth Baptist Church, 1862, Francis D. Lee, Charleston
St. James Church, 1713–1719, Goose Creek
St. Michael's Church, 1752–1761, Samuel Cardy, Charleston
Unitarian Church, 1852–1854, Francis D. Lee, Charleston

TENNESSEE

First Presbyterian Church, 1849–1851, William Strickland, Nashville

TEXAS

San Jose y San Miguel de Aquayo Mission Church, 1768–1782, San Antonio

VERMONT

First Congregational Church, 1804–1805, Lavius Fillmore/ Asher Benjamin, Old Bennington
Old Round Church, 1813, William Rhodes, Richmond

VIRGINIA

Christ Church, 1732, Robert (King) Carter, Lancaster County
Monumental Church, 1812, Robert Mills, Richmond
St. Luke's Church, 1632–1638, Smithfield

WISCONSIN

Annunciation Greek Orthodox Church, 1959, Frank Lloyd Wright, Wauwatosa
Church of St. John Chrysostom, 1851–1853, Richard Upjohn, Delafield
St. Sava Serbian Orthodox Cathedral, 1856–1858, altar screen designed by architects Cambouras and Theodore, Milwaukee

First Baptist Church, 1884–1886, Gothic Revival, Lynchburg, Virginia

List 7–20   Architectural Influences of Various Times and Cultures

AFRICAN INNOVATIONS

camelback shotgun (a second story added across the back of a shotgun house)
carved front doors
covered front porch
double shotgun house (two rooms wide, many rooms deep)
14-ft. high ceilings in shotgun houses
gable-roofed house
low-relief sculpture designs in adobe
"shotgun" house (homes one room wide and several rooms deep—so-named because if a shotgun were fired through the front door, the bullet would go out the back)
square module rooms (10×10 feet or 10×20 feet)
veranda
wattle and daub construction
wide overhangs

ASIAN INNOVATIONS

bright colors used only for royalty
foot-high barrier at base of entrance doors
magnificent tombs
pagoda, a temple built of many stories, each smaller than the one below
rock-cut temples
roofs that come to a peak on the edges
walled square on a north/south axis

EGYPTIAN INNOVATIONS

capitals: lotus and papyrus
engaged columns
fluted columns
frieze
funerary temple
hypostyle hall
mastaba tombs
obelisk
peristyle hall
piers
pilaster
post and lintel
pyramid
rock cut tomb
sphinx
thick engraved column
unified architecture, sculpture, and decorations

GREEK INNOVATIONS

acropolis
bas-relief
caryatids
cella
Classicism
columns: Doric, Ionic, Corinthian
entasis
frieze
pediment
post and lintel
rectangular temples
stoa
theater
widespread use of marble

ROMAN INNOVATIONS

amphitheater
apartment houses
aqueduct
atrium
barrel vault
basilica
bridges
city planning
coffered ceilings
coffered dome
columns with arches
concrete
forum
groin vault
heated baths
mosaic
pilaster
portico
rustication
stadium
triumphal arch

MEDIEVAL INNOVATIONS

baptistery
basilican plan churches
battlements
bay
blind arcade

List 7–20   Continued

MEDIEVAL INNOVATIONS (cont.)
chancel
corbel table
groin vaulting
moats
monasteries
pilaster strip
post and lintel combined with arches
statue-like columns
string course
tall towers
towers over narthex
westwork (narthex transept)

ROMANESQUE INNOVATIONS
apse
decorated arches
interior vaults over crossings
pier buttresses
rectangular ground plans
ribbed vaults
round arches
thick walls
tympanum
variety of columns

RENAISSANCE INNOVATIONS
châteaux
geometry as basis for architecture: circle, square, and
    triangle
decorative colored marble designs
colossal dome
colossal order
ground-floor arcades
multi-tiered façades
Neo-Classical revival
paired columns
Palladian style
symmetry and balance

BAROQUE INNOVATIONS
colonnades
decorative sculpture, inside and out
elaborate public fountains
grand scale
lozenge decorations

mansard roof
niches
ostentatious materials
spherical dome
string courses
undulating façade

NINETEENTH-CENTURY INNOVATIONS
Art Nouveau
cast iron buildings
concrete and metal used together
Gothic revival
introduction of elevator
large exhibition halls and office buildings
metal "skeletons" with glass or concrete walls
Neo-Baroque
Neo-Classicism
prefabricated structural elements
skyscraper
structural steel
Victorian revivals

TWENTIETH-CENTURY INNOVATIONS
air conditioning
Art-Deco
austere box-like skyscrapers
better lighting
buildings adapted to the site
computer-designed architecture
concrete left rough from pouring forms
condominiums
fireproof buildings and factories
flat roofs in homes
geodesic dome
horizontal and vertical setbacks to allow light
industrial materials
international style: steel and glass construction
the mobile home
monumental public sculpture outside buildings
natural materials
parking garages
poured concrete
prefabricated structural parts
renovation of existing structures
sculptural building forms made possible with sky-
    scrapers

List 7–21   American Architectural Characteristics

1600–1750

New England Colonial

eaves close to wall
Elizabethan (1558–1603)
fancy brickwork
half-timbered houses
jetty or overhang
late medieval features
lead-paned casement windows
lean-to on back of house
shingle covering
steep shingled roofs
symmetrical windows
tall, central chimneys
wooden homes hewn and pegged

Burlington, 18th Century, Charles City County, Virginia

Dutch Colonial

brick construction
gambrel roof
stepped-end or straight-sided gables

Spanish Colonial

clerestory windows
flat roofs, with timbers
plain, windowless walls
textured adobe structures

Southern Colonial

brick construction
end chimneys
one-and-a-half stories

GEORGIAN, 1720–1820

Named for three King Georges who ruled from 1714–1820.

Early Georgian, c. 1700–1750

low, hipped roof
pediments above windows, first floor
quoins (square stones at corners and under windows)
swan's neck pediment above door
symmetrical
unbroken (flat) facade

Middle Georgian, c. 1730–1769

decorative features often based on Palladio
double or two-story portico
frequently plain exterior
giant pilasters (square columns with corinthian or ionic capitals)
hipped roof with balustrades and dormer windows
Palladian window (curved at top)
raised basement
shutters on windows

Late Georgian, 1775–1883

breakaway chimneys (end chimneys separated from the house at the top for fire protection)
broken pediment
projecting central pavilion

FEDERAL STYLE, 1770–1890

balustrade on hip roof or porch
Doric columns on porches
entry has sidelights and arched fanlight with tracery
good proportion: square or rectangular design
interiors featured decorative patterns (urns, swags, hexagonal and oval forms)
shallow hipped roof
simple facades with little exterior decoration
six-paneled door
window openings progressively smaller on upper stories

FRENCH COLONIAL, c. 1790

gallery all around house
outside stair leading to rooms on upper floor
raised cottage
steep hipped roof shading gallery

SPANISH BAROQUE, 1784–1797

complex domes and vaults
ornate entrance

AMERICAN NEO-CLASSICISM, 1764–1860

Jeffersonian (Roman Revival)

full-scale cornices
red brick
small Roman portico
symmetry of facade

Roman Classicism, 1790–1830

columns with plain capitals
four-columned portico
lunettes (half-moon shapes above windows)
one-story Roman temple form
portico with pediment
tympanum (half-moon shape above doors)

List 7–21   Continued

AMERICAN NEO-CLASSICISM, 1764–1860 (cont.)

Greek Revival, 1820–1860

carved decorative trim
columns on porches
Doric and Ionic columns
flat corner pilasters
fluted doric columns
frieze, cornice, architrave
horizontal transom over doors
low-pitched roof
pediments
pediment-shaped
      window head
small windows
      around door
wide plain frieze
wide trim in gable

Geodesic Dome

Renaissance Revival, 1840–1890

balcony above cornice
balustrade
paneled pilasters
pedimented windows
rusticated corner stones (quoins)
smaller windows, upper story

Gothic Revival, 1830–1860

carriage porch
colored glass
decorated end gables
full-width or one-story porch
gothic-shaped windows
grouped chimneys
slate roofs
steeply pitched roof
tracery on windows
turrets and battlements
vertical board and batten

Italianate, 1830–1880

balcony
bay windows
Corinthian columns
cupolas
elaborate pediments
groups of three windows
low pyramidal roof lines
round-headed windows
smooth stucco finish
straight vertical, almost square
tall narrow doors
tall tower
wide eaves, large brackets

VICTORIAN ARCHITECTURE, 1870–1900

asymmetrical facades
Georgian and Adamesque features

Greek, Gothic
mixture of styles such as Medieval and Italianate
multi-colored walls
steeply pitched roofs

Octagon, 1850–1870

eight-sided shape (also 6, 10, 12)
two-story
wide eave overhangs

Exotic Revivals, 1835–c. 1890

African

shotgun-style homes
wide, overhanging eaves

Egyptian

"bundled reed" columns
pylon tower
smooth exterior finish
vulture and sun disk symbol

Turkish

ogee arch
onion dome

Oriental

front gables
low-pitched roof
second-floor balcony

Craftsman Style Witchita, Kansas, 1905

Swiss Chalets

gingerbread trim on roof
low-pitched roof
second-floor balcony with flat balustrade

Second Empire, 1855–1890

bay windows
classical columns
decorative cornices
front and side pavilions
mansard roof with dormers
paired and triple windows
paired entry doors
patterned roof
quoins (corner stones)
towers
veranda-like porches

Stick Victorian, 1860–1890

angular and asymmetrical
gingerbread millwork added
patterns made with boards
projecting bay
square bay windows
steep roofs

List 7–21 Continued

Stick/Eastlake, 1870–1890

straight wooden boards
textures in gables
wide, overhanging eaves

Second Empire, 1860–1890

classical columns
front and side pavilions
mansard roof with dormers
paired windows
veranda-like porches

Queen Anne, 1880–1910

contrasting building materials
corner towers with conical roof
finials
fish-scale shingles
full-width porch
horizontal siding
patterned masonry
roof cresting
spindlework and beads
stained glass
steep gabled roof
verandas and balconies

Carpenter Gothic

pointed arches
wood painted to look like stone

Tudor

flattened squared arches

VICTORIAN GOTHIC, 1860–1890

contrasting brick and stone
high-pitched roof lines
pointed arches
polychromatic exteriors
stained
towers
tracery
vertical board and batten

Shingle style, 1880–1900

bay windows, one- or two-
    story
circular turrets
gambrel roof occasionally
horizontal, low buildings
round- or square-headed windows
rusticated stone
shingle covering on most walls
towers
verandas
wavy wall surface

Lionberger House, St. Louis, Missouri, Henry Hobson Richardson, 1886, Richardsonian Romanesque

Richardson Romanesque, 1880–1900

asymmetrical facade
broad hip roof
deeply recessed windows
fortress-like designs
lines of windows
masonry walls
round towers, conical roof
short, squat chimneys
varied colors of stone or brick

Folk Victorian, 1870–1910

combination of styles
decorative scrollwork
porches with spindlework
shingle styles
symmetrical façade
towers

EARLY TWENTIETH-CENTURY, 1900–1920
Late Beaux-Arts (Classicism), 1890–1930

classical revival
free-standing statuary
gigantic paired columns
mixture of styles: Roman, Renaissance
projecting façades or pavilions
variety of stone finishes

Chicago School, 1890–1920

combination of linear and geometric forms
decorative cast iron
escalator
flat roof, decorative cornice at top
framework allowed to show
iron and steel structure
office complexes, 6 to 20 stories
pilaster strips with decorated capital
use of passenger elevator
vertical strips of windows

Mission (Bungalow), 1890–1940

arched roof supports, bell towers
beamed ceilings
combination of materials
large porch
one-story high
wood shingles, stone, brick

Neo-Classicism, 1900–1920

colossal columned portico
few arches or statuary
pilasters on sides
symmetrical features

Prairie Style, 1905–c. 1915

brick or stucco combined with wood
cantilever

List 7–21   Continued

Prairie Style, 1905–c. 1915 (cont.)

horizontal appearance
horizontal bands of casement windows
interior and exterior are coordinated
large, low chimney
low-pitched roof
square porch supports
terraces and balconies
wide, overhanging eaves
windows include stained glass

ARCHITECTURE BETWEEN THE WARS, 1920–1940

Pueblo Revival, 1910–present

flat roof, irregular, rounded edges
roof beams, rough-hewn
stepped-back roof line

Low House, McKim, Meade, and White, 1887, Bristol, Rhode Island
(now demolished), Shingle Style

Craftsman, 1905–1940

beamed ceilings
cobblestone decorations
combination of materials
large porch
low-pitched gabled roof
one-story high
roof rafters exposed
small windows flanking chimney
tapered porch posts to ground level
wood shingles, stone, brick

Art Deco, 1925–1940

concrete, stone, metal
decorative colored mirrors
flat roofs
glazed ceramic ornamentation
hard-edged stylized low reliefs
low-relief geometrical designs
set-back facade
terra cotta and glass ornamentation
vertical emphasis

Art Moderne, 1930–1945

aluminum and stainless steel ornamentation
circular patterns used on doors or glass
curved window glass
flat roofs
horizontal bands of windows
smooth wall finish

International Style, 1920–1945

asymmetrical façade in homes
box-like structure
cantilever
concrete, glass, and steel
curtain walls of windows
eaves boxed in or flush with wall
exposed steel structural elements
flat roof tops
little ornamentation
natural wooden trim
smooth wall surface

ARCHITECTURE OF THE POP CULTURE, 1940–1965

Contemporary Housing

A-frames
apartment living
colonial revival
geodesic domes
mobile homes
ranch house
split level

International Style

box-like skyscrapers
cantilevered building
cast concrete forms
curtain walls of windows
flat roof tops
indoor shopping mall
stainless steel, glass, concrete
structural elements visible

LATE TWENTIETH-CENTURY, 1965–PRESENT

Late Modernism

angular flat-topped buildings
atriums of several stories
curved glass panels
glass, reflections
homes adapted to site and location
modern interpretation of classicism
pre-cast concrete elements
rhythmical set-backs
richness of texture
stretched skin-window walls
vertical, outside supports

Post-Modern

base, shaft, capital, entablature
classical references on skyscrapers
decorative elements and color on skyscrapers
half modern, combined with tradition
moldings, split pediments, keystones
revivals: shingle style, classical, federal

List 7–22   State Capitol Buildings and Their Architects

The buildings listed below are those currently in use in each state, and the architects listed are those who designed the buildings. Because of additions, renovations and reconstructions, most capitol buildings involved a number of architects. Early buildings were often in different locations, and many are now used as museums.

Alabama: Montgomery, 1851, George Nichols; south and north wings designed by Frank Lockwood

Alaska: Juneau, 1929–1931, U.S. Treasury Department Architects

Arizona: Phoenix, 1899–1900, James Reilly Gordon; west wing, 1918–1919, A. J. Gifford

Arkansas: Little Rock, 1899–1914, George R. Mann, Cass Gilbert

California: Sacramento, 1874–1908, Miner F. Butler

Colorado: Denver, 1890–1907, Elijah E. Meyers and Frank E. Edbrooke

Connecticut: Hartford, 1879, Richard M. Upjohn

Delaware: Dover, 1933, William Martin

Florida: Tallahassee, 1902, Frank P. Milburn; new addition, 1977, Edward Durrell Stone

Georgia: Atlanta, 1884–1899, Edbrooke and Burnham

Hawaii: Honolulu, 1965, John Carl Warnecke and Associates

Idaho: Boise, 1906–1912, John Tourtellette

Illinois: Springfield, 1868–1888, John C. Cochrane

Indiana: Indianapolis, 1886, Edwin May/Adolph Scherrer

Iowa: Des Moines, 1871–1886, Cochrane and Pinquenard

Kansas: Topeka, 1866–1903, McDonald Brothers

Kentucky: Frankfort, 1905–1909, F.M. Andrews and Company

Louisiana: Baton Rouge, 1932, Weiss, Dreyfous and Seiferth

Maine: Augusta, 1829–1832, Charles Bulfinch; 1890–1891, John C. Spofford; 1909–1911, G. Henri Desmond

Maryland: Annapolis, 1772–1775, Joseph Clarke

Massachusetts: Boston, 1795, Charles Bulfinch; additions, 1798–1899, William Chapmen, R. Clipston Sturgis, and Robert D. Andrews

Michigan: Lansing, 1873–1878, Elijah E. Myers

Minnesota: St. Paul, 1898–1905, Cass Gilbert

Mississippi: Jackson, 1903, Theodore C. Link

Missouri: Jefferson City, 1917, Tracy and Swarthout

Montana: Helena, 1896–1912, George R. Mann

Nebraska: Lincoln, 1922–1932, Bertram Goodhue

Nevada: Carson City, 1871, Joseph Goseling

New Hampshire: Concord, 1819, Steward James Park

New Jersey: Trenton, 1889, L.H. Broome; additions, 1891, James Moylan and 1907, George E. Poole

New Mexico: Santa Fe, 1966, W.C. Kruger and Associates; 1900 building, I.H. and W.M. Rapp

New York: Albany, 1871–1899, Philip Hooker; renovation, 1911, Thomas Fuller

North Carolina: Raleigh, 1833–1840, Alexander J. Davis

North Dakota: Bismarck, 1883–1902, L.S. Buffington, George Hancock, and Butler Brothers and Ryan; new capitol architects are De Remer, Kurke, Holabird and Root

Ohio: Columbus, 1838–1861, Henry Walter, Martin E. Thompson, and Thomas Cole; annex from 1898–1901

Oklahoma: Oklahoma City, 1917, S.A. Layton and S. Wemyss Smith

Oregon: Salem, 1876, Justus F. Krumbein

Pennsylvania: Harrisburg, 1904–1906, Joseph M. Huston

Rhode Island: Providence, 1891–1903, McKim, Mead, and White

South Carolina: Columbia, 1851–1904, Major John R. Niernsee, J. Crawford Neilson, J. Frank Niernsee, Frank P. Mulburn, and Charles C. Wilson

South Dakota: Pierre, 1908–1910, C.E. Bell; annex, 1932

Tennessee: Nashville, 1845–1855, William Strickland

Texas: Austin, 1885–1888, Colonel E. E. Myers

Utah: Salt Lake City, 1914–1916, Richard K.A. Kletting

Vermont: Montpelier, 1838, Ammi B.Young; 1857–1858, J. R. Richards

Virginia: Richmond, 1785–1792, Thomas Jefferson; wings added, 1902

Washington: Olympia, 1928, Wilder and White

West Virginia: Charleston, 1932, Cass Gilbert

Wisconsin: Madison, 1906–1917, George B. Post and Sons

Wyoming: Cheyenne, 1888–1917, D.W. Gibbs and Company

© 1998 Prentice Hall

List 7–23   American Houses by General Style

ENGLISH COLONIAL

Ashley House, c. 1733, Deerfield, Massachusetts
Bacon's Castle, c. 1655, Surry County, Virginia
Boardman House, 1686, Saugus, Massachusetts

DUTCH COLONIAL

House, 1704, Hackensack, New Jersey
St. Luke's Church, East End, 1632, Isle of Wight County, Virginia

SPANISH COLONIAL

The Alamo, 1744–1757, San Antonio, Texas
Governor's Palace, 1610–1614, Santa Fe, New Mexico
San Estevan, 1610–1614, Acoma, New Mexico

NEW ENGLAND HOMES

Elihu Coleman House, 1722, Nantucket Island, Massachusetts
The Sisters' House, 1743, Ephrata, Pennsylvania

SOUTHERN ARCHITECTURE

Adam Thoroughgood House, 1636–1640, Princess Anne County, Virginia
Burlington, 18th century, Charles City County, Virginia

EARLY GEORGIAN

Williams House, 1706–1707, Old Deerfield, Massachusetts

MIDDLE GEORGIAN

Bries House, 1723, East Greenbush, New York
Dalton House, 1775, Newburyport, Massachusetts
Independence Hall, 1731, Philadelphia, Pennsylvania
Meetinghouse, 1779, Brooklin, Connecticut
Miles Brewton House, 1733, Charleston, South Carolina
Westover, c. 1730–1734, Charles City, Virginia

FEDERAL STYLE, NEO-CLASSICISM

Monticello, 1770–1809, Charlottesville, Virginia
Mount Vernon, 1775, Mount Vernon, Virginia

Monticello, 1768–1809, Classical

French Architectuzre

Home Place, 1801, Charles Parish, Louisiana
Magnolia Mound, c. 1790, Baton Rouge, Louisiana

Spanish Baroque

San Xavier del Bac, 1784–1797, Tucson, Arizona

Gothic Revival

First Baptist Church, 1884–1886, Lynchburg, Virginia

RICHARDSONIAN ROMANESQUE

Lionberger House, 1886, Henry Hobson Richardson, St. Louis, Missouri

SECOND EMPIRE STYLE

Congregational Church, c. 1840, Tallmadge, Ohio
Renwick Gallery, 1859–1861, Washington, DC
Stark House, c. 1820, Louisiana, Missouri

EGYPTIAN REVIVAL

Apthorp House, 1837 Alexander J. Davis, New Haven, Connecticut
Cabell House, 1847, Richmond, Virginia
Egyptian Revival Railroad Station, 1922, Russell Warren, New Bedford, Massachusetts
Washington Monument, 1848–1884, Robert Mills, Washington, DC

QUEEN ANNE STYLE

Gray House, 1891, Santa Cruz, California

SHINGLE STYLE

Low House, 1887, McKim, Meade, and White, Bristol, Rhode Island

SECOND EMPIRE

Cornish House, 1886, Omaha, Nebraska

VICTORIAN EASTLAKE

Rosson House, 1895, Phoenix, Arizona

ART DECO

Butler House, 1937, Kraetsch and Kraetsch, Des Moines, Iowa
Chrysler Building, 1928–1930, William Van Alen, New York City
Commercial Buildings, c. 1930s, Pekin, Illinois
Fox Theater, 1929, C. Howard Crane, St. Louis, Missouri
Knabe Building, 1928, Edward D. Tanner, Kansas City, Missouri
Liberty Memorial, 1921–1926, Harold Van Buren Magonigle, Kansas City, Missouri
Lovell (Health) House, 1929, Richard Neutra, Los Angeles, California
Penobscot Building, 1928, Smith, Hinchman, & Grylls, Detroit, Michigan
White Palace Cafe, 1938, Maben and Son, Gadsden, Alabama

POST-MODERN

Abstract Shingle Style, 1992, Robert Venturi, Maine Coast
Meridian Condominiums, 1988, Maxwell Stockman, San Diego, California
State of Illinois Building, 1985, Helmut Jahn, Chicago, Illinois
Shingle Style Revival, 1989, Robert A.M. Stern, Pottersville, New Jersey
Yale University Art & Architecture Bldg., 1969–1972, Paul Rudolph, New Haven, Connecticut

List 7–24 American Lighthouses

Lighthouses are invariably in beautiful (if lonely) locations, and the towers and buildings are picturesque and worth a visit for the view alone. No attempt is made to list the hundreds of American lighthouses, but simply many of the better-known. The first American lighthouse was in Boston Harbor and went into operation in 1716. Only the earliest date is given, although many of these lighthouses have been rebuilt several times.

ALABAMA

Cape Hatteras, 1873, near Mobile
Middle Bay lighthouse, 1885, Mobile
Mobile Point light, 1822, Fort Morgan near Gulf Shores
Sand Island lighthouse, 1838, near Fort Morgan

ALASKA

Cape Hinchinbrook lighthouse, 1912, Prince William Sound
Cape St. Elias lighthouse, 1916, Kayak Island
Cape Sarichef lighthouse, 1904, Unimak Island
Cape Spencer lighthouse, 1925, Juneau
Eldred Rock lighthouse, 1904, Lynn Canal to Haines and Skagway
Five Finger light station, 1902, Frederick Sound
Scotch Cap lighthouse, 1903, Unimak Island
Sentinel Island light station, 1902, Sentinel Island near Skagway

CALIFORNIA

Anacapa Island light station, 1923, off Ventura
Alcatraz light station, 1854, Alcatraz Island
Battery Point (Old Crescent City) lighthouse, 1856, Crescent City
Cape Mendocino light, 1868, Cape Mendocino
East Brother Island light station, 1874, Richmond
Farallon Islands lighthouse, c. 1859, w. of San Francisco
Fort Point lighthouse, 1853, San Francisco
Los Angeles Harbor (San Pedro Harbor) lighthouse, 1913, Los Angeles
Old Point Loma lighthouse, 1855, San Diego
Piedras Blancas light, 1875, near San Simeon
Pigeon Point lighthouse, 1871–1872, San Mateo
Point Arena light, 1870, Point Arena
Point Bonita light, 1855, San Francisco
Point Cabrillo lighthouse, 1909, Mendocino
Point Fermin lighthouse, 1874, San Pedro
Point Loma lighthouse, 1891, San Diego
Point Pinos light station, 1855, Monterey
Point Reyes lighthouse, 1870, Point Reyes National Seashore
Point Sur lighthouse, 1889, Big Sur
Point Vicente lighthouse, 1926, Point Vicente
Santa Barbara lighthouse, 1856, Santa Barbara
St. George Reef lighthouse, 1856, Crescent City
Trinidad Head light, 1871, Trinidad

Old Point Loma Lighthouse, 1855, San Diego, California

CONNECTICUT

Black Rock Harbor lighthouse, 1809, Fayerweather Island
New Haven Harbor, 1805, Lighthouse Point
New London light, 1760, Thames River
New London Ledge lighthouse, 1909, East side of main channel
Old Lighthouse Museum, 1823, Stonington
Sheffield Island lighthouse, 1868, Norwalk

DELAWARE

Delaware Breakwater lighthouse, 1885, Cape Henlopen
Lighthouse, 1767, Cape Henlopen
Liston Range light, 1876–1877, Delaware River, Biddles Corner
Mispillion lighthouse, 1831, Milford

FLORIDA

Amelia Island light station, 1839, Fernandina Beach
Cape Florida light, c. 1825, Key Biscayne
Cape Canaveral light, 1848, Cape Kennedy
Cape St. George lighthouse, 1833, Cape St. George State Park
Cape san Blas lighthouse, 1847, St. Joe
Carysfort Reef lighthouse, 1852, Key Largo
Cedar Keys lighthouse, 1854, Seahorse Key
Crooked River lighthouse, 1895, Carrabelle
Egmont Key lighthouse, 1848, Egmont Key, St. Petersburg
Fort Jefferson lighthouse, 1825, Key West
Fowey Rocks lighthouse, 1878, Cape Florida
Hillsboro Inlet lighthouse, 1907, Pompano Beach
Jupiter Inlet lighthouse, 1860, Jupiter, near Palm Beach
Key West lighthouse, pre-1825, Key West
Loggerhead Key tower, 1858, Dry Tortugas
Old Pensacola lighthouse, 1835, Santa Rosa Island
Pensacola lighthouse, 1825, Pensacola
Ponce de Leon (Mosquito) lighthouse, 1887, Daytona Beach
Port Boca Grande light station, 1890, Gasparilla Island
Sand Key lighthouse, 1827, near Key West
Sanibel Island lighthouse, 1884, Sanibel Island
St. Augustine lighthouse, 1824, Anastasia Island
St. John's River lighthouse, 1830, Jacksonville
St. Marks (Rear Range) lighthouse, 1831, Newport

GEORGIA

St. Simons lighthouse, 1810, St. Simons Island
Sapelo Island lighthouse, 1820, near Darien
Tybee Museum and lighthouse, 1736, Savannah

HAWAII

Diamond Head lighthouse, 1899, Oahu
Kilauea Point lighthouse, 1913, Kilauea, Kauai
Makapuu Point lighthouse, 1909, Makapuu Point, Oahu
Molokai lighthouse, 1909, Kalaupapa National Historic Park

List 7–24   Continued

ILLINOIS

Chicago Harbor lighthouse, 1832, Chicago
Grosse Point lighthouse, 1873, Evanston

INDIANA

Michigan City lighthouse, 1837, Michigan City
Pierhead light, 1904, Michigan City

LOUISIANA

Chandeleur Island lighthouse, 1848, Chandeleur Island
New Canal lighthouse, 1838, New Orleans
Point au Fer light, 1827, Eugene Island
Pass Manchac lighthouse, 1837, Ponchatoula
Round Island lighthouse, 1833, Pascagoula
Sabine Pass lighthouse, 1856, Sabine Pass
Ship Shoal lighthouse, 1859, Berwick
South Pass tower, 1831, Mississippi Delta
Southwest Reef lighthouse, 1858
Tchefuncte River Rear Range Light, 1838, Madisonville

MAINE

Baker Island lighthouse, 1828, Acadia National Park
Bass Harbor Head lighthouse, 1858, Acadia National Park
Bear Island lighthouse, 1839, Acadia National Park
Brown's Head lighthouse, 1832, Vinalhaven Island
Burnt Island lighthouse, 1821, Boothbay Harbor
Cape Neddick (Nubble) lighthouse, 1879, York Beach
Doubling Point lights, 1898, Bath
Fort Point lighthouse, 1836, Fort Point State Park
Grindel Point lighthouse, 1851, Lincolnville Beach
Isle au Haut lighthouse, 1907, Stonington
Marshall Point lighthouse, 1832, Thomaston
Monhegan Island, 1824, Port Clyde
Owl's Head, 1825, Rockland Harbor
Pemaquid Point lighthouse, 1827, Damariscotta
Perkins Island lighthouse, 1898, Georgeton
Petit Manan lighthouse, 1817, Jonesport
Portland Breakwater lighthouse, 1855–1875, South Portland
Portland Head light, 1787–1791, Cape Elizabeth
Saddleback Ledge lighthouse, 1839, between Vinalhaven and Isle au Haut
Seguin Island lighthouse, 1797, Georgetown
Squirrel Point lighthouse, 1898, Arrowsic Island
Twin light station, 1890s, Matinicus Rock
Two Lights lighthouse, 1828, Cape Elizabeth, Two Lights State Park
West Quoddy Head light, 1808, Quoddy
Whitehead lighthouse, 1804, East side of Whitehead Island

MARYLAND

Cove Point lighthouse, 1828, Solomons
Drum Point lighthouse, 1833, Calvert Marine Museum
Fenwick Island lighthouse, 1859, Route 54 at Maryland border
Havre de Grace (Concord Point) lighthouse, 1827, Havre de Grace
Hooper Strait lighthouse, 1867, Chesapeake Bay Maritime Museum, St. Michaels

Piney Point Lookout lighthouse, 1836, St. Mary's County
Sandy Point, 1883, Chesapeake Bay
Seven Foot Knoll light, 1855, moved from Chesapeake Bay to Baltimore
Thomas Point Shoal lighthouse, 1875, Annapolis
Turkey Point lighthouse, 1833, Elk Neck State Park

MASSACHUSETTS

Annisquan Harbor lighthouse, 1801, Wigwam Point
Bakers Island lighthouse, 1798, Salem Harbor
Bird Island lighthouse, 1819, Marion
Boston Light tower, 1716, Little Brewster Island
Brant Point, 1746, Nantucket Harbor
Butler Flats lighthouse, 1804, New Bedford
Cape Ann Twin lighthouses, 1771, Thacher Island
Cape Cod Highland light, 1859, Truro
Chatham lighthouse, 1808, Chatham
Cleveland Ledge lighthouse, 1943, Bourne (two miles offshore)
Derby Wharf lighthouse, 1871, Salem
East Chop light station, c. 1924, Martha's Vineyard
Eastern Point lighthouse, 1832, Gloucester Harbor
Gay Head lighthouse, 1799, Gay Head, Martha's Vineyard
Highlands lighthouse, 1798, Cape Cod
Long Island Head lighthouse, 1820, North end of Long Island
Long Point, 1827, Provincetown
Lighthouse, 1769, Plymouth
Marblehead Neck lighthouse, 1838, Marblehead
Minots Ledge light, 1850, off shore, Cohasset
Monomoy lighthouse, 1823, Monomoy Island
Nantucket light, 1784, Great Point, Nantucket Island
Nauset Beach lighthouse, 1877, Nauset Beach, North Eastham
Ned Point lighthouse, 1837, Mattapoisett
Newburyport Harbor lighthouse, 1788, Plum Island
Nobska Point lighthouse, 1829, Woods Hole Harbor
Palmer Island lighthouse, 1849, New Bedford Harbor
Plymouth lighthouse (Gurnet), 1769, Plymouth
Race Point lighthouse, 1816, Cape Cod National Seashore
Sankaty Head light, 1850, Nantucket Island
Scituate lighthouse, 1811, Scituate
Ten Pound Island light, 1821, Glouster
Three Sisters lights, 1838, Nauset Beach, North Eastham

MICHIGAN

Au Sable (Big Sable) lighthouse, 1874, Ludington
Beaver Island lighthouse, 1852, Beaver Island, near Charlevoix
Big Bay Point lighthouse, 1896, Big Bay Point
Copper Harbor lighthouse, 1849, Keweenaw Peninsula
Detroit River lighthouse, 1885, South Rockwood
Eagle Harbor light station, 1851, Eagle Harbor
Escanaba (Sand Point) lighthouse, 1868, Escanaba
Fort Gratiot lighthouse, 1825, Port Huron
Forty Mile Point lighthouse, 1897, Presque Isle, near Rogers City
Grand Traverse station, 1853, Northport

List 7–24 Continued

MICHIGAN (cont.)

Holland Harbor South Pierhead lighthouse, 1872, Holland
Huron Island lighthouse, 1868, Skanee
Isle Royale lighthouse, 1875, Menagerie Island
Little Sable lighthouse, 1874, Silver Lake State Park, Hart
Manitou Island lighthouse, 1850, Manitou Island
Marquette Harbor lighthouse, 1853, Marquette
Old Mackinac Point lighthouse, 1892, Mackinaw City
Old Mission Point lighthouse, 1870, Traverse City
Old Presque Isle lighthouse and museum, 1840, Alpena
Passage Island lighthouse, 1882, Passage Island, near Isle Royale
Peninsula Point lighthouse, 1866, Stonington
Point aux Barques lighthouse, 1848, Port Austin
Point Betsie lighthouse, 1858, Frankfort
Point Iroquois lighthouse, 1855, Brimley
Port Sanilac lighthouse, 1886, Port Sanilac
Presque Isle lighthouse, 1871, Presque Isle
Rock Harbor lighthouse, 1855, Isle Royale National Park
Rock of Ages lighthouse, 1908, Isle Royale
Round Island light, 1895, St. Ignace
Seul Choix Point lighthouse, 1892, Seul Choix Point
South Manitou Island lighthouse, 1839, Sleeping Bear Dunes National Seashore
Spectacle Reef light, 1874, Lake Michigan
St. Helena Island light tower, 1874, St. Helena Island
St. James (Beaver Island Harbor) lighthouse, 1856, Charlevoix
Sturgeon Point lighthouse, 1870, Alcona
Tawas Point lighthouse, 1853, Tawas City
Whitefish Point lighthouse, 1848, Whitefish Point
White River light station museum, c. 1875, Whitehall

MINNESOTA

Duluth South Breakwater Inner lighthouse, c. 1906, Duluth
Grand Marais lighthouse, 1885, Grand Marais
Split Rock lighthouse, 1910, Two Harbors

MISSISSIPPI

Biloxi light, 1848, Biloxi
Cat Island light station, 1871, near Gulfport
Round Island lighthouse, 1833, Pascagoula
Ship Island light, 1886, Ship Island

NEW HAMPSHIRE

Isle of Shoals lighthouse, 1821, White Island
Portsmouth light, 1771, Portsmouth Harbor, New Castle Island

NEW JERSEY

Abescon lighthouse, 1857, Atlantic City
Barnegat light, 1835, Barnegat Inlet, North end of Long Beach Island
Cape May lighthouse, 1823, Cape May
Finn's Point Rear Range lighthouse, 1877, Supawna Meadows National Wildlife Refuge
Hereford Inlet lighthouse, 1874, North Wildwood

Navesink (Twin Lights) lighthouses, 1828, Navesink
Sandy Hook light station, 1764, entrance to New York Harbor
Sea Girt lighthouse, 1896, Sea Girt

NEW YORK

Ambrose Channel, 1967, New York
Barcelona lighthouse, 1829, Barcelona
Buffalo Breakwater South End lighthouse, 1903, Buffalo
Buffalo light, 1819, Buffalo
Cedar Island lighthouse, 1839, Sag Harbor
Champlain Memorial lighthouse, 1912, Crown Point
Coney Island lighthouse, 1890, Brooklyn
Eatons Neck light, 1799, Huntington Bay
Esopus Meadows lighthouse, 1839, Esopus
Fire Island light, 1826, Fire Island National Seashore
Fort Niagara lighthouse, 1870, Youngstown
Fort Tompkins light, 1900, Fort Tompkins
Genesee light, 1822, Rochester
Hudson City (Hudson-Athens) lighthouse, 1874, between Hudson and Athens
Jeffrey's Hook lighthouse, 1889, New York City
Kingston (Rondout II) lighthouse, 1880, intersection of Rondout Creek and Hudson River
Montauk Point light station, 1797, Montauk, Long Island
Old Stony Point lighthouse, 1825, Stony Point Battlefield Historic Park
Oswego West Pierhead, 1822, Oswego
Point Gratiot lighthouse, 1875, Dunkirk
Robbins Reef light, c. 1839, upper New York Harbor
Rock Island lighthouse, 1847, Rock Island
Saugerties lighthouse, 1836, Hudson River and Esopus Creek
Selkirk lighthouse, 1838, Pulaski
Sodus Point lighthouse, 1825, Sodus Point
Tarrytown lighthouse, 1883, North Tarrytown
Thirty Mile Point lighthouse, 1876, Somerset
Tibbetts Point lighthouse, 1827, Cape Vincent

NORTH CAROLINA

Bald Head light station (Cape Fear), 1795, Smith Island off Southport
Bodie Island light station, 1848, Bodie Island, Cape Hatteras National Seashore
Cape Hatteras light station, 1803, Cape Hatteras National Seashore, near Buxton
Cape Lookout lighthouse, 1812, Cape Lookout National Seashore
Currituck Beach lighthouse, 1875, Outer Banks, near Kitty Hawk
Light tower, 1958, Oak Island
Ocracoke lighthouse, 1803, Ocracoke

Cape Hatteras Light Station, 1871, North Carolina

List 7–24   Continued

OHIO

Cleveland West Pierhead lighthouse, 1910, Cleveland
Fairport light, 1825, Fairport
Marblehead lighthouse, 1821, Marblehead
Sandusky light, 1821, Sandusky
Toledo Harbor lighthouse, 1904, Toledo
West Sister Island lighthouse, 1848, West Sister Island

OREGON

Cape Arago light station, 1866, Coos Bay
Cape Blanco light, 1870, Port Orford
Cape Meares lighthouse, 1881, Tillamook
Heceta Head lighthouse, 1894, Florence
Tillamook Rock light, 1881, Columbia River
Umpqua River lighthouse, 1857, Reedsport
Yaquina Bay, 1871, Newport
Yaquina Head lighthouse, 1873, Newport

PENNSYLVANIA

Erie Land lighthouse (Old Presque Isle), 1819, Erie
Presque Isle lighthouse, c. 1870, Erie

RHODE ISLAND

Castle Hill lighthouse, 1890, Newport
Dutch Island lighthouse, 1827, Dutch Island
Ida Lewis Rock (Lime Rock light) pre-1881, Newport
Jamestown (Beavertail) light, 1749, Conanicut Island, Narragansett Bay
Newport Harbor lighthouse, 1823, Goat Island
North lighthouse, 1829, New Shoreham, Sandy Point
Point Judith lighthouse, 1810, Point Judith
Prudence Island lighthouse, 1823, Portsmouth
Rose Island light, 1869, Newport
Sakonnet light, 1884, mouth of Saconnet river
Southeast lighthouse, 1873, Block Island
Warwick lighthouse, 1827, Warwick
Watch Hill lighthouse, 1807, Westerly

SOUTH CAROLINA

Cape Romain light, 1827, Raccoon Key off McClellanville
Charleston light station, 1767, Morris Island
Charleston light station, 1962, Sullivan's Island
Georgetown lighthouse, 1801, North Island, off Georgetown
Hunting Island lighthouse, 1859, Beaufort
Harbortown lighthouse, Hilton Head

TEXAS

Aransas Pass light, 1855, Aransas Pass, near Corpus Christi
Galveston Bay light, 1852, Bolivar Point
Lydia Ann lighthouse, 1857, Port Aransas
Point Bolivar lighthouse, 1852, Galveston
Point Isabel lighthouse, 1853, Port Isabel, near Brownsville
Matagorda lighthouse, 1852, Matagorda

VERMONT

Colchester Reef lighthouse, 1871, Shelburne Museum

VIRGINIA

Assateague lighthouse, 1833, Chincoteague National Wildlife Refuge
Cape Charles lighthouse, 1828, Smith Island
Cape Henry lighthouse, 1791, Fort Story, Virginia Beach
Jones Point lighthouse, 1855, Alexandria
New Point Comfort lighthouse, 1805, Mobjack Bay, Mathews County
Old Point Comfort lighthouse, 1802, Fort Monroe, Hampton
Screwpile light, 1855, Point of Shoals

WASHINGTON

Admiralty Head lighthouse, 1903, Coupeville
Cape Disappointment lighthouse, 1856, Ilwaco
Cape Flattery light station, 1858, Neah Bay
Grays Harbor lighthouse, 1900, Westport
Monots Ledge tower, 1851, first lighthouse, Seattle
Mukilteo lighthouse, 1906, Mulkiteo
New Dungeness light Station, 1857, Straits of Juan de Fuca
North Head Light, 1898, Ilwaco
Point Robinson lighthouse, 1885, Vachon Island
Point Wilson lighthouse, 1879, Townsend
West Point lighthouse, 1881, Seattle

WISCONSIN

Baileys Harbor Range Lights, 1870, Baileys Harbor
Cana Island lighthouse, 1870, near Baileys Harbor
Chambers Island lighthouse, 1868, Ephraim
Devil's Island lighthouse, 1891, Devil's Island
Eagle Bluff lighthouse, 1868, Door County
La Pointe, 1858, Chequamegon Bay
Michigan Island lighthouses, 1857, Michigan Island
North Point lighthouse, 1855, North Point
Pilot Island lighthouse, 1850, Pilot Island
Racine Harbor lighthouse, 1866, Racine
Rawley Point lighthouse, 1853, Two Rivers
Sherwood Point lighthouse, 1883 Sherwood Point
Sturgeon Bay Canal lighthouse, 1899, Sturgeon Bay
Wind Point lighthouse, 1880, Wind Point

Two fine field guides may be of interest to the reader. They are:

Holland, Francis Ross, Jr., *America's Lighthouses, an Illustrated History,* Dover Publications, New York, 1981
Holland, F. Ross, *Great American Light Houses,* John Wiley and Sons, Inc., New York, 1994

List 7–25 American Covered Bridges

Although rare in some parts of the country, many covered bridges in America still exist as a part of the romantic past. They originally were probably covered to protect the base structure, and to keep the surface dry for crossing. Dates are given where available.

ALABAMA

Clarkson Covered Bridge, 1904, Clarkson
Coldwater Covered Bridge, c. 1850, Coldwater
Horton Mill Covered Bridge, 1934, Gadsden
Lake Lauralee Bridge, Sterrett
Covered Bridge, Manoc

CALIFORNIA

Bridge over Sheep Pen Creek, 1970s, Jedediah Smith Redwoods State Park
Covered Bridge, 1936, Eureka

CONNECTICUT

Comstock Bridge, Colchester
Cornwall Bridge, 1837, West Cornwall

GEORGIA

Kilgore Mill Covered Bridge, 1874, Winder
Stovall Covered Bridge over Chickamengra Creek, Helen

ILLINOIS

Bureau Creek Bridge, Bureau County

INDIANA

Covered Bridge, 1838, Brown County State Park, Nashville
Covered Bridge, 1868, Bridgeton, Parke County
Covered Bridge, Cataract Falls State Park
Darlington Bridge, 1868, Montgomery County
Mansfield Bridge, 1867, Mansfield
Matthews Covered Bridge, 1876–1877, Marion

Narrows Bridge, Turkey Run State Park
Offutt's Ford Bridge, Rush County
Roann Bridge, Wabash County
Symons Creek Bridge, 1831, Straughn

IOWA

Bridge across North Fork of Skunk River, 1869, Delta
Cutler-Donahoe Bridge, Winterset
Holliwell Bridge, Madison County
Imes Bridge, St. Charles
McBride Bridge, 1870, Madison County

KENTUCKY

Bennett's Mill Bridge, 1855, Ashland
Oldtown Bridge, 1880, Ashland
Bridge over Beech Fork River, 1866, Bardstown

MAINE

Sunday River Bridge (Artist's Bridge), Newry

MASSACHUSETTS

Bissell Bridge, 1880, Charlemont
Chicopee Bridge, 1846, Springfield
Long Bridge, 1853, Charlemont

MICHIGAN

Covered Bridge, Fallasburg

MISSOURI

Bollinger Mill State Historical Site, Burfordville

NEW HAMPSHIRE

Albany Bridge, White Mountain National Forest
Ashuelot Bridge, c. 1840, Ashuelot
Bridge # 37, c. 1820, Stark Village
Cornish-Windsor Bridge, Cornish
Covered Bridge # 51, Jackson
Covered Bridge, Hillsborough County
Haverhill-Bath Covered Bridge, 1827, Woodsville
Passaconway Bridge, White Mountains
Rowell Bridge, West Hopkinton
Saco River Bridge, Conway
Swanzey-Slate Covered Bridge, Westport
Swift River Bridge, Conway

List 7–25   Continued

NEW HAMPSHIRE (cont.)

Swiftwater Bridge, Bath
Tanner Bridge, 1936, Enfield
The Flume, 1886, Franconia Notch State Park
Thompson Bridge, 1832, Swanzey

NEW JERSEY

Forty-five River, Fundy National Park, New Brunswick

NEW YORK

Brasher Falls Bridge, 1861, Brasher Falls
Old Blenheim Bridge, 1855, North Blenheim

NORTH CAROLINA

Reddles River Bridge, (top hat bridge), North Wilkesboro

OHIO

Barrett's Mill Bridge, 1850, Highland County
Bridge over Little Miami River, 1830, Xenia
Covered Bridge, Buckeye Lake State Park
Ferryboat Bridge, 1858, Newtown Falls
New Hope Bridge, 1895, Brown County

OREGON

Five Bridges, Cottage Grove

PENNSYLVANIA

Ackley Bridge, 1832, Green-Washington County line
Bridge No. 212, Haupt's Mill
Bridge, 1856, Earlsville
Clark's Ferry Bridge, Clark's Ferry
Covered Bridge, Chitwood
Covered Bridge, Erwinna
Covered Bridge, Lancaster County
Frankenfeld Bridge, Bucks County
Gallon House Bridge, Silverton
Goodpasture Bridge, Vida
Grave Creek, 1920, Josephine County
Knox Bridge, Valley Forge
Sauk's Bridge over Marsh Creek, 1854, Gettysburg
Short Bridge, 1945, Linn County
South Perkasie Bridge, 1832, Bucks County

Uhlerstown Bridge, Bucks County
Weddle Bridge, Sankey Park, Sweet Home

VERMONT

"Kissing Bridge," Grafton
Baltimore Bridge No. 81, Springfield
Colt's Pond, 1810, Brookfield
Covered Bridge, East Randolph
Covered Bridge, Lyndon
Covered Bridge, North Harland
Covered Bridge, Tunbridge
Covered Bridge, Waitfield
Covered Bridge, Waterville
Covered Bridge, West Arlington
Covered Bridge, West Drummerstone
Covered Bridge, Williamsburg
Covered Bridge, Windsor
Creamery Bridge, 1879, Brattleboro
Lincoln Bridge, 1865, Woodstock
New Middle Bridge, 1969, Woodstock
Scott Covered Bridge, 1870, West Townshend
Slaughterhouse Bridge, Northfield
Swiftwater Bridge, White Mountains
Taftsville Bridge, 1836, Woodstock
Ventilated Bridge, Lake Sunapee
West River Bridge, 1879, West Dummerstone
White Mountain Covered Bridge, Albany

VIRGINIA

Covered Bridge, Weston
Humpback Bridge, 1835, Covington
Meems Bottom Bridge, 1892 and 1979, Meems Bottom

WEST VIRGINIA

Staats Mill Bridge, Jackson County

WASHINGTON

Covered Bridge, Grays River Valley
Manning Bridge, Manning

WISCONSIN

Covered Bridge, Cedarburg

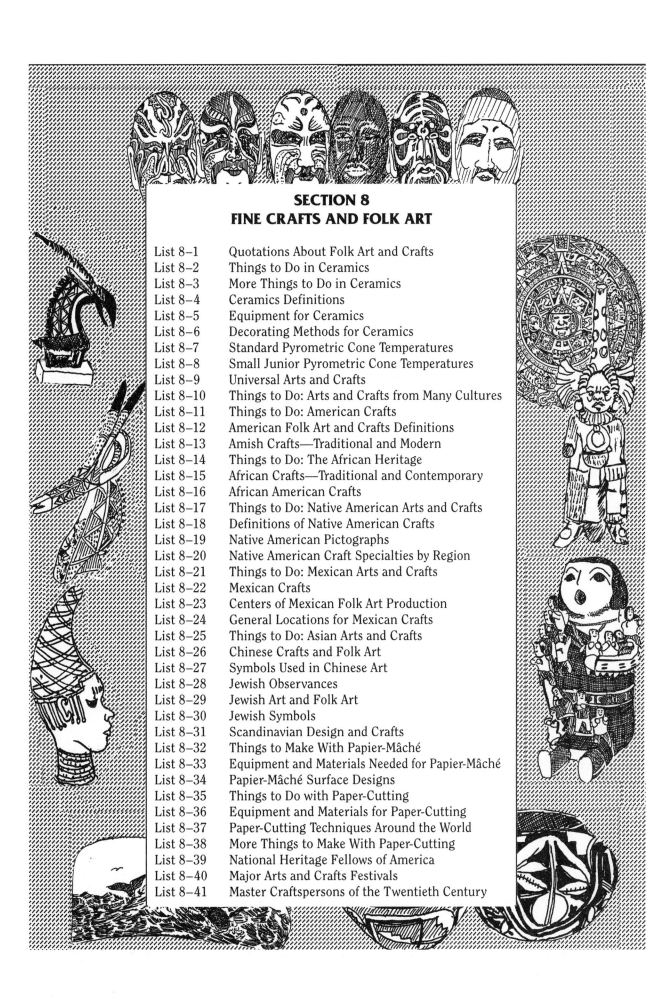

SECTION 8
FINE CRAFTS AND FOLK ART

List 8–1   Quotations About Folk Art and Crafts

"A primitive artist is an amateur whose work sells."

—Grandma Moses (Anna Mary Moses)

"All art is an individual's expression of a culture. Cultures differ, so art looks different."

—Henry Glassie, *The Spirit of Folk Art*

"The hands make the head clever."

—Michael Cardew, potter

"If I didn't start painting, I would have raised chickens."

—Grandma Moses

"Pottery is at once the simplest and the most difficult of all the arts."

—Sir Herbert Read

"Develop an infallible technique and then place yourself at the mercy of inspiration."

—Ralph Rapson

"Technique is cheap."

—Harvey Littleton, glassmaker

"Folk arts are forms of expression passed on within groups of people and thus shared by many . . ."

—Dan Sheehy, Director, Folk & Traditional Arts Program,
National Endowment for the Arts

"Culture is something that evolves out of the simple, enduring elements of everyday life; elements most truthfully expressed in the folk arts and crafts of a nation."

—Thor Hansen

"Art made for the people and by the people, a joy to the maker and user."

—William Morris

"There is more fine abstract design in Navajo rugs than in all these modern paintings."

—Teddy Roosevelt (in speaking of the Armory show)

List 8–2   Things to Do in Ceramics

CARVING

- Create a human figure by carving, using only straight lines and edges (planes); no curved areas.
- Make an abstract sculpture in clay. Begin with a cube and only *remove* clay, leaving no area thicker than one inch.

CASTING

- Make a two-part plaster mold of a large smooth rock; let the opening where the clay is poured become the neck of a pot.
- Model a form in clay, then make a plaster two-part mold. Hold it together with plaster and rubber bands or tape; then pour slip into it, pouring out the excess after it has hardened to ¼ inch.
- Using a purchased mold, pour slip (clay thinned with water) into the mold, and allow the edges to harden to a thickness of ¼ inch before pouring out the excess; allow to dry slightly before handling.

COIL-BUILDING

- Design a serving container that **looks** like your favorite fruit or vegetable.
- Use slab or coil building to make a fantasy or realistic teapot. It must have a handle and a spout.

DRAPING

- After draping a ½-inch thick slab over a large bowl, use a knife to cut out a wedge; trim it and cut decorative openings throughout.
- Drape a slab over a face form (plaster, taped paper, or plastic) to create a ceramic mask.
- Roll out a slab of clay to a thickness of ¼ to ½ inch. Drape it over a mold and allow the sides to hang in folds until the shape is set.

PINCH POTS

- Design a Japanese tea bowl, giving careful attention to the bottom. Impress a weed into the clay around the outside, which will burn away in the firing.
- Make several pinch pots, stacking one on top of another, then hollowing out down the center.

SCULPTING

- Create a gargoyle of clay. Original gargoyles were decorative roof spouts for draining water. They are now used as tabletop decorations and garden ornaments.
- Create a group of figures doing something together (card playing, swimming, playing ball).
- To make a simple figure, roll out a slab, then cut a circle and take out a pie-shaped wedge. Make a cone from the three-quarter circle and add a head, feet, and arms; change the cone, and make the character male or female. Add wings to make an angel.
- Sculpt a domestic or wild animal based on designs of a particular culture or time period (Art Deco, Japanese, Chinese, African).
- Sculpt a portrait bust by working with solid clay; cut it in half with a wire, then hollow it out to a thickness of one inch and rejoin it with slip, being sure to leave a hole in the bottom for air to escape.
- Take inspiration from an ancient culture to create a sculpture of an animal, person, or effigy figure.
- Using a piece of fruit or vegetable for inspiration, transform that fruit or vegetable shape into a person pot by adding features (examples: eggplant, squash, pumpkin, banana).

SLAB-BUILDING

- A gigantic free-standing outdoor mural/sculpture could be created of thick fired and decorated slabs assembled with cement.
- Create a ceramic picture frame suitable for a wedding picture, graduation picture, baby present, a photo of the family pet, or some other momentous occasion.
- Design a fantasy door and entrance (a castle, house of the future, undersea, etc.); make one wall a little larger and angle it out to give it stability.

List 8–2   Continued

- Make a flask by rolling clay approximately ¼-inch thick and cutting out two identical shapes, then joining them at the edges. Put paper in the center to hold them apart in the drying stage. Put holes on the sides for hanging by a leather thong.
- Design a unique group of tiles for a specific place such as around a door or window frame, a kitchen sink, or a fireplace.
- Make a "house" box (your own) or a Victorian-style house by making the four sides and a removable top.
- Make an irregularly shaped squarish slab tile and tell a story on it by incising words and a picture.

WHEEL-THROWING

- After throwing a round pot, deliberately slap it on one side with a paddle to make it irregular.
- Create one complete place setting of dishes for yourself: plate, cup, saucer, bowl, and salad plate.
- Put a handle and lip on a thrown form to create a pitcher.
- Throw a weed pot, with the smallest possible opening for inserting one stem only.
- Throw one or two small tops to be added to a tall four-sided slab-built pot.
- Transform a thrown pot to have the features of a human or animal by adding eyes, nose, and mouth.

List 8–3   More Things to Do in Ceramics

animals	figurines	portrait bust
architectural detail	fountain	sculpture
beads	frames	spice containers
bird bath	gargoyles	tea bowls
bowls	jars	teapot
boxes	jars with lids	tiles
candelabrum	jewelry	trays
candleholders	jug	vases
canisters	lamps	vessels (at least 12 inches)
cups	mugs	weed pot
dinner ware	mural	wind chime
dolls' heads	pitchers	
figure	plates	

List 8–4   Ceramics Definitions

bisque   (sometimes called biscuit ware) a first firing of clay without glazes

bone dry   unfired clay that is free of water and ready to fire

burnish   to polish clay while it is in the greenware stage

casting   to pour clay slip into plaster molds; allows mass reproduction of one form

ceramic   clay products that have been fired for permanence

china   translucent ware fired at 2,230 degrees F; porcelain

clay   a moist earth of decomposed rock; used in products such as pottery, bricks, tiles, and sculpture

coiling   a method of creating pots by building bottom and walls with even, ropelike coils

decal   designs that are transferred to ware before firing; often used in china decorating

earthenware   low-fire pottery, usually red or tan, that has been fired to below 2,000 degrees F

Egyptian paste   low-fire, self-glazing body fires to a gloss or crackle finish

engobe   a glaze made of clay diluted with water that is painted on greenware

firing   making clay products permanent through baking at high temperatures in a kiln

greenware   clay in an unfired state

leather hard   unfired clay that isn't quite dry, yet firm enough to carve or burnish

raku   a low fire often done outdoors that produces dark areas and iridescence

reduction firing   firing with insufficient oxygen; causes interesting color changes in glazes

scoring   making marks on the edges of two pieces of clay before joining with slip

sgraffito   scratching designs through colored slip to allow the body color to show through

slab   clay evenly rolled and formed by draping or joining

slip   clay diluted with water to the consistency of cream; used for joining or as an engobe

stoneware   gray, reddish, or tan clay that has been high fired (cones 5 to 10)

talc   a compound added to white clay

terra cotta   reddish clay that contains grog, commonly used for ceramic sculpture (cones 06 to 5)

throwing   creating vessels on a potter's wheel

turning   completing a piece of ware by rotating on a wheel and trimming with tools

underglaze   colors that can be painted on greenware that will show through a clear glaze

wax resist   the application of melted wax to the foot or body of a clay object to resist the glaze

wedging   kneading moist clay to eliminate air bubbles and produce a uniform texture

List 8–5   Equipment for Ceramics

armature   something to support clay while it is being formed, such as newspaper or a drape mold

bat   a flat plaster of Paris block for drying clay

battens (two) $\frac{1}{4} \times 1\frac{1}{2} \times 12$-inch boards for rolling out even slabs of clay

bead tree   nichrome wire for supporting beads while firing

brushes for glaze   specially designed brushes with extra stiff hair for applying glaze

caliper   measuring tool for checking symmetry and fitting lids to pots

clay   earth with special plastic quality that becomes hard when fired

clay paddles   stick similar to a batten or ruler for paddling coil-built clay for evenness

clay recycling barrels   large covered barrels on wheels or roll-around bases

cone   mixture of clay and glaze with a specific, predetermined melting point; used in firing

decorating wheel   a wheel that will turn to allow for ease in decorating pots

drape molds   molds of plaster for draping a slab of clay until dry

earring holder   specialized wire holder for earrings or pendants for firing on all sides

elephant ear sponge   a specific shape of fine, natural sponge

extruder   a tool that produces specific shapes when clay is forced through a hollow tube

firebrick   coarse brick used for lining kilns

glaze   a finely ground mineral solution painted on bisque ware; when fired, it becomes glassy

grog   fired clay that has been pulverized for adding to clay to reduce shrinkage

hardwood tools   boxwood tools with a variety of end surfaces for modeling clay

heat-resistant gloves   fireproof gloves for removing warm pots from kiln

kiln   a furnace used for firing clay products; electric, gas, or wood-fired

kiln furniture   shelves, posts, and stilts used inside a kiln that support clay products for firing

kiln screen   fire proof curtain on three-fold aluminum frame for screening off the kiln

kiln wash   liquid to be applied to kiln shelves to keep glazeware from sticking

loop tools   tools with ribbons of wire for shaping and trimming ceramic objects

open storage   locking storage with steel-mesh sides to allow air to circulate

plaster of Paris   cilcined gypsum used in bats for drying clay and molds for casting

potter's ribs   shaped pieces of wood or metal for shaping, smoothing wet clay while hand building or throwing

props   kiln shelf supports

pug mill   electric machine for mixing clay or pulverizing dried clay

pyrometer   temperature control for kiln; can allow for automatic shutoff at correct temperature

rolling pins   used in rolling out slabs; also come with carved textures

scale   used for weighing dry clay and mineral glaze formulas

scraper   shaped piece of fine sheet steel for use in forming objects

sinks   special clay traps should be installed in sinks for a ceramic room

slab roller   large flat table with a roller for making consistent clay slabs

spray booth   booth for spraying glazes onto ware

spray bottle   used for spraying ceramic sculpture or other work-in-progress

star stilts   small four pointed stilt to support work in firing

stilts   bar or three-pronged support for holding ceramic wares up from kiln shelf

turntable   decorating or sculpting wheel for turning work while working on it

vent system   may be attached to bottom of kiln, or above kiln, but a necessity

wheel   for making pots; driven by hand, foot, or electric power

List 8–6   Decorating Methods for Ceramics

color oxides rubbed on

combed designs

dip into glaze

glaze: brushed on

glaze: sprayed on

gouge and twist

gouge designs

paddle marks

patterned rolling pins

sgraffito designs scratched through slip

serrated wheel marks

stamped designs

straw imbedded in surface

string rolled into surface, then removed

trailed slip glaze

underglazes painted on greenware, then fired before applying clear glaze

List 8–7   Standard Pyrometric Cone Temperatures

These cones may be placed in a piece of clay and put in front of a kiln hole for visual firings, or placed in a pyrometric "kiln sitter" that shuts off when the cone reaches a specific temperature.

Cone 02	2,048°F	Cone 06	1,830°F
Cone 04	1,940°F	Cone 07	1,803°F
Cone 05	1,915°F		

List 8–8   Small Junior Pyrometric Cone Temperatures

Cone 11	2,437°F	Cone 05	1,944°F
Cone 10	2,426°F	Cone 06	1,873°F
Cone 9	2,403°F	Cone 07	1,846°F
Cone 8	2,372°F	Cone 08	1,801°F
Cone 7	2,307°F	Cone 09	1,751°F
Cone 6	2,291°F	Cone 010	1,686°F
Cone 5	2,230°F	Cone 011	1,680°F
Cone 4	2,208°F	Cone 012	1,650°F
Cone 3	2,185°F	Cone 016	1,517°F
Cone 2	2,154°F	Cone 017	1,443°F
Cone 1	2,154°F	Cone 018	1,386°F
Cone 01	2,152°F	Cone 019	1,333°F
Cone 02	2,098°F	Cone 020	1,231°F
Cone 03	2,068°F	Cone 021	1,189°F
Cone 04	2,008°F	Cone 022	1,165°F

List 8–9   Universal Arts and Crafts

Art forms developed as an outgrowth of human needs such as procuring food, carrying belongings, clothing, storage baskets, cooking pots, shelter, celebrations, and a belief in a supernatural force. These basic needs were universal. As cultures developed, individual differences became more marked, and methods and patterns of decorating became more elaborate. Available materials were a determining force in which art forms became traditional in specific cultures.

apple dolls	glassware	quilling
architectural embellishments	gourd carving	quiltmaking
basketry	jewelry	repoussé
batik	leatherwork	rosemahling
beading	lighting devices	scrimshaw
bookbinding	macramé	silk screening
bronze casting	marbleizing	stenciling
calligraphy	mask making	textiles
cast iron	metalwork	tie dye
ceramics	musical instrument making	tin wares
china painting	needlework	tole painting
collage	painted gourds	toys
copper enameling	papier-mâché	weathervanes
country furniture	paper-cutting	weaving
decoupage	paper flowers	wheat weaving
doll making	papermaking	whittling
fabric block printing	porcelain	wood carving
folk painting	pottery	woodcraft
gem cutting	puppetry	

List 8–10 Things to Do: Arts and Crafts from Many Cultures

- geometric designs *(Islamic):* Make an arabesque design in the manner of mosaics by using a compass to create complex circles or flowerlike designs. After creating interlocking designs, color them with fine-line marker or colored pencils.
- *fraktur (German):* This "certificate" could be to record a wedding, birth, graduation, or engagement. The fancy writing could be in the center. Do calligraphy in the center by hand or on the computer. Then decorate the edges with watercolor and a gold-tipped craft pen. Use hearts, flowers, animals, nature items.
- *molas (Cuna Indians, San Blas Island):* The layered, reverse appliquéd cloth molas created by the Cuna Indians were meant to be worn as blouses. To make a paper mola, use Scratch Art Paper® (which has a black surface, with variegated colors underneath) to draw an animal; then use a nail to scratch lozenge or geometric shapes around and through the animal.
- *Pysanky (Poland):* Pysanky are uniquely decorated eggs done using a batik method. Instead, decorate hollowed-out eggs or wooden eggs with acrylic paints, using the geometric designs.
- *rose painting (rosemahling) (Norway):* Norwegians whiled away long winter hours by painting interior walls and furniture with beautiful designs using flowers or other designs from nature. Get unpainted white tiles and paint designs either with acrylic paint, or with glazes, refiring the tiles.
- *scherenschnitt (German):* Fold black paper in half, then draw a design on one half and cut through both layers at one time with an X-acto® knife. Suitable designs are trees, animals, nature. ***Safety note:*** *When using an X-acto® knife, always hold the non-cutting hand behind the knife.*
- *wycinanki (Poland):* Polish cut-outs are brightly colored, layered paper cut-outs. Using fadeless paper, cut flowers, birds, or trees for the top layer. Build layers of color by cutting and adding paper in other bright colors underneath and on top.

List 8–11 Things to Do: American Crafts

- Make small black-and-white photocopies of birds such as those painted by John James Audubon. Use crayon to enlarge and redraw and color them in bright, unrealistic colors. Paint India ink mixed with liquid detergent over these. Allow them to dry; then, using a ruler, scratch through the ink layer with a nail using vertical lines $\frac{1}{16}$th inch apart.
- *quilting:* Use a computer to make a quilt design. It lends itself easily to such designs as the nine-patch, windmill, and other geometric patterns.
- *scrimshaw:* Use Friendly Plastic® or other white plastic (switchplates, bleach bottles, sheet plastic) as a basis. Use a long nail to scratch a design. Sailing ships, mermaids, flowers, and geometric designs are all suitable for scrimshaw (cross-hatching enhances these designs). Coat with ink or acrylic paint, then wipe off.
- Stencil a floorcloth on canvas by cutting a stencil design from mylar with an X-acto® knife. Apply acrylic paint using either a stencil brush or small piece of sponge. ***Safety note:*** *Remember to always cut on a protected surface, holding the non-cutting hand behind the one with the knife.*
- Use letter stencils, charcoal, conté, or pastels to make a composition much as the Pop artists did. Use only one letter, seeing how many different combinations are possible (or use several stencils to spell out a word). Combine letters with drawings of real objects also. For inspiration, see Jasper Johns, Larry Rivers, Robert Indiana, and Robert Rauschenberg.
- *weathervane:* Make a weathervane by cutting out a cardboard pattern of an animal or bird. Then cut foil slightly larger. Texture the foil with a dull pencil, then affix it to the cardboard backing with tape or glue. Wipe ink on the foil, then wipe off the excess. Glue additional foil on the back to finish.

List 8–12   American Folk Art and Crafts Definitions

BASKETRY

baskets   woven from split-oak, river-cane, honeysuckle, twig and vine, bark, pine needles, sweetgrass, palmetto, and corn shucks

broom making   palmetto, broomcorn, buckeye, and sedge

splint baskets   craftspersons in many parts of the South continue to make baskets from thin splints of wood woven together

FIBERS

album quilt   usually made by several people, involving appliqué and fancy stitching

appliquéd quilt   cut-outs, such as hearts and flowers, were sewn onto a quilt

bed rug   patterned wool blanket, hand woven or hand sewn

counterpane   a fancy hand appliquéd and embroidered bedspread

crazy quilt   quilt made of irregularly cut, embroidered patches of (mostly) silks, satins, and velvets

embroidered quilt   often simple designs done in cross stitch in one color

embroidered sampler   the sampler was a means of teaching young girls how to do various embroidery stitches

hooked rug   these rugs usually had animals, flowers, or geometric designs

macramé   knotted thread; frequently done by sailors to demonstrate knotting ability

net weaving   making fish nets using twine and metal hoops

quilting   sewing layers of cloth together, with pieced designs on the top is an ancient technique that came from the East, but has become a signature of American folk art. Originally old clothing was cut up and pieced together, eventually leading to fancier quilts.

weaving   homespun cloth, coverlets, rag rugs, linsey-woolsey

wool pictures of ships   probably made by sailors because of special attention to rigging

MUSICAL INSTRUMENTS

musical instruments   dulcimers, banjos, fifes made of cane, mandolins and fiddles, accordions, and limberjacks (dancing wooden doll used to beat a rhythm)

PAINTING

overmantle painting   rooms decorated with paintings directly on the wall above a mantle

painted fireboard   a fancy small screen to protect ladies' faces from the fire, sometimes used to cover the fireplace opening when not in use

painted furniture   furniture was often simple, and the tradition of painting it was brought from Europe

painted tin ware   tole painting was used to enhance trays, coffee pots, etc.

SCRIMSHAW

ivory pipe stoppers   for packing tobacco into pipes

scrimshaw knitting needles   sometimes combined with wood or other materials

scrimshaw pie crimpers   serrated wheel with female figure, a hand, a horse, or decorated handle

whale bone yarn swifts   used to turn yarn

whale teeth or whale bone   incised with a sharp instrument (usually done by sailors); used to decorate a whale's tooth or make pie crimpers, corset busks (for making women's waists smaller), umbrella handles, needles

TOYS AND DOLLS

apple doll   the head was a carved, dried apple, placed on a cloth body

corn-husk dolls   these dolls continue in popularity into modern times, though it is unlikely that little girls play with them any more

List 8-12   Continued

dolls   made from cloth, corn cobs, corn husks, cardboard, or paper

puppets   this timeless craft continues, with hand puppets, marionettes, and stick puppets still being used in performances

rag dolls   simple rag dolls are homemade or manufactured, but children still love them

WOODCARVING

carved animals   mostly toys; also carved for carousels: tigers, horses, lions, giraffes

carved figures   the eagle, Uncle Sam, George Washington, Miss Liberty

decoys   carved wooden birds of all types, painted; used to attract real birds for hunters

figureheads   these were at the bows of ships, usually a beautiful woman or a top-hatted man

model ships   intricate ships, complete with rigging; probably made by sailors

tavern sign   usually had the name of the tavern and a painted figure such as a general

Uncle Sam Whirligig, late 19th century, Museum of American Folk Art

trade figure   these figures were sailors, Native Americans, Miss Liberty, Scottish Highlander, Jack Tar

trade signs   wood or metal oversized signs of such things as a tooth, eyeglasses, boot, fish, bread, watch, gun, chair; each designed to tell you what was being sold inside

weathervanes   three-dimensional copper vanes, flat sheet metal, or carved and painted wood; subjects such as trains, angels, fish, bannerets, Indian hunters, roosters, farm animals

whirligig   painted carved figures with moving parts that were activated by the wind

whittling   toys, dolls, whistles, small figures, and animals were whittled out of wood with a knife

woodcarving   in addition to trade signs, trade store figures and figureheads, woodcarvers did decorative carving for ships

OTHER

calligraphy   fancy lettering was done on important family documents; eventually calligraphic strokes were also used to make pictures such as the eagle, a horse, etc.

candlemaking   candles made from animal fat were a necessity

engraved coconuts   this work was done by sailors; similar subjects to those used in scrimshaw

metalsmithing   wrought iron: weathervanes, candleholders, wrought iron utensils, farm implements, gates, fences

pen and ink sampler   boys and girls made samplers in ink on parchment, using alphabets and numbers

pottery   jugs, bowls, pitchers, dishes, etc.

quilling   small pieces of paper were rolled around a needle and these rolls were grouped together to make a fancy picture

saddle making   leather is molded over handmade wooden forms, tooled and stitched

Shaker wooden boxes   these simple round wooden boxes that were used for storage have become collectors' items

silver   craftsmen such as Paul Revere created bowls, porringers, silver services, and napkin rings

squirrel cage   (Colonial) elaborately carved cage with an exercise wheel for the squirrel

stone carving   at first stone carvers made gravestones, but eventually turned to decorative carving for homes, and eventually for monumental work

straw work   straw weaving was a craft brought from Sweden and England; this tradition continues in modern-day Mexico, China, the U.S., and wherever else straw is grown

wheat weaving   wheat was woven into *House Blessings,* ornaments, dolls, other decorations

List 8–13 Amish Crafts—Traditional and Modern

TEXTILES

alphabet samplers

bolster covers, embroidered

braided rugs

clothing: capes, dresses, shirts

doll cradles

doll quilts

door towels (white embroidered towels to be
hung on the back of guest room doors)

family records, embroidered

hand knitted socks

hooked rugs

knitted mittens

memorial samplers

needle case

needlepoint

needlework pictures

pin cushions

potholder sculpture (birds and chickens)

rag dolls

scissors' rest

sewing pockets (roll-ups to keep needles, etc.)

QUILT PATTERNS

Amish quilts are confined to a few patterns, treasured today because of their strong graphic quality and deep colors.

center diamond with nine-patch center

center diamond with sunshine and shadow
center

center square

crazy patch

diamond in the square

double-nine patch

fan quilt

floating bars

floating center diamond

log cabin design

sawtooth diamond

sunshine and shadow

triple Irish chain

FURNITURE

bandbox

baskets

blanket chests

button boxes

candle boxes

chairs

jelly cupboards

lift-top storage boxes

miniature blanket chests

paint-decorated boxes

seed box (resembles a spice cabinet)

sewing boxes

small tables

spoon box

wall cupboards

weathervanes

PAINTINGS

bookplates

frakturs

List 8–14   Things to Do: The African Heritage

- *adinkra cloth:* This African method of printing cloth was done with stamp designs cut from gourds. Use carved artgum erasers to make printing blocks, and print one large cloth with a variety of designs. Or do individual paper or T-shirt designs with repeated stamping.
- Make papier-mâché or Paris-craft masks by forming them over balloons, clay molds, or an egg-shaped wad of paper. Make the basic face, then add cut-out cardboard shapes to make appropriate headdresses on top, securing them firmly before covering with additional paper or Paris-craft strips.
- *people pots:* The tradition of making face vessels is an old one. Form pots using the coil method. Add features so the pot has facial features on one side. Use natural glazes in browns and dark greens.
- *quilting:* Make paper or cloth quilts in the manner of many African American quilters. These have some resemblance to Kenté cloth, with long pieced strips, joined together. Another specialty is appliquéd quilts similar to appliquéd banners found in West Africa.
- *screenwire masks:* These masks, based on the Caribbean tradition, may be formed over each person's face. These should then be painted with features, and mounted to show them off to best advantage, enhancing them with appropriate materials. These masks are also used for the Mardi Gras by Cajuns in the countryside around New Orleans.
- *sculpture:* Make a papier-mâché figure based on African sculpture by wadding and taping newspaper to make a figure, then covering with newspaper strips. Paint the figure either in bright colors or to resemble wood.
- *stick carving:* Hunt for branches that are long and sturdy enough for a walking stick. Use a knife and sandpaper to carve the head to resemble an animal, snake, or person. Remember to make it comfortable enough to fit the hand. Or simply paint animal designs on the stick with acrylic or tempera paint.

List 8–15   African Crafts—Traditional and Contemporary

Because of changing boundaries, these are listed with the name of the modern country, then followed by the names of the former Kingdoms, then by the names of the people. Boundaries of Kingdoms have changed and many of these cultures have vanished. Contemporary crafts include painting, carving, jewelry-making, leatherwork, fabric decorating, and weaving. Modern artists frequently are inspired by traditional techniques and motifs.

REPUBLIC OF BENIN (THE KINGDOM OF DAHOMEY—FON PEOPLE)

appliquéd cloth banners   appliqué techniques for decorating textiles were used by the Fon peoples of Benin, and the Ewe, Fanti, and Ashanti of Ghana

earthen relief murals   wall surfaces embellished with raised designs

figurative wood sculptures   tradition of carved figures

metal sculptures   cast bronze animals, heads, fertility images, bas-relief plaques, and statuary

wattle-and-daub architecture   homes made of mud plastered over a woven wooden framework, or made of adobe-type mud bricks

GHANA (KINGDOM OF ASHANTI—AKAN PEOPLE)

adinkra cloth   designs stamped on plain background fabric with pieces from a carved calabash shell

Ashanti brass goldweights   geometric designs; some illustrated proverbs; animals such as grasshoppers, fish, elephants, crocodiles, leopards, lions

brass-studded wooden chairs

carved stools   elaborately carved stools, often with images of people or animals on the legs

cast gold rings   snails, cocoon, lion

List 8–15   Continued

GHANA (KINGDOM OF ASHANTI—AKAN PEOPLE) (cont.)

fantasy coffins   wooden painted coffins that resemble cars, trucks, fish, animals and birds, airplanes

kente cloth   long narrow strips of cloth; 24 strips joined together were enough for a royal robe

MALI (KINGDOMS OF THE WESTERN SUDAN)

brass and gold castings   goldweights in the shape of animals, jewelry

terra cotta sculptures   elongated heads, pointed chin, equestrian statues, female statues, animals

NIGERIA (ALL INCLUSIVE)

cement tomb figures   painted life-size figures

painted vehicles   sometimes decorated with flowers, animals, and geometric designs

NIGERIA, NORTHERN (HAUSA STATES—HAUSA PEOPLE)

quilted armor for horses

robes created from long woven strips

Antelope, Aribinda region

NIGERIA, NORTH CENTRAL (NOK CULTURE)

bead embroidered headdresses   tall headdresses sometimes had beads hanging down to "cover" the face

chained sets of brass sculpture   Ogboni society

hollow terra-cotta sculpture   men, women, animals

lost wax castings   from Igbo-Ukwu, Nigeria

terra-cotta heads   Owo, Nigeria

NIGERIA, SOUTH CENTRAL (KINGDOM OF BENIN—EDO PEOPLE)

bronze relief plaques   kings, chiefs, and courtiers

bronze sculpture   life-sized portraits (often with an ivory tusk emerging from the top); sometimes used as part of an altar

ivory   carved masks, decorations, jewelry

terra-cotta commemorative heads   models of heads of kings or ancestors were given place of honor because of the African belief that the head is the location of all the senses

NIGERIA, SOUTHWESTERN (YORUBA CULTURE—KINGDOM OF IFE—KINGDOM OF OWO)

bronze heads (Ife)   12th to 16th centuries

bronze roped pots

copper masks   1100–1400

copper seated figures   1100–1400

Ere Ibeji twin cult figures   carved wood; Yoruba peoples have an extraordinary number of twins in their society; in the event of the death of one twin, an effigy of the other is given special attention

lost-wax cast figures   extremely detailed metal figures done by the lost-wax method

ornate paved walkways

terra-cotta sculptures

Yoruba *egungun* masquerade cloth costumes

Yoruba masquerade masks   these carved wooden masks have a long tradition

SIERRA LEONE

Ode-lay costumes   masks, elaborate costumes for masquerade parades and performances

tissue-paper lanterns in fantastic shapes   displayed by Muslims during Ramadan

List 8–16 African American Crafts

Artforms brought from Africa to the Western Hemisphere continue to be based on African traditions. In areas such as Brazil, the Caribbean, and the American South, the African origins are sometimes apparent, with these universal crafts having something in common. These folk art and crafts techniques have been passed from generation to generation.

BASKETS

bark baskets   bark strips held together to make a sturdy basket, sometimes for one-time-use; a basket is made by simply folding birchbark to carry berries

grapevine baskets   wet grapevines manipulated to make sturdy baskets and wreaths

honeysuckle baskets   vine baskets and wreaths

palmetto baskets   palmettos used for woven baskets and hats

pine needle baskets   pine needle baskets constructed in the coil manner, bound with raffia or twine

river cane baskets   coated with pine tar for carrying water

split oak baskets   thin strips of oak soaked, then woven to make sturdy baskets

sweet grass baskets   bundles of grass wrapped in the coil method with raffia to make baskets for church collections, or to hold sewing materials, cakes, or fruit

BROOMS

"broom corn" brooms   brooms are made from the tassels of this plant that resembles a sorghum plant

palmetto brooms   palmetto fronds are split and dried to make a short broom

sedge grass brooms   sedge grass bundled together with wire to make a handle; the feathery ends are supposed to be very effective for picking up dirt

CERAMICS

face vessels   *voodoo pots* or *ugly jugs* were used to hold water; vases without handles were called *goglets;* jugs that had a handle (usually used to hold liquor) were called *monkey jugs*

DOLLS AND TOYS

corn husk dolls   a Colonial craft

rag dolls   a popular variation was the "two headed" doll, with a long (lined) skirt hiding one head; when the doll was upended, it had a different appearance

FIBER ART

African American quilts have a tradition that may have some relationship to African kente cloth or appliquéd storytelling banners. They generally are pieced in strips, or appliquéd. Many combine African and European traditional techniques and motifs.

appliquéd quilts   designs such as animals, people, houses; sun designs were created in the manner of the Dahomey people of Benin

embroidery   often used in quilt making

Mardi Gras "Indian costumes"   elaborate, finely beaded and feathered costumes are worn by African American groups in the Mardi Gras

MUSICAL INSTRUMENTS

fifes (made from cane)   12-inch length of cane hollowed out with a heated poker, and finger holes burned into the sides to make notes

musical instruments   stringed instruments such as a gourd-bodied fiddle, "diddly bow," (one-string instrument using bottles as resonators), drums, gourd banjos, bamboo fifes

WOODCARVING

boats (pirogues)   made of single or multiple hollowed-out logs

figural wooden sculpture   canes with human or animal heads on them; figures for cigar stores; carved wooden chairs; chandeliers; and simply "fine-art" carving of human figures

model birds   carved and brightly colored

painted wood-carved snakes   brightly painted snakes simply painted on found wood that had been cleaned and shaped

walking canes   carved with snakes, figures, or heads on the handle

OTHER

corn shuck bags   corn shucks twisted and knotted with a half hitch

grave decorations   pottery, wrought iron markers, shells

willow chairs   bent green willow furniture has enjoyed a recent revival

wrought iron   tool making, wrought iron decorative gates, fences, balcony railings, decorative panels, window covers

yard sculpture   a few people specialize in yard sculpture using found materials

List 8–17   Things to Do: Native American Arts and Crafts

- *decorating tipis:* Make miniature tipis from brown paper, decorating with appropriate symbols. These can be mounted on sticks or simply rolled into a cone.
- *exploit robes:* Tear a small "robe shape" from brown paper bags or kraft paper. Draw an event in your life, using small figures. Native Americans recorded battles or exploits involving horses and many people.
- *jewelry:* Make a small ball of clay. Flatten it and smooth the edges, then scratch a Native American symbol on it and poke a hole in the top. When it is leather hard, rub an oxide on it, wipe off the excess, then fire it. String it on a leather thong for a pendant.
- *ledger paper drawings:* On 8½ × 11-inch lined paper, record one or more events in your life. Fill the page with drawings of yourself in action.
- *Navajo rug:* Rather than actually weaving a rug, make a Native American rug design on the computer.
- *pottery:* Make a coil pot in the manner of Southwestern pueblo potters. Carve a relief design before polishing the leather-hard pot with a spoon.
- *rock paintings:* Make a "newspaper rock" by working as a group to paint pictographs on a kraft paper background. Or *paint* (pictographs) or *scratch* (petroglyphs) on rocks found by the side of the road or in a stream.
- *sand painting print:* Draw heavily directly on sandpaper with crayon. Turn it over, placing it on white paper; then iron on the back of the sandpaper to create a print.
- *sand painting:* Draw directly on sandpaper with oil pastels, using stylized figures.
- *sand painting:* Make several colors of sand in separate boxes by mixing food color in white sand. Make a small area of design with white glue and dribble sand into that area, dumping off the excess into the original box.
- *weaving:* Use crayon to make a Native American rug design on kraft paper that has been dampened, crumpled, and dried. Tie yarn fringe on the top and bottom.
- *winter count:* Work with friends or family to make a communal *Winter Count* by selecting a symbol to represent the single most important event of each year. These can be on chamois, muslin, or posterboard. The symbols can either be arranged in a spiral or rectangle starting at one corner and moving along to the center.

List 8–18 Definitions of Native American Crafts

Most groups of Native American people had similar rituals, means of hunting, music, and clothing, though their homes varied depending on the climate and available building materials. Model tipis, canoes, bows and arrows, dishes, and dolls were made, perhaps as children's toys, or simply as a pastime. The advent of the train opened up a large market for Native American wares, and many items were created in the 19th century for the tourist trade. These crafts are often distinctive by region, depending on the lifestyle, climate, wildlife, and materials available. Embellishments on everyday items and those made for special occasions reflect the pride of the artisan.

Acoma, c. 1910

Pueblo Acoma Painted Pot

arrowheads   carved of flint, and affixed to a stick with thongs

axes   often made of stone, shaped flat on one end, and attached with thongs to a wooden handle

bandoleer bag   shoulder bag with floral or geometric designs, mostly Canadian or Northeastern

baskets   extraordinary, closely woven baskets were made on the West Coast

belts   woven yarn, beaded leather, leather with silver decorations; a child's belt might be of leather studded with metal, and with beads, pouches, and amulets suspended from it

birchbark boxes   in areas of the Northeast and upper Midwest, boxes and other items of use were decorated by *biting* the bark into interesting designs

bows   bows and arrows are traditionally associated with Native Americans, and many are now featured in museums

bowl   carved wooden bowl used by Woodland Indians and those of the Northwest Coast

breechcloths (or breechclout)   lengths of cloth about 1 ft. × 6 ft; worn by men between the legs with each end tucked into a belt, hanging down front and back; leggings, shirt, and a robe were worn if needed for warmth

button blankets   appliqué totems (animals) on blankets, which are then outlined with buttons; worn by Northwest Coast tribes

chief's blanket   "wearing blankets" featured stripes, geometric designs, and diamonds

clan hat   carved wooden hat with animal totem on top; these were painted, or sometimes embellished with shells; worn by Northwestern tribes

coiled baskets   used for gathering beans, holding grain or trinkets, or created for the tourist market

coiled pottery   generally a specialty of Southwest Native Americans, who continue to create vessels and sculpture in their ancient (and new) traditions

corncob dolls   dressed like adults, with beaded faces, fringed buckskin clothing, and even moccasins

coup stick   coup sticks and lances were carried into battle; the coup stick was used only to touch an enemy in battle, and was decorative, sometimes with a carved head, feathers or other decorations

cradle   flat carrying board for infants was decorated with any combination of wood, textiles, beads, shells, wickerwork (sometimes dyed), buckskin fringes

dance apron   usually was completely covered with beadwork

dresses   traditional dresses vary depending on the climate and available materials; sometimes made of soft leather, beaded and fringed, or woven fabric embellished with cowry shells, or fringed with "bells" made of tin; Seminoles do beautiful patchwork trim on dark clothing

drum   hollow logs with one or both ends covered with skin; an important part of the rituals in Native American life

eagle feathers   only Native Americans have the privilege to use eagle feathers, as it is a protected species

effigy pipe   animals or human figures are carved on the pipe; pipes hold a special place in Indian ceremonies.

List 8–18   Continued

exploit robes   individuals painted scenes of themselves involved in battle or other personal memories on personal tanned-hide exploit robes

feather baskets   often given to commemorate rites of passage; made from brightly colored feathers of meadowlarks, woodpeckers, mallards, and quail

fetishes   combinations of natural objects such as shells, feathers, beads, bones, tied together with thongs, and frequently placed in special areas; some fetishes are carved

figural sculptures   human and animal sculptures found throughout the Native American cultures; some were buried, others kept as prized possessions

fingerweaving   strands of yarn woven together in geometric patterns using the fingers as heddles (to hold strands open); relatively narrow strips (2–3 inches)

frontlets   small animal masks worn at the front of the head, sometimes attached to a headdress

gourd pots   dried gourds with a hole cut in the top to make a pot; sometimes incised with designs and left natural; contemporary artists paint these to resemble traditional ceramic pots

gourd rattles   dried gourds filled with seeds or small stones are used in various ceremonies

headdresses   varied from simple headbands with one eagle feather or leather caps to war bonnets or roach headdresses (horsehair combined with feathers and leather)

kachina   a costumed human dancer who has special powers to the Pueblo Indians; kachina images are replicas of the humans, featuring masks and appropriate dress

knife sheath   made of animal skin, and decorated with quills, beads, and leather fringe

Kokopelli   a humpbacked flute player design found on Southwest pottery; represents rain, harvests, and human fertility

ledger drawings   when animal skins were not available, lined ledger paper used for bookkeeping was used by Native Americans for exploit drawings

leggings   buckskin leg coverings that traditionally had designs to match the moccasins; women's leggings were knee high, and men's reached from hip to ankle

masks   frequently represent animals, and are made of different materials such as carved wood, painted leather, cloth, or cornhusks

medicine bundle   a bag that contains natural materials and images, and can be worn on clothing or attached to a shield, tipi, or horse

moccasins   soft shoes made of cured animal skins; frequently decorated with beads, porcupine quills, or fringe

moose hair embroidery   elaborately embroidered table or seat covers were done with dyed moosehair

musical rattle   elaborately carved rattles for use in special ceremonies by Northwest Native Americans

muslin painting   muslin that was given out by the government was sometimes decorated with exploits and used as tipi linings when animal skins were not available

palette   the Hohokam peoples prepared paint on slate palettes carved to resemble a lizard or other animals

parfleche (bag)   generally has a long strap, frequently decorated with hanging fringes and designs

pictorial blankets   some contemporary Navajo blankets tell stories, which may feature birds, animals, flowers, mountains, trees, or sometimes trains, cars and recreational vehicles (RVs)

pipes   played a special part in ceremonies throughout the continent; style varied depending on the locality; design of the pipe was characteristic of the peoples who used it

pottery   was frequently placed in gravesites in ancient times, often with a hole punched in the bottom for offerings; each pueblo has a different tradition in decoration and technique

poncho   woven blanket with a "keyhole" in the middle for the head is used by some Southwestern peoples

quillwork   before the advent of European glass beads, porcupine quills were flattened, sometimes dyed, and sewn onto clothing, boxes, textiles, and chair covers in decorative patterns

quiver case   leather or birchbark case used to hold arrows

List 8–18   Continued

rattle   carved wooden rattles with "totems" might resemble a fish, bear, raven, sun, or moon

ribbon appliqué   prairie tribes placed appliqué ribbon trim on blankets

roach spreader   decorative headdress of fur and horsehair that stood straight up from the center to the back of the head

rock engravings   Native Americans incised pictographs on rocks throughout America; they are plentiful in Utah, Arizona, and Colorado

sand painting   done by dribbling colored sands through the fingers to create certain patterns; the sand painting process is a religious ceremony, usually conducted by a medicine man

sculpture   stone, wood, and pottery sculptures have been created in all societal groups; subjects vary from human to stylized animal figures

shaman figures   carvings of shamans (medicine men) have been found in graves; their purpose is unknown

silver and turquoise jewelry   plentiful turquoise has made it a favorite of Indian jewelers, who use it plain for beads, or combine it with silver and sometimes coral

storyteller dolls   the figures may be human or animal, but always have their mouths open telling a story to small figures of the same species; not a traditional Native American craft until the 1960s, when Helen Cordova honored her father, who was a clown in a Pueblo society

totem pole   a carved wooden pole, usually topped by a totem that represented the animal favored by a particular tribe of people in the Pacific Northwest; favored totems were the raven, bear, beaver, whale and fish

vest   leather vests usually were worn by Native American males; featured quillwork, beadwork, and fringe

wampum   white and purple clam shells, shaped and with holes drilled in them; used in place of money; Eastern Indians made wampum beads or belts; a treaty or agreement was considered officially sealed when a string or belt of wampum beads accompanied it

war bonnet   contained from 30 to 50 eagle feathers, and was only worn by people who had accumulated honors; each feather was given by one person, and therefore represented a man; an extraordinary honor was to be able to attach buffalo horns to a bonnet

war club   a shaped stone or horn attached to a decorated stick; an ax was sharpened on one end

war shield   used the breast of a bull buffalo that was smoked to cure it; painted with special symbols, and often decorated with feathers and fringes

war shirt   made of leather featuring beads and fringe, and were quite beautiful

weaving   woven bags and blankets were used by most of the Native American peoples

winter count   each year a tribe decided on the single most significant event of their year, and one symbol to represent it was painted on the *winter count* tanned hide

woven blankets   use traditional patterns, techniques, and colors, and continue to be made in modern times

List 8–19   Native American Pictographs

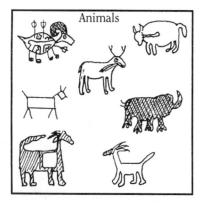

Animals

People

Flowers

Frogs   Rabbit

Owl

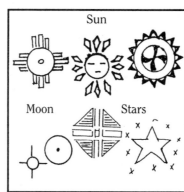

Sun

Moon   Stars

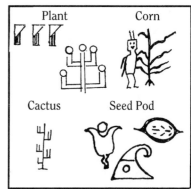

Plant   Corn

Cactus   Seed Pod

Birds

Thunderbirds

Clouds   Rain

Leaf   Squash Blossom

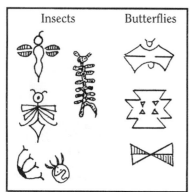

Insects   Butterflies

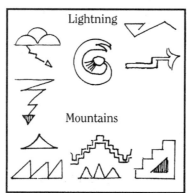

Lightning

Mountains

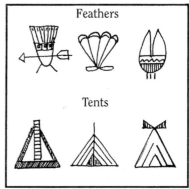

Feathers

Tents

List 8–20   Native American Craft Specialties by Region

ARCTIC, ALASKA, CANADA

appliqué	carved soapstone	metal tools
baskets	carved wood	shaman figures
carved bone	engraved throwing stones	walrus ivory handles for harpoons
carved ivory	masks	

SUBARCTIC

birchbark boxes   birchbark canoes

EASTERN WOODLANDS

This region includes the tribes of the Algonquin, Cree, Delaware, Fox, Iroquois, Mohawk, Oneida, Seneca, Powhatan, Micmac, Conestoga, and Abenaki.

Kiowa, 1904, Smithsonian Institution

beading	cradleboards	porcupine quill decorations
birchbark boxes	embroidery	snowshoes
birchbark patterned by biting	false face masks	woven wampum belt
burden straps	moosehair embroidery	

GREAT LAKES

This area includes the Chippewa, Fox, Kickapoo, Menominee, Ottawa, Penobscot, Potawatomi, Winnebago, Illinois, Shawnee, Mismi, Huron, and Algonquin.

beadwork	moosehair embroidery	quillwork

SOUTHEAST WOODLANDS

Living in this area are the Biloxi, Cherokee, Choctaw, Creek, Seminole, Chickasaw, Natchez, Catawba, and Caddo.

corncob dolls	featherwork	ribbon appliqué
effigy pipes	pottery	Seminole patchwork

NORTHWEST COAST

Here you'll find the tribes of the Bellacoola, Chinook, Chilkat, Cowichan, Haida, Klamath, Kwaikutl, Nootka, Salish, Tlingit, and Tsimshian.

baskets	carved and painted housefronts	masks
beaded tobacco pouches	Chilkat blankets	totem poles
blanket chests	clan hats	whale bone club
button-trimmed robes	dance apron	wooden utensils
carved argillite	drums	
carved fetish rattles	hammered copper plates	

CALIFORNIA

This area includes the Chumash, Hupa, Modoc, Pomo, Cahilla, Karok, and Maidu.

baskets	shell beads	
featherwork		

Tipi model, Cheyenne, 1904, Field Museum of Natural History, Chicago

List 8–20   Continued

SOUTHWEST

The Acoma, Apache, Hopi, Navajo, Papago, Pima, Havasupai, Tesque, San Ildefonso, Santa Clara, Taos, Zia, and Zuni peoples are from this region.

coiled baskets	kachina dolls	story teller dolls
coiled pottery	masks	woven blankets
gourd pots	sand painting	
gourd rattles	silver and turquoise jewelry	

NORTHERN PLATEAU

Here you'll find the Blackfeet, Flathead, Gros Ventre, Nez Perce, Piute, Shoshoni, and Ute.

Arapaho war bonnets	floral beadwork	saddles
bridles	Micmac quill chair cover	Sioux war bonnet
ceremonial rattles	parfleche (decorative bag)	tipis
coup stick	roach spreader (headdress)	tobacco pipes and bags
fingerweaving	rock engravings	

List 8–21   Things to Do: Mexican Arts and Crafts

- *amate paper:* Amate paper is formed from bark. Substitute brown kraft paper or paper bags for painting these simple designs of animals, people, or flowers.
- *ceramics:* Use clay to form bird shapes around a crushed paper oval form. Leave a hole for moisture to escape. When the clay is leather hard, polish with a spoon; glaze with soft colors.
- *gourd designs:* The outer shell of a gourd is either brightly painted with designs such as animals or flowers, or is carved and left in its natural colors (brown and light brown). Make papier-mâché "gourds" on small balloons, with the last coat being brown kraft paper, and then draw designs with brown fine-line marker.
- *aluminum foil masks:* Draw with an empty ball-point pen or dull pencil, using the repoussé technique. This can be done on thin copper foil or heavy-duty aluminum foil. Wipe with permanent ink when finished and wipe off, or "paint" with permanent markers.
- *recycled aluminum drink can masks:* Cut off the top and bottom of aluminum cans **(carefully),** and flatten the sides by rubbing over the edge of a table. Hold horizontal surfaces of three cans together with brads, and make features from the ends of the cans or another cut-up can. These can be colored with permanent markers, decorated with feathers, yarn, sequins, or "jewels." Or take advantage of the colors and designs on the cans. ***Safety note:*** *Wear cotton gloves for cutting off the tops and bottoms to avoid sharp edges.*
- *paper cutting:* Make folded white tissue-paper cuttings similar to those used for decorations for certain times of the year. Use scissors or an X-acto® knife. ***Safety note:*** *When using an X-acto® knife always hold the non-cutting hand behind the knife.*
- *papier-mâché:* Do animal forms or dancing human forms in papier-mâché. Paint in bright colors.
- *tin cutting:* Use scissors to cut soft-drink cans into forms such as stars, layering several cutouts together, and curling the edges to make them three-dimensional. ***Safety note:*** *Wear cotton gloves for cutting to avoid sharp edges.*
- *yarn paintings:* Coat a 5 × 7-inch piece of chipboard with a coat of bee's wax. Make a yarn painting of an animal or other nature motif by placing strands of yarn close together and pressing them into the wax. Or substitute white glue, doing a small amount at a time.

List 8–22   Mexican Crafts

The variety of craft forms in Mexico is due to the diversity of its ethnic mix and geographical features. Fifty-six groups of Indians remain in Mexico, making up approximately 15% of the population, each with its own unique culture. Many of the crafts are made throughout Mexico, while others remain regional. Most can be seen in state-run crafts stores or at regional fairs, but a visit to some of the centers is a worthwhile experience. Traditional techniques are passed from generation to generation, and many of these folk art forms date back to pre-Columbian times.

JEWELRY AND METALSMITHING

acid engraved knife blades

coin necklaces (Yucatán)   coins often combined with beads in necklaces and earrings

earrings (mostly jointed)   worn by men and women, made of beads, coins, gold, lacquer inlaid with abalone shell or painted horn pendants

ex-votos (milagros)   tiny forms represent something for which someone has prayed (often these represent parts of the body (eyes, legs, hands), animals, hearts, houses; these were originally silver, now normally made of nickel or tin

gold and silver work   some areas specialize in forged, cast, and fabricated silver and gold work

hammered copper   specialists make pots, plates, all variety of practical yet decorative items

jade   stone valued more than gold; used for pendants, rings, and death masks

necklaces   seeds and beads of glass and stone combined; some strands are composed of only thin glass beads (papelillo)

painted clay necklaces   death's heads alternating with tigers or leopards

painted tin figures   approximately 4 inches high, these feature repoussé details; subjects are people, animals, birds, fish and butterflies

papier-mâché   used in masks, large lacquered animals, amusing figural sculpture

silver ornaments   buckles, buttons, spurs are decorative features and part of the costume of mariachi bands or cowboys

steel spurs   inlaid with silver

tin ornaments   candlesticks, lanterns, mirror frames, niches for images, plates, and trays

wrought iron   this specialty is used for balconies, doors, fittings for furniture, crosses

TEXTILE ARTS

backstrap loom weaving   narrow bands woven on a backstrap loom are used as sashes, bag handles, or are sewn together to make entire garments

cross stitching   an embroidered area might combine cross stitch and satin stitch

huipil   a loose woven or embroidered tunic, worn by both men and women

machine and hand embroidery   embroidery designs feature animals, flowers, geometric designs, symbols and religious figures

quesquemetl (or queshquemitl)   a diamond-shaped shawl, woven or embroidered

servilleta (cloth)   an embroidered cloth used as a table covering for special occasions

shoulder bags   general purpose bags were woven, painted or beaded

waist sashes   usually made on a backstrap loom

GENERAL

basketry and straw hats   hats made of agave fibers, bamboo, cane, palm, wheatstraw and willow are used throughout Mexico

beading   beaded objects are created by pressing glass beads into a wax-covered surface such as a gourd bowl or square of wood

Day of the Dead objects   specialties for day of the dead include cardboard skeletons, metal-paper death figures, sugar skulls, sugar-paste figures and loaves of "bread of the dead," tissue-paper cut-outs "papel picado"

lacquerware   wood or gourds are carved or incised, gilded, coated with lacquer, and painted in brightly colored designs; a technique that goes back to pre-Columbian times

masks   carved from wood and painted, rough masks of papier-mâché pulp, or smooth, finely lacquered masks; found throughout Mexico

straw painting (popote)   dyed straws are individually stuck down to make a picture

tortoiseshell wares   boxes, bracelets, clasps, earrings, watchstraps, letter openers, ornamental combs are all made from tortoise shell

tree of life (Metepec)   intricate, traditional, brightly-painted clay "tree" includes figures and flowers

yarn pictures   yarn "drawings" are done by pressing yarn into bee's wax coated cardboard or wood

Whistle, Late Classic Maya, 600–900 AD

List 8–23   Centers of Mexican Folk Art Production

Not all states are listed, but these are noted centers of art. This list includes some of the specialties from various cities.

CHIHUAHUA

general   baskets (Tarahumara Indians)

CHIAPAS

Chiapa de Corzo   masks; brilliantly lacquered ware such as gourds and trays

Chiapas   woolen tunics

San Cristobal (Ciudad) de las Casas   wrought-iron crosses and iron fittings for furniture; wax dolls

San Juan Chamula   rag dolls

GUANAJUATO

Celaya   cardboard masks; articulated papier-mâché dolls

Dolores Hidalgo   major center for majolica pots

Guanajuato   majolica

GUERERRO

general   carving in serpentine, malachite and amethyst; miniature wooden painted tiger masks

Acapetlahuaya   lacquered boxes, gourds; carved figures; wooden masks

Acatlán   woven and embroidered textiles

Ameyaltepec (Nahua peoples)   paintings on amate bark paper of daily life or festivals

Olinala   lacquered animal masks; lacquered bowls, wooden chests, trunks, tables, trays

Taxco   silver jewelry production and hollowware

Temalacacingo   wooden figures and animals such as lizards and iguanas, lacquered and painted.

Tenejapa   woolen tunics

HIDALGO

El Nith   lacquerware inlaid with abalone shell; mirrors, boxes, jewelry

Tlahuelompa   beaten copper; bell casting

Zacualtipan   beaten copper; bell casting

JALISCO

general   woven shoulder bags; backstrap weaving; rustic chairs; miniatures carved from horn; yarn pictures

Guadalajara   blown glass; wrought-iron and glass lamps; molded cardboard dolls or animals; spun glass miniatures; chess sets and miniatures of bone, horn, shell, and tortoise shell

San Andres (Huichol Indians)   glass beads netted and made into belts, pectorals (pendants), arm bands, earrings; shoulder bags; yarn pictures; gourds lined with bead pictures

Santa Cruz de las Huertas   figures; Noah's Ark; churches; animals; molded skeletons

Teocaltiche   chess sets; miniatures

Tlaquepaque   Christmas figures: Mary and Joseph, the Magi, shepherds; genre figures, devils; miniature folkloric scenes such as weddings, bullrings, Nativities; glassware

Tonalá   stoneware dinner sets; high-temperature glazed pottery; red pottery decorated with white

MEXICO

general   painted sheet metal; articulated paper skeletons

Chilapa   carved horn combs in the shapes of animals; special combs for wool

Cualac   horn animal figures; horn machete handles

Stone Calendar, 1450–1500, Museum of Archaeology, Mexico City, Mexico

Metepec   tree of life; painted pottery; painted pottery pigs

Mexico City   wire and papier-mâché; wrought-iron and glass lamps; paper dolls with skull heads; "muertos" (toys for the Day of the Dead); carved bone figures; elaborately decorated "skulls"; "Judas figures" of papier-mâché

Ometepec   carved machete handles; small animals

San Antonio la Isla   carved horn combs with painted animal decorations

San Felipe Santiago   cloth dolls dressed in Mazahua Indian costume

San Marcos   horn vessels

Santa Ana   wrapped and woven baskets

Tecomatepec   ceramic pulque mugs, pitchers

Tecpan de Galeana   horn vessels

Tepaltitlan   coiled baskets from dyed palm strands

Toluca   spun-glass miniatures; sugar figures for Day of the Dead

List 8–23 Continued

MICHOACÁN

general rustic chairs; silver; ceramic dinner sets

Ocumicho (Purepecha peoples) painted and varnished ceramics: whistles, banks, devils, skeletons, mermaids, suns, moons; handmade clay figurines and fantasy figures; skull figures on motorcycles

Patamban "pineapples" of clay

Patzcuaro lacquerware; toy cars

San José de Gracia green glazed "pineapples"

Santa Clara del Cobre beaten copper plates and vessels; miniature copper objects

Santa Fe de la Laguna (Purepecha peoples) black glazed ware

Santa Maria Chimetatilan miniatures made of colored palm

Uruapan lacquerware

OAXACA

general geometric designs on woven baskets (Mixtec peoples)

Acatlán polished clay candelabra

Atzompa embroidered dolls

Cayotepec polished black clay vessels, some with openwork

Ixtaltepec cooling jugs

Jamiltepec (Mixtec) painted pottery figures

Oaxaca City silver crosses (Yalalag Indians); jointed crosses; repoussé silver animals often combined with beads; filigree wires worked into gold or silver jewelry; drip-glazed pottery; modeled clay animal figures; painted tin figures, animals, churches; painted wooden toys such as carousels or miniature altars; acid engraved knife blades

Ocotlán large polychrome clay figures

Pinotepa de Don Luis (Mixtec peoples) incised gourds; gourd rattles

Rio Blanco dripped and splattered "everyday" ceramic ware (pottery made exclusively by women)

San Antonio doves made with the blossoms of strawflowers

San Bartolo Coyotepec (Zapotec peoples) burnished black pots

San Martin Tilcajete retablos (small altars); dye-painted animals, figures

San Mateo del Mar wooden carved ornaments used for necklaces

Santa Cruz de las Huertas painted and varnished ceramic tower with figures

Tehuantepec Vishana district: dolls called tanguyus

Teotitlan del Valle woven rugs and blankets

Tonalá painted earthenware

PUEBLA

general miniature animals and kitchens

Acatlán burnished animal sculpture

Amatenango del Valley burnished pots with raised and painted designs

Amozoc silver accessories for mariachi bands and horsemen: spurs, buckles, buttons, stirrups, knife-handles; "blued steel" is inlaid with silver for special spurs

Izucar de Matamoros pottery folk art; majolica vessels

Pahuatlan wooden animals

Puebla City tin-glazed earthenware majolica (called Talavera); rice paper ornaments; small clay painted figures; dolls with wax head and limbs and cloth bodies

San Pablitro (Otomi Indians) paper-cuttings made on amate bark paper; pictures painted on amate paper

San Salvador el Seco stone carving; stone wheels for grinding corn

San Salvador Huixcolotla paper-cuts

Santa Maria Chigmecatitlan interwoven raffia earrings; geometric designed woven baskets

Tecali hollowed and carved onyx vases, boxes, bookends, chess sets, bowls

Tlatlauqui elaborate cast silver ornaments, jointed fish, repoussé

QUERÉTARO

Querétaro wrought iron

TLAXCALA

San Esteban Tizatlan hollowed out and painted walking sticks

San Pablo Apetatitlan wooden masks for carnival

Tlaxcala masks

VERACRUZ

Papantla (Totonac peoples) shops specializing in gold jewelry

Santa Maria Tatecla clay toys

List 8–24   General Locations for Mexican Crafts

If you are looking for specific locations for Mexican crafts, this generalized list may be of value.

clay toys   Santa Maria Tatecla

Day of the Dead specialties   Chilapa, Tecpan de Galeana, Ometepec

glassware   Guadalajara, Texcoco, Monterey, Tlaquepaque, Tonalá, Juárez City, Tijuana

lacquerware   Olinala, Temalacacingo, Acapetlahuaya, Guerrero, Uruapan, Pátzcuaro, Michoacán, Chiapa de Corzo, Chiapas

obsidian   San Francisco Mazapa, San Martin de las Piramides, Taxco

Talavera pottery   Guanajuato, Jalisco, Oaxaca, Aguascalientes

tinplate   Mexico City, Oaxaca, San Miguel de Allende, Puebla, Tlaquepaque, Puente de Ixla

tortoiseshell   La Paz, Campeche, Carmen City, Isla Mujeres

woven palm miniature   Santa Maria Chicmectitlan

wrought-iron locks, nails, furniture fittings   Bajio

List 8–25   Things to Do: Asian Arts and Crafts

The artistic influence of Asia has been carried to many cultures. Changes and adaptations have resulted in unique artistic creations.

- *batik:* Make paper batiks by applying a design with hot wax, then allowing to cool before painting with watercolor or dyes. ***Safety note:*** *Wax will ignite spontaneously at approximately 350 degrees. Keep the wax in a temperature-controlled container or in a coffee can placed in boiling water.*

- *calligraphy:* Paint Japanese or Chinese "sayings" with watercolor on rice paper or handmade paper. Mount the paper on a vertical length of wallpaper with dowels on each end to make a scroll.

- *cloisonné:* This Chinese method of separating colored enamel with silver or copper may be imitated by painting a design on gold wrapping paper with acrylic paint, leaving spaces in between.

- *Japanese fish prints:* Paint a frozen or freshly caught fish with paint or ink. Then use a soft paper such as rice paper, newsprint, or paper towels and lay on the fish, gently pressing to transfer the print. Or make fish prints directly on T-shirts. Metallicized paint is effective.

- *Japanese paste resist dyeing:* Japanese stenciling is quite complex. Instead, cut stencils from file folders, stencil paper, or plastic. Place the stencil on top of white paper, and use a small sponge to dab paint through the open areas. The designs can be as intricate as you wish. Remember to make the design hold together with "bridges." For more than one-time use, oil tagboard stencils with vegetable oil several days in advance.

- *paper cutting:* Japanese *mons* were crests (usually cut within a circle or square) used by families. Create your own *mon* of black paper by selecting a personal motif. All the lines must be connected so it doesn't fall apart. When finished, mount it on contrasting paper.

- *shadow puppets:* Shadow puppets are intricately carved jointed puppets on sticks. Use tagboard or parchment for cutting out shapes, connecting them at the elbows and shoulders with paper fasteners. Tape a dowel to the body and coat-hanger wire to the hands. A "show" may then be performed behind a "screen" of white material stapled to canvas stretchers. Hold the screen upright on a table with a light source behind it.

- Use an X-acto® knife to cut figures from squares of red paper as the Chinese do. Use your own Zodiac sign (books on Zodiacs are available from libraries). ***Safety note:*** *Always hold the non-cutting hand behind the knife.*

List 8–26   Chinese Crafts and Folk Art

Ancient China's artistic heritage is representative of that of many other Asian regions, whose work is similar. Museums contain fine examples of Asian porcelains, carvings, bronzes, paintings, lacquerware, screens, and calligraphy. Asian folk art was created by people who were distanced from the more sophisticated culture of the cities and the court. It evolved when people made utilitarian objects such as baskets, clothing, and decorations for their homes.

BAMBOO

bamboo trinket boxes
baskets
bird cages
coolie hats
folding fans
furniture
silk parasols
sleeping mats

CLAY (CERAMICS)

ceramic animals
ceramic tiles
ceramic tomb guardians
clay figures
masks
model furniture (for tombs)
pottery pillows
teacups
teapots
toys
whistles

CLOTH

blue dye-resist cloth
embroidered children's collars, hats, and shoes
embroidered fans
embroidered stories

IVORY

boats
carved balls within balls
chopsticks

combs
decorative carvings
fans
foo dogs
mahjongg pieces
necklaces
netsuke (toggles for clothing)

JADE

belt buckles
carved chain
carved cups and bowls
decorative carvings
deer
ear "scoop"
earrings
jade bottle
jade screen
pendants
peony
pomegranate
thumb rings
tortoise

METAL

bronze casting
bronze lamps
cloisonné
gold "sleeve weights"
golden armlets
golden earrings
golden hair ornaments
metal bells
silver engraving

PAPER

fans
kites
lanterns
paper cuttings
paper flowers
umbrellas
woodblock prints

STRAW

straw mosaic bookmarks
straw mosaic boxes

OTHER

boat carved from peachstone
calligraphy
carpets, hand knotted and carved
carved peachstone beads
carved seal (chop)
dough figures
lacquer screens
mask making
paintings
papermaking
porcelain
shadow puppets
stone carving
toys
woodcarving

List 8–27   Symbols Used in Chinese Art

In the Asian cultures, traditional symbols were understood by all to represent specific things. Spirits were believed to be involved in people's daily lives.

TWELVE IMPERIAL SYMBOLS

ax
constellations
dragon
flowery bird
fu symbol (bat)
millet and flames
moon
mountain
paired dragons
sun
temple cups
water weed

EIGHT BUDDHIST EMBLEMS

canopy
conch shell
lotus flower
mystic knot
pair of fish
umbrella
vase
wheel of law

FIVE HAPPINESSES (GROUP OF FIVE BATS)

a natural death
health
longevity
love of virtue
officialdom

THREE PERFECTIONS

calligraphy
painting
poetry

NINE PARTS OF A DRAGON

belly of a frog
claws of a hawk
ears of a cow
eyes of a rabbit
head of a camel
horns of a deer
neck of a snake

palm of a tiger
scales of a carp

THREE ABUNDANCES

hands of Buddha: happiness
peaches: longevity
pomegranates: fecundity

MISCELLANEOUS SYMBOLS

bat: good luck
birds: free, wandering spirit
book: learning
butterfly: symbol of joy
carp: determination, good luck
chrysanthemum: autumn, joy
coin: prosperity
crane: longevity
cranes and pine trees together: old age
dragon (five clawed): only used by the emperor
dragon: strength and beauty
fish: plenty, abundance
fu (bat): good luck
gate gods
ingot of gold: riches
kitchen god and his wife: watch daily activities
lotus: purity, creativity
mystic knot: longevity
pair of mandarin ducks: happy marriage
peach: longevity, happy marriage wishes, immortality
peacock: beauty and dignity
peony: spring, joy
phoenix: combination of pheasant and peacock
pine tree: long life
plum blossom: winter and beauty
pomegranate: fertility, numerous descendants
red: life, happiness
teapot: fertility
three-legged toad: spits gold coins, lives on the moon
tiger: ward away evil spirits
tortoise: luck and wisdom
Dragon of Spring: beginning of life, guardian of the East
Phoenix of Summer: peak of life, guardian of the South

List 8–27   Continued

MISCELLANEOUS SYMBOLS (cont.)

Tortoise of Winter: hibernation, luck, guardian of the North

White tiger of Autumn: harvest and death, guardian of the West

Yin: darkness, earth, moon, and quiescence

Yang: light, heaven, sun, and vigor

COLORS

red: joy

white: mourning

BUDDHIST SYMBOLS

angels

demons

devils

THE CHINESE ZODIAC (BASED ON YEAR OF BIRTH)

The Rat: 1924, 1936, 1948, 1960, 1972, 1984, 1996, 2008

The Ox: 1925, 1937, 1949, 1961, 1973, 1985, 1997, 2009

The Tiger: 1926, 1938, 1950, 1962, 1974, 1986, 1998, 2010

The Hare: 1927, 1939, 1951, 1963, 1975, 1987, 1999, 2011

The Dragon: 1928, 1940, 1952, 1964, 1976, 1988, 2000, 2012

The Snake: 1929, 1941, 1953, 1965, 1977, 1989, 2001, 2013

The Horse: 1930, 1942, 1954, 1966, 1978, 1990, 2002, 2014

The Sheep: 1931, 1943, 1955, 1967, 1979, 1991, 2003, 2015

The Monkey: 1932, 1944, 1956, 1968, 1980, 1992, 2004, 2016

The Rooster: 1933, 1945, 1957, 1969, 1981, 1993, 2005, 2017

The Dog: 1934, 1946, 1958, 1970, 1982, 1994, 2006, 2018

The Boar: 1935, 1947, 1959, 1971, 1983, 1995, 2007, 2019

List 8–28   Jewish Observances

To understand the use of many of the objects created in the Jewish culture, definitions of special holiday seasons follow. The Hebrew seasons have specific names, but the actual date varies.

Passover (March–April)   celebrating the Exodus of Israelites from Egypt

Lag B'Omer (April–May)   the thirty-third day between Passover and Shavuot, a special day commemorating two heroes

Shavuot (May–June)   commemoration of the receiving of the Torah on Mount Sinai (seven weeks after Passover)

Tisha B'Av ([Ninth of Av] July–August)   a fast day commemorating the destruction of the temples at Jerusalem

Rosh Hashanah (September–October)   Jewish New Year

Yom Kippur (September–October)   Day of Atonement; a day of fasting and prayer

Sukkot (September–October)   a seven-day feast that commemorates the divine protection the Jews received during their wanderings in the wilderness

Shemini Atzeret (September–October)   a festival that follows the seventh day of Sukkot

Simchat Torah (September–October)   a holiday to observe the annual completion of the reading of the Torah

Chanukkah ([or Hanukkah] November–December)   an eight-day observance of the victory of Judah Maccabee over the Seleucids; one candle is lit on the menorah for each of the days

Tu Bishevat ([Fifteenth of Shevat] January–February)   an agricultural festival

Adar (February–March)   the season for Purim

Purim (February–March)   commemorates the saving of the Persian Jewish community from death

Seder   a special observation of the first night of Passover, which includes specially prepared foods

List 8–29   Jewish Art and Folk Art

Jewish folk art has been created to mark ceremonies and for use in daily rituals. It reflects a 2,000-year period of history. Many beautiful examples of the jeweler's or craftsman's skills are also carefully preserved. The method of decoration frequently reflects the period and culture in which the Jews were living at the time.

amulets for the brit (circumcision ceremony)   paper cut-outs, pillow covers

amulets for women in childbirth   engraved pendants to be worn, or a painting with verses to protect both mothers and children

bags for prayer shawls (embroidered)

challah cover   cover for the special bread made for the Sabbath

dreidel   a spinning top with words on four sides that translate loosely as "nothing," "get," "half," "share," used in a children's game. The symbols mean "A great miracle happened here."

illuminated book   prayerbooks for the High Holy Days were often richly illustrated

itinerarium   an embroidery or painting that shows the main pilgrimage sites of the Holy Land

ketubbah   a formal marriage contract, often richly decorated

kiddush cover   the cover that protects the wine while kiddush is being said on the Sabbath

mappah   an embroidered cover to protect the scrolls of the Torah from the table when it is unrolled and read

Megillat Esther   the story of Esther is one of the five books of the Bible known as the Ketuvim (writings); it is often a beautifully illuminated scroll on one roller, and is read from beginning to end in one session

memento mori   a paper cut-out with verses that remind one of the shortness of life and the imminence of death

mezuzah   a small case to contain biblical passages affixed to the door of a house; made of reeds, glass, silver, ivory, stone, or even embroidered containers (in North Africa)

micrography   miniature writing used to "draw" a picture or decorate around figures

mizrach (East)   paper cut-out, embroidery, drawing, or painting on a Jerusalem-facing wall; it must say mizrach (the place where the sun rises) on it

Omer calendar   a calendar containing a Bible verse for each day of the seven weeks of Omer (the period between Passover and Shavuot); often richly illustrated; sometimes in book form

parokhet   the curtain that hangs behind the door of the Ark, often embroidered

phylacteries (tefillin)   small leather boxes containing Biblical verses, worn during morning prayers

prayer books for women   these contained blessings and prayers for special occasions

quilts   appliquéd wedding quilts or crib quilts rich with symbols

rimmonim   carved finials to ornament the staves on which the Torah scroll is rolled

Seder plates   special serving dishes used for the Sabbath

shiviti (a Biblical saying)   a decorative amulet, embroidered, painted on paper or etched on copper, and usually placed on a Jerusalem-facing wall (generally an East wall)

shpanyer arbeit   Spanish metal thread embroidery

synagogue mosaic pavement   the decorative mosaic pavement of synagogues often includes symbols

tallit   the prayer shawl, with fringes attached to the four corners, is worn during morning prayers; beautifully embroidered bags were sometimes made to contain the shawl

tik   an ornamental container for the Torah used in oriental communities

towel cover   an embroidered cover that was placed over soiled towels

tzitzit   the fringes on four corners of the prayer shawl serve as a reminder to observe the commandments of the Torah

wimpel (torah binder)   strips of cloth used to wrap a newborn son after the circumcision ceremony were richly embroidered, and given to the temple by mothers to be used to protect the Torah

wool embroidery on perforated paper   various amulets or decorations were made in this technique

List 8–30   Jewish Symbols

These symbols frequently appear on artwork, mosaic floors, coins, and illuminated manuscripts.

etrog   a type of lemon used during the harvest celebration of Sukkot

eyes   frequently found on marriage contracts to protect the newlyweds against the evil eye

female busts   the four seasons

fish   fertility symbol

five arches   five is a number with special powers against the evil eye

grape clusters and vine leaf   wine

hand   the hand could be "a guardian against the evil eye"

leviathan   a legendary sea monster, often depicted on handcrafted objects

lion   lion of the tribe of Judah

lulav   a palm branch; one of four species used for the harvest celebration

Magen David   a six-sided star that originated in the sixth century, based on a hexagram

mappah   a binder wrapped around the Torah to keep it from unrolling

menorah   candle holder for the Hanukkah season containing nine candles (the temple menorah contains seven candles)

Messianic meal   jar of manna (bread), fruit of the tree of life, flesh of Leviathan, and blossoming rod of Aaron

rod of Aaron   a blossoming tree branch

shofar   a horn (usually from a ram) that is blown on Rosh Hashanah and other occasions

spice boxes   these boxes of wood or metal often resembled towers, with carved openwork to allow the fragrance to escape

sukkah   a booth that is open at the top to allow stars to be seen; often decorated with branches, decorative paper cutting, and fruits and vegetables; used during the festival of Sukkot

tablets of the law   two tablets of stone bearing the Ten Commandments

Torah   the five books of Moses

Torah Ark   the repository for the scrolls of the law

tree of life   this tree features various animals

twisted columns   reminders of the columns that were in front of the Temple of Solomon

two columns   represent the columns of the temple

zodiac signs   often used on marriage contracts and other formal documents

List 8–31   Scandinavian Design and Crafts

The arts of Denmark, Finland, Norway, and Sweden have a strong tradition. They excel at arts for the home such as fabric, woven tapestries, printed textiles and rugs, furniture design, glassware, ceramics, and silver. These arts are functional, yet noted for their beauty. The tradition is enduring, and specialties from ancient times continue today.

DENMARK

"Danish" furniture   modern, functional design, often in teak or rosewood

paper cutting   intricately cut-paper figures to hang in a window

porcelain   fine china, Royal Copenhagen®, Bing and Grondahl® figures

pottery   functional forms

silver forms   cutlery, tea and coffeepots, jewelry, enameled silver

textiles   block printing on fabric, screen printing

FINLAND

art-glassware   blown glass and engraved glassware

ceramics   wheel thrown and hand formed

textiles   woven textiles, scarves, furniture fabrics

woven rugs and woven bed covers

NORWAY

rose-painting (rosemahling)   rustic painting of roses, patterns, figure motifs on walls, ceilings, ale bowls, trays, wall panels, doors, chests, built-in beds or bed/cupboards, wooden dishes, church interiors

stave churches   churches with intricate architectural structures are national treasures

wood carving   specializing in acanthus leaves, altar screens, boat prows, chests

woven pictorial tapestries

SWEDEN

ceramics   figurines, flower holders, tiles, wall plaques

glassware   acid-etched glass, blown glass, engraved glassware, Orrefors, Kosta-Boda

other   wall paintings, enameled jewelry, amber jewelry

silver   cutlery, cigarette containers, jewelry, buttons, buckles, candleholders, chalices

straw   straw goats, tree ornaments

textiles   block-printed fabric, knitted hats, sweaters, mittens, woven wall hangings and coverlets

wood   carved wood-painted horses, wood inlay furniture, carved murals, wooden stave baskets

wrought iron   door locks, grave crosses, firescreens, candleholders, shop signs, decorative grills for cooking meat

List 8–32   Things to Make with Papier-Mâché

- Alternate newspaper with brown paper or paper towels so you can see areas that need to be covered. New pastes such as Pritt® or Ross® are safer for young students than wallpaper paste (which may have pesticides in it). Paint with tempera or acrylic paints. If you use tempera, you may wish to spray varnish.
- Build up layers of cardboard or balsa wood on heavy cardboard, masonite, or a plywood base to make a building or a group of buildings in a cityscape; cover with tissue; paint.
- Cover an old piece of furniture or a chair in papier-mâché; gesso, then paint with designs; varnish.
- Create an out-of-this-world face of clay; cover it with plastic wrap; then do papier-mâché on it.
- Create animal faces by covering a balloon, then adding ears, noses, eyes, and teeth.
- Create huge heads for a parade with a chicken wire armature (open at the bottom for a person to wear, covering almost the entire body, or at least four times normal size if to be worn on the shoulders).
- Form papier-mâché pulp on the outside or inside of a bowl, sanding afterwards. Cover with gesso before finishing.
- Make a caricature of a public or political figure, working over a balloon or chicken wire armature.
- Make a Greek vase with two soft drink bottles. Cut off the bottom two-thirds of a 1- or 2-quart plastic soft-drink plastic bottle. Invert it and tape the mouth to the whole bottle. Fold a sheet of newspaper and tape on for handles. Cover with papier-mâché; paint.
- Make a mask by half covering a balloon resting on an inverted jar lid (to hold it steady).
- Make a plaster mold for a papier-mâché mask by modeling a form in clay. Place it face-up in a greased box, and pour plaster into the box; when the plaster is set, remove it from the box and remove the clay from the mold. Use it to make a number of identical papier-mâché forms.
- Make a three-dimensional stage set in a box by cutting off the top and halfway back on both sides. Make scenery for a specific scene of a play.
- Make a vase or bowl over a balloon base; cut the bottom off and replace with a flat piece to make it stable. Decorate with acrylic paint.
- Make a wire sculpture of a figure in action (sports, dance, jogging, etc.). Form papier-mâché around the figure, then finish it off with plaster gauze.
- Make an animal armature of aluminum foil; cover with papier-mâché, paint in patterns and bright colors completely unrelated to the actual color of the animal.
- Make bracelets, earrings, pins, and pendants of cardboard covered with papier-mâché and painted. Or make these with papier-mâché pulp.
- Make gargoyles from papier-mâché by taping newspaper forms with masking tape. Further details may be added with plaster gauze. Paint in values of one hue.
- Make giant animals by first making a chicken-wire armature attached to a wooden base. Paint the completed sculpture in unlikely colors or patterns. It will still be a specific animal by its shape.
- Make life-sized figures seated or standing and dress them in regular clothes. Paint them in brightly colored patterns (they will still look like human forms).
- Make mirror frames by mounting the mirror on cardboard, then molding paper pulp around the edges in a design.
- Make papier-mâché furniture by creating oversized figures or body parts (legs, torso, arms) to support a top of glass or wood covered with paper. Use a chicken-wire armature.
- Make papier-mâché pulp to make heads for puppets.
- Make portrait busts by working on a styrofoam base (available from art supply houses); these busts are reusable by cutting the hardened papier-mâché bust in half and rejoining it.
- Oversized vases or umbrella stands can be formed from a chicken-wire armature.
- Start with an old picture frame and add forms made of papier-mâché such as baroque designs, human or animal forms, or any organic object; underpaint, then gild if desired.
- Tie and tape wadded newspaper to make a small armature for an animal. Paint it an unusual color.
- Use tagboard as the basis for a piece of sculpture; cut and make it three dimensional. Then tape it in action and cover it with papier-mâché, then paper towels.
- Use tissue paper saturated with white glue, shaping it into a form such as a tree; paint.
- Work with a group to make a complete dinner of papier-mâché food. Set the table.

List 8–33   Equipment and Materials Needed for Papier-Mâché

For papier-mâché you only need to have two things; newspaper and paste. The items in this list are used for decorative effects and to give greater flexibility.

buckets   for mixing large quantities of paste

cardboard   for additions that need strength

chicken wire   the accepted material for a sculpture armature; usually combined with wood or attached to a base

filler   something such as sawdust or spackle added to newspaper pulp to add bulk

finishes   spray varnish, linseed oil (baked at low temperature), lacquer

gesso   a white opaque undercoat for painting; house paint is an acceptable substitute

glues   cellulose paste, wheat paste, flour and water (¼ cup flour to 6 cups water), white glue (mix 3 parts glue to 1 part water), Pritt®, Ross®, polymer medium

masking tape   used for putting together an armature

oil of wintergreen or oil of cloves   used to keep papier-mâché pulp from becoming moldy

Instant Papier-Mâché®   dried paper pulp to which you add water

other decorative items   silk pieces, copper or brass wire

papers   newspaper, brown grocery bags, kraft paper, newsprint, blotting paper, handmade paper, rice paper, tissue, bogus paper, crepe paper, construction paper

pulp   a mash of newsprint made by soaking overnight, boiling for 20 minutes, and mixing with white glue; use newsprint for coarse pulp and tissue for finer pulp; optional additions to the pulp are linseed oil, oil of wintergreen, whiting (ground chalk), and plaster of Paris

releasing agent   plastic wrap, petroleum jelly, or talcum powder to keep paper from sticking to mold

rolling pin   for rolling out sheets of pulp

sandpaper   for sanding pulp projects smooth

sealers: white glue, gesso, white latex wall paint, varnish, plaster

sieve   used for draining water from pulp

string   used for tying newspaper to create an armature

texturing tools   fork, palette knife, spatula

utility knife   used to cut slots for inserting something such as a handle, or for cutting openings

wire cutters   used when creating a chicken-wire armature

wire whisk   for beating soaked newspaper to make pulp

List 8–34   Papier-Mâché Surface Designs

- Acrylic or tempera paint may be used to paint color on the surface. If using tempera, you may varnish afterwards.
- After gessoing, place brass wire under a final layer of tissue paper that is added to the outside.
- After adding gesso to a sandpapered surface, coat it with different colored layers of paint, sanding after each layer to leave only a small amount of that color showing; varnish.
- Collage materials such as tissue, calligraphy, ticket stubs, gold leaf, colored thread, rice paper, grasses, raffia can be added to a surface.
- Cut designs from cardboard and apply, adding a layer of paper on top that will show the bas-relief.
- Decorate white papier-mâché by gluing on lino-cuts printed on white paper.
- Use photocopies of scientific illustrations on colored paper to glue onto papier-mâché bowls.
- Use string or yarn to create patterns, gluing on top; gesso, then paint.

List 8–35   Things to Do with Paper-Cutting

- Make a colored reverse appliqué or monochromatic cut-out. Use tissue, origami, foil, or fadeless paper to cut out individual pieces to place underneath specific areas of the paper-cut. Select a color scheme, and remember to repeat colors throughout the composition.
- Display cut-outs on a window by attaching them to an acetate folder with a few drops of white glue.
- Make a geometric design on tracing paper. Use ruler, compass, etc. Transfer the design to colored paper and cut out with an X-acto® knife. In making round cuts, turn the paper rather than the knife. ***Safety note:*** *Always keep the non-cutting hand behind the blade.*
- Make a light design on heavy drawing paper, then watercolor areas before making cut-outs (or substitute felt-tipped pens).
- Make a fine line paper cut-out using gold foil gift wrap. Put colored tissue underneath.
- Make a silhouette by taping white paper on the wall, and placing an object such as a ceramic animal in front of a light source (lamp or projector). After making this pattern, transfer it to dark paper and cut it out.
- Make a water-reflection design by folding origami paper in half, and cutting through both layers at once. Leave some "land" between the two cuts. Add waves to the bottom half.
- Mount a paper-cut on a second color, then cut pieces of fadeless or tissue paper and use as accents on top of the two layers.
- Mount the one-color cutout to fadeless paper or variegated tissue paper on mount board.
- Select a photograph to use as a basis for a cut-paper design. Place tracing paper on top of it and draw areas that can be connected to make a paper-cut design. Lines can be varied in thickness. Remove the photograph, make necessary changes, and transfer to colored paper for cutting.
- Spatter-paint watercolor or tissue paper backgrounds before or after placing the monochromatic cut-out in place.
- To make a two-color paper-cut, cut an entire paper-cut from one color; then placing them together, cut portions from the second color. Mount them altogether on a third color.
- Use a black paper-cut on top, lightly draw the openings on white drawing paper, then watercolor in the open areas before mounting the two together.
- Vary appliqué on a monochromatic tissue paper cut-out by tearing paper to go underneath the original paper-cut. For a feathery edge, dip a fine-tipped brush in water and draw around the area before tearing it.

List 8–36   Equipment and Materials for Paper-Cutting

EQUIPMENT

compass

craft knife

glues: paper spray adhesive, wheat glue, wallpaper paste, stick glue

heavy book (for flattening paper)

hole punch

iron (for flattening paper)

masking tape

mat board

metal ruler

needle and thread

paper

pen and ink

pencil

ruler

small bowl

small natural sponge

small, sharp scissors

spoon

tea bags (for instant "aging")

tracing paper

watercolors and brushes

waxed paper

TYPES OF PAPER

bond

calligraphy

fadeless

flint-coated

foil

giftwrap

metallic

mylar®

origami

paper-backed foil

parchment

rice

tissue

Silhouettes by Jean Jacob Hauswirth, Basel, 1860

List 8–37   Paper-Cutting Techniques Around the World

German, Swiss, Pennsylvania Dutch (Deutsch) (scherenschnitte)   usually one-color paper cuttings with intricate scenes

Polish (wycinanki)   designs on brightly colored layers of paper, mostly using flowers, stars, birds, and other motifs from nature

Chinese (k'e-chih)   many layers cut at a time using a knife

Chinese (chien-chih)   individual cuttings made with scissors or knife

English (paper-cutting)   paper mosaics, collage, especially fine botanical illustrations, silhouettes and pin pricking

American (paper-cutting)   nature scenes cut from black paper; mounted on foil or glass

Japanese (mon-kiri)   emblems and crests cut from paper

Japanese (katazome)   stencils cut for use in dyeing

Mexican paper-cutting (papel picado)   intricate white tissue paper cut-outs for holiday decorations

Mayan Otomi Indians, Central America   amate paper symmetrical figures used for rituals

Dutch (knippen, schneiden)   cutwork to decorate commemorative documents

Jewish paper-cuttings   used to commemorate special events; often included written text

List 8–38   More Things to Make with Paper-Cutting

birth announcements
bookmarks
bookplates
chains and streamers
doilies for candles
fraktur: legal documents
gift ribbons
gift tags
greeting cards (one cutting may be photocopied)
haus segen (house blessing)
holiday decorations
labels for jars
picture borders
place cards
shelf paper edges
silhouettes
stencils
valentines

SUBJECTS FOR PAPER-CUTTING

animals
birds

distelfink (bird)
fairy tales
flowers
heraldic designs
human silhouettes
hunting scenes
mythological figures
trees

WAYS TO CHANGE PAPER AFTER CUTTING IT

add calligraphy
add glitter
add iridescent fabric paint
layer one pattern on top of another
punch holes with a paper punch
stain it (tea or instant coffee)
use a pin and prick holes in it
use stencil lettering on it
watercolor it

List 8–39   National Heritage Fellows of America

Since 1982, America's "Living National Treasures" have been recognized at the annual National Heritage Fellowships ceremony on the George Washington University Campus in Washington, DC. Musicians and performance artists are also recognized, but the following names are in the visual arts only. In many cases they are representative of a large group of people who practice the same craft.

"These masters and guardians of folk and traditional arts ensure that America's unique cultural legacy is celebrated and preserved for our children and future generations. Through the National Heritage Fellowships we honor these exceptional artists for their creativity, innovation, and perseverance in revitalizing traditions built by countless others."

—Jane Alexander, Chairperson of the National Endowment for the Arts,
news release, July 8, 1996

1982	Elijah Pierce, African American carver/painter; Columbus, Ohio
1982	George Lopez, Hispanic woodcarver; Cordova, New Mexico
1982	Georgeann Robinson, Osage ribbonworker; Bartlesville, Oklahoma
1982	Duff Severe, saddlemaker and rawhide worker; Pendleton, Oregon
1982	Philip Simmons, African American blacksmith, ornamental ironworker; Charleston, South Carolina
1983	Lanier Meaders, potter; Cleveland, Georgia
1983	Alex Stewart, cooper, woodworker; Sneedville, Tennessee
1983	Ada Thomas, Chitimacha basket maker; Charenton, Louisiana
1983	Lucinda Toomer, African American quilter; Dawson, Georgia
1983	Lem Ward, wildfowl-decoy carver, painter; Crisfield, Maryland
1984	Bertha Cook, knotted-bedspread maker; Boone, North Carolina
1984	Mary Jane Manigault, African American basket maker; Mount Pleasant, South Carolina
1984	Genevieve Nahra Mougin, Lebanese American lace maker; Bettendorf, Iowa
1984	Margaret Tafoya, Santa Clara Pueblo potter; Santa Clara Pueblo, New Mexico
1984	Paul Tiulana, Eskimo mask maker, dancer, singer; Anchorage, Alaska
1985	Mealii Kalama, Hawaiian quilter; Honolulu, Hawaii
1985	Leif Melgaard, Norwegian American woodcarver; Minneapolis, Minnesota
1985	Eppie Archuleta, Hispanic weaver; Alamosa, Colorado
1985	Alice New Holy Blue Legs, Lakota quill artist; Grass Creek, South Dakota
1986	Helen Cordero, Cochiti Pueblo potter; Cochiti Pueblo, New Mexico
1986	Sonia Domsch, Czech American bobbin lace maker; Atwood, Kansas
1986	Ernest Bennett, Anglo American whittler; Indianapolis, Indiana
1986	Jennie Thlunaut, Tlingit Chilkat blanket weaver; Haines, Alaska
1987	Genoveva Castellanoz, Mexican American *corona* maker; Nyssa, Oregon
1987	Juan Alindato, Puerto Rican carnival-mask maker; Ponce, Puerto Rico
1987	Allison "Totie" Montana, Mardi Gras Big Chief, costume maker; New Orleans, Louisiana
1987	Emilio and Senaida Romero, Hispanic tin and embroidery workers; Santa Fe, New Mexico
1987	Newton Washburn, split-ash basket maker; Littleton, New Hampshire
1988	Amber Densmore, quilter; Chelsea, Vermont
1988	Sister Rosalia Haberl, German American bobbin lace maker; Hankinson, North Dakota
1988	Kepka Belton, Czech American egg painter; Ellsworth, Kansas
1988	Yang Fang Nhu, Hmong weaver, embroiderer; Detroit, Michigan

This information was obtained from the National Endowment for the Arts, Folk & Traditional Arts Program.

List 8–39 Continued

1989   Mabel Murphy, Anglo American quilter; Fulton, Missouri

1989   Harry V. Shourds, wildfowl-decoy carver; Seaville, New Jersey

1989   Chesley Goseyun Wilson, Apache fiddle maker; Tucson, Arizona

1990   Em Bun, Cambodian American silk weaver; Harrisburg, Pennsylvania

1990   Maude Kegg, Ojibwa loom beadwork, designer, storyteller, writer; Onamie, Minnesota

1990   Marie McDonald, Hawaiian lei maker; Kamuela, Hawaii

1990   Emilio Rosado, Puerto Rican woodcarver; Utuado, Puerto Rico

1991   George Blake, Hupa-Yurok ceremonial regalia and featherwork craftsman, dugout-canoe builder; Hoopa, California

1991   Rose Frank, Nez Perce cornhusk weaver; Sweetwater, Idaho

1991   Donald L. King, Western saddlemaker; Sheridan, Wyoming

1991   Esther Littlefield, Tlingit beadworker, basket maker; Sitka, Alaska

1991   Gussie Wells and Amber Williams, African American quilters; Oakland, California

1992   Jerry Brown, potter (southern stoneware tradition); Hamilton, Alabama

1992   Belle Deacon, Athabascan basketmaker; Grayling, Alaska

1992   Nora Ezell, African American quilter; Eutaw, Alabama

1992   Gerald R. Hawpetoss, Menominee/Potowatomi regalia maker; Milwaukee, Wisconsin

1993   Nicholas and Elena Charles, Yupik woodcarver/maskmakers, and skin sewers; Bethel, Alaska

1993   Mone & Vanxay, Saenphimmachak Lao weaver/needleworker and loommaker; St. Louis, Missouri

1993   Elmer Miller, bit and spur maker/silversmith; Nampa, Idaho

1994   Mary Mitchell Gabriel, Passamaquoddy basketmaker; Princeton, Maine

1994   Frances Varos Graves, Hispanic American *colcha* embroidery; Ranchos de Taos, New Mexico

1994   Lily Vorperian, Armenian (Marash-style) embroidery; Glendale, California

1995   Mary Holiday Black, Navajo basketmaker; Douglas Mesa, Monument Valley, Utah

1995   Bea Ellis Hensley, blacksmith; Spruce Pine, North Carolina

1995   Nathan Jackson, Native American (Tlingit) carver and metalsmith; Alaska

1995   Nellie Star Boy Menard, Lakota Sioux quilter; Rosebud Reservation, South Dakota

1996   Betty Pisio Christenson, Ukrainian American pysanky (egg decoration); Suring, Wisconsin

1996   Joaquin "Jack" Lujan, Chamorro blacksmith; Barrigada, Territory of Guam

1996   Eva McAdams, Shoshone Native regalia maker; Fort Washakie, Wyoming

1996   Vernon Owens, stoneware potter; Seagrove, North Carolina

1996   Dolly Spencer, Inupiat dollmaker; Homer Alaska

1997   Gladys LeBlanc Clark, Cajun spinner and weaver; Duson, Louisiana

1997   Ramón José López, Santero and metalsmith; Santa Fe, New Mexico

1997   Hystercine Rankin, African American quilter; Lorman, Mississippi

1997   Francis Whitaker, blacksmith/ornamental ironworker, Carbondale, Colorado

List 8–40   Major Arts and Crafts Festivals

Arts and crafts festivals are held almost weekly throughout the United States in small towns and large cities. This list features festivals that have become nationally known.

FEBRUARY

Mid-States Craft Exhibit, Evansville, Indiana

MARCH

Arts and Crafts Festival, Fairhope, Alabama
Heard Museum Indian Fair, Phoenix, Arizona
S.O.F.A. (Sculpture Objects Functional Art), Miami, Florida

APRIL

Folk Festival & Crafts Show, Mountain View, Arkansas

MAY

Kentucky Guild of Artists and Craftsmen's Fair, Berea, Kentucky

JUNE

Contemporary Crafts Market, Santa Monica, California
Frederick Craft Fair, Frederick, Maryland
Mountain Heritage Arts and Crafts Festival, Harpers Ferry, West Virginia
Northeast Crafts Fair, Rhinebeck, New York

JULY

Craftsman's Fair of the Southern Highlands, Asheville, North Carolina
Festival of American Folklife, The Mall, District of Columbia
Mountain State Art and Craft Fair, Ripley, West Virginia
Pacific Northwest Arts and Crafts Festival, Seattle, Washington

AUGUST

Appalachian Arts and Crafts Festival, Beckley, West Virginia
Craftsmen's Fair of the League of New Hampshire, Sunapee State Park, New Hampshire
Georgia Mountain Fair, Hiawassee, Georgia
Santa Fe Indian Market, Santa Fe, New Mexico
Ozark Empire Fair, Springfield, Missouri
South Carolina Arts and Crafts Festival, Easley, South Carolina
United Marine Craftsmen's Fair, Cumberland, Maine
Virginia Highlands Arts and Crafts Festival, Abingdon, Virginia
York State Craft Fair, Ithaca, New York

OCTOBER

The Craftsman's Fall Festival, Gatlinburg, Tennessee
Ozark Arts and Crafts Show, War Eagle Mills, Arkansas
National Festival of Craftsmen, Silver Dollar City, Missouri
S.O.F.A. (Sculpture Objects Functional Art), Chicago, Illinois

NOVEMBER

Southeastern Arts and Crafts Fair, Macon, Georgia

List 8–41   Master Craftspersons of the Twentieth Century

This list cannot possibly include all the artisans who make a living in the crafts field. These are simply a few whose names are included in most books because of the consistency and quality of their work over time. Some of these artists work with the materials of their craft in the traditional way, while others "break the barriers." Unless otherwise noted, the artists are American.

BASKETS

McQueen, John (1943)
Niehues, Sharon (1952) and Leon (1951)
Sauer, Jane (1937)
Seitzman, Lincoln (1923)

CERAMICS

Adams, Hank Murta (1956)
Arneson, Robert (1930–1992)
Ase, Arne (1940, Norway)
Autio, Rudy (1926)
Butterly, Katie
Cliff, Clarice (1899–1972)
Cooper, Susie (1902–1995, England)
de Sainte Phalle, Nikki (1930, France)
de Staebler, Stephen (1933)
DeVore, Richard (1933)
Dillingham, Rick (1952–1994)
Duckworth, Ruth (1919, b. Germany)
Frey, Viola (1933)
Fritz, Robert C. (1920–1986)
Gilhooley, David (1943)
Gill, Andrea (1948)
Higby, Wayne (1943)
Jeck, Douglas (1963)
Karnes, Karen (1925)
Koons, Jeff (1955)
Larocque, Jean-Pierre
Leach, Bernard (1887–1979, England)
Lewis, Lucy (d. 1992)
Lucero, Michael (1953)
MacKenzie-Childs, Richard L.
Martinez, Maria Montoya (1887–1980)
Nagle, Ron (1939)
Nam, Yun-Dong (b. Korea)
Natzler, Gertrud (1935–1971, b. Austria)
Natzler, Otto (1908, b. Austria)
Rossbach, Ed (1914)
Soldner, Paul (1921)

Turner, Robert C. (1913)
Van Briggle, Artis (1869–1904)
Voulkos, Peter (1924)
Warashina, Patti (1940)
Wood, Beatrice (1893)
Wright, Russell (1904–1976)
Youngblood, Nathan (1954)

FIBERS

Blount, Akira (1945)
Constantine, Mildred (1914)
Cook, Lia (1942)
Hicks, Sheila (1934)
Larsen, Jack Lenore (1927)
Ringgold, Faith (1934)
Sauer, Jane (1937)
Tawney, Lenore (1925)
Zeisler, Claire (1903–1991)

GLASS

Abildgaard, Mark (1957)
Barbini, Alfredo (1912, b. Italy)
Brychtova, Jaroslava (1924, Czech Republic)
Castle, Wendell (1932)
Chihuly, Dale (1941)
Ciglar, Vaclav (1929, Czech Republic)
Cyren, Gunnar (b. Sweden)
Dailey, Dan (1947)
Dejonghe, Bernard (1942, France)
Dickenson, Anna (1961, b. England)
Eisch, Erwin (1927, Germany)
Hydman-Vallien, Ulrica (1938, b. Sweden)
Kaplicky, Josef (1899–1962, Czech Republic)
Karel, Marian (1944, Czech Republic)
LaFarge, John (1835–1910)
Leperlier, Antoine (1953, b. France)
Levi, David W. (1951)
Libensky, Stanislav (1921, Czech Republic)
Littleton, Harvey K. (1922)
Marquis, Richard (1945)

List 8–41   Continued

GLASS (cont.)

Myers, Joel Philip (1934)

Patti, Tom (1943)

Reekie, David (1947, b. England)

Tagliapietra, Lino (1934, b. Italy)

Tiffany, Louis Comfort (1848–1933)

Tre, Howard Ben (1949)

Vallien, Bertil (1938, Sweden)

Wolff, Ann (1937, b. Germany)

Zynsky, Mary Ann (Toots) (1951)

JEWELRY AND METALWORK

Aguado, Deborah (1939)

Baldwin, Phillip (1953)

Brandt, Marianne (1893–1983, Germany)

Friedlander, Marguerite (1896–1985, Germany)

Herbst, Gerhard (1959, b. Canada)

Hu, Mary Lee (1943)

Jensen, Georg (1866–1935, Denmark)

Nielsen, Harald (1892–1977, Denmark)

Paley, Albert (1944)

Prip, John (1922)

Scherr, Mary Ann (1931)

Seppa, Heike (1927, b. Sweden)

Smith, Richard (Rick) (1960)

PAPERMAKING

Babcock, John (1941)

Seventy, Sylvia (1947)

WOOD

Castle, Wendell (1932)

Maloof, Sam (1916)

Moulthrop, Edward (1916)

DECORATIVE ARTS

Hoffman, Josef (1870–1956, Austria)

Liebeskind, Daniel

Morris William (1834–1896, England)

Rossetti, Dante Gabriel (1828–1882, Italy)

Ruskin, John (1819–1900, England)

Stickley, Gustave (1858–1942)

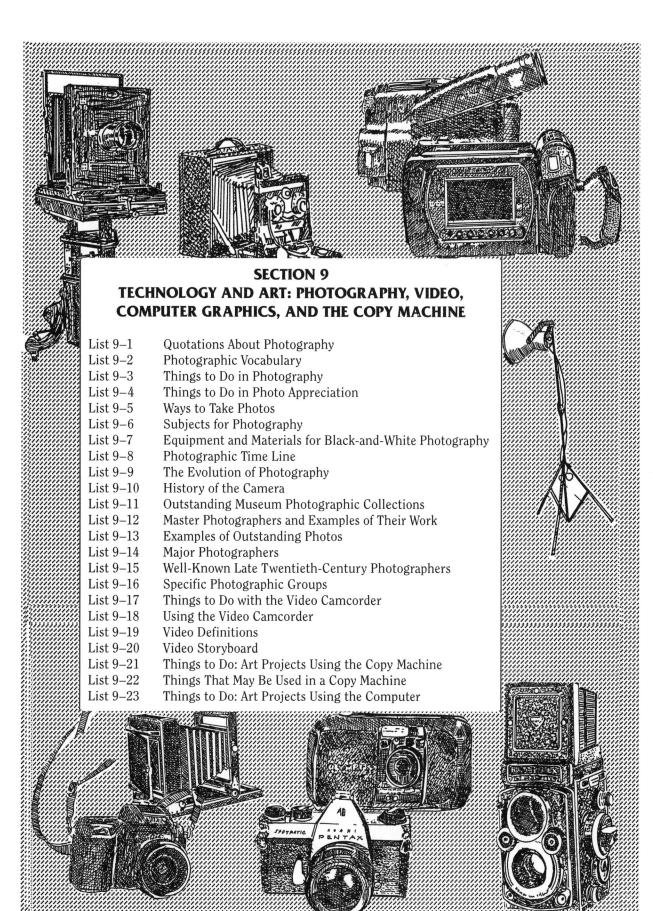

SECTION 9
TECHNOLOGY AND ART: PHOTOGRAPHY, VIDEO, COMPUTER GRAPHICS, AND THE COPY MACHINE

List 9–1   Quotations About Photography

"Photography as a fad is well-nigh on its last legs, thanks principally to the bicycle craze."

—ALFRED STIEGLITZ, 1897

". . . I can't recreate my feelings about how I happened to do this or that, because a lot of my stuff was done without any motivation more than just what I call having a good time and fooling around."

—IMOGEN CUNNINGHAM

"Stieglitz would never say that certain objects of the world were more or less beautiful than others—telegraph poles, for instance, compared with oak trees. He would accept them for what they are, and use the most appropriate object to express his thoughts and convey his vision."

—ANSEL ADAMS

"I pose for papa: 'Don't move . . . stand still . . . don't move . . . Papa counts one . . . two . . . three . . . done!' Yes, it's true, my eyes disobey every time and move around a little bit."

—JACQUES HENRI LARTIGUE (SPEAKING OF HIMSELF AT AGE 7)

"The photogram can be called the key to photography because every good photograph must possess the same fine gradation between the white and black extremes as the photogram."

—LÁSZLÓ MOHOLY-NAGY

". . . after *The Steerage* was printed, I felt satisfied, something I have not been very often. When it was published, I felt that if all my photographs were lost and I were represented only by *The Steerage,* that would be quite all right."

—ALFRED STIEGLITZ

"Stieglitz with his technique and his whole approach to photography was a master and a great man. I like the idea of wrapping something in light, which he did . . ."

—CONSUELO KANAGA, GROUP F.64 MEMBER

"In photography, visual organization can stem only from a developed instinct."

—HENRI CARTIER-BRESSON

"I wish to continue an epic series of photographs of the West begun about 1929; this will include a range from satires on advertising to ranch life, from beach kelp to mountains."

—EDWARD WESTON

Letter to Alfred Stieglitz

"I am only staying on in the hope of meeting you . . . You are the one person in this whole country (and photographically this surely means the world) with whom I wish to [come into] contact at this important time of my life . . ."

—EDWARD WESTON

List 9–2   Photographic Vocabulary

albumen print   an old technique in which salt was beaten into egg white, painted on paper, then sensitized with silver nitrate and dried in the dark; when dry, it was contact-printed

ambrotype   glass was sensitized (with the wet collodion process), and while wet was exposed and developed immediately; this process was in use from 1851 to approximately 1880

aperture   the opening of a camera lens that is expressed in F numbers

ASA (American Standards Association)   a number such as 100, 160, 200, 400, etc., that represents the speed of the film; means the same as ISO

autochrome   material used in early color printing; dyed starch grains over the emulsion

B (bulb)   the shutter speed dial setting that will hold the aperture open as long as the release is pressed; used for low light conditions or time exposures

bellows   light-tight accordion-folded leather sleeve between the lens and the filmboard (mostly found in old cameras) that gives additional depth of field

100 exposure box camera   a simple camera invented in 1888 by George Eastman in which the entire camera was sent in for the film to be developed, reloaded, and returned to the sender

bracketing   taking the same subject several times by doubling and halving the exposure to assure a good print

bulk loader   a holder for film in long rolls (normally 100 ft.) that allows you to roll as many exposures as needed into a cartridge

burning-in   the darkroom process of giving greater exposure to an area that is too light

cable release   a flexible cable that attaches to the shutter release to eliminate camera movement upon exposure; includes a locking mechanism that can be turned to hold the aperture open

calotype (Talbotype)   waxed paper sensitized with silver iodide and developed, then contact printed, invented by William Henry Fox Talbot

carbon prints   made by coating paper with powdered carbon, gelatin, and dichromate before exposing and printing.

camera obscura (literally *dark room*)   a box first used by Aristotle (384–322 BC) to concentrate light onto the back of a dark box through a small opening in the front; a tool used by such artists as Vermeer, Leonardo da Vinci, and Canaletto

carte de visite   basically the first postcard; these photographs were sometimes mailed to friends

cartridge (cassette)   the light-tight metal or plastic container in which film is sold

Cibachrome®   a color reversal process that allows color prints to be made from positive color slides

close-up lens   a lens that is placed on the end of a normal lens to bring small things into focus

contact printing   before the enlarger was invented, photographers placed negatives on sensitized paper under glass, and printed directly onto the paper by exposing to direct sunlight

cyanotype (blueprint)   the process developed by Sir John Herschel to make a print from a high contrast negative

daguerreotype   system originated by Louis Daguerre who coated a polished copper plate with silver iodide, exposed it, then developed it in mercury vapor

depth-of-field   the degree of sharpness of a photograph in front or in back of the area focused on; the smaller the lens opening, the sharper the depth of field

dodging   the darkroom process of holding back light to make an area lighter

double exposure   exposing film or paper twice, with sometimes interesting results

dry plate   a glass plate was coated with light-sensitive chemicals and allowed to dry before exposure

dye transfer   a color printing method that transfers three separate color single-color exposures to a single sheet

emulsion   a light-sensitive solution that is transferred to paper or film

electronic flash   a separate flash unit that is synchronized to go off as the lens opens; varying degrees of flash duration will be used depending on time and distance from the subject

List 9–2 Continued

F stop (aperture)   the size of the lens opening is an F stop; the smaller the opening (F22 for example), the greater the depth of field will be

field camera   camera with lens, bellows, and a spring back that allows a sheet film holder to be inserted between the lensboard and the back of the camera

filters   small glass circles that are screwed to the front of the camera for various purposes: to increase contrast; use with infrared film; convert outdoor film for indoor use; or help eliminate reflections

fish eye lens   an extreme wide-angle lens (180°) that will give a distorted center area

fixer (hypo)   the chemical used in developing that makes an image permanent

grain   irregular clumps of silver on the photographic image; higher ISO gives more grain

gum bichromate   an old coating process for drawing paper that makes it photo-sensitive, giving interesting artistic interpretations in color

high key photo   one that consists mainly of light tones

highlight   a reflection in the eye of a subject; the lightest part of the film

hologram   three-dimensional image of a subject exposed by two laser light beams and exhibited under the same circumstances

incident light   the light that falls on the subject, rather than that reflected from the subject

infrared   special infrared films are used to record the invisible infrared wavelength; the result (done with a red filter) is higher contrasts and green foliage appearing white

ISO (International Standards Organization)   a term interchangeable with ASA that is a rating of the emulsion speed of the film

LED (Light Emitting Diode)   electronic camera operating system

low key photo   a photo that is mostly dark, though it may have some light highlights

macro lens   a lens for close-up work

panning   swinging the camera horizontally as the photo is exposed, causing a moving subject to "stop" while blurring the background, emphasizing the subject's motion

panoramic camera   a swiveling camera that photographed an area of 150°, and was used for large views or photographs of large groups of people

photo floods   light bulbs specially balanced for film, usually used with reflectors on standards

photogram   László Moholy-Nagy and Man Ray were masters of this technique in which objects are placed directly on photo paper which is then exposed to light and developed

photogravure   a positive transparency transferred to a copper plate and then etched; the inked plate is then printed on a printing press

photocollage   created by cutting up photographs and mounting them on a support background

photomontage   a darkroom process in which multiple negatives are printed on the same sheet of paper through masking exposed areas

pinhole camera   a light-tight box (shoe box, oatmeal box, etc.) made into a camera by making a pinhole in a piece of foil, exposing photographic paper or sheet film inside the box

platinum print   photo printed on paper that has been sensitized with iron salts and a platinum compound

Polaroid® Land camera   camera that takes an instant picture

posterization   a technique used with high-contrast film to separate tones

precisionism   a "school" of photography that recorded factories, machinery, and other unromantic subjects; sometimes called the immaculates

props   the backdrop, toys, chairs, columns beloved by Victorian photographers; items such as costumes used in contemporary work to give meaning to a composition

reflected light reading   measurement of the light reflected from the subject to the meter

List 9–2   Continued

reflex camera   through a system of mirrors, the image is reflected on a ground glass screen; reflex cameras are single lens (SLR) or twin lens (TLR)

resin coated (RC) paper   printing paper treated with a synthetic resin; prints and dries faster

reticulation   the effect of crazing caused by developing film in alternating temperature extremes

retouching   applying a dilute color or black to remove flaws

Sabattier effect   named for Armand Sabattier who discovered that exposing a print to light while it is in the developer will cause light tones to become dark and dark tones to become light

salt print   a print made on paper that has been sensitized with ordinary salt, then brushed with silver nitrate, and exposed

sensitized   film or photographic paper is sensitive to light after specific chemicals are applied

shutter release   a mechanical device that exposes the film for a desired time period

shutter speed   the amount of time a shutter is open; this generally ranges from B (which will keep it open indefinitely) to ½₀₀₀ of a second

solarization   a reversal of tones, as in the Sabattier effect, but as a result of prolonged exposure or exposure to an extremely bright light

stereograph   a photo taken with a camera that has two side-by-side lenses that when viewed in a "stereopticon" gives a three-dimensional effect

tintype (ferrotype)   the wet collodion process applied to a black-lacquered tin plate is exposed in the camera and appears as a one-of-a-kind positive image

tripod   a three-legged adjustable stand that screws into the bottom of a camera to hold it steady

view camera (field camera)   term usually applied to a large box camera mounted on a tripod

vignette   to darken or lighten the edges of a photo through adding or holding back light

wet collodion   an early process in which the glass plate was sensitized just before exposure (also called wet plate)

zone system   an exposure system proposed by Ansel Adams that assigns numbers to value differences within various areas of a photograph; Zone 0 is a maximum black, Zone X is pure white; Zone I is gray-black, Zone IX is almost white, etc.; Adams later amended this to include 11 zones

List 9–3   Things to Do in Photography

A beautiful photo, composed in the camera and perfectly printed, is still the primary aim of most photographers. However, contemporary photography often includes manipulated photographs. Ideally, the projects listed here should be done only with perfect photos. In reality, these are good uses for the out-throws that might be over- or underexposed or even slightly stained. **Don't ever throw away a photo.** Even one tiny portion of it may come in handy later.

IN THE CAMERA

- If you have a zoom lens, "zoom" it while an exposure is being made.
- In a darkened room, take a time-exposure of a moving flashlight outlining a human figure.
- Interpret a painted or sculpted art masterpiece by setting up a similar scene and taking a photograph of it.
- Make a pinhole camera using an oatmeal box or shoe box. Paint the inside black. Cut a 1-inch hole in one end or the side, and tape a piece of 2×2-inch aluminum foil over it. Use a needle to make a hole. Tape a piece of black paper over the hole. Place unexposed photo paper inside the box (in a darkroom). When the box is in place to take a photo, lift the black paper on the outside to expose the photo paper (you will have to experiment with times—15 seconds to 5 minutes). Take the paper out of the box in a darkroom, and develop in a darkroom.
- Rubber band a piece of hosiery over the camera lens to get a diffused effect.
- Take a deliberate double exposure by not advancing the film (hold the film release button on the camera) while advancing the lever. Each exposure should receive half the light the meter calls for. Some cameras have built-in capability for double exposures.
- Take nighttime photos by using a tripod and cable release, or rest the camera on a solid surface. Exposure times are available in photo books. It is advisable to bracket the exposures.

CHANGING THE ALREADY-DEVELOPED FILM

- Burn a negative by holding a match under the film until you like what you see. It may burn all the way through, or just bubble the emulsion. **Safety note:** *Do this under controlled circumstances.*
- Draw on a negative with India ink or a fine-line marker, outlining and creating patterns. These areas will print white.
- Select a section of film, and reticulate it by boiling in baking soda. Hold onto one end with tongs, and repeatedly dip it until you see a transformation in the emulsion. Use approximately ½ cup of baking soda per quart of water (it can be stored and reused).
- Use a sharp object and deliberately scratch around the edges of the image on the emulsion side of *dry* film. These areas will print black.

IN THE DARKROOM

- Hold a crumpled cigarette wrapper under the negative in the enlarger. Results are unpredictable, but diffusion results.
- Make a combination print of photogram and negative. Place translucent or opaque objects on an unexposed sheet of photo paper, then expose a negative onto it.
- Make a 35mm high-contrast positive by contact printing a normal negative onto Kodalith® film. Dry it, then make a high-contrast negative using the Kodalith® positive you just made. Print either negative or positive, or do a "line print" by sandwiching them together (taping them slightly offset). Another possibility is to sandwich either one with the normal negative.
- Make a *paper negative* by first printing a photograph using a negative. Then while the print is wet, place it on top of an unexposed wet sheet of photo paper (emulsion to emulsion). Shine light through the back of the print (for a 5×7 print, approximately 45 seconds at F11).
- Make a photomontage by using two or more separate negatives on one print. Make test strips to assure perfect printing of each, then use black construction paper to mask out areas that will be printed. To blend edges, hold the black paper about an inch above the photo paper, moving during exposure.
- Make any image on a computer (words, letters, drawings, patterns, etc.). Print these on an overhead transparency (sometimes these can be done directly in the computer printer), then hold this in place on an unexposed sheet of photographic paper with glass. Expose. Interesting effects can be achieved by combining with a negative at the same time.

List 9–3   Continued

- Place tissue paper over the printing paper, holding it in place with glass before exposing through it. You will get a mottled, softened effect.
- Purchase a precut oval mat. Hold this about an inch above the unexposed paper, keeping it in motion to "vignette" an image such as a portrait. If you prefer a sharper edge, lay it in place directly on the paper. The edges will be light.
- Put a nylon or silk stocking on an embroidery hoop and hold it under the negative. It will diffuse the print.
- Put a roll of paper towels on the enlarger board. Take an unexposed piece of photo paper and drape it over the towels, emulsion side up, holding it in place with a loop of tape underneath each end. This is particularly effective with portraits—gives interesting distortions.
- Put petroleum jelly around the sides of a glass slide or directly on a large sheet of glass, leaving the middle clean. When an image is exposed through this, you will have softened edges.
- Sandwich two negatives together and expose through both. Or print first one, then the other, varying the times of each, so one is the dominant image, while the other may be a lighter gray.
- Solarize a print by flicking on an overhead light for a few seconds when the image can *just* be seen in the developer.
- Tilt an easel holding photo paper by resting one end on the paper towel roll. The result will be a distortion.
- To give an effect of motion, balance the easel on two pencils and roll it along during exposure.
- Use a color transparency positive (a slide) to print a negative photo.

CHANGING THE FINISHED PHOTO

- Cut or purchase a mat for the photo. Cover it with aluminum foil, textured in a pattern, to create a Daguerreotype "case."
- Do a "photo etching" by drawing directly on a black-and-white photo with India ink with a crow-quill or other pen point in a holder. Do cross hatching and intricate textures. Allow to dry overnight. Use Farmers' Reducer® to bleach away the entire photograph, leaving only the ink drawing. Portions of this could be hand-colored with dyes later if you choose.
- For a three-dimensional photo, make three to four identical *quality* prints. Leave one as is for the base. Make separate layers by cutting away portions from the second one, and place it on top of the first, separating them with small pieces of foamcore®. Cut away even more from a third piece, again separating it from the layers below it with foamboard
- Hand color black-and-white photos with dyes, food coloring, watercolor, oil paints, or oil pastels. It is nice to tone these brown before coloring. (Dr. Martins' Dyes® work well.)
- Make a white mat and use pencil or colored pencil on the mat to complement a matted photo. Sometimes just "extending" lines of the photo onto the mat with regular pencil is very effective.
- Photocopy a print onto overhead projector film, then project it onto a wall and draw. Paint the enlarged photocopy.
- Photocopy photos, then cut the photocopy paper to make a photocollage. These are easily colored.
- Print two black-and-white photos, then slice one vertically and one horizontally (½- or 1-inch strips), and weave them together. One of the photos could be toned before slicing. Or cut the photos in a wavy pattern to weave.
- Print two or three identical photos, slice them in ½-inch pieces (either vertically or horizontally), then mount them for an elongated photo.
- Select one photo as a base, then use an X-acto® knife to cut out small selections from other photos or a proof sheet. Affix them to the base with rubber cement. To get a "seamless" collage, rephotograph this photocollage and reprint it. The idea behind a photocollage is fully as important as your skill in cutting. **Safety note:** *Remember to always keep your hand behind a knife when cutting.*
- Tone a photo brown or tone it blue or tone it brown *and* blue. (Use rubber cement to protect areas from an undesired color.)
- Use a Kodalith® transparency or a photocopy on an overhead transparency of a high-contrast print. Do a giant blueprint with the transparency (approximately a three-hour exposure on an overhead projector, six feet away from a 36 × 36-inch blueprint paper). Develop overnight in an inverted large box using a capful of industrial strength ammonia (the blueprint paper develops in the fumes). **Cautionary note:** *Take a deep breath before placing the ammonia in the box or removing the blueprint.*
- Use matte photo paper and color all or part of the photograph with colored pencil.
- Write a poem (preferably non-rhyming) and write it around the edges of a white mat, or even through the picture. Fine-line marker, craft pens, or pencil will do.

List 9–4   Things to Do in Photo Appreciation

APPRECIATION ACTIVITIES

- Compare two photos. Point out similarities and differences. (Look at edges, value differences, use of space, subject, and mood.)
- Divide into groups to analyze one photo. Try to figure out the meaning, why the artist took the photo the way it was taken, what the dominant element is, whether it makes you *feel* anything.
- Do a slide show. Take rolls of slides with a specific theme, and select appropriate music to play while showing the slides. It is also possible to make slides from a book for a slide show.
- Get together in a group to show old cameras (even ones from childhood). Most people don't throw cameras away, and it is interesting to learn about the history of cameras.
- Research the work of one photographer. See if you can relate the work to the attitude of society at that time (politics, literature, music).
- Select a photograph by a known photographer that has special appeal to you. Write about it. You could write a poem, advertisement, or essay based on that photograph.
- Select a photograph that you have taken. Write a story about the circumstances under which it was taken, and why you selected it from all your photos.

ART ELEMENTS USED IN PHOTOGRAPHY

In any analysis of photographs, the elements and principles of art form a major basis for discussion. Here are some sample questions.

Which seems to be the dominant *Element:* line? shape? color? value? texture? space?

Line

What kinds are they? thick, thin, curved, interrupted or parallel lines? What about line direction? Diagonal lines are energetic. Horizontal lines sometimes are restful.

Space

Is there a center of interest? Does space isolate one dominant subject? Does the subject fill the space? Do you feel there is too much space?

Shape

Is there more than one major shape? Is the negative shape (the area around the main subject) interesting?

Texture

How has the photographer used texture? Can you see it? Would you consider it the dominant element? Would the photo be better if there were more textures?

Color

Look at the subject and then decide if the color adds to the idea or detracts from it. Most contemporary photographers use color film to great effect through the use of color filters, taking advantage of atmospheric light, and being aware of the drama of color.

Value

Differences in value are one of the major tools of the photographer. A black-and-white photograph should have a pure black, a pure white, and several tones (eight) in between.

ART PRINCIPLES USED IN PHOTOGRAPHY

Which *Principles* are employed to arrange the elements effectively? repetition? pattern? variety? emphasis? rhythm? contrast?

See if the artist has used *repetition* in shapes, lines, color, etc. The apparently inadvertent *repetition* of one of the elements is what make many classical photographs so dynamic.

There are many kinds of *contrasts:* figure/ground, old/young, rough/smooth, shiny/dull, dark/light, etc. The conscious use of contrast is important.

List 9–4   Continued

Has the artist decided on a *focal point* or *center of interest?* Discover what it is by closing your eyes. Open them, and make note of the first thing you see. That may be the portion that demonstrates the principle of *emphasis.*

Are there *varieties* of lines, shapes or values? Are there *varieties* of texture?

Some photos show *rhythm* through a use of undulating lines and repetition of forms, that lead the eye through the photograph.

Has the photographer taken advantage of patterns found in nature, calling attention to them through composition or point of view?

DISCUSSING PHOTOGRAPHY

Most photographers have preferred subjects. If you are discussing a group of photos (even personal ones), consider putting them in a category. Here are some examples of artists whose work might be categorized.

Conceptual   Man Ray, Sandy Skoglund, Barbara Kruger, Salvador Dali, Cindy Sherman

Design Oriented   Harry Callahan, László Maholy-Nagy, Imogen Cunningham

Documentary   W. Eugene Smith, Robert Capa, Mathew Brady

Landscape   Ansel Adams, Edward Weston, Thomas O'Sullivan, Eliot Porter

Photography as a Tool   Andy Warhol, Eadweard Muybridge, Thomas Eakin

Photojournalism   Weegee (Arthur Fellig), Margaret Bourke-White, Manuel Alvarez Bravo

Pictorialism (fine art)   Paul Strand, Edward Steichen, Julia Margaret Cameron, Alfred Stieglitz

Portraiture   Richard Avedon, Cindy Sherman, Annie Leibovitz

Social Realist   Ben Shahn, Dorothea Lange, Walker Evans, Thomas Annan

Social Reformers   Lewis Hine, Jacob Riis

Still Life   Imogen Cunningham, Robert Mapplethorpe

REACTIONS TO PHOTOGRAPHS

Discuss the reaction you have to a photograph or the work of one individual. Does it leave you:

admiring?	disgusted?	laughing?	saddened?
amazed?	happy?	neutral?	sick?
angered?	interested?	nostalgic?	wondering?
bored?	intrigued?	offended?	
curious?	jealous?	repulsed?	

List 9–5   Ways to Take Photos

Sometimes rather than thinking of *what* to take, it is a good idea to think of *ways* to take photos—it may give a whole new aspect to thinking about photography. Consider some of these.

abstract view of any object	flash photograph	silhouette
back-lit	foreground in focus	stop-action, blurred
background in focus, foreground blurred	high horizon	stop-action, frozen
bird's-eye view	low horizon	studio lighting
close-up	middle ground in focus	three-of-a-kind
dark subject on light background	natural lighting	tic-tac-toe grid (rule of thirds)
double exposure	nighttime photo	unusual viewpoint
figure/background contrast	panning a moving target	vertical
	shooting through a "frame"	worm's-eye view

List 9–6   Subjects for Photography

animals
architectural details
at work
black-on-black
boats
body parts
botanical garden
children
cityscape
clouds
contrasts
cooking
corners
doors
downtown
faces

"faces" in inanimate objects
flowers
frames
geometric arrangement
    (triangular)
hands
high contrast
humor
I simply love _____
    (personal selection)
in the park
landscape
line
machinery
nature
older adults

parts of cars
pattern
people
planes
portrait
product photography
reflections
rhythm
school life
seashore
self portrait
shadows
shape
sitting by the window
space
sports

strong emotion
summer
sunset
supermarket
texture
three of a kind
trains
trees
triangular arrangement
    of shapes
value differences
vehicles
water
weird
white-on-white
winter

List 9–7   Equipment and Materials for Black-and-White Photography

FILM-DEVELOPING EQUIPMENT AND MATERIALS

bottle opener (for taking top from film canister)
chemicals: developer, stop bath, fixer, hypo-clear, Photo Flo®
film processing tank
funnels
graduated cylinder (for measuring)
jugs for chemicals

light-tight changing bag that allows you to load film
reels
scissors
sponges
stirring rod
thermometer

DARKROOM EQUIPMENT

It is possible to put a darkroom anywhere that you can make dark. Prints can be washed in any sink by placing prints in a "holding tray" of water in the darkroom, after fixing, then taking them elsewhere for the washing process.

anti-static cloth or brush
bottles for chemicals
chemicals: developer, stop bath, fixer
easel
electrical outlets
enlarger
funnel
graduated cylinder
grain focuser (critical focus)
paper trimmer
photo-developing trays
print drying rack (screens)

safelight
sink (or holding trays)
squeegee and squeegee board (sheet plastic)
storage for paper, etc.
surface for printing
thermometer
timer
tongs
trash can
ventilation (exhaust fan)
water source, hot and cold

List 9–8   Photographic Time Line

FIRST DISCOVERIES IN PHOTOGRAPHY

1725 Light sensitive silver compounds,
    Johann Heinrich Schulze
c. 1842 self portrait,
    Hippolyte Bayard
1839 First Daguerreotype,
    Louis Daguerre

1816 First negative print,
    Nicéphore Niépce
1841 Calotype,
    William Henry Fox Talbot

1833 Paper negative,
    William Hanry Fox Talbot
1851 Wet collodian process,
1853 Tintype,
1857 Magic lantern (sun-enlarger)

CAMERAS

1845 Daguerreotype camera
1860 View/field camera
1875 Panoramic camera
1861 Stereoscopic camera

1871 Dry plate negatives perfected
1888 100 exposure Kodak
1890 Spy cameras
1891 First telephoto lens, Rudolph Dallmeyer
1905 Color separation camera

EARLY PHOTOGRAPHY

1860–1865 Mathew Brady documents the Civil War
1887 Eadweard Muybridge's motion sequence photographs

DOCUMENTATION, SOCIAL REFORM

1867–1942 Timothy O'Sullivan and W. H. Jackson
    photograph the wild west
1880–1908 Child labor photos, Lewis Hine

TURN OF THE 20TH CENTURY

1883 Negatives exposed on celluloid rather than glass
1890 First motion pictures
1900 Photogravure (halftone reproductions in print)
    Käsebier, Strand, Coburn
1902 Photo Secession movement, Stieglitz, Steichen

1905 Color separation camera
1912 Speed Graphic camera
1925 35mm Leica
1935 Portable electronic flash introduced
1937 Minox
1968 SLR Asahi Pentax

DEVELOPMENTS IN PHOTOGRAPHY

1933 Photography as Art. Photograms—Moholy-Nagy,
    Man Ray
1933–1940 Farm Security Administration Photos (FSA),
    Lange, Shahn, Evans
1932–1936 Group F.64 photographers
1941–1945 World War II photographs,
    Capa, Bourke-White, W. Eugene Smith
1970 Last weekly issue of original *Life* magazine
1971 *Look* magazine folds

1935 Invention of Kodachrome
1941 Color print Kodacolor
1947 Hologram, Dennis Gabor
1948 Polaroid Land Camera
1950s Advent of television
1980s Video camera
1996 Digital cameras

BEYOND THE PHOTOGRAPH

1950s Photo silk screen, Rauschenberg, Warhol
1960s Photo realism in painting, Chuck Close, Audrey Flack, Richard Estes
1970s Old techniques revived: hand coloring, toning, blueprints
1980s Multiple photos on one print, David Hockney
1990s–present Computer enhancement of photos, color copy transfer process

List 9–9   The Evolution of Photography

1560–1600s   Renaissance artists use the camera obscura as an aid in drawing

1725   Johann Heinrich Schulze discovers that some silver compounds are light-sensitive

1802   contact images on paper: Thomas Wedgwood and Sir Humphry Davy

1816   first negative print: Joseph Nicéphore Niépce

1819   hypo-fixer for photo images are discovered by Sir John Frederick Herschel

1824   first photograph: Nicéphore Niépce

1833   paper negative: William Henry Fox Talbot

1837   Hippolyte Bayard works with sensitized paper, exposing it in the camera

1839   first Daguerreotype: Louis Daguerre

1839   first experiments in color photography

1840   lens suitable for portraiture invented: Josepf Max Petzval

1840   first portrait studio is opened in New York by Alexander Wolcott

1841   calotype (Talbotype): William Henry Fox Talbot

1842   cyanotype (blueprint) is perfected by Sir John Frederick Herschel

1845   Daguerreotype camera

1851   collodion wet-plate process, glass is sensitized immediately before exposure: Frederick Scott Archer

1853   tintype: process is originated by Adolphe-Alexandre Martin

1853   sliding-box folding camera for 8×10-inch plates

1853   binocular camera is built by John Benjamin Dancer

1857   enlarger (magic lantern): allows a mirror to reflect sun rays for projecting an image onto paper

1860–1865   Mathew Brady documents Civil War

1861   stereoscopic (side by side lenses), giving two views of one subject

1861   variable aperture is used by William England

1867–1942   Timothy O'Sullivan and William H. Jackson photograph the American West

1871   dry plate coated with gelatin: Richard Leach Maddox

1875   gelatin coating on roll paper: Leon Warnerke

1875   panoramic camera

1878   motion sequence photographs by Eadweard Muybridge

1879   photogravure process is invented

1880–1908   photographs of social consciousness

1882   orthochromatic plates are manufactured

1883   negatives are exposed on celluloid rather than glass

1887   shutter with diaphragm and blades are designed by Edward Bausch

1887   celluloid roll film: Hannibal Goodwin

1888   Kodak box camera (contains 100 exposures): George Eastman

1890   folding box field camera

1890   first motion pictures

1890   spy cameras (concealed in a tie, cane, top hat, beauty case, book)

1891   daylight-loading roll film is introduced by Kodak

1891   first telephoto lens: Thomas Rudolf Dallmeyer

1895   Kodak Bulls Eye No. 2

1898   Jumelle Stereo Camera gives high-speed photography of $1/2000$ of a second

1900   The Mammoth—1,400 pounds, 20-ft long when extended—needs 15 men to operate

1900–1935   Kodak Brownie Series

List 9–9   Continued

1900   halftone reproductions of photographs in magazines, books, and newspapers

1902   Photo secession movement: Alfred Stieglitz, Clarence White, Gertrude Käsebier, Alvin Langdon Coburn, Edward Steichen, Frank Eugene, Joseph Keiley, Karl Struss and others

1905   color separation camera (Lancaster of London)

1908   Lewis Hine (social-realist photographer): child labor in factories

1912   Speed Graphic camera

1920s   advertising photography

1920s, 1930s, 1960s   photojournalistic style

1925   Leica I, Model A., 35mm camera is introduced; designed by Oskar Barnack and Ernst Leitz

1925   flashbulbs are invented

1927   Zeiss Ikon 35mm camera

1928   twin-lens reflex (TLR) Rollieflex camera is manufactured

1932–c. 1936   Group F.64 photographers

1933–1940   Farm Security Administration photographs: Dorothea Lange, Ben Shahn, Walker Evans

1933   Bauhaus in Chicago: Moholy-Nagy creates the photogram

1935   Baby Brownie

1935   portable electronic flash is introduced

1935   Kodachrome color transparency (slide) film is invented

1937   first 35mm single-lens-reflex (SLR) camera, the Exacta

1937   Minox (miniature camera); "You've been minoxed."

1941   Kodacolor (print) film for color negatives and positive prints

1941–1945   World War II photographs: Robert Capa, Eugene Smith, Carl Mydans, Margaret Bourke-White, Gordon Parks

1942   Ektachome positive reversal color film (for slides)

1947   Ektacolor (print) film for color negatives

1947   Hologram: Dennis Gabor

1948   Polaroid Land Camera: Dr. Edwin Land

1950s   Photo silk screens: Andy Warhol, Robert Rauschenberg

1963   Kodak Instamatic

1963   Polaroid instant *color* camera available

1968   Asahi Pentax Spotmatic

1968   Leicaflex Single Lens Reflex

1970   last issue of original *Life* magazine; *Life* photographers: Brassai, Cartier-Bresson, Kertész, Bourke-White

1971   *Look* magazine defunct

1980s   Video camcorders

1990s   Computer enhancement of regular photographs

1996   Kodak Advantix system

1996   Digital cameras

List 9–10   History of the Camera

1853 Sliding-box folding camera
for 8 x 10-inch plates

1861 Stereoscopic (side by side lenses),
giving two views of one subject

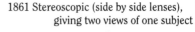

1875 Panoramic camera
1890 Spy cameras (concealed in a tie,
cane, top hat, beauty case, book)
1890 Folding box field camera
1895 Kodak Bulls Eye No. 2
1898 Jumelle Stereo Camera gives
high-speed photography 1/2000 of a second

1888 Kodak 100 exposure box camera

1900–1935 Kodak Brownie Series

1903–1905 Color separation camera
(Lancaster of London)

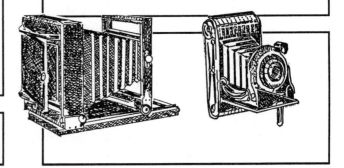

1900 The Mammoth, 1,400 pounds, 20 feet long
when extended, needed 15 men to operate

1912 Speed Graphic Camera

1925 Leica I, model A

1927 Zeiss Ikon 35 mm camera
1931 Twin-lens reflex

1935 Baby Brownie
1937 Minox (miniature camera), "You've been minoxed."
1948 Polaroid Instant Photography
1963 Kodak Instamatic

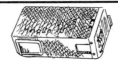

1968 Asahi Pentax Spotmatic

Nikon   Minolta   Olympus

1968 Leicaflex Single Lens

List 9–11   Outstanding Museum Photographic Collections

AMERICA

Ansel Adams Center/Friends of Photography, 250 4th St., San Francisco, California

Art Institute of Chicago, Michigan Avenue at Adams St., Chicago, Illinois

Center for Creative Photography, University of Arizona, Tucson, Arizona

Getty Institute for the Arts, Getty Center Dr., Los Angeles, California

Hallmark Photographic Collection, Kansas City, Missouri

International Center of Photography, Midtown, 1133 Ave. of the Americas, New York City

International Museum of Photography at George Eastman House, Rochester, New York

Library of Congress, 101 Independence Ave. at 1st St., SE, Washington, DC

Metropolitan Museum of Art, 1000 Fifth Ave., New York City

The Museum of Contemporary Photography, Columbia College, 600 S. Michigan Avenue, Chicago, Illinois

Museum of Modern Art, 11 West 53rd St., New York City

Museum of Photographic Arts, Casa de Balboa, Balboa Park, San Diego, California

OTHER

Agfa Foto-Historama im Wallraf-Richartz Museum, Museum Ludwig, Cologne, Germany

British Museum, Great Russell St., London

Musée d'Orsay, 1 Rue de Bellechasse, Paris

National Museum of Photography, Film and Television, Bradford, England

Royal Photographic Society, Bath, England

List 9–12   Master Photographers and Examples of Their Work

ADAMS, ANSEL, 1902–1984, AMERICAN

Possibly the best known of American photographers, Adams created beautiful landscapes of impeccable exposure and printing.

Clearing Winter Storm, Yosemite National Park, California, 1944, Center for Creative Photography, University of Arizona, Tucson

Leaves, Mount Rainier National Park, c. 1942, collection of the artist

Moonrise Over Hernandez, 1941, collection of the Ansel Adams Trust

Winter Sunrise, Sierra Nevada, from Lone Pine, California, 1944, Center for Creative Photography, University of Arizona, Tucson

ARBUS, DIANE, 1923–1971, AMERICAN

Arbus's photographs were often of "outsiders" of society; sensitive, intimate portraits.

Identical Twins, Cathleen and Colleen, 1967, Roselle, New Jersey, Metropolitan Museum of Art, New York City

Man at a Parade on Fifth Avenue, 1969, Museum of Modern Art, New York City

Puerto Rican Woman with a Beauty Mark, 1965, Getty Museum, Los Angeles, California

Untitled, 1970–1971, (People in Masks), Museum of Modern Art, New York City

Xmas Tree in a Living Room, Levittown, NY, 1963, Center for Creative Photography, University of Arizona, Tucson

ATGET, EUGENE, 1857–1927, FRENCH

Atget photographed his surroundings and the people in them; simple, beautifully designed recordings of a time in the past.

Boulevard de Strasbourg, c. 1910, International Museum of Photography at George Eastman House, Rochester, New York

Fête du Trone de Geant, 1925, Art Institute of Chicago, Illinois

Notre Dame, 1925, Museum of Modern Art, New York City

Ragpicker, 1899–1900, Museum of Modern Art, New York City

The Reflecting Pool of the Park at Sceaux, 1925, Bibliothèque Nationale, Paris

AVEDON, RICHARD, 1923, AMERICAN

Avedon, a fashion photographer and portrait artist, compels you to look at his insightful portraits.

Dovina with Elephants, Paris, 1955, Hallmark Photographic Collection, Kansas City, Missouri

Juan Patricio Lobato, Carney, Rocky Ford, Colorado, 8/25/80, collection of the artist

Marilyn Monroe, Actress, New York City, 5/6/57, collection of the artist

Oscar Levant, Pianist, Beverly Hills, California, 4/12/72, Hallmark Photographic Collection, Kansas City, Missouri

BRADY, MATHEW, 1823–1896, AMERICAN

Brady is best known for his portraits of President Lincoln and documentation of the American Civil War. He did not actually take all the photos that are credited to him, but had several photographers working for him.

Abraham Lincoln, 1864, National Archives, Washington, DC

Portrait, c. 1860 (ambrotype), Museum of Modern Art, New York City

Thomas Cole, c. 1845, National Portrait Gallery, Smithsonian Institution, Washington, DC

List 9-12   Continued

BRAVO, MANUEL ALVAREZ, 1902, MEXICAN

Recording the daily lives of Mexican people, using light to its best advantage, his black-and-white photos (frequently sepia toned) were studies in contrast.

How Small the World Is, 1942, Center for Creative Photography, University of Arizona, Tucson

Sparrow, Of Course (Skylight), 1938, International Museum of Photography at George Eastman House, Rochester, New York

CALLAHAN, HARRY, 1912, AMERICAN

Callahan's sense of design was the basis of his many photographs of city streets, nudes, patterns, and deliberate double exposures.

Chicago, c. 1950, Art Institute of Chicago, Illinois

Detroit Street Scene, 1943, Art Institute of Chicago, Illinois

Eleanor, 1949, Hallmark Photography Collection, Kansas City, Missouri

Telephone Wires, c. 1968, Center for Creative Photography, University of Arizona, Tucson

CAMERON, JULIA MARGARET, 1815-1879, BRITISH

Cameron staged her photos, with people sometimes in costume, to resemble the soft, romantic paintings of the period when she worked.

Alice Liddell as Pomona, 1872, Metropolitan Museum of Art, New York City

The Astronomer: Sir John Herschel, 1867, Royal Photographic Society, London

May Prinsep, c. 1865, Metropolitan Museum of Art, New York City

CAPONIGRO, PAUL, 1932, AMERICAN

Caponigro photographed Irish megaliths and other ancient monuments while funded by a Guggenheim grant. He studied under Minor White and Alfred W. Richter.

Avebury Stone Circle, Avebury, Wiltshire, England, 1967, Museum of Modern Art, New York City

Fungus, Ipswich, Massachusetts, 1962, International Museum of Photography at George Eastman House, Rochester, New York

Kilclooney, 1967, International Museum of Photography at George Eastman House, Rochester, New York

Stonehenge, 1967, International Museum of Photography at George Eastman House, Rochester, New York

CARTIER-BRESSON, HENRI, 1908, FRENCH

Cartier-Bresson would wait for what he called "The Decisive Moment" to take a photo, selecting a place to photograph, then waiting for something to happen in that space, timing his photos perfectly.

Alicante, Spain, 1933, Art Institute of Chicago, Illinois

Behind the Gare Saint-Lazare, Paris, 1932, St. Louis Art Museum, Missouri

Hyeres, France, 1932, Art Institute of Chicago, Illinois

Seville, Spain, 1933, Getty Museum, Los Angeles, California

Siphnos, Greece, 1961, Museum of Modern Art, New York City

CUNNINGHAM, IMOGEN, 1883-1976, AMERICAN

Cunningham specialized in scenes of the city, taken with a view camera. A member of F.64 group, her lovely photos of calla lilies and other flowers were known for remarkable clarity.

Snake, 1929, Art Institute of Chicago, Illinois

Two Callas, 1929, The Imogen Cunningham Trust, Berkeley, California

The Unmade Bed, 1957, The Imogen Cunningham Trust, Berkeley, California

Water Hyacinth, c. 1928, St. Louis Art Museum, Missouri

List 9–12   Continued

DAGUERRE, LOUIS JACQUES MANDÉ, 1787–1851, FRENCH

Daguerre developed the process of sensitizing a metal plate and exposing it to create a one-of-a-kind photo. The Daguerreotype bears his name.

Collection of Shells and Miscellany, 1839, Conservatoire Nationale des Arts et Metiers, Paris

Premiere Epreuve fait par Daguerre devant ses Colleagues des Beaux-Arts, 1839, Musée National des Techniques du CNAM—Paris

EVANS, WALKER, 1903–1975, AMERICAN

Evans worked during the 1930s depression for the WPA-FSA. He photographed signs and billboards, often making ironic connections between the out-of-work people posed next to signs showing affluence.

Circus Poster, 1936, Metropolitan Museum of Art, New York City

View of Railroad Station, Edwards, Mississippi, 1936, San Francisco Museum of Modern Art, California

FRANK, ROBERT, 1924, AMERICAN, b. SWITZERLAND

Frank worked as a commercial photographer for a time, then did the photo essay *The Americans* under a Guggenheim grant. Since 1960 he has mostly been a film maker.

Chicago, 1956, St. Louis Art Museum, Missouri

Parade, Hoboken, New Jersey, 1955, Museum of Modern Art, New York City

US 285, New Mexico, c. 1956, Museum of Modern Art, New York City

FRIEDLANDER, LEE, 1934, AMERICAN

Friedlander sometimes photographs monuments that people erect to commemorate a worthy cause. Many books of his work have been published, allowing him artistic freedom that not all photographers have enjoyed.

Galax, Virginia, 1962, Museum of Modern Art, New York City

Gettysburg, 1974, Hallmark Photographic Collection, Kansas City, Missouri

New York City, 1964, Museum of Modern Art, New York City

FRITH, FRANCIS, 1822–1898, ENGLISH

Frith brought the outside world to people through his many travel pictures.

The Approach to Philae, 1859–1860, New York Public Library, New York City

Colossal Sculptures at Philae (Egypt), 1860, New York Public Library, New York City

The Great Pyramid at Giza, From the Plain, 1859, Library of Congress, Washington, DC

The Pyramids of Dahshoor from the East, 1857, Getty Museum, Los Angeles, California

The Pyramids of Sakkarah, From the North East, 1858, New York Public Library, New York City

GILPIN, LAURA, 1891–1979, AMERICAN

Gilpin recorded the life of the Native American in her book *The Enduring Navajo.* At age 81 she took photographs of Canyon de Chelly from the ground and air.

Bryce Canyon #2, 1930, Hallmark Photographic Collection, Kansas City, Missouri

Scissors, String and Two Books, 1930, Amon Carter Museum, Fort Worth, Texas

Sunburst, the Castillo, Chichen Itza, 1932, Amon Carter Museum, Fort Worth, Texas

HINE, LEWIS WICKES, 1874–1940, AMERICAN

Hine took photos that led to social labor reform for workers and children.

The Bar-room in a construction camp on New York State Barge Canal, 1910, New York Public Library, New York City

The Cast/Behind the Footlights/A Modern Inferno (#325), c. 1909, New York Public Library, New York City

Fresh Air for the Baby, Italian Quarter, New York City, 1910, New York Public Library, New York City

Powerhouse Mechanic, c. 1925, Hallmark Photographic Collection, Kansas City, Missouri

List 9–12   Continued

KÄSEBIER, GERTRUDE, 1852–1934, AMERICAN

Käsebier was a portrait photographer and founding member of the Photo-Secession. She was considered one of the leading portrait photographers in the United States.

Baron Adolf de Meyer, 1903, Museum of Modern Art, New York City

The Heritage of Motherhood, c. 1905, International Museum of Photography at George Eastman House, Rochester, New York

Portrait of a Woman, c. 1900, International Museum of Photography at George Eastman House, Rochester, New York

Portrait of Auguste Rodin, 1906, Art Museum, Princeton University, Princeton, New Jersey

KERTÉSZ, ANDRÉ, 1894–1985, AMERICAN, b. HUNGARY

Kertész demonstrated an outstanding sense of design in simple things such as a vase of flowers, or a woman on a couch.

Chairs, The Medici Fountain, 1926, Museum of Fine Arts, Houston, Texas

Chez Mondrian, 1926, Art Institute of Chicago, Illinois

Paris, November 9, 1980, Hallmark Photographic Collection, Kansas City, Missouri

Satiric Dancer, 1926, St. Louis Art Museum, Missouri

LANGE, DOROTHEA, 1895–1965, AMERICAN

During the 1930s Depression, she photographed migrant workers in California for the Works Progress Administration (WPA/FSA).

Funeral Cortege, The End of an Era in a Small Valley Town, California, 1938, Oakland Museum, California

Migrant Mother, Nipomo, California, 1936, Oakland Museum, California

Three Families, Fourteen Children, 1938, St. Louis Art Museum, Missouri

LARTIGUE, JACQUES-HENRI, 1894–1986, FRENCH

Lartigue received his first camera at age 7, and took revealing photographs of French Society at the races, the beach at Deauville, and strolling in the park.

Gerard Willemetz and Dani, 1926, Association des Amis de J.H. Lartigue, Paris

Grand Prix of the Automobile Club of France, 1912, Museum of Modern Art, New York City

Paris, Avenue des Acacias, 1912, Museum of Modern Art, New York City

LEIBOVITZ, ANNIE, 1949, AMERICAN

Leibovitz began as a *Rolling Stone* photographer, specializing in portraits of the famous.

Arnold Schwarzenegger, 1976, photograph for *Pumping Iron*

The Blues Brothers, 1979, *Rolling Stone* cover, February

John Lennon and Yoko Ono, December 8, 1980, 1981, *Rolling Stone* cover

Mick Jagger, 1977, *Rolling Stone* 10th anniversary issue

Mikhail Baryshnikov and Linda Dowdell, 1990, photographed for The White Oak Dance Project

Whoopie Goldberg, Berkeley, California, 1984, *Vanity Fair*

MAPPLETHORPE, ROBERT, 1946–1989, AMERICAN

Mapplethorpe beautifully photographed flowers and other serene subjects, but became a controversial figure through his later graphic exploration of human sexuality.

Ken Moody, 1983, Hallmark Photographic Collection, Kansas City, Missouri

Tulips, 1977, Museum of Modern Art, New York City

List 9–12   Continued

MOHOLY-NAGY, LÁSZLÓ, 1895–1946, AMERICAN, b. HUNGARY

Moholy-Nagy was a founder of the American Bauhaus, especially known for his photograms, or photos taken from unusual viewpoints.

Abstraction, (photogram), 1925, St. Louis Art Museum, Missouri
Berlin Radio Tower, c. 1928, Art Institute of Chicago, Illinois
Oskar Schlemmer, Ascona, 1926, Art Institute of Chicago, Illinois

MUYBRIDGE, EADWEARD, 1830–1904, AMERICAN, b. ENGLAND

Muybridge used consecutive motion photos to demonstrate the process of human and animal motion.

Athletes and Classical Groupings, 1879, Stanford University Museum of Art, Stanford, California
Child Running, c. 1884–1887, New York Public Library, New York City
Cockatoo Flying, c. 1884–1887, New York Public Library, New York City
Daisy Jumping a Hurdle, c. 1885, George Eastman House, Rochester, New York
Nude Men, Motion Study, 1877, Museum of Modern Art, New York City
Valley of the Yosemite from Mosquito Camp, 1872, Museum of Modern Art, New York City

O'SULLIVAN, TIMOTHY H., c. 1840–1882, AMERICAN

O'Sullivan documented the Civil War, and after the war he traveled throughout the West, documenting places that had not been seen before by most of the world.

Ancient Ruins in Canyon de Chelle, N.M., 1873, New York Public Library, New York City
Black Canyon, Colorado River, From Camp 8, Looking Above, 1871, Getty Museum, Los Angeles, California
Field Where General Reynolds Fell, 1863, Art Institute of Chicago, Illinois
A Harvest of Death, Gettysburg, Pennsylvania, July, 1863, New York Public Library, New York City, New York City
Sand Dunes, Carson Desert, 1867, National Archives, Washington DC

PENN, IRVING, 1917, AMERICAN

Penn was known for his still lifes composed in the studio that were used in *Vogue.* He later concentrated on portraiture and monumental nudes.

Duke Ellington, New York, May 19, 1948, Hallmark Photographic Collection, Kansas City, Missouri
Man in White/Woman in Black, Morocco, 1971, collection of the artist
Purple Tulip, 1967, collection of the artist
Woman with Umbrella, New York, 1950, Hallmark Photographic Collection, Kansas City, Missouri

PORTER, ELIOT, 1901–1990, AMERICAN

Porter specialized in photographs of nature, specifically in the Southwest.

Dark Canyon, Glen Canyon, 1965, Art Institute of Chicago, Illinois
Pool in a Brook, Pond Brook, Near Whiteface, New Hampshire, October 1953, Metropolitan Museum of Art, New York City
Red Ossier, 1945, Museum of Modern Art, New York City

RAY, MAN, (EMMANUEL RUDNITSKY), 1890–1976, AMERICAN

Ray mostly made "Rayographs" (his version of the photogram), employing abstract shapes. He was also well known for his solarized photographs, and became a major figure in Dada and Surrealism.

Gala Dali Looking at "The Birth of Liquid Desires," 1935, Museum of Fine Arts, Boston, Massachusetts
Mrs. Henry Rowell, c. 1929, Art Institute of Chicago, Illinois
Portrait of Jean Cocteau, 1922, Getty Museum, Los Angeles, California

List 9–12   Continued

SANDER, AUGUST, 1876–1964, GERMANY

Sander specialized in formal, documentary portraits demonstrating German genetic traits and occupations in the New Objectivity style. His work was published in a book called *People of the Twentieth Century.*

Circus Artists, 1930, collection of John Dunivent, St. Louis, Missouri
Group of Children, Westerwald, 1920, Getty Museum, Los Angeles, California
Persecuted Jew, Mr. Leubsdorf, 1938, Getty Museum, Los Angeles, California
Police Officer, 1925, Museum of Modern Art, New York City
Widower with Sons, 1925, Getty Museum, Los Angeles, California

SHEELER, CHARLES, 1883–1965, AMERICAN

One of the "Immaculates," Sheeler used the stark contrasts in his photographs as inspiration for his paintings of industry and machinery.

Doylestown House—Stairs from Below, 1917, Metropolitan Museum of Art, New York City
Self-Portrait at Easel, 1931–1932, Art Institute of Chicago, Illinois
Wheels, 1939, Museum of Fine Arts, Boston, Massachusetts

SHERMAN, CINDY, 1954, AMERICAN

Sherman's subject is herself, sometimes grotesquely made-up, usually unrecognizable. Her large color photographs are impressive.

Untitled, 1981, Museum of Modern Art, New York City
Untitled, #145, 1985, Metro Pictures, New York City
Untitled Film Still #16, 1978, Hallmark Photographic Collection, Kansas City, Missouri
Untitled Film Still #21, 1978, Metro Pictures, New York City

SMITH, W. EUGENE, 1918–1978, AMERICAN

A war correspondent and *Life* photographer, Smith's photo essays show his involvement with his subjects. One such example was his coverage of the Japanese village of Minamata, whose inhabitants suffered from mercury poisoning.

Tomoko in the Bath, 1972, Museum of Fine Arts, Boston, Massachusetts
Waiting for Survivors of the Andrea Doria Sinking, 1956, Hallmark Photographic Collection, Kansas City, Missouri
Woman with Bread, Spain, 1950, Hallmark Photographic Collection, Kansas City, Missouri

STEICHEN, EDWARD, 1879–1973, AMERICAN

A member of the Photo Secession movement, Steichen is best known for his portraits. He believed that the personality of the photographer should not overshadow the reality of the subject.

After the Grand Prix—Paris, c. 1911, Metropolitan Museum of Art, New York City
Charles Chaplin, 1925, International Museum of Photography at George Eastman House, Rochester, New York
Flatiron, 1907, Metropolitan Museum of Art, New York City
Rodin—The Thinker, 1902, Museum of Modern Art, New York City
Self-Portrait with Brush and Palette, 1902, Art Institute of Chicago, Illinois
Wind Fire: Therese Duncan on the Acropolis, 1921, International Museum of Photography at George Eastman House, Rochester, New York

ALFRED STIEGLITZ, 1864–1946, AMERICAN

Stieglitz is considered the father of American Photography because of his work with *Aperture* magazine, and founding of the Little Galleries of the Photo Secession.

Flatiron, 1902, National Gallery of Art, Washington, DC
Hands, Georgia O'Keeffe, 1920, Metropolitan Museum of Art, New York City

List 9–12   Continued

ALFRED STIEGLITZ, 1864–1946, AMERICAN (cont.)

Music: A Sequence of Ten Cloud Photographs, No. 1, 1922, National Gallery of Art, Washington, DC
The Net Mender, 1894, Art Institute of Chicago, Illinois
The Steerage, 1907, St. Louis Art Museum, Missouri

STRAND, PAUL, 1890–1976, AMERICAN

Strand was both an artist and a documentary photographer, whose work was sometimes quite abstract.

Chair Abstract, Twin Lakes, Connecticut, 1916, San Francisco Museum of Modern Art, California
Church Gateway, Mexico, 1933, St. Louis Art Museum, Missouri
The Family, Luzzara, Italy, 1953, Hallmark Photographic Collection, Kansas City, Missouri
Matchboxes, Bowl and Bottle, Twin Lakes, Connecticut, 1916, Metropolitan Museum of Art, New York City
New York (Wall Street), 1915, Canadian Center for Architecture, Montreal
Photograph, New York (Blind Woman), 1916, Metropolitan Museum of Art, New York City

TALBOT, WILLIAM HENRY FOX, 1800–1877, BRITISH

A pioneer in photography, Talbot was best known for developing the Calotype (sometimes called the Talbotype).

Courtyard Scene, c. 1844, National Museum of American History, Smithsonian Institution, Washington, DC
The Game Keeper, c. 1843, National Museum of American History, Smithsonian Institution, Washington, DC
The Open Door, c. 1844, Gilman Paper Company Collection
Ships at Low Tide, 1844, National Museum of American History, Smithsonian Institution, Washington, DC
Trafalgar Square, 1845, Nelson Column Under Construction, New York Public Library, New York City

UELSMANN, JERRY N., 1934, AMERICAN

Uelsmann specializes in darkroom manipulation, using several negatives on the same black-and-white image. He coined the phrase "post-visualization" to describe this process.

April is the Cruellest Month, 1967, collection of the artist
Small Woods Where I Met Myself, 1967, Hallmark Photographic Collection, Kansas City, Missouri
Untitled (woman reclining on grass/water), 1966, Museum of Modern Art, New York City
Untitled (decaying house with ancient sculpture head), 1964, Museum of Modern Art, New York City
Untitled (office interior with a "cloud" ceiling), 1976, Metropolitan Museum of Art, New York City

WARHOL, ANDY, 1928–1987, AMERICAN

Warhol popularized the use of photo silk screen, with his subjects ranging from film and political figures to starkly realistic electric chairs.

16 Jackies, 1964, collection of Mr. and Mrs. David Pincus
Lana Turner, 1976–1987, Hallmark Photographic Collection, Kansas City, Missouri
Marilyn Monroe, 1967, Museum of Modern Art, New York City

WATKINS, CARLETON E., 1829–1916, AMERICAN

Watkins documented the opening of the West. He was a photographic pioneer, taking his darkroom with him to develop on-site.

Mirror View, El Capitan, No. 38, c. 1866, New York Public Library, New York City
Mirror View, Yosemite Valley, c. 1866, Art Institute of Chicago, Illinois
Multnomah Falls, Columbia River, c. 1870, Art Institute of Chicago, Illinois
The Valley from Mariposa Trail, Yosemite, California, 1863, collection of Daniel Wolf, Inc., New York City
Yosemite Falls, c. 1878–1881, St. Louis Art Museum, Missouri

List 9–12   Continued

WESTON, EDWARD, 1886–1958, AMERICAN

Weston was a member of the Group F.64. His photography included vegetables, nudes, and sometimes vegetables that *looked* like nudes. His stark desert scenes and beach pictures demonstrated his mastery of design.

Drawn from Pepper, 1930, Edward Weston

Armco Steel, Ohio, 1922, San Francisco Museum of Modern Art, California

Burnt Stump, 1937, Center for Creative Photography, University of Arizona, Tucson

Cabbage Leaf, 1931, International Museum of Photography at George Eastman House, Rochester, New York

Dry Salt Pool, Point Lobos, 1939, Art Museum, Princeton University, Princeton, New Jersey

Nude, 1936, International Museum of Photography at George Eastman House, Rochester, New York

Pepper, 1930, Los Angeles County Museum of Art, California

Washstand, 1925, Art Institute of Chicago, Illinois

WHITE, MINOR, 1908–1976, AMERICAN

White was a poet prior to becoming a photographer. He did documentary projects such as the iron-front buildings and waterfront areas of the West Coast, progressing from buildings to landscapes to closeups. His work reflected his commitment to the Asian Zen philosophy.

Face in Door, San Francisco, 1949, International Museum of Photography at George Eastman House, Rochester, New York

Pacific, Devil's Slide, California, 1947, Museum of Modern Art, New York City

Ritual Branch, 1958, Art Museum, Princeton University, Princeton, New Jersey

WINOGRAND, GARRY, 1928–1984, AMERICAN

A photojournalist, Winogrand worked exclusively with the 35mm camera, and was considered a street photographer "par excellence."

Circle Line Ferry, New York, 1971, Museum of Modern Art, New York City

Hard Hat Rally, 1969, Hallmark Photographic Collection, Kansas City, Missouri

Los Angeles, 1964, Museum of Modern Art, New York City

Utah, 1964, Center for Creative Photography, University of Arizona, Tucson

List 9–13   Examples of Outstanding Photos

Abbott, Berenice, *El at Columbus and Broadway,* New York City, 1929, Art Institute of Chicago, Illinois

Adams, Robert, *Summer Nights # 2,* 1982, Hallmark Photographic Collection, Kansas City, Missouri

Annan, James Craig, *Venice from the Lido,* c. 1896, National Galleries of Scotland, Edinburgh

Annan, Thomas, *Close No. 31, Salt Market,* c. 1868–1877, St. Louis Art Museum, Missouri

Annan, Thomas, *The Old Closes and Streets of Glasgow* series, 1900, Kuhn Library and Gallery, University of Maryland, Baltimore

Bourke-White, Margaret, *Nitrogen Plant, I.G. Farben Industry, Leuna, Germany,* 1930, St. Louis Art Museum, Missouri

Bourke-White, Margaret, *The Kremlin, Moscow, Night Bombing by the Germans,* 1941, Hallmark Photographic Collection, Kansas City, Missouri

Brandt, Bill, *Portrait of a Young Girl, Eaton Place, London,* 1955, Museum of Modern Art, New York City

Brassai, (Gyula Halasz), *Bijou of Montmarte,* c. 1932, Museum of Modern Art, New York City

Capa, Robert, *Naples,* 1943, Art Institute of Chicago, Illinois

Coburn, Alvin Langdon, *Williamsburg Bridge,* 1909, University of Texas at Austin

Coburn, Alvin Langdon, *Flatiron Building,* 1912, Museum of Modern Art, New York City

Curtis, Edward S., *Waiting in the Forest—Cheyenne,* 1911, Metropolitan Museum of Art, New York City

Deal, Joe, *San Bernardino, California,* 1978, Hallmark Photographic Collection, Kansas City, Missouri

DeCarava, Roy, *Coltrane No. 24,* 1963, Hallmark Photographic Collection, Kansas City, Missouri

Eakins, Thomas, *Female Nude from the Back,* c. 1880, Metropolitan Museum of Art, New York City

Edgerton, Harold, *Milk Drop Coronet,* 1936, Hallmark Photographic Collection, Kansas City, Missouri

Eggleston, William, *Yellow Flowers, Hillside,* 1974, The Oakland Museum, Oakland, California

Evans, Frederick, *The Sea of Steps, Wells Cathedral: Stairs to the Chapter House and Bridge to Vicar's Close,* 1903, Museum of Modern Art, New York City

Frank, Robert, *U.S. 285 New Mexico,* c. 1956, Museum of Modern Art, New York City

Gardner, Alexander, *Home of a Rebel Sharpshooter, Gettysburg,* 1863, Library of Congress, Washington, DC

Herschel, Sir John Frederick, *Latticed Window of Laycock Abbey,* 1835, Science Museum of London

Hill, David Octavius and Robert Adamson, *Highland Guard,* c. 1844–1845, Royal Photographic Society, Bath, England

Hill, David Octavius and Robert Adamson, *John Henning and Female Audience,* c. 1844, Royal Photographic Society, Bath, England

Hine, Lewis Wickes, *Empire State Building,* 1930–1931, Art Institute of Chicago, Illinois

Hockney, David, *Herrenhausen-Hanover,* 1976, collection of Paul F. Walter, New York City

Koudelka, Josef, *Velka Lomnica, Czechoslovakia,* 1966, Museum of Modern Art, New York City

Kruger, Barbara, *Untitled (Use Only as Directed),* 1988, St. Louis Art Museum, Missouri

Kruger, Barbara, *Untitled (You Get Away with Murder),* 1987, Hallmark Photographic Collection, Kansas City, Missouri

Leibovitz, Annie, *Meryl Streep, New York City,* 1981, Hallmark Photographic Collection, Kansas City, Missouri

Levitt, Helen, *New York,* c. 1942, Hallmark Photographic Collection, Kansas City, Missouri

Mayfield, William, *Orville and His Older Brother Rauchlin Wright at Simines Station,* 1911, Museum of Modern Art, New York City

Meyerowitz, Joel, *Provincetown Porch,* 1977, collection of the artist

Meyerowitz, Joel, *Bay Sky Series, Provincetown,* 1977, Hallmark Photographic Collection, Kansas City, Missouri

Model, Lisette, *Promenade des Anglais, Nice,* 1934, Hallmark Photographic Collection, Kansas City, Missouri

List 9–13 Continued

Morgan, Barbara, *Letter to the World* (Martha Graham), 1994, Museum of Modern Art, New York City

Nadar, (Gaspar-Félix Tournachon), *Auguste Vacquerie,* 1855, Getty Museum, Los Angeles, California

Newman, Arnold, *Igor Stravinsky,* 1946, collection of the artist

Outerbridge, Paul, Jr., *Cheese and Crackers,* 1922, Metropolitan Museum of Art, New York City

Rossler, Jaroslav, *Portrait of a Woman,* 1931, The Richard Sandor Collection

Samaras, Lucas, *Figure,* 1978, (Polaroid print with ink), Hallmark Photographic Collection, Kansas City, Missouri

Simmons, Laurie, *Walking Camera (Jimmy the Camera),* 1987, St. Louis Art Museum, Missouri

Siskind, Aaron, *Pleasures and Terrors of Levitation 99,* 1961, Hallmark Photographic Collection, Kansas City, Missouri

Skoglund, Sandy, *Radioactive Cats,* 1980, St. Louis Art Museum, Missouri

Skoglund, Sandy, *Fox Games,* 1989, Hallmark Photographic Collection, Kansas City, Missouri

Starn, Doug and Mike, *Double Rembrandt with Steps,* 1987, Hallmark Photographic Collection, Kansas City, Missouri

Van Der Zee, James, *Couple in Raccoon Coats,* c. 1929, Art Institute of Chicago, Illinois

Weegee, (Arthur H. Fellig), *Hedda Hopper,* 1953, collection of John Coplans, New York City

Weegee, (Arthur H. Fellig), *The Critic,* 1943, Hallmark Photographic Collection, Kansas City, Missouri

Wegman, William, *Red/Grey-Grey/Red,* 1982, Museum of Modern Art, New York City

Wegman, William, *Ray-O-Vac,* 1973, Museum of Modern Art, New York City

Weston, Edward, *Eroded Rock, Point Lobos,* 1930, Metropolitan Museum of Art, New York City

White, Clarence H., *The Orchard,* 1898, The Toledo Museum of Art, Ohio

White, Minor, *Surf Vertical, San Mateo County, California,* 1947, Art Institute of Chicago, Illinois

List 9–14   Major Photographers

AMERICA

Abbott, Berenice, 1898–1991

Acconci, Vito, 1940

Adams, Ansel, 1902–1984

Adams, Robert, 1937

Anderson, Paul L., 1880–1956

Anthony, Edward, 1818–1888

Arbus, Diane, 1923–1971

Arnold, Charles Dudley, 1844–1917

Austen, E. Alice, 1866–1952

Avedon, Richard, 1923

Bailey, Liberty Hyde, 1858–1954

Baldessari, John, 1931

Baltz, Lewis, 1945

Barnard, George N., 1819–1902

Barney, Tina, 1945

Barrow, Thomas, 1938

Bayer, Herbert, 1900–1986, b. Austria

Bazyk, Dede, 1951

Beckley, Bill, 1946

Bell, William, c. 1830–1910

Benson, Richard, 1943

Berger, Paul, 1948

Berman, Zeke, 1951

Bourke-White, Margaret, 1904–1971

Bradford, William, 1823–1892

Brady, Mathew, 1823–1896

Brigman, Anne, 1869–1950

Brooks, Ellen, 1946

Bruguiere, Francis Joseph, 1879–1945

Bullock, Wynn, 1902–1975

Burden, Chris, 1946

Burson, Nancy, 1948

Callahan, Harry, 1912

Robert Capa, (Andre Friedmann), 1913–1954, b. Hungary

Caponigro, Paul, 1932

Christenberry, William, 1936

Close, Chuck, 1940

Cornelius, Robert, 1809–1893

Cornell, Joseph, 1903–1972

Cosindas, Marie, 1925

Cumming, Robert, 1943

Cunningham, Imogen, 1883–1976

Curtis, Edward Sheriff, 1868–1952

Davidson, Bruce, 1933

Day, F. Holland, 1864–1933

DeCarava, Roy, 1919

Eakins, Thomas, 1844–1916

Easterly, Thomas, 1809–1882

Eastman, George, 1854–1932

Eastman, Michael, 1947

Edgerton, Harold, 1903–1990

Edwards, John Paul, 1883–1958

Eggleston, William, 1939

Eisenstaedt, Alfred, 1898–1995

Evans, Walker, 1903–1975

Eugene, Frank, 1865–1936

Feininger, Andreas, 1906, b. France

Fichter, Robert, 1939

Frank, Robert, 1924, b. Switzerland

Friedlander, Lee, 1934

Gantz, Joe, 1954

Gardner, Alexander, 1821–1882, b. Scotland

Garnett, William A., 1916

Genthe, Arnold, 1869–1942, b. Germany

Gibson, Ralph, 1939

Gilbreth, Frank, 1868–1924

Gilpin, Laura, 1891–1979

Goldin, Nan, 1953

Gowin, Emmet, 1941

Gregor, Harold, 1929

Greene, John Beasely, c. 1832–1856

Groover, Jan, 1943

Haas, Ernst, 1921–1986, b. Austria

Haxton, David, 1943

Hawes, Josiah Johnson, 1808–1908

Heinecken, Robert, 1931

Hillers, John K., 1843–1925, b. Germany

Hine, Lewis Wickes, 1874–1940

Holder, Preston, 1907

Hoyningen-Huene, George, 1900–1968, b. Russia

Jackson, William Henry, 1843–1942

Jacobi, Lotte, 1896–1990, b. Germany

Josephson, Kenneth, 1932

Kanaga, Consuela, 1894–1978

Käsebier, Gertrude, 1852–1934

Kasten, Barbara, 1936

Keaton, Diane, 1946

List 9–14 Continued

Keiley, Joseph, 1869–1914

Kepes, Gyorgy, 1906, b. Hungary

Kertész, André, 1894–1985, b. Hungary

Kiefer, Anselm, 1945

Klein, William, 1928

Klett, Mark, 1952

Koons, Jeff, 1955

Krims, Les, 1942

Kriz, Vilem, 1921, b. Czechoslovakia

Kruger, Barbara, 1945

Lange, Dorothea, 1895–1965

Langenheim, William, 1807–1874, b. Germany

Laughlin, Clarence John, 1905–1985

Lavenson, Alma, 1897–1989

Lee, Russell, 1903–1986

Leibovitz, Annie, 1949

Levine, Sherrie, 1947

Levitt, Helen, 1918

Liberman, Alexander, 1912, b. Russia

Lincoln, Edwin Hale, 1848–1938

Lynes, George Platt, 1907–1955

Lyon, Danny, 1942

Mapplethorpe, Robert, 1946–1989

Mark, Mary Ellen, 1940

Marville, Charles, 1816–c. 1879

Mather, Margrethe, 1885–1952

Metzker, Ray, 1931

Meyer, Baron Adolf de, 1868–1946, b. France

Meyerowitz, Joel, 1938

Michals, Duane, 1932

Model, Lisette, 1906–1985, b. Austria

Moholy-Nagy, László, 1895–1946, b. Hungary

Moon, Karl E., 1878–1948, b. Germany

Moon, Sarah, 1938

Morgan, Barbara, 1900–1992

Muybridge, Eadweard, 1830–1904, b. England

Nettles, Bea, 1946

Newman, Arnold, 1918

Nixon, Nicholas, 1947

Noskowiak, Sonya, 1900–1975

O'Sullivan, Timothy, c. 1840–1882

Outerbridge, Paul, Jr., 1896–1958

Parker, Olivia, 1941

Parks, Gordon, 1912

Penn, Irving, 1917

Pfahl, John, 1939

Porter, Eliot, 1901–1990

Prevost, Victor, 1820–1881, b. France

Ray, Man, (Emmanuel Rudnitsky), 1890–1976

Riis, Jacob, 1849–1914, b. Denmark

Rothstein, Arthur, 1915–1985

Russell, Andrew Joseph, 1830–1902

Ruscha, Edward, 1937

Samaras, Lucas, 1936, b. Greece

Saxton, Joseph, 1799–1873

Serrano, Andres, 1950

Shahn, Ben, 1898–1969, b. Lithuania

Sheeler, Charles, 1883–1965

Sherman, Augustus Francis, 1865–1925

Sherman, Cindy, 1954

Shore, Stephen, 1947

Slavin, Neal, 1941

Sleet, Moneta J., Jr., 1926–1996

Simmons, Laurie, 1949

Siskind, Aaron, 1903–1991

Smith, W. Eugene, 1918–1978

Southworth, Albert Sands, 1811–1894

Starn, Doug and Mike (twins), 1961

Steichen, Edward, 1879–1973

Steiner, Ralph, 1899–1986

Sternfeld, Joel, 1944

Stieglitz, Alfred, 1864–1946

Strand, Paul, 1890–1976

Struss, Carl, 1886–1981

Swift, Henry, 1891–1960

Tietgens, Rolf, 1911–1984, b. Germany

Uelsmann, Jerry, 1934

Ulmann, Doris, 1884–1934

Vachon, John, 1914–1975

Van Dyke, Willard, 1906–1986

Vroman, Adam Clark, 1856–1916

Van Der Zee, James, 1886–1983

Walker, Todd, 1917

Warhol, Andy, 1928–1987

Watkins, Carleton E., 1829–1916

Watkins, Margaret, 1884–1969

Weed, Charles Leander, 1824–1903

Weegee, (Arthur H. Fellig), 1899–1968, b. Hungary

Wegman, William, 1942

Weston, Brett, 1911–1993

List 9–14   Continued

AMERICA (cont.)

Weston, Cole, 1919

Weston, Edward, 1886–1958

White, Clarence H., 1871–1925

White, Minor, 1908–1976

Winogrand, Garry, 1928–1984

Witkin, Joel-Peter, 1939

Wolcott, Marion Post, 1910–1990

Wolff, Paul, 1887–1951, b. Germany

BELGIUM

Broodthaers, Marcel, 1924–1976

CZECH REPUBLIC

Drahos, Tom, 1947

Drtikol, Frantisek, 1878–1961

Hablik, Wenzel August, 1881–1934

Koudelka, Josef, 1938

Sudek, Josef, 1896–1976

ENGLAND

Annan, Thomas, 1829–1887

Arbuthnot, Malcolm, 1874–1968

Archer, Frederick Scott, 1813–1857

Beato, Felice, active c. 1850–1903

Beaton, Cecil, 1904–1980

Bedford, Francis, 1816–1894

Brandt, Bill, 1904–1983

Cameron, Julia Margaret, 1815–1879

Carroll, Lewis, (Charles Lutwidge Dodgson), 1832–1898

Clifford, Charles, 1800–1863

Clifford, Jane, active 1860s

Coburn, Alvin Langdon, 1882–1966, b. USA

Collins, Hannah, 1956

Currey, Francis Edmund, 1814–1896

Delamotte, Phillip Henry, 1820–1889

Emerson, Peter Henry, 1856–1936

Evans, Frederick, 1853–1943

Fenton, Roger, 1819–1869

Filmer, Lady, c. 1840–1903

Frith, Francis, 1822–1898

Gabor, Dennis, 1900–1979

Galton, Francis, 1822–1911

Gilbert and George

   Gilbert Proesch, 1945

   George Passmore, 1942

Grace, John G., 1809–1889

Herschel, Sir John Frederick, 1792–1871

Hockney, David, 1937

Howlett, Robert, 1831–1858

Macpherson, Robert, 1811–1872

Man, Felix, (Hans Baumann), 1893–1985, b. Germany

Price, William Lake, c. 1810–1896

Rejlander, Oscar Gustave, 1813–1875, b. Sweden

Robinson, Henry Peach, 1830–1901

Sutcliffe, Frank Meadow, 1853–1941

Talbot, William Henry Fox, 1800–1877

Whistler, John, 1836–1897

Wilson, George Washington, 1823–1893

FRANCE

Atget, Eugene, 1856–1927

Aubry, Charles Hippolyte, 1811–1877

Baldus, Edouard Denis, 1815–1882

Bayard, Hippolyte, 1801–1877

Bertsch, Auguste-Adolphe, d. 1871

Boubat, Edouard, 1923

Brassai, (Gyula Halasz), 1899–1984, b. Transylvania

Braun, Adolphe, 1811–1877

Carjat, Etienne, 1828–1906

Cartier-Bresson, Henri, 1908

Daguerre, Louis-Jacques Mandé, 1787–1851

Demachy, Robert, 1859–1937

Disderi, Andre A.E., 1819–1889

Doisneau, Robert, 1912–1994

Ducamp, Maxime, 1822–1894

Famin, C., active 1860s–1870s

Faucon, Bernard, 1950

Fernique, Albert, active c. 1870–1904

Hauron, Louis Ducos, 1837–1920

Lartigue, Jacques-Henri, 1894–1986

Le Gray, Gustave, 1820–1882

Le Secq, Henri, 1818–1882

Martin, Adolphe Alexandre, 1824–1886

Marey, Etienne-Jules, 1830–1904

Mieusement, Robert, active c. 1875

Nadar, (Gaspar-Félix Tournachon), 1820–1910

Negre, Charles, 1820–1880

Niépce, Nicéphore, 1765–1833

Robert, Louis, 1810–1882

Salzmann, Auguste, 1842–1872

Vallou de Villeneuve, Julien, 1795–1866

List 9–14   Continued

GERMANY

Albers, Josef, 1888–1976

Anschutz, Ottomar, 1846–1907

Baldus, Edouard-Denis, 1813–1882

Becher, Bernd, 1931

Becher, Hilla Wobeser, 1934

Citroen, Paul, 1896–1983

Degas, Hilaire-Germain-Edgar, 1834–1917

De Meyer, Adolf, 1868–1946

Hausmann, Raoul, 1886–1971

Henri, Florence, 1893–1982

Kiefer, Anselm, 1945

Kuhn, Heinrich, 1866–1944

List, Herbert, 1903–1975

Peterhans, Walter, 1897–1960

Prinz, Bernhard, 1953

Renger-Patzsch, Albert, 1897–1966

Salomon, Dr. Erich, 1886–1944

Sander, August, 1876–1964

Schwitters, Kurt, 1887–1948

Steinert, Otto, 1915–1978

JAPAN

Akiyama, Shotaro, 1920

Akiyama, Ryoji, 1942

Fukuhara, Shinzo, 1883–1948

Hanawa, Gingo, 1957

Nojima, Yasuzo, 1889–1964

Sugimoto, Hiroshi, 1948

MEXICO

Bravo, Manuel Alvarez, 1902

THE NETHERLANDS

Boonstra, Rommert, 1942

Dibbets, Jan, 1941

Evers, Winfred, 1954

Hocks, Teun, 1947

Oorthuys, Cas, 1908–1975

Sixma, Tjarda, 1962

Zwerver, Ton, 1951

SCOTLAND

Adamson, Robert, 1821–1848

Annan, James Craig, 1864–1946

Colvin, Calum, 1961

Hill, David Octavius, 1802–1870

SPAIN

Dali, Salvador, 1904–1989

SWITZERLAND

Bischof, Werner, 1916–1954

Finsler, Hans, 1891–1972

Fischli, Peter, 1952

Schulthess, Emil, 1913

OTHER

Alinari, Leopoldo, 1832–1865, Italy

Karsh, Yousuf, 1908, Armenia/Canada

Lissitzky, El, 1890–1941, Russia

Paolo Gioli, 1942, Italy

Rejlander, Oscar Gustave, 1813–1875, Sweden

Rodchenko, Alexander, 1891–1956, Russia

Shaw, George Bernard, 1856–1950, Ireland

Vishniac, Roman, 1897–1990, Poland

Webb, Boyd, 1947, New Zealand

Weiss, David, 1946, Swiss

Witkiewicz, Stanislaw Ignacy, 1855–1939, Poland

List 9–15   Well-Known Late Twentieth-Century Photographers

AMERICA

Adams, Robert, 1937
Baldessari, John, 1931
Baltz, Lewis, 1945
Barney, Tina, 1945
Barrow, Thomas F., 1938
Benson, Richard, 1943
Berman, Zeke, 1951
Burson, Nancy, 1948
Campus, Peter, 1937
Carter, Keith, 1948
Casebere, James, 1953
Chiarenza, Carl, 1935
Christenberry, William, 1936
Close, Chuck, 1940
Conner, Lois, 1951
Coplans, John, 1920, b. England
Cumming, Robert, 1943
Davis, Lynn, 1944
Deal, Joe, 1947
Devine, Jed, 1944
Eastman, Michael, 1947
Eggleston, William, 1939
Ewald, Wendy, 1951
Gibson, Ralph, 1939
Gossage, John, 1946
Gowin, Emmet, 1941
Groover, Jan, 1943
Heinecken, Robert, 1931
Klett, Mark, 1952
Kruger, Barbara, 1945
Lanker, Brian, 1947
Larson, William, 1942
Leibovitz, Annie, 1949
Levinthal, David, 1949
MacNeil, W. Snyder, 1943

Mann, Sally, 1951
Mapplethorpe, Robert, 1946–1989
Matta-Clark, Gordon, 1943–1978
McDermott, David, 1952
McGough, Peter, 1958
Meyerowitz, Joel, 1938
Misrach, Richard, 1949
Modica, Andrea, 1960
Morell, Abelardo, 1948, b. Cuba
Nixon, Nicholas, 1947
Pfahl, John, 1939
Rice, Leland, 1940
Rogovin, Milton, 1909
Samaras, Lucas, 1936, b. Greece
Serrano, Andres, 1950
Sherman, Cindy, 1954
Skoglund, Sandy, 1946
Starn, Doug and Mike (twins), 1961
Stephenson, David, 1955
Sternfeld, Joel, 1944
Sultan, Larry, 1946
Thorne-Thomsen, Ruth, 1943
Tress, Arthur, 1940
Tseng Kwong Chi, 1950–1990, b. China
Warhol, Andy, 1928–1987
Weems, Carrie Mae, 1950
Witkin, Joel-Peter, 1939
Wojnarowicz, David, 1954–1992
Wolin, Jeffrey, 1951
Woodman, Francesca, 1958–1981

ENGLAND

Armstrong-Jones, Anthony (Lord Snowdon), 1930
Burrows, Larry, 1926–1971
Fuss, Adam, 1961

List 9–16   Specific Photographic Groups

PHOTO SECESSION, 1905–1917

Alfred Steiglitz was the founder of the Little Galleries of the Photo Secession, called Gallery 291. The artists and photographers who exhibited there led the way into modernism in the United States.

Brigman, Anne, 1869–1950

Coburn, Alvin Langdon, 1882–1966

Day, F. Holland, 1864–1933

Eugene, Frank, 1865–1936

Käsebier, Gertrude, 1852–1934

Keiley, Joseph, 1869–1914

Mather, Margrethe, 1885–1952

Steichen, Edward, 1879–1973

Stieglitz, Alfred, 1864–1946

Struss, Carl, 1886–1981

Ulmann, Doris, 1884–1934

Weston, Edward, 1886–1958

White, Clarence, 1871–1925

FARM SECURITY ADMINISTRATION PHOTOGRAPHERS, 1935–c. 1941

The Farm Security Administration, administered by Roy Stryker, employed the following photographers during the Depression to record lives of the American poor: migrant workers and those displaced by dust storms and poverty. The Library of Congress Archives has 250,000 negatives made during this time.

Evans, Walker, 1903–1975

Lange, Dorothea, 1895–1965

Lee, Russell, 1903–1986

Rothstein, Arthur, 1915–1985

Shahn, Ben, 1898–1969, b.Lithuania

Vachon, John, 1914–1975

Wolcott, Marion Post, 1910–1990

GROUP F.64 PHOTOGRAPHERS, 1932–c. 1936

This group of photographers produced work of the highest possible clarity by use of the smallest F-stop on the camera. Most of them went on to become famous photographers.

> "The name[F.64] has come to describe a certain kind of photography characterized by great depth of field, sharp focus, and images that were usually uninfluenced by painting."
>
> —Willard Van Dyke

> "Believe me, a diamond-sharp glossy print does NOT represent F.64 unless there is that most-important-something-else in it—the quality of art in perception and execution . . ."
>
> —Ansel Adams

Adams, Ansel, 1902–1984

Cunningham, Imogen, 1883–1976

Edwards, John Paul, 1883–1958

Noskowiak, Sonya, 1900–1975

Swift, Henry, 1891–1960

Van Dyke, Willard, 1906–1986

Weston, Edward, 1886–1958

Others Who Exhibited with F.64 in 1932

Holder, Preston, 1907

Kanaga, Consuela, 1894–1978

Lavenson (Wahrhaftig), Alma, 1897–1989

Weston, Brett, 1911–1993

List 9–17   Things to Do with the Video Camcorder

Taking pictures with video camcorders is not so different from using regular cameras. You can take "snapshots" that are simply recording family events, or you can make *long format videos* that tell a story or are documentaries.

- Do a "Day in the Life of" long format video about someone you know or your city. These have been done by professional photographers as in *A Day in the Life of the Soviet Union* or *A Day in the Life of America.*
- Do a two-minute self-portrait using a video camera. Tell about what you like, what you do with your spare time, what you can see yourself doing in the future. Perhaps it could be like a one-way conversation with a friend.
- Do a time-capsule video about your life this year. Photograph your home, how you and your friends dress, what you eat, different makes of cars, a headline or two from a newspaper, the inside of a grocery store, etc.
- Get together with two or three friends to do a video presentation about the life of an artist or famous person. Photographs in books can easily be copied and discussed. When photographing pictures in a book, make every effort to eliminate any border by using two L-shaped pieces of black matboard. Set up the picture and record it. Leave the camera on long enough for details in the picture to be seen, then turn it off until you are organized for the next one.
- Make "commercials" about a place or product. Decide what it is that you want to sell, then figure out how you can best do it. Write a storyboard before beginning. As an alternative, make humorous commercials.
- Make a video architectural tour of your region. Decide in advance which buildings will be visited, and what there is about them that will be of interest before you take the pictures. For example, you might want to photograph only Victorian architecture, or Art Deco, or even the worst of the fast-food restaurants in your town.
- Make one "commercial" using three different camera positions.
- Tape an interview with an older family member or someone in your community who is elderly, asking them about their childhood, changes that are seen in the community, about mechanical things, what cars were like, what it was like to be in a hospital back then, etc.
- Tell a human interest story from an objective point of view, as if you were doing a documentary report for television.
- Use the camera from a subjective point of view as if it were your own eyes seeing. You could talk to the camera just as if you were talking to yourself as you observe something.

List 9–18   Using the Video Camcorder

THINGS TO CONSIDER WHEN USING THE VIDEO CAMCORDER

- The camera is normally set on *white balance* to record natural colors. If there is a mixture of light sources (some natural, some artificial), it may be necessary to manually set the white balance by holding a white paper in front of the lens. Shooting on hazy days may give better color results than working in bright sunlight.
- If you are making a long format video, work out how it will be done on a storyboard. (See List 9–20.)
- If recording in the wind, cover the microphone with a piece of cardboard, handkerchief, or other windscreen.
- Make titles. Either use the built-in title functions in a camera, prepare them on a computer, or hand-write them. They should be easily readable, utilizing the same format found on a TV screen (which is in a ratio of 3 units high by 4 units wide).
- Never use a camera move unless there is a reason to do it. Whenever you can, make people move rather than moving the camera.
- Never zoom, tilt, or widen the lens unless there is a reason to do it.
- Decide in advance if you will shoot from an objective point of view (you're a witness to the event) or a subjective point of view (you're part of the event, and the camera's eye acts as your eyes).
- Avoid panning too rapidly.
- Avoid frequent stops and starts.
- Frequently zooming in and out while the camera is on may be disturbing to the viewer.
- Try to have the light behind you rather than shooting into it for best results.

COMPOSITION

- Compose as you would in a still-camera, using the rule of thirds to make composition more interesting.
- Get as close to your subject as you can and still "tell the story."
- Try framing, or use angles that will give a different perspective.
- Use points of view such as extreme high or low angles.

SUGGESTIONS TO HELP HOLD THE CAMERA STEADY

- Use a tripod (you can get rolling tripods to allow you to follow the action).
- Brace the arm holding the camera on the side of your body.
- Sit cross-legged or sit with legs wide-spread for balance.
- Lean against a wall for support.
- Kneel in front of a stool, with your elbows supported while you shoot.
- Lie down to hold the camera, and prop yourself up with both elbows.

FOCUS

- You may prefer to focus manually to have complete control. Be aware that if you use autofocus, the camera may focus on the object nearest the screen or in the exact center of the viewfinder.
- If focusing manually, first adjust at the telephoto end.

TRANSITIONS

- Use the fade or dissolve option to make scene/location/time-transitions.
- Deliberately *rack focus* out the screen when making scene transitions.
- If you plan to edit later, leave an extra five seconds before and after each shot.

List 9–19   Video Definitions

action lines   lines drawn on a storyboard to indicate continued action

aperture   the opening on the lens; controls the amount of light passing through

aspect ratio   the ratio of width to height, as on a TV screen; in most instances the current ratio is 3 to 4 (three units high, four units wide); this is an important ratio to remember when planning a storyboard or title

available light   daylight or ordinary indoor light that is not enhanced by additional lighting

backlighting   light that comes from behind a subject

backlit   a subject is backlit if it is silhouetted against a bright light source such as sunlight; the detail on the subject is likely to be quite dark; will create a halo effect on a person

bust shot   a medium close-up shot of a person from the chest upward

character generation   electronically-generated type or titles on a screen

close up   any detail that fills the frame

continuity   sequence of details from shot to shot, including light level and placement of objects

cut to   two scenes are abruptly butted together (without dissolve or fade)

depth of field   the amount of the image that is in focus is dependent upon the aperture opening; the smaller the opening, the sharper the image

dissolve   a transition that mixes from one shot to another; more pleasing than an abrupt transition

dolly   the camera and tripod move straight in or straight out from the subject

fade up   transition from black or color to a video scene

fade out   from video scene to black or color

key light   the principal light source illuminating a subject

medium shot   for example, if photographing a person, this would be from the waist up

panning   to stand in place and move the camera lens horizontally either to give a panoramic shot or to follow a moving subject

pedestal   move the camera straight up or down

rack focus   to take a shot either in-focus or out-of-focus; usually used for transitions

soundtrack   the background sound while the video is being shot

storyboard   a shot-by-shot plan for shooting videos; opening shots, lighting details, shooting angles

tilt   the camera tilts up or down in a straight line

tracking   the camera follows along, recording movement

transition   part of the editing process, sometimes indicating a change of time, location, or subject by use of rack focus, dissolve, or cut

trucking   sideways action of the camera to follow motion

voice-over   a commentary, usually added after the shot is made

white balance   most cameras are already in white balance; if done manually, a white paper is held in front of the lens

wide shot   a distance shot; a wide angle shot to take in a greater panorama or a full-length figure; if of a person, one would see the entire figure; use a wide-angle lens

zoom   optically bring the subject closer or further away by moving the lens in or out

List 9–20   Video Storyboard

ABBREVIATIONS AND DIRECTIONS FOR THE STORYBOARD

BG: background
CAM: camera
CG: character generation
CU: closeup shot
Cut to: one shot ends and another begins
Dissolve to: one shot mixes into the next shot
E: extreme

ECU: extreme closeup
EWS: extreme wide shot
Fade to Black: move from video scene to black
MCU: medium close up
MS: medium shot
V/O: voice-over; unseen narrator

CAMERA DIRECTIONS

dolly: move camera and tripod toward or away from the subject
pan: move camera lens horizontally
pedestal: move the camera higher or lower

tilt: vertically, from feet to face
truck: move the camera sideways to follow action
zoom: bring subject closer or further away by use of lens

List 9–21   Things to Do:
Art Projects Using the Copy Machine

Copy machines are readily available in most communities. There are numerous art projects that can be done by copying on overhead transparency film or copy paper of various kinds.

ART PROJECTS: OVERHEAD TRANSPARENCY FILM

Transparencies come in colors or clear, and may be printed in a laser printer or copy machine, which means that computer graphics can be printed on them. A transparency may be colored with permanent markers, or mounted on colored fadeless paper.

- Copy a painting or sculpture masterpiece from a book, and enlarge it by projecting onto a wall. Then change it in some way (such as substituting your face for that of the person in the painting, or change tools or clothing).
- Copy Medieval stained-glass windows on a transparency and color the back with permanent markers; mat in black construction paper and hang in a window.
- Do a detailed line drawing on paper with any type of pen or pencil and copy it onto a transparency. Project it onto a large piece of drawing paper. Or project the transparency onto a wall to do a mural.
- Make a blueprint by placing a transparency film image on top of blueprint paper (Diazo black-line positive dry reproduction paper) and holding it in place with a sheet of glass. The blueprint will be properly exposed when the visible area turns from yellow to white (from 10 seconds to 5 minutes, depending on the angle of the sun and the time of the year). Develop the blueprint in ammonia fumes in an inverted large plastic jar (a capful of ammonia is sufficient). **Safety note:** *Keep the opening of the jar down when removing the blueprint.*
- Make a *tintype* by photocopying old family photographs onto an overhead transparency. Place the transparency copy over aluminum foil, then enclose in a mat to hold it in place. The mat could be covered in foil, using a soft pencil or ball-point pen to make repoussé patterns in the manner of a daguerreotype case.
- Make texture screens by printing out computer-generated textures on overhead transparencies. Combine the texture screens with a negative in the darkroom and print onto photo paper, or place them on another type of composition.
- Place a flower between two sheets of transparency film, flatten, and copy it. You will get amazing, interesting detail that can be combined with other materials to make a collage.
- Place a personal photograph or snapshot in the machine and copy it onto a transparency film. To enlarge, place the transparency on an overhead projector and project it onto large canvas. Paint in bright colors with acrylic paint.

ART PROJECTS: PAPER COPIES

- Combine one or two copyright-free illustrations from Dover books with a free-hand drawing.
- Create a collage with magazine cutouts. Select a theme such as flowers, eyes, mouths, hands, etc., then combine the cut-outs with an unlikely object that doesn't quite belong. Photocopy. This can be hand-colored with colored pencil.
- Have a color copy made, then make a *color copy transfer* by dampening a sheet of drawing or watercolor paper with solvent, then placing the treated paper on top of the color copy and burnish on the back with a spoon. Experiment with a variety of solvents to see which works best for you. **Safety note:** *Work in a well-ventilated room.*
- Make 10 copies of a portrait, then trim them and mount them on posterboard. Use colored pencil to color each one with a different set of patterns and colors. (See some Andy Warhol artworks.)
- Make 12 copies of a single subject such as a person, horse, cow, pig, house, flower, etc. (this could be a simple outline drawing). Then use colored pencil to transform that object in the "manner of _____" (your choice of an artist with distinctive style). This is a good project to do with a group of people, comparing changes and trying to guess whose style was used.

List 9–21   Continued

- Make an art object of an ordinary discarded household object (mixer, chair, old toaster, etc.) by covering it with glued-on photocopies. Humor would count for a great deal here, perhaps with one area hand-colored. (An example is a refrigerator that has the entire inside plastered with photocopies of lips.)

- Make copies of family photos and make a rough collage by tearing out the pictures to mount. Use polymer medium or thinned white glue to mount them on heavy drawing paper. Then use acrylic paint or oil pastels to transform the composition, allowing the photography to show through in places.

- Mount a single photocopied image on drawing paper. Use pencil to extend the photo or make it part of a fantasy background.

- Photocopy old-fashioned graphic designs on fluorescent paper. Use three sheets to make a three-dimensional sculpture by folding, curling, cutting. The graphic designs should play a prominent part of the composition.

- Photocopy your own hands or faces. Use these as part of a composition. **Safety note:** *Remember to close eyes, or the light could cause serious damage.*

- Transform a portrait drawing by moving the drawing *as* it is being copied. Then do a drawing based on the distortion and blurs that resulted. (This creative use of a copy machine was developed by art teacher, John Dunivent.)

List 9–22   Materials That May Be Used in a Copy Machine

card stock in many different colors

copy paper in white or colors

drawing paper, cut to 8-½ × 11-inch size

fadeless paper, cut to 8-½ × 11-inch size

fluorescent copy paper (may be bought by the ream)

transparency film, colored or clear

List 9–23   Things to Do:
Art Projects Using the Computer

No attempt is made to describe particular computer graphics software because these change rapidly. The projects listed below are simply *art* projects that use the computer as another way of creating art. An advantage to computer drawing is that each experiment can be saved and the original design retrieved again. Because not everyone has ready access to color screens, printers, or scanners, most of these projects could also be done in black and white, then hand colored with colored pencils.

Computer graphics projects may be printed or *photographed*. To photograph, expose color prints directly from the screen in a darkened room with a 35mm camera at ⅛ of a second (using a tripod and cable release). Fill the camera viewfinder with the screen, allowing the camera to make a proper aperture selection. Or use an 18% gray card (available from a camera store). Make sure there are no reflections. After having the roll of film developed, select a few for printing 8 × 10 or larger on a color copy machine.

- Do a drawing using *line* only, varying direction, width, and types of lines (curved, zig-zag, straight, diagonal, horizontal, vertical). The lines should run off the page in all directions.
- Use all the functions of the computer to make squares, circles, ellipses. Overlap them, enlarge, reduce, and make an entire composition of geometric *shapes*. Fill these in, repeating colors to make an interesting composition.
- Draw a cone, cylinder, and sphere, overlapping them. Use a "spray" function to shade these to show light coming from one direction.
- On a copy of your landscape, incorporate a cone, cylinder, cube, and sphere within the landscape, as if they were giant monuments such as the Egyptian pyramids. These may vary in size (depending on distance away from the viewer), but should fit in as a natural part of the landscape. Show light coming from one direction only.
- Create a composition using only letters of various fonts and sizes. These can be overlapped, filled with texture, turned, repeated, and combined within geometric shapes. Use a lettering book as a reference for letter forms that can be drawn freehand. Allow letters to run off the page.
- Take the "letter" composition, and make a specific color combination, working with five colors only, and incorporating two values of one color, two analogous colors, and a complementary color. Try this with several different schemes. Mount them all together.
- Paint a landscape watercolor on *paper,* working out values. Then do the same project freehand on the computer screen, trying to duplicate your original as precisely as possible.
- Do a line drawing of a landscape, including trees, rocks, etc. (This could be based on a personal photo.) Save this original drawing, and make three variations of it:

    Make the landscape in one color, using different values, and making some areas very dark or light to show value differences.

    Change the colors of the landscape to reflect different times of the day such as early morning or evening.

    Change the colors to reflect a different season such as spring, summer, fall, or winter.

- Design a mask based on celebrations in Native American or African culture. (Obtain books or photocopies of masks to spark ideas.) Leave room on top of the face for a headdress.
- Hex signs on barns are still seen in Eastern regions of the United States. Create a hex sign using concentric circles, and create a five-, six-, or eight-pointed star inside, using color and texture within the divisions. Or make a hex sign with a horse, cow, or rooster.
- Select an animal photo and tape it next to the screen. Draw the animal as realistically as possible. Or scan it if your computer has that capability. Now move the animal to a spot that uses the "rule of thirds" (a "tic-tac-toe" grid intersection), and create an appropriate environment (jungle, desert, swamp, etc.).
- Draw eggs in a bowl and light them from the side. Use a single pale color to show shadow. Add two or three more colors within the shaded areas, gradually darkening them, but allowing some areas to remain white.
- Draw a Victorian House, taking advantage of the computer's functions to make ovals and other geometric shapes. Get a book or photocopies for inspiration. The "gingerbread," stained-glass windows, and trim around doors and porches are very colorful.

List 9–23   Continued

- Select a photograph of an actual city scene. Duplicate the silhouette as nearly as possible with lines and boxes, then fill in with pattern. Add people in the foreground, and use the spray function to create a stormy sky and dark foreground shapes. *Variation:* Take your completed city scene, and cut vertical sections of varying widths, moving them to a different place within the picture for an entirely different effect.
- Create an arabesque based on Islamic design. With the mirrors function, make two or four of the identical design to give the effect of a mosaic tile.
- Create a collage of realistic photos and drawing (if you have a scanner). You can adjust sizes, placement, and color to make an effective composition.
- Use one-point perspective to create a house or block of buildings. Use textures, spray, and fill. Overlap and build up layers to create differences in value.
- Make a kaleidoscope design. Use line to divide the screen horizontally, vertically, and from the four corners, going through the center. Make geometric shapes within these divisions, repeating them as you go around.
- Make a radial design, starting from the center with small ovals or circles. Then make larger and larger ovals and circles as you move out toward the edges of the screen. Use a minimum of 16 shapes, with at least 4 of these shapes overlapped. Fill in, using color and texture to complete the composition.
- Compose a still life using at least 9 objects, overlapping, using color, and filling the entire screen. It may be necessary to do a still-life drawing first, then transfer it.
- Draw a reproduction of a historic masterpiece into the computer. Select one that would allow you to use humor to transform some portion. Leave enough of the original so there is no doubt what your source is, but let artistic license take over, or there is no point in doing it.
- Create computer designs for Navajo blankets, which use a variety of geometric designs. Modern artists also design storytelling pictorial blankets. These are easily done on most computer graphics programs, using appropriate colors and textures.
- Grids on the computer allow for geometric designs such as those based on ancient floor patterns used by the Romans. Design a mosaic floor for your room, creating a border and center design.
- Quilts use mostly geometric pieces, and the computer allows for a great deal of inventiveness in interpreting quilt patterns to be printed or photographed. Begin with simple designs like the nine-patch or windmill. Books or magazines on quilting will be useful.
- Tape an overhead transparency on a mirror and use permanent marker to draw your face on it. Tape this on the computer screen and trace it onto the screen. Use color or texture to complete the drawing.
- Take your face drawing and divide it into planes (using straight line only), making value differences to show its three-dimensional quality. Look for the darkest areas of your face and do them first, then the lightest. You will see these differences by checking the mirror. Or do a pencil drawing first, then work from that.
- Scan a black-and-white photocopy into the computer of a person whom you admire (musician, actress, political figure, scientist, etc.). Think how you can transform the photograph—by cutting out portions, reducing sections, repeating portions of the face, combining line—while moving it about or making an unusual color scheme.
- Make a metamorphosis of one object into another on the computer. For example, begin with something such as an eagle, and in a series of four pictures let it become an airplane. Mount these four pictures side by side to display them.
- This-five step project takes time, but is beautiful when all five projects are printed and displayed side by side. (Project developed by art teacher Timothy Smith.)

  Working from a black-and-white photocopy of a masterpiece, do a line drawing directly on the screen.

  Working in black and white, use textures to make the values approximate those that you see in the black-and-white photocopy.

  Do a color interpretation to make the picture match the original reproduction as closely as possible.

  Do an abstraction of the original reproduction, eliminating detail as much as possible and using as many of the functions of the computer graphics program as possible.

  Cut and paste from your "original reproduction" to make a total abstraction, moving portions from one area to another.

SECTION 10
MUSEUMS

List 10–1   Quotations Related to Museums

"We should comport ourselves with the masterpieces of art as with exalted personages—stand quietly before them and wait till they speak to us."

—ARTHUR SCHOPENHAUER

"Art's whatever you choose to frame."

—FLEUR ADCOCK

"Any art communicates what you're in the mood to receive."

—LARRY RIVERS

"There is no abstract art. You must always start with something."

—PABLO RUIZ Y PICASSO

"A room hung with pictures is a room hung with thoughts."

—SIR JOSHUA REYNOLDS

"I believe that if it were left to artists to choose their own labels, most would choose none."

—BEN SHAHN

"Everyone has talent at twenty-five; the difficulty is to have it at fifty."

—EDGAR DEGAS

"Art is a way of expression that has to be understood by everyone, everywhere."

—RUFINO TAMAYO

List 10–2   Museums Devoted to the Work of One Artist

Benton. *Thomas Hart Benton Home and Studio State Historical Site,* 3616 Belleview, Kansas City, Missouri

Bourdelle. *Musée Bourdelle,* 16 Rue Antoine Bourdelle, Paris

Cezanne. *Atelier de Cezanne,* 9 Ave. Paul-Cezanne, Aix-en-Provence, France

Chagall. *Musée Marc Chagall,* Ave. du Docteur-Menard and Bd. de Cimiez, Nice, France (*Biblical Message* (17 canvases), sketches, gouaches, sculptures, mosaics, engravings)

Corbusier. *Fondation Le Corbusier,* 10 sq. Docteur-Blanche, Paris

Dali. *Salvador Dali Museum,* 100 3rd St. S., St. Petersburg, Florida (paintings, prints, drawings, objet's d'art)

Delacroix. *Musée Eugene-Delacroix,* 6 Rue de Furstemberg, Paris, France (permanent collection of Delacroix's work and that of his contemporaries)

Durer. *Albrecht Durer House,* Am Tiergartnertor, Albrecht-Durer-Strasse 39, Nuremberg (this home from 1509 houses many of Durer's masterpieces, etchings, and woodcuts)

Gorman. *R.C., Navajo Gallery,* 210 Ledoux, Taos, New Mexico (former home of R.C. Gorman, devoted exclusively to his work)

Gross. *Chaim Gross Studio Museum,* 526 LaGuardia Pl., New York City

Hepworth. *Barbara Hepworth Museum and Sculpture Garden,* Barnoon Hill, St. Ives, Cornwall, England

Hopper. *Hopper House,* 82 N. Broadway, Nyack, New York (Edward Hopper memorabilia, changing art exhibitions)

Lehmbruck. *Wilhelm Lehmbruck,* Dusseldorferstrasse 51, 41 Duisburg, Germany (sculpture, painting, drawings and prints from 1905 to 1919)

Milles. *Millesgarden,* Carl Milles vag # 2, Lidingo, S18134 Stockholm, Sweden (Carl Milles' home and studio also includes an outdoor garden)

List 10–2   Continued

Matisse. *Musée Matisse,* 164 Avenue des Arenes, Nice, France (Matisse's studio, including props used in paintings, oils, drawings, engravings)

Miró. *Joan Miró Foundation,* Monjuich, Barcelona, Spain

Monet. *Musée Marmottan* (Claude Monet's Paris Home), 2 Rue Louis-Boilly, Paris, France ("Monet's Monets," the works he reserved for himself and his family)

Monet. *Musée Claude-Monet,* 84 Rue Claude-Monet, Giverny, near Paris, France (gardens, home, studio, *Musée des Impressionistes Americains* [next to Gardens])

Moore. *Henry Moore Foundation,* Dane Tree House, Much Hadham, Hertfordshire, England (home and studio include more than 25 Moore sculptures)

Moreau. *Musée Gustave-Moreau,* 14 Rue de la Rochefoucault, Paris, France (collection of symbolist paintings by Moreau)

Munch. *Munch Museum,* Toyengata 53, Kampen, Oslo, Norway (1,200 paintings, also engravings, woodcuts, drawings, sculptures, documents)

Noguchi. *Isamu Noguchi Garden Museum,* 32–37 Vernon Blvd., Long Island City, New York (sculpture and Archives of Isamu Noguchi)

O'Keeffe. *Georgia O'Keeffe Foundation,* 217 Johnson St., Santa Fe, New Mexico

Picasso. *Musée Picasso,* 5 Rue de Thorigny, Paris, France (200 paintings, 3,000 drawings, sculpture, ceramics, Picasso's personal art collection)

Picasso. *Musée Picasso,* Chateau Grimaldi, Place du Chateau, Antibes, France (23 paintings, drawings, and ceramics, done in the Chateau in 1946, and donated to the museum)

Picasso. *Musée Picasso,* Carrer Montcada 15–19, Barcelona Spain (2,000 artworks done between the ages of 9 and 22)

Rembrandt. *Rembrandthuis,* Jodenbreestraat 4–6, Amsterdam (Rembrandt's home, with printing press)

Remington. *Remington Art Memorial,* Washington and State Sts., Ogdensburg, New York (Frederic Remington's sketchbooks, letters, watercolors, oils, and sculptures)

Rodin. *Rodin Museum,* 22nd Street and Benjamin Franklin Pkwy., Philadelphia (more than 100 Rodin sculptures including *Gates of Hell, The Thinker, Burghers of Calais, The Age of Bronze*)

Rodin. *Rodin Museum,* 77 Rue de Varenne, Paris (the home of Rodin includes his drawings, original casts, garden sculpture)

Rothko. *Rothko Chapel,* 1409 Sul Ross, Houston, Texas (an installation of late paintings by Mark Rothko)

Rubens. *Peter Paul Rubenstraat,* Antwerp, Belgium (Ruben's home complete with original furnishings, garden, and artwork)

Saint-Gaudens. Augustus, *Saint-Gaudens Historic Site,* Route 12A, Cornish, New Hampshire

Toulouse-Lautrec. *Musée Toulouse-Lautrec,* Palais del la Berbi, Albi, France (large collection of Lautrec's work and that of other modern artists)

Twombly. *Cy Twombly Gallery,* The Menil Collection, 1501 Branard, Houston, Texas (permanent installation of Twombly's paintings, sculpture, and works on paper)

van Gogh. *Vincent van Gogh Museum,* Potterstraat 7, Amsterdam (400 paintings, 200 drawings by van Gogh)

van Gogh. *Vincent van Gogh Foundation,* 16 Rond-Point des Arenes, 13200, Arles, France

Vigeland. *Vigeland Sculpture Park,* Vigeland Museum, Nobelsgt 32, Oslo, Norway (the lifework of Gustave Vigeland, 227 sculptures and monumental groupings)

Warhol. *Andy Warhol Museum,* 117 Sandusky St., Pittsburgh, Pennsylvania

Whistler. *Whistler House Museum of Art,* 243 Worthen St., Lowell, Massachusetts (collection of 19th- and 20th-century American paintings and prints, Frank Benson, Thomas B. Lawson, James McNeill Whistler)

Wright. *Frank Lloyd Wright Foundation,* 951 Chicago Ave., Oak Park, Illinois

Wyeth. *Brandywine River Museum,* U.S. Rte. 1, Chadds Ford, Pennsylvania (work by members of the Wyeth family [and other American 19th- and 20th-century landscape painters])

List 10–3   Museums with Special Folk Art Collections

CALIFORNIA

Craft and Folk Art Museum, 5800 Wilshire Blvd., Los Angeles

Mingei International Museum of World Folk Art, La Jolla

CONNECTICUT

The Marine Historical Association, Inc., Mystic Seaport

DELAWARE

The Henry Francis du Pont Winterthur Museum, Winterthur

DISTRICT OF COLUMBIA

Index of American Design, National Gallery of Art, Constitution Ave. at Sixth St., NW, Washington, DC

GEORGIA

High Museum of Folk Art, Georgia Pacific Center, 30 John Wesley Dobbs Ave., Atlanta

MAINE

Bixler Art and Music Center, American Heritage Collection of Folk Art, Waterville

MASSACHUSETTS

Old Sturbridge Village, Sturbridge

Whaling Museum of the Nantucket Historical Association, Broad St., Nantucket

MICHIGAN

Henry Ford Museum and Greenfield Village, Oakwood, Dearborn

NEW MEXICO

Museum of International Folk Art, Museum of New Mexico, Santa Fe

NEW YORK

The Cooper Union Museum, Cooper Sq., New York City

Museum of American Folk Art, Building 2, Lincoln Sq. Columbus Ave. at 65th, New York City

New York State Historical Association, Fenimore House, Cooperstown

The Shaker Museum, Shaker Museum Rd., Old Chatham

NORTH CAROLINA

Old Salem and Museum of Early Southern Decorative Arts, 600 South Main St., Winston-Salem

OKLAHOMA

National Cowboy Hall of Fame and Western Heritage Center, 1700 NE 63rd St., Oklahoma City

SOUTH DAKOTA

Museum of Pioneer Life, 1311 South Duff, Mitchell

TEXAS

Panhandle-Plains Historical Museum, Canyon

UTAH

Chase Home Museum of Utah Folk Art, 617 East South Temple, Salt Lake City

VERMONT

The Bennington Museum, West Main Street, Bennington

Shelburne Museum, U.S. 7, Shelburne

VIRGINIA

Abby Aldrich Rockefeller American Folk Art Collection, South England Street, Williamsburg

The Mariners Museum, Newport News

WISCONSIN

Circus World Museum, 426 Water Street, Baraboo

FOLK ART MUSEUMS IN FOREIGN COUNTRIES

American Museum in Britain, (Claverton Manor), Bath, England

Benaki Museum, Odos Koumbari, Athens, Greece

British Folk Art Collection, Compton Verney, Warwickshire (near Stratford-on-Avon), England (Coptic textiles, Mycenean gold cups, gold jewelry)

National Folklore Museum of Korea, Seoul, Korea

Norsk Folkemuseum, Bygdoy, Museum Veien 10, 2. Oslo

List 10-3 Continued

Drawn after *The Quilting Bee,* 1950, Anna Mary (Grandma) Moses, private collection

List 10-4 American Museums with Special Collections of Ancient and Classical Art

Bowdoin College Museum of Art, Walker Art Building, Brunswick, Maine

Brooklyn Museum, 200 Eastern Pkwy., Brooklyn, New York

California Palace of the Legion of Honor, San Francisco, California

Cleveland Museum of Art, 11150 East Blvd., Cleveland, Ohio

The Cloisters, Fort Tryon Park, New York City

Detroit Institute of Arts, 5200 Woodward Ave., Detroit, Michigan

Fogg Art Museum, 32 Quincy St., Cambridge, Massachusetts

Getty Art Museum, Los Angeles, California

Museum of Fine Arts, 465 Huntington Ave., Boston, Massachusetts

St. Louis Art Museum, 1 Fine Arts Dr., St. Louis, Missouri

List 10-5   American Museums of Late Modern and Contemporary Art

ARIZONA

Museum of Art, 140 N. Main, Tucson

CALIFORNIA

Getty Museum, Los Angeles

Los Angeles County Museum of Art, 5905 Wilshire Blvd., Los Angeles

Museum of Contemporary Art of San Diego, 700 Prospect St., La Jolla

The Museum of Contemporary Art (MOCA), 250 S.Grand Ave., Los Angeles

MOCA at the Temporary Contemporary, 152 N. Central Ave., Los Angeles

Pasadena Museum of Modern Art, Colorado and Orange Grove Blvds., Pasadena

San Francisco Museum of Modern Art, 151 Third St., San Francisco

CONNECTICUT

Housatonic Museum of Art, 510 Barnum Ave., Bridgeport

New England Center for Contemporary Art, Brooklyn

Wadsworth Atheneum, 600 Main St., Hartford

Yale University Art Gallery, 1111 Chapel St., New Haven

DISTRICT OF COLUMBIA

Corcoran Gallery of Art, 17th St. and New York Ave., NW

Hirshhorn Museum and Sculpture Garden, Independence Ave. at 7th St., SW

National Gallery of Art, Constitution Ave. at 4th St., NW

Phillips Collection, 1600 21st St., NW

FLORIDA

Norton Gallery of Art, 1451 S. Olive Ave., West Palm Beach

GEORGIA

Georgia Museum of Art, 2023 University of Georgia, Athens

HAWAII

The Contemporary Museum, 2411 Makiki Heights Dr., Honolulu

ILLINOIS

Art Institute of Chicago, Michigan Avenue at Adams St., Chicago

Museum of Contemporary Art, 237 E. Ontario St., Chicago

INDIANA

Art Gallery, Ball State University, 2000 University Ave., Muncie

Indiana University Art Museum, Indiana University, Bloomington

IOWA

Museum of Art, University of Iowa, Riverside Dr., Iowa City

MAINE

Ogunquit Museum of American Art, 183 Shore Rd. PO Box 815, Ogunquit

Smith College Museum of Art, Elm St. at Bedford Terrace, Northampton

MASSACHUSETTS

Museum of Fine Arts, 49 Chestnut St., Springfield

MICHIGAN

Detroit Institute of Arts, 5200 Woodward Ave., Detroit

MINNESOTA

University Gallery, 333 E. River Rd., Minneapolis

Walker Art Center, Vineland Pl., Minneapolis

MISSOURI

Forum for Contemporary Art, 3540 Washington Ave., St. Louis

Kemper Museum of Contemporary Art and Design, 4420 Warwick Blvd., Kansas City

NEBRASKA

Sheldon Memorial Art Gallery and Sculpture Garden, 12th and R Sts., Lincoln

NEW JERSEY

New Jersey State Museum, 205 W. State St., Trenton

NEW MEXICO

Georgia O'Keeffe Museum, Santa Fe

NEW YORK

Adolf and Esther Gottlieb Foundation, Inc., 380 West Broadway, New York City

Albright-Knox Art Gallery, 1285 Elmwood Ave., Buffalo

Dia Center for the Arts, 542 West 22nd St., New York City

IBM Corporation, Old Orchard Road, Armonk

List 10–5   Continued

NEW YORK (cont.)

Metropolitan Museum of Art, 1000 Fifth Ave., New York City

Munson-Williams-Proctor Institute Museum of Art, 310 Genessee St., Utica

Museum of Modern Art, 11 West 53rd St., New York City

New School for Social Research, 66 West 12th St., New York City

Solomon R. Guggenheim Museum, 1071 5th Ave., New York City

Whitney Museum of American Art, 925 Madison Ave. at 75th St., New York City

Vassar College Art Gallery, Raymond Ave., Poughkeepsie

NORTH CAROLINA

Weatherspoon Art Gallery, University of North Carolina, Spring Garden St. at Tate St., Greensboro

OHIO

Akron Art Museum, 70 E. Market St., Akron

Cleveland Museum of Art, 11150 East Blvd., Cleveland

Dayton Art Institute, 456 Belmonte Park N., Dayton

OREGON

Museum of Art, University of Oregon, Eugene

PENNSYLVANIA

Philadelphia Museum of Art, 26th St. & Benjamin Franklin Pkwy., Philadelphia

TEXAS

Archer M. Huntington Art Gallery, University of Texas, 23rd & San Jacinto Sts., Austin

Dallas Museum of Fine Arts, 1717 N. Harwood, Dallas

Modern Art Museum of Fort Worth, 1309 Montgomery St., Forth Worth

San Antonio Museum of Art, 200 W. Jones Ave., San Antonio

VERMONT

Bundy Art Gallery, Waitsfield

VIRGINIA

Chrysler Museum at Norfolk, 245 W. Olney Road, Norfolk

Hermitage Foundation Museum, 3637 N. Shore Rd., Norfolk

WASHINGTON

Henry Art Gallery, Seattle

WEST VIRGINIA

Huntington Museum of Art, 2033 McCoy Rd., Huntington

WISCONSIN

Milwaukee Art Center, 750 N. Lincoln Memorial Dr., Milwaukee

WYOMING

Fine Arts Center, Rock Springs

List 10–6   Foreign Museums of Contemporary Art

AUSTRALIA

Art Gallery of South Australia, North Terrace, Adelaide 5000

Australian National Gallery, GPO Box 1150, Canberra

AUSTRIA

Graphische Sammlung Albertina, Augustinerstrasse 1, Vienna

Osterreichische Galerie, Prinz-Eugen-Strasse 27, Vienna

BELGIUM

Modern Art Museum/Royal Fine Arts Museums of Belgium, 1 Place Royale, Brussels

Musées Royaux des Beaux-Arts de Belgique, 9 rue du Musée, Brussels

Museum van Hedendaagse Kunst, Hofbouwlaan, Ghent 9000

CANADA

Montreal Museum of Fine Arts, 1379 Sherbrooke St. West, Montreal, Quebec

National Gallery of Canada, 380 Sussex Drive, Ottawa, Ontario

Ydessa Hendeles Art Foundation, 778 King St. W, Toronto, Ontario

DENMARK

Louisiana Museum of Modern Art, Gl Strandvej 13, Humlebaek 3050

ENGLAND

City Art Gallery, Nottingham Castle, Nottingham

Cotton's Atrium, Cotton's Centre, Hays Lane, London

Courtauld Institute Galleries, Somerset House, Strand, London

Fitzwilliam Museum, Trumpington St., Cambridge

Lady Lever Art Gallery, Port Sunlight Village, Bebington

National Gallery, Trafalgar Square, London

Peter Stuyvesant Foundation Limited, Oxford Road, Aylesbury, Bucks

Saatchi Collection, 98A Boundary Rd., London

Salford Art Gallery and Museum, Peel Park, Salford

Southampton City Art Gallery, Civic Centre, Southampton

Tate Gallery, Bankside, London

FRANCE

Musée Cantini, 19 rue Grignan, Marseille 13000

Musée d'Art Moderne de la Ville de Paris, 11 Av. du President Wilson, Paris

Musée de Pontoise, 4 rue Lemercier, Cergy-Pontoise

Musée de Saint-Etienne, 13 bis rue Gambetta, Hotel de Villeneuve, Saint-Etienne

Musée des Beaux-Arts, 10 rue Georges Clemenceau, Nantes

Musée National d'Art Moderne, rue Beaubourg, Paris

GERMANY

Akademie der Kunste, Bildende Kunst, Hanseatenweg 10, Berlin

Goetz Collection, Oberfohringer Strasse 103, 81925 Munich

Kaiser Wilhelm Museum, Karlsplatz 35, Krefeld

Karl Ernst Osthaus-Museum, Hochstrasse 73, Hagen

Kunsthalle Bremen, Am Wall 207, Bremen

Museum Folkwang, Goethestrasse 41, Essen

Staatsgalerie Stuttgart, Konrad-Adenauer Strasse 30–32, Stuttgart

Von der Heydt-Museum, Turmhof 8, Wuppertal

Westfallsches Landesmuseum, Domplatz 10, Munster

ISRAEL

Israel Museum, PO Box 71117, Jerusalem

ITALY

Comitato Tina Modotti, via Mazzini 9, Udine

Fondo Rivetti per l'Arte, via Botticelli 80, Turin

Galleria Nazionale d'Arte Moderna e Contemporanea, vialle Belle Arti 131, Rome

Panza's Villa, Varese (working in conjunction with the Guggenheim in New York)

Peggy Guggenheim Collection, Palazzo Venier dei Leoni, 701 Dorsoduro, Venice

JAPAN

Contemporary Sculpture Centre, 4.20.2. Ebisu Shibuya-Ku, Tokyo

Museum Marugame Hirai, 538 8 Cho-Me, Doki-Cho, Marugame-Shi, Kagawa

Naoshima Museum, Gotanji, Naoshima-cho, Kagawa-gun: Kagawa-ken 761–31

Paleis Huis Ten Bosch, Sasebo City, Nagasaki Prefecture

List 10–6   Continued

MEXICO

Ministry of Education, Republica de Argentina, 18 Colonia Centro, Mexico City

Museo de Arte Moderno, Paseo de la reforma y Ghandi, Mexico City

NETHERLANDS

De Pont Foundation, Wilhelminapark 1, Tilburg

Museum Boymans-van Beuningen, Museumpark 18–20, Rotterdam

Stedelijk Museum of Modern Art, Paulus Potterstraat 13, Amsterdam

SOUTH AMERICA

Museu de Arte Moderna, Av. Infante Dom Henrique 85, Rio de Janeiro, Brazil

SPAIN

Fundacion Caja de Pensiones, Sala de Exposiciones, Calle Serrano 60, Madrid

Guggenheim Museum, Bilbao

IFEMA Collection, Avenida Portugal s/n, Madrid

SWEDEN

Modern Art Museum, Skeppsholmen Island, 111 49, Stockholm

Moderna Museet, Sparvagnshallarna, Box 16392, Stockholm

Nordenhake, Fredsgaten 12, Stockholm

SWITZERLAND

Adolf Wolfli Foundation, Museum of Fine Arts, Hodlerstrasse 12, Berne

Kunsthaus, Heimplatz 1, Zurich

Petit Palais, 2 Terrasse Saint-Victor, Geneva

OTHER

Hermitage Museum, Dworzowaja Nabereshnaja 34–36, St. Petersburg, Russia

Muzeum Sztuki w Lodzi, ut Wieckowskiego 36, Lodz, Poland

Nasjonalgalleriet, Universitetsgaten 13, Oslo, Norway

Rabindra Shavan Archive, Visva-Sharati University, Santini Ketan, West Bengal, India

Scottish National Gallery of Modern Art, Belford Road, Edinburgh, Scotland

Standard Bank Collection, Witwatersrand, University Art Galleries, Private Bag 3, Witwatersrand 2050, Johannesburg, South Africa

State Russian Museum, Michaijlovskij Palace, Inzeneraja ul 4, St. Petersburg, Russia

Waikato Museum of Art and History, Grantham St., Hamilton, Auckland, New Zealand

List 10–7   Museums with Outstanding Photographic Collections

CALIFORNIA

Ansel Adams Center/Friends of Photography, 250 4th St., San Francisco

Getty Museum, Getty Center Drive, Los Angeles

Museum of Photographic Arts, Casa de Balboa, Balboa Park, San Diego

DISTRICT OF COLUMBIA

Library of Congress, 101 Independence Avenue at 1st St., SE, Washington, DC

ILLINOIS

Art Institute of Chicago, Michigan Ave. at Adams St., Chicago

The Museum of Contemporary Photography, Columbia College, 600 S. Michigan Ave., Chicago

Museum of Holography/Chicago, 1134 W. Washington Blvd., Chicago

NEW YORK

International Center of Photography Midtown, 1133 Ave. of the Americas, New York City

International Museum of Photography at George Eastman House, 900 East Ave., Rochester

Metropolitan Museum of Art, 1000 Fifth Ave., New York City

Museum of Modern Art, 11 West 53rd St., New York City

OTHER AMERICAN MUSEUMS WITH SPECIAL PHOTOGRAPHIC COLLECTIONS

Center for Creative Photography, University of Arizona, Tucson

Hallmark Photographic Collection, Kansas City, Missouri

International Photography Hall of Fame and Museum, 2100 NE 52nd St., Oklahoma City, Oklahoma

INTERNATIONAL COLLECTIONS OF PHOTOGRAPHY

Agfa Foto-Historama im Wallraf-Richartz Museum, Museum Ludwig, Cologne, Germany

British Museum, Great Russell St., London, England

Musée d'Orsay, 1 Rue de Bellechasse, Paris

National Museum of Photography, Film and Television, Bradford, England

Royal Photographic Society, Bath, England

Four-panel screen, Drawing from *Fans and Stream,* Sakai Hoitsu, 1820–1828, St. Louis Art Museum

List 10–8   American Museums with Special Emphasis on Asian Art

CALIFORNIA

Asian Art Museum, Golden Gate Park, San Francisco

Fine Arts Gallery, Plaza de Panama, Balboa Park, San Diego

Japanese American National Museum, 369 E. 1st St., Los Angeles

Korean American Museum, 3333 Wilshire Blvd., Los Angeles

M.H. de Young Memorial Museum, Golden Gate Park, San Francisco

Pacific Asia Museum, 46 N. Robles Ave., Palo Alto

CONNECTICUT

Yale Art Gallery, 1111 Chapel St., New Haven

DISTRICT OF COLUMBIA

Arthur M. Sackler Gallery, Smithsonian Institution, 1050 Independence Ave. SW

Freer Gallery, 12th St. and Jefferson Dr., SW

ILLINOIS

Art Institute of Chicago, Michigan Ave. at Adams St., Chicago

Chinese Museum, 2002 S. Wentworth Ave., Chicago

Oriental Institute Museum, 1155 E. 58th St., Chicago

INDIANA

Indianapolis Museum of Art, 1200 W. 38th St., Indianapolis

MASSACHUSETTS

Fogg Art Museum, 32 Quincy St., Cambridge

Mount Holyoke College Art Museum, South Hadley

Museum of Fine Arts, 465 Huntington Ave., Boston

Museum of Fine Arts, 49 Chestnut St., Springfield

Museum of the American China Trade, 215 Adams Street, Milton

Worcester Art Museum, Worcester

MINNESOTA

Minneapolis Institute of Arts, 2400 Third Ave. S., Minneapolis

Minnesota Museum of Art, 75 West 5th, St. Paul

MISSOURI

Nelson-Atkins Museum of Art, 4525 Oak St., Kansas City

NEW JERSEY

Newark Museum, 49 Washington St., Newark

Princeton University Art Museum, Princeton

NEW YORK

The Asia Society Galleries, 725 Park Ave., New York City

Brooklyn Museum, 200 Eastern Pkwy., Brooklyn

Japan Society Gallery, 333 E. 47th St., New York City

Metropolitan Museum of Art, 1000 Fifth Ave., New York City

NORTH CAROLINA

Mint Museum of Art, 2730 Randolph Rd., Charlotte

OHIO

Cleveland Museum of Art, 11150 East Blvd., Cleveland

Dayton Art Institute, 456 Belmonte Park, Dayton

Johnson Museum, Coshocton

Museum of Burmese Arts, Granville

Toledo Museum of Art, Toledo

OREGON

Museum of Art, University of Oregon, Eugene

Portland Art Museum, Portland

PENNSYLVANIA

Everhart Museum, Nay Aug Park, Scranton

University of Pennsylvania Institute of Contemporary Art, 118 S. 36th St., Philadelphia

RHODE ISLAND

Rhode Island School of Design Museum, 224 Benefit St., Providence

Rockefeller Library, Providence

SOUTH CAROLINA

Florence Museum, Florence

TEXAS

Museum of Oriental Cultures, 418 Peoples St., Corpus Christi

VIRGINIA

Hermitage Foundation Museum, 3637 N. Shore Rd., Norfolk

WASHINGTON

Seattle Asian Art Museum, 1400 E. Prospect St., Volunteer Park, Seattle

Wing Luke Asian Museum, 407 Seventh Ave. S., Seattle

List 10-9　Museums Related to the Judaic Culture

AMERICA

Jewish Historical Society of Maryland, 15 Lloyd St., Baltimore, Maryland
The Jewish Museum, 1109 Fifth Ave., New York City
Judah L. Magnes Museum, 2911 Russell St., Berkeley, California
Museum of the Southern Jewish Experience, 4915 I-55 North, Jackson, Mississippi
Skirball Museum, 3077 University Ave., Los Angeles, California
Spertus Museum of Judaica, 618 S. Michigan Ave., Chicago, Illinois
Yeshiva University Museum, 2520 Amsterdam Avenue, New York City

OTHER

Jewish Museum, Woburn House, Tavistock Square, London, WCl, England
Jewish Museum, Jachymova 3, 11001, Prague, Czech Republic

List 10-10　American Museums with Special Emphasis on African American Art

Afro-American Historical and Cultural Museum, 7th and Arch Sts., Philadelphia, Pennsylvania
Banneker-Douglass Museum, 84 Franklin St., Annapolis, Maryland
DuSable Museum of African American History, 740 E. 56th Pl., Chicago, Illinois
Great Plains Black Museum, 2213 Lake St., Omaha, Nebraska
Museum for African Art, 593 Broadway, New York City
Museum of African American Art, 1305 N. Florida Ave., Tampa, Florida
Museum of African American Art, 4005 Crenshaw Blvd., Los Angeles
Museum of African American History, Warren and Brush Sts., Detroit, Michigan
National Museum of African Art, 950 Independence Avenue, SW, Washington, DC
San Francisco African American Historical and Cultural Society, Bldg. C, Fort Mason Center, San Francisco, California
The Studio Museum in Harlem, 144 W. 125th St., New York City
Will T. Murphy African American Museum, 2601 Paul Bryant Drive, Tuscaloosa, Alabama

List 10-11　American Museums with Special Emphasis on Hispanic Art

El Museo del Barrio, 1230 Fifth Ave., New York City
The Florida Museum of Hispanic and Latin American Art, 1 NE 40th St., Miami, Florida
Hispanic Society of America, Broadway between 155th and 156th Sts., New York City
Latino Museum of History, Art, and Culture, 112 South Main, Los Angeles, California
Mexican Fine Arts Center Museum, 1852 W. 19th, Chicago, Illinois
The Mexican Museum, Fort Mason Center, Bldg. D., San Francisco, California
Museo del Grabado Latinoamericano Institute of Puerto Rican Culture, Calle San Sebastian, Old San Juan, Puerto Rico

List 10–12   Museums with Special Emphasis on Native American Art

In most cases, only the nearest town is given, although ruins, etc., may only be near the town.

ALASKA

Alaska State Museum, Juneau
Anchorage Historical and Fine Arts Museum, Anchorage
Besh-Ba-Gowah, south of Glove
Four Story Totem, Juneau
Sheldon Jackson Museum, Sitka
Sitka National Monument, Sitka
Tongass Historical Society Museum, Ketchican

ALABAMA

Indian Mound and Museum, Florence
Mound State Monument, Moundville
Russell Cave National Monument, Bridgeport

Raven Mask, 1992

ARIZONA

Apache Culture Center, Fort Apache
Arizona State Museum, Tucson
Canyon de Chelly, Chinley
Casa Grande Ruins, Coolidge
Colorado River Tribes Indian Museum, Parker
Gila River Indian Museum, Sacaton
Grand Canyon National Park, South Rim and North Rim
Heard Museum, Phoenix
Hopi Museum and Cultural Center, Second Mesa
Kinishba Pueblo, west of Whiteriver
Montezuma Castle National Monument, Camp Verde
Museum of Northern Arizona, Flagstaff
Navajo National Monument, Tonalea
Navajo Tribal Museum, Window Rock
Oraibi Pueblo, southeast of Tuba City
Painted Rocks State Park
Pueblo Grande Museum, Phoenix
Puerco Ruin, Petrified Forest State Park
Signal Mountain, Tucson Mountain Park
Tonto National Monument, Roosevelt
Tuzigoot National Monument, Clarkdale
Walnut Canyon, Flagstaff
Walpi Pueblo, Tuba City
Wupatki National Monument, Flagstaff

ARKANSAS

Caddo Burial Mounds, Murphreesboro
Hampson Memorial Museum of Archaeology, Wilson
Henderson State University Museum, Arkadelphia
University of Arkansas Museum, Fayetteville

CALIFORNIA

Adan E. Treganza Anthropology Museum, San Francisco
Antelope Valley Indian Research Museum, Lancaster
Big and Little Petroglyph Canyons, near China Lake
Bowers Memorial Museum, Santa Ana
Calico Mountains Archaeological Project, Barstow
California State Indian Museum, Sacramento
Catalina Island Museum, Santa Catalina Island
Clarke Memorial Museum, Eureka
Coso Range: Petroglyph Canyon, Renegade Canyon, Sheep Canyon
Coyote Hills Regional Park, Alvarado
Hupa Tribal Museum, Hoopa
Indian Grinding Rock State Historical Monument, Pine Grove
Joshua Tree National Monument, Twentynine Palms
Kern County Museum, Bakersfield
Los Angeles County Museum of History and Science, Los Angeles
Lowie Museum of Anthropology, University of California, Berkeley
Malki Museum, Banning
Oakland Museum, History Division, Oakland
Pioneer Museum and Haggin Galleries, Stockton
Riverside Municipal Museum, Riverside
Sacramento Indian Center, Sacramento
San Bernardino County Museum, Redlands
San Diego Museum of Man, San Diego
Santa Barbara Museum of Natural History, Santa Barbara
Sierra Mono Museum, North Fork
Southwest Museum, Los Angeles
State Lake State Park, Kelseyville
Tulare County Museum, Visalia

COLORADO

Colorado Springs Fine Art Center, Colorado Springs
Colorado State Museum, Denver

List 10–12   Continued

COLORADO (cont.)

Denver Art Museum, Denver
Denver Museum of Natural History, Denver
Gem Village Museum, Bayfield
Koshare Indian Kiva Museum, La Junta
Lowry Pueblo Ruins, Pleasant View
Mesa Verde National Park, Cortez
Pioneers Museum, Colorado Springs
Southern Ute Arts and Crafts, Ignacio
University of Colorado Museum, Boulder
Ute Indian Museum, Montrose

CONNECTICUT

Bruce Museum, Greenwich
Peabody Museum of Natural History, New Haven
Slater Memorial Museum, Norwich
Tantaquidgeon Indian Museum, Uncasville

DISTRICT OF COLUMBIA

Museum of Natural History, Smithsonian Institution
U.S. Department of the Interior Museum

DELAWARE

Island Field Archaeological Museum, South Bowers

FLORIDA

Crystal River State Archaeo-
    logical Site, Crystal River
Florida State Museum,
    Gainesville
Miccosukee Cultural Center
    and Museum, Miami
Museum of Florida History,
    Tallahassee

Zuni Pot, red and black
on white

Seminole Museum, West Hollywood
Seminole Arts and Crafts Center, Fort Lauderdale
Southeast Museum of the North American Indian,
    Marathon
Temple Mound Museum and Park, Fort Walton Beach

GEORGIA

Creek Museum, Indian Springs
Etowah Mounds Archaeological Area, Cartersville
Kolomoki Mounds State Park, Blakely
New Echota Historic Site, Calhoun
Ocmulgee National Monument, Macon

IDAHO

Clothes Horse Trading Post, Fort Hall
Nez Perce National Historic Park, Spalding

ILLINOIS

Cahokia Mounds State Park, East St. Louis
Dickson Mounds Museum of the Illinois Indian, Lewis-
    town
Field Museum of Natural History, Chicago
Illinois State Museum, Springfield
Mitchell Indian Museum, Kendall College, Evanston
Stockade, Galena
University of Illinois Museum of Natural History, Ur-
    bana

INDIANA

Angel Mounds State Memorial, Evansville
Children's Museum, Indianapolis
Eiteljorg Museum of American Indians and Western
    Art, Indianapolis
Indiana University Museum, Bloomington
Mounds State Park, Anderson
Museum of Indian Heritage, Indianapolis
Puterbaugh Museum, Peru

IOWA

Davenport Museum, Davenport
Effigy Mounds National Monument, McGregor

KANSAS

El Quartelejo Indian Kiva Museum, Scott City
Fort Larned National Historic Site, Larned
Huron Indian Cemetery, Huron Park, Kansas City
Indian Burial Pit, Salina
Inscription Rock, Lake Kanpolis State Park, Ellsworth
Kansas Sac and Fox Museum, Highland
Kansas State Historical Society, Topeka
Pawnee Indian Village Museum, Belleville

KENTUCKY

Adena Park, Lexington
Ancient Buried City, Cairo
Museum of Anthropology, U. of Kentucky, Lexington
J.B. Speed Art Museum, Louisville

LOUISIANA

Louisiana State Exhibit Museum, Shreveport
Marksville Prehistoric Indian Park State Monument,
    Marksville

MAINE

Robert Abbe Museum of Stone Age Antiquities, Bar
    Harbor
Wilson Museum, Castine

© 1998 Prentice Hall

List 10–12   Continued

MARYLAND

Baltimore Museum of Art, Baltimore

MASSACHUSETTS

Bronson Museum, Attleboro
Fruitlands Museum, Harvard University, Cambridge
Longhouse Museum, Grafton
Memorial Hall, Deerfield
Peabody Museum, Salem
Peabody Museum of Archaeology and Ethnology, Harvard University, Cambridge
Plimoth Plantation, Inc., Plymouth
Robert S. Peabody Foundation for Archaeology, Andover
Springfield Science Museum, Springfield

MICHIGAN

Chief Blackbird Home Museum, Harbor Springs
Cranbrook Institute of Science, Bloomfield Hills
Fort Wayne Military Museum, Detroit
Grand Rapids Public Museum, Grand Rapids
Great Lakes Indian Museum, Cross Village
Jesse Besser Museum, Alpena
Kingman Museum of Natural History, Battle Creek
Norton Mounds, south of Grand Rapids
University of Michigan Exhibit Museum, Ann Arbor
Wayne State University Museum of Anthropology, Detroit

MINNESOTA

Crow Wing County Historical Society, Brainerd
Mille Lacs State Indian Museum, Mille Lacs
Pipestone National Monument, Pipestone
St. Louis County Historical Society, Duluth
The Science Museum of Minnesota, St. Paul

MISSISSIPPI

Choctaw Museum of the Southern Indian, Philadelphia
Emerald Mound, Natchez
Lauren Rogers Library and Museum, Laurel
Natchez Trace Visitor Center, Tupelo

MISSOURI

Graham Cave State Park, Danville
Kansas City Museum of History and Science, Kansas City
Lyman Archaeological Research Center and Hamilton Field School, (Utz Site), Marshall
Missouri State Museum, Jefferson City
Museum of Anthropology, Columbia
Museum of Science and Natural History, St. Louis

Nelson-Atkins Museum of Art, Kansas City
Ralph Foster Museum, Point Lookout
St. Joseph Museum, St. Joseph
Washington State Park, near DeSoto

MONTANA

Cheyenne Arts and Crafts Shop, Lame Deer
Chief Plenty Coups Museum, Pryor
Custer–Sitting Bull Battlefield Museum, near Hardin

Raven Clan Hat, Chilkat-Tlingit, early 19th century

H. Earl Clack Memorial Museum, Havre
Mac's Museum of Natural History, Broadus
Museum of the Plains Indians, Browning
Pioneer Museum, Glasgow
Poplar Indian Arts and Crafts Museum, Poplar

NEBRASKA

Fort Robinson Museum, Nebraska State Historical Society, Fort Robinson
Fur Trade Museum, Chadron
Nebraska State Historical Society, Lincoln
Pioneers Antelope County Historical Museum, Neligh
University of Nebraska State Museum, Lincoln

NEVADA

Lost City Museum of Archaeology, Lake Mead

NEW HAMPSHIRE

Dartmouth College Museum, Hanover

NEW JERSEY

Hopewell Museum, Hopewell
New Jersey State Museum, Trenton
Newark State Museum, Newark
Paterson Museum, Paterson

NEW MEXICO

Abon State Monument, Albuquerque
Acoma Pueblo, Casa Blanca
American Indian Arts Museum, Santa Fe
Anthropology Museum, Eastern New Mexico University, Portales
Aztec Ruins National Monument, Aztec
Bandelier National Monument, Los Alamos
Bien Mur Indian Market Center, Sandia Pueblo
Chaco Canyon National Monument, Bloomfield

List 10-12   Continued

NEW MEXICO (cont.)

Coronado State Monument, Bernalillo
Gila Cliff Ruins, Gila Hot Springs
Indian Pueblo Cultural Center, Albuquerque
Institute of American Indian Arts Museum, Santa Fe
Jicarilla Arts and Crafts Shop/Museum, Dulce
Kwilleylekia Ruins, Cliff
Maxwell Museum of Anthropology, Albuquerque
Mescalero Apache Cultural Center, Mescalero
Millicent Rogers Museum, Taos
Museum of Navajo Ceremonial Art, Santa Fe
Museum of Indian Arts and Culture, Santa Fe
Museum of New Mexico, Santa Fe
New Mexico State University, Las Cruces
O'ke Oweenge Crafts Cooperative, San Juan Pueblo
Palace of the Governors, Santa Fe
Pecos National Monument, Pecos
Picuris Pueblo, Taos
Puye Cliff Ruins, Santa Clara Reservation, Española
Red Rock Museum, Church Rock
Salmon Ruins Museum, Bloomfield
San Ildefonso Pueblo Museum, Santa Fe
San Juan Pueblo, Española
Sandia Man Cave, Albuquerque
Santa Clara Pueblo, Santa Fe
Taos Pueblo, Taos
Wheelwright Museum of the American Indian, Santa Fe
Zia Pueblo, Santa Ana
Zuni Pueblo, Gallup
Zuni Craftsmen Cooperative Association, Zuni

NEW YORK

Akwesasne Museum, Hogansburg
American Indian Community House Gallery, New York City
American Museum of Natural History, New York City
Brooklyn Museum, Brooklyn
Buffalo and Erie County Historical Society, Buffalo
Buffalo Museum of Science, Buffalo
Canandaigua Historical Society, Canandaigua
Castile Historical Society Museum, Castile
Cayuga Museum of History and Art, Auburn
Chemung County Historical Museum, Elmira

Deer Mask, 800–1400, AD, Key Marco, Florida

Cooperstown Indian Museum, Cooperstown
Fort Plain Museum, Fort Plain
Fort William Henry Restoration and Museum, Lake George
Iroquois Indian Museum, Caverns Road, Howes Cave, New York
Mohawk-Caughnawaga Museum, Fonda
Museum of the American Indian (The Heye Foundation), New York City
New York State Museum and Science Service, Albany
Owasco Indian Village, Owasco
Oysterponds Historical Society, Orient
Rochester Museum and Science Center, Rochester
Six Nations Indian Museum, Onchiota
The Turtle: Native American Center of the Living Arts, Niagara Falls
Yager Museum and Library, Oneonta

NORTH CAROLINA

Museum of the American Indian, Boone
Museum of the Cherokee Indian, Cherokee
Oconaluftee Indian Village, Cherokee
Town Creek Indian Mound, Mount Gilead

NORTH DAKOTA

Three Affiliated Tribes Museum, New Town

OHIO

Allen County Museum, Lima
Butler Institute of American Art, Youngstown
Cincinnati Museum of Natural History, Cincinnati
Cleveland Museum of Art, Cleveland
Cleveland Museum of Natural History, Cleveland
Fort Ancient State Memorial, Lebanon
Indian Museum, Piqua
Johnson-Humrickhouse Memorial Museum, Coshocton
Miamisburg Mound State Memorial, Miamisburg
Mound City Group National Monument, Chillicothe
Ohio Historical Society, Columbus
Ohio State Museum, Columbus
Seip Mound, Bainbridge
Serpent Mound State Memorial, Peebles
Story Mound, Chillicothe
Western Reserve Historical Society, Cleveland

OKLAHOMA

Anadarko Museum, Anadarko
Bacone College, Ataloa Lodge Museum, Muskogee

List 10–12   Continued

OKLAHOMA (Cont.)

Caddo Indian Museum, Caddo

Cherokee Center, Tahlequah

Cherokee History Museum, Tahlequah

Creek Indian Nation Council House, Okmulgee

Five Civilized Tribes Museum, Muskogee

J. Willis Stovall Museum, University of Oklahoma, Norman

Kerr Museum, Poteau

Museum of the Great Plains, Lawton

Oklahoma Historical Society, Oklahoma City

Oklahoma Indian Arts and Crafts Cooperative, Anadarko

Osage Tribal Museum, Pawhuska

Ottawa County Historical Society, Miami

Pawnee Bill Museum, Pawnee

Philbrook Art Center, Tulsa

Ponca City Indian Museum, Ponca City

Red Earth Indian Center, Kirkpatrick Center, Oklahoma City

Seminole Nation Museum, Wewoka

Sequoyah's Home, Sallisaw

Southern Plains Indian Museum, Anadarko

Thomas Gilcrease Institute, Tulsa

Tsa-La-Gi Indian Village, Park Hill

Woolaroc Museum, Bartlesville

OREGON

Collier State Park, Klamath Falls

Coos-Curry Museum, North Bend

Horner Museum, Corvallis

Klamath County Museum, Klamath Falls

Museum of Natural History, University of Oregon, Eugene

Portland Art Museum, Portland

PENNSYLVANIA

American Indian Museum, Harmony

American Indian Museum, Pittsburgh

Carnegie Museum of Natural History, Butler

E.M. Parker Indian Museum, Brookville

Everhard Museum, Scranton

Hershey Museum, Hershey

Indian Steps Museum, east of York

University Museum, Philadelphia

RHODE ISLAND

Haffenreffer Museum, Brown University, Bristol

The Museum of Natural History, Roger Williams Park, Providence

Tomaquag Indian Museum, Exeter

SOUTH DAKOTA

Badlands National Monument, Rapid City

Buechel Memorial Sioux Indian Museum, St. Francis

H.V. Johnston Cultural Center, Eagle Butte

Indian Arts Museum, Martin

Land of the Sioux Museum, Mobridge

Mari Sandoz Museum, Pine Ridge

Museum of the University of South Dakota, Vermillion

Pettigrew Museum, Sioux Falls

Red Cloud Indian Museum, Pine Ridge

Robinson Museum, Pierre

Sioux Indian Museum, Rapid City

TENNESSEE

Chucalissa Indian Town and Museum, Memphis

Lookout Mountain Museum, Lookout Mountain

Frank H. McClung Museum, University of Tennessee, Knoxville

Shiloh Mounds, Shiloh National Military Park, Savannah

TEXAS

Alabama-Coushatta Indian Museum, Livingston

Alibates Flint Quarries National Monument, Sanford

Dallas Museum of Fine Arts, Dallas

El Paso Centennial Museum, University of Texas, El Paso

Fort Concho Preservation and Museum, San Angelo

Fort Worth Museum of Science and History, Fort Worth

Indian Museum, Harwood

Museum of Texas Tech University, Lubbock

Museum of the Big Bend, Alpine

Museum of the Department of Anthropology, University of Texas, Austin

Panhandle-Plains Historical Museum, Canyon

Texas Memorial Museum, University of Texas, Austin

Tigua Indian Reservation Cultural Center, El Paso

The Wilderness Park Museum, El Paso

Ysleta Mission, El Paso

UTAH

Anasazi Indian Village State Historical Site, Escalante

Anthropology Museum, Brigham Young University, Provo

Canyonlands National Park, Moab

List 10–12   Continued

UTAH (cont.)

Dr. and Mrs. William R. Palmer Memorial Museum, Cedar City

Hovenweep National Monument, Hatch Trading Post, Blanding

Information Center and Museum, Salt Lake City

Natural History State Museum, Vernal

Newspaper Rock, Indian Creek State Park, Monticello

Utah Museum of Natural History, University of Utah, Salt Lake City

VIRGINIA

Hampton Institute Museum, Hampton

Valentine Museum, Richmond

WASHINGTON

Anthropology Museum, Washington State University, Seattle

Burke Museum, University of Washington, Seattle

Colville Cultural Museum, Coulee Dam

Daybreak Star Arts Center, Seattle

Eastern Washington State Historical Society, Spokane

Lelooska's, Ariel

Makah Cultural Center and Museum, Neah Bay

Museum of Anthropology, Pullman

Museum of Native American Cultures, Spokane

North Central Indian Museum, Wenatchee

Pacific Northwest Indian Center, Spokane

Roosevelt Petroglyphs, Roosevelt

Seattle Art Museum, Seattle

Suquamish Museum, Suquamish

State Capitol Museum, Olympia

Tacoma Totem Pole, Tacoma

Tulalip Indian Reservation, Marysville

Wanapum Dam Tour Center, Vantage

Washington State Historical Museum, Tacoma

Washington State Museum, University of Washington, Seattle

Yakima Valley Museum, Yakima

Yakima Nation Museum, Toppenish

WEST VIRGINIA

Archaeology Museum, West Virginia University, Morgantown

Grave Creek Mound State Park, Moundsville

WISCONSIN

Aztalan State Park, Aztalan

Kenosha Public Museum, Kenosha

Lizard Mound State Park, West Bend

Logan Museum of Anthropology, Beloit College, Beloit

Museum of Anthropology, Wisconsin State University, Oshkosh

Neville Public Museum, Green Bay

Ojibwa National Museum, Hayward

Oneida Nation Museum, Oneida

Sheboygan Mound Park, Sheboygan

State Historical Society of Wisconsin, Madison

Venne Art Center, Wausau

Winnebago Indian Museum, Wisconsin Dells

WYOMING

Arapahoe Cultural Museum, Ethete

Buffalo Bill Museum and Plains Indian Museum, Cody

Colter Bay Indian Arts Museum, Colter

Fort Bridger Museum, Fort Bridger

Fort Casper Museum and Historic Site, Casper

Fort Laramie National Historic Site, Fort Laramie

Wyoming State Museum, Cheyenne

CANADA

Glenbow Museum, Calgary, Alberta

Kwagiulth Museum and Cultural Center, Quathiaski Cove, B.C.

Lake of the Woods Ojibwa Cultural Center, Kenora, Ontario

Museum of Anthropology, Vancouver, B.C.

Museum of the Woodland Indian, Brantford, Ontario

Royal British Columbia Museum, Victoria, B.C.

U'Mista Cultural Center, Alert Bay, B.C.

List 10–13   Special Southwestern Petroglyph Sites

Within the protected rock art sites listed below, numerous prehistoric southwestern rock art sites may be visited. For specific locations and directions for viewing, state maps are useful. Several field guides appear at the end of the list for specific western regions.

ARIZONA

Canyon de Chelly National Monument, Chinley
Glen Canyon National Recreational Area, Page
Navajo National Monument, Tonalea
Petrified Forest National Park

COLORADO

Mesa Verde National Park, Cortez
Colorado National Monument, Fruita

MINNESOTA

Echo Trail, cliff paintings, Ely

NEVADA

Lehman Caves National Monument, Baker
Red Rock Canyon, Valley of Fire State Park, Moapa

NEW MEXICO

Albuquerque and Santa Fe areas
Bandelier National Monument, Los Alamos
Chaco Canyon National Monument, Bloomfield
El Morro National Monument, Ramah Navajo Indian Reservation
Gila Cliff Dwellings National Monument, Gila Hot Springs
Three Rivers Petroglyph Site, Three Rivers

UTAH

Arches National Park, Moab
Canyonlands National Park, Moab
Capitol Reef National Park, Torrey
Dinosaur National Monument (Utah/Colorado)
Grand Gulch Primitive Area, Hwy. 276
Hovenweep National Monument, Blanding
Natural Bridges National Monument, Lake Powell
Newspaper Rock State Historical Monument, Indian Creek State Park, Monticello
Zion National Park, Springdale

OTHER SITES

Pennacook Tribe Petroglyphs, Bellows Falls, Vermont

Barnes, F.A., *Canyon Country Prehistoric Rock Art,* Wasatch Publishers, Inc., 4460 Ashford Drive, Salt Lake City, Utah, 1982

Patterson, Alex, *A Field Guide to Rock Art Symbols of the Greater Southwest,* Johnson Books, Boulder, Colorado, 1992

Schaafsma, Polly, *The Rock Art of Utah,* University of Utah Press, Salt Lake City, 1971

List 10–14   Museums That Specialize in American Western Art

ARIZONA

Heard Museum, 22 E. Monte Vista Rd., Phoenix

Museum of Northern Arizona, 3001 Fort Valley Rd., Flagstaff

Phoenix Art Museum, 1625 N. Central Ave., Phoenix

CALIFORNIA

Gene Autrey Western Heritage Museum, 4700 Western Heritage Way, Griffith Park, Los Angeles

COLORADO

Colorado Springs Fine Arts Center, 30 W. Dale St., Colorado Springs

Denver Art Museum, 100 W. 14th Ave. Pkwy., Denver

Museum of Western Art, 1727 Tremont Pl., Denver

FLORIDA

John and Mable Ringling Museum, 5401 Bay Shore Rd., Sarasota

IDAHO

Appaloosa Museum and Heritage Center, Moscow-Pullman Hwy., Moscow

MISSOURI

Nelson-Atkins Museum of Art, 4525 Oak St., Kansas City

St. Louis Art Museum, Art Museum Dr., Forest Pk., St. Louis

MONTANA

Montana State University, Museum of the Rockies, Bozeman

NEBRASKA

Buffalo Bill Ranch State Historical Pk., North Platte

Joslyn Art Museum, 2200 Dodge St., Omaha

NEW MEXICO

Harwood Foundation Museum, 238 Ledoux St., Taos

Museum of Fine Arts, 107 W. Palace, Santa Fe

NEW YORK

National Museum of the American Indian, 3753 Broadway & 155th St., New York City

Rockwell Museum, 111 Cedar St., Corning

OKLAHOMA

Cherokee Heritage Center, PO Box 515, Willis Rd., Tahlequah

National Cowboy Hall of Fame and Western Heritage Center, 1700 NE 63rd St., Oklahoma City

Philbrook Museum of Art, PO Box 52510, 2727 S. Rockford Rd., Tulsa

TEXAS

Amon Carter Museum, 3501 Camp Bowie Blvd., Fort Worth

Dallas Museum of Art, 1717 N. Harwood, Dallas

The Huntington Art Gallery, 21st & Guadalupe Sts., University of Texas, Austin

Sid Richardson Collection of Western Art, 309 Main St., Fort Worth

WASHINGTON

Seattle Art Museum, 100 University St., Seattle

WYOMING

Whitney Gallery of Western Art, 720 Sheridan Ave., Cody

Drawn after *Teaching a Pony to Pack Dead Game,* 1895, Nelson Atkins Art Museum, Frederick Remington

List 10–15   Historic Homes Open as Museums

ALABAMA

Arlington Antebellum Home and Gardens, 1820, 331 Cotton Ave., Birmingham (Greek Revival)

Bellingrath Gardens and Home, c. 1920, Bellingrath Hwy., Mobile (800 acres of Garden)

Gaineswood, 1842, 805 S. Cedar St., Demopolis (Greek Revival mansion)

ALASKA

House of Wickersham, 1898, 213 Seventh St., Juneau (Victorian Queen Anne)

Rika's Roadhouse, 1909–1910, Milepost 175 Richardson Hwy., Big Delta State Park, near Fairbanks (log structure)

Totem Bight, reconstructed 1940, North Tongass Hwy. (Ketchikan, reconstruction of Native village, includes clan house and totem poles, Tlingit and Haida peoples)

ARIZONA

Riordan Ranch, 1904, 1300 Riordan Ranch Rd., Flagstaff (Craftsman style)

Rosson House, 1895, 7th and Monroe, Phoenix (Victorian Queen Anne/Eastlake)

Taliesin West, 1938, Paradise Valley, near Phoenix (Wright's western home and school, run much as he did during his lifetime)

ARKANSAS

McCollum-Chidester House, 1847, 926 Washington St. NW, Camden (Civil War era house)

Rosalie House, 1883, 282 Spring St., Eureka Springs (brick Victorian home)

Villa Marre, 1881, 1321 Scott St., Little Rock (Italianate)

CALIFORNIA

Avila Adobe, 1818, 14 Olvera St., Los Angeles (oldest house in Los Angeles/ Spanish Colonial)

Governor's Mansion, 1877, 1526 "H" St., Sacramento (High Victorian/Second Empire)

Haas-Lilienthal House, 1886, 2007 Franklin St., San Francisco (Victorian Queen Anne)

Hearst Castle, 1920s, 750 Hearst Castle Rd., San Simeon (Eclectic/Hispano/Moorish)

Hollyhock House, 1919–1921, 4800 Hollywood Blvd., Los Angeles (Mayan influence, Frank Lloyd Wright

Leland Stanford Mansion, 1856, 802 North St., Sacramento (Italianate/French Second Empire)

COLORADO

Grant-Humphreys Mansion, 1902, 770 Pennsylvania St., Denver (Renaissance Revival/Beaux Arts)

Miramount Castle Museum, 1895, 9 Capitol Hill Ave., Manitou Springs (Gothic and Tudor Revival)

Molly Brown House Museum, 1899, 1340 Pennsylvania St., Denver (Victorian Queen Anne)

CONNECTICUT,

Hill-Stead Museum, 1901, 671 Farmington Ave., Farmington (Colonial Revival) by Stanford White

Mark Twain House, 1874, 351 Farmington Ave., Hartford (Victorian mansion)

Nathan Hale Homestead, 1685–1779, South St., South Coventry (10 room period mansion)

Pardee-Morris House, 1685–1779, 325 Lighthouse Rd., New Haven (American period furnishings)

Stanley-Whitman House, c. 1720, 37 High St., Farmington (18th century frame home)

DELAWARE

Amstel House Museum, 1730, 2 E. 4th St., New Castle (18th century Georgian/Dutch house)

Nemours Mansion and Gardens, 1910, Rockland Rd., Wilmington (modified Louis XVI chateau)

Old Dutch House, c. 1690, 32 E. 3rd St., New Castle (Dutch Colonial)

Winterthur Museum, 1839, Hwy. 52, Wilmington (estate of Henry Francis duPont, large collection of American Antiques and Decorative Arts)

DISTRICT OF COLUMBIA

Christian Heurich Mansion, 1892, 1307 New Hampshire Ave. NW (neo-Renaissance/Victorian)

Decatur House Museum, 1818, 748 Jackson Pl. NW (Federal town house/Adam)

Dumbarton Oaks, 1703 32nd Street NW, (Federal style)

Mount Vernon, c. 1735, Mount Vernon Memorial Hwy., Mount Vernon (Neo-classical)

Tudor Place, 1805, 1644 31st St. NW (Adam/Federal style, original furnishings)

The White House, 1800, 1600 Pennsylvania Ave., NW (English style/Classical Revival)

Woodlawn, 1802, 3 miles from Mount Vernon (late Georgian architecture)

FLORIDA

Ca'd'zan, (John and Mable Ringling home), 5401 Bay Shore Road, Sarasota (Venetian Gothic Palazzo)

List 10–15   Continued

FLORIDA (cont.)

Edison/Ford Winter Estates, 1885, 2350 McGregor Blvd., Fort Myers (winter estates of Thomas Alva Edison and Henry Ford)

Gamble Plantation State Historic Site, 1865, Bradenton (only surviving antebellum home in south Florida)

Vizcaya Museum and Gardens, 1914–1916, 3251 S. Miami Ave., Coconut Grove, near Miami (70 room Italian Renaissance villa)

GEORGIA

Andrew Low House, c. 1848, 329 Abercorn St., Savannah (Victorian/West Indian influence)

Church-Wadel-Brumby House, c. 1820, 280 E. Dougherty St., Athens (Federal-style house)

Harris House, c. 1795, 1822 Broad St., Augusta (period furnishings)

Little White House Historic Site, 1932, Warm Springs (F.D. Roosevelt's summer home)

Taylor-Grady House, 1839, 634 Prince Ave., Athens (Greek Revival mansion)

Telfair Mansion and Art Museum, 1818, 121 Barnard St., Savannah (Regency style)

HAWAII

Chamberlain House Museum, 1831, 553 S. King St., Honolulu (modified Greek Revival)

Hanaiakamalama (Queen Emma Summer Palace), 1848, 2913 Pali Hwy., Oahu (Greek Revival)

Iolani Palace, 1879–1882, 364 South King St., Honolulu (104 rooms, American Florentine/Italian Renaissance)

Maui Historical Society Museum, 19th century Rte. 32 Wailuku and Iao Valley, Maui (Missionary home)

IDAHO

Basque Museum and Cultural Center, 1864, 607 Grove St., Boise (old boarding house for Basque immigrants)

Bishops' House, 1889, 2420 Old Penitentiary Rd., Boise (Victorian Queen Anne)

McConnell Mansion, 1881–1886, 110 South Adams St., Moscow (eclectic Victorian)

Standrod House, 1900, 648 N. Garfield Ave., Pocatello (late Victorian/Queen Anne)

ILLINOIS

Belvedere Mansion and Gardens, 1857, 1008 Park Ave., Galena (Italianate/steamboat Gothic)

Dana-Thomas State Historic Site, 1902, 301 E. Lawrence Ave., Springfield, (Frank Lloyd Wright design, complete with furnishings)

Flanagan House, 1837, 942 NE Glen Oak Ave., Peoria (Federal pre-Civil War)

Lincoln Home, c. 1860, 8th and Jackson St., Springfield (Federal style)

Magnolia Manor, 1869, 2700 Washington Ave., Cairo (Italianate/Victorian)

Robie House, 1909, 5757 South Woodlawn Ave., Chicago (Frank Lloyd Wright's Prairie-style)

INDIANA

Barker Mansion, 1900, 631 Washington St., Michigan City (eclectic, English Manor-style revival)

Governor Hendricks' Home, 1817, 202 E. Walnut, Corydon (original furnishings)

Morris-Butler House Museum, 1859–1862, 1204 N. Park Ave., Indianapolis (eclectic Italianate/Victorian Second Empire)

President Benjamin Harrison Memorial Home, 1874, 1230 N. Delaware St., Indianapolis (Italianate)

William Henry Harrison Mansion, 1804, 3 West Scott St., Vincennes (Georgian)

IOWA

Brucemore, 1886, 2160 Linden Dr. SE, Cedar Rapids (Queen Anne style)

George Wyth House, 1907, 303 Franklin St., Cedar Falls (Prairie style)

Phelps House, c. 1850, 521 Columbia St., Burlington (Italianate/Victorian)

Salisbury House, 4025 Tonawanda Dr., Des Moines (replica of king's house in Salisbury, England)

Scholte House, 728 Washington, Pella (oldest dwelling in Pella, French and Italian furniture)

KANSAS

Brown Mansion, 1897, 2019 Walnut St., Coffeyville (Victorian)

Carroll Mansion, 1867, 1128 Fifth Ave., Leavenworth (Victorian)

Grinter Place, 1857, 1420 South 78th St., Kansas City, Kansas (Georgian/Greek Revival)

KENTUCKY

Farmington, 1810, 3033 Bardstown Rd., Louisville (Federal style)

Federal Hill, 1795, My Old Kentucky Home State Pk., US 150, Bardstown (Georgian)

Hunt-Morgan House, c. 1812, 201 N. Mill St., Lexington (Georgian)

Old Governors' Mansion, 1798, 420 High St., Frankfort (Georgian style)

List 10–15 Continued

KENTUCKY (cont.)

Owensboro Museum of Fine Art, pre-Civil War, 901 Frederica St., Owensboro (restored mansion now used as an art museum)

Riverview, 1857, 1100 W. Main Ave., Bowling Green (Italianate style)

LOUISIANA

Homeplace, 1801, Charles Parish (French Colonial)

Magnolia Mound, c. 1790, Baton Rouge, Louisiana (French architecture)

Homeplace Plantation, c. 1800, Hahnville, Louisiana

Pontalba Apartments, Jackson Sq., 19th century, New Orleans (Greek Revival style)

Shadows-on-the-Teche, 1834, East Main St., New Iberia (French Colonial/Greek Revival)

MAINE

Lady Pepperell House, 1760, Route 103, Kittery (late Georgian)

Morse House, 1858, Park and Danforth Sts., Portland (Italian villa style),

Wadsworth-Longfellow House, 1785, 487 Congress St., Portland (old brick three-story house)

Wedding Cake House, c. 1820, Kennebunk Landing, Kennebunk (Adamesque-Federal)

MARYLAND

Chase-Lloyd House, 1769, 22 Maryland Ave., Annapolis (period furnishings, Georgian)

Hammond-Harwood House, 1774, 19 Maryland Ave., Annapolis (late Georgian)

Homewood House, 1803, Charles and 34th Sts., Baltimore (Federal Period)

William Paca House, 1763, Prince George St., Annapolis (William Buckland carvings, Georgian)

MASSACHUSETTS

Boardman House, 1686, Saugus, Massachusetts (Postmedieval English)

Elihu Coleman House, 1722, Nantucket Island (early New England "saltbox")

Boardman House, Saugus, Massachusetts, 1686, New England type

Hadwen House, c. 1770, 96 Main St., Nantucket (Greek Revival)

Harrison Gray Otis House, 1795, 141 Cambridge St., Boston (Adamesque house)

House of the Seven Gables, 1668, 54 Turner St., Salem (Postmedieval English)

John Ward House, 1684, 132–34 Essex St., Salem (Jacobean house)

John Whipple House, 1640, 53 S. Main St., Ipswich (Medieval)

Nichols House Museum, early 19th century, 55 Mount Vernon St., Boston (Federal)

Old Ship Meetinghouse, 1681, 21 Lincoln St., Hingham (American Colonial)

Paul Revere House, c. 1676, North Square, Boston (Colonial, two-story gable-roofed row house)

Pierce-Nichols House, 1782, 80 Federal St., Salem (late Georgian)

Pingree House, 1804, Essex St. next to the Essex Institute, Salem (furnished in period pieces)

Williams House, 1706–1707, Old Deerfield, Massachusetts (early Georgian)

MICHIGAN

Cranbrook House, 1908, 380 Lone Pine Rd., Bloomfield Hills (Craftsman-style decorative arts)

Friant House, 1892, Heritage Hill District, Grand Rapids (Queen Anne/Medieval Revival)

Honolulu House Museum, 1860, 107 N. Kalamazoo Ave., Marshall (Italianate/plantation style)

Kempf House, 1853, 312 S. Division, Ann Arbor (Greek Revival architecture)

Kimball House Museum, 1886, 196 Capital Ave. NE, Battle Creek (Victorian home)

Meyer May House, 1908, 450 Madison St. SE (Frank Lloyd Wright-designed home)

MINNESOTA

Alexander Ramsey House, 1872, 265 S. Exchange St., St. Paul (French Renaissance)

Charles A. Lindbergh House, 1906–1920, 1200 Lindbergh Dr. S., Little Falls (modified Craftsman bungalow)

Mayowood, 1911, Rte. 125, Rochester, home of Dr. Charles Mayo (Eclectic)

Hubbard House, 1871, 606 S. Broad St., Mankato (Victorian home)

Olaf Swensson Farm Museum, County Rd. 5, Granite Falls (brick farmhouse and farm)

MISSISSIPPI

Beauvoir, c. 1850, 2244 Beach Blvd., Biloxi (southern French architecture)

The Briers, 1812–1815, Irvine Ave., Natchez (Southern planter style)

Governor's Mansion, 1842, 300 E. Capitol St., Jackson (Greek Revival style)

Homewood, c. 1836, Columbus (Greek Revival)

List 10–15   Continued

MISSISSIPPI (cont.)

Longwood, 1855–1861, Lower Woodville Rd., Natchez (octagonal house, Victorian eclectic)

Magnolia Hall, 1858, S. Pearl at Washington (Greek Revival mansion)

Rosalie, 1820–1823, South end of Broadway, Natchez (Greek Revival antebellum style)

MISSOURI

Balduc House Museum, 1770, 125 S. Maine St., Sainte Genevieve (French -Colonial style log home)

Campbell House Museum, c. 1850, 1508 Locust St., St. Louis (Mid-Victorian town house)

Chatillon-De Menil House, 1848, 3352 De Menil Pl., St. Louis (Greek Revival antebellum mansion)

Rockcliffe Mansion, c. 1900, 1000 Bird St., Hannibal (Beaux-arts mansion)

Tower Grove House, c. 1850, Missouri Botannical Garden, St. Louis (Victorian furnishings)

MONTANA

Daly Mansion, c. 1886, County 169, Hamilton (42-room eclectic Colonial mansion)

Grant-Kohrs Ranch National Historic Site, 19th century, north edge of Deer Lodge (Greek Revival)

Moss Mansion Museum, 1901, 914 Division St., Billings (Eclectic Renaissance Revival)

Original Governor's Mansion, 1888, 304 N. Ewing St., Helena (22-room brick home)

William Andrews Clark House, 1884, 219 West Granite St., Butte (high Victorian Queen Anne)

NEBRASKA

General Crook House, 1878, 30th and Fort Sts., Omaha (period furnishings)

Louis E. May Historical Museum, 1874, 1643 N. Nye Ave., Fremont (Victorian home)

Cornish House, Omaha, Nebraska, 1886, Second Empire

NEVADA

Bowers Mansion, 1864, 4005 Old Highway 395 North, Carson City (Italianate)

House of the Silver Door Knobs, 1868, 70 South "B" St., Virginia City (Second Empire)

MacKay Mansion, 1860, 129 South "D" St., Virginia City (modified Italianate)

NEW HAMPSHIRE

Governor John Langdon Mansion, 1784, 143 Pleasant Street, Portsmouth (Colonial Revival)

John Paul Jones House, 1758, Middle and State Sts., Portsmouth (gambrel-roof, early Georgian)

Macphaedris-Warner House, 1718–1732, 150 Daniels St., Portsmouth (Queen Anne style)

Richard Jackson House, 1664, 76 Northwest St., Portsmouth (Medieval style)

Wentworth-Gardner House, 1760, Mechanic St., Portsmouth (Georgian style)

Wheeler House, 1814–1815, Orford (Federal Style)

NEW JERSEY

Ackerman House, 1704, Hackensack, New Jersey (Dutch Colonial)

Boxwood Hall State Historic Site, c. 1755, 1073 E. Jersey St., Elizabeth (New England Classical)

Covenhoven House, 18th century house. 150 W. Main St., Freehold

Ackerman House, Hackensack, New Jersey, 1704, Dutch Colonial, Gambrel roof

The Hermitage, 1760, 335 N. Franklin Tpke., Hohokus (stone Victorian house)

Steuben House State Historic Site, 1713, Hacksensack (Dutch Colonial)

Schuyler-Hamilton House, 1760, 5 Olyphant Pl., Morristown (Colonial, white clapboard)

NEW MEXICO

El Zaguan, pre 1850, 545 Canyon Rd., Santa Fe (adobe Spanish Colonial)

Ernest L. Blumenschein Home, 1797, 13 Ledoux St., Taos (Adobe/Spanish Colonial)

Governor's Palace, 1610–1614, Santa Fe, N.M. (Spanish/Indian Colonial

La Hacienda de Don Antonio Severino Martinez, 1804, Ranchitos Rd. and Route 240, near Taos (Spanish Colonial)

NEW YORK

Boscobel, 1807, State 9D between Garrison and Cold Spring (Adamesque architecture)

Falaise, c. 1923, Sands Point, Long Island (mansion with electic European influence)

Hempstead House, c. 1900, Sands Point, Long Island (early 20th century, Wedgewood collection)

Lyndhurst, 1838, 635 S. Broadway, Tarrytown (Gothic Revival)

List 10–15   Continued

NEW YORK (CONT.)

Morris-Jumel Mansion, 1765, 1765 Jumel Terrace at 160th, New York City (Federal style)

Schuyler Mansion, 1761, 32 Catherine St., Albany (Georgian)

Van Cortlandt Mansion, 1748, Broadway at 242nd St., New York City (Georgian manor house, 17th and 18th century furnishings)

Wilcox Mansion, c. 1890s, 641 Delaware Ave., Buffalo (Greek Revival)

NORTH CAROLINA

Biltmore, 1890–1895, Route 25, Asheville (French chateau, 250 room mansion for the Vanderbilts)

Newbold-White House, 1680s, US 17 Bypass to Hartford, Edenton (oldest house in the state)

Washington Duke Homestead, 1852, Duke Homestead Rd., Durham

NORTH DAKOTA

Chateau de Mores State Historic Site, 1883, US 10/I-94, Medora (French chateau-style)

Governors' Mansion State Historic Site, 1884, 4th St. & B Ave., Bismarck

OHIO

John Hauck House, 19th century, 812 Dayton St., Cincinnati (Italianate)

Perkins Mansion, 1837, 550 Copley Rd., Akron (Greek Revival style)

Stan Hywet Hall and Gardens, 1912, 714 N. Portage Path, Akron (Tudor Revival, 65 rooms)

Taft Museum, 1820, 316 Pike St., Cincinnati (Federal-Period mansion)

OKLAHOMA

Frank Phillips Mansion, 1908, 1107 S. Cherokee Ave., Bartlesville (eclectic Neoclassical/Greek Revival)

Hefner family mansion, 1917, 201 NW 14th St., Oklahoma City (Eclectic Neoclassical)

Murray-Lindsay Mansion, 1880, Erin Springs (Classic-Revival)

Overholser Mansion, 1902–1904, 405 NW 15th St., Oklahoma City (late Victorian/Queen Anne)

OREGON

Captain George Flavel House Museum, 1884, 441 Eighth St., Astoria (Queen Anne/Italianate)

Captain John C. Ainsworth House, 1850, 19195 S. Leland Rd., Oregon City

Deepwood Estate, 1894, 1116 Mission St., SE, Salem (Queen Anne)

Pittock Mansion, 1914, 3929 NW Pittock Dr., Portland (French Renaissance chateau)

PENNSYLVANIA

The Cloister, 1741–1743, 632 W. Main, Ephrata (Medieval dormitories for communal living)

Fallingwater, Mill Run, 1936, near Connellsville (Frank Lloyd Wright design)

Fox Hunter Mansion, 1786, 5300 N. Front St., Harrisburg (Federal-style stone mansion)

Landingford Plantation, 1683, 15 Race St., Chester, Caleb Pusey Home (early Colonial)

Mount Pleasant, 1761, Fairmont Pk., Philadelphia (18th century High Georgian house)

Woodford, 1756, 33rd and Dauphin Sts., Philadelphia (Colonial)

RHODE ISLAND

The Breakers, 1895, Ochre Point Rd., Newport (Italian Renaissance Vanderbilt "cottage")

John Brown House, 1786, 52 Power St. at Benefit, Providence (Georgian)

Colony House, 1739–1743, Washington Sq., Newport (Colonial Classical/pre-Revolutionary Capitol building)

Governor Stephens Hopkins House, 1707–1742, Benefit and Hopkins St., Providence (Colonial)

Marble House, 1892, Bellevue, Newport (French style)

SOUTH CAROLINA

Heyward-Washington House, 1772, 87 Church St., Charleston (Georgian townhouse)

John Mark Verdier House Museum, c. 1790, 801 Bay St., Beaufort (Federal period)

Joseph Manigault House, 1803, 350 Meeting St., Charleston (Adamesque-Federal style)

Miles Brewton House, 1733, 27 King St., 18th Century, Charleston (Georgian, Pre-Revolutionary)

SOUTH DAKOTA

Mellette House, 1883, 421 5th Ave. NW, Watertown (Victorian brick home)

Pettigrew Home and Museum, 1889, 8th St. and Duluth Ave., Sioux Falls (Queen-Anne)

TENNESSEE

Governor William Blount Mansion, 1792, 200 W. Hill Ave., Knoxville (two-story frame house)

James K. Polk's Ancestral Home, 1816, 301 W. 7th St., Columbia (Federal style)

Mallory-Neely House, c. 1852, 652 Adams Ave., Memphis (Italianate)

List 10–15   Continued

TENNESSEE (cont.)

Woodruff-Fontaine House, 1870, 680 Adams Ave., Memphis (Second Empire/Victorian)

TEXAS

Ashton Villa, 1859, 2328 Broadway, Galveston (Italianate)

DeGolyer House, 1939, 8525 Garland Rd., Dallas (Spanish Eclectic)

Mission San Francisco de la Espada, 1731, 10040 Espada Rd., San Antonio

Mission San Juan Capistrano, 1731, 9102 Graf Rd., San Antonio

Moody Mansion, 1893, 2618 Broadway, Galveston (Richardsonian Romanesque)

Spanish Governor's Palace, 1749, 105 Plaza de Armas, San Antonio (Spanish Colonial)

Steves Homestead, 1876, 509 King William St., San Antonio (Italianate/Second Empire)

UTAH

Alfred McCune Home, 1901, 200 North Main St., Salt Lake City (Tudor Revival with East Asian influence)

Beehive House, 1853–1855, 67 East South Temple St., Salt Lake City (Greek Revival, Brigham Young's home)

Kearns Mansion, 1902, 603 East South Temple, Salt Lake City (eclectic Renaissance)

VERMONT

Dana House, 1807, 26 Elm St., Woodstock (fine early 19th century home, period furnishings)

Dutton House, 1782, Route 7, Shelburne (Colonial Salt box)

Historic Hildene, 1904, Manchester (Robert Todd Lincoln's Home, Georgian manor house with original furnishings)

John Strong Mansion, 1795, West Addison, Vergennes (Federal-style House)

VIRGINIA

Adam Thoroughgood House, 1636–1640, 1636 Parish Rd., Norfolk (Postmedieval English)

Bacon's Castle, c. 1655, 465 Bacon's Castle Trail, Surry County, (Postmedieval English)

Governor's Palace, 1706–1720, Williamsburg (Colonial Georgian style)

Gunston Hall, 1755, 10709 Gunston Rd., Alexandria (Chinese to Gothic influence, Palladian dining room)

Monticello, 1770–1809, State 53, Charlottesville (early Classical)

Oatlands, 1803, Leesburg (Classical revival)

Stratford, 1725, 40 miles southeast of Fredericksburg (plantation house on Potomac River)

Wythe House, 1752–1754, Williamsburg (Colonial Georgian)

WASHINGTON

Chateau Ste. Michelle, 1930, I-405, 205 W. 5th St., Sunnyside

Henderson House Museum, 1905, I-5, Tumwater Historic Pk., Olympia (Carpenter Gothic style)

Hoquiam's Castle, 1897, 515 Chenault Ave., Hoquiam (Victorian Queen Anne)

Maryhill Museum of Art, c. 1920, 35 Maryhill Museum Dr., Goldendale (mansion featuring exhibitions of Rodin sculpture, chess collection, Native American baskets)

WEST VIRGINIA

General Adam Stephen House, 1789, 309 E. John St., Martinsburg (period furnishings, stone house)

Governor's Mansion, 1925, 1716 Kanawha Blvd., Charleston (Georgian style)

Stealey-Goff Vance House, 1807, 123 W. Main St., Clarksburg

WISCONSIN

Captain Frederick Pabst Mansion, 1893, 2000 W. Wisconsin Ave., Milwaukee

Charles A. Grignon Mansion, 1837, 1313 Augustine St., Appleton (Greek Revival style)

Falling Water, 1936, Mill Run, Pennsylvania

Cotton House, 2632 S. Webster Ave., Green Bay (Greek Revival)

Kilbourntown House, 1844, Estabrook Park, Milwaukee (Greek Revival)

Lincoln-Tallman House, 1855–1857, 440 N. Jackson, Janesville (antebellum mansion, Italianate design)

Octagon House, 1856, 276 Linden St., Fond du Lac (period furnishings)

Octagon House, 1854, 919 Charles St., Watertown (Victorian mansion, eight-sided house)

WYOMING

Historic *Governors' Mansion,* 1904, 300 E. 21st St., Cheyenne (Colonial Revival, Georgian)

Ivinson Mansion, 1892, 603 Ivinson Ave., Laramie (Victorian Queen Anne-Eastlake)

Trail End Historic Site, 1908–1913, 400 Clarendon Ave., Sheridan (Colonial Revival, Flemish/Neoclassical)

List 10–16   American Museum Towns

These cities may be authentically restored (such as Williamsburg), or contain some homes and restored buildings, brought together in one place to preserve the heritage of the past.

CALIFORNIA
Bodie State Historic Park, Bridgeport
Columbia State Historic Park, Columbia
Solvang Village, Solvang "Scandinavian" town

CONNECTICUT
Mystic Seaport, Mystic

FLORIDA
Historic St. Augustine, St. Augustine

GEORGIA
Westville Village, Lumpkin

HAWAII
Polynesian Cultural Center, Laie, Oahu

ILLINOIS
Bishop Hill, near Galesburg
Lincoln's New Salem State Historic Site, Springfield
Naper Settlement, Aurora Avenue, Naperville
Nauvoo Historic District, Nauvoo

INDIANA
New Harmony, founded by Harmonie Society members, 19th
century

IOWA
Amana Colonies, US 151 & IA 220, Amish Colonies

KENTUCKY
Shakertown at Pleasant Hill, Harrodsburg

MAINE
Old Town, Augusta
Shaker Village, Poland Spring

MASSACHUSETTS
Deerfield Village, Deerfield
Hancock Shaker Village, Pittsfield
Nantucket Island
Plimoth Plantation, Plymouth
Old Sturbridge Village, Sturbridge
Storrowton Village, West Springfield
Salem, historic district

MICHIGAN
Henry Ford Museum and Greenfield Village, Dearborn

MINNESOTA
Lumbertown, U.S.A., Brainerd

MISSOURI
Faust Park Historic Village, St. Louis County

NEBRASKA
Harold Warp Pioneer Village, Minden
Stuhr Museum of the Prairie Pioneer, Grand Island

NEW HAMPSHIRE
Canterbury Shaker Village, Canterbury
Strawbery Banke Museum, Portsmouth

NEW JERSEY
Batsto Historic Site, Hammonton
Historic Towne, Smithville
Waterloo Village, Waterloo

NEW MEXICO
Santa Fe, adobe buildings
Socorro Village, Socorro
Taos Pueblo, Taos

NEW YORK
Farmer's Museum and Village Crossroads, Cooperstown
Genesee Country Museum, Mumford
Richmondtown Restoration, New York City

NORTH CAROLINA
Old Salem, Winston-Salem

OHIO
Geuga County Pioneer Village, Burton
Schoenbrunn Village State Memorial, New Philadelphia
Sharon Woods Village, Cincinnati
Zoar Village State Memorial, Zoar

PENNSYLVANIA
Ephrata Cloister, Ephrata
Farm Museum of Landis Valley, Lancaster
Historic Fallsington, Fallsington
Hopewell Furnace National Historic Site, Elverson
Old Economy Village, Ambridge

SOUTH DAKOTA
Prairie Village, Madison

TEXAS
Heritage Garden Village, Woodville

VERMONT
Shelburne Museum, Shelburne

VIRGINIA
Colonial Williamsburg, Williamsburg
Jamestown Festival Park, Jamestown
Yorktown, Yorktown

WASHINGTON
Old Mission Pioneer Village, Cashmere

WEST VIRGINIA
Harpers Ferry, Harpers Ferry

WISCONSIN
Stonefield, Cassville

List 10–17   Museums in America

Although a number of these museums are in other lists, they are organized here by state. A few major university art museums are included.

ALABAMA

Birmingham Museum of Art, 2000 8th Ave. North, Birmingham (comprehensive collection of European, American and Asian Art, 12th century to present, Wedgwood collection, Remington bronzes)

Mobile Museum of Art, 4850 Museum Dr., Mobile (southern furniture, contemporary American crafts, American and European art)

Montgomery Museum of Fine Arts, One Museum Dr., Montgomery (southern regional art, 19th- and 20th-century American art)

ALASKA

Alaska State Museum, 395 Whittier, Juneau (Eskimo, Aleut, Northwest Coast, Athabaskan art, Alaskan fine art)

Anchorage Museum of History and Art, 121 W. Seventh Ave., Anchorage (comprehensive Alaskan art collection)

University of Alaska Museum, 907 Yukon Dr., Fairbanks (photography, Native American art)

ARIZONA

Heard Museum, 22 East Monte Vista Rd., Phoenix (Native American jewelry, pots, paintings, baskets, weavings, Kachina dolls, annual Native American art exhibition, Jaune Quick-to-See Smith, Kay WalkingStick)

Phoenix Art Museum, 1625 North Central Ave., Phoenix (Asian collection, 20th-century art, European and American paintings)

ARKANSAS

Arkansas Arts Center, MacArthur Pk., 9th and Commerce Sts., Little Rock (contemporary crafts, American and European drawings, 19th- and 20th-century paintings)

CALIFORNIA

Asian Art and Culture Center/Avery Brundage Collection, Golden Gate Pk., San Francisco (*Bronze Rhinoceros Vessel,* Kmer sculpture, painted scrolls, pottery T'ang *Camel,* 12,000 objects over 6,000 years)

California Palace of the Legion of Honor, Lincoln Pk., San Francisco (Harnett's *After the Hunt,* Lorenzo Lotto's *Portrait of a Man,* Fragonard's *Self Portrait,* large collection of Rodin bronzes: *The Thinker, Burghers of Calais, The Age of Bronze,* print collection)

Fine Arts Gallery, Plaza de Panama, Balboa Pk., San Diego (Rembrandt's *Young Man With a Cock's Feather in His Hat,* Titian's *Portrait of the Doge Francesco Donato,* Rubens' *Holy Family With St. Francis*)

Henry E. Huntington Art Gallery, 1151 Oxford Rd., San Marino (Gainsborough's *Blue Boy,* Thomas Lawrence's *Pinkie,* Joshua Reynolds' *Sarah Siddons as The Tragic Muse*)

Getty Museum, 1200 Getty Center Drive, Los Angeles (Classical vases and sculpture, photographs, illuminated manuscripts, paintings, drawings, sculpture, French furniture, Tintoretto's *Toilet of Venus,* Pierre Bonnard's *Nude,* Van Gogh's *Irises*)

Los Angeles County Museum of Art, 5905 Wiltshire Blvd., Los Angeles (De Hooch's *Woman Giving Money to Her Servant Girl,* Holbein's *Young Woman With a White Coif,* Rembrandt's *Portrait of Maarten Looten,* Cezanne's *Still Life With Cherries and Apricots,* Giorgione's *Head of a Woman,* Hockney's *Mulholland Drive: The Road to the Studio*)

M.H. De Young Memorial Museum, Golden Gate Pk., San Francisco (ancient Asian bronzes, Cranach's *Madonna and Child,* Cellini's bust of *Cosimo de Medici,* El Greco's *St. John the Baptist,* Bellini's *Doge Leonardo Loredano,* Rubens' *The Tribute Money,* American art, textiles)

The Museum of Contemporary Art (MOCA), 250 S. Grand Ave., Los Angeles (Claes Oldenburg's and Coosje van Bruggen's *Knife Ship II,* 20th-century art in all media, including sculpture and painting)

Norton Simon Museum of Art, 411 W. Colorado Blvd., Pasadena (Botticelli, Degas, Goya, Manet, Matisse, Rembrandt, van Gogh, Zurbaran)

List 10–17   Continued

CALIFORNIA (cont.)

Oakland Art Museum, 1000 Oak St., Oakland (California artists, Diebenkorn, Viola Frey, Dorothea Lange, Eadweard Muybridge)

Pasadena Art Museum, 46 North Los Robles Ave., Pasadena (Klee's *Refuge,* Kandinsky's *Severe in Sweet,* Feininger's *Blue Skyscraper*)

San Diego Museum of Art, Balboa Pk., San Diego (German Expressionists, European and American paintings, Mark Rothko, Paul Gauguin)

San Francisco Museum of Modern Art, 151 Third St., San Francisco (Diego Rivera's *Flower Vendor,* Braque's *The Table,* Matisse's *Woman with the Hat,* 20th-century modernist and contemporary art)

Santa Barbara Museum of Art, 1130 State St., Santa Barbara (Sumerian *Head of Gudea,* comprehensive collection of American, Asian, and 19th-century French art)

Timken Art Gallery, Plaza de Panama, Balboa Pk., San Diego (Bosch's *Christ Taken Captive,* Canaletto's *Bacino di San Marco, Tribute Money*)

University of California at Berkeley, 2626 Bancroft Way, Berkeley (Soviet, Japanese and American avant-garde film and video, 20th-century American and European paintings, sculpture, drawings and prints)

COLORADO

Colorado Springs Fine Arts Center, 30 W. Dale St., Colorado Springs (Walt Kuhn's *Trio,* Arthur Dove's *Fog Horns,* American and Native American art, large collection of Santos, Southwestern and Hispanic Colonial art)

Denver Art Museum, 100 West Fourteenth Ave. Pkwy., Denver (Giuseppi Arcimboldo's *Summer,* Degas' *Examen de Danse,* collection of Santos, collection of Western art, contemporary art, and photography)

CONNECTICUT

The New Britain Museum of American Art, 56 Lexington St., New Britain (Benton's *The Arts of Life in America,* Harnett's *Still Life With Violin,* Eakins' *Old Lady Sewing,* Eastman Johnson's *Hollyhocks,* American art from 1740 to present)

Wadsworth Atheneum, 600 Main St., Hartford (Bierstadt's *In the Yosemite Valley,* Copley's *Portrait of Mrs. Seymore Fort,* Goya's *Gossiping Women,* Rubens' *Tiger Hunt,* Zurbaran's *St. Serapion,* African American collection, 20th-century masters)

Yale Center for British Art, 1080 Chapel St., New Haven (16th- to 20th-century British paintings, sculpture, prints, drawings)

Yale University Art Gallery, 1111 Chapel St., New Haven (13th- to 20th-century European art, prints, drawings, photographs, 20th-century American painting, van Gogh's *The Night Cafe,* Eakins' *John Biglen in a Single Scull,* Brancusi's *Yellow Bird,* Moore's *Draped Seated Woman,* Ralph Earl's *Roger Sherman,* Trumbull's *Surrender of Burgoyne,* Joseph Stella's *Battle of Light, Coney Island* and *Brooklyn Bridge*)

DELAWARE

Delaware Art Museum, 2301 Kentmere Pkwy., Wilmington (American art: Hopper, Gorky, Homer, John Sloan, Howard Pyle)

The Henry Francis du Pont Winterthur Museum, Rte. 52, Winterthur (Stuart's *George Washington,* West's *Peace Treaty Between England and the American Colonies,* American furniture, silver)

DISTRICT OF COLUMBIA

Corcoran Gallery of Art, 17th St. and New York Ave. NW (Samuel F.B. Morse's *The Old House of Representatives,* Bierstadt's *The Last of the Buffalo,* Bellow's *Forty-two Kids,* Frankenthaler, Sargent, Warhol, Copley, Frederic Edwin Church's *Niagara Falls*)

Freer Gallery, 12th Street and Jefferson Drive, SW (Persian miniature paintings, *A Buddhist Procession,* Whistler's *The Peacock Room* and *Nocturne—Blue and Gold*)

Hirshhorn Museum and Sculpture Garden, Independence Ave. at 7th St. SW (19th- and 20th-century contemporary paintings and sculpture, outdoor sculpture garden, Rodin, Matisse, de Kooning, Picasso, Stuart Davis, Horace Pippin)

List 10–17   Continued

DISTRICT OF COLUMBIA (cont.)

National Gallery of Art, 4th St. and Constitution Ave. (Raphael's *Alba Madonna,* Titian's *Venus with a Mirror,* Vermeer's *A Woman Weighing Gold,* Toulouse-Lautrec's *Quadrille at the Moulin Rouge,* Titian's *Doge Andrea Gritti,* Rembrandt's *The Mill* and *Lady with an Ostrich Fan,* Van Eyck's *The Annunciation,* Renoir's *A Girl with Watering Can*)

National Museum of African Art, 950 Independence Ave. SW (African gold collection, masks, ivory sculpture, wood carvings, Central African pottery)

National Museum of American Art, Smithsonian Institution, 8th and G Sts. NW (American art from 18th century to present, George Catlin, Albert Bierstadt, John LaFarge, Edmonia Lewis, Hiram Powers, Albert Pinkham Ryder)

National Museum of Women in the Arts, 1250 New York Ave., NW (over 1200 works from over 400 women artists from 28 countries, Rosa Bonheur, Judy Chicago, Helen Frankenthaler, Frida Kahlo, Berthe Morisot, Louise Nevelson)

Renwick Gallery, 1859–1861, Second Empire Style, Washington, DC

National Portrait Gallery, Smithsonian Institution, 8th and F Sts. NW (portraits of persons important in the history of the United States, important Catlin collection)

The Phillips Collection, 1600 21st St. NW (Bonnard's *The Open Window,* Marin's *Maine Islands,* Picasso's *The Blue Room,* Corot's *View from the Farnese Gardens,* Klee's *Arab Song,* Arthur Dove's *Cows in Pasture,* Renoir's *Luncheon of the Boating Party*)

Renwick Gallery, National Museum of American Art, Smithsonian Institution, Pennsylvania Avenue and 17th St. NW (American contemporary crafts and decorative arts)

United States Capitol Art Collection, Capitol Building (744 works of American art: portraits, marble and bronze busts, frescoes, murals, lunettes dealing with American history)

FLORIDA

The Charles Hosmer Morse Museum of American Art, 445 Park Ave. N., Winter Park (Cecilia Beaux, Robert Henri, Maxfield Parrish, Tiffany lamps, vases, leaded windows)

John and Mabel Ringling Museum of Art, 5401 Bay Shore Rd., Sarasota (Rubens' *Meeting of Abraham and Mechizedek,* Cranach's *Cardinal Albrecht as St. Jerome,* collection of circus wagons and other memorabilia)

Museum of Fine Arts, 255 Beach Dr. NE, St. Petersburg (O'Keeffe's *Poppy,* Jacobean and Georgian period rooms, Steuben crystal, sculpture courts)

Norton Gallery, Pioneer Pk., West Palm Beach (Degas' *Little Dancer,* Brancusi's *Mme. Pogany,* Braque's *Still Life on Red Tablecloth,* El Greco's *Purification of the Temple*)

Salvador Dali Museum, 1003rd St. S., St. Petersburg (collection of Dali's paintings, prints, drawings)

Tampa Museum of Art, 600 N. Ashley Dr., Tampa (contemporary American painting and photography, classical antiquities)

The Wolfsonian, 1001 Washington Ave., Miami Beach (founded 1996, 70,000 objects including books, furniture, games, and works on paper, machine-influenced designs since 1885, Art Deco movie-theater window grille, radios, etc.)

GEORGIA

Georgia Museum of Art, Jackson St., University of Georgia, Athens (Max Weber's *Drapeau,* Stuart Davis' *Snow on the Mountain*)

High Museum of Art, 1280 Peachtree St., NE, Atlanta (Faith Ringgold's *Church Picnic Story Quilt,* comprehensive collection, American artists, Harnett, Childe Hassam, Jacob Lawrence, John Marin, John Singer Sargent)

HAWAII

The Contemporary Museum, 2411 Makiki Heights Dr., Honolulu (sculpture garden, permanent collection from 1940s to present)

Honolulu Academy of the Arts, 900 S. Beretania St., Honolulu (Asian, European and American art, Kress and Michener collections, Oceanic and African art)

List 10–17   Continued

IDAHO

Boise Art Museum, 670 S. Julia Davis Dr., Boise (American Realism and contemporary Northwest art)

ILLINOIS

Art Institute of Chicago, Michigan Ave. at Adams St., Chicago (Toulouse-Lautrec's *At the Moulin Rouge,* Renoir's *Rower's Lunch,* Seurat's *Sunday Afternoon on the Island of La Grande Jatte,* Cassatt's *La Toilette,* Monet's *Gare St. Lazare,* Hans Memling's diptych of *Madonna and Child and Donor*)

Field Museum of Natural History, Roosevelt Rd. and Lake Shore Dr., Chicago (archaeological treasures, important Egyptian exhibition and tomb)

Museum of Contemporary Art, 237 East Ontario St., Chicago (post World War II art, Pop Art, Surrealism, [Magritte's *The Wonders of Nature*] Minimalism)

Oriental Institute, University of Chicago, 1155 E. 58th St., Chicago (*Colossal Portrait of Tutankhamen,* Assyrian *Winged Bull,* Persian *Bull's Head and Man-Bull* capital)

Terra Museum of American Art, 666 N. Michigan Ave., Chicago (American painters: Bingham, Audubon, Cassatt, Copley, Hassam, Prendergast, Whistler)

INDIANA

Indianapolis Museum of Art, 1200 W. 38th St., Indianapolis (Asian, Pre-Columbian, African, American, European, J.M.W. Turner collection)

University of Indiana Art Museum, Indiana University, Bloomington (Greek and Roman art, Laurent's *Birth of Venus,* Maillol's *Nude,* and Barlach's *Singing Man*)

IOWA

Cedar Rapids Museum of Art, 410 Third Ave. SE, Cedar Rapids (Grant Wood, Mauricio Lazansky collections, 19th- to 20th-century sculpture, Malvina Hoffman, regional artists)

Des Moines Art Center, Greenwood Pk., Des Moines (Yasuo Kuniyoshi's *Amazing Juggler,* Calder *Mobile,* Prendergast, Bellows, Burchfield, Hassam, Hopper, Shahn, Max Weber, Jasper Johns, Brancusi, Cindy Sherman)

KANSAS

Spencer Museum of Art, University of Kansas, Lawrence (comprehensive collection of ancient artifacts, quilts, Japanese prints and Edo paintings)

Wichita Art Museum, 619 Stackman Dr., Wichita (18th- to 20th-century American painting, John Steuart Curry's *Kansas Cornfield,* Marin, Hopper, Walt Kuhn, Gaston Lachaise)

KENTUCKY

University of Kentucky Art Museum, Rose and Euclid Sts., Lexington (African and pre-Columbian, American and European art)

LOUISIANA

New Orleans Museum of Art, 1 Collins Diboll Circle, City Park, New Orleans (Naum Gabo's *Construction in Space,* Veronese's *Sacred Conversation,* photographs, art of the Americas, Fabergé Gallery, 13th- to 19th-century European painting)

MAINE

Bowdoin College Museum of Fine Arts, Walker Art Building, Brunswick (Stuart's *Jefferson* and *Madison,* sculpture by French and Saint-Gaudens, ancient artifacts, Colonial painters Copley, Earl, Feke, Smibert, Trumbull, and Stuart)

Ogunquit Museum of American Art, 183 Shore Rd., Ogunquit (Charles Burchfield, Charles Demuth, Jack Levine, John Marin, Reginald Marsh, Marsden Hartley)

MARYLAND

Baltimore Museum of Art, Art Museum Dr., Baltimore (French Post-Impressionist collection: van Gogh's *The Shoes,* Gauguin's *Woman With a Mango,* Lipchitz's *Gertrude Stein,* Matisse's *The Blue Nude,* Cezanne's *Mont Ste. Victoire Seen from Bibemus Quarry,* Asian, Pre-Columbian, American, European decorative arts)

Peale Museum, 225 N. Holliday St., Baltimore (Charles Willson Peale's *Exhuming the Mastodon,* Rembrandt Peale's *Roman Daughter,* Sarah Miriam Peale's *Self Portrait*)

Walters Art Gallery, Charles and Centre Sts., Baltimore (Ingres' *Interior of a Harem with Odalisque,* Manet's *Le Cafe-Concert,* Daumier's *Second-Class Railway Carriage,* sculpture collection, Medieval objects)

MASSACHUSETTS

Addison Gallery of American Art, Phillips Academy, Andover (Eakins' *Professor Rowland,* Homer's *Eight Bells,* Ryder's *Toilers of the Sea,* Luks' *The Spielers*)

Fine Arts Museum, 465 Huntington Ave., Boston (paintings and sculpture from India, Old Kingdom Egyptian sculpture, American, European, and Asian decorative arts)

Fogg Art Museum, 32 Quincy St., Cambridge (Ingres' *Odalisque with a Slave,* Degas' *Cotton Merchants,* Sheeler's *Upper Deck,* Copley's *Portrait of Mrs. Thomas Boylston,* T'ang Dynasty *Adoring Bodhisattva,* print and drawing collection)

Isabella Stewart Gardner Museum, 280 The Fenway, Boston (Botticelli's *Madonna and Child of the Eucharist,* Titian's *The Rape of Europa,* Velazquez's *Philip IV,* Raphael's *Portrait of Count Tomamaso Inghirami,* John Singer Sargent's *El Jaleo*)

Museum of Fine Arts, 49 Chestnut St., Springfield (Erastus Field's *Historic Monument of the American Republic,* Gericault's *The Madman-Kidnapper,* 19th-century American prints, *Self-Portrait,* American artists, 20th-century, prints, sculpture, Tiffany glass)

Smith College Museum of Art, Northampton (American and European Paintings)

Sterling and Francine Clark Art Institute, 225 South St., Williamstown (old master paintings, Degas' *Self-Portrait* and bronze *Ballet Dancer,* Piero Della Francesca's *Madonna and Child With Four Angels,* Homer's *The Bridle Path*)

Worcester Art Museum, 55 Salisbury St., Worcester (comprehensive collection of Egyptian and classical antiquities to Impressionist paintings, Pop Art, Clouet's *Diane de Poitiers,* Gainsborough's *The Artist's Daughters,* Sheeler's *City Interior*)

MICHIGAN

Detroit Institute of Arts, 5200 Woodward Ave., Detroit (Brueghel's *The Wedding Dance,* da Vinci's *The Adoration With Two Angels,* Whistler's *Nocturne in Black and Gold: The Falling Rocket,* Sheeler's *Home Sweet Home,* graphic arts and photography)

MINNESOTA

Minneapolis Institute of Arts, 2400 Third Ave. S., Minneapolis (painting, sculpture, decorative arts, period rooms, Beckmann's *Blindman's Bluff,* Munch's *Jealousy,* Gauguin's *Tahitian Mountains,* Seurat's *Port-en-Bessin,* Larry Rivers' *The Studio, Pieta* by the Master of the St. Lucy Legend, Degas' *Portrait of Mlle. Hortense Valpincon*)

Walker Art Center, Vineland Pl., Minneapolis (Stuart Davis' *Colonial Cubism,* Franz Marc's *Blue Horses,* Jacques Lipchitz's *Prometheus and the Vulture,* contemporary painting, sculpture garden)

MISSISSIPPI

Mississippi Museum of Art, 201 E. Pascagoula St., Jackson (19th- and 20th-century American, Southern, and Mississippi art, old master to contemporary paintings, Asian and Native American art)

MISSOURI

Kemper Museum of Contemporary Art and Design, 4420 Warwick Blvd., Kansas City (Deborah Butterfield's *Horse,* Janet Fish, William Wegman, Nancy Graves)

List 10–17   Continued

MISSOURI (cont.)

Nelson-Atkins Museum of Art, 4525 Oak St., Kansas City (Thomas Hart Benton paintings, strong Asian collection, Goya's *Don Ignacio Omulryan y Rourera,* Caravaggio's *St. John the Baptist,* Rodin's *The Thinker,* Henry Moore's sculpture, Raphaelle Peale's *After the Bath,* Memling's *Madonna and Child Enthroned*)

St. Louis Art Museum, 1 Fine Arts Dr., Forest Park, St. Louis (German Expressionists, including many paintings by Max Beckmann, John Greenwood's *Sea Captains Carousing at Suriname,* George Caleb Bingham's *Raftsmen Playing Cards,* van Gogh's *Stairway at Auvers,* de Hooch's *A Game of Skittles,* Hals' *Portrait of a Woman*)

St. Louis Art Museum, 1904, Cass Gilbert, Beaux Artes

Washington University Gallery of Art, One Brookings Dr., St. Louis (Guston's *Fable,* varied collection of European drawings and paintings)

MONTANA

Montana Historical Society, 225 N. Roberts, Helena (Western art, Montana history, Charles M. Russell, Phimister Proctor)

NEBRASKA

Joslyn Art Museum, 2200 Dodge St., Omaha (collections of Western art by George Catlin, Seth Eastman, Card Bodmer, Thomas Hart Benton's *Hailstorm,* Grant Wood's *Stone City,* Pollock's *Galaxy,* 19th- and 20th-century art)

NEVADA

Nevada Museum of Art, 160 W. Liberty St., Reno (19th- and 20th-century American art, paintings of the Great Basin region)

NEW HAMPSHIRE

Hood Museum of Art, Dartmouth College, Hanover (American and European paintings, Asian, African, Oceanic and Pre-Columbian artifacts)

NEW JERSEY

The Art Museum, Princeton University, Princeton (classical, Chinese, Pre-Columbian, American collection, sculpture court, Medieval art)

Newark Museum, 43–49 Washington St., Newark (American painting and sculpture, Joseph Stella's *Brooklyn Bridge,* 20th-century American paintings, Tibetan artifacts)

NEW MEXICO

Georgia O'Keeffe Foundation, 217 Johnson St., Santa Fe (O'Keeffe's watercolors, sculpture, and oils)

Museum of Fine Arts, 107 W. Palace Ave., Palace of the Governors, Santa Fe (20th-century American art, Native American, Hispanic, work by Georgia O'Keeffe)

University of New Mexico, Harwood Foundation Museum, 238 Ledoux St., Taos (20th-century art of Taos and surrounding areas)

NEW YORK

Albright-Knox Art Gallery, 1285 Elmwood Ave., Buffalo (Gauguin's *The Yellow Christ,* Gorky's *The Liver is the Cock's Comb,* Moore's carved *Reclining Nude,* Lehmbruck's *Kneeling Woman,* David Smith's *Tank Totem IV,* 20th-century American art)

American Craft Museum, 40 W. 53rd St., New York City (contemporary American crafts from mid-20th century, changing exhibitions)

Brooklyn Museum, 200 Eastern Pkwy., Brooklyn (comprehensive collection of artifacts from ancient times, period rooms, costumes and textiles, Ralph Blakelock's *Moonlight,* Hiram Powers' *The Greek Slave,* Bingham's *Shooting for the Beef,* Hopi *Kachina* dolls, Oceania Ancestor figures, African masks and sculpture)

The Cloisters, Fort Tyron Pk., New York City (Medieval treasures, including portions of an actual cloister, stone and wood carvings, stained glass, *Unicorn Tapestries*)

List 10–17   Continued

NEW YORK (cont.)

Cooper Hewitt Museum of Design, 2 E. 91st St., New York City (historic and contemporary collection, changing exhibitions)

Corning Museum of Glass, One Museum Way, Corning (outstanding collection of glass from 1500 BC to present, demonstrations of glass blowing)

Everson Museum of Art, 401 Harrison St., Syracuse (American paintings, ceramics, prints, photography and sculpture, African and Asian art)

Frick Collection, 1 East 70th St., New York City (Constable's *Salisbury Cathedral,* Van Eyck's *Virgin and Child with Saints and a Donor,* Fragonard's *The Progress of Love,* La Tour's *The Education of the Virgin,* Rembrandt's *The Polish Rider* and *Self-Portrait,* Boucher, El Greco, Gainsborough, Van Dyck)

The Herbert F. Johnson Museum of Art, Cornell University, Ithaca (print collection: Baskin, Hassam, Marin, Pennell and Whistler, 115 Tiffany glass pieces)

Hyde Collection, 161 Warren St., Glen Falls (Eakins' *In The Studio,* Rubens' *Head of a Negro,* Rembrandt's *Christ,* Peto's *Still Life,* Leonardo, Degas, Homer, Picasso, Renoir, van Gogh, Whistler)

Metropolitan Museum of Art, 1000 Fifth Ave., New York City (5000 years of art, Egyptian temple, Demuth's *I Saw the Figure 5 in Gold,* Sargent's *Madame X,* El Greco's *View of Toledo,* Memling's *Tommaso and Maria Portinari,* Rembrandt's *Aristotle Contemplating the Bust of Homer*)

Munson-Williams-Proctor Institute, 310 Genesee St., Utica (American paintings; Charles Burchfield, Arthur Dove, Arshile Gorky, Morris Graves)

Museum of Modern Art, 11 W. 53rd St., New York City (outstanding modern collection, sculpture garden, Picasso's *Three Musicians* and *Les Demoiselles d'Avignon,* Rodin's *Monument to Balzac,* de Chirico's *Nostalgia of the Infinite,* Braque's *Woman With a Mandolin,* Monet's *Waterlilies,* van Gogh's *Starry Night*)

National Academy of Design, 1083 5th Ave., New York City (19th- and 20th-century American art)

New York Historical Society Museum, 170 Central Pk. West, New York City (18th- to 20th-century American paintings, drawings, prints, Audubon's *Birds of America,* Thomas Cole's *The Course of Empire,* Bierstadt, Charles Willson Peale, Louis Comfort Tiffany)

Pierpont Morgan Library, 29 E. 36th St., New York City (Medieval and Renaissance manuscripts, drawings, prints)

Rochester Memorial Art Gallery, University of Rochester, Rochester (American collection, Copley, Homer, Eakins, Ryder, Stuart Davis, Elie Nadelman, Isamu Noguchi)

Solomon R. Guggenheim Museum, 1071 Fifth Ave., New York City (Leger's *The Great Parade,* Cezanne's *The Clock Maker,* 120 paintings by Kandinsky, Toulouse-Lautrec, Giacometti, Paul Gauguin, Paul Klee, Georges Braque)

Whitney Museum of American Art, Madison Ave. at 75th St., New York City (20th-century American paintings, sculpture, Alexander Calder's *Circus,* Ben Shahn's *The Passion of Sacco and Vanzetti,* Max Weber's *Adoration of the Moon,* Edward Hopper's *Early Sunday Morning*)

The Solomon R. Guggenheim Museum, 1957–1959, New York, Frank Lloyd Wright

NORTH CAROLINA

North Carolina Museum of Art, 2110 Blue Ridge Rd., Raleigh (14th- to 19th-century European and American paintings, classical sculpture, Boucher's *The Abduction of Europa,* Rembrandt's *Esther's Feast,* Bellotto's *Views of Dresden*)

NORTH DAKOTA

North Dakota Museum of Art, Box 7305 University Station, Grand Forks (contemporary art by regional, national, and international artists)

OHIO

Allen Memorial Art Museum, Oberlin College, Main and Lorrain Sts., Oberlin (17th-century Dutch paintings, 14th- to 20th-century European and American painting and sculpture, Japanese print collection)

List 10–17   Continued

OHIO (cont.)

Butler Institute of American Art, 524 Wick Ave., Youngstown (American paintings, drawings, and prints from 1719 to present, Hopper's *Pennsylvania Coal Town,* Homer's *Snap the Whip*)

Cincinnati Art Museum, Eden Pk., Cincinnati (500 years of art; Botticelli's *Judith With the Head of Holofernes,* Joos van Cleve's *Francis I,* Cezanne's *Bread and Eggs,* Grant Wood's *Daughters of the Revolution,* Sir Henry Raeburn's *The Elphinstone Children,* Frank Duveneck's *Whistling Boy*)

Cleveland Museum of Art, 11150 East Blvd., Cleveland (arts of the ancient Mediterranean, Egypt, Greece, and Rome, J.M.W. Turner's *Burning of the Houses of Parliament,* George Bellows' *Stag at Sharkey's,* Manet's *Portrait of Berthe Morisot,* Berthe Morisot's *Young Lady in White,* Japanese treasures)

Columbus Museum of Art, 480 E. Broad St., Columbus (Impressionism and American Modernism, paintings by George Bellows, John Marin, Charles Demuth, Maurice Prendergast, Jules Pascin, Monet, O'Keeffe, Pissaro, Renoir)

Taft Museum, 316 Pike St., Cincinnati (Duncan Phyfe furniture [25 pieces], Robert S. Duncanson paintings, Corot, Gainsborough, Hals, Ingres, Rembrandt, Sargent, Whistler, Turner)

Toledo Museum of Art, Monroe Street at Scottwood Ave., Toledo (Thomas Cole's *The Architect's Dream,* Hopper's *Two on the Aisle,* Rubens' *Crowning of St. Catherine,* Jacques Louis David's *Oath of the Horatii,* large collection of glass; Wyeth, Frank Stella, Hopper, Feininger)

OKLAHOMA

Gilcrease Museum, 1400 Gilcrease Museum Rd., Tulsa (American sculpture and painting, Native American artifacts and art, Remington, Charles M. Russell, Albert Bierstadt, Thomas Eakins)

Oklahoma City Art Museum, 3113 Pershing Blvd., Oklahoma City (regional, American, and European art, George Bellows, Eugene Boudin, Alexander Calder, Sam Francis, Andy Warhol, Robert Indiana)

Philbrook Museum of Art, 2727 S. Rockford Rd., Tulsa (18th- and 19th-century European and American painting, Italian Renaissance sculpture and painting, paintings by Durer, Goya, Tiepolo)

OREGON

Portland Art Museum, 1219 Southwest Pk., Portland (Northwestern Coast collection: masks, baskets, contemporary art, Bronzino's *Madonna and Child With the Infant St. John the Baptist*)

PENNSYLVANIA

Barnes Foundation, 300 North Latch's Lane, Merion Station (collection of Impressionists, old masters, African, Asian, and primitive art, Cezanne's *Les Grandes Baigneuses,* Matisse's *Three Sisters* triptych, Renoir's *Bathers of 1918,* Seurat's *Les Poseuses*)

Brandywine River Museum, U.S. Rte. 1, Chadds Ford (work by members of the Wyeth family, American 19th- and 20th-century landscape paintings)

Carnegie Institute Art Museum, 4400 Forbes Ave., Pittsburgh (Oriental art, photography, paintings, sculpture, prints, drawings, Rouault's *Old King,* Kokoschka's *Thomas Masary*)

Frick Art Museum, 7227 Reynolds St., Pittsburgh (Italian Renaissance, Flemish and French paintings; bronzes, tapestries)

Historical Society of Pennsylvania, Philadelphia (Philadelphia furniture, 500 pieces of silver, early Colonial painters: Hesselius, Peale family, Sully, West, Copley)

Pennsylvania Academy of Fine Arts, 118 N. Broad St., Philadelphia (18th- to 20th-century, American painting, sculpture, drawings, and prints, Charles Willson Peale's *The Artist in His Museum,* Benjamin West's *Penn's Treaty With the Indians,* Eakins' *Portrait of Walt Whitman*)

Philadelphia Museum of Art, Benjamin Franklin Pkwy. at 26th St., Philadelphia (Brancusi's *Bird in Space,* Duchamp's *Nude Descending a Staircase,* Peale's *Staircase Group,* Oriental collection: Persian, Indian, Chinese and Japanese artifacts, Picasso's *Three Musicians,* Rousseau's *Carnival Evening,* van Gogh's *Sunflowers,* Cezanne's *Bathers,* 40 paintings by Thomas Eakins, Ruben's *Prometheus Bound*)

List 10–17   Continued

PENNSYLVANIA (cont.)

University of Pennsylvania Museum, 33rd and Spruce Sts., Philadelphia (extensive archaeological treasures: Mid-Eastern, East African, American, and Oceanic)

RHODE ISLAND

Newport Art Museum, 76 Bellevue Ave., Newport (permanent collection of New England and Newport artists, contemporary and historical)

Rhode Island School of Design Museum of Art, 224 Benefit St., Providence (antiquity to 20th-century collection, classical Greek sculpture, Degas' *Six Friends of the Artist* and *Before the Race*)

SOUTH CAROLINA

Bob Jones University Museum of Sacred Art, Wade Hampton Blvd., Greenville (13th- to 19th-century French, Flemish, Italian, Dutch, Spanish art: Botticelli, Rubens, Tintoretto, Titian, Van Dyck)

Columbia Museum of Art, 1112 Bull St., Columbia (Botticelli's *Nativity,* Canaletto's *View of Venice,* Joachim Patinir's *The Flight into Egypt* Tiffany glass, 13th- to 20th-century European and American paintings, sculpture, graphic arts)

SOUTH DAKOTA

Civic Fine Arts Center, 235 W. 10th St., Sioux Falls (regional, American, and International artists, paintings, sculpture, other media)

TENNESSEE

Dixon Gallery and Gardens, 4339 Park Ave., Memphis (German porcelain, French Impressionists, pewter)

Memphis Brooks Museum of Art, Overton Pk., 1934 Poplar Ave., Memphis (European painting from 13th to 20th centuries, English and American decorative arts, collection of Greek vases)

TEXAS

Amon Carter Museum, 3501 Camp Bowie Blvd., Fort Worth (19th- and 20th-century American art, Remington's *The Old Stage Coach of the Plains*)

Dallas Museum of Fine Arts, 1717 N. Harwood, Dallas (contemporary, pre-Columbian, American and European paintings, Morris Graves' *Bird,* Matisse's *Collage,* Pollock's *Cathedral,* Rufino Tamayo's *El Hombre*)

El Paso Museum of Art, 1211 Montana Ave., El Paso (Kress collection of 14th- to 17th-century European, 19th- to 20th-century American paintings, Spanish and Hispanic art)

Kimbell Art Museum, 3333 Camp Bowie Blvd., Fort Worth (Asian, African, Mesoamerican, prehistoric to 20th-century art, Matisse, Rubens, Velazquez, Caravaggio's *The Cardsharps,* Cezanne, Fra Angelico)

Menil Collection, 1515 Sul Ross, Houston (antiquities, Byzantine, tribal, and 20th-century collection, Magritte's *Golconda*)

Modern Art Museum of Forth Worth, 1309 Montgomery St., Fort Worth (20th-century artists, Avery, Diebenkorn, Donald Judd, Kandinsky, Motherwell, Pollock, Picasso, Rauschenberg, Clyfford Still)

Museum of Fine Arts, 1001 Bissonnet, Houston (more than 27,000 works of art from prehistoric artifacts to contemporary art, Cezanne's *Madame Cezanne in Blue*)

UTAH

Brigham Young University Museum of Fine Arts, North Campus Dr., Provo (Hudson River School, American Realism, American Impressionism)

VERMONT

Shelburne Museum, Webb Art Gallery, U.S. 7, Burlington (18th- and19th-century American art, Church, Cole, Bierstadt, Quidor, Homer, folk art collection)

St. Johnsbury Athenaeum, 30 Main St., St. Johnsbury (19th-century American landscapes, Hudson River School)

List 10–17 Continued

VIRGINIA

Virginia Museum of Fine Arts, Grove Ave. and North Blvd., Richmond (ancient, Medieval, and contemporary art, five Faberge *Imperial Easter Eggs,* Copley's *Mrs. Isaac Royall,* Francesco Guardi's *Piazza San Marco,* Henry Moore's *Reclining Figure,* sculpture court)

WASHINGTON

Charles and Emma Frye Art Museum, 704 Terry Ave., Seattle (German and 19th-century American paintings, Alaskan and Russia American collections)

Maryhill Museum of Art, 35 Maryhill Museum Dr., Goldendale (Rodin collection, Russian icons, Native American baskets and other artifacts, outdoor full-sized reproduction of Stonehenge)

Seattle Art Museum, 100 University St., Seattle (20,000 works of art covering 5,000 years, Native American art, Asian art, Ming Dynasty *Camels,* Mark Tobey's *Forms Follow Man,* Morris Graves' *Sea Fish and Constellation*)

Tacoma Art Museum, 1123 Pacific Ave., Tacoma (19th- and 20th-century art, Dale Chihuly, Jacob Lawrence, Robert Motherwell, Renoir, Raphael Soyer, Mark Tobey)

WEST VIRGINIA

Huntington Museum of Art, 2033 McCoy Rd., Huntington (French, English and American paintings, Frank Benson, George Inness, Willard Metcalf, Alfred Stieglitz)

Sunrise Art Museum, 746 Myrtle Rd., Charleston (regional art, contemporary sculpture, 19th- to 20th-century American paintings, Chuck Close, Stuart Davis, Viola Frey, Nancy Graves, Larry Rivers, Ben Shahn)

WISCONSIN

Milwaukee Art Center, 750 N. Lincoln Memorial Drive, Milwaukee (20th-century American and European painting and sculpture, ancient art, decorative arts, film, video)

WYOMING

Buffalo Bill Historical Center, 750 Sheridan Ave., Cody (gallery of Western art, Plains Indian Museum)

National Museum of Wildlife Art, Rungius Rd., Jackson Hole (sculpture and paintings of North American wildlife, artists exhibited: Audubon, Catlin, A. Phimister Procter, Charles M. Russell)

List 10–18   Major International Museums

Most major museums in the world began when one person's personal art collection was made available for the public to see. Additional personal collections, museum purchases, and individually-donated artworks built the museum. A nation's cultural history is represented by its art, and most of these museums take great pride in their displays of regional art and artifacts. A minimal overview of the collection and addresses are given in the event you might wish to write for further information. Museums from the United States are given in List 10–17.

AFGHANISTAN

Kabul Museum, Darul Aman, Kabul (5000 years of Afghanistan's history, Islamic collection, Buddhist paintings)

AFRICA

Johannesburg Art Gallery, Joubert Pk., Johannesburg (South African art, 19th-century French painting and sculpture, British works)

Jos Museum, Jos, Benue-Plateau State, Nigeria (Nok culture, contemporary Nigerian art, architecture and archaeology of Nigeria)

National Museum, Museum Hill, Nairobi (ancient and contemporary African art)

South African National Gallery, Government Avenue, Cape Town (Dutch and English paintings, German Expressionism, modern European schools of art)

ARGENTINA

Juan B. Castagnino Municipal Museum of Fine Arts, Avenida Pelligrini 2202, Rosario (Argentine artists, European painters)

AUSTRALIA

Adelaide, Art Gallery of South Australia, North Terrace, Adelaide (Australian and English art)

Art Gallery of New South Wales, Art Gallery Rd., The Domain, Sydney (traditional and modern European art, Australian painters, Aboriginal artworks)

Museum of Contemporary Art, Circular Quay West, Sydney (DuChamp, Christo, Warhol, Aboriginal art)

National Gallery of Victoria, 180 St. Kilda Rd., Melbourne (Aboriginal, colonial Australian, Asian, and European works, Tom Robert's *Shearing the Rams,* Frederick McCubbin's *The Pioneer*)

AUSTRIA

Albertina Collection, Augustinerstrasse I, Vienna (prints, drawings, watercolors, Durer's *Praying Hands,* Rembrandt's etchings)

Kunsthistorisches Museum, Maria Theresienplatz, Vienna (Hapsburg collections, Brueghel's *Tower of Babel* and *Peasant Wedding,* Velazquez's *Infanta Margarita,* Vermeer's *The Artist in His Studio, The Gemma Augustea* (Roman Cameo), Cellini's *Saliera* (salt cellar), Holbein's *Jane Seymore,* Cranach's *Young Woman*)

BELGIUM

Ancient Art Museum, Royal Fine Arts Museums of Belgium, 3 Rue de la Regence, Brussels (Van Dyck, Rubens, Jordaens, Van der Weyden, Master of Flemalle, Brueghel, Rubens)

Antwerp Fine Arts Museum, Leopold de Waelplein, 1000, Antwerp (Van Eyck, Van der Weyden, Van Dyck, Rubens, Ensor, Permeke, Delvaux)

Modern Art Museum/Royal Fine Arts Museums of Belgium, 1 Place Royale, Brussels (19th-century Belgian from 1860–present, Ensor, Delvaux, Magritte, Jacques-Louis David)

Municipal Fine Arts Museum, Dyver 12, 8000 Bruges (early Flemish Masters: Van Eyck, Memling, Van Der Weyden, Bosch, Gerard David)

Royal Museums of Art and History, Avenue des Nerviens, 10 Parc du Cinquantenaire, Brussels (armor, Oriental ceramics, Belgian lace and tapestries, ancient mid-Eastern and European artifacts)

Rubenshuis Museum, Rubenstraat, Antwerp (Rubens' home has original furnishings)

List 10–18   Continued

CANADA

Art Gallery of Greater Victoria, 1040 Moss St., Victoria, British Columbia (Japanese and Chinese artworks, European painting and sculpture, 15th- to 20th-century art)

Art Gallery of Ontario, Grange Pk., Toronto 133, Ontario (Rubens' *The Elevation of the Cross,* Gainsborough's *The Harvest Wagon,* Moore's *Working Model for Three-Piece Sculpture No. 3—Vertebrae,* New York School collection)

National Gallery of Canada, Elgin St., Ottawa, Ontario (Benjamin West's *The Death of General Wolfe,* Memling, Martini, Rembrandt, El Greco, Corot)

Royal Ontario Museum, 100 Queen's Pk., Toronto 5, Ontario (outstanding Oriental collections, Canadian paintings and furniture)

Winnipeg Art Gallery, 30 Memorial Blvd., Winnipeg, Manitoba (Eskimo carvings, Dufy's *The Jetty at Trouville,* North German panel: *Flagellation of Christ*)

CHINA

Shanghai Museum, People's Square, Shanghai (bronze vessels, paintings, ceramics, furniture, jade, seals, and coins)

DENMARK

Ny Carlsberg Glyptothek, Dantes Plads, 1556 Copenhagen (Egyptian and Greek collections, Gauguin and other Impressionists)

Rosenborg Castle Collections, 1606, Ostervoldegade 4a, 1350 Copenhagen (crown jewels, ivory *Coronation Chair,* life-size silver lions, Venetian glass, silver furniture)

Royal Museum of Fine Arts, 1307 Solvgade, Copenhagen (Rembrandt, *Sappo at Emmaus,* 20th century, French art, large selection of Danish art)

CZECH REPUBLIC

National Gallery, Hradcanske Namesti 15, Prague 1 (Bohemian Master, Brueghel's *Haymakers,* Kokoschka, *The Charles Bridge, Prague*)

EGYPT

Egyptian Museum, Midan El Tahrir, Cairo (Egyptian antiquities from 1800 BC, King Tut treasures, gold, sculpture, mummies)

ENGLAND

Apsley House, 149 Picadilly, London (Lord Wellington's restored home, collection of Sevres, Canalettos, Rubens)

Ashmolean Museum, Beaumont Street, Oxford (Minoan, Mycenaean and Cycladic, Egyptian collections, *Bodleian Bowl,* armor)

Barber Institute of Fine Arts, The University, Birmingham (English and European collections)

Birmingham Museum and Art Gallery, Congreve St., Birmingham (Italian collection, tapestries, furniture, mid-east archaeological collection)

Bristol Art Gallery, Queen's Rd., Bristol (Oriental collection, Chinese glass, wide European collection of paintings and prints)

British Museum, Great Russell St., London (*Elgin Marbles* (Parthenon), *Lindisfarne Gospels, Rosetta Stone, Magna Carta,* Egyptian sphinxes and other ancient treasures from around the world)

Courtauld Institute Galleries, Somerset House Strand, London (Manet's *Bar at the Folies-Bergere,* many other Impressionists, old masters)

Fitzwilliam Museum, Trumpington St., Cambridge (Egyptian, Greek and Roman antiquities, European paintings, medieval manuscripts and music collection)

Manchester City Art Gallery, Mosley St., Manchester (Dutch 17th century, sculpture, glass, furniture, pre-Raphaelite paintings, Turner)

List 10–18   Continued

ENGLAND (cont.)

National Gallery, Trafalgar Sq., London (Italian masters, Rembrandt, Velasquez, Cezanne, Van Eyck, Botticelli)

National Portrait Gallery, 2 St. Martin's Pl., London (portraits of important figures in English history)

Tate Gallery, Millbank, London (Turner, Picasso, Rothko, Stubbs, Constable, Blake, Gainsborough, Epstein, Moore)

Tate Gallery, Porthmeor Beach, St. Ives (artists from St. Ives, 20th-century work from the Tate Gallery, London)

Victoria and Albert Museum, Cromwell Rd., South Kensington, London (fine and applied arts, arms and armor, musical instruments, woodwork, sculpture)

Walker Art Gallery, William Brown St., Liverpool (English art, 15th-century, 19th- and 20th-century English paintings, Italian primitives)

Wallace Collection, Hertford House, Manchester Sq., London (Boucher, Watteau, Fragonard, Sevres, Rembrandt, Titian, Rubens, Reynolds, Canaletto)

FINLAND

Ateneum Art Museum, Kaivokatu 1–4, Helsinki (European and Finnish collection of old masters to present-day painters)

FRANCE

Condé Museum, Chateau de Chantilly, Chantilly (Regence woodwork, Chantilly porcelain, Flemish and Italian Primitives, Memling, Clouet, *Les Tres Riches Heures du Duc de Berry*)

Louvre, Palais du Louvre, Paris (Egyptian, Leonardo's *Mona Lisa*, Whistler's *Portrait of the Artist's Mother*, Van Dyck's *Charles I of England*, Holbein's *Portrait of Emmaus*, Rembrandt's *Bathsheba Bathing, Nike of Samothrace, Venus de Milo, Code of Hammurabi, Frieze from the Parthenon, The Seated Scribe*)

Maeght Foundation, Saint Paul de Vence (20th-century French art, Braque, Chagall, Kandinsky, Miró, and Giacometti)

Musée D'Orsay, 1 Rue de Lille, Paris (French Impressionists, 19th-century sculpture, photography, applied arts, van Gogh collection)

Musée de Cluny, 6 Place Paul Painleve, Paris (Medieval art in a Gothic residence, applied arts, tapestries, altars, Limoges enamels)

Musée de l'Homme, Arts, et Civilisations, Palais de Trocadero, Paris (due to open in 2002, African and Oceanic collections)

Musée de la Reine Mathilde, Rue Lambert Leonard Leforestier, Calvados, Bayeux (*Bayeux Tapestry*)

Musée des Arts Decoratifs, 107 Rue de Rivoli, Paris (collection of furniture, paintings, textiles, weapons, jewelry, glassware, toys, carpets, posters, Art Nouveau, Art Deco)

Musée Jeu de Paume, Place de la Concorde, Paris (contemporary works by such French artists as Dubuffet, Takis, and Broodthears)

Musée National d'Art Moderne, Place Georges-Pompidou, Beaubourg (Modigliani, Utrillo, Vuillard, Derain, Delaunay, Braque, Dufy, Leger, Matisse, Picasso's *Harlequin*)

Orangerie, Palais du Louvre, Place de la Concord and Quai de Tuileries, Paris (large collection of Monet's *Waterlilies*)

GERMANY

Alte Pinakothek, Barerstrasse 27, Munich (Van Der Weyden's *The Adoration of the Magi*, Durer's *Self Portrait in Fur Coat*)

Art Gallery of the Old Masters, Zwinger, 801 Dresden (Rembrandt, Vermeer, Holbein, van Eyck, Velasquez, Giorgione, Raphael)

Art Museum of Dusseldorf, 4 Dusseldorf-Nord, Ehrenhof (Art Nouveau collection, German Expressionists, Dutch paintings)

Bode Museum, Monbijoubrucke am Kupfergraben, Berlin (early Christian, Byzantine, and Egyptian art, Ravenna mosaics, Cranach's *Doomsday*)

List 10–18   Continued

GERMANY (cont.)

Bremen Art Gallery, Am Wall 207, D28 Bremen (15th- to 20th-century European paintings, emphasis on 19th-century French and German)

Charlottenburg Palace Museums, Berlin (head of *Nefertiti, Guelph Treasure,* Egyptian, Greek, and Roman antiquities, Egyptian, early Christian, Byzantine, and sculpture collection, European paintings, Cranach, Elsheimer, Ravenna *Mosaics,* Donatello)

Dahlem Museum, Arnimallee 23/27, Berlin (collection of European and Far Eastern art, Durer, Cranach, Holbein, van Eyck, van der Weyden, Vermeer Hals, Rembrandt)

Hamburg Art Gallery, 1 Glockengiesserwall, 2000 Hamburg (Kirschner's *Self Portrait with Model,* Beckmann's *Odysseus and Calypso,* Corinth's *At the Hairdresser,* van Dyck's *The Adoration of the Shepherds*)

Herzog Anton Ulrich Museum, 33 Braunschweig, Museumstrasse 1, Brunswick (ducal collection of antiquities, European paintings, clocks, ceramics, carvings)

Kaiser Friedrich Museum, Museum Island, Berlin (Prussian Royal collections, sculpture, print, and drawing collections)

National Gallery, Potsdamer Strasse 50, Berlin (Modern art, Renoir, Manet, Munch, Kokoschka, Klee, Beckmann)

National Gallery, Prezihova ulica 1, Laibach, formerly Ljubjana, Yugoslavia (Slovenian art from the 13th century to the early 20th century)

State Museums, am Kupfergraben, Berlin (Greek and Roman antiquities, *Pergamon Altar, Ishtar Gate, Facade of Mshatta*)

Wallraf-Richartz Museum, Cologne (German, Dutch, Flemish primitives, Hals' *Hille Bobbe,* German Expressionists)

GREECE

Acropolis Museum, southeast corner of the Acropolis, Athens (*The Calf-Bearer,* The *Critius Boy, Parthenon* fragments, *Caryatids, The Rampin Rider*)

Benaki Museum, Odos Koumbari, Athens (Coptic textiles, Mycenean gold cups, gold jewelry)

Delphi Museum, Delphi (Archaic sculpture from the *Temple of Apollo, The Sphinx,* 6th century BC)

National Museum of Athens, 28 October Street, Athens (gold *Death mask, Vaphio Cups, Funeral Stele,* bronze *Poseidon, Artemis from Delos*)

HUNGARY

Fine Arts Museum, Dozsa Gy ut 41, Budapest (Italian, Esterhazy Collection of European masterworks, Leonardo da Vinci's *Model of an Equestrian Statue,* Rembrandt, Goya, Raphael, Giorgione)

INDIA

Asutosh Museum of Indian Art, Calcutta University, College Square, Calcutta 12 (Eastern India and Bengal collections, stone sculpture, textiles, scrolls, coins, seals, ivory)

Baroda Museum and Picture Gallery, Sayaji Park, Baroda (ancient and modern Indian and other Asian art and a small European collection)

Government Museum Egmore, Madras (stone and bronze sculpture, wood carvings, metalwork, pottery, armor, coins and paintings)

National Gallery of Modern Art, Jaipur House, New Delhi (contemporary Indian art)

Prince of Wales Museum Fort, Bombay (sculpture, ivories, Indian and European paintings)

IRAN

Archaeological Museum, Avenue de Musée, Teheran (Persian gold, sculpture and artifacts from Persepolis, carpets, silver, porcelain)

IRAQ

Iraq Museum, Baghdad (Mesopotamian antiquities, *Neanderthal Man,* pair of *Winged Bulls, Lyre with Gold Bull's Head*)

List 10–18   Continued

IRELAND

National Gallery of Ireland, Merrion Square, Dublin (paintings)

National Museum of Ireland, Kildare St. and Merrion St., Dublin (stone age antiquities, shrines, handicrafts)

ISRAEL

Israel Museum, Hakirya, Jerusalem (*Dead Sea Scrolls, Torah Scrolls* and ornaments, *Menorahs,* contemporary Israeli artists)

ITALY

Accademia, Venice (Venetian painting from 14th to 18th centuries, Giorgione's *The Tempest,* Veronese's *The Feast in the House of Levi,* Titian's *Presentation of the Virgin at the Temple*)

Bargello National Museum, Via del Proconsolo 4, Florence (Donatello's *David,* Cellini, Bernini, Brunelleschi, Della Robbia)

Borghese Gallery, Piazzale Scipione Borghese 5, Rome (Canova's *Paolina Borghese as Venus,* Bernini's *Apollo and Daphne,* Caravaggio's *St. Jerome,* Raphael's *The Deposition,* Cranach's *Venus and Cupid With a Honeycomb*)

Brera Picture Gallery, Via Brera 28, Milan (Mantegna's *The Dead Christ,* Carvaggio's *Supper at Emmaus,* Guardi, Bramante)

Capitoline Museums, Piazza del Campidoglio, Rome (Michelangelo's *Staircase and Piazza,* ancient Greek, Etruscan, and Italian vases, *She-Wolf, The Dying Gaul,* Titian's *Baptism of Christ*)

Capodimonte National Museum and Gallery, Parco di Capodimonte, Naples (Titian *Danae and the Shower of Gold,* Brueghel's *Parable of the Blind Leading the Blind*)

Civic Museum of Ancient Art, Palazzo Madama, Piazzo Castello, Turin (Roman and Barbarian jewelry, *The Turin Hours (Tres Belles Heures du Duc de Berry),* Messina's *Portrait of an Unknown Man,* Della Robbia's *Annunciation*)

Galleria Accademia, Via Ricasoli 60, Florence (Michelangelo's *David,* other works by Michelangelo, Italian primitives)

National Museum, Piazza Museu, Naples (sculptures, cameos, *Farnese Cup, Farnese Bull* [restored by Michelangelo])

National Museum of Rome, Viale delle Terme di Diocleziano, Rome (ancient art, frescoes from *Villa of Livia,* Roman sarcophagi, *The Discus Thrower*)

Palazzo Bianco Gallery, Via Garibaldi II, Genoa (Zurbaran, Gerard David, Rubens, Genoese painters from 15th to 17th centuries)

Pitti Palace, Piazza Pitti, Florence (*Boboli* gardens, Raphael, Titian, Tintoretto, Rubens, van Dyck, Fra Filippo Lippi, Veronese, Brueghel, Velasquez)

Poldi Pezzoli Museum, Via Manzoni 12, Milan (Pollaiuolo, Botticelli, Bellini, Mantegna, Tiepolo, Murano glass collection)

Uffizi Gallery, loggiato degli Uffizi, Florence (Botticelli, Leonardo da Vinci, Michelangelo, Memling, Raphael, Caravaggio, Giotto)

Vatican Museums, Viale Vaticano, Vatican City (Rome) (Michelangelo's *Sistine Chapel, Last Judgment,* Raphael's *School of Athens,* Ancient sculpture: *Apollo Belvedere, Laocoön Group,* Giotto's *Stefanaschi Polyptych,*)

Villa Giulia National Museum, Piazza di Villa Giulia 9, Rome (Etruscan art, sculptures from Veii, *Sarcophagus of the Bride and Bridegroom,* Ambrosiana Picture Gallery, Piazza Pio XI)

JAPAN

Bridgestone Museum of Art, 1–1 Kyobashi, Chuo-ku, Tokyo (Western Art: Cezanne, Renoir, De Chirico, Rouault, Rousseau, Sisley, Manet)

National Museum of Tokyo, Ueno Park, Tokyo (Japanese art from pre 551 BC to present, Japanese national treasures)

Yamato Bunkakan Museum, 1-11-6 Gakuen Minami, Nara (Japanese national treasures, Japanese and Chinese painting, sculpture, ceramics)

List 10–18   Continued

KOREA

National Central Museum of Korea, Sejong-no, Seoul (metallurgic art, ceramics, paintings, Buddhist paintings, central Asian art)

LEBANON

Archaeological Museum of the American University of Beirut, Beirut (archaeological finds from Middle Eastern cultures, Stone Age through Bronze and Iron ages)

MEXICO

Modern Art Museum, Bosque de Chapultepec, Mexico City (Tamayo, O'Gorman, Camarena, Mexican paintings and sculpture)

National Museum of Anthropology, Calla de la Milla, Mexico City (Mayan, Olmec, Teotihuacan, Toltec, Aztec, *Jade mask*)

THE NETHERLANDS

Boymans-Van Beuningen Museum, Mathenesserlaan 18–20, Rotterdam (Bosch, Brueghel, Steen, van Gogh's *Armand Roulin,* Kandinsky, De Stael, Hubert and Jan van Eyck's *The Three Marys at the Sepulchre,* Hals' *Portrait of a Man*)

Frans Hals Museum, Groot Heligland 62, Haarlem (Hals and other Haarlem School painters)

Mauritshuis Royal Picture Gallery, Plein 29, The Hague (Vermeer, Steen, Van Dyck, Van der Weyden, Rubens, Rembrandt, Hals, Memling)

Rijksmuseum Kroller-Mueller, Otterlo (van Gogh collection, Impressionists, Seurat, Moore, Hepworth, Mondrian)

Rijksmuseum, Stadhouderskade 42, Amsterdam (Vermeer, Hals, Ruisdael, prints, Rembrandt's *The Night Watch,* Hals' *The Merry Toper*)

Stedelijk Museum, Paulus Potterstraat 13, Amsterdam (modern art, mostly from 1950 to present)

Vincent van Gogh Museum, Potterstraat 7, Amsterdam (400 paintings, 200 drawings by van Gogh)

NEW ZEALAND

Auckland City Art Gallery, Kitchener Street, Auckland (European and New Zealand paintings)

Auckland War Memorial Museum, Auckland (*Maori Meeting House, Storage House, War Canoe,* wood and stone carvings)

National Art Gallery, Buckle Street, Wellington (Australian and British artists, Hepworth's *Oval Form*)

National Museum, Buckle Street, Wellington (Maori collection, European and New Zealand paintings)

NORWAY

National Gallery, Universitetsgaten 13, Oslo (Norwegian paintings, Manet, Renoir, Russian icons, El Greco)

Munch Museum, Toyengata 53, Kampen, Oslo (large collection of Munch's paintings)

POLAND

National Museum at Warsaw, Aleje Jerozelimskie 3, Warsaw (Polish art, European, Egyptian and Greek art, Canaletto's *26 Views of Warsaw*)

Wawelu Castle State Art Collections, Krakow (Flemish tapestries, coronation sword, gold chalice, arms and armor, European paintings)

PORTUGAL

Gulbenkian Museum, Calouste Gulbenkian Park, Avenida Berne, Lisbon (eclectic collection of Western and Eastern antiquities, paintings, ceramics, bronzes)

ROMANIA

Art Museum of the Socialist Republic of Romania, 1 Strada Stirbei Voda, Bucharest (10th- to 18th-century Romanian painting, sculpture and decorative arts, Brancusi)

List 10–18   Continued

RUSSIA

Hermitage Museum, Dworzowaja Nabereshnaja 34–36, St. Petersburg (Scythian gold objects, 6th–4th-century BC Pazyryk Tumuli objects, magnificent collection of old European masters, French Impressionists)

Pushkin Museum of Fine Arts, Volkhoncha 12, Moscow (Western European paintings from 15th to 20th centuries, antiquities)

Russian State Museum, Inzhenernaya, St. Petersburg (collection of Russian art: painting, sculpture, folk art)

Tretiakov Gallery, Lavrushinski per 10, Moscow (Russian art, icons, sculpture, miniatures)

SCOTLAND

National Gallery of Scotland, The Mound, Edinburgh (Raphael, El Greco, Degas, Claude Lorraine, Tiepolo, Constable, Ramsay)

SOUTH AMERICA

Fine Arts Museum, Los Caobos, Caracas, Venezuela (Venezuelan art, 20th-century Latin American sculpture, pre-Columbian and Egyptian art)

Modern Art Museum, Avenida Beira Mar, Aterro, Rio de Janeiro, Brazil (Brancusi's *Mlle Pogany,* Picasso's *Cubist Head,* Vieira Da Silva's *The Terraces*)

Museo National, São Paulo, Avenida Paulista, Brazil (traditional and modern European collection)

National Museum of Fine Arts, Avenida del Libertador 1473, Buenos Aires, Argentina (Argentine art, European paintings, prints, drawings, furniture, musical instruments)

SPAIN

Museo Pablo Picasso, calle de Montcada 15–17, Barcelona (some of Picasso's finest artworks)

Prado Museum, Paseo del Prado, Madrid (Rubens, Velazquez, El Greco, Brueghel, Goya, Zurbaran, Murillo, Bosch's *Garden of Earthly Delights*)

SWEDEN

Gothenburg Art Gallery, Gotaplatsen S-41256, Gothenburg (Northern European paintings, modern Swedish and other Scandinavian artists)

Modern Art Museum, Skeppsholmen Island, 111 49, Stockholm (Brancusi's *The Newborn Child,* Calder's *The Four Elements,* Picasso's *The Guitar Player,* Kienholz's *The State Hospital,* Rauschenberg's *Monogram,* Matisse's *Moroccan Landscape*)

National Museum, Box 16176 S. Blasieholmshamnen, Stockholm (Royal collections, Swedish paintings, Durer's *Young Girl,* Delacroix's *The Lion Hunting,* La Tour's *St. Jerome in Penitence,* Raphael's *Adoration of the Shepherds*)

SWITZERLAND

Basle Fine Arts Museum, St. Albangraben 16, Basle (Holbein, Grunewald, Cranach, Rousseau, Klee, Gauguin, Marc, Miró)

Berne Museum of Fine Arts, 12 Hodlerstrasse, CH-3011, Berne (Klee, Swiss works of art from 15th to 20th centuries, early Italian paintings, Cubist art)

Fine Arts Museum, Heimplatz I, Zurich (Munch's *Lueck Harbour,* 100 works by Giacometti including *The Chariot Bronze,* Toulouse Lautrec's *Bar,* Rousseau's *Portrait of Pierre Loti*)

TAIWAN

National Palace Museum, Wai-shuang-hsi, Shi-lin (comprehensive collections of bronzes, porcelains, hanging scrolls covering 3,600 years)

THAILAND

National Museum, Bangkok (Thailand's religious, cultural, and archaeological treasures)

List 10–18   Continued

TUNISIA

National Museum of Bardo, Le Bardo, Tunis (Phoenician, Roman, early Christian and Moslem antiquities, Arab museum, Roman mosaics)

TURKEY

Ankara Archaeological Museum, Ulus, Ankara (Hittite remains excavated in Turkey and Ephesus)

Ephesus Museum, Province of Izmir, Selcuk (Ephesus antiquities: *Head of Eros,* Roman sundial, Mycenaean vases, sculptures)

Topkapi Palace Museum, Istanbul (Sultan's treasures: jewels, thrones, Oriental porcelain, mosaics, illuminated manuscripts)

WALES

National Museum of Wales, Cardiff (archaeology, art, geology, botany, Welsh and British paintings, Richard Wilson)

FEDERAL REPUBLIC OF YUGOSLAVIA

Belgrade National Museum (Narodni Musej Beograd), Trg Republike Sq., Belgrade, Serbia-Montenegro (archaeological collection from prehistory, Serbian art, European collection)